CONTEMPORARY
DRAMA

Thirteen Plays

Contemporary Drama

THIRTEEN PLAYS

Second Edition

SELECTED AND EDITED

by

STANLEY A. CLAYES

Loyola University, Chicago

and

DAVID G. SPENCER

California State College, Bakersfield

CHARLES' SCRIBNER'S SONS

NEW YORK

CONTENTS

PREFACE

The plays in *Contemporary Drama: 13 Plays* are representative of the variety of the realistic-naturalistic tradition and some reactions against it. The second edition differs from the first in the substitution of three plays, in the inclusion of the complete preface to *Miss Julie,* and in the addition of Arthur Miller's introduction to the two-act version of *A View from the Bridge.*

The realism of Ibsen, Chekhov, Shaw, and Strindberg, which John Gassner calls the modern classicism, may be viewed as the basis for such successful later plays as those included in this anthology by O'Casey, Odets, Williams and Miller. But the crystallization of tradition creates reaction against it, and this tendency in drama is illustrated here by the fantasy in Giraudoux' *Ondine,* the poetic drama of Lorca's *The House of Bernarda Alba,* the episodic structure of Brecht's epic drama *The Caucasian Chalk Circle* and the highly successful expressionistic techniques of van Itallie's *America Hurrah* and Bullins' *A Son, Come Home.*

The introductory comments that accompany each of these plays, with the exception of the reviews, were written by the playwrights themselves. In these comments the playwrights explain their general aims as writers, they discuss technique or ideas, or they comment upon the general tendency of modern drama; they do not explain their plays. These comments, while they will tend to elucidate some practices of the playwrights, will raise as many questions as they answer about technique, critical standards, and the final statement made by each play. They may also provide the student with a certain amount of source material for drawing comparisons between the intentions and achievements of certain playwrights, and between one play and another.

Since the aim of the introductory material is to present students with what might have been the fruits of their own research, we have not regularized or made more conventional the spelling and punctuation that we found in the original. The student will find British spellings and *theater* and *Chekhov* in the common variant spellings, and we have resisted whenever possible the temptation to call attention with *sic* to other departures from convention in the work of highly competent writers and translators. We have, however, put into italic type the titles of plays where three authors had used quotation marks, but even here we have made an exception of Shaw whose reasoned and consistent policy was to designate titles neither by quotation marks nor by italics.

Our gratitude goes chiefly to the pleasant and charitable women in New York publishing houses and agencies who toil thanklessly to reconcile the demands of their employers and the authors they represent and editors like ourselves who never close a transaction but just keep writing letters about it. Those who have been most kind this time are Leah Daniels at Random House, Else B. Lorch at New Directions, Judith Schmidt at Grove Press, who wrote a great many letters refusing everything we asked permission for, and many others who did the extraordinary thing of answering promptly. We are also grateful to many colleagues (particularly Paul Hummert, Rita Clarkson, and William Hiebel) who discussed with us the highly variable topics of teachability and student interest.

S. A. C.

D. G. S.

TO THE STUDENT

The plays in this book are representative of the diversity in style, attitude and resolution that characterizes modern drama. Though tradition, reaction and revolt characterize its history, modern drama began in revolt: revolt against the romantic melodrama that preceded it, and against the rigidities of conventional 19th century attitudes toward religion, idealism, love, sexual morality and justice. These attitudes found expression as the themes of modern drama, and these themes recur in variation in all the plays in this book. While the themes provide some means for discussing the plays, they are not necessarily the most significant feature of the plays, which are of literary interest on other grounds as well. First they are realistic, but the essence of their realism is not that they picture life with photographic accuracy (none of these plays attempt that). "Drama purely imitative of life isn't drama at all," says O'Casey in "The Green Goddess of Realism." To state the real aim of the best playwrights O'Casey quotes Allardyce Nicoll: "The great art of the theater is to suggest, not to tell openly; to dilate the mind by symbols, not by actual things; to express in Lear a world's sorrow, and in Hamlet the grief of humanity." These modern plays attempt to dilate the mind by symbols, but the essence of their realism is to stress the modern relevance, universal though it may be, of the real conflicts they portray. As Shaw in a reckless moment put it, "Ibsen supplies the want left by Shakespear. He gives us not only ourselves but our situations."

Although Shakespeare's achievement as a dramatic poet is unapproachable by dramatists of lesser genius writing in twentieth-century colloquial prose, another essential part of the realism illustrated in most of these plays is their authors' various attempts to both accept and transcend the limitations of realistic dialogue. Eric Bentley, implying the essential problem of a non-poetic drama, praised Ibsen for his "imaginative use of unimaginative language." With the exception of Lorca, who wrote poetic drama, these playwrights find individual solutions to the problem of creating a prose style suitable for drama. Chekhov's language, praised in an essay here by Arthur Miller, is better, more natural and more universal in its implications, than Ibsen's language, which is heavy with portent and symbol. Shaw gave his own wit to all his characters. Others through style and the search for colorful generic speech idiom found a distinctive voice as well as a distinctive dramatic form. All have labored with language to make it at least seem realistic.

Like even the greatest drama, the plays in this book are constructed from conflicts of attitudes. Each play, rich in the detailed experience and situation of its own particular ethnic background (Chekhov's provincial Russia, O'Casey's Dublin, Miller's Italian New York), develops to crisis and resolution a conflict of attitude. Understanding the plays is a matter of understanding the attitudes of the characters and then of understanding the ironies of their authors' attitudes toward them. Seeing a play's greatness, its importance, or merely its craftsmanship, is far more complex. For both perceptions the introductory selections should be of some help.

The introductory selections, with the exception of a few reviews, are written by the playwrights themselves, and should provide the student with a first-hand statement suggesting the various authors' particular concerns in matters of technique and attitude. They are not exhaustive explanations, and they do not explain what the plays "mean" as students would often like them to do, but they should provide some basis that will enable the student to confront these plays on the authors' terms.

Because the authors' concerns are diverse, the introductory selections usually explain only one aspect of them. Giraudoux and Lorca, both in practice concerned to develop a distinctive dramatic style, speak of the theatre as a school for instructing the public, a position which would seem to put them close to Shaw and Brecht. Yet how different in dramatic style these four authors are. Lorca worked for the style and effect of classical tragedy. Giraudoux, equally unconcerned with realistic surfaces, is equally willing to risk the charge of melodrama and sentimentality to achieve a tragic style, frankly fantastic, that might be acceptable to moderns. Brecht, who describes his epic drama in "Theatre for Pleasure or Theatre for Instruction," rejects not only the sentimental but all sympathetic identification by the audience with his characters, a theoretical alienation that does not always work in productions of his plays. Of the four only Shaw, however much a moralist, seems most conventionally modern. Introducing Ibsen to England and continuing his dramatic style, Shaw was the first important writer in the major tradition of the Anglo-American theatre.

"My task," Ibsen said in his letter of 1874, "has been the description of humanity." Certainly *The Wild Duck* and the letters printed here do not support the common idea that Ibsen was simply a dramatist with a thesis even though we find ideas in his plays. For Ibsen, as for Strindberg and Chekhov, however differently, the problem was to create a dramatic design that put human passions, ideas and attitudes in a perspective that revealed ("described") them truly. The truth revealed, however, is invariably limited to the ability of the author to see and dramatize.

When early realistic plays showed individuals simply as products and victims of the forces of heredity, instinct, society and environment, the term naturalistic seems more appropriate than the term realistic to denote the tradition. Naturalism is a special form of realism, but in practice the terms are used somewhat interchangeably. Objectivity, not the naturalistic thesis, was the aim of the realists. The plays and introductory comments by O'Casey, Odets, Williams, and Miller, all of whom continue the tradition and discuss aspects of it, reveal that truth and not polemic nor moral was their aim. Even Shaw, with all his concern for his message, though less objective than Ibsen, described humanity with more objectivity than he realized. The tradition that these plays illustrate in much of its variety explores the relationship of a fairly restricted group of characters. Their motivation, with the effects of environment documented, are explored; their illusions, their weaknesses and their strengths are revealed. Though such a study of motive may make the naturalists' point, the best plays have less narrow aims. Avoiding the excesses O'Casey deplores in his essay, the stage is set realistically, the detail often symbolic. Characters leave the stage with an announced destination and return for a reason. They speak to each other in idiomatic modern language, often heavy with the color of their cultural background, but with more wit, more style or more design than in real life.

It is that tradition that the "Foreword to Miss Julie," though naturalistic, began a reaction against. Strindberg called for a less realistic, more imaginative theatrical effect. He called for monologue, mime, ballet, music and special lighting effects. In his later dream plays he led the revolution against the little family scene of modern realism. We can find the restrained use of music in Chekhov, the frank use of fantasy in Giraudoux and the use of monologue in O'Neill. The attempt to make plays more theatrical than realistic (or naturalistic) led to wide ranging experiment including the poetic, the expressionistic, the epic, and the absurd. Because the important absurd plays of Albee, Beckett, Genet, Ionesco, and Pinter were not available for this anthology, only the poetic (*The House of Bernarda Alba*), the epic (*The Caucasian Chalk Circle*) and the expressionistic (*America Hurrah*) are represented.

The differences among the plays and the introductory selections raise a number of questions about style, attitude, and literary or theatrical quality. Although a variety of contemporary dramatic styles are represented in the plays, most are written in the realistic manner. To what extent are their virtues and defects the result of the concerns their authors discuss? How have the individual playwrights solved for themselves the problems of style and language discussed by Giraudoux and Miller? If the combined aim discussed by these authors is to create a realistic theater for both pleasure and instruction, one that tells the truth about human beings and tells it with intelligence, passion, imagination and style, who is the most successful? Whose dramatic image is most vivid and most likely to last? Whose truth is most important and most universal? Which play is most skillful with character and language, richest in atmospheric detail? Is the most realistic play here necessarily the best play?

HENRIK IBSEN

LETTER to Frederik Hegel [1]

Grossensass, 2nd September 1884

Dear Mr. Hegel,—Along with this letter I send you the manu-
script of my new play, *The Wild Duck*. For the last four
months I have worked at it every day; and it is not without a
certain feeling of regret that I part from it. Long, daily association with the persons in this play has endeared them to me,
in spite of their manifold failings; and I am not without hope
that they may find good and kind friends among the great
reading public, and more particularly among the actor tribe—
to whom they offer roles which will well repay the trouble
spent on them. The study and representation of these characters will not be an easy task; therefore it is desirable that the
book should be offered to the theaters as early as possible in the
season; I shall send the letters, which you will be good enough
to despatch along with the different copies.

In some ways this new play occupies a position by itself
among my dramatic works; in its method it differs in several
respects from my former ones. But I shall say no more on this
subject at present. I hope that my critics will discover the
points alluded to; they will, at any rate, find several things to
squabble about and several things to interpret. I also think that
The Wild Duck may very probably entice some of our young
dramatists into new paths; and this I consider a result to be
desired. . . .

SPEECH at the Festival of the Norwegian Women's Rights League,
Christiania, *May 26th, 1898* [2]

I am not a member of the Women's Rights League. Whatever I have written is without any conscious thought of
making propaganda. I have been more poet and less social
philosopher than people generally seem inclined to believe.

[1] *The Correspondence of Henrik Ibsen,* trans. and ed. Mary Morison
(London, 1905), pp. 383-384. Reprinted by permission of Hodder
and Stoughton Ltd.
[2] This speech and the following three speeches are reprinted from
Speeches and New Letters of Henrik Ibsen, trans. Arne Kildal (Boston,
1909), pp. 57, 59, 65.

I thank you for the toast, but must disclaim the honor of having consciously worked for the women's rights movement. I am not even quite clear as to just what this women's rights movement really is. To me, it has seemed a problem of humanity in general. And if you read my books carefully you will understand this. True enough, it is desirable to solve the problem of women's rights, along with all the others; but that has not been the whole purpose. My task has been the *description of humanity*. To be sure, whenever such description is felt to be reasonably true, the reader will insert his own feelings and sentiments into the work of the poet. These are attributed to the poet; but incorrectly so. Every reader remolds it so beautifully and nicely, each according to his own personality. Not only those who write, but also those who read are poets; they are collaborators; they are often more poetical than the poet himself.

SPEECH to the Norwegian Students, *September 10th, 1874*

And what is it then that constitutes a poet? As for me, it was a long time before I realized that to be a poet, that is chiefly to see, but mark well, to see in such a manner that the thing seen is perceived by his audience just as the poet saw it. . . .

I have thought when I say this to you, to the students, it will reach exactly its right address. It will be understood as it is to be understood; for a student has essentially the same task as the poet: to make clear to himself and thereby to others, the temporal and eternal questions which are astir in the age and in the community to which he belongs. . . .

SPEECH at the Banquet in Christiania, *March 23d, 1898*—in celebration of Ibsen's 70th birthday

. . . *The* young writers do not any longer have to write for a narrow circle. They have a public, an entire people to whom they may speak and to whom they may direct their thoughts and feelings. Whether they meet *opposition* or *adherence*—that is immaterial. It is only the *inability,* the *unwillingness to hear* which is evil. That have *I* felt. . . .

SPEECH at the Banquet in Stockholm, *September 24th, 1887*

It has been said of me on different occasions that I am a pessimist. And so I am in so far as I do not believe in the everlasting-

4

ness of human ideals. But I am also an optimist in so far as I firmly believe in the capacity for procreation and development of ideals. Especially, to be more definite, am I of the opinion that the ideals of our time, while disintegrating, are tending towards what in my play *Emperor and Galilean* I indicated by the name of "The Third Kingdom." Therefore, permit me to drink a toast to that which is in the process of formation,—to that which is to come.

HENRIK IBSEN

The Wild Duck

A Play in Five Acts

CHARACTERS

WERLE, *a merchant, manufacturer, etc.*
GREGERS WERLE, his son.
OLD EKDAL.
HIALMAR EKDAL, *his son, a photographer.*
GINA EKDAL, *Hialmar's wife.*
HEDVIG, *their daughter, a girl of fourteen.*
MRS. SÖRBY, *Werle's housekeeper.*
RELLING, *a doctor.*
MOLVIK, *ex-student of theology.*

GRÅBERG, *Werle's bookkeeper.*
PETTERSEN, *Werle's servant.*
JENSEN, *a hired waiter.*
A FLABBY GENTLEMAN.
A THIN-HAIRED GENTLEMAN.
A SHORT-SIGHTED GENTLEMAN.
Six *other gentlemen, guests at Werle's dinner-party.*
Several *hired waiters.*

The first act passes in Werle's house, the remaining acts at Hialmar Ekdal's.

Pronunciation of Names: Gregers Werle = Grayghers Verlë; Hialmar Ekdal = Yalmar Aykdal; Gina = Gheena; Gråberg = Groberg; Jensen = Yensen.

ACT FIRST

At WERLE's *house. A richly and comfortably furnished study; book-cases and upholstered furniture; a writing-table, with papers and documents, in the centre of the room; lighted lamps with green shades, giving a subdued light. At the back, open folding-doors with curtains drawn back. Within is seen a large and handsome room, brilliantly lighted with lamps and branching candlesticks. In front, on the right (in the study), a small baize door leads into* WERLE's *office. On the left, in front, a fireplace with a glowing coal fire, and farther back a double door leading into the dining-room.*

WERLE's *servant,* PETTERSEN, *in livery, and* JENSEN, *the hired waiter, in black, are putting the study in order. In the large room, two or three other hired waiters are moving about, arranging things and lighting more candles. From the dining-room, the hum of conversation and laughter of many voices are heard; a glass is tapped with a knife; silence follows, and a toast is proposed; shouts of "Bravo!" and then again a buzz of conversation.*

PETTERSEN: [*Lights a lamp on the chimney-place and places a shade over it.*] Hark to them, Jensen! now the old man's on his legs holding a long palaver about Mrs. Sörby.

JENSEN: [*Pushing forward an arm-chair.*] Is it true, what folks say, that they're—very good friends, eh?

PETTERSEN: Lord knows.

JENSEN: I've heard tell as he's been a lively customer in his day.

PETTERSEN: May be.

JENSEN: And he's giving this spread in honour of his son, they say.

PETTERSEN: Yes. His son came home yesterday.

JENSEN: This is the first time I ever heard as Mr. Werle had a son.

PETTERSEN: Oh yes, he has a son, right enough. But he's a fixture, as you might say, up at the Höidal works. He's never once come to town all the years I've been in service here.

A WAITER: [*In the doorway of the other room.*] Pettersen, here's an old fellow wanting——

PETTERSEN: [*Mutters.*] The devil—who's this now?

[OLD EKDAL *appears from the right, in the inner room. He is dressed in a threadbare overcoat with a high collar; he wears woollen mittens, and carries in his hand a stick and a fur cap. Under his arm, a brown paper parcel. Dirty red-brown wig and small grey moustache.*]

PETTERSEN: [*Goes towards him.*] Good Lord—what do you want here?

EKDAL: [*In the doorway.*] Must get into the office, Pettersen.

PETTERSEN: The office was closed an hour ago, and——

EKDAL: So they told me at the front door. But Gråberg's in there still. Let me slip in this way, Pettersen; there's a good fellow. [*Points towards the baize door.*] It's not the first time I've come this way.

PETTERSEN: Well, you may pass. [*Opens the door.*] But mind you go out again the proper way, for we've got company.

EKDAL: I know, I know—h'm! Thanks, Pettersen, good old friend! Thanks! [*Mutters softly.*] Ass!

[*He goes into the office;* PETTERSEN *shuts the door after him.*]

JENSEN: Is he one of the office people?

PETTERSEN: No, he's only an outside hand that does odd jobs of copying. But he's been a tip-topper in his day, has old Ekdal.

JENSEN: You can see he's been through a lot.

PETTERSEN: Yes; he was an army officer, you know.

JENSEN: You don't say so?

PETTERSEN: No mistake about it. But then he went into the timber trade or something of the sort. They say he once played Mr. Werle a very nasty trick. They were partners in the Höidal works at the time. Oh, I know old Ekdal well, I do. Many a nip of bitters and bottle of ale we two have drunk at Madam Eriksen's.

JENSEN: He don't look as if he'd much to stand treat with.

PETTERSEN: Why, bless you, Jensen, it's me that stands treat. I always think there's no harm in being a bit civil to folks that have seen better days.

JENSEN: Did he go bankrupt then?

PETTERSEN: Worse than that. He went to prison.

JENSEN: To prison!

PETTERSEN: Or perhaps it was the Penitentiary. [Listens.] Sh! They're leaving the table.

[The dining-room door is thrown open from within, by a couple of waiters. MRS. SÖRBY comes out conversing with two gentlemen. Gradually the whole company follows, amongst them WERLE. Last come HIALMAR EKDAL and GREGERS WERLE.]

MRS. SÖRBY: [In passing, to the servant.] Tell them to serve the coffee in the music-room, Pettersen.

PETTERSEN: Very well, Madam.

[She goes with the two Gentlemen into the inner room, and thence out to the right. PETTERSEN and JENSEN go out the same way.]

A FLABBY GENTLEMAN: [To a THIN-HAIRED GENTLEMAN.] Whew! What a dinner!—It was no joke to do it justice!

THE THIN-HAIRED GENTLEMAN: Oh, with a little good-will one can get through a lot in three hours.

THE FLABBY GENTLEMAN: Yes, but afterwards, afterwards, my dear Chamberlain!

A THIRD GENTLEMAN: I hear the coffee and maraschino are to be served in the music-room.

THE FLABBY GENTLEMAN: Bravo! Then perhaps Mrs. Sörby will play us something.

THE THIN-HAIRED GENTLEMAN: [In a low voice.] I hope Mrs. Sörby mayn't play us a tune we don't like, one of these days!

THE FLABBY GENTLEMAN: Oh no, not she! Bertha will never turn against her old friends.

[They laugh and pass into the inner room.]

WERLE: [In a low voice, dejectedly.] I don't think anybody noticed it, Gregers.

GREGERS: [Looks at him.] Noticed what?

WERLE: Did you not notice it either?

GREGERS: What do you mean?

WERLE: We were thirteen at table.

GREGERS: Indeed? Were there thirteen of us?

WERLE: [Glances towards HIALMAR EKDAL.] Our usual party is twelve. [To the others.] This way, gentlemen!

[WERLE and the others, all except HIALMAR and GREGERS, go out by the back, to the right.]

HIALMAR: [Who has overhead the conversation.] You ought not to have invited me, Gregers.

GREGERS: What! Not ask my best and only friend to a party supposed to be in my honour——?

HIALMAR: But I don't think your father likes it. You see I am quite outside his circle.

GREGERS: So I hear. But I wanted to see you and have a talk with you, and I certainly shan't be staying long.—Ah, we two old schoolfellows have drifted far apart from each other. It must be sixteen or seventeen years since we met.

HIALMAR: Is it so long?

GREGERS: It is indeed. Well, how goes it with you? You look well. You have put on flesh, and grown almost stout.

HIALMAR: Well, "stout" is scarcely the word; but I daresay I look a little more of a man than I used to.

GREGERS: Yes, you do; your outer man is in first-rate condition.

HIALMAR: [In a tone of gloom.] Ah, but the inner man! That is a very different matter, I can tell you! Of course you know of the terrible catastrophe that has befallen me and mine since last we met.

GREGERS: [More softly.] How are things going with your father now?

HIALMAR: Don't let us talk of it, old fellow. Of course my poor unhappy father lives with me. He hasn't another soul in the world to care for him. But you can understand that this is a miserable subject for me.—Tell me, rather, how you have been getting on up at the works.

GREGERS: I have had a delightfully lonely time of it—plenty of leisure to think and think about things. Come over here; we may as well make ourselves comfortable.

[He seats himself in an arm-chair by the fire and draws HIALMAR down into another alongside of it.]

HIALMAR: [Sentimentally.] After all, Gregers, I thank you for inviting me to your father's table; for I take it as a sign that you have got over your feeling against me.

GREGERS: [*Surprised.*] How could you imagine I had any feeling against you?

HIALMAR: You had at first, you know.

GREGERS: How at first?

HIALMAR: After the great misfortune. It was natural enough that you should. Your father was within an ace of being drawn into that—well, that terrible business.

GREGERS: Why should that give me any feeling against you? Who can have put that into your head?

HIALMAR: I know it did, Gregers; your father told me so himself.

GREGERS: [*Starts.*] My father! Oh indeed. H'm.—Was that why you never let me hear from you?—not a single word.

HIALMAR: Yes.

GREGERS: Not even when you made up your mind to become a photographer?

HIALMAR: Your father said I had better not write to you at all, about anything.

GREGERS: [*Looking straight before him.*] Well well, perhaps he was right.—But tell me now, Hialmar: are you pretty well satisfied with your present position?

HIALMAR: [*With a little sigh.*] Oh yes, I am; I have really no cause to complain. At first, as you may guess, I felt it a little strange. It was such a totally new state of things for me. But of course my whole circumstances were totally changed. Father's utter, irretrievable ruin,—the shame and disgrace of it, Gregers—

GREGERS: [*Affected.*] Yes, yes; I understand.

HIALMAR: I couldn't think of remaining at college; there wasn't a shilling to spare; on the contrary, there were debts—mainly to your father I believe——

GREGERS: H'm——

HIALMAR: In short, I thought it best to break, once for all, with my old surroundings and associations. It was your father that specially urged me to it; and since he interested himself so much in me——

GREGERS: My father did?

HIALMAR: Yes, you surely knew that, didn't you? Where do you suppose I found the money to learn photography, and to furnish a studio and make a start? All that costs a pretty penny, I can tell you.

GREGERS: And my father provided the money?

HIALMAR: Yes, my dear fellow, didn't you know? I understood him to say he had written to you about it.

GREGERS: Not a word about his part in the business. He must have forgotten it. Our correspondence has always been purely a business one. So it was my father that——!

HIALMAR: Yes, certainly. He didn't wish it to be generally known; but he it was. And of course it was he, too, that put me in a position to marry. Don't you—don't you know about that either?

GREGERS: No, I haven't heard a word of it. [*Shakes him by the arm.*] But, my dear Hialmar, I can't tell you what pleasure all this gives me—pleasure, and self-reproach. I have perhaps done my father injustice after all—in some things. This proves that he has a heart. It shows a sort of compunction——

HIALMAR: Compunction——?

GREGERS: Yes, yes—whatever you like to call it. Oh, I can't tell you how glad I am to hear this of father.—So you are a married man, Hialmar! That is further than I shall ever get. Well, I hope you are happy in your married life?

HIALMAR: Yes, thoroughly happy. She is as good and capable a wife as any man could wish for. And she is by no means without culture.

GREGERS: [*Rather surprised.*] No, of course not.

HIALMAR: You see, life is itself an education. Her daily intercourse with me—— And then we know one or two rather remarkable men, who come a good deal about us. I assure you, you would hardly know Gina again.

GREGERS: Gina?

HIALMAR: Yes; had you forgotten that her name was Gina?

GREGERS: Whose name? I haven't the slightest idea——

HIALMAR: Don't you remember that she used to be in service here?

GREGERS: [*Looks at him.*] Is it Gina Hansen——?

HIALMAR: Yes, of course it is Gina Hansen.

GREGERS: ——who kept house for us during the last year of my mother's illness?

HIALMAR: Yes, exactly. But, my dear friend, I'm quite sure your father told you that I was married.

GREGERS: [*Who has risen.*] Oh yes, he mentioned it; but not that——[*Walking about the room.*] Stay—perhaps he did—now that I think of it. My father always writes such short letters. [*Half seats himself on the arm of the chair.*] Now, tell me,

Hialmar—this is interesting—how did you come to know Gina—your wife?

HIALMAR: The simplest thing in the world. You know Gina did not stay here long; everything was so much upset at that time, owing to your mother's illness and so forth, that Gina was not equal to it all; so she gave notice and left. That was the year before your mother died—or it may have been the same year.

GREGERS: It was the same year. I was up at the works then. But afterwards——?

HIALMAR: Well, Gina lived at home with her mother, Madam Hansen, an excellent hard-working woman, who kept a little eating-house. She had a room to let too; a very nice comfortable room.

GREGERS: And I suppose you were lucky enough to secure it?

HIALMAR: Yes; in fact, it was your father that recommended it to me. So it was there, you see, that I really came to know Gina.

GREGERS: And then you got engaged?

HIALMAR: Yes. It doesn't take young people long to fall in love——; h'm——

GREGERS: [Rises and moves about a little.] Tell me: was it after your engagement —was it then that my father—I mean was it then that you began to take up photography?

HIALMAR: Yes, precisely. I wanted to make a start, and to set up house as soon as possible; and your father and I agreed that this photography business was the readiest way. Gina thought so too. Oh, and there was another thing in its favour, by-the-bye: it happened, luckily, that Gina had learnt to retouch.

GREGERS: That chimed in marvellously.

HIALMAR: [Pleased, rises.] Yes, didn't it? Don't you think it was a marvelous piece of luck?

GREGERS: Oh, unquestionably. My father seems to have been almost a kind of providence for you.

HIALMAR: [With emotion.] He did not forsake his old friend's son in the hour of his need. For he has a heart, you see.

MRS. SÖRBY: [Enters, arm-in-arm with WERLE.] Nonsense, my dear Mr. Werle; you mustn't stop there any longer staring at all the lights. It's very bad for you.

WERLE: [Lets go her arm and passes his hand over his eyes.] I daresay you are right.

[PETTERSEN and JENSEN carry round refreshment trays.]

MRS. SÖRBY: [To the Guests in the other room.] This way, if you please, gentlemen. Whoever wants a glass of punch must be so good as to come in here.

THE FLABBY GENTLEMAN: [Comes up to MRS. SÖRBY.] Surely, it isn't possible that you have suspended our cherished right to smoke?

MRS. SÖRBY: Yes. No smoking here, in Mr. Werle's sanctum, Chamberlain.

THE THIN-HAIRED GENTLEMAN: When did you enact these stringent amendments on the cigar law, Mrs. Sörby?

MRS. SÖRBY: After the last dinner, Chamberlain, when certain persons permitted themselves to overstep the mark.

THE THIN-HAIRED GENTLEMAN: And may one never overstep the mark a little bit, Madame Bertha? Not the least little bit?

MRS. SÖRBY: Not in any respect whatsoever, Mr. Balle.

[Most of the Guests have assembled in the study; servants hand round glasses of punch.]

WERLE: [To HIALMAR, who is standing beside a table.] What are you studying so intently, Ekdal?

HIALMAR: Only an album, Mr. Werle.

THE THIN-HAIRED GENTLEMAN: [Who is wandering about.] Ah, photographs! They are quite in your line of course.

THE FLABBY GENTLEMAN: [In an armchair.] Haven't you brought any of your own with you?

HIALMAR: No, I haven't.

THE FLABBY GENTLEMAN: You ought to have; it's very good for the digestion to sit and look at pictures.

THE THIN-HAIRED GENTLEMAN: And it contributes to the entertainment, you know.

THE SHORT-SIGHTED GENTLEMAN: And all contributions are thankfully received.

MRS. SÖRBY: The Chamberlains think that when one is invited out to dinner, one ought to exert oneself a little in return, Mr. Ekdal.

THE FLABBY GENTLEMAN: Where one dines so well, that duty becomes a pleasure.

THE THIN-HAIRED GENTLEMAN: And when it's a case of the struggle for existence, you know——

MRS. SÖRBY: I quite agree with you!

[They continue the conversation, with laughter and joking.]

GREGERS: [Softly.] You must join in, Hialmar.

HIALMAR: [Writhing.] What am I to talk about?

THE FLABBY GENTLEMAN: Don't you think, Mr. Werle, that Tokay may be considered one of the more wholesome sorts of wine?

WERLE: [By the fire.] I can answer for the Tokay you had to-day, at any rate; it's one of the very finest seasons. Of course you would notice that.

THE FLABBY GENTLEMAN: Yes, it had a remarkably delicate flavour.

HIALMAR: [Shyly.] Is there any difference between the seasons?

THE FLABBY GENTLEMAN: [Laughs.] Come! That's good!

WERLE: [Smiles.] It really doesn't pay to set fine wine before you.

THE THIN-HAIRED GENTLEMAN: Tokay is like photographs, Mr. Ekdal: they both need sunshine. Am I not right?

HIALMAR: Yes, light is important no doubt.

MRS. SÖRBY: And it's exactly the same with Chamberlains—they, too, depend very much on sunshine, [1] as the saying is.

THE THIN-HAIRED GENTLEMAN: Oh fie! That's a very threadbare sarcasm!

THE SHORT-SIGHTED GENTLEMAN: Mrs. Sörby is coming out——

THE FLABBY GENTLEMAN: ——and at our expense, too. [Holds up his finger reprovingly.] Oh, Madame Bertha, Madame Bertha!

MRS. SÖRBY: Yes, and there's not the least doubt that the seasons differ greatly. The old vintages are the finest.

THE SHORT-SIGHTED GENTLEMAN: Do you reckon me among the old vintages?

MRS. SÖRBY: Oh, far from it.

THE THIN-HAIRED GENTLEMAN: There now! But me, dear Mrs. Sörby——?

THE FLABBY GENTLEMAN: Yes, and me? What vintage should you say that we belong to?

MRS. SÖRBY: Why, to the sweet vintages, gentlemen.

[She sips a glass of punch. The gentlemen laugh and flirt with her.]

WERLE: Mrs. Sörby can always find a loop-hole—when she wants to. Fill your glasses, gentlemen! Pettersen, will you see to it——! Gregers, suppose we have a glass together. [GREGERS does not move.] Won't you join us, Ekdal? I found no opportunity of drinking with you at table.

[GRÅBERG, the Bookkeeper, looks in at the baize door.]

GRÅBERG: Excuse me, sir, but I can't get out.

WERLE: Have you been locked in again?

GRÅBERG: Yes, and Flakstad has carried off the keys.

WERLE: Well, you can pass out this way.

GRÅBERG: But there's some one else——

WERLE: All right; come through, both of you. Don't be afraid.

[GRÅBERG and OLD EKDAL come out of the office.]

WERLE: [Involuntarily.] Ugh!

[The laughter and talk among the Guests cease. HIALMAR starts at the sight of his father, puts down his glass, and turns towards the fireplace.]

EKDAL: [Does not look up, but makes little bows to both sides as he passes, murmuring.] Beg pardon, come the wrong way. Door locked—door locked. Beg pardon.

[He and GRÅBERG go out by the back, to the right.]

WERLE: [Between his teeth.] That idiot Gråberg!

GREGERS: [Open-mouthed and staring, to HIALMAR.] Why surely that wasn't——!

THE FLABBY GENTLEMAN: What's the matter? Who was it?

GREGERS: Oh, nobody, only the bookkeeper and some one with him.

THE SHORT-SIGHTED GENTLEMAN: [To HIALMAR.] Did you know that man?

HIALMAR: I don't know—I didn't notice——

THE FLABBY GENTLEMAN: What the deuce has come over every one?

[He joins another group who are talking softly.]

MRS. SÖRBY: [Whispers to the Servant.] Give him something to take with him; something good, mind.

PETTERSEN: [Nods.] I'll see to it. [Goes out.]

GREGERS: [Softly and with emotion, to HIALMAR.] So that was really he!

HIALMAR: Yes.

GREGERS: And you could stand there and deny that you knew him!

HIALMAR: [Whispers vehemently.] But how could I——!

GREGERS: ——acknowledge your own father?

HIALMAR: [With pain.] Oh, if you were in my place——

[The conversation amongst the Guests,

---

[1] The "sunshine" of Court favour.

which has been carried on in a low tone, now swells into constrained joviality.]

THE THIN-HAIRED GENTLEMAN: [*Approaching* HIALMAR *and* GREGERS *in a friendly manner.*] Aha! Reviving old college memories, eh? Don't you smoke, Mr. Ekdal? May I give you a light? Oh, by-the-bye, we mustn't——

HIALMAR: No, thank you, I won't——

THE FLABBY GENTLEMAN: Haven't you a nice little poem you could recite to us, Mr. Ekdal? You used to recite so charmingly.

HIALMAR· I am sorry I can't remember anything.

THE FLABBY GENTLEMAN: Oh, that's a pity. Well, what shall we do, Balle?

[*Both Gentlemen move away and pass into the other room.*]

HIALMAR: [*Gloomily.*] Gregers—I am going! When a man has felt the crushing hand of Fate, you see—— Say good-bye to your father for me.

GREGERS: Yes, yes. Are you going straight home?

HIALMAR: Yes. Why?

GREGERS: Oh, because I may perhaps look in on you later.

HIALMAR: No, you mustn't do that. You must not come to my home. Mine is a melancholy abode, Gregers; especially after a splendid banquet like this. We can always arrange to meet somewhere in the town.

MRS. SÖRBY: [*Who has quietly approached.*] Are you going, Ekdal?

HIALMAR: Yes.

MRS. SÖRBY: Remember me to Gina.

HIALMAR: Thanks.

MRS. SÖRBY: And say I am coming up to see her one of these days.

HIALMAR: Yes, thank you. [*To* GREGERS.] Stay here; I will slip out unobserved.

[*He saunters away, then into the other room, and so out to the right.*]

MRS. SÖRBY: [*Softly to the Servant, who has come back.*] Well, did you give the old man something?

PETTERSEN: Yes; I sent him off with a bottle of cognac.

MRS. SÖRBY: Oh, you might have thought of something better than that.

PETTERSEN: Oh no, Mrs. Sörby; cognac is what he likes best in the world.

THE FLABBY GENTLEMAN: [*In the doorway with a sheet of music in his hand.*] Shall we play a duet, Mrs. Sörby?

MRS. SÖRBY: Yes, suppose we do.

THE GUESTS: Bravo, bravo!

[*She goes with all the Guests through the back room, out to the right.* GREGERS *remains standing by the fire.* WERLE *is looking for something on the writing table, and appears to wish that* GREGERS *would go; as* GREGERS *does not move,* WERLE *goes towards the door.*]

GREGERS: Father, won't you stay a moment?

WERLE: [*Stops.*] What is it?

GREGERS: I must have a word with you.

WERLE: Can it not wait till we are alone?

GREGERS: No, it cannot; for perhaps we shall never be alone together.

WERLE: [*Drawing nearer.*] What do you mean by that?

[*During what follows, the pianoforte is faintly heard from the distant music-room.*]

GREGERS: How has that family been allowed to go so miserably to the wall?

WERLE: You mean the Ekdals, I suppose?

GREGERS: Yes, I mean the Ekdals. Lieutenant Ekdal was once so closely associated with you.

WERLE: Much too closely; I have felt that to my cost for many a year. It is thanks to him that I—yes I—have had a kind of slur cast upon my reputation.

GREGERS: [*Softly.*] Are you sure that he alone was to blame?

WERLE: Who else do you suppose——?

GREGERS: You and he acted together in that affair of the forests——

WERLE: But was it not Ekdal that drew the map of the tracts we had bought—that fraudulent map! It was he who felled all that timber illegally on Government ground. In fact, the whole management was in his hands. I was quite in the dark as to what Lieutenant Ekdal was doing.

GREGERS: Lieutenant Ekdal himself seems to have been very much in the dark as to what he was doing.

WERLE: That may be. But the fact remains that he was found guilty and I acquitted.

GREGERS: Yes, I know that nothing was proved against you.

WERLE: Acquittal is acquittal. Why do you rake up these old miseries that turned my hair grey before its time? Is that the sort of thing you have been brooding over up there, all these years? I can assure you, Gregers, here in the town the whole story has been forgotten long ago—so far as *I* am concerned.

GREGERS: But that unhappy Ekdal family——

WERLE: What would you have had me do for the people? When Ekdal came out of prison he was a broken-down being, past all help. There are people in the world who dive to the bottom the moment they get a couple of slugs in their body, and never come to the surface again. You may take my word for it, Gregers, I have done all I could without positively laying myself open to all sorts of suspicion and gossip——

GREGERS: Suspicion——? Oh, I see.

WERLE: I have given Ekdal copying to do for the office, and I pay him far, far more for it than his work is worth——

GREGERS: [*Without looking at him.*] H'm; that I don't doubt.

WERLE: You laugh? Do you think I am not telling you the truth? Well, I certainly can't refer you to my books, for I never enter payments of that sort.

GREGERS: [*Smiles coldly.*] No, there are certain payments it is best to keep no account of.

WERLE: [*Taken aback.*] What do you mean by that?

GREGERS: [*Mustering up courage.*] Have you entered what it cost you to have Hialmar Ekdal taught photography?

WERLE: I? How "entered" it?

GREGERS: I have learnt that it was you who paid for his training. And I have learnt, too, that it was you who enabled him to set up house so comfortably.

WERLE: Well, and yet you talk as though I had done nothing for the Ekdals! I can assure you these people have cost me enough in all conscience.

GREGERS: Have you entered any of these expenses in your books?

WERLE: Why do you ask?

GREGERS: Oh, I have my reasons. Now tell me: when you interested yourself so warmly in your old friend's son—it was just before his marriage, was it not?

WERLE: Why, deuce take it—after all these years, how can I——?

GREGERS: You wrote me a letter about that time—a business letter, of course; and in a postscript you mentioned—quite briefly—that Hialmar Ekdal had married a Miss Hansen.

WERLE: Yes, that was quite right. That was her name.

GREGERS: But you did not mention that this Miss Hansen was Gina Hansen—our former housekeeper.

WERLE: [*With a forced laugh of derision.*] No; to tell the truth, it didn't occur to me that you were so particularly interested in our former housekeeper.

GREGERS: No more I was. But [*Lowers his voice.*] there were others in this house who were particularly interested in her.

WERLE: What do you mean by that? [*Flaring up.*] You are not alluding to me, I hope?

GREGERS: [*Softly but firmly.*] Yes, I am alluding to you.

WERLE: And you dare—— You presume to—— How can that ungrateful hound—that photographer fellow—how dare he go making such insinuations!

GREGERS: Hialmar has never breathed a word about this. I don't believe he has the faintest suspicion of such a thing.

WERLE: Then where have you got it from? Who can have put such notions in your head?

GREGERS: My poor unhappy mother told me; and that the very last time I saw her.

WERLE: Your mother! I might have known as much! You and she—you always held together. It was she who turned you against me, from the first.

GREGERS: No, it was all that she had to suffer and submit to, until she broke down and came to such a pitiful end.

WERLE: Oh, she had nothing to suffer or submit to; not more than most people, at all events. But there's no getting on with morbid, overstrained creatures—that I have learnt to my cost.—And you could go on nursing such a suspicion—burrowing into all sorts of old rumours and slanders against your own father! I must say, Gregers, I really think that at your age you might find something more useful to do.

GREGERS: Yes, it is high time.

WERLE: Then perhaps your mind would be easier than it seems to be now. What can be your object in remaining up at the works, year out and year in, drudging away like a common clerk, and not drawing a farthing more than the ordinary monthly wage? It is downright folly.

GREGERS: Ah, if I were only sure of that.

WERLE: I understand you well enough. You want to be independent; you won't be beholden to me for anything. Well, now there happens to be an opportunity for you to become independent, your own master in everything.

GREGERS: Indeed? In what way——?

WERLE: When I wrote you insisting on your coming to town at once—h'm——

GREGERS: Yes, what is it you really want of me? I have been waiting all day to know.

WERLE: I want to propose that you should enter the firm, as partner.

GREGERS: I? Join your firm? As partner?

WERLE: Yes. It would not involve our being constantly together. You could take over the business here in town, and I should move up to the works.

GREGERS: You would?

WERLE: The fact is, I am not so fit for work as I once was. I am obliged to spare my eyes, Gregers; they have begun to trouble me.

GREGERS: They have always been weak.

WERLE: Not as they are now. And besides, circumstances might possibly make it desirable for me to live up there—for a time, at any rate.

GREGERS: That is certainly quite a new idea to me.

WERLE: Listen, Gregers: there are many things that stand between us; but we are father and son after all. We ought surely to be able to come to some sort of understanding with each other.

GREGERS: Outwardly, you mean, of course?

WERLE: Well, even that would be something. Think it over, Gregers. Don't you think it ought to be possible? Eh?

GREGERS: [Looking at him coldly.] There is something behind all this.

WERLE: How so?

GREGERS: You want to make use of me in some way.

WERLE: In such a close relationship as ours, the one can always be useful to the other.

GREGERS: Yes, so people say.

WERLE: I want very much to have you at home with me for a time. I am a lonely man, Gregers; I have always felt lonely, all my life through; but most of all now that I am getting up in years. I feel the need of some one about me——

GREGERS: You have Mrs. Sörby.

WERLE: Yes, I have her; and she has become, I may say, almost indispensable to me. She is lively and even-tempered; she brightens up the house; and that is a very great thing for me.

GREGERS: Well then, you have everything just as you wish it.

WERLE: Yes, but I am afraid it can't last. A woman so situated may easily find herself in a false position, in the eyes of the world. For that matter it does a man no good, either.

GREGERS: Oh, when a man gives such dinners as you give, he can risk a great deal.

WERLE: Yes, but how about the woman, Gregers? I fear she won't accept the situation much longer; and even if she did—even if, out of attachment to me, she were to take her chance of gossip and scandal and all that——? Do you think, Gregers—you with your strong sense of justice——

GREGERS: [Interrupts him.] Tell me in one word: are you thinking of marrying her?

WERLE: Suppose I were thinking of it? What then?

GREGERS: That's what I say: what then?

WERLE: Should you be inflexibly opposed to it!

GREGERS: Not at all. Not by any means.

WERLE: I was not sure whether your devotion to your mother's memory——

GREGERS: I am not overstrained.

WERLE: Well, whatever you may or may not be, at all events you have lifted a great weight from my mind. I am extremely pleased that I can reckon on your concurrence in this matter.

GREGERS: [Looking intently at him.] Now I see the use you want to put me to.

WERLE: Use to put you to? What an expression!

GREGERS: Oh, don't let us be nice in our choice of words—not when we are alone together, at any rate. [With a short laugh.] Well well! So this is what made it absolutely essential that I should come to town in person. For the sake of Mrs. Sörby, we are to get up a pretence at family life in the house—a tableau of filial affection! That will be something new indeed.

WERLE: How dare you speak in that tone!

GREGERS: Was there ever any family life here? Never since I can remember. But now, forsooth, your plans demand something of the sort. No doubt it will have an excellent effect when it is reported that the son has hastened home, on the wings of filial piety, to the grey-haired father's wedding-feast. What will then remain of all the rumours as to the wrongs the poor dead mother had to submit to? Not a vestige. Her son annihilates them at one stroke.

WERLE: Gregers—I believe there is no one in the world you detest as you do me.

GREGERS: [Softly.] I have seen you at too close quarters.

WERLE: You have seen me with your mother's eyes. [Lowers his voice a little.] But you should remember that her eyes were—clouded now and then.

GREGERS: [Quivering.] I see what you are hinting at. But who was to blame for mother's unfortunate weakness? Why you, and all those——! The last of them was this woman that you palmed off upon Hialmar Ekdal, when you were—— Ugh!

WERLE: [Shrugs his shoulders.] Word for word as if it were your mother speaking!

GREGERS: [Without heeding.] And there he is now, with his great, confiding, child-like mind, compassed about with all this treachery—living under the same roof with such a creature, and never dreaming that what he calls his home is built upon a lie! [Comes a step nearer.] When I look back upon your past, I seem to see a battle-field with shattered lives on every hand.

WERLE: I begin to think the chasm that divides us is too wide.

GREGERS: [Bowing, with self-command.] So I have observed; and therefore I take my hat and go.

WERLE: You are going! Out of the house?

GREGERS: Yes. For at last I see my mission in life.

WERLE: What mission?

GREGERS: You would only laugh if I told you.

WERLE: A lonely man doesn't laugh so easily, Gregers.

GREGERS: [Pointing towards the background.] Look, father,—the Chamberlains are playing blind-man's-buff with Mrs. Sörby.—Good-night and good-bye.

[He goes out by the back to the right. Sounds of laughter and merriment from the Company, who are now visible in the outer room.]

WERLE: [Muttering contemptuously after GREGERS.] Ha——! Poor wretch—and he says he is not overstrained!

ACT SECOND

HIALMAR EKDAL'S studio, a good-sized room, evidently in the top storey of the building. On the right, a sloping roof of large panes of glass, half-covered by a blue curtain. In the right-hand corner, at the back, the entrance door; farther forward, on the same side, a door leading to the sitting-room. Two doors on the opposite side, and between them an iron stove. At the back, a wide double sliding-door. The studio is plainly but comfortably fitted up and furnished. Between the doors on the right, standing out a little from the wall, a sofa with a table and some chairs; on the table a lighted lamp with a shade; beside the stove an old arm-chair. Photographic instruments and apparatus of different kinds lying about the room. Against the back wall, to the left of the double door, stands a bookcase contain-ing a few books, boxes, and bottles of chemicals, instruments, tools, and other objects. Photographs and small articles, such as camel's-hair pencils, paper, and so forth, lie on the table.

GINA EKDAL sits on a chair by the table, sewing. HEDVIG is sitting on the sofa, with her hands shading her eyes and her thumbs in her ears, reading a book.

GINA: [Glances once or twice at HEDVIG, as if with secret anxiety; then says:] Hedvig!

HEDVIG: [Does not hear.]

GINA: [Repeats more loudly.] Hedvig!

HEDVIG: [Takes away her hands and looks up.] Yes, mother?

GINA: Hedvig dear, you mustn't sit reading any longer now.

HEDVIG: Oh mother, mayn't I read a little more? Just a little bit?

GINA: No no, you must put away your book now. Father doesn't like it; he never reads hisself in the evening.

HEDVIG: [*Shuts the book.*] No, father doesn't care much about reading.

GINA: [*Puts aside her sewing and takes up a lead pencil and a little account-book from the table.*] Can you remember how much we paid for the butter to-day?

HEDVIG: It was one crown sixty-five.

GINA: That's right. [*Puts it down.*] It's terrible what a lot of butter we get through in this house. Then there was the smoked sausage, and the cheese—let me see— [*Writes.*]—and the ham— [*Adds up.*] Yes, that makes just——

HEDVIG: And then the beer.

GINA: Yes, to be sure. [*Writes.*] How it do mount up! But we can't manage with no less.

HEDVIG: And then you and I didn't need anything hot for dinner, as father was out.

GINA: No; that was so much to the good. And then I took eight crowns fifty for the photographs.

HEDVIG: Really! So much as that?

GINA: Exactly eight crowns fifty.

[*Silence.* GINA *takes up her sewing again,* HEDVIG *takes paper and pencil and begins to draw, shading her eyes with her left hand.*]

HEDVIG: Isn't it jolly to think that father is at Mr. Werle's big dinner-party?

GINA: You know he's not really Mr. Werle's guest. It was the son invited him. [*After a pause.*] We have nothing to do with that Mr. Werle.

HEDVIG: I'm longing for father to come home. He promised to ask Mrs. Sörby for something nice for me.

GINA: Yes, there's plenty of good things going in that house, I can tell you.

HEDVIG: [*Goes on drawing.*] And I believe I'm a little hungry too.

[OLD EKDAL, *with the paper parcel under his arm and another parcel in his coat pocket, comes in by the entrance door.*]

GINA: How late you are to-day, grandfather!

EKDAL: They had locked the office door. Had to wait in Gråberg's room. And then they let me through—h'm.

HEDVIG: Did you get some more copying to do, grandfather?

EKDAL: This whole packet. Just look.

GINA: That's capital.

HEDVIG: And you have another parcel in your pocket.

EKDAL: Eh? Oh never mind, that's noth-

ing. [*Puts his stick away in a corner.*] This work will keep me going a long time, Gina. [*Opens one of the sliding-doors in the back wall a little.*] Hush! [*Peeps into the room for a moment, then pushes the door carefully to again.*] Hee-hee! They're fast asleep, all the lot of them. And she's gone into the basket herself. Hee-hee!

HEDVIG: Are you sure she isn't cold in that basket, grandfather?

EKDAL: Not a bit of it! Cold? With all that straw? [*Goes towards the farther door on the left.*] There are matches in here, I suppose.

GINA: The matches is on the drawers.

[EKDAL *goes into his room.*]

HEDVIG: It's nice that grandfather has got all that copying.

GINA: Yes, poor old father; it means a bit of pocket-money for him.

HEDVIG: And he won't be able to sit the whole forenoon down at that horrid Madam Eriksen's.

GINA: No more he won't.

[*Short silence.*]

HEDVIG: Do you suppose they are still at the dinner-table?

GINA: Goodness knows; as like as not.

HEDVIG: Think of all the delicious things father is having to eat! I'm certain he'll be in splendid spirits when he comes. Don't you think so, mother?

GINA: Yes; and if only we could tell him that we'd got the room let——

HEDVIG: But we don't need that this evening.

GINA: Oh, we'd be none the worse of it, I can tell you. It's no use to us as it is.

HEDVIG: I mean we don't need it this evening, for father will be in a good humour at any rate. It is best to keep the letting of the room for another time.

GINA: [*Looks across at her.*] You like having some good news to tell father when he comes home in the evening?

HEDVIG: Yes; for then things are pleasanter somehow.

GINA: [*Thinking to herself.*] Yes, yes, there's something in that.

[OLD EKDAL *comes in again and is going out by the foremost door to the left.*]

GINA: [*Half turning in her chair.*] Do you want something out of the kitchen, grandfather?

EKDAL: Yes, yes, I do. Don't you trouble. [*Goes out.*]

GINA: He's not poking away at the fire, is

he? [*Waits a moment.*] Hedvig, go and see what he's about.

[EKDAL *comes in again with a small jug of steaming hot water.*]

HEDVIG: Have you been getting some hot water, grandfather?

EKDAL: Yes, hot water. Want it for something. Want to write, and the ink has got as thick as porridge—h'm.

GINA: But you'd best have your supper, first, grandfather. It's laid in there.

EKDAL: Can't be bothered with supper, Gina. Very busy, I tell you. No one's to come to my room. No one—h'm.

[*He goes into his room;* GINA *and* HEDVIG *look at each other.*]

GINA: [*Softly.*] Can you imagine where he's got money from?

HEDVIG: From Gråberg, perhaps.

GINA: Not a bit of it. Gråberg always sends the money to me.

HEDVIG: Then he must have got a bottle on credit somewhere.

GINA: Poor grandfather, who'd give him credit?

[HIALMAR EKDAL, *in an overcoat and grey felt hat, comes in from the right.*]

GINA: [*Throws down her sewing and rises.*] Why, Ekdal. Is that you already?

HEDVIG: [*At the same time jumping up.*] Fancy your coming so soon, father!

HIALMAR: [*Taking off his hat.*] Yes, most of the people were coming away.

HEDVIG: So early?

HIALMAR: Yes, it was a dinner-party, you know. [*Is taking off his overcoat.*]

GINA: Let me help you.

HEDVIG: Me too.

[*They draw off his coat;* GINA *hangs it up on the back wall.*]

HEDVIG: Were there many people there, father?

HIALMAR: Oh no, not many. We were about twelve or fourteen at table.

GINA: And you had some talk with them all?

HIALMAR: Oh yes, a little; but Gregers took me up most of the time.

GINA: Is Gregers as ugly as ever?

HIALMAR: Well, he's not very much to look at. Hasn't the old man come home?

HEDVIG: Yes, grandfather is in his room, writing.

HIALMAR: Did he say anything?

GINA: No, what should he say?

HIALMAR: Didn't he say anything about——? I heard something about his

having been with Gråberg. I'll go in and see him for a moment.

GINA: No, no, better not.

HIALMAR: Why not? Did he say he didn't want me to go in?

GINA: I don't think he wants to see nobody this evening——

HEDVIG: [*Making signs.*] H'm—h'm!

GINA: [*Not noticing.*] ——he has been in to fetch hot water——

HIALMAR: Aha! Then he's——

GINA: Yes, I suppose so.

HIALMAR: Oh God! my poor old white-haired father!—Well, well; there let him sit and get all the enjoyment he can.

[OLD EKDAL, *in an indoor coat and with a lighted pipe, comes from his room.*]

EKDAL: Got home? Thought it was you I heard talking.

HIALMAR: Yes, I have just come.

EKDAL: You didn't see me, did you?

HIALMAR: No; but they told me you had passed through—so I thought I would follow you.

EKDAL: H'm, good of you, Hialmar.—Who were they, all those fellows?

HIALMAR: Oh, all sorts of people. There was Chamberlain Flor, and Chamberlain Balle, and Chamberlain Kaspersen, and Chamberlain—this, that, and the other—I don't know who all——

EKDAL: [*Nodding.*] Hear that, Gina! Chamberlains every one of them!

GINA: Yes, I hear as they're terrible genteel in that house nowadays.

HEDVIG: Did the Chamberlains sing, father? Or did they read aloud?

HIALMAR: No, they only talked nonsense. They wanted me to recite something for them; but I knew better than that.

EKDAL: You weren't to be persuaded, eh?

GINA: Oh, you might have done it.

HIALMAR: No; one mustn't be at everybody's beck and call. [*Walks about the room.*] That's not my way, at any rate.

EKDAL: No no; Hialmar's not to be had for the asking, he isn't.

HIALMAR: I don't see why I should bother myself to entertain people on the rare occasions when I go into society. Let the others exert themselves. These fellows go from one great dinner-table to the next and gorge and guzzle day out and day in. It's for them to bestir themselves and do something in return for all the good feeding they get.

GINA: But you didn't say that?

HIALMAR: [*Humming.*] Ho-ho-ho—; faith, I gave them a bit of my mind.

EKDAL: Not the Chamberlains?

HIALMAR: Oh, why not? [*Lightly.*] After that, we had a little discussion about Tokay.

EKDAL: Tokay! There's a fine wine for you!

HIALMAR: [*Comes to a standstill.*] It may be a fine wine. But of course you know the vintages differ; it all depends on how much sunshine the grapes have had.

GINA: Why, you know everything, Ekdal.

EKDAL: And did they dispute that?

HIALMAR: They tried to; but they were requested to observe that it was just the same with Chamberlains—that with them, too, different batches were of different qualities.

GINA: What things you do think of!

EKDAL: Hee-hee! So they got that in their pipes too?

HIALMAR: Right in their teeth.

EKDAL: Do you hear that, Gina? He said it right in the very teeth of all the Chamberlains.

GINA: Fancy—! Right in their teeth!

HIALMAR: Yes, but I don't want it talked about. One doesn't speak of such things. The whole affair passed off quite amicably of course. They were nice, genial fellows; I didn't want to wound them—not I!

EKDAL: Right in their teeth, though—!

HEDVIG: [*Caressingly.*] How nice it is to see you in a dress-coat! It suits you so well, father.

HIALMAR: Yes, don't you think so? And this one really sits to perfection. It fits almost as if it had been made for me;—a little tight in the arm-holes perhaps;—help me, Hedvig. [*Takes off the coat.*] I think I'll put on my jacket. Where is my jacket, Gina?

GINA: Here it is. [*Brings the jacket and helps him.*]

HIALMAR: That's it! Don't forget to send the coat back to Molvik first thing to-morrow morning.

GINA: [*Laying it away.*] I'll be sure and see to it.

HIALMAR: [*Stretching himself.*] After all, there's a more homely feeling about this. A free-and-easy indoor costume suits my whole personality better. Don't you think so, Hedvig?

HEDVIG: Yes, father.

HIALMAR: When I loosen my necktie into a pair of flowing ends—like this—eh?

HEDVIG: Yes, that goes so well with your moustache and the sweep of your curls.

HIALMAR: I should not call them curls exactly; I should rather say locks.

HEDVIG: Yes, they are too big for curls.

HIALMAR: Locks describes them better.

HEDVIG: [*After a pause, twitching his jacket.*] Father.

HIALMAR: Well, what is it?

HEDVIG: Oh, you know very well.

HIALMAR: No, really I don't——

HEDVIG: [*Half laughing, half whimpering.*] Oh yes, father; now don't tease me any longer!

HIALMAR: Why, what do you mean?

HEDVIG: [*Shaking him.*] Oh what nonsense; come, where are they, father? All the good things you promised me, you know?

HIALMAR: Oh—if I haven't forgotten all about them!

HEDVIG: Now you're only teasing me, father! Oh, it's too bad of you! Where have you put them?

HIALMAR: No, I positively forgot to get anything. But wait a little! I have something else for you, Hedvig. [*Goes and searches in the pockets of the coat.*]

HEDVIG: [*Skipping and clapping her hands.*] Oh mother, mother!

GINA: There, you see; if you only give him time——

HIALMAR: [*With a paper.*] Look, here it is.

HEDVIG: That? Why, that's only a paper.

HIALMAR: That is the bill of fare, my dear; the whole bill of fare. Here you see: "Menu"—that means bill of fare.

HEDVIG: Haven't you anything else?

HIALMAR: I forgot the other things, I tell you. But you may take my word for it, these dainties are very unsatisfying. Sit down at the table and read the bill of fare, and then I'll describe to you how the dishes taste. Here you are, Hedvig.

HEDVIG: [*Gulping down her tears.*] Thank you.

[*She seats herself, but does not read;* GINA *makes signs to her;* HIALMAR *notices it.*]

HIALMAR: [*Pacing up and down the room.*] It's monstrous what absurd things the father of a family is expected to think of; and if he forgets the smallest trifle, he is treated to sour faces at once. Well, well, one gets used to that too. [*Stops near the stove, by the old man's chair.*] Have you peeped in there this evening, father?

EKDAL: Yes, to be sure I have. She's gone into the basket.

HIALMAR: Ah, she has gone into the basket. Then she's beginning to get used to it.

EKDAL: Yes; just as I prophesied. But you know there are still a few little things——

HIALMAR: A few improvements, yes.

EKDAL: They've got to be made, you know.

HIALMAR: Yes, let us have a talk about the improvements, father. Come, let us sit on the sofa.

EKDAL: All right. H'm—think I'll just fill my pipe first. Must clean it out, too. H'm.

[He goes into his room.]

GINA: [Smiling to HIALMAR.] His pipe!

HIALMAR: Oh yes yes, Gina; let him alone—the poor shipwrecked old man.— Yes, these improvements—we had better get them out of hand to-morrow.

GINA: You'll hardly have time to-morrow, Ekdal.

HEDVIG: [Interposing.] Oh yes he will, mother!

GINA: ——for remember them prints that has to be retouched; they've sent for them time after time.

HIALMAR: There now! those prints again! I shall get them finished all right! Have any new orders come in?

GINA: No, worse luck; to-morrow I have nothing but those two sittings, you know.

HIALMAR: Nothing else? Oh no, if people won't set about things with a will——

GINA: But what more can I do? Don't I advertise in the papers as much as we can afford?

HIALMAR: Yes, the papers, the papers; you see how much good they do. And I suppose no one has been to look at the room either?

GINA: No, not yet.

HIALMAR: That was only to be expected. If people won't keep their eyes open——. Nothing can be done without a real effort, Gina!

HEDVIG: [Going towards him.] Shall I fetch you the flute, father?

HIALMAR: No; no flute for me; I want no pleasures in this world. [Pacing about.] Yes, indeed I will work to-morrow; you shall see if I don't. You may be sure I shall work as long as my strength holds out.

GINA: But my dear good Ekdal, I didn't mean it in that way.

HEDVIG: Father, mayn't I bring in a bottle of beer?

HIALMAR: No, certainly not. I require nothing, nothing—— [Comes to a standstill.] Beer? Was it beer you were talking about?

HEDVIG: [Cheerfully.] Yes, father; beautiful fresh beer.

HIALMAR: Well—since you insist upon it, you may bring in a bottle.

GINA: Yes, do; and we'll be nice and cosy.

[HEDVIG runs towards the kitchen door.]

HIALMAR: [By the stove, stops her, looks at her, puts his arm round her neck and presses her to him.] Hedvig, Hedvig!

HEDVIG: [With tears of joy.] My dear, kind father!

HIALMAR: No, don't call me that. Here have I been feasting at the rich man's table, —battening at the groaning board——! And I couldn't even——!

GINA: [Sitting at the table.] Oh nonsense, nonsense, Ekdal.

HIALMAR: It's not nonsense! And yet you must'nt be too hard upon me. You know that I love you for all that.

HEDVIG: [Throwing her arms round him.] And we love you, oh so dearly, father!

HIALMAR: And if I am unreasonable once in a while,—why then—you must remember that I am a man beset by a host of cares. There, there! [Dries his eyes.] No beer at such a moment as this. Give me the flute.

[HEDVIG runs to the bookcase and fetches it.]

HIALMAR: Thanks! That's right. With my flute in my hand and you two at my side— ah——!

[HEDVIG seats herself at the table near GINA; HIALMAR paces backwards and forwards, pipes up vigorously, and plays a Bohemian peasant dance, but in a slow plaintive tempo, and with sentimental expression.]

HIALMAR: [Breaking off the melody, holds out his left hand to GINA, and says with emotion.] Our roof may be poor and humble, Gina; but it is home. And with all my heart I say: here dwells my happiness.

[He begins to play again; almost immediately after, a knocking is heard at the entrance door.]

GINA. [Rising.] Hush, Ekdal,—I think there's some one at the door.

HIALMAR: [*Laying the flute on the book-case.*] There! Again!

[*Gina goes and opens the door.*]

GREGERS WERLE: [*In the passage.*] Excuse me——

GINA: [*Starting back slightly.*] Oh!

GREGERS: ——does not Mr. Ekdal, the photographer, live here?

GINA: Yes, he does.

HIALMAR: [*Going towards the door.*] Gregers! You here after all? Well, come in then.

GREGERS: [*Coming in.*] I told you I would come and look you up.

HIALMAR: But this evening——? Have you left the party?

GREGERS: I have left both the party and my father's house.—Good evening, Mrs. Ekdal. I don't know whether you recognise me?

GINA: Oh yes; it's not difficult to know young Mr. Werle again.

GREGERS: No, I am like my mother; and no doubt you remember her.

HIALMAR: Left your father's house, did you say?

GREGERS: Yes, I have gone to a hotel.

HIALMAR: Indeed. Well, since you're here, take off your coat and sit down.

GREGERS: Thanks.

[*He takes off his overcoat. He is now dressed in a plain grey suit of a countrified cut.*]

HIALMAR: Here, on the sofa. Make yourself comfortable.

[GREGERS *seats himself on the sofa;* HIALMAR *takes a chair at the table.*]

GREGERS: [*Looking around him.*] So these are your quarters, Hialmar—this is your home.

HIALMAR: This is the studio, as you see——

GINA: But it's the largest of our rooms, so we generally sit here.

HIALMAR: We used to live in a better place; but this flat has one great advantage: there are such capital outer rooms——

GINA: And we have a room on the other side of the passage that we can let.

GREGERS: [*To* HIALMAR.] Ah—so you have lodgers too?

HIALMAR: No, not yet. They're not so easy to find, you see; you have to keep your eyes open. [*To* HEDVIG.] What about that beer, eh?

[HEDVIG *nods and goes out into the kitchen.*]

GREGERS: So that is your daughter?

HIALMAR: Yes. that is Hedvig.

GREGERS: And she is your only child?

HIALMAR: Yes, the only one. She is the joy of our lives, and—[*lowering his voice*]—at the same time our deepest sorrow, Gregers.

GREGERS: What do you mean?

HIALMAR: She is in serious danger of losing her eyesight.

GREGERS: Becoming blind?

HIALMAR: Yes. Only the first symptoms have appeared as yet, and she may not feel it much for some time. But the doctor has warned us. It is coming, inexorably.

GREGERS: What a terrible misfortune! How do you account for it?

HIALMAR: [*Sighs.*] Hereditary, no doubt.

GREGERS: [*Starting.*] Hereditary?

GINA: Ekdal's mother had weak eyes.

HIALMAR: Yes, so my father says; I can't remember her.

GREGERS: Poor child! And how does she take it?

HIALMAR: Oh, you can imagine we haven't the heart to tell her of it. She dreams of no danger. Gay and careless and chirping like a little bird, she flutters onward into a life of endless night. [*Overcome.*] Oh, it is cruelly hard on me, Gregers.

[HEDVIG *brings a tray with beer and glasses, which she sets upon the table.*]

HIALMAR: [*Stroking her hair.*] Thanks, thanks, Hedvig.

[HEDVIG *puts her arm round his neck and whispers in his ear.*]

HIALMAR: No, no bread and butter just now. [*Looks up.*] But perhaps you would like some, Gregers.

GREGERS: [*With a gesture of refusal.*] No, no thank you.

HIALMAR: [*Still melancholy.*] Well, you can bring in a little all the same. If you have a crust, that is all I want. And plenty of butter on it, mind.

[HEDVIG *nods gaily and goes out into the kitchen again.*]

GREGERS: [*Who has been following her with his eyes.*] She seems quite strong and healthy otherwise.

GINA: Yes. In other ways there's nothing amiss with her, thank goodness.

GREGERS: She promises to be very like you, Mrs. Ekdal. How old is she now?

GINA: Hedvig is close on fourteen; her birthday is the day after to-morrow.

GREGERS: She is pretty tall for her age, then.

GINA: Yes, she's shot up wonderful this last year.

GREGERS: It makes one realise one's own age to see these young people growing up. —How long is it now since you were married?

GINA: We've been married—let me see— just on fifteen years.

GREGERS: Is it so long as that?

GINA: [*Becomes attentive; looks at him.*] Yes, it is indeed.

HIALMAR: Yes, so it is. Fifteen years all but a few months. [*Changing his tone.*] They must have been long years for you, up at the works, Gregers.

GREGERS: They seemed long while I was living them; now they are over, I hardly know how the time has gone.

[OLD EKDAL *comes from his room without his pipe, but with his old-fashioned uniform cap on his head; his gait is somewhat unsteady.*]

EKDAL: Come now, Hialmar, let's sit down and have a good talk about this—h'm —what was it again?

HIALMAR: [*Going towards him.*] Father, we have a visitor here—Gregers Werle.—I don't know if you remember him.

EKDAL: [*Looking at* GREGERS, *who has risen.*] Werle? Is that the son? What does he want with me?

HIALMAR: Nothing; it's me he has come to see.

EKDAL: Oh! Then there's nothing wrong?

HIALMAR: No, no, of course not.

EKDAL: [*With a large gesture.*] Not that I'm afraid, you know; but——

GREGERS: [*Goes over to him.*] I bring you a greeting from your old hunting-grounds, Lieutenant Ekdal.

EKDAL: Hunting-grounds?

GREGERS: Yes, up in Höidal, about the works, you know.

EKDAL: Oh, up there. Yes, I knew all those places well in the old days.

GREGERS: You were a great sportsman then.

EKDAL: So I was, I don't deny it. You're looking at my uniform cap. I don't ask anybody's leave to wear it in the house. So long as I don't go out in the streets with it——

[HEDVIG *brings a plate of bread and butter, which she puts upon the table.*]

HIALMAR: Sit down, father, and have a glass of beer. Help yourself, Gregers.

[EKDAL *mutters and stumbles over to the sofa.* GREGERS *seats himself on the chair nearest to him,* HIALMAR *on the other side of* GREGERS. GINA *sits a little way from the table, sewing;* HEDVIG *stands beside her father.*]

GREGERS: Can you remember, Lieutenant Ekdal, how Hialmar and I used to come up and visit you in the summer and at Christmas?

EKDAL: Did you? No, no, no; I don't remember it. But sure enough I've been a tidy bit of a sportsman in my day. I've shot bears too. I've shot nine of 'em, no less.

GREGERS: [*Looking sympathetically at him.*] And now you never get any shooting?

EKDAL: Can't just say that, sir. Get a shot now and then perhaps. Of course not in the old way. For the woods you see—the woods, the woods——! [*Drinks.*] Are the woods fine up there now?

GREGERS: Not so fine as in your time. They have been thinned a good deal.

EKDAL: Thinned? [*More softly, and as if afraid.*] It's dangerous work that. Bad things come of it. The woods revenge themselves.

HIALMAR: [*Filling up his glass.*] Come— a little more, father.

GREGERS: How can a man like you— such a man for the open air—live in the midst of a stuffy town, boxed within four walls?

EKDAL: [*Laughs quietly and glances at* HIALMAR.] Oh, it's not so bad here. Not at all so bad.

GREGERS: But don't you miss all the things that used to be a part of your very being—the cool sweeping breezes, the free life in the woods and on the uplands, among beasts and birds——?

EKDAL: [*Smiling.*] Hialmar, shall we let him see it?

HIALMAR: [*Hastily and a little embarrassed.*] Oh no no, father; not this evening.

GREGERS: What does he want to show me?

HIALMAR: Oh, it's only something—you can see it another time.

GREGERS: [*Continues, to the old man.*] You see I have been thinking, Lieutenant Ekdal, that you should come up with me to the works; I am sure to be going back soon. No doubt you could get some copying there too. And here, you have nothing on earth to interest you—nothing to liven you up.

EKDAL: [*Stares in astonishment at him.*] Have *I* nothing on earth to——!

GREGERS: Of course you have Hialmar; but then he has his own family. And a man like you, who has always had such a passion for what is free and wild——

EKDAL: [*Thumps the table.*] Hialmar, he shall see it!

HIALMAR: Oh, do you think it's worth while, father? It's all dark.

EKDAL: Nonsense; it's moonlight. [*Rises.*] He shall see it, I tell you. Let me pass! Come and help me, Hialmar.

HEDVIG: Oh yes, do, father!

HIALMAR: [*Rising.*] Very well then.

GREGERS: [*To* GINA.] What is it?

GINA: Oh, nothing so very wonderful, after all.

[EKDAL *and* HIALMAR *have gone to the back wall and are each pushing back a side of the sliding door;* HEDVIG *helps the old man;* GREGERS *remains standing by the sofa;* GINA *sits still and sews. Through the open doorway a large, deep irregular garret is seen with odd nooks and corners; a couple of stove-pipes running through it, from rooms below. There are skylights through which clear moonbeams shine in on some parts of the great room; others lie in deep shadow.*]

EKDAL: [*To* GREGERS.] You may come close up if you like.

GREGERS: [*Going over to them.*] Why, what is it?

EKDAL: Look for yourself. H'm.

HIALMAR: [*Somewhat embarrassed.*] This belongs to father, you understand.

GREGERS: [*At the door, looks into the garret.*] Why, you keep poultry, Lieutenant Ekdal.

EKDAL: Should think we did keep poultry. They've gone to roost now. But you should just see our fowls by daylight, sir!

HEDVIG: And there's a——

EKDAL: Sh—sh! don't say anything about it yet.

GREGERS: And you have pigeons too, I see.

EKDAL: Oh yes, haven't we just got pigeons! They have their nest-boxes up there under the rooftree; for pigeons like to roost high, you see.

HIALMAR: They aren't all common pigeons.

EKDAL: Common! Should think not indeed! We have tumblers, and a pair of pouters, too. But come here! Can you see that hutch down there by the wall?

GREGERS: Yes; what do you use it for?

EKDAL: That's where the rabbits sleep, sir.

GREGERS: Dear me; so you have rabbits too?

EKDAL: Yes, you may take my word for it, we have rabbits! He wants to know if we have rabbits, Hialmar! H'm! But now comes the thing, let me tell you! Here we have it! Move away, Hedvig. Stand here; that's right,—and now look down there.—Don't you see a basket with straw in it?

GREGERS: Yes. And I can see a fowl lying in the basket.

EKDAL: H'm—"a fowl"——

GREGERS: Isn't it a duck?

EKDAL: [*Hurt.*] Why, of course it's a duck.

HIALMAR: But what kind of duck, do you think?

HEDVIG: It's not just a common duck——

EKDAL: Sh!

GREGERS: And it's not a Muscovy duck either.

EKDAL: No, Mr.—Werle; it's not a Muscovy duck; for it's a wild duck!

GREGERS: Is it really? A wild duck?

EKDAL: Yes, that's what it is. That "fowl" as you call it—is the wild duck. It's our wild duck, sir.

HEDVIG: My wild duck. It belongs to me.

GREGERS: And can it live up here in the garret? Does it thrive?

EKDAL: Of course it has a trough of water to splash about in, you know.

HIALMAR: Fresh water every other day.

GINA: [*Turning towards* HIALMAR.] But my dear Ekdal, it's getting icy cold here.

EKDAL: H'm, we had better shut up then. It's as well not to disturb their night's rest, too. Close up, Hedvig.

[HIALMAR *and* HEDVIG *push the garret doors together.*]

EKDAL: Another time you shall see her properly. [*Seats himself in the arm-chair by the stove.*] Oh, they're curious things, these wild ducks, I can tell you.

GREGERS: How did you manage to catch it, Lieutenant Ekdal?

EKDAL: *I* didn't catch it. There's a certain man in this town whom we have to thank for it.

GREGERS: [*Starts slightly.*] That man was not my father, was he?

EKDAL: You've hit it. Your father and no one else. H'm.

HIALMAR: Strange that you should guess that, Gregers.

GREGERS: You were telling me that you owed so many things to my father; and so I thought perhaps——

GINA: But we didn't get the duck from Mr. Werle himself——

EKDAL: It's Håkon Werle we have to thank for her, all the same, Gina. [*To* GREGERS.] He was shooting from a boat, you see, and he brought her down. But your father's sight is not very good now. H'm; she was only wounded.

GREGERS: Ah! She got a couple of slugs in her body, I suppose.

HIALMAR: Yes, two or three.

HEDVIG: She was hit under the wing, so that she couldn't fly.

GREGERS: And I suppose she dived to the bottom, eh?

EKDAL: [*Sleepily, in a thick voice.*] Of course. Always do that, wild ducks do. They shoot to the bottom as deep as they can get, sir—and bite themselves fast in the tangle and seaweed—and all the devil's own mess that grows down there. And they never come up again.

GREGERS: But your wild duck came up again, Lieutenant Ekdal.

EKDAL: He had such an amazingly clever dog, your father had. And that dog—he dived in after the duck and fetched her up again.

GREGERS: [*Who has turned to* HIALMAR.] And then she was sent to you here?

HIALMAR: Not at once; at first your father took her home. But she wouldn't thrive there; so Pettersen was told to put an end to her——

EKDAL: [*Half asleep.*] H'm—yes—Pettersen—that ass——

HIALMAR: [*Speaking more softly.*] That was how we got her, you see; for father knows Pettersen a little; and when he heard about the wild duck he got him to hand her over to us.

GREGERS: And now she thrives as well as possible in the garret there?

HIALMAR: Yes, wonderfully well. She has got fat. You see, she has lived in there so long now that she has forgotten her natural wild life; and it all depends on that.

GREGERS: You are right there, Hialmar. Be sure you never let her get a glimpse of the sky and the sea——. But I mustn't stay any longer; I think your father is asleep.

HIALMAR: Oh, as for that——

GREGERS: But, by-the-bye—you said you had a room to let—a spare room?

HIALMAR: Yes; what then? Do you know of anybody——?

GREGERS: Can I have that room?

HIALMAR: You?

GINA: Oh no, Mr. Werle, you——

GREGERS: May I have the room? If so, I'll take possession first thing to-morrow morning.

HIALMAR: Yes, with the greatest pleasure——

GINA: But, Mr. Werle, I'm sure it's not at all the sort of room for you.

HIALMAR: Why, Gina! how can you say that?

GINA: Why, because the room's neither large enough nor light enough, and——

GREGERS: That really doesn't matter, Mrs. Ekdal.

HIALMAR: I call it quite a nice room, and not at all badly furnished either.

GINA: But remember the pair of them underneath.

GREGERS: What pair?

GINA: Well, there's one as has been a tutor——

HIALMAR: That's Molvik—Mr. Molvik, B.A.

GINA: And then there's a doctor, by the name of Relling.

GREGERS: Relling? I know him a little; he practised for a time up in Höidal.

GINA: They're a regular rackety pair, they are. As often as not, they're out on the loose in the evenings; and then they come home at all hours, and they're not always just——

GREGERS: One soon gets used to that sort of thing. I daresay I shall be like the wild duck——

GINA: H'm; I think you ought to sleep upon it first, anyway.

GREGERS: You seem very unwilling to have me in the house, Mrs. Ekdal.

GINA: Oh no! What makes you think that?

HIALMAR: Well, you really behave strangely about it, Gina. [*To* GREGERS.] Then I suppose you intend to remain in the town for the present?

GREGERS: [*Putting on his overcoat.*] Yes, now I intend to remain here.

HIALMAR: And yet not at your father's? What do you propose to do, then?

GREGERS: Ah, if I only knew that, Hialmar, I shouldn't be so badly off! But when one has the misfortune to be called Gregers—! "Gregers"—and then "Werle" after it; did you ever hear anything so hideous?

HIALMAR: Oh, I don't think so at all.

GREGERS: Ugh! Bah! I feel I should like to spit upon the fellow that answers to such a name. But when a man is once for all doomed to be Gregers—Werle in this world, as I am——

HIALMAR: [Laughs.] Ha ha! If you weren't Gregers Werle, what would you like to be?

GREGERS: If I could choose, I should like best to be a clever dog.

GINA: A dog!

HEDVIG: [Involuntarily.] Oh no!

GREGERS; Yes, an amazingly clever dog; one that goes to the bottom after wild ducks when they dive and bite themselves fast in tangle and sea-weed, down among the ooze.

HIALMAR: Upon my word now, Gregers —I don't in the least know what you're driving at.

GREGERS: Oh well, you might not be much the wiser if you did. It's understood, then, that I move in early to-morrow morning. [To GINA.] I won't give you any trouble; I do everything for myself. [To HIALMAR.] We can talk about the rest to-morrow.—Good-night, Mrs. Ekdal. [Nods to HEDVIG.] Good-night.

GINA: Good-night, Mr. Werle.

HEDVIG: Good-night.

HIALMAR: [Who has lighted a candle.] Wait a moment; I must show you a light; the stairs are sure to be dark.

[GREGERS and HIALMAR go out by the passage door.]

GINA: [Looking straight before her, with her sewing in her lap.] Wasn't that queer-like talk about wanting to be a dog?

HEDVIG: Do you know, mother—I believe he meant something quite different by that.

GINA: Why, what should he mean?

HEDVIG: Oh, I don't know; but it seemed to me he meant something different from what he said—all the time.

GINA: Do you think so? Yes, it was sort of queer.

HIALMAR: [Comes back.] The lamp was still burning. [Puts out the candle and sets it down.] Ah, now one can get a mouthful of food at last. [Begins to eat the bread and butter.] Well, you see, Gina—if only you keep your eyes open——

GINA: How, keep your eyes open——?

HIALMAR: Why, haven't we at last had the luck to get the room let? And just think —to a person like Gregers—a good old friend.

GINA: Well, I don't know what to say about it.

HEDVIG: Oh mother, you'll see; it'll be such fun!

HIALMAR: You're very strange. You were so bent upon getting the room let before and now you don't like it.

GINA: Yes I do, Ekdal; if it had only been to some one else—— But what do you suppose Mr. Werle will say?

HIALMAR: Old Werle? It doesn't concern him.

GINA: But surely you can see that there's something amiss between them again, or the young man wouldn't be leaving home. You know very well those two can't get on with each other.

HIALMAR: Very likely not, but——

GINA: And now Mr. Werle may fancy it's you that has egged him on——

HIALMAR: Let him fancy so, then! Mr. Werle has done a great deal for me; far be it from me to deny it. But that doesn't make me everlastingly dependent upon him.

GINA: But, my dear Ekdal, maybe grandfather 'll suffer for it. He may lose the little bit of work he gets from Gråberg.

HIALMAR: I could almost say: so much the better! Is it not humiliating for a man like me to see his grey-haired father treated as a pariah? But now I believe the fulness of time is at hand. [Takes a fresh piece of bread and butter.] As sure as I have a mission in life, I mean to fulfil it now!

HEDVIG: Oh yes, father, do!

GINA: Hush! Don't wake him!

HIALMAR: [More softly.] I will fulfil it, I say. The day shall come when—— And that is why I say it's a good thing we have let the room; for that makes me more independent. The man who has a mission in life must be independent. [By the arm-chair, with emotion.] Poor old white-haired father! Rely on your Hialmar. He has broad shoulders—strong shoulders, at any rate. You shall yet wake up some fine day and—— [To GINA.] Do you not believe it?

GINA: [Rising.] Yes, of course I do; but in the meantime suppose we see about getting him to bed.

HIALMAR: Yes, come.

[They take hold of the old man carefully.]

ACT THIRD

HIALMAR EKDAL'S *studio. It is morning: the daylight shines through the large window in the slanting roof; the curtain is drawn back.*

HIALMAR *is sitting at the table, busy retouching a photograph; several others lie before him. Presently* GINA, *wearing her hat and cloak, enters by the passage door; she has a covered basket on her arm.*

HIALMAR: Back already, Gina?

GINA: Oh yes, one can't let the grass grow under one's feet. [*Sets her basket on a chair, and takes off her things.*]

HIALMAR: Did you look in at Gregers' room?

GINA: Yes, that I did. It's a rare sight, I can tell you;· he's made a pretty mess to start off with.

HIALMAR: How so?

GINA: He was determined to do everything for himself, he said; so he sets to work to light the stove, and what must he do but screw down the damper till the whole room is full of smoke. Ugh! There was a smell fit to——

HIALMAR: Well, really!

GINA: But that's not the worst of it; for then he thinks he'll put out the fire, and goes and empties his water-jug into the stove, and so makes the whole floor one filthy puddle.

HIALMAR: How annoying!

GINA: I've got the porter's wife to clear up after him, pig that he is! But the room won't be fit to live in till the afternoon.

HIALMAR: What's he doing with himself in the meantime?

GINA: He said he was going out for a little while.

HIALMAR: I looked in upon him too, for a moment—after you had gone.

GINA: So I heard. You've asked him to lunch.

HIALMAR: Just to a little bit of early lunch, you know. It's his first day—we can hardly do less. You've got something in the house, I suppose?

GINA: I shall have to find something or other.

HIALMAR: And don't cut it too fine, for I fancy Relling and Molvik are coming up too. I just happened to meet Relling on the stairs, you see; so I had to——

GINA: Oh, are we to have those two as well?

HIALMAR: Good Lord—a couple more or less can't make any difference.

OLD EKDAL: [*Opens his door and looks in.*] I say, Hialmar—— [*Sees* GINA.] Oh!

GINA: Do you want anything, grandfather?

EKDAL: Oh no, it doesn't matter. H'm! [*Retires again.*]

GINA: [*Takes up the basket.*] Be sure you see that he doesn't go out.

HIALMAR: All right, all right. And, Gina, a little herring-salad wouldn't be a bad idea; Relling and Molvik were out on the loose again last night.

GINA: If only they don't come before I'm ready for them——

HIALMAR: No, of course they won't; take your own time.

GINA: Very well; and meanwhile you can be working a bit.

HIALMAR: Well, I am working! I am working as hard as I can!

GINA: Then you'll have that job off your hands, you see.

[*She goes out to the kitchen with her basket.* HIALMAR *sits for a time pencilling away at the photograph, in an indolent and listless manner.*]

EKDAL: [*Peeps in, looks round the studio, and says softly:*] Are you busy?

HIALMAR: Yes I'm toiling at these wretched pictures——

EKDAL: Well well, never mind,—since you're so busy—h'm!

[*He goes out again; the door stands open.*]

HIALMAR: [*Continues for some time in silence; then he lays down his brush and goes over to the door.*] Are you busy, father?

EKDAL: [*In a grumbling tone, within.*] If you're busy, I'm busy too. H'm!

HIALMAR: Oh, very well, then. [*Goes to his work again.*]

EKDAL: [*Presently, coming to the door again.*] H'm; I say, Hialmar, I'm not so very busy, you know.

HIALMAR: I thought you were writing.

EKDAL: Oh, devil take it! can't Gråberg wait a day or two? After all, it's not a matter of life and death.

HIALMAR: No; and you're not his slave either.

EKDAL: And about that other business in there——

HIALMAR: Just what I was thinking of. Do you want to go in. Shall I open the door for you?

EKDAL: Well, it wouldn't be a bad notion.

HIALMAR: [*Rises.*] Then we'd have that off our hands.

EKDAL: Yes, exactly. It's got to be ready first thing to-morrow. It is to-morrow, isn't it? H'm?

HIALMAR: Yes, of course it's to-morrow. [HIALMAR *and* EKDAL *push aside each his half of the sliding door. The morning sun is shining in through the skylights; some doves are flying about; others sit cooing, upon the perches; the hens are heard clucking now and then, further back in the garret.*]

HIALMAR: There; now you can get to work, father.

EKDAL: [*Goes in.*] Aren't you coming too?

HIALMAR: Well really, do you know——; I almost think—— [*Sees* GINA *at the kitchen door.*] I? No; I haven't time; I must work. —But now for our new contrivance——

[*He pulls a cord, a curtain slips down inside, the lower part consisting of a piece of old sailcloth, the upper part of a stretched fishing net. The floor of the garret is thus no longer visible.*]

HIALMAR: [*Goes to the table.*] So! Now, perhaps I can sit in peace for a little while.

GINA: Is he rampaging in there again?

HIALMAR: Would you rather have had him slip down to Madam Eriksen's. [*Seats himself.*] Do you want anything? You know you said——

GINA: I only wanted to ask if you think we can lay the table for lunch here?

HIALMAR: Yes; we have no early appointment, I suppose?

GINA: No, I expect no one to-day except those two sweethearts that are to be taken together.

HIALMAR: Why the deuce couldn't they be taken together another day!

GINA: Don't you know, I told them to come in the afternoon, when you are having your nap.

HIALMAR: Oh, that's capital. Very well, let us have lunch here then.

GINA: All right; but there's no hurry about laying the cloth; you can have the table for a good while yet.

HIALMAR: Do you think I am not sticking to my work? I'm at it as hard as I can!

GINA: Then you'll be free later on, you know. [*Goes out into the kitchen again. Short pause.*]

EKDAL: [*In the garret doorway, behind the net.*] Hialmar!

HIALMAR: Well?

EKDAL: Afraid we shall have to move the water-trough, after all.

HIALMAR: What else have I been saying all along?

EKDAL: H'm—h'm—h'm. [*Goes away from the door again.*]

[HIALMAR *goes on working a little; glances toward the garret and half rises.* HEDVIG *comes in from the kitchen.*]

HIALMAR: [*Sits down again hurriedly.*] What do you want?

HEDVIG: I only wanted to come in beside you, father.

HIALMAR. [*After a pause.*] What makes you go prying around like that? Perhaps you are told off to watch me?

HEDVIG: No, no.

HIALMAR: What is your mother doing out there?

HEDVIG: Oh, mother's in the middle of making the herring-salad. [*Goes to the table.*] Isn't there any little thing I could help you with, father?

HIALMAR: Oh no. It is right that I should bear the whole burden—so long as my strength holds out. Set your mind at rest, Hedvig; if only your father keeps his health——

HEDVIG: Oh no, father! You mustn't talk in that horrid way.

[*She wanders about a little, stops by the doorway and looks into the garret.*]

HIALMAR: Tell me, what is he doing?

HEDVIG: I think he's making a new path to the water-trough.

HIALMAR: He can never manage that by himself! And here am I doomed to sit——!

HEDVIG: [*Goes to him.*] Let me take the brush, father; I can do it, quite well.

HIALMAR: Oh nonsense; you will only hurt your eyes.

HEDVIG: Not a bit. Give me the brush.

HIALMAR: [*Rising.*] Well, it won't take more than a minute or two.

HEDVIG: Pooh, what harm can it do then? [*Takes the brush.*] There! [*Seats herself.*] I can begin upon this one.

HIALMAR: But mind you don't hurt your eyes! Do you hear? *I* won't be answerable; you do it on your own responsibility— understand that.

HEDVIG: [*Retouching.*] Yes yes, I understand.

HIALMAR: You are quite clever at it, Hedvig. Only a minute or two, you know. [*He slips through by the edge of the curtain into the garret.* HEDVIG *sits at her work.* HIALMAR *and* EKDAL *are heard disputing inside.*]

HIALMAR: [*Appears behind the net.*] I say, Hedvig—give me those pincers that are lying on the shelf. And the chisel. [*Turns away inside.*] Now you shall see, father. Just let me show you first what I mean! [HEDVIG *has fetched the required tools from the shelf, and hands them to him through the net.*]

HIALMAR: Ah, thanks. I didn't come a moment too soon. [*Goes back from the curtain again; they are heard carpentering and talking inside.* HEDVIG *stands looking in at them. A moment later there is a knock at the passage door; she does not notice it.*]

GREGERS WERLE: [*Bareheaded, in indoor dress, enters and stops near the door.*] H'm——!

HEDVIG: [*Turns and goes towards him.*] Good morning. Please come in.

GREGERS: Thank you. [*Looking towards the garret.*] You seem to have workpeople in the house.

HEDVIG: No, it is only father and grandfather. I'll tell them you are here.

GREGERS: No no, don't do that; I would rather wait a little. [*Seats himself on the sofa.*]

HEDVIG: It looks so untidy here—[*Begins to clear away the photographs.*]

GREGERS: Oh, don't take them away. Are those prints that have to be finished off?

HEDVIG: Yes, they are a few I was helping father with.

GREGERS: Please don't let me disturb you.

HEDVIG: Oh no. [*She gathers the things to her and sits down to work;* GREGERS *looks at her, meanwhile, in silence.*]

GREGERS: Did the wild duck sleep well last night?

HEDVIG: Yes, I think so, thanks.

GREGERS: [*Turning towards the garret.*] It looks quite different by day from what it did last night in the moonlight.

HEDVIG: Yes, it changes ever so much. It looks different in the morning and in the afternoon; and it's different on rainy days from what it is in fine weather.

GREGERS: Have you noticed that?

HEDVIG: Yes, how could I help it?

GREGERS: Are you, too, fond of being in there with the wild duck?

HEDVIG: Yes, when I can manage it——

GREGERS: But I suppose you haven't much spare time; you go to school, no doubt.

HEDVIG: No, not now; father is afraid of my hurting my eyes.

GREGERS: Oh; then he reads with you himself?

HEDVIG: Father has promised to read with me; but he has never had time yet.

GREGERS: Then is there nobody else to give you a little help?

HEDVIG: Yes, there is Mr. Molvik; but he is not always exactly—quite——

GREGERS: Sober?

HEDVIG: Yes, I suppose that's it!

GREGERS: Why, then you must have any amount of time on your hands. And in there I suppose it is a sort of world by itself?

HEDVIG: Oh yes, quite. And there are such lots of wonderful things.

GREGERS: Indeed?

HEDVIG: Yes, there are big cupboards full of books; and a great many of the books have pictures in them.

GREGERS: Aha!

HEDVIG: And there's an old bureau with drawers and flaps, and a big clock with figures that go out and in. But the clock isn't going now.

GREGERS: So time has come to a standstill in there—in the wild duck's domain.

HEDVIG: Yes. And then there's an old

paint-box and things of that sort; and all the books.

GREGERS: And you read the books, I suppose?

HEDVIG: Oh yes, when I get the chance. Most of them are English though, and I don't understand English. But then I look at the pictures.—There is one great big book called "Harrison's History of London." [1] It must be a hundred years old; and there are such heaps of pictures in it. At the beginning there is Death with an hour-glass and a woman. I think that is horrid. But then there are all the other pictures of churches, and castles, and streets, and great ships sailing on the sea.

GREGERS: But tell me, where did all those wonderful things come from?

HEDVIG: Oh, an old sea captain once lived here, and he brought them home with him. They used to call him "The Flying Dutchman." That was curious, because he wasn't a Dutchman at all.

GREGERS: Was he not?

HEDVIG: No. But at last he was drowned at sea; and so he left all those things behind him.

GREGERS: Tell me now—when you are sitting in there looking at the pictures, don't you wish you could travel and see the real world for yourself?

HEDVIG: Oh no! I mean always to stay at home and help father and mother.

GREGERS: To retouch photographs?

HEDVIG: No, not only that. I should love above everything to learn to engrave pictures like those in the English books.

GREGERS: H'm. What does your father say to that?

HEDVIG: I don't think father likes it; father is strange about such things. Only think, he talks of my learning basket-making, and straw-plaiting! But I don't think that would be much good.

GREGERS: Oh no, I don't think so either.

HEDVIG: But father was right in saying that if I had learnt basket-making I could have made the new basket for the wild duck.

GREGERS: So you could; and it was you that ought to have done it, wasn't it?

HEDVIG: Yes, for it's my wild duck.

GREGERS: Of course it is.

HEDVIG: Yes, it belongs to me. But I lend it to father and grandfather as often as they please.

GREGERS: Indeed? What do they do with it?

HEDVIG: Oh, they look after it, and build places for it, and so on.

GREGERS: I see; for no doubt the wild duck is by far the most distinguished inhabitant of the garret?

HEDVIG: Yes, indeed she is; for she is a real wild fowl, you know. And then she is so much to be pitied; she has no one to care for, poor thing.

GREGERS: She has no family, as the rabbits have——

HEDVIG: No. The hens too, many of them, were chickens together; but she has been taken right away from all her friends. And then there is so much that is strange about the wild duck. Nobody knows her, and nobody knows where she came from either.

GREGERS: And she has been down in the depths of the sea.

HEDVIG: [*With a quick glance at him, represses a smile and asks.*] Why do you say "the depths of the sea"?

GREGERS: What else should I say?

HEDVIG: You could say "the bottom of the sea." [1]

GREGERS: Oh, mayn't I just as well say the depths of the sea?

HEDVIG: Yes; but it sounds so strange to me when other people speak of the depths of the sea.

GREGERS: Why so? Tell me why?

HEDVIG: No, I won't; it's so stupid.

GREGERS: Oh no, I am sure it's not. Do tell me why you smiled.

HEDVIG: Well, this is the reason: whenever I come to realise suddenly—in a flash—what is in there, it always seems to me that the whole room and everything in it should be called "the depths of the sea."—But that is so stupid.

GREGERS: You mustn't say that.

HEDVIG: Oh yes, for you know it is only a garret.

GREGERS: [*Looks fixedly at her.*] Are you so sure of that?

HEDVIG: [*Astonished.*] That it's a garret?

---

[1] *A New and Universal History of the Cities of London and Westminster*, by Walter Harrison. London, 1775, folio.

[1] Gregers here uses the old-fashioned expression "havsens bund," while Hedvig would have him use the more common-place "havets bund" or "havbunden."

GREGERS: Are you quite certain of it?
[HEDVIG *is silent, and looks at him open-mouthed.* GINA *comes in from the kitchen with the table things.*]
GREGERS: [*Rising.*] I have come in upon you too early.
GINA: Oh, you must be somewhere; and we're nearly ready now, any way. Clear the table, Hedvig.
[HEDVIG *clears away her things; she and* GINA *lay the cloth during what follows.* GREGERS *seats himself in the arm-chair and turns over an album.*]
GREGERS: I hear you can retouch, Mrs. Ekdal.
GINA: [*With a side glance.*] Yes, I can.
GREGERS: That was exceedingly lucky.
GINA: How—lucky?
GREGERS: Since Ekdal took to photography, I mean.
HEDVIG: Mother can take photographs too.
GINA: Oh, yes; I was bound to learn that.
GREGERS: So it is really you that carry on the business, I suppose?
GINA: Yes, when Ekdal hasn't time himself——
GREGERS: He is a great deal taken up with his old father, I daresay.
GINA: Yes; and then you can't expect a man like Ekdal to do nothing but take car-de-visits of Dick, Tom and Harry.
GREGERS: I quite agree with you; but having once gone in for the thing——
GINA: You can surely understand, Mr. Werle, that Ekdal's not like one of your common photographers.
GREGERS: Of course not; but still——
[*A shot is fired within the garret.*]
GREGERS: [*Starting up.*] What's that?
GINA: Ugh! now they're firing again!
GREGERS: Have they firearms in there?
HEDVIG: They are out shooting.
GREGERS: What! [*At the door of the garret.*] Are you shooting, Hialmar?
HIALMAR: [*Inside the net.*] Are you there? I didn't know; I was so taken up—— [*To* HEDVIG.] Why did you not let us know? [*Comes into the studio.*]
GREGERS: Do you go shooting in the garret?
HIALMAR: [*Showing a double-barrelled pistol.*] Oh, only with this thing.
GINA: Yes, you and grandfather will do yourselves a mischief some day with that there pigstol.

HIALMAR: [*With irritation.*] I believe I have told you that this kind of firearm is called a pistol.
GINA: Oh, that doesn't make it much better, that I can see.
GREGERS: So you have become a sportsman too, Hialmar?
HIALMAR: Only a little rabbit-shooting now and then. Mostly to please father, you understand.
GINA: Men are strange beings; they must always have something to pervert theirselves with.
HIALMAR: [*Snappishly.*] Just so; we must always have something to divert ourselves with.
GINA: Yes, that's just what I say.
HIALMAR: H'm. [*To* GREGERS.] You see the garret is fortunately so situated that no one can hear us shooting. [*Lays the pistol on the top shelf of the bookcase.*] Don't touch the pistol, Hedvig! One of the barrels is loaded; remember that.
GREGERS: [*Looking through the net.*] You have a fowling-piece too, I see.
HIALMAR: That is father's old gun. It's of no use now; something has gone wrong with the lock. But it's fun to have it all the same; for we can take it to pieces now and then, and clean and grease it, and screw it together again.—Of course, it's mostly father that fiddle-faddles with all that sort of thing.
HEDVIG: [*Beside* GREGERS.] Now you can see the wild duck properly.
GREGERS: I was just looking at her. One of her wings seems to me to droop a bit.
HEDVIG: Well, no wonder; her wing was broken, you know.
GREGERS: And she trails one foot a little. Isn't that so?
HIALMAR: Perhaps a very little bit.
HEDVIG: Yes, it was by that foot the dog took hold of her.
HIALMAR: But otherwise she hasn't the least thing the matter with her; and that is simply marvellous for a creature that has a charge of shot in her body, and has been between a dog's teeth——
GREGERS: [*With a glance at* HEDVIG.] ——and that has lain in the depths of the sea—so long.
HEDVIG: [*Smiling.*] Yes.
GINA: [*Laying the table.*] That blessëd wild duck! What a lot of fuss you do make over her.

HIALMAR: H'm;—will lunch soon be ready?

GINA: Yes, directly. Hedvig, you must come and help me now.

[GINA *and* HEDVIG *go out into the kitchen.*]

HIALMAR: [*In a low voice.*] I think you had better not stand there looking in at father; he doesn't like it. [GREGERS *moves away from the garret door.*] Besides I may as well shut up before the others come. [*Claps his hands to drive the fowls back.*] Ssh—ssh, in with you! [*Draws up the curtain and pulls the doors together.*] All the contrivances are my own invention. It's really quite amusing to have things of this sort to potter with, and to put to rights when they get out of order. And it's absolutely necessary, too; for Gina objects to having rabbits and fowls in the studio.

GREGERS: To be sure; and I suppose the studio is your wife's special department?

HIALMAR: As a rule, I leave the everyday details of business to her; for then I can take refuge in the parlour and give my mind to more important things.

GREGERS: What things may they be, Hialmar?

HIALMAR: I wonder you have not asked that question sooner. But perhaps you haven't heard of the invention?

GREGERS: The invention? No.

HIALMAR: Really? Have you not? Oh no, out there in the wilds——

GREGERS: So you have invented something, have you?

HIALMAR: It is not quite completed yet; but I am working at it. You can easily imagine that when I resolved to devote myself to photography, it wasn't simply with the idea of taking likenesses of all sorts of commonplace people.

GREGERS: No; your wife was saying the same thing just now.

HIALMAR: I swore that if I consecrated my powers to this handicraft, I would so exalt it that it should become both an art and a science. And to that end I determined to make this great invention.

GREGERS: And what is the nature of the invention? What purpose does it serve?

HIALMAR: Oh, my dear fellow, you mustn't ask for details yet. It takes time, you see. And you must not think that my motive is vanity. It is not for my own sake that I am working. Oh no; it is my life's mission that stands before me night and day.

GREGERS: What is your life's mission?

HIALMAR: Do you forget the old man with the silver hair?

GREGERS: Your poor father? Well, but what can you do for him?

HIALMAR: I can raise up his self-respect from the dead, by restoring the name of Ekdal to honour and dignity.

GREGERS: Then that is your life's mission?

HIALMAR: Yes. I will rescue the shipwrecked man. For shipwrecked he was, by the very first blast of the storm. Even while those terrible investigations were going on, he was no longer himself. That pistol there—the one we use to shoot rabbits with—has played its part in the tragedy of the house of Ekdal.

GREGERS: The pistol? Indeed?

HIALMAR: When the sentence of imprisonment was passed—he had the pistol in his hand——

GREGERS: Had he——?

HIALMAR: Yes; but he dared not use it. His courage failed him. So broken, so demoralised was he even then! Oh, can you understand it? He, a soldier; he, who had shot nine bears, and who was descended from two lieutenant-colonels—one after the other of course. Can you understand it, Gregers?

GREGERS: Yes, I understand it well enough.

HIALMAR: I cannot. And once more the pistol played a part in the history of our house. When he had put on the grey clothes and was under lock and key—oh, that was a terrible time for me, I can tell you. I kept the blinds drawn down over both my windows. When I peeped out, I saw the sun shining as if nothing had happened. I could not understand it. I saw people going along the street, laughing and talking about indifferent things. I could not understand it. It seemed to me that the whole of existence must be at a standstill—as if under the eclipse.

GREGERS: I felt like that too, when my mother died.

HIALMAR: It was in such an hour that Hialmar Ekdal pointed the pistol at his own breast.

GREGERS: You too thought of——!

HIALMAR: Yes.

GREGERS: But you did not fire?

HIALMAR: No. At the decisive moment I won the victory over myself. I remained in life. But I can assure you it takes some courage to choose life under circumstances like those.

GREGERS: Well, that depends on how you look at it.

HIALMAR: Yes, indeed, it takes courage. But I am glad I was firm: for now I shall soon perfect my invention; and Dr. Relling thinks, as I do myself, that father may be allowed to wear his uniform again. I will demand that as my sole reward.

GREGERS: So that is what he meant about his uniform——?

HIALMAR: Yes, that is what he most yearns for. You can't think how my heart bleeds for him. Every time we celebrate any little family festival—Gina's and my wedding day, or whatever it may be—in comes the old man in the lieutenant's uniform of happier days. But if he only hears a knock at the door—for he daren't show himself to strangers, you know— he hurries back to his room again as fast as his old legs can carry him. Oh, it's heart-rending for a son to see such things!

GREGERS: How long do you think it will take you to finish your invention?

HIALMAR: Come now, you mustn't expect me to enter into particulars like that. An invention is not a thing completely under one's own control. It depends largely on inspiration—on intuition—and it is almost impossible to predict when the inspiration may come.

GREGERS: But it's advancing?

HIALMAR: Yes, certainly, it is advancing. I turn it over in my mind every day; I am full of it. Every afternoon, when I have had my dinner, I shut myself up in the parlour, where I can ponder undisturbed. But I can't be goaded to it; it's not a bit of good; Relling says so too.

GREGERS: And you don't think that all that business in the garret draws you off and distracts you too much?

HIALMAR: No no no; quite the contrary. You mustn't say that. I cannot be everlastingly absorbed in the same laborious train of thought. I must have something alongside of it to fill up the time of waiting. The inspiration, the intuition, you see—when it comes, it comes, and there's an end of it.

GREGERS: My dear Hialmar, I almost think you have something of the wild duck in you.

HIALMAR: Something of the wild duck? How do you mean?

GREGERS: You have dived down and bitten yourself fast in the undergrowth.

HIALMER: Are you alluding to the well-nigh fatal shot that has broken my father's wing—and mine too?

GREGERS: Not exactly to that. I don't say that your wing has been broken; but you have strayed into a poisonous marsh, Hialmar; an insidious disease has taken hold of you, and you have sunk down to die in the dark.

HIALMAR: I? To die in the dark? Look here, Gregers, you must really leave off talking such nonsense.

GREGERS: Don't be afraid; I shall find a way to help you up again. I too have a mission in life now; I found it yesterday.

HIALMAR: That's all very well; but you will please leave me out of it. I can assure you that—apart from my very natural melancholy, of course—I am as contented as any one can wish to be.

GREGERS: Your contentment is an effect of the marsh poison.

HIALMAR: Now, my dear Gregers, pray do not go on about disease and poison; I am not used to that sort of talk. In my house nobody ever speaks to me about unpleasant things.

GREGERS: Ah, that I can easily believe.

HIALMAR: It's not good for me you see. And there are no marsh poisons here, as you express it. The poor photographer's roof is lowly, I know—and my circumstances are narrow. But I am an inventor, and I am the breadwinner of a family. That exalts me above my mean surroundings. —Ah, here comes lunch!

[GINA and HEDVIG bring bottles of ale, a decanter of brandy, glasses, etc. At the same time, RELLING and MOLVIK enter from the passage; they are both without hat or overcoat. MOLVIK is dressed in black.]

GINA: [Placing the things upon the table.] Ah, you two have come in the nick of time.

RELLING: Molvik got it into his head that he could smell herring-salad, and then there was no holding him.—Good morning again, Ekdal.

HIALMAR: Gregers, let me introduce you

to Mr. Molvik. Doctor—— Oh, you know Relling, don't you?

GREGERS: Yes, slightly.

RELLING: Oh, Mr. Werle, junior! Yes, we two have had one or two little skirmishes up at the Höidal works. You've just moved in?

GREGERS: I moved in this morning.

RELLING: Molvik and I live right under you; so you haven't far to go for the doctor and the clergyman, if you should need anything in that line.

GREGERS: Thanks, it's not quite unlikely; for yesterday we were thirteen at table.

HIALMAR: Oh, come now, don't let us get upon unpleasant subjects again!

RELLING: You may make your mind easy, Ekdal; I'll be hanged if the finger of fate points to you.

HIALMAR: I should hope not, for the sake of my family. But let us sit down now, and eat and drink and be merry.

GREGERS: Shall we not wait for your father?

HIALMAR: No, his lunch will be taken into him later. Come along!

[*The men seat themselves at table, and eat and drink.* GINA *and* HEDVIG *go in and out and wait upon them.*]

RELLING: Molvik was frightfully screwed yesterday, Mrs. Ekdal.

GINA: Really? Yesterday again?

RELLING: Didn't you hear him when I brought him home last night.

GINA: No, I can't say I did.

RELLING: That was a good thing, for Molvik was disgusting last night.

GINA: Is that true, Molvik?

MOLVIK: Let us draw a veil over last night's proceedings. That sort of thing is totally foreign to my better self.

RELLING: [*To* GREGERS.] It comes over him like a sort of possession, and then I have to go out on the loose with him. Mr. Molvik is dæmonic, you see.

GREGERS: Dæmonic?

RELLING: Molvik is dæmonic, yes.

GREGERS: H'm.

RELLING: And dæmonic natures are not made to walk straight through the world; they must meander a little now and then.— Well, so you still stick up there at those horrible grimy works?

GREGERS: I have stuck there until now.

RELLING: And did you ever manage to collect that claim you went about presenting?

GREGERS: Claim? [*Understands him.*] Ah, I see.

HIALMAR: Have you been presenting claims, Gregers?

GREGERS: Oh, nonsense.

RELLING: Faith, but he has, though! He went round to all the cottars' cabins presenting something he called "the claim of the ideal."

GREGERS: I was young then.

RELLING: You're right; you were very young. And as for the claim of the ideal—you never got it honoured while I was up there.

GREGERS: Nor since either.

RELLING: Ah, then you've learnt to knock a little discount off, I expect.

GREGERS: Never, when I have a true man to deal with.

HIALMAR: No, I should think not, indeed. A little butter, Gina.

RELLING: And a slice of bacon for Molvik.

MOLVIK: Ugh! not bacon!

[*A knock at the garret door.*]

HIALMAR: Open the door, Hedvig; father wants to come out.

[HEDVIG *goes over and opens the door a little way;* EKDAL *enters with a fresh rabbit-skin; she closes the door after him.*]

EKDAL: Good morning, gentlemen! Good sport to-day. Shot a big one.

HIALMAR: And you've gone and skinned it without waiting for me——!

EKDAL: Salted it too. It's good tender meat, is rabbit; it's sweet; it tastes like sugar. Good appetite to you, gentlemen! [*Goes into his room.*]

MOLVIK: [*Rising.*] Excuse me——; I can't——; I must get downstairs immediately——

RELLING: Drink some soda water, man!

MOLVIK: [*Hurrying away.*] Ugh—ugh! [*Goes out by the passage door.*]

RELLING: [*To* HIALMAR.] Let us drain a glass to the old hunter.

HIALMAR: [*Clinks glasses with him.*] To the undaunted sportsman who has looked death in the face!

RELLING: To the grey-haired—— [*Drinks.*] By-the-bye, is his hair grey or white?

HIALMAR: Something between the two, I fancy; for that matter, he has very few hairs left of any colour.

RELLING: Well well, one can get through

the world with a wig. After all, you are a happy man, Ekdal; you have your noble mission to labour for——

HIALMAR: And I do labour, I can tell you.

RELLING: And then you have your excellent wife, shuffling quietly in and out in her felt slippers, with that see-saw walk of hers, and making everything cosy and comfortable about you.

HIALMAR: Yes, Gina—[Nods to her.]—you are a good help-mate on the path of life.

GINA: Oh, don't sit there cricketizing me.

RELLING: And your Hedvig too, Ekdal!

HIALMAR: [Affected.] The child, yes! The child before everything! Hedvig, come here to me. [Strokes her hair.] What day is it to-morrow, eh?

HEDVIG: [Shaking him.] Oh no, you're not to say anything, father.

HIALMAR: It cuts me to the heart when I think what a poor affair it will be; only a little festivity in the garret——

HEDVIG: Oh, but that's just what I like!

RELLING: Just you wait till the wonderful invention sees the light, Hedvig!

HIALMAR: Yes indeed—then you shall see——! Hedvig, I have resolved to make your future secure. You shall live in comfort all your days. I will demand—something or other—on your behalf. That shall be the poor inventor's sole reward.

HEDVIG: [Whispering, with her arms round his neck.] Oh you dear, kind father!

RELLING: [To GREGERS.] Come now, don't you find it pleasant, for once in a way, to sit at a well-spread table in a happy family circle?

HIALMAR: Ah yes, I really prize these social hours.

GREGERS: For my part, I don't thrive in marsh vapours.

RELLING: Marsh vapours?

HIALMAR: Oh, don't begin with that stuff again!

GINA: Goodness knows there's no vapours in this house, Mr. Werle; I give the place a good airing every blessed day.

GREGERS: [Leaves table.] No airing you can give will drive out the taint I mean.

HIALMAR: Taint!

GINA: Yes, what do you say to that, Ekdal!

RELLING: Excuse me—may it not be you yourself that have brought the taint from those mines up there?

GREGERS: It is like you to call what I bring into this house a taint.

RELLING: [Goes up to him.] Look here, Mr. Werle, junior: I have a strong suspicion that you are still carrying about that "claim of the ideal" large as life, in your coat-tail pocket.

GREGER: I carry it in my breast.

RELLING: Well, wherever you carry it, I advise you not to come dunning us with it here, so long as I am on the premises.

GREGERS: And if I do so none the less?

RELLING: Then you'll go head-foremost down the stairs; now I've warned you.

HIALMAR: [Rising.] Oh, but Relling——!

GREGERS: Yes, you may turn me out——

GINA: [Interposing between them.] We can't have that, Relling. But I must say, Mr. Werle, it ill becomes you to talk about vapours and taints, after all the mess you made with your stove.

[A knock at the passage door.]

HEDVIG: Mother, there's somebody knocking.

HIALMAR: There now, we're going to have a whole lot of people!

GINA: I'll go—— [Goes over and opens the door, starts, and draws back.] Oh—oh dear!

[WERLE, in a fur coat, advances one step into the room.]

WERLE: Excuse me; but I think my son is staying here.

GINA: [With a gulp.] Yes.

HIALMAR: [Approaching him.] Won't you do us the honour to——?

WERLE: Thank you, I merely wish to speak to my son.

GREGERS: What is it? Here I am.

WERLE: I want a few words with you, in your room.

GREGERS: In my room? Very well—— [About to go.]

GINA: No, no, your room's not in a fit state——

WERLE: Well then, out in the passage here; I want to have a few words with you alone.

HIALMAR: You can have them here, sir. Come into the parlour, Relling.

[HIALMAR and RELLING go off to the right. GINA takes HEDVIG with her into the kitchen.]

GREGERS: [After a short pause.] Well, now we are alone.

WERLE: From something you let fall last evening, and from your coming to lodge with the Ekdals, I can't help inferring that you intend to make yourself unpleasant to me, in one way or another.

GREGERS: I intend to open Hialmar Ekdal's eyes. He shall see his position as it really is—that is all.

WERLE: Is that the mission in life you spoke of yesterday?

GREGERS: Yes. You have left me no other.

WERLE: Is it I, then, that have crippled your mind, Gregers?

GREGERS: You have crippled my whole life. I am not thinking of all that about mother—— But it's thanks to you that I am continually haunted and harassed by a guilty conscience.

WERLE: Indeed! It is your conscience that troubles you, is it?

GREGERS: I ought to have taken a stand against you when the trap was set for Lieutenant Ekdal. I ought to have cautioned him; for I had a misgiving as to what was in the wind.

WERLE: Yes, that was the time to have spoken.

GREGERS: I did not dare to, I was so cowed and spiritless. I was mortally afraid of you—not only then, but long afterwards.

WERLE: You have got over that fear now, it appears.

GREGERS: Yes, fortunately. The wrong done to old Ekdal, both by me and by—others, can never be undone; but Hialmar I can rescue from all the falsehood and deception that are bringing him to ruin.

WERLE: Do you think that will be doing him a kindness?

GREGERS: I have not the least doubt of it.

WERLE: You think our worthy photographer is the sort of man to appreciate such friendly offices?

GREGERS: Yes, I do.

WERLE: H'm—we shall see.

GREGERS: Besides, if I am to go on living, I must try to find some cure for my sick conscience.

WERLE: It will never be sound. Your conscience has been sickly from childhood. That is a legacy from your mother, Gregers —the only one she left you.

GREGERS: [With a scornful half-smile.] Have you not yet forgiven her for the mistake you made in supposing she would bring you a fortune?

WERLE: Don't let us wander from the point.—Then you hold to your purpose of setting young Ekdal upon that which you imagine to be the right scent?

GREGERS: Yes, that is my fixed resolve.

WERLE: Well, in that case I might have spared myself this visit; for of course it is useless to ask whether you will return home with me?

GREGERS: Quite useless.

WERLE: And I suppose you won't enter the firm either?

GREGERS: No.

WERLE: Very good. But as I am thinking of marrying again, your share in the property will fall to you at once.[1]

GREGERS: [Quickly.] No, I do not want that.

WERLE: You don't want it?

GREGERS: No, I dare not take it, for conscience' sake.

WERLE: [After pause.] Are you going up to the works again?

GREGERS: No; I consider myself released from your service.

WERLE: But what are you going to do?

GREGERS: Only to fulfil my mission; nothing more.

WERLE: Well, but afterwards? What are you going to live upon?

GREGERS: I have laid by a little out of my salary.

WERLE: How long will that last?

GREGERS: I think it will last my time.

WERLE: What do you mean?

GREGERS: I shall answer no more questions.

WERLE: Good-bye then, Gregers.

GREGERS: Good-bye.

[WERLE goes.]

HIALMAR: [Peeping in.] He's gone, isn't he?

GREGERS: Yes.

[HIALMAR and RELLING enter; also GINA and HEDVIG from the kitchen.]

RELLING: That luncheon-party was a failure.

GREGERS: Put on your coat, Hialmar; I want you to come for a long walk with me.

HIALMAR: With pleasure. What was it your father wanted? Had it anything to do with me?

GREGERS: Come along. We must have a

[1] By Norwegian law, before a widower can marry again, a certain proportion of his property must be settled on his children by his former marriage.

talk. I'll go and put on my overcoat. [*Goes out by the passage door.*]

GINA: You shouldn't go out with him, Ekdal.

RELLING: No, don't you do it. Stay where you are.

HIALMAR: [*Gets his hat and overcoat.*] Oh, nonsense! When a friend of my youth feels impelled to open his mind to me in private——

RELLING: But devil take it—don't you see that the fellow's mad, cracked, demented!

GINA: There, what did I tell you! His mother before him had crazy fits like that sometimes.

HIALMAR: The more need for a friend's watchful eye. [*To* GINA.] Be sure you have dinner ready in good time. Good-bye for the present. [*Goes out by the passage door.*]

RELLING: It's a thousand pities the fellow didn't go to hell through one of the Höidal mines.

GINA: Good Lord! what makes you say that?

RELLING: [*Muttering.*] Oh, I have my own reasons.

GINA: Do you think young Werle is really mad?

RELLING: No, worse luck; he's no madder than most other people. But one disease he has certainly got in his system.

GINA: What is it that's the matter with him?

RELLING: Well, I'll tell you, Mrs. Ekdal. He is suffering from an acute attack of integrity.

GINA: Integrity?

HEDVIG: Is that a kind of disease?

RELLING: Yes, it's a national disease; but it only appears sporadically. [*Nods to* GINA.] Thanks for your hospitality.

[*He goes out by the passage door.*]

GINA: [*Moving restlessly to and fro.*] Ugh, that Gregers Werle—he was always a wretched creature.

HEDVIG: [*Standing by the table, and looking searchingly at her.*] I think all this is very strange.

ACT FOURTH

HIALMAR EKDAL's *studio. A photograph has just been taken; a camera with the cloth over it, a pedestal, two chairs, a folding table, etc., are standing out in the room. Afternoon light; the sun is going down; a little later it begins to grow dusk.*

GINA *stands in the passage doorway, with a little box and a wet glass plate in her hand, and is speaking to somebody outside.*

GINA: Yes, certainly. When I make a promise I keep it. The first dozen shall be ready on Monday. Good afternoon.

[*Some one is heard going downstairs.* GINA *shuts the door, slips the plate into the box, and puts it into the covered camera.*]

HEDVIG: [*Comes in from the kitchen.*] Are they gone?

GINA: [*Tidying up.*] Yes, thank goodness, I've got rid of them at last.

HEDVIG: But can you imagine why father hasn't come home yet?

GINA: Are you sure he's not down in Relling's room?

HEDVIG: No, he's not; I ran down the kitchen stair just now and asked.

GINA: And his dinner standing and getting cold, too.

HEDVIG: Yes, I can't understand it. Fa-

ther's always so careful to be home to dinner!

GINA: Oh, he'll be here directly, you'll see.

HEDVIG: I wish he would come; everything seems so queer to-day.

GINA: [*Calls out.*] There he is!

[HIALMAR EKDAL *comes in at the passage door.*]

HEDVIG: [*Going to him.*] Father! Oh what a time we've been waiting for you!

GINA: [*Glancing sidelong at him.*] You've been out a long time, Ekdal.

HIALMAR: [*Without looking at her.*] Rather long, yes.

[*He takes off his overcoat;* GINA *and* HEDVIG *go to help him; he motions them away.*]

GINA: Perhaps you've had dinner with Werle?

HIALMAR: [*Hanging up his coat.*] No.

GINA: [*Going towards the kitchen door.*] Then I'll bring some in for you.

HIALMAR: No; let the dinner alone. I want nothing to eat.

HEDVIG: [*Going nearer to him.*] Are you not well, father?

HIALMAR: Well? Oh yes, well enough. We have had a tiring walk, Gregers and I.

GINA: You didn't ought to have gone so far, Ekdal; you're not used to it.

HIALMAR: H'm; there's many a thing a man must get used to in this world. [*Wanders about the room.*] Has any one been here whilst I was out?

GINA: Nobody but the two sweethearts.

HIALMAR: No new orders?

GINA: No, not to-day.

HEDVIG: There will be some to-morrow, father, you'll see.

HIALMAR: I hope there will; for to-morrow I am going to set to work in real earnest.

HEDVIG: To-morrow! Don't you remember what day it is to-morrow?

HIALMAR: Oh yes, by-the-bye——. Well, the day after, then. Henceforth I mean to do everything myself; I shall take all the work into my own hands.

GINA: Why, what can be the good of that, Ekdal? It'll only make your life a burden to you. I can manage the photography all right; and you can go on working at your invention.

HEDVIG: And think of the wild duck, father,—and all the hens and rabbits and——!

HIALMAR: Don't talk to me of all that trash! From to-morrow I will never set foot in the garret again.

HEDVIG: Oh but, father, you promised that we should have a little party——

HIALMAR: H'm, true. Well then, from the day after to-morrow. I should almost like to wring that cursëd wild duck's neck!

HEDVIG: [*Shrieks.*] The wild duck!

GINA: Well I never!

HEDVIG: [*Shaking him.*] Oh no, father; you know it's my wild duck!

HIALMAR: That is why I don't do it. I haven't the heart to—for your sake, Hedvig. But in my inmost soul I feel that I ought to do it. I ought not to tolerate under my roof a creature that has been through those hands.

GINA: Why, good gracious, even if grandfather did get it from that poor creature, Pettersen——

HIALMAR: [*Wandering about.*] There are certain claims—what shall I call them? —let me say claims of the ideal—certain obligations, which a man cannot disregard without injury to his soul.

HEDVIG: [*Going after him.*] But think of the wild duck, —the poor wild duck!

HIALMAR: [*Stops.*] I tell you I will spare it—for your sake. Not a hair of its head shall be—I mean, it shall be spared. There are greater problems than that to be dealt with. But you should go out a little now, Hedvig, as usual; it is getting dusk enough for you now.

HEDVIG: No, I don't care about going out now.

HIALMAR: Yes do; it seems to me your eyes are blinking a great deal; all these vapours in here are bad for you. The air is heavy under this roof.

HEDVIG: Very well then, I'll run down the kitchen stair and go for a little walk. My cloak and hat?—oh, they're in my own room. Father—be sure you don't do the wild duck any harm whilst I'm out.

HIALMAR: Not a feather of its head shall be touched. [*Draws her to him.*] You and I, Hedvig—we two——! Well, go along.

[HEDVIG *nods to her parents and goes out through the kitchen.*]

HIALMAR: [*Walks about without looking up.*] Gina.

GINA: Yes?

HIALMAR: From to-morrow—or, say, from the day after tomorrow—I should like to keep the household account-book myself.

GINA: Do you want to keep the accounts too, now?

HIALMAR: Yes; or to check the receipts at any rate.

GINA: Lord help us! that's soon done.

HIALMAR: One would hardly think so; at any rate you seem to make the money go a very long way. [*Stops and looks at her.*] How do you manage it?

GINA: It's because me and Hedvig, we need so little.

HIALMAR: Is it the case that father is very liberally paid for the copying he does for Mr. Werle?

GINA: I don't know as he gets anything out of the way. I don't know the rates for that sort of work.

HIALMAR: Well, what does he get, about? Let me hear!

GINA: Oh, it varies; I daresay it'll come

to about as much as he costs us, with a little pocket-money over.

HIALMAR: As much as he costs us! And you have never told me this before!

GINA: No, how could I tell you? It pleased you so much to think he got everything from you.

HIALMAR: And he gets it from Mr. Werle.

GINA: Oh well, he has plenty and to spare, he has.

HIALMAR: Light the lamp for me, please!

GINA: [Lighting the lamp.] And of course we don't know as it's Mr. Werle himself; it may be Gråberg——

HIALMAR: Why attempt such an evasion?

GINA: I don't know; I only thought——

HIALMAR: H'm!

GINA: It wasn't me that got grandfather that copying. It was Bertha, when she used to come about us.

HIALMAR: It seems to me your voice is trembling.

GINA: [Putting the lamp-shade on.] Is it?

HIALMAR: And your hands are shaking, are they not?

GINA: [Firmly.] Come right out with it, Ekdal. What has he been saying about me?

HIALMAR: Is it true—can it be true that—that there was an—an understanding between you and Mr. Werle, while you were in service there?

GINA: That's not true. Not at that time. Mr. Werle did come after me, that's a fact. And his wife thought there was something in it, and then she made such a hocus-pocus and hurly-burly, and she hustled me and bustled me about so, that I left her service.

HIALMAR: But afterwards, then?

GINA: Well, then I went home. And mother—well, she wasn't the woman you took her for, Ekdal; she kept on worrying and worrying at me about one thing and another—for Mr. Werle was a widower by that time.

HIALMAR: Well, and then?

GINA: I suppose you've got to know it. He gave me no peace until he'd had his way.

HIALMAR: [Striking his hands together.] And this is the mother of my child! How could you hide this from me?

GINA: Yes, it was wrong of me; I ought certainly to have told you long ago.

HIALMAR: You should have told me at the very first;—then I should have known the sort of woman you were.

GINA: But would you have married me all the same?

HIALMAR: How can you dream that I would?

GINA: That's just why I didn't dare tell you anything, then. For I'd come to care for you so much, you see; and I couldn't go and make myself utterly miserable——

HIALMAR: [Walks about.] And this is my Hedvig's mother. And to know that all I see before me—[Kicks at a chair.]—all that I call my home—I owe to a favoured predecessor! Oh that scoundrel Werle!

GINA: Do you repent of the fourteen—the fifteen years as we've lived together?

HIALMAR: [Placing himself in front of her.] Have you not every day, every hour, repented of the spider's-web of deceit you have spun around me? Answer me that! How could you help writhing with penitence and remorse?

GINA: Oh, my dear Ekdal, I've had all I could do to look after the house and get through the day's work——

HIALMAR: Then you never think of reviewing your past?

GINA: No; Heaven knows I'd almost forgotten those old stories.

HIALMAR: Oh, this dull, callous contentment! To me there is something revolting about it. Think of it—never so much as a twinge of remorse!

GINA: But tell me, Ekdal—what would have become of you if you hadn't had a wife like me?

HIALMAR: Like you——!

GINA: Yes; for you know I've always been a bit more practical and wide-awake than you. Of course I'm a year or two older.

HIALMAR: What would have become of me!

GINA: You'd got into all sorts of bad ways when first you met me; that you can't deny.

HIALMAR: "Bad ways" do you call them? Little do you know what a man goes through when he is in grief and despair—especially a man of my fiery temperament.

GINA: Well, well, that may be so. And I've no reason to crow over you, neither; for you turned a moral of a husband, that you did, as soon as ever you had a house and home of your own.—And now we'd got everything so nice and cosy about us; and me and Hedvig was just thinking we'd soon be able to let ourselves go a bit, in the way of both food and clothes.

HIALMAR: In the swamp of deceit, yes.

GINA: I wish to goodness that detestable being had never set his foot inside our doors!

HIALMAR: And I, too, thought my home such a pleasant one. That was a delusion. Where shall I now find the elasticity of spirit to bring my invention into the world of reality? Perhaps it will die with me; and then it will be your past, Gina, that will have killed it.

GINA: [*Nearly crying.*] You musn't say such things, Ekdal. Me, that has only wanted to do the best I could for you, all my days!

HIALMAR: I ask you, what becomes of the breadwinner's dream? When I used to lie in there on the sofa and brood over my invention, I had a clear enough presentiment that it would sap my vitality to the last drop. I felt even then that the day when I held the patent in my hand—that day—would bring my—release. And then it was my dream that you should live on after me, the dead inventor's well-to-do widow.

GINA: [*Drying her tears.*] No, you mustn't talk like that, Ekdal. May the Lord never let me see the day I am left a widow!

HIALMAR: Oh, the whole dream has vanished. It is all over now. All over!

[GREGERS WERLE *opens the passage door cautiously and looks in.*]

GREGERS: May I come in?

HIALMAR: Yes, come in.

GREGERS: [*Comes forward, his face beaming with satisfaction, and holds out both his hands to them.*] Well, dear friends——! [*Looks from one to the other, and whispers to* HIALMAR.] Have you not done it yet?

HIALMAR: [*Aloud.*] It is done.

GREGERS: It is?

HIALMAR: I have passed through the bitterest moments of my life.

GREGERS: But also, I trust, the most ennobling.

HIALMAR: Well, at any rate, we have got through it for the present.

GINA: God forgive you, Mr. Werle.

GREGERS: [*In great surprise.*] But I don't understand this.

HIALMAR: What don't you understand?

GREGERS: After so great a crisis—a crisis that is to be the starting-point of an entirely new life—of a communion founded on truth, and free from all taint of deception

——

HIALMAR: Yes yes, I know; I know that quite well.

GREGERS: I confidently expected, when I entered the room, to find the light of transfiguration shining upon me from both husband and wife. And now I see nothing but dulness, oppression, gloom——

GINA: Oh, is that it? [*Takes off the lampshade.*]

GREGERS: You will not understand me, Mrs. Ekdal. Ah well, you, I suppose, need time to——. But you, Hialmar? Surely you feel a new consecration after the great crisis.

HIALMAR: Yes, of course I do. That is—in a sort of way.

GREGERS: For surely nothing in the world can compare with the joy of forgiving one who has erred, and raising her up to oneself in love.

HIALMAR: Do you think a man can so easily throw off the effects of the bitter cup I have drained?

GREGERS: No, not a common man, perhaps. But a man like you——!

HIALMAR: Good God! I know that well enough. But you must keep me up to it, Gregers. It takes time, you know.

GREGERS: You have much of the wild duck in you, Hialmar.

[RELLING *has come in at the passage door.*]

RELLING: Oho! is the wild duck to the fore again?

HIALMAR: Yes; Mr. Werle's wing-broken victim.

RELLING: Mr. Werle's——? So it's him you are talking about?

HIALMAR: Him and—ourselves.

RELLING: [*In an undertone to* GREGERS.] May the devil fly away with you!

HIALMAR: What is that you are saying?

RELLING: Only uttering a heartfelt wish that this quacksalver would take himself off. If he stays here, he is quite equal to making an utter mess of life, for both of you.

GREGERS: These two will not make a mess of life, Mr. Relling. Of course I won't speak of Hialmar—him we know. But she, too, in her innermost heart, has certainly something loyal and sincere——

GINA: [*Almost crying.*] You might have let me alone for what I was, then.

RELLING: [*To* GREGERS.] Is it rude to ask what you really want in this house?

GREGERS: To lay the foundations of a true marriage.

RELLING: So you don't think Ekdal's marriage is good enough as it is?

GREGERS: No doubt it is as good a marriage as most others, worse luck. But a true marriage it has yet to become.

HIALMAR: You have never had eyes for the claims of the ideal, Relling.

RELLING: Rubbish, my boy!—But excuse me, Mr. Werle: how many—in round numbers—how many true marriages have you seen in the course of your life?

GREGERS: Scarcely a single one.

RELLING: Nor I either.

GREGERS: But I have seen innumerable marriages of the opposite kind. And it has been my fate to see at close quarters what ruin such a marriage can work in two human souls.

HIALMAR: A man's whole moral basis may give away beneath his feet; that is the terrible part of it.

RELLING: Well, I can't say I've ever been exactly married, so I don't pretend to speak with authority. But this I know, that the child enters into the marriage problem. And you must leave the child in peace.

HIALMAR: Oh—Hedvig! my poor Hedvig!

RELLING: Yes, you must be good enough to keep Hedvig outside of all this. You two are grown-up people; you are free, in God's name, to make what mess and muddle you please of your life. But you must deal cautiously with Hedvig, I tell you; else you may do her a great injury.

HIALMAR: An injury!

RELLING: Yes, or she may do herself an injury—and perhaps others too.

GINA: How can you know that, Relling?

HIALMAR: Her sight is in no immediate danger, is it?

RELLING: I am not talking about her sight. Hedvig is at a critical age. She may be getting all sorts of mischief into her head.

GINA: That's true—I've noticed it already! She's taken to carrying on with the fire, out in the kitchen. She calls it playing at house-on-fire. I'm often scared for fear she really sets fire to the house.

RELLING: You see; I thought as much.

GREGERS: [To RELLING.] But how do you account for that?

RELLING: [Sullenly.] Her constitution's changing, sir.

HIALMAR: So long as the child has me——! So long as I am above ground——!
[A knock at the door.]

GINA: Hush, Ekdal; there's some one in the passage. [Calls out.] Come in!

[MRS. SÖRBY, in walking dress, comes in.]

MRS. SÖRBY: Good evening.

GINA: [Going towards her.] Is it really you, Bertha?

MRS. SÖRBY: Yes, of course it is. But I'm disturbing you, I'm afraid?

HIALMAR: No, not at all; an emissary from that house——

MRS. SÖRBY: [To GINA.] To tell the truth, I hoped your men-folk would be out at this time. I just ran up to have a little chat with you, and to say good-bye.

GINA: Good-bye? Are you going away, then?

MRS. SÖRBY: Yes, to-morrow morning,—up to Höidal. Mr. Werle started this afternoon. [Lightly to GREGERS.] He asked me to say good-bye for him.

GINA: Only fancy——!

HIALMAR: So Mr. Werle has gone? And now you are going after him?

MRS. SÖRBY: Yes, what do you say to that, Ekdal?

HIALMAR: I say: beware!

GREGERS: I must explain the situation. My father and Mrs. Sörby are going to be married.

HIALMAR: Going to be married!

GINA: Oh Bertha! So it's come to that at last!

RELLING: [His voice quivering a little.] This is surely not true?

MRS. SÖRBY: Yes, my dear Relling, it's true enough.

RELLING: You are going to marry again?

MRS. SÖRBY: Yes, it looks like it. Werle has got a special license, and we are going to be married quite quietly, up at the works.

GREGERS: Then I must wish you all happiness, like a dutiful stepson.

MRS. SÖRBY: Thank you very much—if you mean what you say. I certainly hope it will lead to happiness, both for Werle and for me.

RELLING: You have every reason to hope that. Mr. Werle never gets drunk—so far as I know; and I don't suppose he's in the habit of thrashing his wives, like the late lamented horse-doctor.

MRS. SÖRBY: Come now, let Sörby rest in peace. He had his good points too.

RELLING: Mr. Werle has better ones, I have no doubt.

MRS. SÖRBY: He hasn't frittered away all that was good in him, at any rate. The man who does that must take the consequences.

RELLING: I shall go out with Molvik this evening.

MRS. SÖRBY: You mustn't do that, Relling. Don't do it—for my sake.

RELLING: There's nothing else for it. [*To* HIALMAR.] If you're going with us, come along.

GINA: No, thank you. Ekdal doesn't go in for that sort of dissertation.

HIALMAR: [*Half aloud, in vexation.*] Oh, do hold your tongue!

RELLING: Good-bye, Mrs.—Werle. [*Goes out through the passage door.*]

GREGERS: [*To* MRS. SÖRBY.] You seem to know Dr. Relling pretty intimately.

MRS. SÖRBY: Yes, we have known each other for many years. At one time it seemed as if things might have gone further between us.

GREGERS: It was surely lucky for you that they did not.

MRS. SÖRBY: You may well say that. But I have always been wary of acting on impulse. A woman can't afford absolutely to throw herself away.

GREGERS: Are you not in the least afraid that I may let my father know about this old friendship?

MRS. SÖRBY: Why, of course I have told him all about it myself.

GREGERS: Indeed?

MRS. SÖRBY: Your father knows every single thing that can, with any truth, be said about me. I have told him all; it was the first thing I did when I saw what was in his mind.

GREGERS: Then you have been franker than most people, I think.

MRS. SÖRBY: I have always been frank. We women find that the best policy.

HIALMAR: What do you say to that, Gina?

GINA: Oh, we're not all alike, us women aren't. Some are made one way, some another.

MRS. SÖRBY: Well, for my part, Gina, I believe it's wisest to do as I've done. And Werle has no secrets either, on his side. That's really the great bond between us, you see. Now he can talk to me as openly as a child. He has never had the chance to do that before. Fancy a man like him, full of health and vigour, passing his whole youth and the best years of his life in listening to nothing but penitential sermons! And very often the sermons had for their text the most imaginary offences—at least so I understand.

GINA: That's true enough.

GREGERS: If you ladies are going to follow up this topic, I had better withdraw.

MRS. SÖRBY: You can stay so far as that's concerned. I shan't say a word more. But I wanted you to know that I had done nothing secretly or in an underhand way. I may seem to have come in for a great piece of luck; and so I have, in a sense. But after all, I don't think I am getting any more than I am giving. I shall stand by him always, and I can tend and care for him as no one else can, now that he is getting helpless.

HIALMAR: Getting helpless?

GREGERS: [*To* MRS. SÖRBY.] Hush, don't speak of that here.

MRS. SÖRBY: There is no disguising it any longer, however much he would like to. He is going blind.

HIALMAR: [*Starts.*] Going blind? That's strange. He too going blind!

GINA: Lots of people do.

MRS. SÖRBY: And you can imagine what that means to a business man. Well, I shall try as well as I can to make my eyes take the place of his. But I mustn't stay any longer; I have such heaps of things to do.— Oh, by-the-bye, Ekdal, I was to tell you that if there is anything Werle can do for you, you must just apply to Gråberg.

GREGERS: That offer I am sure Hialmar Ekdal will decline with thanks.

MRS. SÖRBY: Indeed? I don't think he used to be so——

GINA: No, Bertha, Ekdal doesn't need anything from Mr. Werle now.

HIALMAR: [*Slowly, and with emphasis.*] Will you present my compliments to your future husband, and say that I intend very shortly to call upon Mr. Gråberg——

GREGERS: What! You don't really mean that?

HIALMAR: To call upon Mr. Gråberg, I say, and obtain an account of the sum I owe his principal. I will pay that debt of honour —ha ha ha! a debt of honour, let us call it! In any case, I will pay the whole, with five per cent. interest.

GINA: But, my dear Ekdal, God knows we haven't got the money to do it.

HIALMAR: Be good enough to tell your future husband that I am working assiduously at my invention. Please tell him that what sustains me in this laborious task is the wish to free myself from a torturing burden of debt. That is my reason for proceeding with the invention. The entire profits shall be devoted to releasing me from my pecuniary obligations to your future husband.

MRS. SÖRBY: Something has happened here.

HIALMAR: Yes, you are right.

MRS. SÖRBY: Well, good-bye. I had something else to speak to you about, Gina; but it must keep till another time. Good-bye.

[HIALMAR and GREGERS *bow silently.* GINA *follows* MRS. SÖRBY *to the door.*]

HIALMAR: Not beyond the threshold, Gina!

[MRS. SÖRBY *goes;* GINA *shuts the door after her.*]

HIALMAR: There now, Gregers; I have got that burden of debt off my mind.

GREGERS: You soon will, at all events.

HIALMAR: I think my attitude may be called correct.

GREGERS: You are the man I have always taken you for.

HIALMAR: In certain cases, it is impossible to disregard the claim of the ideal. Yet, as the breadwinner of a family, I cannot but writhe and groan under it. I can tell you it is no joke for a man without capital to attempt the repayment of a long-standing obligation, over which, so to speak, the dust of oblivion had gathered. But it cannot be helped: the Man in me demands his rights.

GREGERS: [*Laying his hand on* HIALMAR'S *shoulder.*] My dear Hialmar—was it not a good thing I came?

HIALMAR: Yes.

GREGERS: Are you not glad to have had your true position made clear to you?

HIALMAR: [*Somewhat impatiently.*] Yes, of course I am. But there is one thing that is revolting to my sense of justice.

GREGERS: And what is that?

HIALMAR: It is that—but I don't know whether I ought to express myself so unreservedly about your father.

GREGERS: Say what you please, so far as I am concerned.

HIALMAR: Well then, is it not exasperating to think that it is not I, but he, who will realise the true marriage?

GREGERS: How can you say such a thing?

HIALMAR: Because it is clearly the case. Isn't the marriage between your father and Mrs. Sörby founded upon complete confidence, upon entire and unreserved candour on both sides? They hide nothing from each other, they keep no secrets in the background; their relation is based, if I may put it so, on mutual confession and absolution.

GREGERS: Well, what then?

HIALMAR: Well, is not that the whole thing? Did you not yourself say that this was precisely the difficulty that had to be overcome in order to found a true marriage?

GREGERS: But this is a totally different matter, Hialmar. You surely don't compare either yourself or your wife with those two ——? Oh, you understand me well enough.

HIALMAR: Say what you like, there is something in all this that hurts and offends my sense of justice. It really looks as if there were no just providence to rule the world.

GINA: Oh no, Ekdal; for God's sake don't say such things.

GREGERS: H'm; don't let us get upon those questions.

HIALMAR: And yet, after all, I cannot but recognise the guiding finger of fate. He is going blind.

GINA: Oh, you can't be sure of that.

HIALMAR: There is no doubt about it. At all events there ought not to be; for in that very fact lies the righteous retribution. He has hoodwinked a confiding fellow creature in days gone by——

GREGERS: I fear he has hoodwinked many.

HIALMAR: And now comes inexorable, mysterious Fate, and demands Werle's own eyes.

GINA: Oh, how dare you say such dreadful things! You make me quite scared.

HIALMAR: It is profitable, now and then, to plunge deep into the night side of existence.

[HEDVIG, *in her hat and cloak, comes in by the passage door. She is pleasurably excited, and out of breath.*]

GINA: Are you back already?

HEDVIG: Yes, I didn't care to go any farther. It was a good thing, too; for I've just met some one at the door.

HIALMAR: It must have been that Mrs. Sörby.

HEDVIG: Yes.

HIALMAR: [*Walks up and down.*] I hope you have seen her for the last time.

[*Silence.* HEDVIG, *discouraged, looks first at one and then at the other, trying to divine their frame of mind.*]

HEDVIG: [*Approaching, coaxingly.*] Father.

HIALMAR: Well—what is it, Hedvig?

HEDVIG: Mrs. Sörby had something with her for me.

HIALMAR: [*Stops.*] For you?

HEDVIG: Yes. Something for to-morrow.

GINA: Bertha has always given you some little thing on your birthday.

HIALMAR: What is it?

HEDVIG: Oh, you mustn't see it now. Mother is to give it to me to-morrow morning before I'm up.

HIALMAR: What is all this hocus-pocus that I am to be kept in the dark about!

HEDVIG: [Quickly.] Oh no, you may see it if you like. It's a big letter. [Takes the letter out of her cloak pocket.]

HIALMAR: A letter too?

HEDVIG: Yes, it is only a letter. The rest will come afterwards, I suppose. But fancy —a letter! I've never had a letter before. And there's "Miss" written upon it. [Reads.] "Miss Hedvig Ekdal." Only fancy—that's me!

HIALMAR: Let me see that letter.

HEDVIG: [Hands it to him.] There it is.

HIALMAR: That is Mr. Werle's hand.

GINA: Are you sure of that, Ekdal?

HIALMAR: Look for yourself.

GINA: Oh, what do I know about such-like things?

HIALMAR: Hedvig, may I open the letter —and read it?

HEDVIG: Yes, of course you may, if you want to.

GINA: No, not to-night, Ekdal; it's to be kept till to-morrow.

HEDVIG: [Softly.] Oh, can't you let him read it! It's sure to be something good; and then father will be glad, and everything will be nice again.

HIALMAR: I may open it then?

HEDVIG: Yes do, father. I'm so anxious to know what it is.

HIALMAR: Well and good. [Opens the letter, takes out a paper, reads it through, and appears bewildered.] What is this——!

GINA: What does it say?

HEDVIG: Oh yes, father—tell us!

HIALMAR: Be quiet. [Reads it through again; he has turned pale, but says with self-control.] It is a deed of gift, Hedvig.

HEDVIG: Is it? What sort of gift am I to have?

HIALMAR: Read for yourself.

[HEDVIG goes over and reads for a time by the lamp.]

HIALMAR: [Half-aloud, clenching his hands.] The eyes! The eyes—and then that letter!

HEDVIG: [Leaves off reading.] Yes, but it seems to me that it's grandfather that's to have it.

HIALMAR: [Takes the letter from her.] Gina—can you understand this?

GINA: I know nothing whatever about it; tell me what's the matter.

HIALMAR: Mr. Werle writes to Hedvig that her old grandfather need not trouble himself any longer with the copying, but that he can henceforth draw on the office for a hundred crowns a month——

GREGERS: Aha!

HEDVIG: A hundred crowns, mother! I read that.

GINA: What a good thing for grandfather!

HIALMAR: ——a hundred crowns a month so long as he needs it—that means, of course, so long as he lives.

GINA: Well, so he's provided for, poor dear.

HIALMAR: But there is more to come. You didn't read that, Hedvig. Afterwards this gift is to pass on to you.

HEDVIG: To me! The whole of it?

HIALMAR: He says that the same amount is assured to you for the whole of your life. Do you hear that, Gina?

GINA: Yes, I hear.

HEDVIG: Fancy—all that money for me! [Shakes him.] Father, father, aren't you glad——?

HIALMAR: [Eluding her.] Glad! [Walks about.] Oh what vistas—what perspectives open up before me! It is Hedvig, Hedvig that he showers these benefactions upon!

GINA: Yes, because it's Hedvig's birth-day——

HEDVIG: And you'll get it all the same, father! You know quite well I shall give all the money to you and mother.

HIALMAR: To mother, yes! There we have it.

GREGERS: Hialmar, this is a trap he is setting for you.

HIALMAR: Do you think it's another trap?

GREGERS: When he was here this morning he said: Hialmar Ekdal is not the man you imagine him to be.

HIALMAR: Not the man——!

GREGERS: That you shall see, he said.

HIALMAR: He meant you should see that I would let myself be bought off——!

HEDVIG: Oh mother, what does all this mean?

GINA: Go and take off your things.

[HEDVIG goes out by the kitchen door, half-crying.]

GREGERS: Yes, Hialmar—now is the time to show who was right, he or I.

HIALMAR: [*Slowly tears the paper across, lays both pieces on the table, and says:*] Here is my answer.

GREGERS: Just what I expected.

HIALMAR: [*Goes over to* GINA, *who stands by the stove, and says in a low voice:*] Now please make a clean breast of it. If the connection between you and him was quite over when you—came to care for me, as you call it—why did he place us in a position to marry?

GINA: I suppose he thought as he could come and go in our house.

HIALMAR: Only that? Was not he afraid of a possible contingency?

GINA: I don't know what you mean.

HIALMAR: I want to know whether—your child has the right to live under my roof.

GINA: [*Draws herself up; her eyes flash.*] You ask that!

HIALMAR: You shall answer me this one question: Does Hedvig belong to me—or ——? Well!

GINA: [*Looking at him with cold defiance.*] I don't know.

HIALMAR: [*Quivering a little.*] You don't know!

GINA: How should I know? A creature like me——

HIALMAR: [*Quietly turning away from her.*] Then I have nothing more to do in this house.

GREGERS: Take care, Hialmar! Think what you are doing!

HIALMAR: [*Puts on his overcoat.*] In this case, there is nothing for a man like me to think twice about.

GREGERS: Yes indeed, there are endless things to be considered. You three must be together if you are to attain the true frame of mind for self-sacrifice and forgiveness.

HIALMAR: I don't want to attain it. Never, never! My hat! [*Takes his hat.*] My home has fallen in ruins about me. [*Bursts into tears.*] Gregers, I have no child!

HEDVIG: [*Who has opened the kitchen door.*] What is that you're saying? [*Coming to him.*] Father, father!

GINA: There, you see!

HIALMAR: Don't come near me, Hedvig! Keep far away. I cannot bear to see you. Oh! those eyes——! Good-bye. [*Makes for the door.*]

HEDVIG: [*Clinging close to him and screaming loudly.*] No! no! Don't leave me!

GINA: [*Cries out.*] Look at the child, Ekdal! Look at the child!

HIALMAR: I will not! I cannot! I must get out—away from all this!

[*He tears himself away from* HEDVIG, *and goes out by the passage door.*]

HEDVIG: [*With despairing eyes.*] He is going away from us, mother! He is going away from us! He will never come back again!

GINA: Don't cry, Hedvig. Father's sure to come back again.

HEDVIG: [*Throws herself sobbing on the sofa.*] No, no, he'll never come home to us any more.

GREGERS: Do you believe I meant all for the best, Mrs. Ekdal?

GINA: Yes, I daresay you did; but God forgive you, all the same.

HEDVIG: [*Lying on the sofa.*] Oh, this will kill me! What have I done to him? Mother, you must fetch him home again!

GINA: Yes yes yes; only be quiet, and I'll go out and look for him. [*Puts on her outdoor things.*] Perhaps he's gone in to Relling's. But you mustn't lie there and cry. Promise me!

HEDVIG: [*Weeping convulsively.*] Yes, I'll stop, I'll stop; if only father comes back!

GREGERS: [*To* GINA, *who is going.*] After all, had you not better leave him to fight out his bitter fight to the end?

GINA: Oh, he can do that afterwards. First of all, we must get the child quieted. [*Goes out by the passage door.*]

HEDVIG: [*Sits up and dries her tears.*] Now you must tell me what all this means. Why doesn't father want me any more?

GREGERS: You mustn't ask that till you are a big girl—quite grown-up.

HEDVIG: [*Sobs.*] But I can't go on being as miserable as this till I'm grown-up.—I think I know what it is.—Perhaps I'm not really father's child.

GREGERS: [*Uneasily.*] How could that be?

HEDVIG: Mother might have found me. And perhaps father has just got to know it; I've read of such things.

GREGERS: Well, but if it were so——

HEDVIG: I think he might be just as fond of me for all that. Yes, fonder almost. We got the wild duck in a present, you know, and I love it so dearly all the same.

GREGERS: [*Turning the conversation.*] Ah, the wild duck, by-the-bye! Let us talk about the wild duck a little, Hedvig.

HEDVIG: The poor wild duck! He doesn't want to see it any more either. Only think, he wanted to wring its neck!

GREGERS: Oh, he won't do that.

HEDVIG: No; but he said he would like to. And I think it was horrid of father to say it; for I pray for the wild duck every night, and ask that it may be preserved from death and all that is evil.

GREGERS: [Looking at her.] Do you say your prayers every night?

HEDVIG: Yes.

GREGERS: Who taught you to do that?

HEDVIG: I myself; one time when father was very ill, and had leeches on his neck, and said that death was staring him in the face.

GREGERS: Well?

HEDVIG: Then I prayed for him as I lay in bed; and since then I have always kept it up.

GREGERS: And now you pray for the wild duck too?

HEDVIG: I thought it was best to bring in the wild duck; for she was so weakly at first.

GREGERS: Do you pray in the morning, too?

HEDVIG: No, of course not.

GREGERS: Why not in the morning as well?

HEDVIG: In the morning it's light, you know, and there's nothing in particular to be afraid of.

GREGERS: And your father was going to wring the neck of the wild duck that you love so dearly?

HEDVIG: No; he said he ought to wring its neck, but he would spare it for my sake; and that was kind of father.

GREGERS: [Coming a little nearer.] But suppose you were to sacrifice the wild duck of your own free will for his sake.

HEDVIG: [Rising.] The wild duck!

GREGERS: Suppose you were to make a free-will offering, for his sake, of the dearest treasure you have in the world!

HEDVIG: Do you think that would do any good?

GREGERS: Try it, Hedvig.

HEDVIG: [Softly, with flashing eyes.] Yes, I will try it.

GREGERS: Have you really the courage for it, do you think?

HEDVIG: I'll ask grandfather to shoot the wild duck for me.

GREGERS: Yes, do. But not a word to your mother about it.

HEDVIG: Why not?

GREGERS: She doesn't understand us.

HEDVIG: The wild duck! I'll try it to-morrow morning.

[GINA comes in by the passage door.]

HEDVIG: [Going towards her.] Did you find him, mother?

GINA: No, but I heard as he had called and taken Relling with him.

GREGERS: Are you sure of that?

GINA: Yes, the porter's wife said so. Molvik went with them too, she said.

GREGERS: This evening, when his mind so sorely needs to wrestle in solitude——!

GINA: [Takes off her things.] Yes, men are strange creatures, so they are. The Lord only knows where Relling has dragged him to! I ran over to Madam Eriksen's, but they weren't there.

HEDVIG: [Struggling to keep back her tears.] Oh, if he should never come home any more!

GREGERS: He will come home again. I shall have news to give him to-morrow; and then you shall see how he comes home. You may rely upon that, Hedvig, and sleep in peace. Good-night.

[He goes out by the passage door.]

HEDVIG: [Throws herself sobbing on GINA's neck.] Mother, mother!

GINA: [Pats her shoulder and sighs.] Ah yes; Relling was right, he was. That's what comes of it when crazy creatures go about presenting the claims of the—what-you-may-call-it.

ACT FIFTH

HIALMAR EKDAL's *studio. Cold, grey, morning light. Wet snow lies upon the large panes of the sloping roof-window.*

GINA *comes from the kitchen with an apron and bib on, and carrying a dusting-brush and a duster; she goes towards the sitting-room door. At the same moment* HEDVIG *comes hurriedly in from the passage.*

GINA: [*Stops.*] Well?

HEDVIG: Oh, mother, I almost think he's down at Relling's——

GINA: There, you see!

HEDVIG: ——because the porter's wife says she could hear that Relling had two people with him when he came home last night.

GINA: That's just what I thought.

HEDVIG: But it's no use his being there, if he won't come up to us.

GINA: I'll go down and speak to him at all events.

[OLD EKDAL, *in dressing-gown and slippers, and with a lighted pipe, appears at the door of his room.*]

EKDAL: Hialmar—— Isn't Hialmar at home?

GINA: No, he's gone out.

EKDAL: So early? And in such a tearing snowstorm? Well well; just as he pleases; I can take my morning walk alone.

[*He slides the garret door aside;* HEDVIG *helps him; he goes in; she closes it after him.*]

HEDVIG: [*In an undertone.*] Only think, mother, when poor grandfather hears that father is going to leave us.

GINA: Oh, nonsense; grandfather mustn't hear anything about it. It was a heaven's mercy he wasn't at home yesterday in all that hurly-burly.

HEDVIG: Yes, but——

[GREGERS *comes in by the passage door.*]

GREGERS: Well, have you any news of him?

GINA: They say he's down at Relling's.

GREGERS: At Relling's! Has he really been out with those creatures?

GINA: Yes, like enough.

GREGERS: When he ought to have been yearning for solitude, to collect and clear his thoughts——

GINA: Yes, you may well say so.

[RELLING *enters from the passage.*]

HEDVIG: [*Going to him.*] Is father in your room?

GINA: [*At the same time.*] Is he there?

RELLING: Yes, to be sure he is.

HEDVIG: And you never let us know!

RELLING: Yes; I'm a brute. But in the first place I had to look after the other brute; I mean our dæmonic friend, of course; and then I fell so dead asleep that——

GINA: What does Ekdal say to-day?

RELLING: He says nothing whatever.

HEDVIG: Doesn't he speak?

RELLING: Not a blessed word.

GREGERS: No no; I can understand that very well.

GINA: But what's he doing then?

RELLING: He's lying on the sofa, snoring.

GINA: Oh is he? Yes, Ekdal's a rare one to snore.

HEDVIG: Asleep? Can he sleep?

RELLING: Well, it certainly looks like it.

GREGERS: No wonder, after the spiritual conflict that has rent him——

GINA: And then he's never been used to gadding about out of doors at night.

HEDVIG: Perhaps it's a good thing that he's getting sleep, mother.

GINA: Of course it is; and we must take care we don't wake him up too early. Thank you, Relling. I must get the house cleaned up a bit now, and then—— Come and help me, Hedvig.

[GINA *and* HEDVIG *go into the sitting-room.*]

GREGERS: [*Turning to* RELLING.] What is your explanation of the spiritual tumult that is now going on in Hialmar Ekdal?

RELLING: Devil a bit of a spiritual tumult have *I* noticed in him.

GREGERS: What! Not at such a crisis, when his whole life has been placed on a new foundation——? How can you think that such an individuality as Hialmar's——?

RELLING: Oh, individuality—he! If he

ever had any tendency to the abnormal developments you call individuality, I can assure you it was rooted out of him while he was still in his teens.

GREGERS: That would be strange indeed, —considering the loving care with which he was brought up.

RELLING: By those two high-flown, hysterical maiden aunts, you mean?

GREGERS: Let me tell you that they were women who never forgot the claim of the ideal—but of course you will only jeer at me again.

RELLING: No, I'm in no humour for that. I know all about those ladies; for he has ladled out no end of rhetoric on the subject of his "two soul-mothers." But I don't think he has much to thank them for. Ekdal's misfortune is that in his own circle he has always been looked upon as a shining light——

GREGERS: Not without reason, surely. Look at the depth of his mind!

RELLING: *I* have never discovered it. That his father believed in it I don't so much wonder; the old lieutenant has been an ass all his days.

GREGERS: He has had a child-like mind all his days; that is what you cannot understand.

RELLING: Well, so be it. But then, when our dear, sweet Hialmar went to college, he at once passed for the great light of the future amongst his comrades too! He was handsome, the rascal—red and white—a shop-girl's dream of manly beauty; and with his superficially emotional temperament, and his sympathetic voice, and his talent for declaiming other people's verses and other people's thoughts——

GREGERS: [*Indignantly.*] Is it Hialmar Ekdal you are talking about in this strain?

RELLING: Yes, with your permission; I am simply giving you an inside view of the idol you are grovelling before.

GREGERS: I should hardly have thought I was quite stone blind.

RELLING: Yes you are—or not far from it. You are a sick man, too, you see.

GREGERS: You are right there.

RELLING: Yes. Yours is a complicated case. First of all there is that plaguy integrity-fever; and then—what's worse—you are always in a delirium of hero-worship; you must always have something to adore, outside yourself.

GREGERS: Yes, I must certainly seek it outside myself.

RELLING: But you make such shocking mistakes about every new phœnix you think you have discovered. Here again you have come to a cotter's cabin with your claim of the ideal; and the people of the house are insolvent.

GREGERS: If you don't think better than that of Hialmar Ekdal, what pleasure can you find in being everlastingly with him?

RELLING: Well, you see, I'm supposed to be a sort of a doctor—save the mark! I can't but give a hand to the poor sick folk who live under the same roof with me.

GREGERS: Oh, indeed! Hialmar Ekdal is sick too, is he!

RELLING: Most people are, worse luck.

GREGERS: And what remedy are you applying in Hialmar's case?

RELLING: My usual one. I am cultivating the life-illusion [1] in him.

GREGERS: Life—illusion? I didn't catch what you said.

RELLING: Yes, I said illusion. For illusion, you know, is the stimulating principle.

GREGERS: May I ask with what illusion Hialmar is inoculated?

RELLING: No, thank you; I don't betray professional secrets to quacksalvers. You would probably go and muddle his case still more than you have already. But my method is infallible. I have applied it to Molvik as well. I have made him "dæmonic." That's the blister I have to put on his neck.

GREGERS: Is he not really dæmonic then?

RELLING: What the devil do you mean by dæmonic! It's only a piece of gibberish I've invented to keep up a spark of life in him. But for that, the poor harmless creature would have succumbed to self-contempt and despair many a long year ago. And then the old lieutenant! But he has hit upon his own cure, you see.

GREGERS: Lieutenant Ekdal? What of him?

RELLING: Just think of the old bear-hunter shutting himself up in that dark garret to shoot rabbits! I tell you there is not a happier sportsman in the world than that old man pottering about in there among all that rubbish. The four or five withered Christmas-trees he has saved up are the same to him as the whole great fresh Höidal forest; the cock and the hens are big game-birds in the fir-tops; and the rabbits that flop about the garret floor are the bears he

---

[1] "Livslögnen," literally "the life-lie."

has to battle with—the mighty hunter of the mountains!

GREGERS: Poor unfortunate old man! Yes; he has indeed had to narrow the ideals of his youth.

RELLING: While I think of it, Mr. Werle, junior—don't use that foreign word: ideals. We have the excellent native word: lies.

GREGERS: Do you think the two things are related?

RELLING: Yes, just about as closely as typhus and putrid fever.

GREGERS: Dr. Relling, I shall not give up the struggle until I have rescued Hialmar from your clutches!

RELLING: So much the worse for him. Rob the average man of his life-illusion, and you rob him of his happiness at the same stroke. [*To* HEDVIG, *who comes in from the sitting-room.*] Well, little wild-duck-mother, I'm just going down to see whether papa is still lying meditating upon that wonderful invention of his. [*Goes out by the passage door.*]

GREGERS: [*Approaches* HEDVIG.] I can see by your face that you have not yet done it.

HEDVIG: What? Oh, that about the wild duck! No.

GREGERS: I suppose your courage failed when the time came.

HEDVIG: No, that wasn't it. But when I awoke this morning and remembered what we had been talking about, it seemed so strange.

GREGERS: Strange?

HEDVIG: Yes, I don't know——. Yesterday evening, at the moment, I thought there was something so delightful about it; but since I have slept and thought of it again, it somehow doesn't seem worth while.

GREGERS: Ah, I thought you could not have grown up quite unharmed in this house.

HEDVIG: I don't care about that, if only father would come up——

GREGERS: Oh, if only your eyes had been opened to that which gives life its value— if you possessed the true, joyous, fearless spirit of sacrifice, you would soon see how he would come up to you.—But I believe in you still, Hedvig.

[*He goes out by the passage door.*]

[HEDVIG *wanders about the room for a time; she is on the point of going into the kitchen when a knock is heard at the garret door.* HEDVIG *goes over and opens it a little;* OLD EKDAL *comes out; she pushes the door to again.*]

EKDAL: H'm, it's not much fun to take one's morning walk alone.

HEDVIG: Wouldn't you like to go shooting, grandfather?

EKDAL: It's not the weather for it to-day. It's so dark there, you can scarcely see where you're going.

HEDVIG: Do you never want to shoot anything besides the rabbits?

EKDAL: Do you think the rabbits aren't good enough?

HEDVIG: Yes, but what about the wild duck?

EKDAL: Ho-ho! are you afraid I shall shoot your wild duck? Never in the world. Never.

HEDVIG: No, I suppose you couldn't; they say it's very difficult to shoot wild ducks.

EKDAL: Couldn't! Should rather think I could.

HEDVIG: How would you set about it, grandfather?—I don't mean with my wild duck, but with others?

EKDAL: I should take care to shoot them in the breast, you know; that's the surest place. And then you must shoot against the feathers, you see—not the way of the feathers.

HEDVIG: Do they die then, grandfather?

EKDAL: Yes, they die right enough— when you shoot properly. Well, I must go and brush up a bit. H'm—understand— h'm. [*Goes into his room.*]

[HEDVIG *waits a little, glances towards the sitting-room door, goes over to the bookcase, stands on tip-toe, takes the double-barrelled pistol down from the shelf, and looks at it.* GINA, *with brush and duster, comes from the sitting-room.* HEDVIG *hastily lays down the pistol, unobserved.*]

GINA: Don't stand raking amongst father's things, Hedvig.

HEDVIG: [*Goes away from the bookcase.*] I was only going to tidy up a little.

GINA: You'd better go into the kitchen, and see if the coffee's keeping hot; I'll take his breakfast on a tray, when I go down to him.

[HEDVIG *goes out.* GINA *begins to sweep and clean up the studio. Presently the passage door is opened with hesitation, and* HIALMAR EKDAL *looks in. He has on his overcoat, but not his hat; he is unwashed, and his hair is dishevelled*

*and unkempt. His eyes are dull and
heavy.*]

GINA: [*Standing with the brush in her
hand, and looking at him.*] Oh, there now,
Ekdal—so you've come after all?

HIALMAR: [*Comes in and answers in a
toneless voice.*] I come—only to depart again
immediately.

GINA: Yes, yes, I suppose so. But, Lord
help us! what a sight you are!

HIALMAR: A sight?

GINA: And your nice winter coat too!
Well, that's done for.

HEDVIG: [*At the kitchen door.*] Mother,
hadn't I better——? [*Sees* HIALMAR, *gives
a loud scream of joy, and runs to him.*] Oh,
father, father!

HIALMAR: [*Turns away and makes a
gesture of repulsion.*] Away, away, away!
[*To* GINA.] Keep her away from me, I say!

GINA: [*In a low tone.*] Go into the sitting-
room, Hedvig.

[HEDVIG *does so without a word.*]

HIALMAR: [*Fussily pulls out the table-
drawer.*] I must have my books with me.
Where are my books?

GINA: Which books?

HIALMAR: My scientific books, of course;
the technical magazines I require for my
invention.

GINA: [*Searches in the bookcase.*] Is it
these here paper-covered ones?

HIALMAR: Yes, of course.

GINA: [*Lays a heap of magazines on the
table.*] Shan't I get Hedvig to cut them for
you?

HIALMAR: I don't require to have them
cut for me.

[*Short silence.*]

GINA: Then you're still set on leaving us,
Ekdal?

HIALMAR: [*Rummaging amongst the
books.*] Yes, that is a matter of course, I
should think.

GINA: Well, well.

HIALMAR: [*Vehemently.*] How can I
live here, to be stabbed to the heart every
hour of the day?

GINA: God forgive you for thinking such
vile things of me.

HIALMAR: Prove——!

GINA: I think it's you as has got to prove.

HIALMAR: After a past like yours? There
are certain claims—I may almost call them
claims of the ideal——

GINA: But what about grandfather?
What's to become of him, poor dear?

HIALMAR: I know my duty; my helpless
father will come with me. I am going out
into the town to make arrangements——.
H'm—[*Hesitatingly.*] has any one found my
hat on the stairs?

GINA: No. Have you lost your hat?

HIALMAR: Of course I had it on when I
came in last night; there's no doubt about
that; but I couldn't find it this morning.

GINA: Lord help us! where have you been
to with those two ne'er-do-weels?

HIALMAR: Oh, don't bother me about
trifles. Do you suppose I am in the mood to
remember details?

GINA: If only you haven't caught cold,
Ekdal. [*Goes out into the kitchen.*]

HIALMAR: [*Talks to himself in a low
tone of irritation, whilst he empties the
table-drawer.*] You're a scoundrel, Relling!
—You're a low fellow!—Ah, you shameless
tempter!—I wish I could get some one to
stick a knife into you!

[*He lays some old letters on one side,
finds the torn document of yesterday,
takes it up and looks at the pieces;
puts it down hurriedly as* GINA *enters.*]

GINA: [*Sets a tray with coffee, etc., on
the table.*] Here's a drop of something hot,
if you'd fancy it. And there's some bread
and butter and a snack of salt meat.

HIALMAR: [*Glancing at the tray.*] Salt
meat? Never under this roof! It's true I have
not had a mouthful of solid food for nearly
twenty-four hours; but no matter.—My
memoranda! The commencement of my autobiography! What has become of my diary,
and all my important papers? [*Opens the
sitting-room door but draws back.*] She is
there too!

GINA: Good Lord! the child must be
somewhere!

HIALMAR: Come out.

[*He makes room,* HEDVIG *comes, scared,
into the studio.*]

HIALMAR: [*With his hand upon the door-
handle, says to* GINA:] In these, the last moments I spend in my former home, I wish
to be spared from interlopers—— [*Goes
into the room.*]

HEDVIG: [*With a bound towards her
mother, asks softly, trembling.*] Does that
mean me?

GINA: Stay out in the kitchen, Hedvig;
or, no—you'd best go into your own room.
[*Speaks to* HIALMAR *as she goes in to him.*]
Wait a bit, Ekdal; don't rummage so in the
drawers; I know where everything is.

HEDVIG: [*Stands a moment immovable, in terror and perplexity, biting her lips to keep back the tears; then she clenches her hands convulsively, and says softly.*] The wild duck.

[*She steals over and takes the pistol from the shelf, opens the garret door a little way, creeps in, and draws the door to after her.* HIALMAR *and* GINA *can be heard disputing in the sitting-room.*]

HIALMAR: [*Comes in with some manu-script books and old loose papers, which he lays upon the table.*] That portmanteau is of no use! There are a thousand and one things I must drag with me.

GINA: [*Following with the portmanteau.*] Why not leave all the rest for the present, and only take a shirt and a pair of woollen drawers with you?

HIALMAR: Whew!—all these exhausting preparations——! [*Pulls off his overcoat and throws it upon the sofa.*]

GINA: And there's the coffee getting cold.

HIALMAR: H'm. [*Drinks a mouthful with-out thinking of it, and then another.*]

GINA: [*Dusting the backs of the chairs.*] A nice job you'll have to find such another big garret for the rabbits.

HIALMAR: What! Am I to drag all those rabbits with me too?

GINA: You don't suppose grandfather can get on without his rabbits.

HIALMAR: He must just get used to doing without them. Have not *I* to sacrifice very much greater things than rabbits!

GINA: [*Dusting the bookcase.*] Shall I put the flute in the portmanteau for you?

HIALMAR: No. No flute for me. But give me the pistol!

GINA: Do you want to take the pigstol with you?

HIALMAR: Yes. My loaded pistol.

GINA: [*Searching for it.*] It's gone. He must have taken it in with him.

HIALMAR: Is he in the garret?

GINA: Yes, of course he's in the garret.

HIALMAR: H'm—poor lonely old man.

[*He takes a piece of bread and butter, eats it, and finishes his cup of coffee.*]

GINA: If we hadn't have let that room, you could have moved in there.

HIALMAR: And continued to live under the same roof with——! Never,—never!

GINA: But couldn't you put up with the sitting-room for a day or two? You could have it all to yourself.

HIALMAR: Never within these walls!

GINA: Well then, down with Relling and Molvik.

HIALMAR: Don't mention those wretches' names to me! The very thought of them al-most takes away my appetite.—Oh no, I must go out into the storm and the snow-drift,—go from house to house and seek shelter for my father and myself.

GINA: But you've got no hat, Ekdal! You've been and lost your hat, you know.

HIALMAR: Oh those two brutes, those slaves of all the vices! A hat must be pro-cured. [*Takes another piece of bread and butter.*] Some arrangement must be made. For I have no mind to throw away my life, either. [*Looks for something on the tray.*]

GINA: What are you looking for?

HIALMAR: Butter.

GINA: I'll get some at once. [*Goes out into the kitchen.*]

HIALMAR: [*Calls after her.*] Oh it doesn't matter; dry bread is good enough for me.

GINA: [*Brings a dish of butter.*] Look here; this is fresh churned.

[*She pours out another cup of coffee for him; he seats himself on the sofa, spreads more butter on the already but-tered bread, and eats and drinks awhile in silence.*]

HIALMAR: Could I, without being sub-ject to intrusion—intrusion of any sort—could I live in the sitting-room there for a day or two?

GINA: Yes, to be sure you could, if you only would.

HIALMAR: For I see no possibility of get-ting all father's things out in such a hurry.

GINA: And besides, you've surely got to tell him first as you don't mean to live with us others no more.

HIALMAR: [*Pushes away his coffee cup.*] Yes, there is that too; I shall have to lay bare the whole tangled story to him——. I must turn matters over; I must have breathing-time; I cannot take all these burdens on my shoulders in a single day.

GINA: No, especially in such horrible weather as it is outside.

HIALMAR: [*Touching* WERLE'S *letter.*] I see that paper is still lying about here.

GINA: Yes, I haven't touched it.

HIALMAR: So far as I am concerned it is mere waste paper——

GINA: Well, *I* have certainly no notion of making any use of it.

HIALMAR: ——but we had better not let

it get lost all the same;—in all the upset when I move, it might easily——

GINA: I'll take good care of it, Ekdal.

HIALMAR: The donation is in the first instance made to father, and it rests with him to accept or decline it.

GINA: [Sighs.] Yes, poor old father——

HIALMAR: To make quite safe—— Where shall I find some gum?

GINA: [Goes to the bookcase.] Here's the gum-pot.

HIALMAR: And a brush?

GINA: The brush is here too. [Brings him the things.]

HIALMAR: [Takes a pair of scissors.] Just a strip of paper at the back——[Clips and gums.] Far be it from me to lay hands upon what is not my own—and least of all upon what belongs to a destitute old man—and to—the other as well.—There now. Let it lie there for a time; and when it is dry, take it away. I wish never to see that document again. Never!

[GREGERS WERLE enters from the passage.]

GREGERS: [Somewhat surprised.] What, —are you sitting here, Hialmar?

HIALMAR: [Rises hurriedly.] I had sunk down from fatigue.

GREGERS: You have been having breakfast, I see.

HIALMAR: The body sometimes makes its claims felt too.

GREGERS: What have you decided to do?

HIALMAR: For a man like me, there is only one course possible. I am just putting my most important things together. But it takes time, you know.

GINA: [With a touch of impatience.] Am I to get the room ready for you, or am I to pack your portmanteau?

HIALMAR: [After a glance of annoyance at GREGERS.] Pack—and get the room ready!

GINA: [Takes the portmanteau.] Very well; then I'll put in the shirt and the other things. [Goes into the sitting-room and draws the door to after her.]

GREGERS: [After a short silence.] I never dreamed that this would be the end of it. Do you really feel it a necessity to leave house and home?

HIALMAR: [Wanders about restlessly.] What would you have me do?—I am not fitted to bear unhappiness, Gregers. I must feel secure and at peace in my surroundings.

GREGERS: But can you not feel that here?

Just try it. I should have thought you had firm ground to build upon now—if only you start afresh. And remember, you have your invention to live for.

HIALMAR: Oh don't talk about my invention. It's perhaps still in the dim distance.

GREGERS: Indeed.

HIALMAR: Why, great heavens, what would you have me invent? Other people have invented almost everything already. It becomes more and more difficult every day——

GREGERS: And you have devoted so much labour to it.

HIALMAR: It was that blackguard Relling that urged me to it.

GREGERS: Relling?

HIALMAR: Yes, it was he that first made me realise my aptitude for making some notable discovery in photography.

GREGERS: Aha—it was Relling!

HIALMAR: Oh, I have been so truly happy over it! Not so much for the sake of the invention itself, as because Hedvig believed in it—believed in it with a child's whole eagerness of faith.—At least, I have been fool enough to go and imagine that she believed in it.

GREGERS: Can you really think that Hedvig has been false towards you?

HIALMAR: I can think anything now. It is Hedvig that stands in my way. She will blot out the sunlight from my whole life.

GREGERS: Hedvig! Is it Hedvig you are talking of? How should she blot out your sunlight?

HIALMAR: [Without answering.] How unutterably I have loved that child! How unutterably happy I have felt every time I came home to my humble room, and she flew to meet me, with her sweet little blinking eyes. Oh, confiding fool that I have been! I loved her unutterably;—and I yielded myself up to the dream, the delusion, that she loved me unutterably in return.

GREGERS: Do you call that a delusion?

HIALMAR: How should I know? I can get nothing out of Gina; and besides, she is totally blind to the ideal side of these complications. But to you I feel impelled to open my mind, Gregers. I cannot shake off this frightful doubt—perhaps Hedvig has never really and honestly loved me.

GREGERS: What would you say if she were to give you a proof of her love? [Lis-

tens.] What's that? I thought I heard the wild duck——?

HIALMAR: It's the wild duck quacking. Father's in the garret.

GREGERS: Is he? [*His face lights up with joy.*] I say you may yet have proof that your poor misunderstood Hedvig loves you!

HIALMAR: Oh, what proof can she give me? I dare not believe in any assurances from that quarter.

GREGERS: Hedvig does not know what deceit means.

HIALMAR: Oh Gregers, that is just what I cannot be sure of. Who knows what Gina and that Mrs. Sörby may many a time have sat here whispering and tattling about? And Hedvig usually has her ears open, I can tell you. Perhaps the deed of gift was not such a surprise to her, after all. In fact, I'm not sure but that I noticed something of the sort.

GREGERS: What spirit is this that has taken possession of you?

HIALMAR: I have had my eyes opened. Just you notice;—you'll see, the deed of gift is only a beginning. Mrs. Sörby has always been a good deal taken up with Hedvig; and now she has the power to do whatever she likes for the child. They can take her from me whenever they please.

GREGERS: Hedvig will never, never leave you.

HIALMAR: Don't be so sure of that. If only they beckon to her and throw out a golden bait——! And oh! I have loved her so unspeakably! I would have counted it my highest happiness to take her tenderly by the hand and lead her, as one leads a timid child through a great dark empty room!—I am cruelly certain now that the poor photographer in his humble attic has never really and truly been anything to her. She has only cunningly contrived to keep on a good footing with him until the time came.

GREGERS: You don't believe that yourself, Hialmar.

HIALMAR: That is just the terrible part of it—I don't know what to believe,—I never can know it. But can you really doubt that it must be as I say? Ho-ho, you have far too much faith in the claim of the ideal, my good Gregers! If those others came, with the glamour of wealth about them, and called to the child:—"Leave him: come to us: here life awaits you——!"

GREGERS: [*Quickly.*] Well, what then?

HIALMAR: If I then asked her: Hedvig, are you willing to renounce that life for me? [*Laughs scornfully.*] No thank you! You would soon hear what answer I should get.

[*A pistol shot is heard from within the garret.*]

GREGERS: [*Loudly and joyfully.*] Hialmar!

HIALMAR: There now; he must needs go shooting too.

GINA: [*Comes in.*] Oh Ekdal, I can hear grandfather blazing away in the garret by hisself.

HIALMAR: I'll look in——

GREGERS: [*Eagerly, with emotion.*] Wait a moment! Do you know what that was?

HIALMAR: Yes, of course I know.

GREGERS: No you don't know. But *I* do. That was the proof!

HIALMAR: What proof?

GREGERS: It was a child's free-will offering. She has got your father to shoot the wild duck.

HIALMAR: To shoot the wild duck!

GINA: Oh, think of that——!

HIALMAR: What was that for?

GREGERS: She wanted to sacrifice to you her most cherished possession; for then she thought you would surely come to love her again.

HIALMAR: [*Tenderly, with emotion.*] Oh, poor child!

GINA: What things she does think of!

GREGERS: She only wanted your love again, Hialmar. She could not live without it.

GINA: [*Struggling with her tears.*] There, you can see for yourself, Ekdal.

HIALMAR: Gina, where is she?

GINA: [*Sniffs.*] Poor dear, she's sitting out in the kitchen, I dare say.

HIALMAR: [*Goes over, tears open the kitchen door, and says:*] Hedvig, come, come in to me! [*Looks round.*] No, she's not here.

GINA: Then she must be in her own little room.

HIALMAR: [*Without.*] No, she's not here either. [*Comes in.*] She must have gone out.

GINA: Yes, you wouldn't have her anywheres in the house.

HIALMAR: Oh, if she would only come home quickly, so that I can tell her—— Everything will come right now, Gregers; now I believe we can begin life afresh.

GREGERS: [*Quietly.*] I knew it; I knew the child would make amends.

[OLD EKDAL *appears at the door of his*

room; he is in full uniform, and is busy buckling on his sword.]

HIALMAR: [*Astonished.*] Father! Are you there?

GINA: Have you been firing in your room?

EKDAL: [*Resentfully, approaching.*] So you go shooting alone, do you, Hialmar?

HIALMAR: [*Excited and confused.*] Then it wasn't you that fired that shot in the garret?

EKDAL: Me that fired? H'm.

GREGERS: [*Calls out to* HIALMAR.] She has shot the wild duck herself!

HIALMAR: What can it mean? [*Hastens to the garret door, tears it aside, looks in and calls loudly:*] Hedvig!

GINA: [*Runs to the door.*] Good God, what's that!

HIALMAR: [*Goes in.*] She's lying on the floor!

GREGERS: Hedvig! lying on the floor! [*Goes in to* HIALMAR.]

GINA: [*At the same time.*] Hedvig! [*Inside the garret.*] No, no, no!

EKDAL: Ho-ho! does she go shooting too, now?

[HIALMAR, GINA, *and* GREGERS *carry* HEDVIG *into the studio; in her dangling right hand she holds the pistol fast clasped in her fingers.*]

HIALMAR: [*Distracted.*] The pistol has gone off. She has wounded herself. Call for help! Help!

GINA: [*Runs into the passage and calls down.*] Relling! Relling! Doctor Relling; come up as quick as you can!

[HIALMAR *and* GREGERS *lay* HEDVIG *down on the sofa.*]

EKDAL: [*Quietly.*] The woods avenge themselves.

HIALMAR: [*On his knees beside* HEDVIG.] She'll soon come to now. She's coming to——; yes, yes, yes.

GINA: [*Who has come in again.*] Where has she hurt herself? I can't see anything—— [RELLING *comes hurriedly, and immediately after him* MOLVIK; *the latter without his waistcoat and necktie, and with his coat open.*]

RELLING: What's the matter here?

GINA: They say Hedvig has shot herself.

HIALMAR: Come and help us!

RELLING: Shot herself! [*He pushes the table aside and begins to examine her.*]

HIALMAR: [*Kneeling and looking anxiously up at him.*] It can't be dangerous?

Speak, Relling! She is scarcely bleeding at all. It can't be dangerous?

RELLING: How did it happen?

HIALMAR: Oh, we don't know——!

GINA: She wanted to shoot the wild duck.

RELLING: The wild duck?

HIALMAR: The pistol must have gone off.

RELLING: H'm. Indeed.

EKDAL: The woods avenge themselves. But I'm not afraid, all the same. [*Goes into the garret and closes the door after him.*]

HIALMAR: Well, Relling,—why don't you say something?

RELLING: The ball has entered the breast.

HIALMAR: Yes, but she's coming to!

RELLING: Surely you can see that Hedvig is dead.

GINA: [*Bursts into tears.*] Oh my child, my child.

GREGERS: [*Huskily.*] In the depths of the sea——

HIALMAR: [*Jumps up.*] No, no, she must live! Oh, for God's sake, Relling—only a moment—only just till I can tell her how unspeakably I loved her all the time!

RELLING: The bullet has gone through her heart. Internal hemorrhage. Death must have been instantaneous.

HIALMAR: And I! I hunted her from me like an animal! And she crept terrified into the garret and died for love of me! [*Sobbing.*] I can never atone to her! I can never tell her——! [*Clenches his hands and cries, upwards.*] O thou above——! If thou indeed! Why hast thou done this thing to me?

GINA: Hush, hush, you mustn't go on that awful way. We had no right to keep her, I suppose.

MOLVIK: The child is not dead, but sleepeth.

RELLING: Bosh!

HIALMAR: [*Becomes calm, goes over to the sofa, folds his arms, and looks at* HEDVIG.] There she lies so stiff and still.

RELLING: [*Tries to loosen the pistol.*] She's holding it so tight, so tight.

GINA: No, no, Relling, don't break her fingers; let the pigstol be.

HIALMAR: She shall take it with her.

GINA: Yes, let her. But the child mustn't lie here for a show. She shall go to her own room, so she shall. Help me, Ekdal.

[HIALMAR *and* GINA *take* HEDVIG *between them.*]

HIALMAR: [*As they are carrying her.*] Oh Gina, Gina, can you survive this!

GINA: We must help each other to bear it. For now at least she belongs to both of us.

MOLVIK: [*Stretches out his arms and mumbles.*] Blessed be the Lord; to earth thou shalt return; to earth thou shalt re-turn——

RELLING: [*Whispers.*] Hold your tongue, you fool; you're drunk.

[HIALMAR *and* GINA *carry the body out through the kitchen door.* RELLING *shuts it after them.* MOLVIK *slinks out into the passage.*]

RELLING: [*Goes over to* GREGERS *and says.*] No one shall ever convince me that the pistol went off by accident.

GREGERS: [*Who has stood terrified, with convulsive twitchings.*] Who can say how the dreadful thing happened?

RELLING: The powder has burnt the body of her dress. She must have pressed the pistol right against her breast and fired.

GREGERS: Hedvig has not died in vain. Did you not see how sorrow set free what is noble in him?

RELLING: Most people are ennobled by the actual presence of death. But how long do you suppose this nobility will last in him?

GREGERS: Why should it not endure and increase throughout his life?

RELLING: Before a year is over, little Hedvig will be nothing to him but a pretty theme for declamation.

GREGERS: How dare you say that of Hialmar Ekdal?

RELLING: We will talk of this again, when the grass has first withered on her grave. Then you'll hear him spouting about "the child too early torn from her father's heart;" then you'll see him steep himself in a syrup of sentiment and self-admiration and self-pity. Just you wait!

GREGERS: If you are right and I am wrong, then life is not worth living.

RELLING: Oh, life would be quite tolerable, after all, if only we could be rid of the confounded duns that keep on pestering us, in our poverty, with the claim of the ideal.

GREGERS: [*Looking straight before him.*] In that case, I am glad that my destiny is what it is.

RELLING: May I inquire,—what is your destiny?

GREGERS: [*Going.*] To be the thirteenth at table.

RELLING: The devil it is.

THE END

ANTON CHEKHOV

LETTER to S. P. Diaguilev [1]

Yalta, Dec. 30, 1902

You write that we talked about a serious religious movement in Russia. We talked not of a Russian but of an intellectual movement. About Russia I won't say anything, and as for the intellectuals, they are at present only playing at religion, chiefly from lack of anything else to do. Of the cultured part of our public, it may be said that it has moved away from religion and is moving further and further away from it, whatever else may be said and whatever religious and philo-sophic societies may be formed. Whether that is a good or a bad thing I cannot decide; I will only say that the religious movement of which you write is one thing, and all modern culture is another, and it is impossible to place the latter in casual dependence on the former. Modern culture is but the beginning of a work for a great future, a work that will go on, perhaps, for tens of thousands of years, in order that mankind may, even in the remote future, come to know the truth of a real God—that is, not by guessing, not by seeking in Dostoevsky, but by perceiving clearly, as one perceives that twice two is four. Modern culture is only the beginning of a work, but the religious movement of which we spoke is a survival, almost the end of what has ceased, or is ceasing to exist. But it is a long story; one can't put it all into a letter. . . .

LETTER to O. L. Knipper [2]

Yalta, September 30, 1899

At your command I hasten to answer your letter in which you ask me about Astrov's last scene with Elena.

You write that Astrov addresses Elena in that scene like

[1] *The Life and Letters of Anton Tchekov*, trans. and ed. S. S. Kotelian-sky and Philip Tomlinson (New York, 1925), p. 282. Reprinted by permission of Cassell and Company Ltd., London.
[2] This letter and the following three to A. S. Suvorin are reprinted from *The Letters of Anton Chekhov to his Family and Friends*, trans. and ed. Constance Garnett (New York, 1920), pp. 368, 114–118, 99–100. Reprinted by permission of David Garnett and A. P. Watt and Son, London.

the most ardent lover, "clutches at his feeling like a drowning man at a straw."

But that's not right, not right at all! Astrov likes Elena, she attracts him by her beauty; but in the last act he knows already that nothing will come of it, and he talks to her in that scene in the same tone as of the heat in Africa, and kisses her quite casually, to pass the time. If Astrov takes that scene violently, the whole mood of the fourth act—quiet and despondent—is lost. . . .

LETTER to A. S. Suvorin

December 30, 1888

. . . Disappointment, apathy, nervous limpness and exhaustion are the inevitable consequence of extreme excitability, and such excitability is extremely characteristic of our young people. . . . Over-tired people never lose the capacity for becoming extremely excited, but cannot keep it up for long, and each excitement is followed by still greater apathy. . . .
. . . In my description of Ivanov there often occurs the word "Russian." Don't be cross about it. When I was writing the play I had in mind only the things that really matter— that is, only the typical Russian characteristics. Thus the extreme excitability, the feeling of guilt, the liability to become exhausted are purely Russian. Germans are never excited, and that is why Germany knows nothing of disappointed, superfluous, or over-tired people. . . . The excitability of the French is always maintained at one and the same level, and makes no sudden bounds or falls, and so a Frenchman is normally excited down to a decrepit old age. In other words, the French do not have to waste their strength in over-excitement; they spend their powers sensibly, and do not go bankrupt.

LETTER to A. S. Suvorin

Sumy, Madame Lintvaryov's Estate, May 30, 1888

. . . It seems to me it is not for writers of fiction to solve such questions as that of God, of pessimism, etc. The writer's business is simply to describe who has been speaking about God or about pessimism, how, and in what circumstances. The artist must be not the judge of his characters and of their conversations, but merely an impartial witness. I have heard a desultory conversation of two Russians about pessimism—a conversation which settles nothing—and I must report that conversation as I heard it; it is for the jury, that is, for the readers, to decide on the value of it. My business is merely to be talented—*i.e.*, to know how to distinguish important statements from unimportant, how to throw light on the characters, and to speak their language. Shtcheglov-Leontyev blames me for finishing the story with the words, "There's no making out anything in this world." He thinks a writer who is a good psychologist ought to be able to make it out— that is what he is a psychologist for. But I don't agree with him. It is time that writers, especially those who are artists, recognized that there is no making out anything in this world, as once Socrates recognized it, and Voltaire, too.

LETTER to A. S. Suvorin

Moscow, October 27, 1888

. . . In conversation with my literary colleagues I always insist that it is not the artist's business to solve problems that require a specialist's knowledge. It is a bad thing if a writer tackles a subject he does not understand. We have specialists for dealing with special questions: It is their business to judge of the commune, of the future of capitalism, of the evils of drunkenness, of boots, of the diseases of women. An artist must only judge of what he understands, his field is just as limited as that of any other specialist—I repeat this and insist on it always. That in his sphere there are no questions, but only answers, can only be maintained by those who have never written and have had no experience of thinking in images. An artist observes, selects, guesses, combines—and this in itself presupposes a problem: unless he had set himself a problem from the very first there would be nothing to conjecture and nothing to select. To put it briefly, I will end by using the language of psychiatry: if one denies that creative work involves problems and purposes, one must admit that an artist creates without premeditation or intention, in a state of aberration; therefore, if an author boasted to me of having written a novel without a preconceived design, under a sudden inspiration, I should call him mad.

You are right in demanding that an artist should take an intelligent attitude to his work, but you confuse two things: *solving a problem* and *stating a problem correctly*. It is only the second that is obligatory for the artist. In *Anna Karenin* and *Evgeny Onyegin* not a single problem is solved, but they satisfy you completely because all the problems are correctly stated in them. It is the business of the judge to put the right questions, but the answers must be given by the jury according to their own lights.

ANTON CHEKHOV

Uncle Vanya

CHARACTERS

SEREBRIAKOFF, ALEXANDER VLADIMIROVICH, *a retired professor.*

ELENA ANDREEVNA, *his wife, twenty-seven years old.*

SOFIA ALEXANDROVNA (SONIA), *his daughter by a first marriage.*

VOINITSKAYA, MARIA VASILIEVNA, *widow of a privy councillor, mother of the first wife of the professor.*

VOINITSKY, IVAN PETROVICH, *her son* (UNCLE VANYA).

ASTROFF, MIKHAIL LVOVICH, *a doctor.*

TELEGIN, ILYA ILYICH, *an impoverished landowner.*

MARINA, *an old nurse.*

A WORKMAN.

The action takes place on the estate of Serebriakoff.

Anton Chekhov, "Uncle Vanya," *Best Plays by Chekhov,* trans. Stark Young (New York, 1956). Copyright © 1956 by Stark Young. Reprinted by permission of the Estate of Stark Young, and Leah Salisbury, Inc.

ACT ONE

A garden. A part of the house, and its terrace, can be seen. Under an old poplar in the alley a table is set for tea. There are benches and chairs; a guitar lies on one of the benches. Not far from the table, there is a swing. It is past two in the afternoon of a cloudy day.

MARINA, *a plain, small old woman, sits near the samovar without moving, and knits on a stocking.* ASTROFF *walks to and fro near her.*

MARINA: [*Pouring a glass.*] Drink some tea, son, please.

ASTROFF: [*Accepts the glass unwillingly.*] Somehow I don't feel like it.

MARINA: Maybe you'll drink a little vodka?

ASTROFF: No. I don't drink vodka every day. Besides, it's very sultry today. [*A pause.*] Nurse, how long have we known each other?

MARINA: [*Thinking it over.*] How long? May God help me to remember. . . . You came here to these parts . . . When? . . . Vera Petrovna was still alive, little Sonia's mother. In her time you were here for two winters . . . so it comes to about eleven years in all. [*Pausing to think.*] And maybe even more. . . .

ASTROFF: Have I changed much since then?

MARINA: Much. Then you were young and handsome, and now you have aged. And your good looks now are not what they were. And what's more, might we say . . . you drink a little vodka.

ASTROFF: Yes. . . . In ten years I have become a different man. And what is the reason? I am overworked, nurse. From morning till night, always on your feet, don't know what rest is, and at night you lie under a blanket and are afraid you might be dragged off to see some sick man. During all the time we have known each other I have not had one free day. How can anybody not grow old? And life itself is boring, stupid, dirty . . . it strangles you, this life. Around you only odd people, without exception, odd people; and having lived with them two or three years, little by little you get to be odd yourself. It's unavoidable fate. [*Twirling his long mustache.*] Look how I've grown this enormous mustache . . . it's a silly mustache. I've grown odd. Nurse . . . I haven't grown stupider; my brains, thank God, are in the right place, but my feelings somehow have grown numb. There's nothing I want, nothing I need, nobody I love. . . . Maybe it's only you that I love. [*Kissing her head.*] When I was little I had a nurse like you.

MARINA: Maybe you'd like something to eat.

ASTROFF: No. The third week of Lent I went to Malitskoye to an epidemic . . . typhus. . . . The huts were stacked full of people. Filth, stench, smoke, calves running around the floor among the sick . . . and pigs too. . . . I was hard at it all day, never sat down, didn't have a bite to eat and when I came home, they wouldn't let me rest— they brought in a railroad switchman; I put him on the table to perform an operation, and he ups and dies on me under the chloroform. And just when I didn't need any feelings, my feelings woke up, my conscience was stricken, as if I had killed him deliberately. . . . I sat down, closed my eyes—like this—and I thought: those who will live one or two hundred years after us, and those we blaze the trail for now, will they remember us with a kind word? But they won't, Nurse.

MARINA: People won't remember but God will remember.

ASTROFF: Thank you very much. That was well said.

[VOINITSKY *comes out of the house; he has had a nap after lunch and looks rumpled. He sits down on the bench as he arranges his stylish necktie.*]

VOINITSKY: Yes. . . . [*A pause.*] Yes. . . .

ASTROFF: Had enough sleep?

VOINITSKY: Yes . . . Very much so.

60

[*Yawns.*] Since the Professor and his spouse came to live here, life is off the track . . . I sleep at odd hours, for lunch and dinner I eat a lot of highly-spiced dishes, drink wine . all that is not good for your health. We never used to have a free minute, Sonia and I worked—I can tell you that—and now it's only Sonia who works, and I sleep, eat, drink. . . . There's no good in it.

MARINA: [*Shaking her head.*] No order to anything around here. The Professor gets up at twelve o'clock, but the samovar has been boiling since early morning, waiting for him. Without them here we used to have dinner right after noon as people do everywhere, and with them here it is nearly seven. At night the Professor reads and writes, and suddenly when it's after one at night there's a ring. . . . What is it, sir? Tea! Wake up people for him, start the samovar. [*Scornfully.*] What order!

ASTROFF: And will they stay here long?

VOINITSKY: A hundred years. The Professor has decided to settle down here.

MARINA: There now. You see. The samovar has already been two hours on the table, and they are gone walking.

VOINITSKY: Here they are, here they are. . . . Don't get upset.

[*Voices are heard; from the depths of the garden, returning from a walk, come* SEREBRIAKOFF, ELENA ANDREEVNA, SONIA *and* TELEGIN.]

SEREBRIAKOFF: Wonderful, wonderful. . . . Wonderful views!

TELEGIN: Remarkable, your Excellency.

SONIA: We'll go into the woods tomorrow, Papa. Would you like to?

VOINITSKY: Ladies and gentlemen, tea!

SEREBRIAKOFF: Send my tea into my study, be so kind, my friends. I have something more that I must do today.

SONIA: And you will surely like the woods.

[ELENA ANDREEVNA, SEREBRIAKOFF, *and* SONIA *go into the house;* TELEGIN *goes to the table and sits down near* MARINA.]

VOINITSKY: It's hot. stifling really, but our great scientist has an overcoat on, rubbers. an umbrella and gloves.

ASTROFF: That means he is preserving his health.

VOINITSKY: But how beautiful she is! How beautiful! In all my life I have never seen a lovelier woman.

TELEGIN: [*His speech is high-pitched and pretentious.*] Whether I ride in the field, Marina Timofeevna, walk in the shady garden, or look at this table, I experience inexplicable delight! The weather is charming, the little birds sing, we all live in this world in harmony—what more could we have! [*Accepting a glass of tea.*] I am deeply grateful to you!

VOINITSKY: [*Dreamily.*] What eyes. . . . Wonderful woman!

ASTROFF: Talk about something, Ivan Petrovich.

VOINITSKY: [*Listlessly.*] What shall I talk ˙ about?

ASTROFF: Isn't there anything new?

VOINITSKY: Nothing. Everything is an old story. I am the same as I always was, grown worse very likely, since I'm getting lazy; I do nothing and only make a fuss like any old grumbler. My old magpie *Maman* is still babbling about the emancipation of women; with one eye she looks into the grave and with the other she rummages through her learned books for the dawn of a new life.

ASTROFF: And the Professor?

VOINITSKY: And the Professor as usual sits from morning till late at night in his study and writes. As the poet says, "Straining our brain, knitting our brow, we keep writing, writing odes, but neither we nor they hear any praise anywhere." Poor paper! It would be better if he wrote his autobiography. What a capital subject that would be! A retired professor, you under stand, an old crust, a learned old dried mackerel. Gout, rheumatism, migraine, and his liver swollen with jealousy and envy. . . . So this mackerel lives on the estate of his first wife, lives there against his will because he cannot afford to live in town. Forever complains of his misfortunes, though as a matter of fact, he is unusually lucky. [*Nervously.*] You just think what luck! He was the son of a humble sacristan, he was a simple theological student, and attained to a university degree and a professor's chair, became his Excellency, the son-in-law of a Senator, *et cetera, et cetera.* All that is unimportant, however; this is the point: a man for exactly twenty-five years reads and writes about art, and understands exactly nothing about art. Twenty-five years he chews over some other man's thoughts about realism, naturalism, and all the other nonsense, twenty-five years reads and writes about what intelligent people already know and stupid people are not interested in—which means that for twenty-five years he pours from empty to empty. And along with it what conceit! What pretense! He retired, and he is not known to a single living soul, he is absolutely unknown; which just means that for those twenty-five years he was occupying somebody else's place. But, mind you, he strides about like a demigod!

ASTROFF: Well, it seems you are envious.

VOINITSKY: Yes, I am envious! Look at his success with women! No Don Juan ever knew such complete success as he's had. His first wife, my sister—she was a beautiful, gentle creature, pure as this blue sky, noble, generous, who had more admirers than he had students—she loved him as only pure angels might love those who are as pure and beautiful as they are. His mother-in-law, my mother, still adores him, and he still inspires her with holy awe. His second wife, a beauty, clever—you just saw her—married him when he was already old, gave him her youth, beauty, freedom, brilliance. For what? Why?

ASTROFF: Is she faithful to the professor?

VOINITSKY: Unfortunately, yes.

ASTROFF: And why unfortunately?

VOINITSKY: Faithfulness like this is false from beginning to end; it has a fine sound but no logic. To be unfaithful to an old husband you cannot bear—is immoral; but to try to silence within yourself your poor youth and your live feelings—that is quite moral.

TELEGIN: [In a tearful voice.] Vanya, I don't like it when you say that. Really, now . . . anybody who is unfaithful to wife or to husband, is, it means so to me, an unfaithful person, who can even be unfaithful to his country!

VOINITSKY: [Annoyed.] Oh, turn off your tap, Waffles!

TELEGIN: Allow me, Vanya—my wife ran off with her lover the day after our wedding [Pompously.] because of my unattractive appearance. After that I have not shirked my duty. I still, up till now, love her and am faithful to her, help her with what I can, and gave up my property to educate the little children she begot with her lover. Happiness I am robbed of, but I still have pride. And she? Her youth is

gone, her beauty, under the influence of the laws of nature, is faded, her lover has passed away. . . . What has she left?

[Enter SONIA and ELENA ANDREEVNA; a little later enter MARIA VASILIEVNA with a book; she sits down and reads; she is served tea and she drinks it without looking up.]

SONIA: [Rapidly to nurse.] There, Nurse, the peasants have come. Go talk to them, and I'll pour the tea. [Pours tea.]

[The nurse leaves, ELENA takes her cup and drinks, sitting in the swing.]

ASTROFF: [To ELENA.] I really came to see your husband. You wrote that he is very sick, rheumatism and something else, but apparently he is quite well.

ELENA: Yesterday evening he was down in the dumps, complained of pains in his legs, and today he is quite fit.

ASTROFF: And with me, breaking my neck, galloping thirty versts. Well, it's all right, and it's not the first time. Just for that I'll stay with you till tomorrow and, at least, will sleep quantum satis.

SONIA: Wonderful! You so very seldom spend the night with us. Very likely you haven't had any dinner?

ASTROFF: No, I have not.

SONIA: So then you shall have dinner as well. We now dine after six o'clock. [Drinking.] The tea's cold!

TELEGIN: In the samovar the temperature has already lowered considerably.

ELENA: Very well, Ivan Ivanovich, we will drink it cold.

TELEGIN: Excuse me . . . Not Ivan Ivanovich, but Ilya Ilyich . . . Ilya Ilyich Telegin, or, as some people call me with my pock-marked face, Waffles. Once upon a time it was I who christened Sonia, and his Excellency, your spouse, knows me very well. I live with you now on this estate. . . . If you have deigned to notice, I have dinner with you every day.

SONIA: Ilya Ilyich is our helper, our right hand. [Tenderly.] Let me pour you some more, Godfather.

MARIA VOINITSKAYA: Oh!

SONIA: What is it, Grandmother?

MARIA VOINITSKAYA: I forgot to tell Alexander . . . I forgot something. . . . I received a letter today from Kharkoff from Pavel Alexeevich. . . . He sent his new pamphlet.

ASTROFF: Is it interesting?

MARIA VOINITSKAYA: Interesting, but it's

strange somehow. He disapproves of what seven years ago he himself defended. It's terrible!

VOINITSKY: There is nothing terrible in that. Drink, Mama, drink your tea.

MARIA VOINITSKAYA: But I want to talk!

VIONITSKY: But for fifty years now we talk and talk, and read pamphlets. It's high time to stop.

MARIA VOINITSKAYA: You seem to find it hard to listen when I talk. Forgive me, Jean, but during the last year you have changed so that I absolutely do not recognize you. . . . You used to be a man of strong convictions, a bright personality.

VOINITSKY: Oh, yes! I used to be a bright personality that didn't give light to anybody. [*A pause.*] I used to be a bright personality! . . . That couldn't be more venomous! I am forty-seven years old. Up to last year, I deliberately tried just as you do to blind my eyes with this pedantry of yours and not to see real life—and I thought I was doing well. And now, if you only knew! I don't sleep nights because of disappointment, and anger that I so stupidly let time slip by, when now I could have had everything that my old age denies me!

SONIA: Uncle Vanya, that's boring.

MARIA VOINITSKAYA: [*To her son.*] It looks as if you are challenging your former convictions. . . . But they are not guilty, it's you are guilty. You keep forgetting that a conviction in itself is nothing, it's a dead letter. . . . You should have been doing something.

VOINITSKY: Doing something? Not everybody is capable of being a *perpetuum mobile* writing, like your *Herr* professor.

MARIA VOINITSKAYA: What do you mean by that?

SONIA: [*Imploringly.*] Grandmother! Uncle Vanya! I beg you!

VOINITSKY: I am silent. Silent and apologizing. [*A pause.*]

ELENA: And fine weather today . . . Not hot. . . . [*A pause.*]

VOINITSKY: It's fine weather to hang yourself. . . .

[TELEGIN *tunes the guitar.* MARINA *walks near the house and calls the chickens.*]

MARINA: Here, Chick, Chick, Chick. . . .

SONIA: Nurse, why have the peasants come? . . .

MARINA: Still the same old thing, still about the waste plot of land. Here, Chick, Chick, Chick. . . .

SONIA: Which one are you calling?

MARINA: Spotty! She's gone off with her chicks. . . . The crows might get them. [*Goes out.*]

[TELEGIN *plays a polka; everyone listens silently;* A WORKMAN *enters.*]

WORKMAN: Master Doctor here? [*To* ASTROFF.] Please, Mikhail Lvovich, we came to get you.

ASTROFF: From where?

WORKMAN: From the factory.

ASTROFF: [*Annoyed.*] I thank you humbly. Then, I must go. [*Looks around for his cap.*] Bother, the devil take it. . . . Where is that cap?

SONIA: How tiresome it is, really . . . to come from the factory to dinner!

ASTROFF: No. It will be too late. Where . . . Where to . . . [*To the* WORKMAN.] Here's what, slip me a glass of vodka, my good fellow, anyhow. [WORKMAN *goes out.*] Where . . . where to. . . . [*Finds his cap.*] Ostroffsky in some play of his has a man with a big mustache and small abilities. . . . That's me. Well, I have the honor to bid you good-by, ladies and gentlemen. [*To* ELENA.] If you would look in on me some time, you and Sonia here, I'd be very glad—truly. I have a tiny little estate, in all about thirty acres, but, if it interests you, a model garden and nursery, such as you won't find around here in a thousand miles. Next to me is the state forestry. . . . The forester there is old, always sick, and the truth is I handle all the work that's done.

ELENA: They have told me that you love the woods very much. Of course, one can be very useful, but doesn't it interfere with your real calling? After all you are a doctor.

ASTROFF: God only knows what is our real calling.

ELENA: And is it interesting?

ASTROFF: Yes, it's an interesting business.

VOINITSKY: [*Ironically.*] Very!

ELENA: [*To* ASTROFF.] You are still a young man, you look . . . well thirty-six or -seven years old . . . and it must not be quite so interesting as you say, with always the trees and the trees and the trees. I think it's monotonous.

SONIA: No, it is extremely interesting. Every year Mikhail Lvovich plants new wood plots and they have already sent him a bronze medal and a diploma. He petitioned not to have the old ones destroyed. If you would only hear him out you would agree with him completely. He says that forests adorn the earth, that they teach a man to understand the beautiful and inspire him to lofty moods. Forests soften a severe climate. In countries where the climate is mild, you spend less effort in the struggle with nature, and so man there is gentler and tenderer; people are beautiful there, lively, easily excited, their speech is exquisite, their movements are graceful. Their sciences and arts blossom, their philosophy is not gloomy, their relation to a woman is full of exquisite nobility . . .

VOINITSKY: [Laughing.] Bravo, bravo! All this is darling, but not convincing, and so [To ASTROFF.] allow me, my friend, to go on heating stoves with wood and building barns out of wood.

ASTROFF: You can heat stoves with peat moss, and build barns with stones. Well, I admit you may cut woods out of some need, but why destroy them? Russian woods are creaking under the ax, milliards of trees perish, dwellings of beasts and birds are emptied, rivers go shallow and dry, wonderful landscapes vanish, never to be brought back again, and all because lazy man hasn't sense enough to bend down and pick up fuel from the ground. [To ELENA.] Isn't that the truth, my lady? He must be a reckless barbarian to burn this beauty in his stove, destroy what we cannot create again. Man is endowed with intellect and creative powers so that he may multiply what is given to him, but up to now he has not created, he has destroyed. Forests are fewer and fewer, rivers dry up, game becomes extinct, the climate is ruined, and every day the earth gets poorer and uglier. [To VOINITSKY.] Here you are with that mocking look in your eyes, and all I say seems to you not very serious and . . . and, indeed it may be foolishness; but, when I pass the peasants' woods that I have saved from being chopped down, or when I hear the sound of my young wood rustling, the stand I planted with my own hands, I realize that climate too is a little in my power, and that a thousand years from now if man should be happy, why, then I'll be a small part of that too. When I plant a birch and see it later on burst into green and wave in the wind, my soul fills with pride, and I . . . [Seeing the WORKMAN,

who has brought a tray with a glass of vodka.] However . . . [Drinks.] it's time. The whole thing very likely is only foolishness after all. I have the honor to bid you good-by. [Going toward the house.]

SONIA: [Taking his arm and going along with him.] When will you come to see us?

ASTROFF: I don't know.

SONIA: Again after a month?

[ASTROFF and SONIA go into the house; MARIA VASILIEVNA and TELEGIN remain near the table; ELENA and VOINITSKY go toward the terrace.]

ELENA: And you, Ivan Petrovich, you behaved yourself impossibly again. Did you have to annoy Maria Vasilievna, talking of perpetuum mobile! And today at lunch you argued with Alexander again. How small of you that is!

VOINITSKY: But what if I detest him!

ELENA: There is nothing to detest Alexander for, he is the same as you all are. Not any worse than you are.

VOINITSKY: If you could see your face, your movements. . . . How lazy your life is! Oh, how lazy!

ELENA: Oh, both lazy and bored! Everybody blames my husband, everybody looks at me with pity: miserable creature, she has an old husband! This concern over me—oh, how I understand it! Just as Astroff said: you all go on ruining our woods recklessly and soon there will be nothing left on earth. In the same way you ruin man recklessly and soon, thanks to you, soon there will be no faithfulness, no purity, no capacity for sacrifice left on earth. Why can't you look at a woman with indifference if she is not yours? Because—the doctor was right—in all of you sits the demon of destruction. You have no pity either for woods or birds, or women, or for each other.

VOINITSKY: I don't like this philosophy. [A pause.]

ELENA: This doctor has a tired, nervous face. An interesting face. It's obvious Sonia likes him, she is in love with him, and I understand her. While I have been here he has been here three times already, but I am shy and have not really talked to him once even, and haven't been kind to him. He thought I had a grudge against him. It's quite possible that the reason you and I are such friends, Ivan, is that both of us are tiresome, boring people! Tiresome!

Don't look at me that way, I don't like it.

VOINITSKY: How can I look at you differently if I love you? You are my joy, my life, my youth! I know my chance of any return is just about nil, but I don't want anything, just let me look at you, hear your voice. . . .

ELENA: Hush they might hear you!

[*They go toward the house.*]

VOINITSKY: [*Following her.*] Don't drive me away, let me talk about my love, and just that will be the greatest happiness for me.

ELENA: This is painful. [*Both enter the house.*]

[TELEGIN *strums some chords and plays a polka;* MARIA VASILIEVNA *is jotting something down on the margins of the pamphlet.*]

CURTAIN

ACT TWO

Dining room in SEREBRIAKOFF'S *house. It is night; you can hear the watchman tapping in the garden.* SEREBRIAKOFF *is sitting in an easy chair in front of an open window, dozing.* ELENA ANDREEVNA *sits near him and is also dozing.*

SEREBRIAKOFF: [*Awakening suddenly.*] Who is there? Sonia, you?

ELENA: This is me.

SEREBRIAKOFF: You, Lenotchka. . . . This unbearable pain!

ELENA: Your robe has fallen on the floor. [*Bundles up his legs.*] I'll shut the window, Alexander.

SEREBRIAKOFF: No, not for me, to me it's stuffy. I just now dozed off and dreamed that my left leg did not belong to me. An excruciating pain woke me up. No, this is not the gout, it's rheumatism, more likely. What time is it now?

ELENA: Twenty minutes past midnight. [*A pause.*]

SEREBRIAKOFF: In the morning look in the library for Batyushkov. It seems to me we have him.

ELENA: What?

SEREBRIAKOFF: Look for Batyushkov in the morning. I seem to remember we had him. But why is it so hard for me to breathe?

ELENA: You are tired. Not sleeping a second night.

SEREBRIAKOFF: They say that Turgenev developed angina from gout. I am afraid it might be that way with me. This damned, disgusting old age, the devil take it! When I got old I began to be revolting to myself. And you all, I dare say, find it revolting to look at me.

ELENA: You speak of your old age as if we were all guilty of your being old.

SEREBRIAKOFF: And you are the first one to be revolted. [ELENA *moves away and sits down farther away from him.*] Of course, you are right. I am not stupid and I understand. You are young, healthy, beautiful, you want to live, and I am an old man, almost a corpse. So? As if I didn't understand? And, of course, it's stupid of me to be still alive. But wait a little, soon I'll set you all free. It won't be much longer now that I shall have to drag myself around.

ELENA: I can't bear it. . . . For God's sake, be quiet.

SEREBRIAKOFF: It looks as if nobody can bear it, thanks to me; everyone is bored, everyone is ruining their youth, I am the only one. I'm the only one who's enjoying life and is content. Yes, of course!

ELENA: [*In tears.*] Be quiet! You have me all worn out.

SEREBRIAKOFF: I am torturing everybody. Of course.

ELENA: [*Through her tears.*] It's unbearable! Tell me, what do you want from me?

SEREBRIAKOFF: Nothing.

ELENA: Well, then, be quiet. I beg you.

SEREBRIAKOFF: It's a strange thing, Ivan Petrovich begins to talk or that old idiot, Maria Vasilievna—and it's quite all right with everybody listening; but if I say just one word, look how everybody begins to be miserable. Even my voice is revolting. Well, let us suppose I am revolting, I am an egoist, I am a despot—but don't I really, even in my old age, have some right to egotism?

As if I have not earned it? As if, is what I'm asking you, I have no right to a quiet old age, to some attention from people?

ELENA: Nobody is disputing your rights. [*A window is banging in the wind.*] A wind has come up, I'll close the window. [*Closing it.*]. It will rain soon. Nobody is disputing your rights.

[*A pause; the watchman in the garden is tapping and singing a song.*]

SEREBRIAKOFF: To work all your life for learning, grow used to your desk, to your auditorium, to your esteemed colleagues—and suddenly, for no reason, to find yourself in this morgue, to see here every day stupid people, to listen to flat conversations. . . . I want to live, I love success, I love fame, applause—and then here—here I am like an exile. To grieve over your past every minute, to watch the success of the others, to fear death . . . I can't! I haven't the strength for it! And here they are, they won't even forgive me for being old.

ELENA: Wait, do have patience: in five or six years I'll be old too.

[*Enter* SONIA.]

SONIA: Papa, you yourself gave orders to fetch Doctor Astroff, and when he got here you refused to see him. That is not very nice. We have just bothered a man for nothing.

SEREBRIAKOFF: What do I need your Astroff for? He understands just about as much of medicine as I understand of astronomy.

SONIA: We can't with your gout summon the entire medical faculty.

SEREBRIAKOFF: I wouldn't even talk to that imbecile.

SONIA: As you like. [*Sitting down.*] It's all the same to me.

SEREBRIAKOFF: What time is it now?

ELENA: Past midnight.

SEREBRIAKOFF: I'm suffocating—Sonia, fetch me the drops from the table!

SONIA: Certainly, at once. [*She hands him the drops.*]

SEREBRIAKOFF: [*With annoyance.*] Ach, not those! You can't even ask—you can't even ask for anything!

SONIA: I beg you, don't be capricious. It might please some people, but not me; kindly leave me out of it. I don't like it. Besides I have no time to waste. I have to get up early tomorrow, I've got hay to cut.

[*Enter* VOINITSKY *in a dressing gown, with a candle.*]

VOINITSKY: A storm is gathering outside. [*Lightning.*] There, now! Elena and Sonia, go to sleep, I have come to take your place.

SEREBRIAKOFF: [*Alarmed.*] No, no! Don't leave me with him! No. He'll talk my head off.

VOINITSKY: But we must give them some rest! It is the second night now they have not had any sleep.

SEREBRIAKOFF: Let them go to sleep, but you go away too. Thank you. I implore you. For the sake of our former friendship, don't protest. We'll talk later.

VOINITSKY: [*Smiling ironically.*] Our former friendship . . . former . . . !

SONIA: Be quiet, Uncle Vanya.

SEREBRIAKOFF: [*To his wife.*] My dear, don't leave me with him! He'll talk my head off.

VOINITSKY: Really, this is just getting to be laughable.

[*Enter* MARINA *with a candle.*]

SONIA: You ought to lie down, Nurse. It's already late.

MARINA: The samovar hasn't been cleared from the table yet. How can you very well lie down?

SEREBRIAKOFF: Everybody doesn't sleep, everybody can't bear it, only I, I alone am blissfully happy.

MARINA: [*Comes to* SEREBRIAKOFF, *tenderly.*] What is it, dear sir? Does it hurt? My legs throb too, how they throb! [*Arranging the robe.*] This is your old ailment. Vera Petrovna, Sonia's dear mother, used to spend sleepless nights, killing herself, pitying you. She loved you so. [*A pause.*] Old ones like young ones want somebody to feel sorry for them, but nobody feels sorry for the old. [*Kisses* SEREBRIAKOFF *on his shoulder.*] Dear sir, let's go to bed. . . . Let's go, my dear. . . . I will give you some linden tea to drink, it will warm up your feet. . . . I'll pray to God for you.

SEREBRIAKOFF: [*Very much touched.*] Let us go, Marina.

MARINA: My legs throb so, throb so! [*She and* SONIA *are leading him.*] Your Vera Petrovna, Sonia's mother, was always killing herself with pity, always crying. . . . You were still small and foolish, Sonia, then. Come, come, dear sir.

[SEREBRIAKOFF, SONIA *and* MARINA *go out.*]

ELENA: I am worn out with him. I can hardly stand up.

VOINITSKY: You with him, I with myself. It's the third night now I have not slept.

ELENA: Things are not going very well in this house. Your mother hates everything except her pamphlets and the Professor; the Professor is cross, he won't trust me, and is afraid of you; Sonia is angry at her father, she is angry at me and hasn't spoken to me for two weeks now; you hate my husband and openly scorn your mother; I am irritable and twenty times today have been ready to cry. . . . Things are not going very well in this house.

VOINITSKY: Let's leave philosophy out of it!

ELENA: Ivan, you are educated and intelligent and you must understand that the world is going to ruin not from robbing, not from fires, but from hate, enmity, from all this petty squabbling. . . . Your business should not be to grumble, but to make peace among us all.

VOINITSKY: First of all you make me make peace with myself! My darling . . . [Seizing her hand.]

ELENA: Stop it! [Takes away her hand.] Go away!

VOINITSKY: The rain will be over now and everything in nature will be fresh and breathing. Only I will not be refreshed by the storm. Day and night like a fiend at my throat is the thought that my life is hopelessly lost. No past, it was stupidly spent on trifles, and the present with all its absurdity is frightful. Here they are: my life and my love: where shall I put them, what shall I do with them? This feeling of mine is dying in vain, like a ray of sunlight that has strayed into a pit, and I myself am dying.

ELENA: When you talk to me of your love, I get numb somehow and don't know what to say. Forgive me, there is really nothing I can say to you. [She wants to go.] Good night.

VOINITSKY: [Barring her way.] And if only you knew how I suffer from the thought that next to me in the same house another life is dying—yours! Your life. What are you waiting for? What curst philosophy is it in your way? Do understand, understand . . .

ELENA: [Looking at him closely.] Ivan Petrovich, are you drunk?

VOINITSKY: Perhaps, perhaps . . .

ELENA: Where is the doctor?

VOINITSKY: He is there spending the night with me. Perhaps, perhaps. . . . Anything is possible!

ELENA: And today you were drinking? Why is that?

VOINITSKY: Because it is like living. Somehow—like living. Don't stand in my way, Elena!

ELENA: You never used to drink and never used to talk so much. Go to bed! I am bored with you.

VOINITSKY: [Seizing her hand.] My darling . . . My beautiful!

ELENA: [Annoyed.] Let me alone. After all, it is revolting. [Goes out.]

VOINITSKY: [Alone.] She is gone. [A pause.] Ten years ago I used to meet her at my dear sister's. She was seventeen then and I was thirty-seven years old. Why didn't I fall in love with her then and propose to her? It was so possible. And by now she would have been my wife . . . Yes . . . Now we both would have been awakened by the storm; she would have been frightened by the thunder and I would have held her in my arms and whispered: "Don't be afraid, I am here." Oh, beautiful thoughts, how wonderful, I am even smiling . . . but, my God, thoughts are getting tangled up in my head. . . . Why am I old? Why doesn't she understand me? Her rhetoric, her idle moralizing, her foolish, idle thoughts about the end of the world—all that is hateful to me. [A pause.] Oh, how I was deceived! I adored that Professor, that pitiful, gouty creature, I worked for him like an ox! Sonia and I squeezed out of this estate its last drop of juice; like thrifty peasants we sold vegetable oil, beans, cottage cheese, went hungry ourselves so that out of pennies and halfpennies we might pile up thousands and send them to him. I used to be proud of him and his learning, I lived and breathed it! All he wrote and uttered seemed to me genius. . . . God, and now here he is retired, and you can see now the whole sum of his life. After he is gone there won't be a single page of his work left behind; he is absolutely unknown, he is nothing! A soap bubble! And I've been fooled . . . I can see . . . stupid . . . fooled . . .

[Enter ASTROFF in a Prince Albert coat without a waistcoat and without *a necktie; he is a bit tipsy; after him* TELEGIN *with a guitar.*]

ASTROFF: Play!

[TELEGIN *strums softly.*]

ASTROFF: [*To* VOINITSKY.] Are you alone here? No ladies?

[*Hands on hips, sings softly.*]
"Go away hut, go away stove,
The master has no room to lie down . . ."
And I was awakened by the storm. A downright, soaking rain it was. What time is it now?

VOINITSKY: Ah, the devil only knows.

ASTROFF: It seems to me I heard the voice of Elena Andreevna.

VOINITSKY: She was just here.

ASTROFF: Superb woman! [*Looking at the medicine bottles on the table.*] Medicines. Every sort of prescription. From Kharkov, and Moscow, and Tula. . . . All the towns in Russia have had enough of his gout. Is he ill or is he pretending to be?

VOINITSKY: Ill. He's ill.

[*A pause.*]

ASTROFF: Why are you sad today? Is it the Professor you are sorry for, perhaps?

VOINITSKY: Leave me alone.

ASTROFF: And in love with the Professor's wife perhaps?

VOINITSKY: She is my friend.

ASTROFF: Already?

VOINITSKY: What does that mean—"already"?

ASTROFF: A woman can be a man's friend only in some such sequence as this: first, a companion, then a mistress, and then after that a friend.

VOINITSKY: That's a vulgar philosophy.

ASTROFF: So that's it. Yes . . . I must confess I'm getting to be a vulgarian. You can see too I'm drunk. Usually I get drunk only once a month. When I'm like that I get very brazen and impertinent to the very limit. Then anything goes. I undertake the most difficult operations and do them beautifully; I paint the broadest plans for the future; at such times I don't look like a fool to myself any more, and believe that I am bringing an enormous boon to humanity . . . enormous! . . . At such times I have my own system of philosophy, and all of you, my little brothers, seem to me such very small insects . . . microbes. [*To* TELEGIN.] Waffles, play!

TELEGIN: My good friend, with all my soul, I should be glad to, but do understand—they are asleep in the house!

ASTROFF: Play!

[TELEGIN *strums softly.*]

ASTROFF: I need a drink. Come on, we still seem to have some cognac left. And as soon as it begins to grow light we will go to my place. All rightie? I have a medical orderly who never says "all right" but "all rightie." A terrible rascal. So, all rightie? [*Seeing* SONIA *enter.*] Pardon me, I am without a necktie.

[*Goes out quickly;* TELEGIN *goes out after him.*]

SONIA: And you, Uncle Vanya, you got drunk again with the doctor. Struck up a friendship, you bright hawks. That one is always like this, but why you? At your age, it's not becoming.

VOINITSKY: Age has nothing to do with it. When one has no real life, one lives in illusions. After all, that's better than nothing.

SONIA: All our hay is mowed, it rains every day, everything is rotting and you occupy yourself with illusions. You have neglected the farming completely—I'm the only one that works, and I have no strength left. [*Alarmed.*] Uncle, you have tears in your eyes!

VOINITSKY: What tears? There's nothing . . . nonsense . . . You looked at me just now as your dead mother used to. My dear . . . [*Kissing her hands and her face.*] My sister . . . my dear sister . . . Where is she now? If she knew! Ah, if she knew!

SONIA: What? Uncle, knew what?

VOINITSKY: It's very hard, I'm not well . . . Nothing . . . Later . . . It's nothing. I will go. . . . [*Goes out.*]

SONIA: [*Knocking at the door.*] Mikhail Lvovich! Aren't you asleep? Just one minute!

ASTROFF: [*From behind the door.*] Right away! [*A little later, he comes in; he is already in his vest and necktie.*] What is your command?

SONIA: You go ahead and drink if it is not revolting to you, but I implore you, don't let Uncle drink. It is bad for him.

ASTROFF: Very well. We shall not drink any more. [*A pause.*] I will go home now. Resolved and signed. By the time they hitch up my team it will be dawn.

SONIA: It's raining. Wait till morning.

ASTROFF: The storm is passing by, only a fringe will hit us. I'm going. And, please, don't ask me any more to see your father. I say to him—gout, and he says rheumatism; I tell him to lie down, he sits up. And today he wouldn't even talk to me.

SONIA: He is spoiled. [*Going to the sideboard.*] Would you like a little bite of something?

ASTROFF: Well, I think I will.

SONIA: I like to have a bite at night, and it seems there's something on the sideboard. In his time, they say, he had great success with women, and the ladies spoiled him. Here take some cheese.

[*Both stand by the sideboard and eat.*]

ASTROFF: I haven't eaten anything today, I only drank. Your father has a difficult character. [*Getting a bottle out of the sideboard.*] May I? [*He drinks a glass.*] Nobody is here and one can speak out straight. You know, it seems to me you know I could not live through a month in your house, I'd suffocate in this air . . . Your father, who is all absorbed in his gout and books, Uncle Vanya, with his hypochondria, your grandmother, and, to top it all, your stepmother. . . .

SONIA: What about my stepmother?

ASTROFF: In a human being everything ought to be beautiful: face and clothes, and soul and thoughts. She is beautiful, no disputing that, but she merely eats and sleeps and walks and charms us all with her beauty—and nothing more. She has no responsibilities whatever, other people work for her . . . isn't it so? An idle life can't be right. [*A pause.*] However, perhaps I'm too hard on her. I am not satisfied by life, just as your Uncle Vanya is not, and we both are getting to be nothing but grumblers.

SONIA: And you are not content with your life?

ASTROFF: On the whole, I like life, but our rural Russsian, average man's life, I can't bear it, with all the strength in my soul I have a contempt for it, and as far as my own personal life goes, there is, so help me God, absolutely nothing good in it. You know how it is when you are walking in the woods on a dark night and see far off a little light burning. You don't mind either the fatigue, or the darkness or the branches scratching you in the face. I work—as you know very well—as nobody else does in the district, fate never lets up her blow on me, at times what I go through

is unbearable, but for me there is no little light in the distance. For myself I am not expecting anything any more, I don't like people. . . . It's a long time since I loved anyone.

SONIA: No one?

ASTROFF: No one. Only toward your nurse I feel a certain tenderness for old memories' sake. Peasants are all alike, monotonous, primitive, living in dirt. And it is hard to get on with the intelligentsia. They tire one. They all, all our good friends, will have shallow thoughts, shallow feelings and will not see farther than their noses—the simple fact is they are stupid. And those that are cleverer and more important, are hysterical, absorbed with analyzing themselves—they whine, they despise everything, they slander people cruelly, they approach a man sideways, look at him out of the corner of an eye and decide: "Oh, he is a psychopath!" or: "He is a phrase-maker!" And when they don't know which label to stick on to my forehead, they say: "He's an odd one, odd!" I love the woods, that is odd; I don't eat meat—that's odd too. There is no longer any spontaneous, pure, free kinship to nature or to people. . . . No and no!

[*He is about to drink.*]

SONIA: [*Stopping him.*] No, I beg you, I implore you, don't drink any more.

ASTROFF: Why?

SONIA: It is so unbecoming to you! You are refined, you have such a gentle voice. . . . More than that you are like nobody among the people I know, like nobody else—you are beautiful. Then why do you want to look like ordinary people who drink and play cards? Oh, don't do that, I implore you! You always say that people don't create but merely destroy that that's given to them from above. Then why, why, are you destroying yourself? Don't, don't, I entreat you, I implore you!

ASTROFF: [*Holding out his hand to her.*] I won't drink any more.

SONIA: Give me your word.

ASTROFF: Word of honor.

SONIA: [*Shaking his hand vigorously.*] Thank you!

ASTROFF: Basta! I have sobered up. See, I am already completely sober and will stay like this to the end of my days. [*Looking at his watch.*] And so, let's go on. I say: my time has already passed, it's too late for me . . . I am aged, overworked, I've become common, all my feelings have become blunted and I never seem able to attach myself to anyone. I don't love anybody and . . . I'm already past loving anybody. What still enthralls me is beauty. I am not indifferent to it. It seems to me that if Elena Andreevna only wanted to, in one day she could set my head in a whirl. . . . But that is not love, it's not belonging to someone—not [Covering his eyes with his hand and shuddering.]

SONIA: What is the matter with you?

ASTROFF: Well. . . . During Lent my patient died under chloroform.

SONIA: It is time to forget about that. [A pause.] Tell me, Mikhail Lvovich. . . . If I had a friend, or a younger sister, and if you learned that she . . . well, let us say, loved you, just what way would you take it?

ASTROFF: [Shrugging his shoulders.] I don't know. Very likely no way. I would let her understand that I cannot fall in love with her. . . . Besides, I have other things on my mind. Be that as it may, it's already time for me to leave. Good-by, my dear, or else we won't sleep till morning. [Shaking her hand.] I'll go through the living room, if you will let me—I am afraid your uncle might get hold of me. [Leaves.]

SONIA: [Alone.] He didn't say anything to me. . . . His soul and heart are still hidden from me; but why do I feel so happy? [Laughing from happiness.] I said to him: You are refined, noble, you have such a gentle voice. . . . Was it the wrong moment for just that? His voice trembles, caresses you— Here I feel him in the air. And when I told him about a younger sister, he didn't understand. . . . [Wringing her hands.] Oh, how terrible it is that I am not pretty! How terrible! And I know I am not pretty, I know, I know. . . . Last Sunday as we were leaving church, I heard them talking about me and one woman said: "She is kind, generous, but it's a pity she is not pretty." . . . not pretty.

[Enter ELENA.]

ELENA: [Opening the windows.] The storm has passed. What fine air! [A pause.] Where is the doctor?

SONIA: Gone. [A pause.]

ELENA: Sofia!

SONIA: What?

ELENA: How long will you be cross with me? We haven't done each other any

wrong. Why then should we be enemies? Enough is enough.

SONIA: I myself wanted to . . . [Embracing her.] Yes, enough of our being angry.

ELENA: Excellent. [Both are excited.]

SONIA: Papa is lying down?

ELENA: No, he is sitting in the living room. . . . We don't speak to each other for whole weeks, you and I. God knows why. [Seeing that the sideboard is open.] What is that?

SONIA: Mikhail Lvovich had supper.

ELENA: And there is some wine. . . . Let us drink bruderschaft.

SONIA: Let's.

ELENA: Out of one glass . . . [Pours.] That's better. [They drink and kiss.]

SONIA: It's a long time I wanted to make peace, but somehow I felt embarrassed . . . [Crying.]

ELENA: Why are you crying?

SONIA: Nothing, no special reason.

ELENA: Well, there—there—[Crying.] You foolish creature, and I am crying too. . . . [A pause.] You resent me because it looks as if I married your father calculatingly. . . . Then, if you believe in oaths, I swear to you—I married him for love. I was infatuated with him as a learned and famous man. My love was not real; my love was artificial, but it seemed real to me then. I am not guilty. And you from the very day of the wedding have never stopped accusing me with your intelligent, suspecting eyes.

SONIA: Well, peace, peace! Let us forget.

ELENA: Don't look at it like that—'tisn't like you . . . One must have faith in everybody, otherwise life is impossible.

[A pause.]

SONIA: Tell me in all honesty, as a friend . . . are you happy?

ELENA: No.

SONIA: I knew it. Here's one more question. Tell me frankly—would you have liked to have a young husband?

ELENA: What a child you still are. Of course I should have. [Laughing.] Now, ask me something else, ask me . . .

SONIA: Do you like the doctor?

ELENA: Yes, very much.

SONIA: [Laughing.] I have a silly face . . . haven't I? Here he is, gone, and I keep hearing his voice and his steps, and when I look at a dark window I see his face there. Let me try to say what I mean

—but I can't talk so loud, I am ashamed. Let's go to my room, there we'll talk. Do I seem silly to you? Confess . . . tell me something about him. . . .

ELENA: But what?

SONIA: He is clever. . . . He can do anything, is able to do anything. . . . He heals the sick and he plants woodlands.

ELENA: It isn't a matter of woods and medicine. . . . My dear, understand, it's the genius! And do you know what genius means? Bravery, a free mind, a broad sweep. When he plants a little tree, he is already imagining what it will be like in a thousand years, he is already dreaming of the happiness of mankind. Such people are rare, one must love them. . . . He drinks, he is sometimes rude—but what harm is there in that! A genius in Russia can't be too much of a saint. Think yourself what a life that doctor has! Impassable mud on the roads, frost, blinding snow, enormous distances, people crude and wild, poverty all around, diseases. In such a setting it is hard for anyone who works and struggles day after day to keep himself steady and sober at forty. . . . [Kisses her.] From the bottom of my soul I wish you— you deserve happiness. . . . [Getting up.] —I am a tedious, passing face—in music, and in my husband's house, in all the novels —the truth is, everywhere I was merely a passing face. The truth is, Sonia, when you stop and think of it, I am very, very unhappy! [Walking on the stage excitedly.] There's no happiness for me in this world. No! Why are you laughing?

SONIA: [Laughing, covering her face.] I am so happy . . . so happy!

ELENA: I feel like playing . . . I would like to play something now.

SONIA: Do play. [Embraces her.] I cannot sleep. . . . Do play!

ELENA: Right away. Your father is not asleep. When he is ill music irritates him. Go ask. If he is quite well then I'll play. Go on.

SONIA: Right away. [Goes out.]

[The watchman is tapping in the garden.]

ELENA: It is a long time since I've played. I shall play and cry—cry like a fool. [Through the window.] Is it you tapping, Efim?

THE VOICE OF THE WATCHMAN: Me!

ELENA: Don't tap, the master is not well.

THE VOICE OF THE WATCHMAN: I'll go right away! [Whistles.] Hey, you, Nicky! Boris! Nicky! [Another whistle.] [A pause.]

SONIA: [Returning.] No, you cannot!

CURTAIN

ACT THREE

Living room in the house of SEREBRIAKOFF. *Three doors: to the right, to the left, and in the middle. Daytime.*

VOINITSKY, SONIA *are sitting down, and* ELENA ANDREEVNA *is walking around the room, busy with her thoughts.*

VOINITSKY: Herr Professor deigned to express a wish, that we all gather today in this living room by one o'clock. [Looks at the clock.] Quarter to one. He wished to disclose something to the world.

ELENA: Perhaps some kind of business.

VOINITSKY: He hasn't got any business. He writes nonsense, grumbles, and is jealous, and nothing else.

SONIA: [Reproachfully.] Uncle!

VOINITSKY: Well, well, sorry. [Pointing to ELENA.] Do admire: she walks around and sways a bit from laziness. Very sweet! Very!

ELENA: All day long you buzz, always buzzing—aren't you tired of it. [With anguish.] I am dying of boredom, I don't know what to do.

SONIA: [Shrugging her shoulders.] Isn't there enough to do? If you wanted to.

ELENA: For example?

SONIA: Occupy yourself with running the house, teaching the children, caring for the sick. Is that so little? When you and Papa were not here, Uncle Vanya and I went to the market ourselves to sell the flour.

ELENA: I don't know how. Besides it is not interesting. It is only in sociological novels they teach and cure sick peasants, and how can I suddenly for no reason go to curing and teaching them?

SONIA: And in the same way I don't understand how not to go and not to teach. Wait, and you will get used to it. [*Embracing her.*] Don't be bored, darling. [*Laughing.*] You are bored, you can't find a place for yourself, and boredom and idleness are infectious. Look how Uncle Vanya does nothing but walk behind you, like a shadow. I dropped my work and ran here to talk with you. I am getting lazy, I can't do anything. Doctor Mikhail Lvovich used to come to us very seldom, once a month, it was hard to coax him and now he drives here every day, he has forsaken both his woods and his medicine. You must be a witch.

VOINITSKY: Why are you wilting away? [*With animation.*] Now, my darling, my magnificent one, be a good girl! In your veins flows the blood of a water nymph, so be it a water nymph! Let yourself go if only for once in your life, hurry and fall in love with some River God up to your ears—and plunge head foremost into a whirlpool, so that Herr Professor and all of us hold up our hands we are so astonished.

ELENA: [*Angrily.*] Leave me alone! How cruel it is!

[*She wants to go.*]

VOINITSKY: [*Preventing her.*] Now, now, my joy, forgive me . . . I apologize [*Kissing her hand.*] Be patient.

ELENA: An angel wouldn't have the patience—you must agree . . .

VOINITSKY: As a token of peace and harmony, I'll bring a bouquet of roses, now; I made it for you this morning. . . . Autumn roses—charming, sad roses . . . [*Goes out.*]

SONIA: Autumn roses—charming, sad roses.

[*Both of them look out of the window.*]

ELENA: And September is already with us. How will we live through the winter here! [*A pause.*] Where's the doctor?

SONIA: In Uncle Vanya's room. Writing something. I am glad Uncle Vanya went out, I must talk to you.

ELENA: About what?

SONIA: About what? [*Puts her head on* ELENA'S *breast.*]

ELENA: Well, there, there . . . [*Stroking her hair.*] Enough.

SONIA: I am not pretty.

ELENA: You have beautiful hair.

SONIA: No! [*Looking back to glance at herself in the mirror.*] No! When a woman is not pretty they tell her: "You have beautiful eyes, you have beautiful hair." I have loved him now for six years, loved him more than my own mother; every minute I hear his voice, feel the touch of his hand; and I watch the door, waiting; it always seems to me that he will be coming in. And here, you see I keep looking for you, to talk about him. He is here every day now but does not look at me, doesn't see me. . . . It's such agony! I haven't any hope, no, no! [*In despair.*] Oh, God, grant me strength. . . . I prayed all night. . . . I often come to him, start talking to him myself, look into his eyes. . . . I have no more pride, I've no power to control myself. . . . I could not contain myself and yesterday I confessed to Uncle Vanya, that I am in love . . . and all the servants know I love him. Everybody knows.

ELENA: And he?

SONIA: No. He never notices me.

ELENA: [*Meditating.*] A strange man he is . . . Do you know what? Let me, I'll talk to him . . . Carefully, by hinting. . . . [*A pause.*] Really, how long can you be in some uncertain state! Do let me! [SONIA *nods her head to agree.*] That's wonderful. He loves you or he doesn't love you —that won't be hard to find out. Don't be embarrassed, my little dove, don't worry— I'll question him carefully, he won't even know. All we want is to find out: Yes or No? [*A pause.*] If no, then let him stop coming here. Isn't that so? [SONIA *nods her head to agree.*] Easier when you don't see him. We won't file it away in a box; we'll question him right now. He intended to show me some sketches. . . . Go tell him I want to see him.

SONIA: [*In great excitement.*] You will tell me the whole truth?

ELENA: Yes, of course. It seems to me the truth, whatever it is, is not so frightful as uncertainty after all. You may count on me, little dove.

SONIA: Yes, yes . . . I'll tell him that you want to see his charts—[*Going, she stops near the door.*] No, uncertainty is better . . . After all, there is hope—

ELENA: What is it?

SONIA: Nothing. [*Goes out.*]

ELENA: [*Alone.*] There is nothing worse

than when you know someone's secret and are no help. [*Meditating.*] He is not in love with her—that is clear, but why doesn't he marry her? She is not pretty but for a country doctor, at his age she would be a fine wife. Intelligent, so kind, true. . . . No, it isn't that, not that. . . . [*A pause.*] I understand this poor girl. She lives in the midst of uninterrupted boredom. Instead of people she has some sort of gray shadows, wandering around her, what they say is trifling, all they know is that they eat and they drink, and they sleep. And then sometimes he comes, not like the others, handsome, interesting, charming, as if in the twilight rises a bright moon. . . . Oh, to give in to the charm of such a man, to forget yourself. . . . It looks as if I were a little carried away myself. Yes, I am bored without him; here I am smiling, when I think of him. . . . Uncle Vanya says that in my veins perhaps flows the blood of a water nymph. "Let yourself go at least once in your life. . . ." What then? Perhaps, it must be so . . . To fly away like a free bird, away from you all, from your sleepy faces, from your conversations, to forget that you exist in the world . . . But I am cowardly, I'm shy . . . I'll be tortured by my conscience . . . You see. He comes here every day, I can guess why he is here and I already feel myself guilty, I'm ready to fall on my knees before Sonia and ask her forgiveness, and to cry . . .

ASTROFF: [*Enters with a chart.*] Good morning. [*Shaking her hand.*] You'd like to see my . . .

ELENA: You promised yesterday to show me your work . . . are you free?

ASTROFF: Oh, of course. [*Spreads the chart on the card table and fastens it with thumb tacks.*] Where were you born?

ELENA: [*Helping him with the chart.*] In Petersburg.

ASTROFF: And received your education?

ELENA: In the conservatory.

ASTROFF: This may not interest you.

ELENA: Why? It's true I don't know the country, but I read a great deal.

ASTROFF: Here in the house I have my own table . . . In Ivan's room. When I'm utterly tired out, and in a complete torpor, I drop everything and run to this house, and amuse myself with this thing here an hour or so . . . Ivan and Sonia do the accounts and I sit near them at my own table dabbling, and I feel warm, at peace, and the cricket chirps. But this pleasure I don't allow myself often, not often, once a month. . . . [*Pointing it out on the chart.*] Now look here at this. The picture of our district as it was fifty years ago. The dark green and light green colors are forests; half of the whole area is forests. The red crosslines on the green show where elks and goats used to be—I am showing here both *flora* and *fauna*. On this lake used to live swans, geese, ducks and, as the old men say, a powerful lot of all kinds of birds; you saw nothing but birds. They floated like a cloud. Besides the villages and small towns, you see various settlements were scattered, farms, monasteries, water-mills. . . . There were a great many cattle and horses; you can tell by the blue color. For example, in this district the blue is thick; whole herds were there, and each farm owned three horses. [*A pause.*] Now we'll look lower down. What there was twenty-five years ago. Only a third of the whole area is woodland. There are no longer any goats, but there are elks. The green and the blue colors are already paler. And so on, and so forth. Now here's the third part: a picture of the district today. The green comes here and there, but not solid, only in spots; the elks have disappeared, the swans, and the grouse. . . . Of the villages, settlements, monasteries, mills, there is not even a trace. On the whole a picture of gradual, plain degeneration, which apparently needs only some ten or fifteen years more to be complete. You will say that there are cultural influences at work here, that the old life must naturally have yielded place to the new. Yes, I understand that if in place of these destroyed forests, roads were laid out, railroads, if there were mills, factories, schools—people would become healthier, richer, more intelligent; but there is nothing of the kind! In the district the same swamps, mosquitoes, the same absence of roads, poverty, typhus, diphtheria, fires. . . . We have here a case of degeneration that results from a struggle that's beyond men's strength for existence; degeneration caused by sloth, by ignorance, by the complete absence of any conscience, when a cold, hungry, sick man to save what life he has left, for his children, instinctively, subconsciously grabs at everything that might satisfy his hunger, or warm him, destroys everything, without a thought of tomorrow. Nearly everything is already destroyed and in its place there is nothing created. [*Coldly.*] I can see by your face that this is not interesting to you. . . .

ELENA: But I understand so little of that. . . .

ASTROFF: There is nothing to understand, it's simply uninteresting.

ELENA: To be frank, my mind is not on that. Forgive me. I must do a little cross-questioning and I am embarrassed and don't know how to begin.

ASTROFF: A cross-examination?

ELENA: Yes, a cross-examination, but . . . rather innocent. Let's sit down! [*They sit down.*] The matter concerns one young person. We shall talk like honest people, as friends, without beating about the bush. We shall talk and then forget what the talk was about. Yes?

ASTROFF: Yes.

ELENA: The matter concerns my step-daughter Sonia. Do you like her?

ASTROFF: Yes, I respect her.

ELENA: Do you like her as a woman?

ASTROFF: [*Not at once.*] No.

ELENA: Two or three words more—and that's the end of it. Have you noticed nothing?

ASTROFF: Nothing.

ELENA: [*Taking his hand.*] You don't love her, I see it in your eyes . . . she's suffering—understand it and . . . stop coming here.

ASTROFF: [*Getting up.*] My season has already passed. . . . Besides, I have no time. . . . [*Shrugging his shoulders.*] When can I find it. [*He is embarrassed.*]

ELENA: Pooh, what a disagreeable conversation! I am as upset as if I were dragging twenty tons. Well, thank God, we have finished. Let us forget, as if we had not talked at all, and . . . and you ride away. You are an intelligent man, you will understand. . . . [*A pause.*] I am blushing red all over.

ASTROFF: If you had told me a month or two ago, then I possibly would have considered it, but now. . . . [*Shrugs his shoulders.*] And, if she is suffering, then, of course. . . . There is only one thing I do not understand: Why did you have to have this cross-examination? [*Looks into her eyes and moves a finger from side to side.*] You are sly!

ELENA: What does that mean?

ASTROFF: [*Laughing.*] Sly! Let us suppose, Sonia is suffering. I readily admit it, but why this cross-examination of yours?

[*With much animation, not letting her talk.*] Permit me, don't make an astonished face, you know very well why I come here every day . . . Why and for whose sake I come, that you know very well. You darling bird of prey, don't look at me like that, I am a wise old sparrow. . . .

ELENA: [*Incredulous.*] Bird of prey? I don't understand a bit of it.

ASTROFF: A beautiful, fluffy little thing . . . you must have victims! Here I am already a whole month not doing anything, I have dropped everything, I look greedily for you—and this you like hugely. Well, then? I am conquered, you knew it even without the questioning. [*Folds his arms and bows his head.*] I give up. Here, eat me!

ELENA: Have you lost your mind?

ASTROFF: [*Laughing through his teeth.*] You are sly.

ELENA: Oh, I am better and more superior than you think! I swear to you! [*Wants to go.*]

ASTROFF: [*Barring her way.*] I will leave today, I will not be here again, but . . . [*Taking her hand, looking around.*] Where are we going to see each other? Tell me quickly: Where? Someone might come in here, tell me quickly . . . [*Passionately.*] What a wonderful, luscious . . . One kiss . . . For me just to kiss your fragrant hair . . .

ELENA: I swear to you . . .

ASTROFF: [*Not letting her talk.*] Why swear? Mustn't swear. No use for needless words . . . Oh, how beautiful! What hands! [*Kisses her hands.*]

ELENA: But that's enough, after all . . . go away . . . [*Withdraws her hands.*] You forget yourself.

ASTROFF: Tell me, tell me where will we see each other tomorrow? [*Holds her by the waist.*] You can see, it can't be escaped, we've got to see each other.

[*He kisses her; at that point* VOINITSKY *enters with a bouquet of roses and stops at the door.*]

ELENA: [*Not seeing* VOINITSKY.] Have mercy . . . leave me alone. . . . [*Puts her head on* ASTROFF's *breast.*] No! [*She moves to go.*]

ASTROFF: [*Restraining her by the waist.*] Come tomorrow to the wood . . . about two o'clock . . . Yes? Yes? You will come?

ELENA: [*Noticing* VOINITSKY.] Let me go! [*In great embarrassment moves to the window.*] This is terrible.

VOINITSKY: [*Puts the bouquet on the chair; excitedly wipes his face and behind his collar with a handkerchief.*] So? . . . Yes . . . So?

ASTROFF: [*With false nonchalance.*] Today, much esteemed Ivan Petrovich, the weather is not bad. In the morning it was cloudy, as if it would rain, and now the sun's shining. Honestly speaking, autumn turned out beautiful . . . and the winter crop not bad. [*Folds the chart into a cylinder.*] Except for one thing: the days are getting short. . . . [*Goes out.*]

ELENA: [*Quickly goes to* VOINITSKY.] You will try, you will use all your influence, so that my husband and I can go away from here today even! Do you hear me? Today!

VOINITSKY: [*Wiping his face.*] Ah? Well, yes . . . very well. Elena, I saw everything, everything . . .

ELENA: [*Nervously.*] Do you hear me? I must leave here this very day!

[*Enter* SEREBRIAKOFF, SONIA, TELEGIN, *and* MARINA.]

TELEGIN: I myself somehow your excellency, am not entirely well. It is two days now I have been ailing. My head somehow . . .

SEREBRIAKOFF: But where are the others? I don't like this house. A sort of labyrinth. Twenty-six enormous rooms, everybody scatters and can never find anybody. [*Rings.*] Ask Maria Vasilievna and Elena Andreevna here.

ELENA: I am here.

SEREBRIAKOFF: I beg you, ladies and gentlemen, sit down.

SONIA: [*Approaching* ELENA, *impatiently.*] What did he say?

ELENA: Later.

SONIA: You are trembling. You are upset. [*Peering inquisitively into her face.*] I understand . . . He said, that he will not be here any more . . . yes? [*A pause.*] Say it: Yes?

[ELENA *nods her head.*]

SEREBRIAKOFF: [*To* TELEGIN.] One can still make peace with illness, no matter what, but what I cannot digest is this regime of country life. I have a feeling as if I had fallen from the earth on to some foreign planet. Sit down, ladies and gentlemen, I beg you. Sonia! [SONIA *does not hear him, she stands with her head down, sadly.*] Sonia! [*A pause.*] She doesn't hear. [*To* MARINA.] And you, Nurse, sit down. [NURSE *sits down and knits on a stocking.*]

I beg you, ladies and gentlemen. Hang your ears, so to speak, on a peg of attention. [*He laughs.*]

VOINITSKY: [*Excitedly.*] Maybe I'm not needed. Shall I leave?

SEREBRIAKOFF: No, you are needed here more than anybody.

VOINITSKY: What do you want from me?

SEREBRIAKOFF: You . . . But why are you angry? [*A pause.*] If I am guilty in your eyes of anything, then pardon me please.

VOINITSKY: Drop that tone. Let's proceed with business . . . What do you need?

[*Enter* MARIA VASILIEVNA.]

SEREBRIAKOFF: Here is Mama. I'll begin, ladies and gentlemen. [*A pause.*] I invited you, ladies and gentlemen, so that I might explain that the Inspector General is on his way. However, jokes aside. It is a serious matter. I, ladies and gentlemen, gathered you together, to ask you for help and advice, and, knowing your undying courtesy, I hope I will get it. I am a learned man, a bookworm, and have always been a stranger to practical life. Do without directions of well-informed people, I cannot, and I beg you, Ivan Petrovich, and you here, Ilya Ilyich, and you, *Maman*. . . . The fact is *manet omnes una nox*, that is: we are all mortal; I am old, sick, and therefore find it timely to regulate my property terms in so far as that concerns my family. My life is already finished, I am not thinking of myself, but I have a young wife, a maiden-daughter. [*A pause.*] To go on living in the country is impossible for me. We are not made for country life. Yet to live in town on the income we get from this estate, is impossible. If we sell, let's say, a wood, that would be an unusual measure which we cannot do every year. One must find such measures as would guarantee us a permanent, more or less definite figure of income. I have thought of one such measure and have the honor to propose it for your discussion. Aside from details, I will state it along general lines. Our estate gives an average of not more than two percent. I propose to sell it. If the proceeds we convert into interest-bearing paper, then we will receive from four to five percent, and I think there will even be a surplus of several thousand, which will allow us to buy a small villa in Finland.

VOINITSKY: Wait . . . my ears must be deceiving me. Repeat what you said.

SEREBRIAKOFF: To convert money into

interest-bearing paper, and with the surplus, what is left, buy a villa in Finland.

VOINITSKY: Not Finland . . . You said something else.

SEREBRIAKOFF: I propose to sell the estate.

VOINITSKY: That's it. You will sell the estate, excellent, a fine idea . . . and where would you order me to go with my old mother and with Sonia here?

SEREBRIAKOFF: All this we will discuss in good time. Not everything at once.

VOINITSKY: Wait. Apparently, up to now I have had not a drop of common sense. Up to now I was so stupid as to think that this estate belongs to Sonia. My late father bought this estate as a dowry for my sister. Up to now I have been naïve, have understood that this was not a Turkish law but Russian; I thought that the estate passed from my sister to Sonia.

SEREBRIAKOFF: Yes. The estate belongs to Sonia. Who is arguing that? Without Sonia's consent I would not decide to sell. Besides what I propose to do is for Sonia's benefit.

VOINITSKY: This is incomprehensible, incomprehensible! Either I have lost my mind, or . . . or . . .

MARIA VASILIEVNA: Jean, don't contradict Alexander. You must believe he knows better than we do what is good and what is bad.

VOINITSKY: No, let me have some water. [Drinking the water.] Say whatever you want to, whatever you want to!

SEREBRIAKOFF: I don't understand why you excite yourself. I don't say that my project is ideal. If everybody finds it unsuitable then I will not insist.

[A pause.]

TELEGIN: [Confusedly.] Your Excellency, I nourish toward learning not only reverence, but feelings of kinship as well. My brother, Gregory Ilyich's wife's brother, perhaps you know him, Konstantine Trofimovich Lakedemonov, was a magistrate . . .

VOINITSKY: Hold on there, Waffles, we are talking about business. . . . Wait, later on . . . [To SEREBRIAKOFF.] Here, you ask him. This estate was bought from his uncle.

SEREBRIAKOFF: Ah, and why should I ask? What for?

VOINITSKY: This estate was bought with

things as they were at that time for ninety-five thousand. Father paid down only seventy and there was a debt left of twenty-five thousand. Now listen . . . This estate would not have been bought had I not given up my inheritance in favor of my sister, whom I loved deeply. As if that were not enough, for ten years I worked like an ox, and paid off the entire debt . . .

SEREBRIAKOFF: I regret that I began this conversation.

VOINITSKY: The estate is clear of debts and intact only because of my personal efforts. And here when I have grown old, they want to throw me out on my neck!

SEREBRIAKOFF: I don't understand what you are driving at.

VOINITSKY: For twenty-five years I have managed this estate, worked, sent you money, like a most conscientious clerk, and during all that time you not once thanked me. All the time—both in my youth and now—you paid me five hundred roubles a year for wages—fit for a beggar—and you never once thought of increasing it by even one rouble!

SEREBRIAKOFF: Ivan Petrovich, how could I know? I am not a practical man and understand nothing. You could have yourself increased it as much as you wanted to . . .

VOINITSKY: Why didn't I steal? Why don't you all hold me in contempt for not having stolen? It would have been just and now I would not be a beggar!

MARIA VASILIEVNA: [Sternly.] Jean!

TELEGIN: [Excitedly.] Vanya, my friend, don't, don't. . . . I am trembling. . . . Why spoil good relations? [Kissing him.] Don't!

VOINITSKY: For twenty-five years with this mother here I sat like a mole inside these four walls. All our thoughts and feelings belonged to you alone. In the daytime we talked of you, of your works, felt proud of you, pronounced your name with reverence; the nights we wasted reading magazines and books, which I now despise from the depths.

TELEGIN: Don't, Vanya, don't . . . I cannot . . .

SEREBRIAKOFF: [Indignantly.] I don't unstand, what do you want?

VOINITSKY: You were to us a creature of the highest order and your articles we knew by heart . . . But now my eyes are open!

I see everything! You write about art, but you understand nothing of art! All your works, that I used to love, are not worth a brass penny! You fooled us!

SEREBRIAKOFF: Ladies and gentlemen! Do make him stop, after all! I shall go!

ELENA ANDREEVNA: Ivan Petrovich, I demand that you stop talking! Do you hear?

VOINITSKY: I will not stop talking! [*Barring* SEREBRIAKOFF'S *way.*] Wait, I haven't finished! You have ruined my life! I have not lived, have not lived! Thanks to you I destroyed, swept away, the best years of my life! You are my worst enemy!

TELEGIN: I cannot . . . cannot . . . I'll go . . . [*Leaves in great agitation.*]

SEREBRIAKOFF: What do you want from me? And what right have you to talk to me in such a tone? Imbecile! If the estate is yours, then take it, I don't need it.

ELENA: This very minute I'm going away from this hell! [*Shouting.*] I can't bear it any longer.

VOINITSKY: My life is lost to me! I am talented, intelligent, brave . . . Had I lived a normal life, there might have come out of me a Schopenhauer, a Dostoevski . . . I am through with keeping accounts, making reports. I am losing my mind. . . . Mother, I am in despair! Mother!

MARIA VASILIEVNA: [*Sternly.*] Listen to Alexander!

SONIA: [*Kneels down before the nurse and huddles close to her.*] Nurse, darling! Nurse, darling!

VOINITSKY: Mother! What am I to do? Don't, don't I know myself what I should do! [*To* SEREBRIAKOFF.] You will remember me! [*Goes out through the middle door.*]

[MARIA VASILIEVNA *goes after him.*]

SEREBRIAKOFF: Ladies and gentlemen, but what is it, after all? Take this madman away from me! I cannot live with him under the same roof! He lives there [*Pointing to the middle door.*] almost next to me . . . Let him move to the village, into some cottage, or I will move away from here, but remain with him in the same house I cannot.

ELENA: [*To her husband.*] We will go away from here today! We must make arrangements at once.

SEREBRIAKOFF: Contemptible you are!

SONIA: [*Kneeling, turns to her father; nervously, through her tears.*] One must be merciful, Papa! Uncle Vanya and I are so miserable! [*Controlling her despair.*] One must be merciful! Try to remember when you were younger, Uncle Vanya and Grandmother translated books for you at night, copied your papers . . . every night, every night! Uncle Vanya and I worked without any rest, we were afraid to spend a penny on ourselves and sent everything to you . . . We did not eat our bread free. I am not saying the right thing, not the right thing I am saying, but you have to understand us, Papa. One must be merciful!

ELENA: [*Excited, to her husband.*] Alexander, for God's sake, have it out with him . . . I implore you.

SEREBRIAKOFF: Very well, I shall have it out with him. I am not accusing him of anything, I am not angry, but, please agree with me, his conduct is at least strange. As you wish, I will go to him. [*Goes out through the middle door.*]

ELENA: Be gentler with him, quiet him. . . . [*Goes out after him.*]

SONIA: [*Nestling against* MARINA.] Nurse! Nurse!

MARINA: It's all right, my child. The geese will cackle—and then stop . . . cackle—and stop.

SONIA: Nurse!

MARINA: [*Patting her head.*] You are shivering, as if it were frost! Well, well, my little orphan, God is merciful. Some linden tea or some raspberry, and it will pass, you'll forget it. Don't be sad, my little orphan . . . [*Looking at the middle door, fiercely.*] There, you geese—

[*Offstage there is a shot; one hears* ELENA *scream;* SONIA *shudders.*]

MARINA: Oh, you!

SEREBRIAKOFF: [*Runs in, swaying with fright.*] Hold him! Hold him! He has lost his mind.

[ELENA *and* VOINITSKY *struggle in the doorway.*]

ELENA: [*Trying to grab the revolver from him.*] Give it to me! Give it to me, I tell you!

VOINITSKY: Let me go, Elena! Let me go! [*Freeing himself, runs in and looks around for* SEREBRIAKOFF.] Where is he? Ah, there he is! [*Shoots at him.*] Bang! [*A pause.*] Didn't hit? Missed again? [*Angrily.*] Ah, the devil, devil . . . devil take you. . . .

[*Beating the revolver on the floor and sitting down exhausted in a chair.*

SEREBRIAKOFF *is stunned;* ELENA *leaning against the wall is fainting.*]

ELENA: Take me away from here! Take me away, kill me, but . . . I cannot stay here, cannot!

VOINITSKY: [*In despair.*] Oh, what am I doing! What am I doing.

SONIA: [*Softly.*] Nurse, darling! Nurse, darling!

CURTAIN

ACT FOUR

IVAN PETROVICH'S *room. It is his bedroom, and also is the office of the estate. Near the window a large table with books for cash accounts, and papers of all kinds, a desk, bookcases, scales. A smaller table for* ASTROFF; *on this table there are paints and drawing instruments; next to them a portfolio. There is a bird cage with a starling. On the wall a map of Africa, which apparently is of no use to anyone here. There's an enormous sofa, upholstered in oilcloth. To the left—a door leading into bedrooms; to the right— a door leading into a passage; at the door to the right a mat is spread so that the peasants won't muddy up the floor.*

It is an autumn evening; all is tranquil. TELEGIN *and* MARINA *sit facing each other and wind wool for stockings.*

TELEGIN: You be faster, Marina Timofeevna, because they will be calling us right away to say good-by. They've already ordered the horses brought.

MARINA: [*Trying to wind faster.*] There is not much left.

TELEGIN: To Kharkov they are going. And there they will live.

MARINA: And it is better so.

TELEGIN: Got scared . . . Elena, she says, "I do not wish to live here one hour," she says . . . "let us go, and let us go . . . Let's live," she says, "in Kharkov, we'll look around and then we will send for our things," she says. Going away light, no goods to carry. It means, Marina Timofeevna, that it's not their fate to live here. Not their fate . . . [*Somewhat pompously.*] A fatal predestination.

MARINA: And it is better so. Just a while ago they raised a racket firing, what a shame!

TELEGIN: Yes, it's a subject worthy of the brush of Aivazovski.

MARINA: I'd hope my eyes could not see it. [*A pause.*] We'll live again, the way it used to be in the old days. In the morning shortly after seven the tea, shortly after noon the dinner, in the evening sit down to supper; everything in its proper order, the way people have them, Christian-like. [*With a sigh.*] It is a long time since I, sinner that I am, have eaten noodle soup.

TELEGIN: Yes, for a long time they have not made noodle soup here. [*A pause.*] A long time. . . . This morning, Marina Timofeevna, I walked through the village, and the storekeeper shouted after me: "Hey, you sponger!" And very bitter I began to feel!

MARINA: And don't you pay attention, friend. All of us are spongers on God. Like you, like Sonia, like Ivan—nobody sits doing nothing, we are all working! Everybody. . . . Where is Sonia?

TELEGIN: In the garden. Keeps walking with the doctor, looking for Ivan. They are afraid he might lay hands on himself.

MARINA: And where is his pistol?

TELEGIN: [*Whispering.*] I hid it in the cellar!

MARINA: [*With a smile.*] Oh, our sins!

[*Enter from outside* VOINITSKY *and* ASTROFF.]

VOINITSKY: Leave me alone. [*To* MARINA *and* TELEGIN.] Go away from here, leave me alone if only for one hour! I cannot stand being treated like someone's ward. I don't need a guardian.

TELEGIN: Right off, Vanya. [*Goes out on tiptoes.*]

MARINA: You geese—goo—goo— [*Gathers up the wool and goes out.*]

VOINITSKY: Leave me alone!

ASTROFF: With much pleasure, I should have left here a long time ago, but, I repeat,

I am not leaving till you return what you took from me.

VOINITSKY: I did not take anything from you.

ASTROFF: Seriously—I mean it—don't detain me. I should have left a long time ago.

VOINITSKY: I took nothing from you.

[*Both sit down.*]

ASTROFF: Yes? Well then, I shall wait a little, and then, excuse me, I'll have to use force. We will tie you up and search you. I am saying this seriously, absolutely.

VOINITSKY: As you wish. [*A pause.*] To play such a fool: to fire twice and not to hit even once! That I'll never forgive myself for!

ASTROFF: Well, if you feel like shooting, why not fire at your own forehead?

VOINITSKY: [*Shrugging his shoulders.*] Strange. I attempted a murder, and they don't arrest me, don't prosecute me. That means they consider me insane. [*He gives an angry laugh.*] I—insane, and they are not insane. They are not insane who under the guise of a professor, a learned wizard, hide their lack of talent and their stupidity and crying heartlessness. They are not insane who marry old men and then in front of everybody's eyes deceive them. I saw, saw, how you embraced her!

ASTROFF: Yes-s, embraced her—and this for you. [*Thumbs his nose.*]

VOINITSKY: [*Looking at the door.*] No, it's the earth that still holds you.

ASTROFF: And that is silly.

VOINITSKY: Why not—I am insane, irresponsible, I have the right to say silly things.

ASTROFF: That's an old story. You are not insane, you are simply odd. A little clown. There was a time when I too regarded every person who was odd as sick, abnormal, and now I am of the opinion that the normal state of man is to be odd. You are entirely normal.

VOINITSKY: [*Covering his face with his hands.*] I'm ashamed! If you knew how ashamed I am! This sharp feeling of shame is not like just pain. It's unbearable! [*Bending down on the table.*] What am I to do? What am I to do?

ASTROFF: Nothing.

VOINITSKY: Give me something! Oh, my God . . . I am forty-seven years old; if—suppose I'll live till sixty—if so I still have thirteen years left. That long! How shall I live through these thirteen years? What will I do, what will I fill them with? Oh, do you understand. . . . [*Convulsively pressing ASTROFF's hand.*] Do you understand, if I could only live through what is left of life somehow differently. To wake up on a clear, quiet morning and to feel that you have begun to live anew, that all the past˙ is forgotten, faded away, like smoke. [*Crying.*] To begin a new life . . . teach me how to begin . . . from what to begin . . .

ASTROFF: [*Annoyed, sharply.*] Eh, you! What new life is there? Our situation, yours and mine, is hopeless.

VOINITSKY: Yes?

ASTROFF: I am convinced of that.

VOINITSKY: Give me something . . . [*Pointing to his heart.*] Here inside me it burns.

ASTROFF: [*Angrily.*] Stop it! [*Relenting.*] Those who will live a hundred, two hundred years after us and who will despise us because we have lived our lives so stupidly and so without any taste—those, perhaps, will find the way how to be happy. And there's but one hope for you and me. The hope that when we'll be sleeping in our coffins, we might be visited by dreams, perhaps even pleasant ones. [*Sighing.*] Yes, brother. In the whole district there were only two decent, cultured men: you and I. But in some ten years, narrow-minded life, despised life, has strangled us with its rotten fumes. It has poisoned our blood and we have become just as much vulgarians as the rest of them. [*In a lively voice.*] But, however, you stop trying to talk the toothache away. Give me back, you, what you took from me.

VOINITSKY: I did not take anything from you.

ASTROFF: You took from my traveling medicine chest a jar of morphine. [*A pause.*] Listen, if you, no matter what, want to commit suicide, then go into the woods and shoot yourself there. The morphine, however, give it back to me, or there will be talk, guesses, they will think I gave it to you. As for me, it is enough that I will have to cut you open. Do you think that would be interesting?

[*Enter* SONIA.]

VOINITSKY: Leave me alone.

ASTROFF: [*To* SONIA.] Sonia, your uncle stole a jar of morphine from my medicine chest and won't give it back. Tell him that after all that's not very intelligent of him. Besides I haven't time for it, it's time for me to go.

SONIA: Uncle Vanya, did you take the morphine?

[*A pause.*]

ASTROFF: He took it. I am certain of that.

SONIA: Give it back. Why do you want to frighten us? [*Tenderly.*] Give it back, Uncle Vanya! I am just as unhappy as you are, maybe, but I don't despair. I bear it and I will bear it till the end of my life. Then you bear it too. [*A pause.*] Give it back! [*Kisses his hand.*] My dear, nice Uncle, darling, give it back! [*Crying.*] You are kind, you will take pity on us and give it back. You bear it too, Uncle! Bear it!—

VOINITSKY: [*Gets the jar from the table and gives it to* ASTROFF.] Here, take it! [*To* SONIA.] But we must get to work quickly, quickly do something, or else I cannot . . . cannot . . .

SONIA: Yes, yes, to work. As soon as we see them off, we will sit down to work. . . . [*Nervously handling the papers on the desk.*] We have let everything go.

ASTROFF: [*Putting the jar into his medicine chest and fastening the straps.*] Now I can start off.

ELENA: [*Entering.*] Ivan, are you here? We are leaving now. Go to Alexander, he wants to tell you something.

SONIA: Go on, Uncle Vanya. [*Taking* VOINITSKY *by the arm.*] Let's go. Papa and you must make peace. You really must.

[SONIA *and* VOINITSKY *go out.*]

ELENA: I am leaving. [*Proffers her hand to* ASTROFF.]

ASTROFF: Already?

ELENA: They have already brought the horses.

ASTROFF: Good-by.

ELENA: Today you promised me that you would go away from here.

ASTROFF: I remember. I am leaving now. [*A pause.*] Were you frightened? [*Takes her hand.*] Is it really so alarming?

ELENA: Yes.

ASTROFF: And maybe you would stay! Would you? Tomorrow at the forester's. . . .

ELENA: No. . . . I've already decided . . . and that is why I look at you so bravely, because our departure is already decided. . . . I ask you one thing: think better of me. I want you to respect me.

ASTROFF: Ah! [*With a gesture of impatience.*] Stay here, I beg you. Confess that you have nothing to do in this world, you have no aim whatsoever, you have nothing to occupy your attention with, and sooner or later anyhow you'll give up to your feelings—you can't escape it. So it is better not in Kharkov and not somewhere in Kursk but here in nature's bosom—at least it is poetic, very beautiful even. . . . Here at the forester's there are houses that are half in ruins, quite to Turgenev's taste.

ELENA: How funny you are . . . I am angry with you, but yet. . . . I'll be thinking of you with pleasure. You are an interesting, original man. We shall never see each other again, and so why hide it? I was even carried away a little by you. So let us shake each other's hand and part as friends. Don't think evil of me.

ASTROFF: [*Shaking her hand.*] Yes, go away from here . . . [*Meditating.*] It seems you are a good, sincere person, but it seems also there is something strange in your whole nature. You came here with your husband, and everyone who worked here, bustling about or building something, had to drop work and for the entire summer they occupied themselves with your husband's gout and you. Both of you, he and you—infected us with your idleness. I was carried away, I have not done anything for a whole month, and during that time people were ailing, and the peasants were grazing their cattle in my woods, so that no matter where you and your husband went, you brought destruction everywhere. I am joking, of course, yet . . . it's strange how I am convinced that if you should stay on, there would be an enormous devastation. And I would perish, and you too would not survive. Well, go away. *Finita la commedia.*

ELENA: [*Takes a pencil from his desk and hides it quickly.*] I am taking this pencil to remember you by.

ASTROFF: It's odd somehow. . . . We have known each other, and suddenly for some reason—we will never see each other again. And that's how it is in this world . . . While no one is here, until Uncle Vanya comes in with a bouquet, let me . . . kiss you . . . for good-by . . . Yes? [*Kissing her cheek.*] So there . . . it's all beautiful.

ELENA: I wish you the best of everything. [*Glancing around quickly.*] No matter what, once in a lifetime! [*Embracing him impetu-*

ously. They both back away from each other.] I must go.

ASTROFF: Go away quickly. If the horses are ready, then start right off.

ELENA: They seem to be coming.

[*They stand there listening.*]

ASTROFF: *Finita!*

[*Enter* SEREBRIAKOFF, VOINITSKY, MARIA VASILIEVNA *with a book,* TELEGIN *and* SONIA.]

SEREBRIAKOFF: [*To* VOINITSKY.] He who remembers the past should have his eye plucked out. After what happened, in those few hours I have lived through so much and have thought so much that it seems to me I could write an entire treatise for the edification of posterity on how one should live. I accept your apologies willingly and beg you myself to forgive me. Good-by!

[*Exchanges kisses with* VOINITSKY *three times.*]

VOINITSKY: You will receive what you used to receive accurately. Everything will be as always.

[ELENA *embraces* SONIA.]

SEREBRIAKOFF: [*Kissing* MARIA VASILIEVNA's *hand.*] Mama . . .

MARIA VASILIEVNA: [*Kissing him.*] Alexander, have another picture taken and send it to me. You know, how dear you are to me.

TELEGIN: Good-by, Your Excellency! Don't forget us!

SEREBRIAKOFF: [*Having kissed his daughter.*] Good-by . . . Everybody good-by! [*Offering his hand to* ASTROFF.] Thank you for the pleasant company. . . . I respect your trend of thought, your fascinations, your impulses, but allow an old man to add to his farewell salutations just one remark: One must, ladies and gentlemen, do something. One must do something! [*Bowing to all in general.*] The best of everything to you.

[*Goes out;* MARIA VASILIEVNA *and* SONIA *follow him.*]

VOINITSKY: [*Kissing* ELENA's *hand fervently.*] Good-by. . . . Forgive me. . . . Never, we'll never meet again.

ELENA: [*Touched.*] Good-by, my dear. [*She kisses his head and goes out.*]

ASTROFF: [*To* TELEGIN.] Tell them, Waffles, to bring my horses too at the same time.

TELEGIN: At your service, my friend. [*Goes out. Only* ASTROFF *and* VOINITSKY *remain.*]

ASTROFF: [*Taking his paints from the* table *and putting them into his suitcase.*] Why aren't you going to see them off?

VOINITSKY: Let them go, and I . . . I can't. I feel very low, I must busy myself quickly with something . . . Work, work! [*He fumbles with the papers on the desk.*]

[*A pause. Bells are heard.*]

ASTROFF: They are gone. The Professor is glad to go. Nothing could tempt him back here.

MARINA: [*Entering.*] They are gone. [*Sitting down in an armchair and knitting on a stocking.*]

SONIA: [*Enters.*] They are gone. [*Wiping her eyes.*] God grant everything will be well with them. Well, Uncle Vanya, let's do something.

VOINITSKY: To work, to work. . . .

SONIA: It's a long, long time now we haven't sat together at this table. [*Lighting a lamp on the table.*] There seems to be no ink. . . . [*She takes the inkwell, goes to the cupboard, and pours out some ink.*] And I feel sad that they are gone.

MARIA VASILIEVNA: [*Entering slowly.*] They are gone!

[*She sits down and buries herself in her reading.*]

SONIA: [*Sitting down at the table and turning the pages of an account book.*] Up the bills first of all, Uncle Vanya. In our hands that's been terribly neglected. They sent again today for a bill. Write. You write one bill, I'll write another.

VOINITSKY: [*Writing.*] "The bill . . . to Mr. . . ."

[*Both write silently.*]

MARINA: [*Yawning.*] I'm getting sleepy. . . .

ASTROFF: It is quiet. Pens are scratching, crickets are chirping. It's warm and cozy . . . I don't feel like leaving here. [*There is the sound of bells.*] There, they are bringing the horses. . . . That means that all there is left is for me to tell you good-by, my dear friends, and say good-by to my table and—be off!

[*Puts the charts into the portfolio.*]

MARINA: And why are you fidgeting? You could sit down.

ASTROFF: I can't.

VOINITSKY: [*Writing.*] "And of the old debt there remains two seventy-five . . ."

[*Enter* A WORKMAN.]

THE WORKMAN: Mikhail Lvovich, the horses are ready.

ASTROFF: I heard it. [*Giving him the*

traveling medicine chest, the suitcase, and the portfolio.] Here, take this. See that you don't crumple the portfolio.

THE WORKMAN: I'll see to it.

[*He goes out.*]

ASTROFF: Well . . . [*He starts saying good-by.*]

SONIA: When will we see each other?

ASTROFF: Not before summer very likely. I doubt during the winter. . . . Obviously, if anything should happen, then let me know—I will come. [*Shaking hands.*] Thanks for bread, for salt, for kindness . . . in a word, for everything. [*Goes to the nurse and kisses her on the head.*] Good-by, good-by, old one.

MARINA: And so you will leave without tea?

ASTROFF: I don't want any, Nurse.

MARINA: Maybe you will drink a little vodka?

ASTROFF: [*Undecided.*] Well maybe . . .

[*MARINA goes out.*]

ASTROFF: [*After a pause.*] My side horse is lame for some reason. I noticed it even yesterday when Peter led him to water.

VOINITSKY: Must change his shoe.

ASTROFF: I will have to stop by at the blacksmith's in Rojhdestvenoy. There's no dodging it. [*He goes to the map of Africa and looks at it.*] And it must be burning hot in this very Africa—that's something hellish.

VOINITSKY: Yes, very likely.

MARINA: [*Returning with a tray on which there is a glass of vodka and a piece of bread.*] Drink please.

[*ASTROFF drinks the vodka.*]

MARINA: To your health, Son. [*Bowing low.*] And why not a bite of bread.

ASTROFF: No, just that . . . And now, the best of everything. [*To MARINA.*] Don't see me off, Nurse. Don't.

[*He goes out; SONIA follows him with a candle, to light the way; MARINA sits down in her armchair.*]

VOINITSKY: [*Writing.*] "Second of February, vegetable oil twenty pounds . . . sixteenth of February again vegetable oil twenty pounds . . . Buckwheat . . ."

[*A pause. There is the sound of bells.*]

MARINA: He is gone.

[*A pause.*]

SONIA: [*Returning and putting the candle on the table.*] He is gone . . .

VOINITSKY: [*Adding on the abacus and writing down the sum.*] That makes . . . fifteen . . . twenty-five . . .

[*SONIA sits down and begins writing.*]

MARINA: [*Yawning.*] A-ah, our sins . . .

[*TELEGIN enters on tiptoes, sits down near the door and quietly tunes the guitar.*]

VOINITSKY: [*To SONIA, stroking her hair with his hand.*] My child, how heavy this is on me. Oh, if you knew how heavy it is!

SONIA: What can we do, we must live! [*A pause.*] We shall live, Uncle Vanya. We'll live through a long, long line of days, endless evenings; we'll bear patiently the trials fate sends us; we'll work for others now and in our old age without ever knowing any rest, and when our hour comes, we'll die humbly and there beside the coffin we'll say that we suffered, that we cried, that we felt bitter, and God will take pity on us, and you and I, Uncle, darling Uncle, shall see life bright, beautiful, fine, we shall be happy and will look back tenderly with a smile on these misfortunes we have now—and we shall rest. I have faith, I believe warmly, passionately . . . [*Kneeling before him and putting her head on his hands; in a tired voice.*] We shall rest!

[*TELEGIN plays the guitar quietly.*]

SONIA: We shall rest! We shall hear the angels, we shall see the whole sky all diamonds, we shall see how all earthly evil, all our sufferings, are drowned in the mercy that will fill the whole world. And our life will grow peaceful, tender, sweet as a caress. I believe, I do believe . . . [*Wipes away his tears with a handkerchief.*] Poor, dear Uncle Vanya, you are crying . . . [*Through her tears.*] In your life you haven't known what joy was; but wait, Uncle Vanya, wait. . . . We shall rest. . . . [*Embraces him.*] We shall rest! [*The night watchman taps. TELEGIN is strumming quietly; MARIA VASILIEVNA is writing on the margins of a pamphlet; MARINA is knitting on a stocking.*]

SONIA: We shall rest!

THE CURTAIN FALLS SLOWLY.

AUGUST STRINDBERG

FOREWORD to *Miss Julie* [1]

Theatre has long seemed to me—in common with much other art—a *Biblia Pauperum,* a Bible in pictures for those who cannot read what is written or printed; and I see the playwright as a lay preacher peddling the ideas of his time in popular form, popular enough for the middle-classes, mainstay of theatre audiences, to grasp the gist of the matter without troubling their brains too much. For this reason theatre has always been an elementary school for the young, the semi-educated and for women who still have a primitive capacity for deceiving themselves and letting themselves be deceived— who, that is to say, are susceptible to illusion and to suggestion from the author. I have therefore thought it not unlikely that in these days, when that rudimentary and immature thought-process operating through fantasy appears to be developing into reflection, research and analysis, that theatre, like religion, might be discarded as an outworn form for whose appreciation we lack the necessary conditions. This opinion is confirmed by the major crisis still prevailing in the theatres of Europe, and still more by the fact that in those countries of culture, producing the greatest thinkers of the age, namely England and Germany, drama—like other fine arts—is dead.

Some countries, it is true, have attempted to create a new drama by using the old forms with up-to-date contents, but not only has there been insufficient time for these new ideas to be popularized, so that the audience can grasp them, but also people have been so wrought up by the taking of sides that pure, disinterested appreciation has become impossible. One's deepest impressions are upset when an applauding or a hissing majority dominates as forcefully and openly as it can in the theatre. Moreover, as no new form has been devised for these new contents, the new wine has burst the old bottles.

In this play I have not tried to do anything new, for this cannot be done, but only to modernize the form to meet the

August Strindberg, "Foreword to *Miss Julie," Six Plays of Strindberg,* trans. Elizabeth Sprigge (New York, 1955), pp. 61–73. Copyright 1955 by Elizabeth Sprigge. Reprinted by permission of Collins-Knowlton-Wing, Inc.

demands which may, I think, be made on this art today. To this end I chose—or surrendered myself to—a theme which claims to be outside the controversial issues of today, since questions of social climbing or falling, of higher or lower, better or worse, of man and woman, are, have been and will be of lasting interest. When I took this theme from a true story told me some years ago, which made a deep impression, I saw it as a subject for tragedy, for as yet it is tragic to see one favoured by fortune go under, and still more to see a family heritage die out, although a time may come when we have grown so developed and enlightened that we shall view with indifference life's spectacle, now seeming so brutal, cynical and heartless. Then we shall have dispensed with those inferior, unreliable instruments of thought called feelings, which become harmful and superfluous as reasoning develops.

The fact that my heroine rouses pity is solely due to weakness; we cannot resist fear of the same fate overtaking us. The hyper-sensitive spectator may, it is true, go beyond this kind of pity, while the man with belief in the future may actually demand some suggestion for remedying the evil—in other words some kind of policy. But, to begin with, there is no such thing as absolute evil; the downfall of one family is the good fortune of another, which thereby gets a chance to rise, and, fortune being only comparative, the alternation of rising and falling is one of life's principal charms. Also, to the man of policy, who wants to remedy the painful fact that the bird of prey devours the dove, and lice the bird of prey, I should like to put the question: why should it be remedied? Life is not so mathematically idiotic as only to permit the big to eat the small; it happens just as often that the bee kills the lion or at least drives it mad.

That my tragedy depresses many people is their own fault. When we have grown strong as the pioneers of the French revolution, we shall be happy and relieved to see the national parks cleared of ancient rotting trees which have stood too long in the way of others equally entitled to a period of growth—as relieved as we are when an incurable invalid dies.

My tragedy "The Father" was recently criticised for being too sad—as if one wants cheerful tragedies! Everybody is clamouring for this supposed "joy of life," and theatre managers demand farces, as if the joy of life consisted in being ridiculous and portraying all human beings as suffering from St. Vitus's dance or total idiocy. I myself find the joy of life in its strong and cruel struggles, and my pleasure in learning, in adding to my knowledge. For this reason I have chosen for this play an unusual situation, but an instructive one—an exception, that is to say, but a great exception, one proving the rule, which will no doubt annoy all lovers of the commonplace. What will offend simple minds is that my plot is not simple, nor its point of view single. In real life an action—this, by the way, is a somewhat new discovery—is generally caused by a whole series of motives, more or less fundamental, but as a rule the spectator chooses just one of these—the one which his mind can most easily grasp or that does most credit to his intelligence. A suicide is committed. Business troubles, says the man of affairs. Unrequited love, say the women. Sickness, says the invalid. Despair, says the down-and-out. But it is possible that the motive lay in all or none of these directions, or that the dead man concealed his actual motive by revealing quite another, likely to reflect more to his glory.

I see Miss Julie's tragic fate to be the result of many circumstances: the mother's character, the father's mistaken upbringing of the girl, her own nature, and the influence of her fiancé on a weak, degenerate mind. Also, more directly, the festive mood of Midsummer Eve, her father's absence, her monthly indisposition, her pre-occupation with animals, the excitement of dancing, the magic of dusk, the strongly aphrodisiac influence of flowers, and finally the chance that drives the couple into a room alone—to which must be added the urgency of the excited man.

My treatment of the theme, moreover, is neither exclusively physiological nor psychological. I have not put the blame wholly on the inheritance from her mother, nor on her physical condition at the time, nor on immorality. I have not even preached a moral sermon; in the absence of a priest I leave this to the cook.

I congratulate myself on this multiplicity of motives as being up-to-date, and if others have done the same thing before me, then I congratulate myself on not being alone in my "paradoxes," as all innovations are called.

In regard to the drawing of the characters, I have made my people somewhat "characterless" for the following reasons. In the course of time the word character has assumed manifold meanings. It must have originally signified the dominating trait of the soul-complex, and this was confused with temperament. Later it became the middle-class term for the automaton, one whose nature had become fixed or who had adapted himself to a particular rôle in life. In fact a person who had ceased to grow was called a character, while one continuing to develop— the skilful navigator of life's river, sailing not with sheets set fast, but veering before the wind to luff again—was called characterless, in a derogatory sense, of course, because he was so hard to catch, classify and keep track of. This middle-class conception of the immobility of the soul was transferred to the stage where the middle-class has always ruled. A character came to signify a man fixed and finished: one who invariably appeared either drunk or jocular or melancholy, and characterization required nothing more than a physical defect such as a club-foot, a wooden leg, a red nose; or the fellow might be made to repeat some such phrase as: "That's capital!" or: "Barkis is willin'!" This simple way of regarding human beings still survives in the great Molière. Harpagon is nothing but a miser, although Harpagon might have been not only a miser, but also a first-rate financier, an excellent father and a good citizen. Worse still, his "failing" is a distinct advantage to his son-in-law and his daughter, who are his heirs, and who therefore cannot criticise him, even if they have to wait a while to get to bed. I do not believe, therefore, in simple stage characters; and the summary judgments of authors—this man is stupid, that one brutal, this jealous, that stingy, and so forth—should be challenged by the Naturalists who know the richness of the soul-complex and realise that vice has a reverse side very much like virtue.

Because they are modern characters, living in a period of transition more feverishly hysterical than its predecessor at least, I have drawn my figures vacillating, disintegrated, a blend of old and new. Nor does it seem to me unlikely that, through newspapers and conversations, modern ideas may have filtered down to the level of the domestic servant.

My souls (characters) are conglomerations of past and present stages of civilization, bits from books and newspapers, scraps of humanity, rags and tatters of fine clothing, patched together as is the human soul. And I have added a little evolutionary history by making the weaker steal and repeat the words of the stronger, and by making the characters borrow ideas or "suggestions" from one another.

Miss Julie is a modern character, not that the half-woman, the man-hater, has not existed always, but because now that she has been discovered she has stepped to the front and begun to make a noise. The half-woman is a type who thrusts herself forward, selling herself nowadays for power, decorations, distinctions, diplomas, as formerly for money. The type implies degeneration; it is not a good type and it does not endure; but it can unfortunately transmit its misery, and degenerate men seem instinctively to choose their mates from among such women, and so they breed, producing offspring of indeterminate sex to whom life is torture. But fortunately they perish, either because they cannot come to terms with reality, or because their repressed instincts break out uncontrollably, or again because their hopes of catching up with men are shattered. The type is tragic, revealing a desperate fight against nature, tragic too in its Romantic inheritance now dissipated by Naturalism, which wants nothing but happiness—and for happiness strong and sound species are required.

But Miss Julie is also a relic of the old warrior nobility now giving way to the new nobility of nerve and brain. She is a victim of the discord which a mother's "crime" has produced in a family, a victim too of the day's complaisance, of circumstances, of her own defective constitution, all of which are equivalent to the Fate or Universal Law of former days. The Naturalist has abolished guilt with God, but the consequences of the action—punishment, imprisonment or the fear of it—he cannot abolish, for the simple reason that they remain whether he is acquitted or not. An injured fellow-being is not so complacent as outsiders, who have not been injured, can afford to be. Even if the father had felt impelled to take no vengeance, the daughter would have taken vengeance on herself, as she does here, from that innate or acquired sense of honour which the upper-classes inherit—whether from Barbarism or Aryan forebears, or from the chivalry of the Middle Ages, who knows? It is a very beautiful thing, but it has become a danger nowadays to the preservation of the race. It is the nobleman's *harakiri*, the Japanese law of inner conscience which compels him to cut his own stomach open at the insult of another, and which survives in modified form in the duel, a privilege of the nobility. And so the valet Jean lives on, but Miss Julie cannot live without honour. This is the thrall's advantage over the nobleman, that he lacks this fatal preoccupation with honour. And in all of us Aryans there is something of the nobleman, or the Don Quixote, which makes us sympathize with the man who commits suicide because he has done something ignoble and lost his honour. And we are noblemen enough to suffer at the sight of fallen greatness littering the earth like a corpse— yes, even if the fallen rise again and make restitution by honourable deeds. Jean, the valet, is a race-builder, a man of marked characteristics. He was a labourer's son who has educated himself towards becoming a gentleman. He has learnt easily, through his well-developed senses (smell, taste, vision)— and he also has a sense of beauty. He has already bettered himself, and is thick-skinned enough to have no scruples about using other people's services. He is already foreign to his associates, despising them as part of the life he has turned his back on, yet also fearing and fleeing from them because they know his secrets, pry into his plans, watch his rise with envy, and look forward with pleasure to his fall. Hence his dual, indeterminate character, vacillating between love of the heights and hatred of those who have already achieved them. He is, he says himself, an aristocrat; he has learned the secrets of good society. He is polished, but vulgar within; he already wears his tails with taste, but there is no guarantee of his personal cleanliness.

He has some respect for his young lady, but he is frightened of Kristin, who knows his dangerous secrets, and he is sufficiently callous not to allow the night's events to wreck his plans for the future. Having both the slave's brutality and the master's lack of squeamishness, he can see blood without fainting and take disaster by the horns. Consequently he emerges from the battle unscathed, and probably ends his days as a hotel-keeper. And even if *he* does not become a Roumanian Count, his son will doubtless go to the university and perhaps become a county attorney.

The light which Jean sheds on a lower-class conception of life, life seen from below, is on the whole illuminating—when he speaks the truth, which is not often, for he says what is favourable to himself rather than what is true. When Miss Julie suggests that the lower-classes must be oppressed by the attitude of their superiors, Jean naturally agrees, as his object is to gain her sympathy; but when he perceives the advantage of separating himself from the common herd, he at once takes back his words.

It is not because Jean is now rising that he has the upper hand of Miss Julie, but because he is a man. Sexually he is the aristocrat because of his virility, his keener senses and his capacity for taking the initiative. His inferiority is mainly due to the social environment in which he lives, and he can probably shed it with his valet's livery.

The slave mentality expresses itself in his worship of the Count (the boots), and his religious superstition; but he worships the Count chiefly because he holds that higher position for which Jean himself is striving. And this worship remains even when he has won the daughter of the house and seen how empty is that lovely shell.

I do not believe that a love relationship in the "higher" sense could exist between two individuals of such different quality, but I have made Miss Julie imagine that she is in love, so as to lessen her sense of guilt, and I let Jean suppose that if his social position were altered he would truly love her. I think love is like the hyacinth which has to strike roots in darkness *before* it can produce a vigorous flower. In this case it shoots up quickly, blossoms and goes to seed all at the same time, which is why the plant dies so soon.

As for Kristin, she is a female slave, full of servility and sluggishness acquired in front of the kitchen fire, and stuffed full of morality and religion, which are her cloak and scapegoat. She goes to church as a quick and easy way of unloading her household thefts on to Jesus and taking on a fresh cargo of guiltlessness. For the rest she is a minor character, and I have therefore sketched her in the same manner as the Pastor and the Doctor in "The Father," where I wanted ordinary human beings, as are most country pastors and provincial doctors. If these minor characters seem abstract to some people this is due to the fact that ordinary people are to a certain extent abstract in pursuit of their work; that is to say, they are without individuality, showing, while working, only one side of themselves. And as long as the spectator does not feel a need to see them from other sides, there is nothing wrong with my abstract presentation.

In regard to the dialogue, I have departed somewhat from tradition by not making my characters catechists who ask stupid questions in order to elicit a smart reply. I have avoided the symmetrical, mathematical construction of French dialogue, and let people's minds work irregularly, as they do in real life where, during a conversation, no topic is drained to the dregs, and one mind finds in another a chance cog to engage in. So too the dialogue wanders, gathering in the opening scenes material which is later picked up, worked over, repeated, expounded and developed like the theme in a musical composition.

The plot speaks for itself, and as it really only concerns two people, I have concentrated on these, introducing only one minor character, the cook, and keeping the unhappy spirit of the father above and behind the action. I have done this because it seems to me that the psychological process is what interests people most today. Our inquisitive souls are no longer satisfied with seeing a thing happen; we must also know how it happens. We want to see the wires themselves, to watch the machinery, to examine the box with the false bottom, to take hold of the magic ring in order to find the join, and look at the cards to see how they are marked.

In this connection I have had in view the documentary novels of the brothers de Goncourt, which appeal to me more than any other modern literature.

As far as the technical side of the work is concerned I have made the experiment of abolishing the division into acts. This is because I have come to the conclusion that our capacity for illusion is disturbed by the intervals, during which the audience has time to reflect and escape from the suggestive influence of the author-hypnotist. My play will probably take an hour and a half, and as one can listen to a lecture, a sermon or a parliamentary debate for as long as that or longer, I do not think a theatrical performance will be fatiguing in the same length of time. As early as 1872, in one of my first dramatic attempts, "The Outlaw," I tried this concentrated form, although with scant success. The play was written in five acts, and only when finished did I become aware of the restless, disjointed effect that it produced. The script was burnt and from the ashes rose a single well-knit act—fifty pages of print, playable in one hour. The form of the present play is, therefore, not new, but it appears to be my own, and changing tastes may make it timely. My hope is one day to have an audience educated enough to sit through a whole evening's entertainment in one act, but one would have to try this out to see. Meanwhile, in order to provide respite for the audience and the players, without allowing the audience to escape from the illusion, I have introduced three art forms: monologue, mime and ballet. These are all part of drama, having their origins in classic tragedy, monody having become monologue and the chorus, ballet.

Monologue is now condemned by our realists as unnatural, but if one provides motives for it one makes it natural, and then can use it to advantage. It is, surely, natural for a public speaker to walk up and down the room practicing his speech, natural for an actor to read his part aloud, for a servant girl to talk to her cat, a mother to prattle to her child, an old maid to chatter to her parrot, and a sleeper to talk in his sleep. And in order that the actor may have a chance, for once, of working independently, free from the author's direction, it is better that the monologue should not be written, but only indicated. For since it is of small importance what is said in one's sleep or to the parrot or to the cat—none of it influences the action— a talented actor, identifying himself with the atmosphere and the situation, may improvise better than the author, who cannot calculate how much may be said or how long taken without waking the audience from the illusion.

Some Italian theatres have, as we know, returned to improvisation, thereby producing actors who are creative, although within the bounds set by the author. This may well be a step forward, or even the beginning of a new art-form worthy to be called *productive*.

In places where monologue would be unnatural I have used mime, leaving here an even wider scope for the actor's imagination, and more chance for him to win independent laurels. But so as not to try the audience beyond endurance, I have introduced music—fully justified by the Midsummer Eve dance—to exercise its powers of persuasion during the dumb show. But I beg the musical director to consider carefully his choice of compositions, so that conflicting moods are not induced by selections from the current operetta or dance show, or by folk-tunes of too local a character.

The ballet I have introduced cannot be replaced by the usual kind of "crowd-scene," for such scenes are too badly played—a lot of grinning idiots seizing the opportunity to show off and thus destroying the illusion. And as peasants cannot improvise their taunts, but use ready-made phrases with a double meaning, I have not composed their lampoon, but taken a little-known song and dance which I myself noted down in the Stockholm district. The words are not quite to the point, but this too is intentional, for the cunning, i.e. weakness, of the slave prevents him from direct attack. Nor can there be clowning in a serious action, or coarse joking in a situation which nails the lid on a family coffin.

As regards the scenery, I have borrowed from impressionist painting its asymmetry and its economy; thus, I think, strengthening the illusion. For the fact that one does not see the whole room and all the furniture leaves scope of conjecture—that is to say imagination is roused and complements what is seen. I have succeeded too in getting rid of those tiresome exits through doors, since scenery doors are made of canvas, and rock at the slightest touch. They cannot even express the wrath of an irate head of the family who, after a bad dinner, goes out slamming the door behind him, "so that the whole house shakes." On the stage it rocks. I have also kept to a single set, both in order to let the characters develop in their métier and to break away from over-decoration. When one has only one set, one may expect it to be realistic; but as a matter of fact nothing is harder than to get a stage room that looks something like a room, however easily the scene painter can produce flaming volcanoes and water-falls. Presumably the walls must be of canvas; but it seems about time to dispense with painted shelves and cooking utensils. We are asked to accept so many stage conventions that we might as least be spared the pain of painting pots and pans.

I have set the back wall and the table diagonally so that the actors may play full-face and in half-profile when they are sitting opposite one another at the table. In the opera AÏDA I saw a diagonal background, which led the eye to unfamiliar perspectives and did not look like mere reaction against boring straight lines.

Another much needed innovation is the abolition of foot-lights. This lighting from below is said to have the purpose of making the actors' faces fatter. But why, I ask, should all actors have fat faces? Does not this underlighting flatten out all the subtlety of the lower part of the face, specially the jaw, falsify the shape of the nose and throw shadows up over the eyes? Even if this were not so, one thing is certain: that the lights hurt the performers' eyes, so that the full play of their expression is lost. The foot-lights strike part of the retina usually protected—except in sailors who have to watch sunlight on water—and therefore one seldom sees anything other than a crude rolling of the eyes, either sideways or up towards the gallery, showing their whites. Perhaps this too causes that tiresome blinking of the eyelashes, especially by actresses. And when anyone on the stage wants to speak with his eyes, the only thing he can do is to look straight at the audience, with whom he or she then gets into direct communication, outside the framework of the set—a habit called, rightly or wrongly, "greeting one's friends."

Would not sufficiently strong side-lighting, with some kind of reflectors, add to the actor's powers of expression by allowing him to use the face's greatest asset:—the play of the eyes?

I have few illusions about getting the actors to play *to* the audience instead of *with* it, although this is what I want. That I shall see an actor's back throughout a critical scene is beyond my dreams, but I do wish crucial scenes could be played, not in front of the prompter's box, like duets expecting applause, but in the place required by the action. So, no revolutions, but just some small modifications, for to make the stage into a real room with the fourth wall missing would be too upsetting altogether.

I dare not hope that the actresses will listen to what I have to say about make-up, for they would rather be beautiful than life-like, but the actor might consider whether it is to his advantage to create an abstract character with grease-paints, and cover his face with it like a mask. Take the case of a man who draws a choleric charcoal line between his eyes and then, in this fixed state of wrath, has to smile at some repartee. What a frightful grimace the result is! And equally, how is that false forehead, smooth as a billiard ball, to wrinkle when the old man loses his temper?

In a modern psychological drama, where the subtlest reactions of a character need to be mirrored in the face rather than expressed by sound and gesture, it would be worth while experimenting with powerful side-lighting on a small stage and a cast without make-up, or at least with the minimum.

If, in addition, we could abolish the visible orchestra, with its distracting lamps and its faces turned toward the audience; if we could have the stalls raised so that the spectators' eyes were higher than the players' knees; if we could get rid of the boxes (the centre of my target), with their tittering diners and supper-parties, and have total darkness in the auditorium during the performance; and if, first and foremost, we could have a *small* stage and a *small* house, then perhaps a new dramatic art might arise, and theatre once more become a place of entertainment for educated people. While waiting for such a theatre it is as well for us to go on writing so as to stock that repertory of the future.

I have made an attempt. If it has failed, there is time enough to try again.

AUGUST STRINDBERG

Miss Julie

CHARACTERS

MISS JULIE, *aged 25*
JEAN, *the valet, aged 30*
KRISTIN, *the cook, aged 35*

August Strindberg, "Miss Julie," *Six Plays of Strindberg,* trans. Elizabeth Sprigge (New York, 1955). Copyright 1955, by Elizabeth Sprigge. Reprinted by permission of Collins-Knowlton-Wing, Inc.

Scene: The large kitchen of a Swedish manor house in a country district in the eighties.

Midsummer eve.

The kitchen has three doors, two small ones into JEAN's *and* KRISTIN's *bedrooms, and a large, glass-fronted double one, opening on to a courtyard. This is the only way to the rest of the house.*

Through these glass doors can be seen part of a fountain with a cupid, lilac bushes in flower and the tops of some Lombardy poplars. On one wall are shelves edged with scalloped paper on which are kitchen utensils of copper, iron and tin.

To the left is the corner of a large tiled range and part of its chimney-hood, to the right the end of the servants' dinner table with chairs beside it.

The stove is decorated with birch boughs, the floor strewn with twigs of juniper. On the end of the table is a large Japanese spice jar full of lilac.

There are also an ice-box, a scullery table and a sink. Above the double door hangs a big old-fashioned bell; near it is a speaking-tube.

A fiddle can be heard from the dance in the barn near-by. KRISTIN *is standing at the stove, frying something in a pan. She wears a light-coloured cotton dress and a big apron.*

JEAN *enters, wearing livery and carrying a pair of large riding-boots with spurs, which he puts in a conspicuous place.*

JEAN: Miss Julie's crazy again to-night, absolutely crazy.

KRISTIN: Oh, so you're back, are you?

JEAN: When I'd taken the Count to the station, I came back and dropped in at the Barn for a dance. And who did I see there but our young lady leading off with the gamekeeper. But the moment she sets eyes on me, up she rushes and invites me to waltz with her. And how she waltzed—I've never seen anything like it! She's crazy.

KRISTIN: Always has been, but never so bad as this last fortnight since the engagement was broken off.

JEAN: Yes, that was a pretty business, to be sure. He's a decent enough chap, too, even if he isn't rich. Oh, but they're choosy! [*Sits down at the end of the table.*] In any case, it's a bit odd that our young—er—lady would rather stay at home with the yokels than go with her father to visit her relations.

KRISTIN: Perhaps she feels a bit awkward, after that bust-up with her fiancé.

JEAN: Maybe. That chap had some guts, though. Do you know the sort of thing that was going on, Kristin? I saw it with my own eyes, though I didn't let on I had.

KRISTIN: You saw them . . . ?

JEAN: Didn't I just! Came across the pair of them one evening in the stable-yard. Miss Julie was doing what she called "training" him. Know what that was? Making him jump over her riding-whip—the way you teach a dog. He did it twice and got a cut each time for his pains, but when it came to the third go, he snatched the whip out of her hand and broke it into smithereens. And then he cleared off.

KRISTIN: What goings on! I never did!

JEAN: Well, that's how it was with that little affair . . . Now, what have you got for me, Kristin? Something tasty?

KRISTIN: [*Serving from the pan to his plate.*] Well, it's just a little bit of kidney I cut off their joint.

JEAN: [*Smelling it.*] Fine! That's my

special delice. [*Feels the plate.*] But you might have warmed the plate.

KRISTIN: When you choose to be finicky you're worse than the Count himself. [*Pulls his hair affectionately.*]

JEAN: [*Crossly.*] Stop pulling my hair. You know how sensitive I am.

KRISTIN: There, there! It's only love, you know.

[JEAN *eats.* KRISTIN *brings a bottle of beer.*]

JEAN: Beer on Midsummer Eve? No thanks! I've got something better than that. [*From a drawer in the table brings out a bottle of red wine with a yellow seal.*] Yellow seal, see! Now get me a glass. You use a glass with a stem of course when you're drinking it straight.

KRISTIN: [*Giving him a wine-glass.*] Lord help the woman who gets you for a husband, you old fusser! [*She puts the beer in the ice-box and sets a small saucepan on the stove.*]

JEAN: Nonsense! You'll be glad enough to get a fellow as smart as me. And I don't think it's done you any harm people calling me your fiancé. [*Tastes the wine.*] Good. Very good indeed. But not quite warmed enough. [*Warms the glass in his hand.*] We bought this in Dijon. Four francs the litre without the bottle, and duty on top of that. What are you cooking now? It stinks.

KRISTIN: Some bloody muck Miss Julie wants for Diana.

JEAN: You should be more refined in your speech, Kristin. But why should you spend a holiday cooking for that bitch? Is she sick or what?

KRISTIN: Yes, she's sick. She sneaked out with the pug at the lodge and got in the usual mess. And that, you know, Miss Julie won't have.

JEAN: Miss Julie's too high-and-mighty in some respects, and not enough in others, just like her mother before her. The Countess was more at home in the kitchen and cowsheds than anywhere else, but would she ever go driving with only one horse? She went round with her cuffs filthy, but she had to have the coronet on the cuff-links. Our young lady—to come back to her—hasn't any proper respect for herself or her position. I mean she isn't refined. In the Barn just now she dragged the gamekeeper away from Anna and made him dance with her—no waiting to be asked. We wouldn't do a thing like that. But that's what hap-

pens when the gentry try to behave like the common people—they become common . . . Still she's a fine girl. Smashing! What shoulders! And what—er—etcetera!

KRISTIN: Oh come off it! I know what Clara says, and she dresses her.

JEAN: Clara? Pooh, you're all jealous! But I've been out riding with her . . . and as for her dancing!

KRISTIN: Listen, Jean. You will dance with me, won't you, as soon as I'm through.

JEAN: Of course I will.

KRISTIN: Promise?

JEAN: Promise? When I say I'll do a thing I do it. Well, thanks for the supper. It was a real treat. [*Corks the bottle.*]

[JULIE *appears in the doorway, speaking to someone outside.*]

JULIE: I'll be back in a moment. Don't wait.

[JEAN *slips the bottle into the drawer and rises respectfully.* JULIE *enters and joins* KRISTIN *at the stove.*]

Well, have you made it? [KRISTIN *signs that* JEAN *is near them.*]

JEAN: [*Gallantly.*] Have you ladies got some secret?

JULIE: [*Flipping his face with her handkerchief.*] You're very inquisitive.

JEAN: What a delicious smell! Violets.

JULIE: [*Coquettishly.*] Impertinence! Are you an expert of scent too? I must say you know how to dance. Now don't look. Go away. [*The music of a schottische begins.*]

JEAN: [*With impudent politeness.*] Is it some witches' brew you're cooking on Midsummer Eve? Something to tell your stars by, so you can see your future?

JULIE: [*Sharply.*] If you could see that you'd have good eyes. [*To* KRISTIN.] Put it in a bottle and cork it tight. Come and dance this schottische with me, Jean.

JEAN: [*Hesitating.*] I don't want to be rude, but I've promised to dance this one with Kristin.

JULIE: Well, she can have another, can't you, Kristin? You'll lend me Jean, won't you?

KRISTIN: [*Bottling.*] It's nothing to do with me. When you're so condescending, Miss, it's not his place to say no. Go on, Jean, and thank Miss Julie for the honour.

JEAN: Frankly speaking, Miss, and no offence meant, I wonder if it's wise for you to dance twice running with the same partner, specially as those people are so ready to jump to conclusions.

JULIE: [*Flaring up.*] What did you say? What sort of conclusions? What do you mean?

JEAN: [*Meekly.*] As you choose not to understand, Miss Julie, I'll have to speak more plainly. It looks bad to show a preference for one of your retainers when they're all hoping for the same unusual favour.

JULIE: Show a preference! The very idea! I'm surprised at you. I'm doing the people an honour by attending their ball when I'm mistress of the house, but if I'm really going to dance, I mean to have a partner who can lead and doesn't make me look ridiculous.

JEAN: If those are your orders, Miss, I'm at your service.

JULIE: [*Gently.*] Don't take it as an order. To-night we're all just people enjoying a party. There's no question of class. So now give me your arm. Don't worry, Kristin. I shan't steal your sweetheart.

[JEAN *gives* JULIE *his arm and leads her out.*]

[*Left alone,* KRISTIN *plays her scene in an unhurried, natural way, humming to the tune of the schottische, played on a distant violin. She clears* JEAN'S *place, washes up and puts things away, then takes off her apron, brings out a small mirror from a drawer, props it against the jar of lilac, lights a candle, warms a small pair of tongs and curls her fringe. She goes to the door and listens, then turning back to the table finds* MISS JULIE'S *forgotten handkerchief. She smells it, then meditatively smooths it out and folds it.*]

[*Enter* JEAN.]

JEAN: She really *is* crazy. What a way to dance! With people standing grinning at her too from behind the doors. What's got into her, Kristin?

KRISTIN: Oh, it's just her time coming on. She's always queer then. Are you going to dance with me now?

JEAN: Then you're not wild with me for cutting that one.

KRISTIN: You know I'm not—for a little thing like that. Besides, I know my place.

JEAN: [*Putting his arm round her waist.*] You're a sensible girl, Kristin, and you'll make a very good wife . . .

[*Enter* JULIE, *unpleasantly surprised.*]

JULIE: [*With forced gaiety.*] You're a fine beau—running away from your partner.

JEAN: Not away, Miss Julie, but as you see back to the one I deserted.

JULIE: [*Changing her tone.*] You really can dance, you know. But why are you wearing your livery on a holiday. Take it off at once.

JEAN: Then I must ask you to go away for a moment, Miss. My black coat's here. [*Indicates it hanging on the door to his room.*]

JULIE: Are you so shy of me——just over changing a coat? Go into your room then— or stay here and I'll turn my back.

JEAN: Excuse me then, Miss. [*He goes to his room and is partly visible as he changes his coat.*]

JULIE: Tell me, Kristin, is Jean your fiancé? You seem very intimate.

KRISTIN: My fiancé? Yes, if you like. We call it that.

JULIE: Call it?

KRISTIN: Well, you've had a fiancé yourself, Miss, and . . .

JULIE: But we really were engaged.

KRISTIN: All the same it didn't come to anything.

[JEAN *returns in his black coat.*]

JULIE: Très gentil, Monsieur Jean. Très gentil.

JEAN: Vous voulez plaisanter, Madame.

JULIE: Et vous voulez parler français. Where did you learn it?

JEAN: In Switzerland, when I was sommelier at one of the biggest hotels in Lucerne.

JULIE: You look quite the gentleman in that get-up. Charming. [*Sit at the table.*]

JEAN: Oh, you're just flattering me!

JULIE: [*Annoyed.*] Flattering you?

JEAN: I'm too modest to believe you would pay real compliments to a man like me, so I must take it you are exaggerating— that this is what's known as flattery.

JULIE: Where on earth did you learn to make speeches like that? Perhaps you've been to the theatre a lot.

JEAN: That's right. And travelled a lot too.

JULIE: But you come from this neighbourhood, don't you?

JEAN: Yes, my father was a labourer on the next estate—the District Attorney's place. I often used to see you, Miss Julie, when you were little, though you never noticed me.

JULIE: Did you really?

JEAN: Yes. One time specially I remember . . . but I can't tell you about that.

JULIE: Oh do! Why not? This is just the time.

JEAN: No, I really can't now. Another time perhaps.

JULIE: Another time means never. What harm in now?

JEAN: No harm, but I'd rather not. [*Points to* KRISTIN, *now fast asleep.*] Look at her.

JULIE: She'll make a charming wife, won't she? I wonder if she snores.

JEAN: No, she doesn't, but she talks in her sleep.

JULIE: [*Cynically.*] How do you know she talks in her sleep?

JEAN: [*Brazenly.*] I've heard her. [*Pause. They look at one another.*]

JULIE: Why don't you sit down?

JEAN: I can't take such a liberty in your presence.

JULIE: Supposing I order you to.

JEAN: I'll obey.

JULIE: Then sit down. No, wait a minute. Will you get me a drink first?

JEAN: I don't know what's in the ice-box. Only beer, I expect.

JULIE: There's no only about it. My taste is so simple I prefer it to wine.

[JEAN *takes a bottle from the ice-box, fetches a glass and plate and serves the beer.*]

JEAN: At your service.

JULIE: Thank you. Won't you have some yourself?

JEAN: I'm not really a beer-drinker, but if it's an order . . .

JULIE: Order? I should have thought it was ordinary manners to keep your partner company.

JEAN: That's a good way of putting it. [*He opens another bottle and fetches a glass.*]

JULIE: Now drink my health. [*He hesitates.*] I believe the man really is shy.

[JEAN *kneels and raises his glass with mock ceremony.*]

JEAN: To the health of my lady!

JULIE: Bravo! Now kiss my shoe and everything will be perfect. [*He hesitates, then boldly takes hold of her foot and lightly kisses it.*] Splendid. You ought to have been an actor.

JEAN: [*Rising.*] We can't go on like this, Miss Julie. Someone might come in and see us.

JULIE: Why would that matter?

JEAN: For the simple reason that they'd talk. And if you knew the way their tongues were wagging out there just now, you . . .

JULIE: What were they saying? Tell me. Sit down.

JEAN: [*Sitting.*] No offence meant, Miss, but . . . well, their language wasn't nice, and they were hinting . . . oh, you know quite well what. You're not a child, and if a lady's seen drinking alone at night with a man—and a servant at that—then . . .

JULIE: Then what? Besides, we're not alone. Kristin's here.

JEAN: Yes, asleep.

JULIE: I'll wake her up. [*Rises.*] Kristin, are you asleep? [KRISTIN *mumbles in her sleep.*] Kristin! Goodness, how she sleeps!

KRISTIN: [*In her sleep.*] The Count's boots are cleaned—put the coffee on—yes, yes, at once. . . . [*Mumbles incoherently.*]

JULIE: [*Tweaking her nose.*] Wake up, can't you!

JEAN: [*Sharply.*] Let her sleep.

JULIE: What?

JEAN: When you've been standing at the stove all day you're likely to be tired at night. And sleep should be respected.

JULIE: [*Changing her tone.*] What a nice idea. It does you credit. Thank you for it. [*Holds out her hand to him.*] Now come out and pick some lilac for me.

[*During the following* KRISTIN *goes sleepily in to her bedroom.*]

JEAN: Out with you, Miss Julie?

JULIE: Yes.

JEAN: It wouldn't do. It really wouldn't.

JULIE: I don't know what you mean. You can't possibly imagine that . . .

JEAN: I don't, but others do.

JULIE: What? That I'm in love with the valet?

JEAN: I'm not a conceited man, but such a thing's been known to happen, and to these rustics nothing's sacred.

JULIE: You, I take it, are an aristocrat.

JEAN: Yes, I am.

JULIE: And I am coming down in the world.

JEAN: Don't come down, Miss Julie. Take my advice. No one will believe you came down of your own accord. They'll all say you fell.

JULIE: I have a higher opinion of our

people than you. Come and put it to the test. Come on. [*Gazes into his eyes.*]

JEAN: You're very strange, you know.

JULIE: Perhaps I am, but so are you. For that matter everything is strange. Life, human beings, everything, just scum drifting about on the water until it sinks—down and down. That reminds me of a dream I sometimes have, in which I'm on top of a pillar and can't see any way of getting down. When I look down I'm dizzy; I have to get down but I haven't the courage to jump. I can't stay there and I long to fall, but I don't fall. There's no respite. There can't be any peace at all for me until I'm down, right down on the ground. And if I did get to the ground I'd want to be under the ground . . . Have you ever felt like that?

JEAN: No. In my dream I'm lying under a great tree in a dark wood. I want to get up, up to the top of it, and look out over the bright landscape where the sun is shining and rob that high nest of its golden eggs. And I climb and climb, but the trunk is so thick and smooth and it's so far to the first branch. But I know if I can once reach that first branch I'll go to the top just as if I'm on a ladder. I haven't reached it yet, but I shall get there, even if only in my dreams.

JULIE: Here I am chattering about dreams with you. Come on. Only into the park. [*She takes his arm and they go towards the door.*]

JEAN: We must sleep on nine midsummer flowers tonight; then our dreams will come true, Miss Julie. [*They turn at the door. He has a hand to his eye.*]

JULIE: Have you got something in your eye? Let me see.

JEAN: Oh, it's nothing. Just a speck of dust. It'll be gone in a minute.

JULIE: My sleeve must have rubbed against you. Sit down and let me see to it. [*Takes him by the arm and makes him sit down, bends his head back and tries to get the speck out with the corner of her handkerchief.*] Keep still now, quite still. [*Slaps his hand.*] Do as I tell you. Why, I believe you're trembling, big, strong man though you are! [*Feels his biceps.*] What muscles!

JEAN: [*Warning.*] Miss Julie!

JULIE: Yes, Monsieur Jean?

JEAN: Attention. Je ne suis qu'un homme.

JULIE: Will you stay still! There now. It's out. Kiss my hand and say thank you.

JEAN: [*Rising.*] Miss Julie, listen. Kristin's gone to bed now. Will you listen?

JULIE: Kiss my hand first.

JEAN: Very well, but you'll have only yourself to blame.

JULIE: For what?

JEAN: For what! Are you still a child at twenty-five? Don't you know it's dangerous to play with fire?

JULIE: Not for me. I'm insured.

JEAN: [*Bluntly.*] No, you're not. And even if you are, there's still stuff here to kindle a flame.

JULIE: Meaning yourself?

JEAN: Yes. Not because I'm me, but because I'm a man and young and . . .

JULIE: And good-looking? What incredible conceit! A Don Juan perhaps? Or a Joseph? Good Lord, I do believe you are a Joseph!

JEAN: Do you?

JULIE: I'm rather afraid so.

[JEAN *goes boldly up and tries to put his arms round her and kiss her. She boxes his ears.*]

How dare you!

JEAN: Was that in earnest or a joke?

JULIE: In earnest.

JEAN: Then what went before was in earnest too. You take your games too seriously and that's dangerous. Anyhow I'm tired of playing now and beg leave to return to my work. The Count will want his boots first thing and it's past midnight now.

JULIE: Put those boots down.

JEAN: No. This is my work, which it's my duty to do. But I never undertook to be your playfellow and I never will be. I consider myself too good for that.

JULIE: You're proud.

JEAN: In some ways—not all.

JULIE: Have you even been in love?

JEAN: We don't put it that way, but I've been gone on quite a few girls. And once I went sick because I couldn't have the one I wanted. Sick, I mean, like those princes in the Arabian Nights who couldn't eat or drink for love.

JULIE: Who was she? [*No answer.*] Who was she?

JEAN: You can't force me to tell you that.

JULIE: If I ask as an equal, ask as a— friend? Who was she?

JEAN: You.

JULIE: [*Sitting.*] How absurd!

JEAN: Yes, ludicrous if you like. That's the story I wouldn't tell you before, see, but now I will . . . Do you know what the world looks like from below? No, you don't. No more than the hawks and falcons do whose backs one hardly ever sees because they're always soaring up aloft. I lived in a labourer's hovel with seven other children and a pig, out in the grey fields where there isn't a single tree. But from the window I could see the wall round the Count's park with apple-trees above it. That was the Garden of Eden, guarded by many terrible angels with flaming swords. All the same I and the other boys managed to get to the tree of life. Does all this make you despise me?

JULIE: Goodness, all boys steal apples!

JEAN: You say that now, but all the same you do despise me. However, one time I went into the Garden of Eden with my mother to weed the onion beds. Close to the kitchen garden there was a Turkish pavilion hung all over with jasmine and honeysuckle. I hadn't any idea what it was used for, but I'd never seen such a beautiful building. People used to go in and then come out again, and one day the door was left open. I crept up and saw the walls covered with pictures of kings and emperors, and the windows had red curtains with fringes—you know now what the place was, don't you? I. . . . [*Breaks off a piece of lilac and holds it for* JULIE *to smell. As he talks, she takes it from him.*] I had never been inside the manor, never seen anything but the church, and this was more beautiful. No matter where my thoughts went, they always came back—to that place. The longing went on growing in me to enjoy it fully, just once. Enfin, I sneaked in, gazed and admired. Then I heard someone coming. There was only one way out for the gentry, but for me there was another and I had no choice but to take it. [JULIE *drops the lilac on the table.*] Then I took to my heels, plunged through the raspberry canes, dashed across the strawberry beds and found myself on the rose terrace. There I saw a pink dress and a pair of white stockings—it was you. I crawled into a weed pile and lay there right under it among prickly thistles and damp rank earth. I watched you walking among the roses and said to myself: "If it's true that a thief can get to heaven and be with the angels, it's pretty strange that a labourer's child here on God's earth mayn't come in the park and play with the Count's daughter."

JULIE: [*Sentimentally.*] Do you think all poor children feel the way you did?

JEAN: [*Taken aback, then rallying.*] All poor children? . . . Yes, of course they do. Of course.

JULIE: It must be terrible to be poor.

JEAN: [*With exaggerated distress.*] Oh yes, Miss Julie, yes. A dog may lie on the Countess's sofa, a horse may have his nose stroked by a young lady, but a servant. . . . [*Change of tone.*] well, yes, now and then you meet one with guts enough to rise in the world, but how often? Anyhow, do you know what I did? Jumped in the millstream with my clothes on, was pulled out and got a hiding. But the next Sunday, when Father and all the rest went to Granny's, I managed to get left behind. Then I washed with soap and hot water, put my best clothes on and went to church so as to see you. I did see you and went home determined to die. But I wanted to die beautifully and peacefully, without any pain. Then I remembered it was dangerous to sleep under an elder bush. We had a big one in full bloom, so I stripped it and climbed into the oats-bin with the flowers. Have you ever noticed how smooth oats are? Soft to touch as human skin . . . Well, I closed the lid and shut my eyes, fell asleep, and when they woke me I was very ill. But I didn't die, as you see. What I meant by all that I don't know. There was no hope of winning you—you were simply a symbol of the hopelessness of ever getting out of the class I was born in.

JULIE: You put things very well, you know. Did you go to school?

JEAN: For a while. But I've read a lot of novels and been to the theatre. Besides, I've heard educated folk talking—that's what's taught me most.

JULIE: Do you stand round listening to what we're saying?

JEAN: Yes, of course. And I've heard quite a bit too! On the carriage box or rowing the boat. Once I heard you, Miss Julie, and one of your young lady friends . . .

JULIE: Oh! Whatever did you hear?

JEAN: Well, it wouldn't be nice to repeat it. And I must say I was pretty startled. I couldn't think where you had learnt such words. Perhaps, at bottom, there isn't as much difference between people as one's led to believe.

JULIE: How dare you! We don't behave as you do when we're engaged.

JEAN: [*Looking hard at her.*] Are you sure? It's no use making out so innocent to me.

JULIE: The man I gave my love to was a rotter.

JEAN: That's what you always say—afterwards.

JULIE: Always?

JEAN: I think it must be always. I've heard the expression several times in similar circumstances.

JULIE: What circumstances?

JEAN: Like those in question. The last time . . .

JULIE: [*Rising.*] Stop. I don't want to hear any more.

JEAN: Nor did *she*—curiously enough. May I go to bed now please?

JULIE: [*Gently.*] Go to bed on Midsummer Eve?

JEAN: Yes. Dancing with that crowd doesn't really amuse me.

JULIE: Get the key of the boathouse and row me out on the lake. I want to see the sun rise.

JEAN: Would that be wise?

JULIE: You sound as though you're frightened for your reputation.

JEAN: Why not? I don't want to be made a fool of, nor to be sent packing without a character when I'm trying to better myself. Besides, I have Kristin to consider.

JULIE: So now it's Kristin.

JEAN: Yes, but it's you I'm thinking about too. Take my advice and go to bed.

JULIE: Am I to take orders from you?

JEAN: Just this once, for your own sake. Please. It's very late and sleepiness goes to one's head and makes one rash. Go to bed. What's more, if my ears don't deceive me, I hear people coming this way. They'll be looking for me, and if they find us here, you're done for.

[*The* CHORUS *approaches, singing. During the following dialogue the song is heard in snatches, and in full when the peasants enter.*]

Out of the wood two women came,
Tridiri-ralla, tridiri-ra.
The feet of one were bare and cold,
Tridiri-ralla-la.

The other talked of bags of gold,
Tridiri-ralla, tridiri-ra.
But neither had a sou to her name,
Tridiri-ralla-la.

The bridal wreath I give to you,
Tridiri-ralla, tridiri-ra.
But to another, I'll be true,
Tridiri-ralla-la.

JULIE: I know our people and I love them, just as they do me. Let them come. You'll see.

JEAN: No, Miss Julie, they don't love you. They take your food, then spit at it. You must believe me. Listen to them, just listen to what they're singing . . . No, don't listen.

JULIE: [*Listening.*] What are they singing?

JEAN: They're mocking—you and me.

JULIE: Oh no! How horrible! What cowards!

JEAN: A pack like that's always cowardly. But against such odds there's nothing we can do but run away.

JULIE: Run away? Where to? We can't get out and we can't go in to Kristin's room.

JEAN: Into mine then. Necessity knows no rules. And you can trust me. I really am your true and devoted friend.

JULIE: But supposing . . . supposing they were to look for you in there?

JEAN: I'll bolt the door, and if they try to break in I'll shoot. Come on. [*Pleading.*] Please come.

JULIE: [*Tensely.*] Do you promise . . . ?

JEAN: I swear!

[JULIE *goes quickly into his room and he excitedly follows her.*]
[*Led by the fiddler, the peasants enter in festive attire with flowers in their hats. They put a barrel of beer and a keg of spirits, garlanded with leaves, on the table, fetch glasses and begin to carouse. The scene becomes a ballet. They form a ring and dance and sing and mime: "Out of the wood two women came." Finally they go out, still singing.*]
[JULIE *comes in alone. She looks at the havoc in the kitchen, wrings her hands, then takes out her powder puff and powders her face.*]
[JEAN *enters in high spirits.*]

JEAN: Now you see! And you heard, didn't you? Do you still think it's possible for us to stay here?

JULIE: No, I don't. But what can we do?

JEAN: Run away. Far away. Take a journey.

JULIE: Journey? But where to?

JEAN: Switzerland. The Italian lakes. Ever been there?

JULIE: No. Is it nice?

JEAN: Ah! Eternal summer, oranges, evergreens . . . ah!

JULIE: But what would we do there?

JEAN: I'll start a hotel. First-class accommodation and first-class customers.

JULIE: Hotel?

JEAN: There's life for you. New faces all the time, new languages—no time for nerves or worries, no need to look for something to do—work rolling up of its own accord. Bells ringing night and day, trains whistling, buses coming and going, and all the time gold pieces rolling on to the counter. There's life for you!

JULIE: For you. And I?

JEAN: Mistress of the house, ornament of the firm. With your looks, and your style . . . oh, it's bound to be a success! Terrific! You'll sit like a queen in the office and set your slaves in motion by pressing an electric button. The guests will file past your throne and nervously lay their treasure on your table. You've no idea the way people tremble when they get their bills. I'll salt the bills and you'll sugar them with your sweetest smiles. Ah, let's get away from here! [Produces a time-table.] At once, by the next train. We shall be at Malmö at six-thirty, Hamburg eight-forty next morning, Frankfurt-Basle the following day, and Como by the St. Gothard pass in —let's see—three days. Three days!

JULIE: That's all very well. But Jean, you must give me courage. Tell me you love me. Come and take me in your arms.

JEAN: [Reluctantly.] I'd like to, but I daren't. Not again in this house. I love you—that goes without saying. You can't doubt that, Miss Julie, can you?

JULIE: [Shyly, very feminine.] Miss? Call me Julie. There aren't any barriers between us now. Call me Julie.

JEAN: [Uneasily.] I can't. As long as we're in this house, there are barriers between us. There's the past and there's the Count. I've never been so servile to anyone as I am to him. I've only got to see his gloves on a chair to feel small. I've only to hear his bell and I shy like a horse. Even now, when I look at his boots, standing there so proud and stiff, I feel my back beginning to bend. [Kicks the boots.] It's those old, narrow-minded notions drummed into us as children . . . but they can soon be forgotten. You've only got to get to another country, a republic, and people will bend themselves double before my porter's livery. Yes, double they'll bend themselves, but I shan't. I wasn't born to bend. I've got guts, I've got character, and once I reach that first branch, you'll watch me climb. Today I'm valet, next year I'll be proprietor, in ten years I'll have made a fortune, and then I'll go to Roumania, get myself decorated and I may, I only say may, mind you, end up as a Count.

JULIE: [Sadly.] That would be very nice.

JEAN: You see in Roumania one can buy a title, and then you'll be a Countess after all. My Countess.

JULIE: What do I care about all that? I'm putting those things behind me. Tell me you love me, because if you don't . . . if you don't, what am I?

JEAN: I'll tell you a thousand times over—later. But not here. No sentimentality now or everything will be lost. We must consider this thing calmly like reasonable people. [Takes a cigar, cuts and lights it.] You sit down there and I'll sit here and we'll talk as if nothing has happened.

JULIE: My God, have you no feelings at all?

JEAN: Nobody has more. But I know how to control them.

JULIE: A short time ago you were kissing my shoe. And now . . .

JEAN: [Harshly.] Yes, that was then. Now we have something else to think about.

JULIE: Don't speak to me so brutally.

JEAN: I'm not. Just sensibly. One folly's been committed, don't let's have more. The Count will be back at any moment and we've got to settle our future before that. Now, what do you think of my plans? Do you approve?

JULIE: It seems a very good idea—but just one thing. Such a big undertaking would need a lot of capital. Have you got any?

JEAN: [Chewing his cigar.] I certainly have. I've got my professional skill, my wide experience and my knowledge of foreign languages. That's capital worth having, it seems to me.

JULIE: But it won't buy even one railway ticket.

JEAN: Quite true. That's why I need a backer to advance some ready cash.

JULIE: How could you get that at a moment's notice?

JEAN: You must get it, if you want to be my partner.

JULIE: I can't. I haven't any money of my own. [*Pause.*]

JEAN: Then the whole thing's off.

JULIE: And . . . ?

JEAN: We go on as we are.

JULIE: Do you think I'm going to stay under this roof as your mistress? With everyone pointing at me. Do you think I can face my father after this? No. Take me away from here, away from this shame, this humiliation. Oh my God, what have I done? My God, my God! [*Weeps.*]

JEAN: So that's the tune now, is it? What have you done? Same as many before you.

JULIE: [*Hysterically.*] And now you despise me. I'm falling, I'm falling.

JEAN: Fall as far as me and I'll lift you up again.

JULIE: Why was I so terribly attracted to you? The weak to the strong, the falling to the rising? Or was it love? Is that love? Do you know what love is?

JEAN: Do I? You bet I do. Do you think I never had a girl before?

JULIE: The things you say, the things you think!

JEAN: That's what life's taught me, and that's what I am. It's no good getting hysterical or giving yourself airs. We're both in the same boat now. Here, my dear girl, let me give you a glass of something special. [*Opens the drawer, takes out the bottle of wine and fills two used glasses.*]

JULIE: Where did you get that wine?

JEAN: From the cellar.

JULIE: My father's burgundy.

JEAN: Why not, for his son-in-law?

JULIE: And I drink beer.

JEAN: That only shows your taste's not so good as mine.

JULIE: Thief!

JEAN: Are you going to tell on me?

JULIE: Oh God! The accomplice of a petty thief! Was I blind drunk? Have I dreamt this whole night? Midsummer Eve, the night for innocent merrymaking.

JEAN: Innocent, eh?

JULIE: Is anyone on earth as wretched as I am now?

JEAN: Why should *you* be? After such a conquest. What about Kristin in there? Don't you think she has any feelings?

JULIE: I did think so, but I don't any longer. No. A menial is a menial . . .

JEAN: And a whore is a whore.

JULIE: [*Falling to her knees, her hands clasped.*] O God in heaven, put an end to my miserable life! Lift me out of this filth in which I'm sinking. Save me! Save me!

JEAN: I must admit I'm sorry for you. When I was in the onion bed and saw you up there among the roses, I . . . yes, I'll tell you now . . . I had the same dirty thoughts as all the boys.

JULIE: You, who wanted to die because of me?

JEAN: In the oats-bin? That was just talk.

JULIE: Lies, you mean.

JEAN: [*Getting sleepy.*] More or less. I think I read a story in some paper about a chimney-sweep who shut himself up in a chest full of lilac because he'd been summonsed for not supporting some brat . . .

JULIE: So this is what you're like.

JEAN: I had to think up something. It's always the fancy stuff that catches the women.

JULIE: Beast!

JEAN: Merde!

JULIE: Now you have seen the falcon's back.

JEAN: Not exactly it's *back*.

JULIE: I was to be the first branch.

JEAN: But the branch was rotten.

JULIE: I was to be a hotel sign.

JEAN: And I the hotel.

JULIE: Sit at your counter, attract your clients and cook their accounts.

JEAN: I'd have done that myself.

JULIE: That any human being can be so steeped in filth!

JEAN: Clean it up then.

JULIE: Menial! Lackey! Stand up when I speak to you.

JEAN: Menial's whore, lackey's harlot, shut your mouth and get out of here! Are you the one to lecture me for being coarse? Nobody of my kind would ever be as coarse as you were tonight. Do you think any servant girl would throw herself at a man that way? Have you ever seen a girl of my class asking for it like that? I haven't. Only animals and prostitutes.

JULIE: [*Broken.*] Go on. Hit me, trample on me—it's all I deserve. I'm rotten.

But help me! If there's any way out at all, help me.

JEAN: [*More gently.*] I'm not denying myself a share in the honour of seducing you, but do you think anybody in my place would have dared look in your direction if you yourself hadn't asked for it? I'm still amazed . . .

JULIE: And proud.

JEAN: Why not? Though I must admit the victory was too easy to make me lose my head.

JULIE: Go on hitting me.

JEAN: [*Rising.*] No. On the contrary I apologise for what I've said. I don't hit a person who's down—least of all a woman. I can't deny there's a certain satisfaction in finding that what dazzled one below was just moonshine, that the falcon's back is grey after all, that there's powder on the lovely cheek, that polished nails can have black tips, that the handkerchief is dirty although it smells of scent. On the other hand it hurts to find that what I was struggling to reach wasn't high and isn't real. It hurts to see you fallen so low you're far lower than your own cook. Hurts like when you see the last flowers of summer lashed to pieces by rain and turned to mud.

JULIE: You're talking as if you're already my superior.

JEAN: I am. I might make you a Countess, but you could never make me a Count, you know.

JULIE: But I am the child of a Count, and you could never be that.

JEAN: True, but I might be the father of Counts if. . . .

JULIE: You're a thief. I'm not.

JEAN: There are worse things than being a thief—much lower. Besides, when I'm in a place I regard myself as a member of the family to some extent, as one of the children. You don't call it stealing when children pinch a berry from overladen bushes. [*His passion is roused again.*] Miss Julie, you're a glorious woman, far too good for a man like me. You were carried away by some kind of madness, and now you're trying to cover up your mistake by persuading yourself you're in love with me. You're not, although you may find me physically attractive, which means your love's no better than mine. But I wouldn't be satisfied with being nothing but an animal

for you, and I could never make you love me.

JULIE: Are you sure?

JEAN: You think there's a chance? Of my loving you, yes, of course. You're beautiful, refined [*Takes her hand.*] educated, and you can be nice when you want to be. The fire you kindle in a man isn't likely to go out. [*Puts his arm round her.*] You're like mulled wine, full of spices, and your kisses. . . . [*He tries to pull her to him, but she breaks away.*]

JULIE: Let go of me! You won't win me that way.

JEAN: Not that way, how then? Not by kisses and fine speeches, not by planning the future and saving you from shame? How then?

JULIE: How? How? I don't know. There isn't any way. I loathe you—loathe you as I loathe rats, but I can't escape from you.

JEAN: Escape with me.

JULIE: [*Pulling herself together.*] Escape? Yes, we must escape. But I'm so tired. Give me a glass of wine. [*He pours it out. She looks at her watch.*] First we must talk. We still have a little time. [*Empties the glass and holds it out for more.*]

JEAN: Don't drink like that. You'll get tipsy.

JULIE: What's that matter?

JEAN: What's it matter? It's vulgar to get drunk. Well, what have you got to say?

JULIE: We've got to run away, but we must talk first—or rather, I must, for so far you've done all the talking. You've told me about your life, now I want to tell you about mine, so that we really know each other before we begin this journey together.

JEAN: Wait. Excuse my saying so, but don't you think you may be sorry afterwards if you give away your secrets to me?

JULIE: Aren't you my friend?

JEAN: On the whole. But don't rely on me.

JULIE: You can't mean that. But anyway everyone knows my secrets. Listen. My mother wasn't well-born; she came of quite humble people, and was brought up with all those new ideas of sex-equality and women's rights and so on. She thought marriage was quite wrong. So when my

father proposed to her, she said she would
never become his *wife* . . . but in the
end she did. I came into the world, as far
as I can make out, against my mother's will,
and I was left to run wild, but I had to
do all the things a boy does—to prove
women are as good as men. I had to wear
boys' clothes; I was taught to handle
horses—and I wasn't allowed in the dairy.
She made me groom and harness and go
out hunting; I even had to try to plough.
All the men on the estate were given the
women's jobs, and the women the men's,
until the whole place went to rack and
ruin and we were the laughing-stock of
the neighbourhood. At last my father seems
to have come to his senses and rebelled.
He changed everything and ran the place
his own way. My mother got ill—I don't
know what was the matter with her, but she
used to have strange attacks and hide herself in the attic or the garden. Sometimes
she stayed out all night. Then came the
great fire which you have heard people
talking about. The house and the stables
and the barns—the whole place burnt to
the ground. In very suspicious circumstances. Because the accident happened the
very day the insurance had to be renewed,
and my father had sent the new premium,
but through some carelessness the messenger it arrived too late. [*Refills her glass
and drinks.*]

JEAN: Don't drink any more.

JULIE: Oh, what does it matter? We
were destitute and had to sleep in the
carriages. My father didn't know how to
get money to rebuild, and then my mother
suggested he should borrow from an old
friend of hers, a local brick manufacturer.
My father got the loan and, to his surprise,
without having to pay interest. So the place
was rebuilt. [*Drinks.*] Do you know who
set fire to it?

JEAN: Your lady mother.

JULIE: Do you know who the brick
manufacturer was?

JEAN: Your mother's lover?

JULIE: Do you know whose the money
was?

JEAN: Wait . . . no, I don't know
that.

JULIE: It was my mother's.

JEAN: In other words the Count's, unless
there was a settlement.

JULIE: There wasn't any settlement. My
mother had a little money of her own which

she didn't want my father to control, so
she invested it with her—friend.

JEAN: Who grabbed it.

JULIE: Exactly. He appropriated it. My
father came to know all this. He couldn't
bring an action, couldn't pay his wife's
lover, nor prove it was his wife's money.
That was my mother's revenge because he
made himself master in his own house. He
nearly shot himself then—at least there's
a rumour he tried and didn't bring it off.
So he went on living, and my mother had
to pay dearly for what she'd done. Imagine
what those five years were like for me.
My natural sympathies were with my
father, yet I took my mother's side, because
I didn't know the facts. I'd learnt from her
to hate and distrust men—you know how
she loathed the whole male sex. And I
swore to her I'd never become the slave of
any man.

JEAN: And so you got engaged to that
attorney.

JULIE: So that he should be my slave.

JEAN: But he wouldn't be.

JULIE: Oh yes, he wanted to be, but he
didn't have the chance. I got bored with
him.

JEAN: Is that what I saw—in the stable-
yard?

JULIE: What did you see?

JEAN: What I saw was him breaking
off the engagement.

JULIE: That's a lie. It was I who broke
it off. Did he say it was him? The cad.

JEAN: He's not a cad. Do you hate men,
Miss Julie?

JULIE: Yes . . . most of the time. But
when that weakness comes, oh . . . the
shame!

JEAN: Then do you hate me?

JULIE: Beyond words. I'd gladly have
you killed like an animal.

JEAN: Quick as you'd shoot a mad dog,
eh?

JULIE: Yes.

JEAN: But there's nothing here to shoot
with—and there isn't a dog. So what do
we do now?

JULIE: Go abroad.

JEAN: To make each other miserable
for the rest of our lives?

JULIE: No, to enjoy ourselves for a day
or two, for a week, for as long as enjoyment lasts, and then—to die . . .

JEAN: Die? How silly! I think it would
be far better to start a hotel.

JULIE: [*Without listening.*] . . . die on the shores of Lake Como, where the sun always shines and at Christmas time there are green trees and glowing oranges.

JEAN: Lake Como's a rainy hole and I didn't see any oranges outside the shops. But it's a good place for tourists. Plenty of villas to be rented by—er—honeymoon couples. Profitable business that. Know why? Because they all sign a lease for six months and all leave after three weeks.

JULIE: [*Naïvely.*] After three weeks? Why?

JEAN: They quarrel, of course. But the rent has to be paid just the same. And then it's let again. So it goes on and on, for there's plenty of love although it doesn't last long.

JULIE: You don't want to die with me?

JEAN: I don't want to die at all. For one thing I like living and for another I consider suicide's a sin against the Creator who gave us life.

JULIE: You believe in God—*you*?

JEAN: Yes, of course. And I go to church every Sunday. Look here, I'm tired of all this. I'm going to bed.

JULIE: Indeed! And do you think I'm going to leave things like this? Don't you know what you owe the woman you've ruined?

JEAN: [*Taking out his purse and throwing a silver coin on the table.*] There you are. I don't want to be in anybody's debt.

JULIE: [*Pretending not to notice the insult.*] Don't you know what the law is?

JEAN: There's no law unfortunately that punishes a woman for seducing a man.

JULIE: But can you see anything for it but to go abroad, get married and then divorce?

JEAN: What if I refuse this mésalliance?

JULIE: Mésalliance?

JEAN: Yes, for me. I'm better bred than you, see! Nobody in my family committed arson.

JULIE: How do you know?

JEAN: Well, you can't prove otherwise, because we haven't any family records outside the Registrar's office. But I've seen your family tree in that book on the drawing-room table. Do you know who the founder of your family was? A miller who let his wife sleep with the King one night during the Danish war. I haven't any ancestors like that. I haven't any ancestors at all, but I might become one.

JULIE: This is what I get for confiding in someone so low, for sacrificing my family honour . . .

JEAN: Dishonour! Well, I told you so. One shouldn't drink, because then one talks. And one shouldn't talk.

JULIE: Oh, how ashamed I am, how bitterly ashamed! If at least you loved me!

JEAN: Look here—for the last time—what do you want? Am I to burst into tears? Am I to jump over your riding whip? Shall I kiss you and carry you off to Lake Como for three weeks, after which . . . What am I to do? What do you want? This is getting unbearable, but that's what comes of playing around with women. Miss Julie, I can see how miserable you are; I know you're going through hell, but I don't understand you. We don't have scenes like this; we don't go in for hating each other. We make love for fun in our spare time, but we haven't all day and all night for it like you. I think you must be ill. I'm sure you're ill.

JULIE: Then you must be kind to me. You sound almost human now.

JEAN: Well, be human yourself. You spit at me, then won't let me wipe it off—on you.

JULIE: Help me, help me! Tell me what to do, where to go.

JEAN: Jesus, as if I knew!

JULIE: I've been mad, raving mad, but there must be a way out.

JEAN: Stay here and keep quiet. Nobody knows anything.

JULIE: I can't. People do know. Kristin knows.

JEAN: They don't know and they wouldn't believe such a thing.

JULIE: [*Hesitating.*] But—it might happen again.

JEAN: That's true.

JULIE: And there might be—consequences.

JEAN: [*In panic.*] Consequences! Fool that I am I never thought of that. Yes, there's nothing for it but to go. At once. I can't come with you. That would be a complete giveaway. You must go alone—abroad—anywhere.

JULIE: Alone? Where to? I can't.

JEAN: You must. And before the Count gets back. If you stay, we know what will happen. Once you've sinned you feel you might as well go on, as the harm's done. Then you get more and more reckless and in the end you're found out. No. You must go abroad. Then write to the Count and tell him everything, except that it was me. He'll never guess that—and I don't think he'll want to.

JULIE: I'll go if you come with me.

JEAN: Are you crazy, woman? "Miss Julie elopes with valet." Next day it would be in the headlines, and the Count would never live it down.

JULIE: I can't go. I can't stay. I'm so tired, so completely worn out. Give me orders. Set me going. I can't think any more, can't act . . .

JEAN: You see what weaklings you are. Why do you give yourselves airs and turn up your noses as if you're the lords of creation? Very well, I'll give you your orders. Go upstairs and dress. Get money for the journey and come down here again.

JULIE: [Softly.] Come up with me.

JEAN: To your room? Now you've gone crazy again. [Hesitates a moment.] No! Go along at once. [Takes her hand and pulls her to the door.]

JULIE: [As she goes.] Speak kindly to me, Jean.

JEAN: Orders always sound unkind. Now you know. Now you know.

[Left alone, JEAN sighs with relief, sits down at the table, takes out a note-book and pencil and adds up figures, now and then aloud. Dawn begins to break. KRISTIN enters dressed for church, carrying his white dickey and tie.]

KRISTIN: Lord Jesus, look at the state the place is in! What have you been up to? [Turns out the lamp.]

JEAN: Oh, Miss Julie invited the crowd in. Did you sleep through it? Didn't you hear anything?

KRISTIN: I slept like a log.

JEAN: And dressed for church already.

KRISTIN: Yes, you promised to come to Communion with me today.

JEAN: Why, so I did. And you've got my bib and tucker, I see. Come on then. [Sits. KRISTIN begins to put his things on. Pause. Sleepily.] What's the lesson today?

KRISTIN: It's about the beheading of John the Baptist, I think.

JEAN: That's sure to be horribly long. Hi, you're choking me! Oh Lord, I'm so sleepy, so sleepy!

KRISTIN: Yes, what have you been doing up all night? You look absolutely green.

JEAN: Just sitting here talking with Miss Julie.

KRISTIN: She doesn't know what's proper, that one. [Pause.]

JEAN: I say, Kristin.

KRISTIN: What?

JEAN: It's queer really, isn't it, when you come to think of it? Her.

KRISTIN: What's queer?

JEAN: The whole thing. [Pause.]

KRISTIN: [Looking at the half-filled glasses on the table.] Have you been drinking together too?

JEAN: Yes.

KRISTIN: More shame you. Look me straight in the face.

JEAN: Yes.

KRISTIN: Is it possible? Is it possible?

JEAN: [After a moment.] Yes, it is.

KRISTIN: Oh! This I would never have believed. How low!

JEAN: You're not jealous of her, surely?

KRISTIN: No, I'm not. If it had been Clara or Sophie I'd have scratched your eyes out. But not of her. I don't know why; that's how it is though. But it's disgusting.

JEAN: You're angry with her then.

KRISTIN: No. With you. It was wicked of you, very very wicked. Poor girl. And, mark my words, I won't stay here any longer now—in a place where one can't respect one's employers.

JEAN: Why should one respect them?

KRISTIN: You should know since you're so smart. But you don't want to stay in the service of people who aren't respectable, do you? I wouldn't demean myself.

JEAN: But it's rather a comfort to find out they're no better than us.

KRISTIN: I don't think so. If they're no better there's nothing for us to live up to. Oh and think of the Count! Think of him. He's been through so much already. No, I won't stay in the place any longer. A fellow like you too! If it had been that attorney now or somebody of her own class . . .

JEAN: Why, what's wrong with . . .

KRISTIN: Oh, you're all right in your own way, but when all's said and done there is a difference between one class and another. No, this is something I'll never be able to stomach. That our young lady who was so proud and so down on men you'd never believe she'd let one come near her should go and give herself to one like you. She who wanted to have poor Diana shot for running after the lodge-keeper's pug. No, I must say . . . ! Well, I won't stay here any longer. On the twenty-fourth of October I quit.

JEAN: And then?

KRISTIN: Well, since you mention it, it's about time you began to look around, if we're ever going to get married?

JEAN: But what am I to look for? I shan't get a place like this when I'm married.

KRISTIN: I know you won't. But you might get a job as porter or caretaker in some public institution. Government rations are small but sure, and there's a pension for the widow and children.

JEAN: That's all very fine, but it's not in my line to start thinking at once about dying for my wife and children. I must say I had rather bigger ideas.

KRISTIN: You and your ideas! You've got obligations too, and you'd better start thinking about them.

JEAN: Don't *you* start pestering me about obligations. I've had enough of that. [*Listens to a sound upstairs.*] Anyway we've plenty of time to work things out. Go and get ready now and we'll be off to church.

KRISTIN: Who's that walking about upstairs?

JEAN: Don't know—unless it's Clara.

KRISTIN: [*Going.*] You don't think the Count could have come back without our hearing him?

JEAN: [*Scared.*] The Count? No, he can't have. He'd have rung for me.

KRISTIN: God help us! I've never known such goings on. [*Exits.*]

[*The sun has now risen and is shining on the treetops. The light gradually changes until it slants in through the windows.* JEAN *goes to the door and beckons.* JULIE *enters in travelling clothes, carrying a small bird-cage covered with a cloth which she puts on a chair.*]

JULIE: I'm ready.

JEAN: Hush! Kristin's up.

JULIE: [*In a very nervous state.*] Does she suspect anything?

JEAN: Not a thing. But, my God, what a sight you are!

JULIE: Sight? What do you mean?

JEAN: You're white as a corpse and—pardon me—your face is dirty.

JULIE: Let me wash then. [*Goes to the sink and washes her face and hands.*] There. Give me a towel. Oh! The sun is rising!

JEAN: And that breaks the spell.

JULIE: Yes. The spell of Midsummer Eve . . . But listen, Jean. Come with me. I've got the money.

JEAN: [*Sceptically.*] Enough?

JULIE: Enough to start with. Come with me. I can't travel alone today. It's Midsummer Day, remember. I'd be packed into a suffocating train among crowds of people who'd all stare at me. And it would stop at every station while I yearned for wings. No, I can't do that, I simply can't. There will be memories too; memories of Midsummer Days when I was little. The leafy church—birch and lilac—the gaily spread dinner table, relatives, friends—evening in the park—dancing and music and flowers and fun. Oh, however far you run away—there'll always be memories in the baggage car—and remorse and guilt.

JEAN: I will come with you, but quickly now then, before it's too late. At once.

JULIE: Put on your things. [*Picks up the cage.*]

JEAN: No luggage, mind. That would give us away.

JULIE: No, only what we can take with us in the carriage.

JEAN: [*Fetching his hat.*] What on earth have you got there? What is it?

JULIE: Only my greenfinch. I don't want to leave it behind.

JEAN: Well, I'll be damned! We're to take a bird-cage along, are we? You're crazy. Put that cage down.

JULIE: It's the only thing I'm taking from my home. The only living creature who cares for me since Diana went off like that. Don't be cruel. Let me take it.

JEAN: Put that cage down, I tell you—and don't talk so loud. Kristin will hear.

JULIE: No, I won't leave it in strange hands. I'd rather you killed it.

JEAN: Give the little beast here then and I'll wring its neck.

JULIE: But don't hurt it, don't . . . no, I can't.

JEAN: Give it here. I *can.*

JULIE: [*Taking the bird out of the cage and kissing it.*] Dear little Serena, must you die and leave your mistress?

JEAN: Please don't make a scene. It's *your* life and future we're worrying about. Come on, quick now!

[*He snatches the bird from her, puts it on a board and picks up a chopper.* JULIE *turns away.*]

You should have learnt how to kill chickens instead of target-shooting. Then you wouldn't faint at a drop of blood.

JULIE: [Screaming.] Kill me too! Kill me! You who can butcher an innocent creature without a quiver. Oh, how I hate you, how I loathe you! There is blood between us now. I curse the hour I first saw you. I curse the hour I was conceived in my mother's womb.

JEAN: What's the use of cursing. Let's go.

JULIE: [Going to the chopping-block as if drawn against her will.] No, I won't go yet. I can't . . . I must look. Listen! There's a carriage. [Listens without taking her eyes off the board and chopper.] You don't think I can bear the sight of blood. You think I'm so weak. Oh, how I should like to see your blood and your brains on a chopping-block! I'd like to see the whole of your sex swimming like that in a sea of blood. I think I could drink out of your skull, bathe my feet in your broken breast and eat your heart roasted whole. You think I'm weak. You think I love you, that my womb yearned for your seed and I want to carry your offspring under my heart and nourish it with my blood. You think I want to bear your child and take your name. By the way, what is your name? I've never heard your surname. I don't suppose you've got one. I should be "Mrs. Hovel" or "Madam Dunghill." You dog wearing my collar, you lackey with my crest on your buttons! I share you with my cook; I'm my own servant's rival! Oh! Oh! Oh! . . . You think I'm a coward and will run away. No, now I'm going to stay—and let the storm break. My father will come back . . . find his desk broken open . . . his money gone. Then he'll ring that bell— twice for the valet—and then he'll send for the police . . . and I shall tell everything. Everything. Oh how wonderful to make an end of it all—a real end! He has a stroke and dies and that's the end of all of us. Just peace and quietness . . . eternal rest. The coat of arms broken on the coffin and the Count's line extinct . . . But the valet's line goes on in an orphanage, wins laurels in the gutter and ends in jail.

JEAN: There speaks the noble blood! Bravo, Miss Julie. But now, don't let the cat out of the bag.

[KRISTIN enters dressed for church, carrying a prayer-book. JULIE rushes to her and flings herself into her arms for protection.]

JULIE: Help me, Kristin! Protect me from this man!

KRISTIN: [Unmoved and cold.] What goings-on for a feast day morning! [Sees the board.] And what a filthy mess. What's it all about? Why are you screaming and carrying on so?

JULIE: Kristin, you're a woman and my friend. Beware of that scoundrel!

JEAN: [Embarrassed.] While you ladies are talking things over, I'll go and shave. [Slips into his room.]

JULIE: You must understand. You must listen to me.

KRISTIN: I certainly don't understand such loose ways. Where are you off to in those travelling clothes? And he had his hat on, didn't he, eh?

JULIE: Listen, Kristin. Listen, I'll tell you everything.

KRISTIN: I don't want to know anything.

JULIE: You must listen.

KRISTIN: What to? Your nonsense with Jean? I don't care a rap about that; it's nothing to do with me. But if you're thinking of getting him to run off with you, we'll soon put a stop to that.

JULIE: [Very nervously.] Please try to be calm, Kristin, and listen. I can't stay here, nor can Jean—so we must go abroad.

KRISTIN: Hm, hm!

JULIE: [Brightening.] But you see, I've had an idea. Supposing we all three go— abroad—to Switzerland and start a hotel together . . . I've got some money, you see . . . and Jean and I could run the whole thing—and I thought you would take charge of the kitchen. Wouldn't that be splendid? Say yes, do. If you come with us everything will be fine. Oh do say yes! [Puts her arms round KRISTIN.]

KRISTIN: [Coolly thinking.] Hm, hm!

JULIE: [Presto tempo.] You've never travelled, Kristin. You should go abroad and see the world. You've no idea how nice it is travelling by train—new faces all the time and new countries. On our way through Hamburg we'll go to the zoo— you'll love that—and we'll go to the theatre and the opera too . . . and when we get to Munich there'll be the museums, dear, and pictures by Rubens and Raphael—the great painters, you know . . . You've heard of Munich, haven't you? Where King Ludwig lived—you know, the king who went mad. . . . We'll see his castles—some of his castles are still just like in fairy-tales . . . and from there it's not far to Switzerland—and the Alps. Think of the Alps, Kristin dear, covered with snow in the middle of summer . . . and there are oranges there and trees that are green the whole year round . . .

[JEAN *is seen in the door of his room, sharpening his razor on a strop which he holds with his teeth and his left hand. He listens to the talk with satisfaction and now and then nods approval.* JULIE *continues, tempo prestissimo.*]

And then we'll get a hotel . . . and I'll sit at the desk, while Jean receives the guests and goes out marketing and writes letters . . . There's life for you! Trains whistling, buses driving up, bells ringing upstairs and downstairs . . . and I shall make out the bills—and I shall cook them too . . . you've no idea how nervous travellers are when it comes to paying their bills. And you—you'll sit like a queen in the kitchen . . . of course there won't be any standing at the stove for you. You'll always have to be nicely dressed and ready to be seen, and with your looks—no, I'm not flattering you—one fine day you'll catch yourself a husband . . . some rich Englishman, I shouldn't wonder—they're the ones who are easy [*Slowing down.*] to catch . . . and then we'll get rich and build ourselves a villa on Lake Como . . . of course it rains there a little now and then—but—[*Dully.*]—the sun must shine there too sometimes—even though it seems gloomy—and if not—then we can come home again—come back [*Pause.*] here—or somewhere else . . .

KRISTIN: Look here, Miss Julie, do you believe all that yourself?

JULIE: [*Exhausted.*] Do I believe it?

KRISTIN: Yes.

JULIE: [*Wearily.*] I don't know. I don't believe anything any more. [*Sinks down on the bench; her head in her arms on the table.*] Nothing. Nothing at all.

KRISTIN: [*Turning to* JEAN.] So you meant to beat it, did you?

JEAN: [*Disconcerted, putting the razor on the table.*] Beat it? What are you talking about? You've heard Miss Julie's plan, and

though she's tired now with being up all night, it's a perfectly sound plan.

KRISTIN: Oh, is it? If you thought I'd work for that . . .

JEAN: [*Interrupting.*] Kindly use decent language in front of your mistress. Do you hear?

KRISTIN: Mistress?

JEAN: Yes.

KRISTIN: Well, well, just listen to that!

JEAN: Yes, it would be a good thing if you did listen and talked less. Miss Julie is your mistress and what's made you lose your respect for her now ought to make you feel the same about yourself.

KRISTIN: I've always had enough self-respect—

JEAN: To despise other people.

KRISTIN: —not to go below my own station. Has the Count's cook ever gone with the groom or the swineherd? Tell me that.

JEAN: No, you were lucky enough to have a high-class chap for your beau.

KRISTIN: High-class all right—selling the oats out of the Count's stable.

JEAN: You're a fine one to talk—taking a commission on the groceries and bribes from the butcher.

KRISTIN: What the devil . . . ?

JEAN: And now you can't feel any respect for your employers. You, you!

KRISTIN: Are you coming to church with me? I should think you need a good sermon after your fine deeds.

JEAN: No, I'm not going to church today. You can go alone and confess your own sins.

KRISTIN: Yes, I'll do that and bring back enough forgiveness to cover yours too. The Saviour suffered and died on the cross for all our sins, and if we go to Him with faith and a penitent heart, He takes all our sins upon Himself.

JEAN: Even grocery thefts?

JULIE: Do you believe that, Kristin?

KRISTIN: That is my living faith, as sure as I stand here. The faith I learnt as a child and have kept ever since, Miss Julie. "But where sin abounded, grace did much more abound."

JULIE: Oh, if I had your faith! Oh, if . . .

KRISTIN: But you see you can't have it without God's special grace, and it's not given to all to have that.

JULIE: Who is it given to then?

KRISTIN: That's the great secret of the workings of grace, Miss Julie. God is no respecter of persons, and with Him the last shall be first . . .

JULIE: Then I suppose He does respect the last.

KRISTIN: [*Continuing.*] . . . and it is easier for a camel to go through the eye of a needle than for a rich man to enter into the kingdom of God. That's how it is, Miss Julie. Now I'm going—alone, and on my way I shall tell the groom not to let any of the horses out, in case anyone should want to leave before the Count gets back. Goodbye. [*Exit.*]

JEAN: What a devil! And all on account of a greenfinch.

JULIE: [*Wearily.*] Never mind the greenfinch. Do you see any way out of this, any end to it?

JEAN: [*Pondering.*] No.

JULIE: If you were in my place, what would you do?

JEAN: In your place? Wait a bit. If I was a woman—a lady of rank who had—fallen. I don't know. Yes, I do know now.

JULIE: [*Picking up the razor and making a gesture.*] This?

JEAN: Yes. But I wouldn't do it, you know. There's a difference between us.

JULIE: Because you're a man and I'm a woman? What is the difference?

JEAN: The usual difference—between man and woman.

JULIE: [*Holding the razor.*] I'd like to. But I can't. My father couldn't either, that time he wanted to.

JEAN: No, he didn't want to. He had to be revenged first.

JULIE: And now my mother is revenged again, through me.

JEAN: Didn't you ever love your father, Miss Julie?

JULIE: Deeply, but I must have hated him too—unconsciously. And he let me be brought up to despise my own sex, to be half woman, half man. Whose fault is what's happened? My father's, my mother's or my own? My own? I haven't anything that's my own. I haven't one single thought that I didn't get from my father, one emotion that didn't come from my mother, and as for this last idea—about all people being equal—I got that from him, my fiancé—that's why I call him a cad. How can it be my fault? Push the responsibility on to Jesus, like Kristin does? No, I'm too proud

and—thanks to my father's teaching—too intelligent. As for all that about a rich person not being able to get into heaven, it's just a lie, but Kristin, who has money in the savings-bank, will certainly not get in. Whose fault is it? What does it matter whose fault it is? In any case I must take the blame and bear the consequences.

JEAN: Yes, but . . . [*There are two sharp rings on the bell.* JULIE *jumps to her feet.* JEAN *changes into his livery.*] The Count is back. Supposing Kristin . . . [*Goes to the speaking-tube, presses it and listens.*]

JULIE: Has he been to his desk yet?

JEAN: This is Jean, sir. [*Listens.*] Yes, sir. [*Listens.*] Yes, sir, very good, sir. [*Listens.*] At once, sir? [*Listens.*] Very good, sir. In half an hour.

JULIE: [*In panic.*] What did he say? My God, what did he say?

JEAN: He ordered his boots and his coffee in half an hour.

JULIE: Then there's half an hour . . . Oh, I'm so tired! I can't do anything. Can't be sorry, can't run away, can't stay, can't live—can't die. Help me. Order me, and I'll obey like a dog. Do me this last service —save my honour, save his name. You know what I ought to do, but haven't the strength to do. Use your strength and order me to do it.

JEAN: I don't know why—I can't now— I don't understand . . . It's just as if this coat made me—I can't give you orders— and now that the Count has spoken to me —I can't quite explain, but . . . well, that devil of a lackey is bending my back again. I believe if the Count came down now and ordered me to cut my throat, I'd do it on the spot.

JULIE: Then pretend you're him and I'm you. You did some fine acting before, when you knelt to me and played the aristocrat. Or . . . Have you ever seen a hypnotist at the theatre? [*He nods.*] He says to the person "Take the broom," and he takes it. He says "Sweep," and he sweeps . . .

JEAN: But the person has to be asleep.

JULIE: [*As if in a trance.*] I am asleep already . . . the whole room has turned to smoke—and you look like a stove—a stove like a man in black with a tall hat— your eyes are glowing like coals when the fire is low—and your face is a white patch like ashes. [*The sunlight has now reached the floor and lights up* JEAN.] How nice and warm it is! [*She holds out her hands as though warming them at a fire.*] And so light—and so peaceful.

JEAN: [*Putting the razor in her hand.*] Here is the broom. Go now while it's light —out to the barn—and. . . . [*Whispers in her ear.*]

JULIE: [*Waking.*] Thank you. I am going now—to rest. But just tell me that even the first can receive the gift of grace.

JEAN: The first? No, I can't tell you that. But wait . . . Miss Julie, I've got it! You aren't one of the first any longer. You're one of the last.

JULIE: That's true. I'm one of the very last. I *am* the last. Oh! . . . But now I can't go. Tell me again to go.

JEAN: No, I can't now either. I can't.

JULIE: And the first shall be last.

JEAN: Don't think, don't think. You're taking my strength away too and making me a coward. What's that? I thought I saw the bell move . . . To be so frightened of a bell! Yes, but it's not just a bell. There's somebody behind it—a hand moving it— and something else moving the hand—and if you stop your ears—if you stop your ears —yes, then it rings louder than ever. Rings and rings until you answer—and then it's too late. Then the police come - and . . . and. . . . [*The bell rings twice loudly.* JEAN *flinches, then straightens himself up.*] It's horrible. But there's no other way to end it . . . Go!

[JULIE *walks firmly out through the door.*]

CURTAIN

FEDERICO GARCÍA LORCA

A TALK ABOUT THE THEATRE [1]

Instead of testimonials for poets and playwrights I would organize attacks and dares in which we should be challenged cavalierly and with real rage: "I bet you don't have the courage to do this!" "I bet you're not able to express the ocean's anguish in one character!" "I bet you don't dare recount the despair of the enemy soldiers in a war!" Demands and struggling, upon a basis of stern love, temper the soul of the artist, while facile praise makes it effeminate and destroys it. The theatres are full of deceiving sirens crowned with hothouse roses, and the public is satisfied, and it applauds sawdust hearts and speeches spoken from the teeth out; but the dramatic poet, if he wants to save himself from oblivion, dares not forget fields of roses dampened by the morning where suffer the tiller of the soil and that dove, wounded by a mysterious hunter, which agonizes amidst the rushes, without anyone hearing its plaint.

* * * * * *

. . . The theatre is one of the most expressive and useful instruments for the edification of a nation, and the barometer which marks its greatness or descent. A theatre perceptive and well oriented in all its branches, from tragedy to vaudeville, can change a country's sensibility in a few years; and a debased theatre, one in which hoofs substitute for wings, can degrade and dull an entire nation.

The theatre is a school of tears and laughter and a free rostrum where men can expose to view outworn or mistaken moralities and elucidate with living examples eternal norms of man's heart and sentiment.

* * * * * *

The delicious light theatre of reviews, vaudeville and farce, classes to which I am an addicted spectator, could defend and even save itself; but verse drama, the historical genre, and

[1] Federico García Lorca, from "A Talk About the Theatre," *Obras Completas,* 2nd ed., (Buenos Aires, 1949), VII, 183–187. This selection translated by James Graham-Luján. Reprinted by permission of James Graham-Luján.

the so-named Spanish *zarzuela* will suffer more reverses each day because they are the most exacting classes and those in which the true innovations are due; and there is no authority nor spirit of sacrifice to impose them upon a public which one must highhandedly tame and, on many occasions, contradict and attack. The theatre must instruct the public and not the public the theatre. In order to achieve this, authors and actors must once again vest themselves, at cost of blood, in great authority, for the theatre public is like the children at a school: it adores the grave and austere master who demands justice and who defines it, and it covers with cruel tacks the chairs where timid and toadying teachers sit—those who neither teach nor make room for teaching.

The public can be taught—note that I say public and not people; it can be taught, for I saw Debussy and Ravel trampled years ago and later was present at the clamorous ovations that a popular public gave to the works formerly rejected. These composers were imposed by a criterion of authority superior to that of the current taste, just as Wedekind in Germany, Pirandello in Italy, and many others were.

* * * * * *

Art above everything else. Most noble art; and you, beloved actors, artists above everything else. Artists from head to foot since you have come up to the feigned and painful world of the stage out of love and vocation. Artists by occupation and preoccupation. In the most modest theatre and in the proudest, the word "Art" must be written in halls and dressing rooms, for otherwise we shall have to place there the word "Commerce" or some other which I do not dare utter. And hierarchy, discipline and sacrifice and love.

I do not wish to give you a lesson, since I am in the position of receiving some. My words are dictated by enthusiasm and certainty. I am not a deluded person. I have thought a great deal—and done so coldly—what I am thinking —and, like a good Andalusian, I possess the secret of being able to think coldly because my blood is ancient. I know that the truth is not held by him who, eating his bread by the fireside, says "today, today, today," but by him who serenely watches the faraway first light in the countryside's daybreak.

I know that he who says "right now, now, now," with his eyes fixed on the small jaws of the box office is not right— but he who says "tomorrow, tomorrow, tomorrow," and perceives the arrival of the new life which settles upon the world.

FEDERICO GARCÍA LORCA

The House of Bernarda Alba

A DRAMA ABOUT WOMEN IN THE VILLAGES OF SPAIN
TRANSLATED BY
JAMES GRAHAM-LUJÁN AND RICHARD L. O'CONNELL

CHARACTERS

BERNARDA, *age 60.*
MARIA JOSEFA, *Bernarda's mother, age 80.*
ANGUSTIAS, *Bernarda's daughter, age 39.*
MAGDALENA, *Bernarda's daughter, age 30.*
AMELIA, *Bernarda's daughter, age 27.*
MARTIRIO, *Bernarda's daughter, age 24.*

ADELA, *Bernarda's daughter, age 20.*
A MAID, *age 50.*
LA PONCIA, *a maid, age 60.*
PRUDENCIA, *age 50.*
WOMEN IN MOURNING.

*The writer states that these Three Acts are intended as a
photographic document.*

ACT I

A very white room in Bernarda Alba's house. The walls are white. There are arched doorways with jute curtains tied back with tassels and ruffles. Wicker chairs. On the walls, pictures of unlikely landscapes full of nymphs or legendary kings.

It is summer. A great brooding silence fills the stage. It is empty when the curtain rises. Bells can be heard tolling outside.

FIRST SERVANT: [*Entering.*] The tolling of those bells hits me right between the eyes.

PONCIA: [*She enters, eating bread and sausage.*] More than two hours of mumbo jumbo. Priests are here from all the towns. The church looks beautiful. At the first responsory for the dead, Magdalena fainted.

FIRST SERVANT: She's the one who's left most alone.

PONCIA: She's the only one who loved her father. Ay! Thank God we're alone for a little. I came over to eat.

FIRST SERVANT: If Bernarda sees you . . . !

PONCIA: She's not eating today so she'd just as soon we'd all die of hunger! Domineering old tyrant! But she'll be fooled! I opened the sausage crock.

FIRST SERVANT: [*With an anxious sadness.*] Couldn't you give me some for my little girl, Poncia?

PONCIA: Go ahead! and take a fistful of peas too. She won't know the difference today.

VOICE: [*Within.*] Bernarda!

PONCIA: There's the grandmother! Isn't she locked up tight?

FIRST SERVANT: Two turns of the key.

PONCIA: You'd better put the cross-bar up too. She's got the fingers of a lock-picker!

VOICE: [*Within.*] Bernarda!

PONCIA: [*Shouting.*] She's coming! [*To THE SERVANT.*] Clean everything up good. If Bernarda doesn't find things shining, she'll pull out the few hairs I have left.

SERVANT: What a woman!

PONCIA: Tyrant over everyone around her. She's perfectly capable of sitting on your heart and watching you die for a whole year without turning off that cold little smile she wears on her wicked face. Scrub, scrub those dishes!

SERVANT: I've got blood on my hands from so much polishing of everything.

PONCIA: She's the cleanest, she's the decentest, she's the highest everything! A good rest her poor husband's earned!

[*The bells stop.*]

SERVANT: Did all the relatives come?

PONCIA: Just hers. His people hate her. They came to see him dead and make the sign of the cross over him; that's all.

SERVANT: Are there enough chairs?

PONCIA: More than enough. Let them sit on the floor. When Bernarda's father died people stopped coming under this roof. She doesn't want them to see her in her "domain." Curse her!

SERVANT: She's been good to you.

PONCIA: Thirty years washing her sheets. Thirty years eating her leftovers. Nights of watching when she had a cough. Whole days peeking through a crack in the shutters to spy on the neighbors and carry her the tale. Life without secrets one from the other. But in spite of that—curse her! May the "pain of the piercing nail" [1] strike her in the eyes.

SERVANT: Poncia!

PONCIA: But I'm a good watchdog! I bark when I'm told and bite beggars' heels when she sics me on 'em. My sons work in her fields—both of them already married, but one of these days I'll have enough.

SERVANT: And then . . . ?

PONCIA: Then I'll lock myself up in a room with her and spit in her face—a

---

[1] "pain of the piercing nail" i.e. pain of the cross.

whole year. "Bernarda, here's for this, that
and the other!" Till I leave her—just like a
lizard the boys have squashed. For that's
what she is—she and her whole family! Not
that I envy her her life. Five girls are left
her, five ugly daughters—not counting
Angustias the eldest, by her first husband,
who has money—the rest of them, plenty of
eyelets to embroider, plenty of linen petticoats, but bread and grapes when it comes
to inheritance.

SERVANT: Well, I'd like to have what
they've got!

PONCIA: All we have is our hands and a
hole in God's earth.

SERVANT: And that's the only earth
they'll ever leave to us—to us who have
nothing!

PONCIA: [At the cupboard.] This glass
has some specks.

SERVANT: Neither soap nor rag will take
them off.

[The bells toll.]

PONCIA: The last prayer! I'm going over
and listen. I certainly like the way our
priest sings. In the Pater Noster his voice
went up, and up—like a pitcher filling with
water little by little. Of course, at the end
his voice cracked, but it's glorious to hear
it. No, there never was anybody like the old
Sacristan—Tronchapinos. At my mother's
Mass, may she rest in peace, he sang. The
walls shook—and when he said "Amen,"
it was as if a wolf had come into the church.
[Imitating him.] A-a-a-men! [She starts
coughing.]

SERVANT: Watch out—you'll strain your
windpipe!

PONCIA: I'd rather strain something else!
[Goes out laughing.]

[THE SERVANT scrubs. The bells toll.]

SERVANT: [Imitating the bells.] Dong,
dong, dong. Dong, dong, dong. May God
forgive him!

BEGGAR WOMAN: [At the door, with a
little girl.] Blesséd be God! [2]

SERVANT: Dong, dong, dong. I hope he
waits many years for us! Dong, dong, dong.

BEGGAR: [Loudly, a little annoyed.]
Blesséd be God!

SERVANT: [Annoyed.] Forever and ever!

BEGGAR: I came for the scraps.

[The bells stop tolling.]

SERVANT: You can go right out the way
you came in. Today's scraps are for me.

BEGGAR: But you have somebody to take
care of you—and my little girl and I are all
alone!

SERVANT: Dogs are alone too, and they
live.

BEGGAR: They always give them to me.

SERVANT: Get out of here! Who let you
in anyway? You've already tracked up the
place. [THE BEGGAR WOMAN and LITTLE
GIRL leave. THE SERVANT goes on scrubbing.] Floors finished with oil, cupboards,
pedestals, iron beds—but us servants, we
can suffer in silence—and live in mud huts
with a plate and a spoon. I hope someday
not a one will be left to tell it. [The bells
sound again.] Yes, yes—ring away. Let
them put you in a coffin with gold inlay
and brocade to carry it on—you're no less
dead than I'll be, so take what's coming to
you, Antonio María Benavides—stiff in
your broadcloth suit and your high boots—
take what's coming to you! You'll never
again lift my skirts behind the corral door!

[From the rear door, two by two,
women in mourning with large shawls
and black skirts and fans, begin to enter. They come in slowly until the
stage is full.]

SERVANT: [Breaking into a wail.] Oh,
Antonio María Benavides, now you'll never
see these walls, nor break bread in this
house again! I'm the one who loved you
most of all your servants. [Pulling her hair.]
Must I live on after you've gone? Must I
go on living?

[The two hundred women finish coming in, and Bernarda and her five
daughters enter. BERNARDA leans on a
cane.]

BERNARDA: [To THE SERVANT.] Silence!

SERVANT: [Weeping.] Bernarda!

BERNARDA: Less shrieking and more
work. You should have had all this cleaner
for the wake. Get out. This isn't your place.

[THE SERVANT goes off crying.]

The poor are like animals—they seem to
be made of different stuff.

FIRST WOMAN: The poor feel their sor-
rows too.

BERNARDA: But they forget them in front
of a plateful of peas.

FIRST GIRL: [Timidly.] Eating is necessary for living.

[2] "Blessed be God" a ritual phrase to which the
expected answer is—in this case—"Forever and
ever!"

BERNARDA: At your age one doesn't talk in front of older people.

FIRST WOMAN: Be quiet, child.

BERNARDA: I've never taken lessons from anyone. Sit down. Magdalena, don't cry. If you want to cry, get under your bed. Do you hear me?

SECOND WOMAN: [*To* BERNARDA.] Have you started to work the fields?

BERNARDA: Yesterday.

THIRD WOMAN: The sun comes down like lead.

FIRST WOMAN: I haven't known heat like this for years.

[*Pause. They all fan themselves.*]

BERNARDA: Is the lemonade ready?

PONCIA: Yes, Bernarda.

[*She brings in a large tray full of little white jars which she distributes.*]

BERNARDA: Give the men some.

PONCIA: They're already drinking in the patio.

BERNARDA: Let them get out the way they came in. I don't want them walking through here.

A GIRL: [*To* ANGUSTIAS.] Pepe el Romano was with the men during the service.

ANGUSTIAS: There he was.

BERNARDA: His mother was there. She saw his mother. Neither she nor I saw Pepe . . .

GIRL: I thought . . .

BERNARDA: The one who *was* there was Darajalí, the widower. Very close to your Aunt. We all of us saw him.

SECOND WOMAN: [*Aside, in a low voice.*] Wicked, worse than wicked woman!

THIRD WOMAN: A tongue like a knife!

BERNARDA: Women in church shouldn't look at any man but the priest—and him only because he wears skirts. To turn your head is to be looking for the warmth of corduroy.

FIRST WOMAN: Sanctimonious old snake!

PONCIA: [*Between her teeth.*] Itching for a man's warmth.

BERNARDA: [*Beating with her cane on the floor.*] Blesséd be God! [3]

ALL: [*Crossing themselves.*] Forever blesséd and praised.

BERNARDA: Rest in peace with holy company at your head.

ALL: Rest in peace!

BERNARDA: With the Angel Saint Michael, and his sword of justice.

ALL: Rest in peace!

BERNARDA: With the key that opens, and the hand that locks.

ALL: Rest in peace!

BERNARDA: With the most blesséd, and the little lights of the field.

ALL: Rest in peace!

BERNARDA: With our holy charity, and all souls on land and sea.

ALL: Rest in peace!

BERNARDA: Grant rest to your servant, Antonio María Benavides, and give him the crown of your blesséd glory.

ALL: Amen.

BERNARDA: [*She rises and chants.*] Requiem aeternam donat eis domine.

ALL: [*Standing and chanting in the Gregorian fashion.*] Et lux perpetua luce ab eis. [4]

[*They cross themselves.*]

FIRST WOMAN: May you have health to pray for his soul.

[*They start filing out.*]

THIRD WOMAN: You won't lack loaves of hot bread.

SECOND WOMAN: Nor a roof for your daughters.

[*They are all filing in front of* BERNARDA *and going out.* ANGUSTIAS *leaves by the door to the patio.*]

FOURTH WOMAN: May you go on enjoying your wedding wheat.

PONCIA: [*She enters, carrying a money bag.*] From the men—this bag of money for Masses.

BERNARDA: Thank them—and let them have a glass of brandy.

GIRL: [*To* MAGDALENA.] Magdalena . . .

BERNARDA: [*To* MAGDALENA *who is starting to cry.*] Sh-h-h-h! [*She beats with her cane on the floor.*]

[*All the women have gone out.*]

BERNARDA: [*To the women who have just left.*] Go back to your houses and criticize everything you've seen! I hope it'll be many years before you pass under the archway of my door again.

[3] "Blessed be God" the passage which follows is in part litany and in part folk phrase.

[4] "Requiem aeternam . . . ab eis" Bernarda and the others misquote a passage from the Burial Mass. "Requiem aeternam dona eis Domine: et lux perpetua luceat eis." "Eternal rest give unto them, O Lord: and let perpetual light shine upon them."

PONCIA: You've nothing to complain about. The whole town came.

BERNARDA: Yes, to fill my house with the sweat from their wraps and the poison of their tongues.

AMELIA: Mother, don't talk like that.

BERNARDA: What other way is there to talk about this curséd village with no river —this village full of wells where you drink water always fearful it's been poisoned?

PONCIA: Look what they've done to the floor!

BERNARDA: As though a herd of goats had passed through. [PONCIA cleans the floor.] Adela, give me a fan.

ADELA: Take this one. [She gives her a round fan with green and red flowers.]

BERNARDA: [Throwing the fan on the floor.] Is that the fan to give to a widow? Give me a black one and learn to respect your father's memory.

MARTIRIO: Take mine.

BERNARDA: And you?

MARTIRIO: I'm not hot.

BERNARDA: Well, look for another, because you'll need it. For the eight years of mourning, not a breath of air will get in this house from the street. We'll act as if we'd sealed up doors and windows with bricks. That's what happened in my father's house —and in my grandfather's house. Meantime, you can all start embroidering your hope-chest linens. I have twenty bolts of linen in the chest from which to cut sheets and coverlets. Magdalena can embroider them.

MAGDALENA: It's all the same to me.

ADELA: [Sourly.] If you don't want to embroider them—they can go without. That way yours will look better.

MAGDALENA: Neither mine nor yours. I know I'm not going to marry. I'd rather carry sacks to the mill. Anything except sit here day after day in this dark room.

BERNARDA: That's what a woman is for.

MAGDALENA: Cursed be all women.

BERNARDA: In this house you'll do what I order. You can't run with the story to your father any more. Needle and thread for women. Whiplash and mules for men. That's the way it has to be for people who have certain obligations.

[ADELA goes out.]

VOICE: Bernarda! Let me out!

BERNARDA: [Calling.] Let her out now!

[THE FIRST SERVANT enters.]

FIRST SERVANT: I had a hard time holding her. In spite of her eighty years, your mother's strong as an oak.

BERNARDA: It runs in the family. My grandfather was the same way.

SERVANT: Several times during the wake I had to cover her mouth with an empty sack because she wanted to shout out to you to give her dishwater to drink at least, and some dogmeat, which is what she says you feed her.

MARTIRIO: She's mean!

BERNARDA: [To SERVANT.] Let her get some fresh air in the patio.

SERVANT: She took her rings and the amethyst earrings out of the box, put them on, and told me she wants to get married.

[The daughters laugh.]

BERNARDA: Go with her and be careful she doesn't get near the well.

SERVANT: You don't need to be afraid she'll jump in.

BERNARDA: It's not that—but the neighbors can see her there from their windows.

[THE SERVANT leaves.]

MARTIRIO: We'll go change our clothes.

BERNARDA: Yes, but don't take the 'kerchiefs from your heads.

[ADELA enters.]

And Angustias?

ADELA: [Meaningfully.] I saw her looking out through the cracks of the back door. The men had just gone.

BERNARDA: And you, what were you doing at the door?

ADELA: I went there to see if the hens had laid.

BERNARDA: But the men had already gone!

ADELA: [Meaningfully.] A group of them were still standing outside.

BERNARDA: [Furiously.] Angustias! Angustias!

ANGUSTIAS: [Entering.] Did you want something?

BERNARDA: For what—and at whom— were you looking?

ANGUSTIAS: Nobody.

BERNARDA: Is it decent for a woman of your class to be running after a man the day of her father's funeral? Answer me! Whom were you looking at?

[Pause.]

ANGUSTIAS: I . . .

BERNARDA: Yes, you!

ANGUSTIAS: Nobody.

BERNARDA: Soft! Honeytongue! [She strikes her.]

PONCIA: [*Running to her.*] Bernarda, calm down! [*She holds her.* ANGUSTIAS *weeps.*]

BERNARDA: Get out of here, all of you! [*They all go out.*]

PONCIA: She did it not realizing what she was doing—although it's bad, of course. It really disgusted me to see her sneak along to the patio. Then she stood at the window listening to the men's talk which, as usual, was not the sort one should listen to.

BERNARDA: That's what they come to funerals for. [*With curiosity.*] What were they talking about?

PONCIA: They were talking about Paca la Roseta. Last night they tied her husband up in a stall, stuck her on a horse behind the saddle, and carried her away to the depths of the olive grove.

BERNARDA: And what did she do?

PONCIA: She? She was just as happy— they say her breasts were exposed and Maximiliano held on to her as if he were playing a guitar. Terrible!

BERNARDA: And what happened?

PONCIA: What had to happen. They came back almost at daybreak. Paca la Roseta with her hair loose and a wreath of flowers on her head.

BERNARDA: She's the only bad woman we have in the village.

PONCIA: Because she's not from here. She's from far away. And those who went with her are the sons of outsiders too. The men from here aren't up to a thing like that.

BERNARDA: No, but they like to see it, and talk about it, and suck their fingers over it.

PONCIA: They were saying a lot more things.

BERNARDA: [*Looking from side to side with a certain fear.*] What things?

PONCIA: I'm ashamed to talk about them.

BERNARDA: And my daughter heard them?

PONCIA: Of course!

BERNARDA: That one takes after her Aunts: white and mealy-mouthed and casting sheep's eyes at any little barber's compliment. Oh, what one has to go through and put up with so people will be decent and not too wild!

PONCIA: It's just that your daughters are of an age when they ought to have husbands. Mighty little trouble they give you. Angustias must be much more than thirty now.

BERNARDA: Exactly thirty-nine.

PONCIA: Imagine. And she's never had a beau . . .

BERNARDA: [*Furiously.*] None of them has ever had a beau and they've never needed one! They get along very well.

PONCIA: I didn't mean to offend you.

BERNARDA: For a hundred miles around there's no one good enough to come near them. The men in this town are not of their class. Do you want me to turn them over to the first shepherd?

PONCIA: You should have moved to another town.

BERNARDA: That's it. To sell them!

PONCIA: No, Bernarda, to change. . . . Of course, any place else, they'd be the poor ones.

BERNARDA: Hold your tormenting tongue!

PONCIA: One can't even talk to you. Do we, or do we not share secrets?

BERNARDA: We do not. You're a servant and I pay you. Nothing more.

PONCIA: But . . .

SERVANT: [*Entering.*] Don Arturo's here. He's come to see about dividing the inheritance.

BERNARDA: Let's go. [*To* THE SERVANT.] You start whitewashing the patio. [*To* LA PONCIA.] And you start putting all the dead man's clothes away in the chest.

PONCIA: We could give away some of the things.

BERNARDA: Nothing—not a button even! Not even the cloth we covered his face with.

[*She goes out slowly, leaning on her cane. At the door she turns to look at the two servants. They go out. She leaves.*]

[AMELIA *and* MARTIRIO *enter.*]

AMELIA: Did you take the medicine?

MARTIRIO: For all the good it'll do me.

AMELIA: But you took it?

MARTIRIO: I do things without any faith, but like clockwork.

AMELIA: Since the new doctor came you look livelier.

MARTIRIO: I feel the same.

AMELIA: Did you notice? Adelaida wasn't at the funeral.

MARTIRIO: I know. Her sweetheart doesn't let her go out even to the front doorstep. Before, she was gay. Now, not even powder on her face.

AMELIA: These days a girl doesn't know whether to have a beau or not.

MARTIRIO: It's all the same.

AMELIA: The whole trouble is all these wagging tongues that won't let us live. Adelaida has probably had a bad time.

MARTIRIO: She's afraid of our mother. Mother is the only one who knows the story of Adelaida's father and where he got his lands. Everytime she comes here, Mother twists the knife in the wound. Her father killed his first wife's husband in Cuba so he could marry her himself. Then he left her there and went off with another woman who already had one daughter, and then he took up with this other girl, Adelaida's mother, and married her after his second wife died insane.

AMELIA: But why isn't a man like that put in jail?

MARTIRIO: Because men help each other cover up things like that and no one's able to tell on them.

AMELIA: But Adelaida's not to blame for any of that.

MARTIRIO: No. But history repeats itself. I can see that everything is a terrible repetition. And she'll have the same fate as her mother and grandmother—both of them wife to the man who fathered her.

AMELIA: What an awful thing!

MARTIRIO: It's better never to look at a man. I've been afraid of them since I was a little girl. I'd see them in the yard, yoking the oxen and lifting grain sacks, shouting and stamping, and I was always afraid to grow up for fear one of them would suddenly take me in his arms. God has made me weak and ugly and has definitely put such things away from me.

AMELIA: Don't say that! Enrique Humanas was after you and he liked you.

MARTIRIO: That was just people's ideas! One time I stood in my nightgown at the window until daybreak because he let me know through his shepherd's little girl that he was going to come, and he didn't. It was all just talk. Then he married someone else who had more money than I.

AMELIA: And ugly as the devil.

MARTIRIO: What do men care about ugliness? All they care about is lands, yokes of oxen, and a submissive bitch who'll feed them.

AMELIA: Ay!

[MAGDALENA enters.]

MAGDALENA: What are you doing?

MARTIRIO: Just here.

AMELIA: And you?

MAGDALENA: I've been going through all the rooms. Just to walk a little, and look at Grandmother's needlepoint pictures—the little woolen dog, and the black man wrestling with the lion—which we liked so much when we were children. Those were happier times. A wedding lasted ten days and evil tongues weren't in style. Today people are more refined. Brides wear white veils, just as in the cities, and we drink bottled wine, but we rot inside because of what people might say.

MARTIRIO: Lord knows what went on then!

AMELIA: [To MAGDALENA.] One of your shoelaces has come untied.

MAGDALENA: What of it?

AMELIA: You'll step on it and fall.

MAGDALENA: One less!

MARTIRIO: And Adela?

MAGDALENA: Ah! She put on the green dress she made to wear for her birthday, went out to the yard, and began shouting: "Chickens! Chickens, look at me!" I had to laugh.

AMELIA: If Mother had only seen her!

MAGDALENA: Poor little thing! She's the youngest one of us and still has her illusions. I'd give something to see her happy.

[Pause. ANGUSTIAS crosses the stage, carrying some towels.]

ANGUSTIAS: What time is it?

MAGDALENA: It must be twelve.

ANGUSTIAS: So late?

AMELIA: It's about to strike.

[ANGUSTIAS goes out.]

MAGDALENA: [Meaningfully.] Do you know what? [Pointing after ANGUSTIAS.]

AMELIA: No.

MAGDALENA: Come on!

MARTIRIO: I don't know what you're talking about!

MAGDALENA: Both of you know it better than I do, always with your heads together, like two little sheep, but not letting anybody else in on it. I mean about Pepe el Romano!

MARTERIO: Ah!

MAGDALENA: [Mocking her.] Ah! The whole town's talking about it. Pepe el Romano is coming to marry Angustias. Last night he was walking around the house and I think he's going to send a declaration soon.

MARTIRIO: I'm glad. He's a good man.

AMELIA: Me too. Angustias is well off.

MAGDALENA: Neither one of you is glad.

MARTIRIO: Magdalena! What do you mean?

MAGDALENA: If he were coming because of Angustias' looks, for Angustias as a woman, I'd be glad too, but he's coming for her money. Even though Angustias is our sister, we're her family here and we know she's old and sickly, and always has been the least attractive one of us! Because if she looked like a dressed-up stick at twenty, what can she look like now, now that she's forty?

MARTIRIO: Don't talk like that. Luck comes to the one who least expects it.

AMELIA: But Magdalena's right after all! Angustias has all her father's money; she's the only rich one in the house and that's why, now that Father's dead and the money will be divided, they're coming for her.

MAGDALENA: Pepe el Romano is twenty-five years old and the best looking man around here. The natural thing would be for him to be after you, Amelia, or our Adela, who's twenty—the least likely one in this house, a woman who, like her father, talks through her nose.

MARTIRIO: Maybe he likes that!

MAGDALENA: I've never been able to bear your hypocrisy.

MARTIRIO: Heavens!

[ADELA enters.]

MAGDALENA: Did the chickens see you?

ADELA: What did you want me to do?

AMELIA: If Mother sees you, she'll drag you by your hair!

ADELA: I had a lot of illusions about this dress. I'd planned to put it on the day we were going to eat watermelons at the well. There wouldn't have been another like it.

MARTIRIO: It's a lovely dress.

ADELA: And one that looks very good on me. It's the best thing Magdalena's ever cut.

MAGDALENA: And the chickens, what did they say to you?

ADELA: They presented me with a few fleas that riddled my legs.

[They laugh.]

MARTIRIO: What you can do is dye it black.

MAGDALENA: The best thing you can do is give it to Angustias for her wedding with Pepe el Romano.

ADELA: [With hidden emotion.] But Pepe el Romano . . .

AMELIA: Haven't you heard about it?

ADELA: No.

MAGDALENA: Well, now you know!

ADELA: But it can't be!

MAGDALENA: Money can do anything.

ADELA: Is that why she went out after the funeral and stood looking through the door? [Pause.] And that man would . . .

MAGDALENA: Would do anything.

[Pause.]

MARTIRIO: What are you thinking, Adela?

ADELA: I'm thinking that this mourning has caught me at the worst moment of my life for me to bear it.

MAGDALENA: You'll get used to it.

ADELA: [Bursting out, crying with rage.] I will not get used to it! I can't be locked up. I don't want my skin to look like yours. I don't want my skin's whiteness lost in these rooms. Tomorrow I'm going to put on my green dress and go walking in the streets. I want to go out!

[THE FIRST SERVANT enters.]

MAGDALENA: [In a tone of authority.] Adela!

SERVANT: The poor thing! How she misses her father. . . .

[She goes out.]

MARTIRIO: Hush!

AMELIA: What happens to one will happen to all of us.

[ADELA grows calm.]

MAGDALENA: The servant almost heard you.

SERVANT: [Entering.] Pepe el Romano is coming along at the end of the street.

[AMELIA, MARTIRIO and MAGDALENA run hurriedly.]

MAGDALENA: Let's go see him!

[They leave rapidly.]

SERVANT: [To Adela.] Aren't you going?

ADELA: It's nothing to me.

SERVANT: Since he has to turn the corner, you'll see him better from the window of your room.

[THE SERVANT goes out. ADELA is left on the stage, standing doubtfully; after a moment, she also leaves rapidly, going toward her room. BERNARDA and LA PONCIA come in.]

BERNARDA: Damned portions and shares.

PONCIA: What a lot of money is left to Angustias!

BERNARDA: Yes.

PONCIA: And for the others, considerably less.

BERNARDA: You've told me that three times now, when you know I don't want it mentioned! Considerably less; a lot less! Don't remind me any more.

[ANGUSTIAS *comes in, her face heavily made up.*]

Angustias!

ANGUSTIAS: Mother.

BERNARDA: Have you dared to powder your face? Have you dared to wash your face on the day of your father's death?

ANGUSTIAS: He wasn't my father. Mine died a long time ago. Have you forgotten that already?

BERNARDA: You owe more to this man, father of your sisters, than to your own. Thanks to him, your fortune is intact.

ANGUSTIAS: We'll have to see about that first!

BERNARDA: Even out of decency! Out of respect!

ANGUSTIAS: Let me go out, Mother!

BERNARDA: Let you go out? After I've taken that powder off your face, I will. Spineless! Painted hussy! Just like your Aunts! [*She removes the powder violently with her handkerchief.*] Now get out!

PONCIA: Bernarda, don't be so hateful!

BERNARDA: Even though my mother is crazy, I still have my five senses and I know what I'm doing.

[*They all enter.*]

MAGDALENA: What's going on here?

BERNARDA: Nothing's "going on here"!

MAGDALENA: [*To* ANGUSTIAS.] If you're fighting over the inheritance, you're the richest one and can hang on to it all.

ANGUSTIAS: Keep your tongue in your pocketbook!

BERNARDA: [*Beating on the floor.*] Don't fool yourselves into thinking you'll sway me. Until I go out of this house feet first I'll give the orders for myself and for you!

[*Voices are heard and* MARIA JOSEFA, BERNARDA'S *mother, enters. She is very old and has decked out her head and breast with flowers.*]

MARIA JOSEFA: Bernarda, where is my mantilla? Nothing, nothing of what I own will be for any of you. Not my rings nor my black moiré dress. Because not a one of you is going to marry—not a one. Bernarda, give me my necklace of pearls.

BERNARDA: [*To* THE SERVANT.] Why did you let her get in here?

SERVANT: [*Trembling.*] She got away from me!

MARIA JOSEFA: I ran away because I want to marry—I want to get married to a beautiful manly man from the shore of the sea. Because here the men run from women.

BERNARDA: Hush, hush, Mother!

MARIA JOSEFA: No, no—I won't hush. I don't want to see these single women, longing for marriage, turning their hearts to dust; and I want to go to my home town. Bernarda, I want a man to get married to and be happy with!

BERNARDA: Lock her up!

MARIA JOSEFA: Let me go out, Bernarda!

[THE SERVANT *seizes* MARIA JOSEFA.]

BERNARDA: Help her, all of you!

[*They all grab the old woman.*]

MARIA JOSEFA: I want to get away from here! Bernarda! To get married by the shore of the sea—by the shore of the sea!

QUICK CURTAIN

ACT II

A white room in BERNARDA'S *house. The doors on the left lead to the bedrooms.*

BERNARDA'S DAUGHTERS *are seated on low chairs, sewing.* MAGDALENA *is embroidering.* LA PONCIA *is with them.*

ANGUSTIAS: I've cut the third sheet.

MARTIRIO: That one goes to Amelia.

MAGDALENA: Angustias, shall I put Pepe's initials here too?

ANGUSTIAS: [*Dryly.*] No.

MAGDALENA: [*Calling.*] Adela, aren't you coming?

AMELIA: She's probably stretched out on the bed.

PONCIA: Something's wrong with that one. I find her restless, trembling, frightened—as if a lizard were between her breasts.

MARTIRIO: There's nothing, more or less, wrong with her than there is with all of us.

MAGDALENA: All of us except Angustias.

ANGUSTIAS: I feel fine, and anybody who doesn't like it can pop.

MAGDALENA: We all have to admit the nicest things about you are your figure and your tact.

ANGUSTIAS: Fortunately, I'll soon be out of this hell.

MAGDALENA: Maybe you won't get out!

MARTIRIO: Stop this talk!

ANGUSTIAS: Besides, a good dowry is better than dark eyes in one's face!

MAGDALENA: All you say just goes in one ear and out the other.

AMELIA: [To LA PONCIA.] Open the patio door and see if we can get a bit of a breeze.

[LA PONCIA opens the door.]

MARTIRIO: Last night I couldn't sleep because of the heat.

AMELIA: Neither could I.

MAGDALENA: I got up for a bit of air. There was a black storm cloud and a few drops even fell.

PONCIA: It was one in the morning and the earth seemed to give off fire. I got up too. Angustias was still at the window with Pepe.

MAGDALENA: [With irony.] That late? What time did he leave?

ANGUSTIAS: Why do you ask, if you saw him?

AMELIA: He must have left about one-thirty.

ANGUSTIAS: Yes. How did you know?

AMELIA: I heard him cough and heard his mare's hoofbeats.

PONCIA: But I heard him leave around four.

ANGUSTIAS: It must have been someone else!

PONCIA: No, I'm sure of it!

AMELIA: That's what it seemed to me, too.

MAGDALENA: That's very strange!

[Pause.]

PONCIA: Listen, Angustias, what did he say to you the first time he came by your window?

ANGUSTIAS: Nothing. What should he say? Just talked.

MARTIRIO: It's certainly strange that two people who never knew each other should suddenly meet at a window and be engaged.

ANGUSTIAS: Well, I didn't mind.

AMELIA: I'd have felt very strange about it.

ANGUSTIAS: No, because when a man comes to a window he knows, from all the busybodies who come and go and fetch and carry, that he's going to be told "yes."

MARTIRIO: All right, but he'd have to ask you.

ANGUSTIAS: Of course!

AMELIA: [Inquisitively.] And how did he ask you?

ANGUSTIAS: Why, no way:—"You know I'm after you. I need a good, well brought up woman, and that's you—if it's agreeable."

AMELIA: These things embarrass me!

ANGUSTIAS: They embarrass me too, but one has to go through it!

PONCIA: And did he say anything more?

ANGUSTIAS: Yes, he did all the talking.

MARTIRIO: And you?

ANGUSTIAS: I couldn't have said a word. My heart was almost coming out of my mouth. It was the first time I'd ever been alone at night with a man.

MAGDALENA: And such a handsome man.

ANGUSTIAS: He's not bad looking.

PONCIA: Those things happen among people who have an idea how to do things, who talk and say and move their hand. The first time my husband, Evaristo the Short-tailed, came to my window . . . Ha! Ha! Ha!

AMELIA: What happened?

PONCIA: It was very dark. I saw him coming along and as he went by he said, "Good evening." "Good evening," I said. Then we were both silent for more than half an hour. The sweat poured down my body. Then Evaristo got nearer and nearer as if he wanted to squeeze in through the bars and said in a very low voice—"Come here and let me feel you!"

[They all laugh. AMELIA gets up, runs, and looks through the door.]

AMELIA: Ay, I thought Mother was coming!

MAGDALENA: What she'd have done to us!

[They go on laughing.]

AMELIA: Sh-h-h! She'll hear us.

PONCIA: Then he acted very decently. Instead of getting some other idea, he went to raising birds, until he died. You aren't married but it's good for you to know, anyway, that two weeks after the wedding a man gives up the bed for the table, then the table for the tavern, and the woman who doesn't like it can just rot, weeping in a corner.

AMELIA: You liked it.

PONCIA: I learned how to handle him!

MARTIRIO: Is it true that you sometimes hit him?

PONCIA: Yes, and once I almost poked out one of his eyes!

MAGDALENA: All women ought to be like that!

PONCIA: I'm one of your mother's school. One time I don't know what he said to me, and then I killed all his birds—with the pestle!

[*They laugh.*]

MAGDALENA: Adela, child! Don't miss this.

AMELIA: Adela!

[*Pause.*]

MAGDALENA: I'll go see!

[*She goes out.*]

PONCIA: That child is sick!

MARTIRIO: Of course. She hardly sleeps!

PONCIA: What *does* she do, then?

MARTIRIO: How do I know what she does?

PONCIA: You probably know better than we do, since you sleep with just a wall between you.

ANGUSTIAS: Envy gnaws on people.

AMELIA: Don't exaggerate.

ANGUSTIAS: I can tell it in her eyes. She's getting the look of a crazy woman.

MARTIRIO: Don't talk about crazy women. This is one place you're not allowed to say that word.

[MAGDALENA *and* ADELA *enter.*]

MAGDALENA: Didn't you say she was asleep?

ADELA: My body aches.

MARTIRIO: [*With a hidden meaning.*] Didn't you sleep well last night?

ADELA: Yes.

MARTIRIO: Then?

ADELA: [*Loudly.*] Leave me alone. Awake or asleep, it's no affair of yours. I'll do whatever I want to with my body.

MARTIRIO: I was just concerned about you!

ADELA: Concerned?—curious! Weren't you sewing? Well, continue! I wish I were invisible so I could pass through a room without being asked where I was going!

SERVANT: [*Entering.*] Bernarda is calling you. The man with the laces is here.

[*All but* ADELA *and* LA PONCIA *go out, and as* MARTIRIO *leaves, she looks fixedly at* ADELA.]

ADELA: Don't look at me like that! If you want, I'll give you my eyes, for they're younger, and my back to improve that hump you have, but look the other way when I go by.

PONCIA: Adela, she's your sister, and the one who most loves you besides!

ADELA: She follows me everywhere. Sometimes she looks in my room to see if I'm sleeping. She won't let me breathe, and always, "Too bad about that face!" "Too bad about that body! It's going to waste!" But I won't let that happen. My body will be for whomever I choose.

PONCIA: [*Insinuatingly, in a low voice.*] For Pepe el Romano, no?

ADELA: [*Frightened.*] What do you mean?

PONCIA: What I said, Adela!

ADELA: Shut up!

PONCIA: [*Loudly.*] Don't you think I've noticed?

ADELA: Lower your voice!

PONCIA: Then forget what you're thinking about!

ADELA: What do you know?

PONCIA: We old ones can see through walls. Where do you go when you get up at night?

ADELA: I wish you were blind!

PONCIA: But my head and hands are full of eyes, where something like this is concerned. I couldn't possibly guess your intentions. Why did you sit almost naked at your window, and with the light on and the window open, when Pepe passed by the second night he came to talk with your sister?

ADELA: That's not true!

PONCIA: Don't be a child! Leave your sister alone. And if you like Pepe el Romano, keep it to yourself. [ADELA *weeps.*] Besides, who says you can't marry him? Your sister Angustias is sickly. She'll die with her first child. Narrow waisted, old—and out of my experience I can tell you she'll die. Then Pepe will do what all widowers do in these parts: he'll marry the youngest and most beautiful, and that's you. Live on that hope, forget him, anything; but don't go against God's law.

ADELA: Hush!

PONCIA: I won't hush!

ADELA: Mind your own business. Snooper, traitor!

PONCIA: I'm going to stick to you like a shadow!

ADELA: Instead of cleaning the house and then going to bed and praying for the dead, you root around like an old sow about go-ings on between men and women—so you can drool over them.

PONCIA: I keep watch; so people won't spit when they pass our door.

ADELA: What a tremendous affection you've suddenly conceived for my sister.

PONCIA: I don't have any affection for any of you. I want to live in a decent house. I don't want to be dirtied in my old age!

ADELA: Save your advice. It's already too late. For I'd leap not over you, just a ser-vant, but over my mother to put out this fire I feel in my legs and my mouth. What can you possibly say about me? That I lock myself in my room and will not open the door? That I don't sleep? I'm smarter than you! See if you can catch the hare with your hands.

PONCIA: Don't defy me, Adela, don't defy me! Because I can shout, light lamps, and make bells ring.

ADELA: Bring four thousand yellow flares and set them about the walls of the yard. No one can stop what has to happen.

PONCIA: You like him that much?

ADELA: That much! Looking in his eyes I seem to drink his blood in slowly.

PONCIA: I won't listen to you.

ADELA: Well, you'll have to! I've been afraid of you. But now I'm stronger than you!

[ANGUSTIAS enters.]

ANGUSTIAS: Always arguing!

PONCIA: Certainly. She insists that in all this heat I have to go bring her I don't know what from the store.

ANGUSTIAS: Did you buy me the bottle of perfume?

PONCIA: The most expensive one. And the face powder. I put them on the table in your room.

[ANGUSTIAS goes out.]

ADELA: And be quiet!

PONCIA: We'll see!

[MARTIRIO and AMELIA enter.]

MARTIRIO: [To ADELA.] Did you see the laces?

AMELIA: Angustias', for her wedding sheets, are beautiful.

ADELA: [To MARTIRIO, who is carrying some lace.] And these?

MARTIRIO: They're for me. For a night-gown.

ADELA: [With sarcasm.] One needs a sense of humor around here!

MARTIRIO: [Meaningfully.] But only for me to look at. I don't have to exhibit my-self before anybody.

PONCIA: No one ever sees us in our nightgowns.

MARTIRIO: [Meaningfully, looking at ADELA.] Sometimes they don't! But I love nice underwear. If I were rich, I'd have it made of Holland Cloth. It's one of the few tastes I've left.

PONCIA: These laces are beautiful for babies' caps and christening gowns. I could never afford them for my own. Now let's see if Angustias will use them for hers. Once she starts having children, they'll keep her running night and day.

MAGDALENA: I don't intend to sew a stitch on them.

AMELIA: And much less bring up some stranger's children. Look how our neigh-bors across the road are—making sacrifices for four brats.

PONCIA: They're better off than you. There at least they laugh and you can hear them fight.

MARTIRIO: Well, you go work for them, then.

PONCIA: No, fate has sent me to this nunnery!

[Tiny bells are heard distantly as though through several thicknesses of wall.]

MAGDALENA: It's the men going back to work.

PONCIA: It was three o'clock a minute ago.

MARTIRIO: With this sun!

ADELA: [Sitting down.] Ay! If only we could go out in the fields too!

MAGDALENA: [Sitting down.] Each class does what it has to!

MARTIRIO: [Sitting down.] That's it!

AMELIA: [Sitting down.] Ay!

PONCIA: There's no happiness like that in the fields right at this time of year. Yes-terday morning the reapers arrived. Forty or fifty handsome young men.

MAGDALENA: Where are they from this year?

PONCIA: From far, far away. They came from the mountains! Happy! Like weath-ered trees! Shouting and throwing stones! Last night a woman who dresses in sequins and dances, with an accordion, arrived, and fifteen of them made a deal with her to take her to the olive grove. I saw them from far away. The one who talked with her was a boy with green eyes—tight knit as a sheaf of wheat.

AMELIA: Really?

ADELA: Are you sure?

PONCIA: Years ago another one of those women came here, and I myself gave my eldest son some money so he could go. Men need things like that.

ADELA: Everything's forgiven *them*.

AMELIA: To be born a woman's the worst possible punishment.

MAGDALENA: Even our eyes aren't our own.

[*A distant song is heard, coming nearer.*]

PONCIA: There they are. They have a beautiful song.

AMELIA: They're going out to reap now.

CHORUS:
The reapers have set out
Looking for ripe wheat;
They'll carry off the hearts
Of any girls they meet.

[*Tambourines and carrañacas* [5] *are heard. Pause. They all listen in the silence cut by the sun.*]

AMELIA: And they don't mind the sun!

MARTIRIO: They reap through flames.

ADELA: How I'd like to be a reaper so I could come and go as I pleased. Then we could forget what's eating us all.

MARTIRIO: What do you have to forget?

ADELA: Each one of us has something.

MARTIRIO: [*Intensely.*] Each one!

PONCIA: Quiet! Quiet!

CHORUS: [*Very distantly.*]
Throw wide your doors and windows,
You girls who live in the town.
The reaper asks you for roses
With which to deck his crown.

PONCIA: What a song!

MARTIRIO: [*With nostalgia.*]
Throw wide your doors and windows,
You girls who live in the town.

ADELA: [*Passionately.*]
The reaper asks you for roses
With which to deck his crown.

[*The song grows more distant.*]

PONCIA: Now they're turning the corner.

ADELA: Let's watch them from the window of my room.

PONCIA: Be careful not to open the shutters too much because they're likely to give them a push to see who's looking.

[5] "Carrañacas" rattles, noisemakers.

[*The three leave.* MARTIRIO *is left sitting on the low chair with her head between her hands.*]

AMELIA: [*Drawing near her.*] What's wrong with you?

MARTIRIO: The heat makes me feel ill.

AMELIA: And it's no more than that?

MARTIRIO: I was wishing it were November, the rainy days, the frost—anything except this unending summertime.

AMELIA: It'll pass and come again.

MARTIRIO: Naturally. [*Pause.*] What time did you go to sleep last night?

AMELIA: I don't know. I sleep like a log. Why?

MARTIRIO: Nothing. Only I thought I heard someone in the yard.

AMELIA: Yes?

MARTIRIO: Very late.

AMELIA: And weren't you afraid?

MARTIRIO: No. I've heard it other nights.

AMELIA: We'd better watch out! Couldn't it have been the shepherds?

MARTIRIO: The shepherds come at six.

AMELIA: Maybe a young, unbroken mule?

MARTIRIO: [*To herself, with double meaning.*] That's it! That's it! An unbroken little mule.

AMELIA: We'll have to set a watch.

MARTIRIO: No. No. Don't say anything. It may be I've just imagined it.

AMELIA: Maybe.

[*Pause.* AMELIA *starts to go.*]

MARTIRIO: Amelia!

AMELIA: [*At the door.*] What?

[*Pause.*]

MARTIRIO: Nothing.

[*Pause.*]

AMELIA: Why did you call me?

[*Pause.*]

MARTIRIO: It just came out. I didn't mean to.

[*Pause.*]

AMELIA: Lie down for a little.

ANGUSTIAS: [*She bursts in furiously, in a manner that makes a great contrast with previous silence.*] Where's that picture of Pepe I had under my pillow? Which one of you has it?

MARTIRIO: No one.

AMELIA: You'd think he was a silver St. Bartholomew.

ANGUSTIAS: Where's the picture?

[PONCIA, MAGDALENA *and* ADELA *enter.*]

ADELA: What picture?

ANGUSTIAS: One of you has hidden it on me.

MAGDALENA: Do you have the effrontery to say that?

ANGUSTIAS: I had it in my room, and now it isn't there.

MARTIRIO: But couldn't it have jumped out into the yard at midnight? Pepe likes to walk around in the moonlight.

ANGUSTIAS: Don't joke with me! When he comes I'll tell him.

PONCIA: Don't do that! Because it'll turn up. [Looking at ADELA.]

ANGUSTIAS: I'd like to know which one of you has it.

ADELA: [Looking at MARTIRIO.] Somebody has it! But not me!

MARTIRIO: [With meaning.] Of course not you!

BERNARDA: [Entering, with her cane.] What scandal is this in my house in the heat's heavy silence? The neighbors must have their ears glued to the walls.

ANGUSTIAS: They've stolen my sweetheart's picture!

BERNARDA: [Fiercely.] Who? Who?

ANGUSTIAS: They have!

BERNARDA: Which one of you? [Silence.] Answer me! [Silence.] [To LA PONCIA.] Search their rooms! Look in their beds. This comes of not tying you up with shorter leashes. But I'll teach you now! [To ANGUSTIAS.] Are you sure?

ANGUSTIAS: Yes.

BERNARDA: Did you look everywhere?

ANGUSTIAS: Yes, Mother.

[They all stand in an embarrassed silence.]

BERNARDA: At the end of my life—to make me drink the bitterest poison a mother knows. [To PONCIA.] Did you find it?

PONCIA: Here it is.

BERNARDA: Where did you find it?

PONCIA: It was . . .

BERNARDA: Say it! Don't be afraid.

PONCIA: [Wonderingly.] Between the sheets in Martirio's bed.

BERNARDA: [To MARTIRIO.] Is that true?

MARTIRIO: It's true.

BERNARDA: [Advancing on her, beating her with her cane.] You'll come to a bad end yet, you hypocrite! Trouble maker!

MARTIRIO: [Fiercely.] Don't hit me, Mother!

BERNARDA: All I want to!

MARTIRIO: If I let you! You hear me? Get back!

PONCIA: Don't be disrespectful to your mother!

ANGUSTIAS: [Holding BERNARDA.] Let her go, please!

BERNARDA: Not even tears in your eyes.

MARTIRIO: I'm not going to cry just to please you.

BERNARDA: Why did you take the picture?

MARTIRIO: Can't I play a joke on my sister? What else would I want it for?

ADELA: [Leaping forward, full of jealousy.] It wasn't a joke! You never liked to play jokes. It was something else bursting in her breast—trying to come out. Admit it openly now.

MARTIRIO: Hush, and don't make me speak; for if I should speak the walls would close together one against the other with shame.

ADELA: An evil tongue never stops inventing lies.

BERNARDA: Adela!

MAGDALENA: You're crazy.

AMELIA: And you stone us all with your evil suspicions.

MARTIRIO: But some others do things more wicked!

ADELA: Until all at once they stand forth stark naked and the river carries them along.

BERNARDA: Spiteful!

ANGUSTIAS: It's not my fault Pepe el Romano chose me!

ADELA: For your money.

ANGUSTIAS: Mother!

BERNARDA: Silence!

MARTIRIO: For your fields and your orchards.

MAGDALENA: That's only fair.

BERNARDA: Silence, I say! I saw the storm coming but I didn't think it'd burst so soon. Oh, what an avalanche of hate you've thrown on my heart! But I'm not old yet— I have five chains for you, and this house my father built, so not even the weeds will know of my desolation. Out of here!

[They go out. BERNARDA sits down desolately. LA PONCIA is standing close to the wall. BERNARDA recovers herself, and beats on the floor.]

I'll have to let them feel the weight of my hand! Bernarda, remember your duty!

PONCIA: May I speak?

BERNARDA: Speak. I'm sorry you heard.

A stranger is always out of place in a family.

PONCIA: What I've seen, I've seen.

BERNARDA: Angustias must get married right away.

PONCIA: Certainly. We'll have to get her away from here.

BERNARDA: Not her, him!

PONCIA: Of course. He's the one to get away from here. You've thought it all out.

BERNARDA: I'm not thinking. There are things that shouldn't and can't be thought out. I give orders.

PONCIA: And you think he'll be satisfied to go away?

BERNARDA: [Rising.] What are you imagining now?

PONCIA: He will, of course, marry Angustias.

BERNARDA: Speak up! I know you well enough to see that your knife's out for me.

PONCIA: I never knew a warning could be called murder.

BERNARDA: Have you some "warning" for me?

PONCIA: I'm not making any accusations, Bernarda. I'm only telling you to open your eyes and you'll see.

BERNARDA: See what?

PONCIA: You've always been smart, Bernarda. You've seen other people's sins a hundred miles away. Many times I've thought you could read minds. But, your children are your children, and now you're blind.

BERNARDA: Are you talking about Martirio?

PONCIA: Well, yes—about Martirio . . . [With curiosity.] I wonder why she hid the picture?

BERNARDA: [Shielding her daughter.] After all, she says it was a joke. What else could it be?

PONCIA: [Scornfully.] Do you believe that?

BERNARDA: [Sternly.] I don't merely believe it. It's so!

PONCIA: Enough of this. We're talking about your family. But if we were talking about your neighbor across the way, what would it be?

BERNARDA: Now you're beginning to pull the point of the knife out.

PONCIA: [Always cruelly.] No, Bernarda. Something very grave is happening here. I don't want to put the blame on your shoulders, but you've never given your daughters any freedom. Martirio is lovesick, I don't care what you say. Why didn't you let her marry Enrique Humanas? Why, on the very day he was coming to her window, did you send him a message not to come?

BERNARDA: [Loudly.] I'd do it a thousand times over! My blood won't mingle with the Humanas' while I live! His father was a shepherd.

PONCIA: And you see now what's happening to you with these airs!

BERNARDA: I have them because I can afford to. And you don't have them because you know where you came from!

PONCIA: [With hate.] Don't remind me! I'm old now. I've always been grateful for your protection.

BERNARDA: [Emboldened.] You don't seem so!

PONCIA: [With hate, behind softness.] Martirio will forget this.

BERNARDA: And if she doesn't—the worse for her. I don't believe this is that "very grave thing" that's happening here. Nothing's happening here. It's just that you wish it would! And if it should happen one day, you can be sure it won't go beyond these walls.

PONCIA: I'm not so sure of that! There are people in town who can also read hidden thoughts, from afar.

BERNARDA: How you'd like to see me and my daughters on our way to a whorehouse!

PONCIA: No one knows her own destiny!

BERNARDA: I know my destiny! And my daughters! The whorehouse was for a certain woman, already dead. . . .

PONCIA: [Fiercely.] Bernarda, respect the memory of my mother!

BERNARDA: Then don't plague me with your evil thoughts!

[Pause.]

PONCIA: I'd better stay out of everything.

BERNARDA: That's what you ought to do. Work and keep your mouth shut. The duty of all who work for a living.

PONCIA: But we can't do that. Don't you think it'd be better for Pepe to marry Martirio or . . . yes! . . . Adela?

BERNARDA: No, I don't think so.

PONCIA: [With meaning.] Adela! She's Romano's real sweetheart!

BERNARDA: Things are never the way we want them!

PONCIA: But it's hard work to turn them from their destined course. For Pepe to be with Angustias seems wrong to me—and to other people—and even to the wind. Who knows if they'll get what they want?

BERNARDA: There you go again! Sneaking up on me—giving me bad dreams. But I won't listen to you, because if all you say should come to pass—I'd scratch your face.

PONCIA: Frighten someone else with that.

BERNARDA: Fortunately, my daughters respect me and have never gone against my will!

PONCIA: That's right! But, as soon as they break loose they'll fly to the rooftops!

BERNARDA: And I'll bring them down with stones!

PONCIA: Oh, yes! You were always the bravest one!

BERNARDA: I've always enjoyed a good fight!

PONCIA: But aren't people strange. You should see Angustias' enthusiasm for her lover, at her age! And he seems very smitten too. Yesterday my oldest son told me that when he passed by with the oxen at four-thirty in the morning they were still talking.

BERNARDA: At four-thirty?

ANGUSTIAS: [Entering.] That's a lie!

PONCIA: That's what he told me.

BERNARDA: [To ANGUSTIAS.] Speak up!

ANGUSTIAS: For more than a week Pepe has been leaving at one. May God strike me dead if I'm lying.

MARTIRIO: [Entering.] I heard him leave at four too.

BERNARDA: But did you see him with your eyes?

MARTIRIO: I didn't want to look out. Don't you talk now through the side window?

ANGUSTIAS: We talk through my bedroom window.

[ADELA appears at the door.]

MARTIRIO: Then . . .

BERNARDA: What's going on here?

PONCIA: If you're not careful, you'll find out! At least Pepe was at one of your windows—and at four in the morning too!

BERNARDA: Are you sure of that?

PONCIA: You can't be sure of anything in this life!

ADELA: Mother, don't listen to someone who wants us to lose everything we have.

BERNARDA: I know how to take care of myself! If the townspeople want to come bearing false witness against me, they'll run into a stone wall! Don't any of you talk

about this! Sometimes other people try to stir up a wave of filth to drown us.

MARTIRIO: I don't like to lie.

PONCIA: So there must be something.

BERNARDA: There won't be anything. I was born to have my eyes always open. Now I'll watch without closing them 'til I die.

ANGUSTIAS: I have the right to know.

BERNARDA: You don't have any right except to obey. No one's going to fetch and carry for me. [To LA PONCIA.] And don't meddle in our affairs. No one will take a step without my knowing it.

SERVANT: [Entering.] There's a big crowd at the top of the street, and all the neighbors are at their doors!

BERNARDA: [To PONCIA.] Run see what's happening!

[The Girls are about to run out.] Where are you going? I always knew you for window-watching women and breakers of your mourning. All of you, to the patio!

[They go out. BERNARDA leaves. Distant shouts are heard. MARTIRIO and ADELA enter and listen, not daring to step farther than the front door.]

MARTIRIO: You can be thankful I didn't happen to open my mouth.

ADELA: I would have spoken too.

MARTIRIO: And what were you going to say? Wanting isn't doing!

ADELA: I do what I can and what happens to suit me. You've wanted to, but haven't been able.

MARTIRIO: You won't go on very long.

ADELA: I'll have everything!

MARTIRIO: I'll tear you out of his arms!

ADELE: [Pleadingly.] Martirio, let me be!

MARTIRIO: None of us will have him!

ADELA: He wants me for his house!

MARTIRIO: I saw how he embraced you!

ADELA: I didn't want him to. It's as if I were dragged by a rope.

MARTIRIO: I'll see you dead first!

[MAGDALENA and ANGUSTIAS look in. The tumult is increasing. THE SERVANT enters with BERNARDA. PONCIA also enters from another door.]

PONCIA: Bernarda!

BERNARDA: What's happening?

PONCIA: Librada's daughter, the unmarried one, had a child and no one knows whose it is!

ADELA: A child?

PONCIA: And to hide her shame she killed

it and hid it under the rocks, but the dogs, with more heart than most Christians, dug it out and, as though directed by the hand of God, left it at her door. Now they want to kill her. They're dragging her through the streets—and down the paths and across the olive groves the men are coming, shouting so the fields shake.

BERNARDA: Yes, let them all come with olive whips and hoe handles—let them all come and kill her!

ADELA: No, not to kill her!

MARTIRIO: Yes—and let us go out too!

BERNARDA: And let whoever loses her decency pay for it!

[Outside a woman's shriek and a great clamor is heard.]

ADELA: Let her escape! Don't you go out!

MARTIRIO: [Looking at ADELA.] Let her pay what she owes!

BERNARDA: [At the archway.] Finish her before the guards come! Hot coals in the place where she sinned!

ADELA: [Holding her belly.] No! No!

BERNARDA: Kill her! Kill her!

CURTAIN

ACT III

Four white walls, lightly washed in blue, of the interior patio of BERNARDA ALBA's *house. The doorways, illuminated by the lights inside the rooms, give a tenuous glow to the stage.*

At the center there is a table with a shaded oil lamp about which BERNARDA *and her* DAUGHTERS *are eating.* LA PONCIA *serves them.* PRUDENCIA *sits apart. When the curtain rises, there is a great silence interrupted only by the noise of plates and silverware.*

PRUDENCIA: I'm going. I've made you a long visit. [She rises.]

BERNARDA: But wait, Prudencia. We never see one another.

PRUDENCIA: Have they sounded the last call to rosary?

PONCIA: Not yet.

[PRUDENCIA sits down again.]

BERNARDA: And your husband, how's he getting on?

PRUDENCIA: The same.

BERNARDA: We never see him either.

PRUDENCIA: You know how he is. Since he quarrelled with his brothers over the inheritance, he hasn't used the front door. He takes a ladder and climbs over the back wall.

BERNARDA: He's a real man! And your daughter?

PRUDENCE: He's never forgiven her.

BERNARDA: He's right.

PRUDENCIA: I don't know what he told you. I suffer because of it.

BERNARDA: A daughter who's disobedient stops being a daughter and becomes an enemy.

PRUDENCIA: I let water run. The only consolation I've left is to take refuge in the church, but, since I'm losing my sight,

I'll have to stop coming so the children won't make fun of me.

[A heavy blow is heard against the walls.]

What's that?

BERNARDA: The stallion. He's locked in the stall and he kicks against the wall of the house. [Shouting.] Tether him and take him out in the yard! [In a lower voice.] He must be too hot.

PRUDENCIA: Are you going to put the new mares to him?

BERNARDA: At daybreak.

PRUDENCIA: You've known how to increase your stock.

BERNARDA: By dint of money and struggling.

PONCIA: [Interrupting.] And she has the best herd in these parts. It's a shame that prices are low.

BERNARDA: Do you want a little cheese and honey?

PRUDENCIA: I have no appetite.

[The blow is heard again.]

PONCIA: My God!

PRUDENCIA: It quivered in my chest!

BERNARDA: [Rising, furiously.] Do I have to say things twice? Let him out to roll on the straw. [Pause. Then, as though *speaking to the Stableman.*] Well, then lock the mares in the corral, but let him run free or he may kick down the walls. [*She returns to the table and sits again.*] Ay, what a life!

PRUDENCIA: You have to fight like a man.

BERNARDA: That's it.

[ADELA *gets up from the table.*] Where are you going?

ADELA: For a drink of water.

BERNARDA: [*Raising her voice.*] Bring a pitcher of cool water. [*To* ADELA.] You can sit down.

[ADELA *sits down.*]

PRUDENCIA: And Angustias, when will she get married?

BERNARDA: They're coming to ask for her within three days.

PRUDENCIA: You must be happy.

ANGUSTIAS: Naturally!

AMELIA: [*To* MAGDALENA.] You've spilled the salt!

MAGDALENA: You can't possibly have worse luck than you're having.

AMELIA: It always brings bad luck.

BERNARDA: That's enough!

PRUDENCIA: [*To* ANGUSTIAS.] Has he given you the ring yet?

ANGUSTIAS: Look at it. [*She holds it out.*]

PRUDENCIA: It's beautiful. Three pearls. In my day, pearls signified tears.

ANGUSTIAS: But things have changed now.

ADELA: I don't think so. Things go on meaning the same. Engagement rings should be diamonds.

PONCIA: The most appropriate.

BERNARDA: With pearls or without them, things are as one proposes.

MARTIRIO: Or as God disposes.

PRUDENCIA: I've been told your furniture is beautiful.

BERNARDA: It cost sixteen thousand *reales.*

PONCIA: [*Interrupting.*] The best is the wardrobe with the mirror.

PRUDENCIA: I never saw a piece like that.

BERNARDA: We had chests.

PRUDENCIA: The important thing is that everything be for the best.

ADELA: And that you never know.

BERNARDA: There's no reason why it shouldn't be.

[*Bells are heard very distantly.*]

PRUDENCIA: The last call. [*To* ANGUSTIAS.] I'll be coming back to have you show me your clothes.

ANGUSTIAS: Whenever you like.

PRUDENCIA: Good evening—God bless you!

BERNARDA: Good-bye, Prudencia.

ALL FIVE DAUGHTERS: [*At the same time.*] God go with you!

[*Pause,* PRUDENCIA *goes out.*]

BERNARDA: Well, we've eaten.

[*They rise.*]

ADELA: I'm going to walk as far as the gate to stretch my legs and get a bit of fresh air.

[MAGDALENA *sits down in a low chair and leans against the wall.*]

AMELIA: I'll go with you.

MARTIRIO: I too.

ADELA: [*With contained hate.*] I'm not going to get lost!

AMELIA: One needs company at night.

[*They go out.* BERNARDA *sits down.* ANGUSTIAS *is clearing the table.*]

BERNARDA: I've told you once already! I want you to talk to your sister Martirio. What happened about the picture was a joke and you must forget it.

ANGUSTIAS: You know she doesn't like me.

BERNARDA: Each one knows what she thinks inside. I don't pry into anyone's heart, but I want to put up a good front and have family harmony. You understand?

ANGUSTIAS: Yes.

BERNARDA: Then that's settled.

MAGDALENA: [*She is almost asleep.*] Besides, you'll be gone in no time. [*She falls asleep.*]

ANGUSTIAS: Not soon enough for me.

BERNARDA: What time did you stop talking last night?

ANGUSTIAS: Twelve-thirty.

BERNARDA: What does Pepe talk about?

ANGUSTIAS: I find him absent-minded. He always talks to me as though he were thinking of something else. If I ask him what's the matter, he answers—"We men have our worries."

BERNARDA: You shouldn't ask him. And when you're married, even less. Speak if he speaks, and look at him when he looks at you. That way you'll get along.

ANGUSTIAS: But, Mother, I think he's hiding things from me.

BERNARDA: Don't try to find out. Don't ask him, and above all, never let him see you cry.

ANGUSTIAS: I should be happy, but I'm not.

BERNARDA: It's all the same.

ANGUSTIAS: Many nights I watch Pepe very closely through the window bars and he seems to fade away—as though he were hidden in a cloud of dust like those raised by the flocks.

BERNARDA: That's just because you're not strong.

ANGUSTIAS: I hope so!

BERNARDA: Is he coming tonight?

ANGUSTIAS: No, he went into town with his mother.

BERNARDA: Good, we'll get to bed early. Magdalena!

ANGUSTIAS: She's asleep.

[ADELA, MARTIRIO and AMELIA enter.]

AMELIA: What a dark night!

ADELA: You can't see two steps in front of you.

MARTIRIO: A good night for robbers, for anyone who needs to hide.

ADELA: The stallion was in the middle of the corral. White. Twice as large. Filling all the darkness.

AMELIA: It's true. It was frightening. Like a ghost.

ADELA: The sky has stars as big as fists.

MARTIRIO: This one stared at them till she almost cracked her neck.

ADELA: Don't you like them up there?

MARTIRIO: What goes on over the roof doesn't mean a thing to me. I have my hands full with what happens under it.

ADELA: Well, that's the way it goes with you!

BERNARDA: And it goes the same for you as for her.

ANGUSTIAS: Good night.

ADELA: Are you going to bed now?

ANGUSTIAS: Yes, Pepe isn't coming tonight.

[She goes out.]

ADELA: Mother, why, when a star falls or lightning flashes, does one say:

Holy Barbara, blessed on high
May your name be in the sky
With holy water written high?

BERNARDA: The old people know many things we've forgotten.

AMELIA: I close my eyes so I won't see them.

ADELA: Not I. I like to see what's quiet and been quiet for years on end, running with fire.

MARTIRIO: But all that has nothing to do with us.

BERNARDA: And it's better not to think about it.

ADELA: What a beautiful night! I'd like to stay up till very late and enjoy the breeze from the fields.

BERNARDA: But we have to go to bed. Magdalena!

AMELIA: She's just dropped off.

BERNARDA: Magdalena!

MAGDALENA: [Annoyed.] Leave me alone!

BERNARDA: To bed!

MAGDALENA: [Rising, in a bad humor.] You don't give anyone a moment's peace!

[She goes off grumbling.]

AMELIA: Good night!

[She goes out.]

BERNARDA: You two get along, too.

MARTIRIO: How is it Angustias' sweetheart isn't coming tonight?

BERNARDA: He went on a trip.

MARTIRIO: [Looking at ADELA.] Ah!

ADELA: I'll see you in the morning!

[She goes out. MARTIRIO drinks some water and goes out slowly, looking at the door to the yard. LA PONCIA enters.]

PONCIA: Are you still here?

BERNARDA: Enjoying this quiet and not seeing anywhere the "very grave thing" that's happening here—according to you.

PONCIA: Bernarda, let's not go any further with this.

BERNARDA: In this house there's no question of a yes or a no. My watchfulness can take care of anything.

PONCIA: Nothing's happening outside. That's true, all right. Your daughters act and are as though stuck in a cupboard. But neither you nor anyone else can keep watch inside a person's heart.

BERNARDA: My daughters breathe calmly enough.

PONCIA: That's your business, since you're their mother. I have enough to do just with serving you.

BERNARDA: Yes, you've turned quiet now.

PONCIA: I keep my place—that's all.

BERNARDA: The trouble is you've nothing to talk about. If there were grass in this house, you'd make it your business to put the neighbors' sheep to pasture here.

PONCIA: I hide more than you think.

BERNARDA: Do your sons still see Pepe at four in the morning? Are they still repeating this house's evil litany?

PONCIA: They say nothing.

BERNARDA: Because they can't. Because there's nothing for them to sink their teeth in. And all because my eyes keep constant watch!

PONCIA: Bernarda, I don't want to talk about this because I'm afraid of what you'll do. But don't you feel so safe.

BERNARDA: Very safe!

PONCIA: Who knows, lightning might strike suddenly. Who knows but what all of a sudden, in a rush of blood, your heart might stop.

BERNARDA: Nothing will happen here. I'm on guard now against all your suspicions.

PONCIA: All the better for you.

BERNARDA: Certainly, all the better!

SERVANT: [Entering.] I've just finished with the dishes. Is there anything else, Bernarda?

BERNARDA: [Rising.] Nothing. I'm going to get some rest.

PONCIA: What time do you want me to call you?

BERNARDA: No time. Tonight I intend to sleep well.

[She goes out.]

PONCIA: When you're powerless against the sea, it's easier to turn your back on it and not look at it.

SERVANT: She's so proud! She herself pulls the blindfold over her eyes.

PONCIA: I can do nothing. I tried to head things off, but now they frighten me too much. You feel this silence?—in each room there's a thunderstorm—and the day it breaks, it'll sweep all of us along with it. But I've said what I had to say.

SERVANT: Bernarda thinks nothing can stand against her, yet she doesn't know the strength a man has among women alone.

PONCIA: It's not all the fault of Pepe el Romano. It's true last year he was running after Adela; and she was crazy about him—but she ought to keep her place and not lead him on. A man's a man.

SERVANT: And some there are who believe he didn't have to talk many times with Adela.

PONCIA: That's true. [In a low voice.] And some other things.

SERVANT: I don't know what's going to happen here.

PONCIA: How I'd like to sail across the sea and leave this house, this battleground, behind!

SERVANT: Bernarda's hurrying the wedding and it's possible nothing will happen.

PONCIA: Things have gone much too far already. Adela is set no matter what comes, and the rest of them watch without rest.

SERVANT: Martirio too . . . ?

PONCIA: That one's the worst. She's a pool of poison. She sees El Romano is not for her, and she'd sink the world if it were in her hand to do so.

SERVANT: How bad they all are!

PONCIA: They're women without men, that's all. And in such matters even blood is forgotten. Sh-h-h-h! [She listens.]

SERVANT: What's the matter?

PONCIA: [She rises.] The dogs are barking.

SERVANT: Someone must have passed by the back door.

[ADELA enters wearing a white petticoat and corselet.]

PONCIA: Aren't you in bed yet?

ADELA: I want a drink of water. [She drinks from a glass on the table.]

PONCIA: I imagined you were asleep.

ADELIA: I got thirsty and woke up. Aren't you two going to get some rest?

SERVANT: Soon now.

[ADELA goes out.]

PONCIA: Let's go.

SERVANT: We've certainly earned some sleep. Bernarda doesn't let me rest the whole day.

PONCIA: Take the light.

SERVANT: The dogs are going mad.

PONCIA: They're not going to let us sleep.

[They go out. The stage is left almost dark. MARIA JOSEFA enters with a lamb in her arms.]

MARIA JOSEFA: [Singing.]
Little lamb, child of mine,
Let's go to the shore of the sea,
The tiny ant will be at his doorway,
I'll nurse you and give you your bread.
Bernarda, old leopard-face,
And Magdalena, hyena-face,
Little lamb . . .
Rock, rock-a-bye,
Let's go to the palms at Bethlehem's gate.
[She laughs.]
Neither you nor I would want to sleep
The door will open by itself
And on the beach we'll go and hide
In a little coral cabin.
Bernarda, old leopard-face,
And Magdalena, hyena-face,
Little lamb . . .
Rock, rock-a-bye,

Let's go to the palms at Bethlehem's gate.

[*She goes off singing.*]

[ADELA *enters. She looks about cautiously and disappears out the door leading to the corral.* MARTIRIO *enters by another door and stands in anguished watchfulness near the center of the stage. She also is in petticoats. She covers herself with a small black scarf.* MARIA JOSEFA *crosses before her.*]

MARTIRIO: Grandmother, where are you going?

MARIA JOSEFA: You are going to open the door for me? Who are you?

MARTIRIO: How did you get out here?

MARIA JOSEFA: I escaped. You, who are you?

MARTIRIO: Go back to bed.

MARIA JOSEFA: You're Martirio. Now I see you. Martirio, face of a martyr. And when are you going to have a baby? I've had this one.

MARTIRIO: Where did you get that lamb?

MARIA JOSEFA: I know it's a lamb. But can't a lamb be a baby? It's better to have a lamb than not to have anything. Old Bernarda, leopard-face, and Magdalena, hyena-face!

MARTIRIO: Don't shout.

MARIA JOSEFA: It's true. Everything's very dark. Just because I have white hair you think I can't have babies, but I can— babies and babies and babies. This baby will have white hair, and I'd have *this* baby, and another, and this *one* other; and with all of us with snow white hair we'll be like the waves—one, then another, and another. Then we'll all sit down and all of us will have white heads, and we'll be seafoam. Why isn't there any seafoam here? Nothing but mourning shrouds here.

MARTIRIO: Hush, hush.

MARIA JOSEFA: When my neighbor had a baby, I'd carry her some chocolate and later she'd bring me some, and so on—always and always and always. You'll have white hair, but your neighbors won't come. Now I have to go away, but I'm afraid the dogs will bite me. Won't you come with me as far as the fields? I don't like fields. I like houses, but open houses, and the neighbor women asleep in their beds with their little tiny tots, and the men outside sitting in their chairs. Pepe el Romano is a giant. All of you love him. But he's going to devour you because you're grains of wheat. No, not grains of wheat. Frogs with no tongues!

MARTIRIO: [*Angrily.*] Come, off to bed with you. [*She pushes her.*]

MARIA JOSEFA: Yes, but then you'll open the door for me, won't you?

MARTIRIO: Of course.

MARIA JOSEFA: [*Weeping.*]
Little lamb, child of mine,
Let's go to the shore of the sea,
The tiny ant will be at his doorway,
I'll nurse you and give you your bread.

[MARTIRIO *locks the door through which* MARIA JOSEFA *came out and goes to the yard door. There she hesitates, but goes two steps farther.*]

MARTIRIO: [*In a low voice.*] Adela! [*Pause. She advances to the door. Then, calling.*] Adela!

[ADELA *enters. Her hair is disarranged.*]

ADELA: And what are you looking for me for?

MARTIRIO: Keep away from him.

ADELA: Who are you to tell me that?

MARTIRIO: That's no place for a decent woman.

ADELA: How you wish *you'd* been there!

MARTIRIO: [*Shouting.*] This is the moment for me to speak. This can't go on.

ADELA: This is just the beginning. I've had strength enough to push myself forward—the spirit and looks you lack. I've seen death under this roof, and gone out to look for what was mine, what belonged to me.

MARTIRIO: That soulless man came for another woman. You pushed yourself in front of him.

ADELA: He came for the money, but his eyes were always on me.

MARTIRIO: I won't allow you to snatch him away. He'll marry Angustias.

ADELA: You know better than I he doesn't love her.

MARTIRIO: I know.

ADELA: You know because you've seen— he loves me, me!

MARTIRIO: [*Desperately.*] Yes.

ADELA: [*Close before her.*] He loves me, *me!* He loves me, *me!*

MARTIRIO: Stick me with a knife if you like, but don't tell me that again.

ADELA: That's why you're trying to fix it so I won't go away with him. It makes no difference to you if he puts his arms around a woman he doesn't love. Nor does it to me. He could be a hundred years with Angustias, but for him to have his arms around me seems terrible to you—because you too love him! You love him!

MARTIRIO: [*Dramatically.*] Yes! Let me say it without hiding my head. Yes! My breast's bitter, bursting like a pomegranate. I love him!

ADELA: [*Impulsively, hugging her.*] Martirio, Martirio, I'm not to blame!

MARTIRIO: Don't put your arms around me! Don't try to smooth it over. My blood's no longer yours, and even though I try to think of you as a sister, I see you as just another woman. [*She pushes her away.*]

ADELA: There's no way out here. Whoever has to drown—let her drown. Pepe is mine. He'll carry me to the rushes along the river bank. . . .

MARTIRIO: He won't!

ADELA: I can't stand this horrible house after the taste of his mouth. I'll be what he wants me to be. Everybody in the village against me, burning me with their fiery fingers; pursued by those who claim they're decent, and I'll wear, before them all, the crown of thorns that belongs to the mistress of a married man.

MARTIRIO: Hush!

ADELA: Yes, yes. [*In a low voice.*] Let's go to bed. Let's let him marry Angustias. I don't care any more, but I'll go off alone to a little house where he'll come to see me whenever he wants, whenever he feels like it.

MARTIRIO: That'll never happen! Not while I have a drop of blood left in my body.

ADELA: Not just weak you, but a wild horse I could force to his knees with just the strength of my little finger.

MARTIRIO: Don't raise that voice of yours to me. It irritates me. I have a heart full of a force so evil that, without my wanting to be, I'm drowned by it.

ADELA: You show us the way to love our sisters. God must have meant to leave me alone in the midst of darkness, because I can see you as I've never seen you before.

[*A whistle is heard and* ADELA *runs toward the door, but* MARTIRIO *gets in front of her.*]

MARTIRIO: Where are you going?

ADELA: Get away from that door!

MARTIRIO: Get by me if you can!

ADELA: Get away!

[*They struggle.*]

MARTIRIO: [*Shouts.*] Mother! Mother!

ADELA: Let me go!

[BERNARDA *enters. She wears petticoats and a black shawl.*]

BERNARDA: Quiet! Quiet! How poor I am without even a man to help me!

MARTIRIO: [*Pointing to* ADELA.] She was with him. Look at those skirts covered with straw!

BERNARDA: [*Going furiously toward* ADELA.] That's the bed of a bad woman!

ADELA: [*Facing her.*] There'll be an end to prison voices here!

[ADELA *snatches away her mother's cane and breaks it in two.*]

This is what I do with the tyrant's cane. Not another step. No one but Pepe commands me!

[MAGDALENA *enters.*]

MAGDALENA: Adela!

[LA PONCIA *and* ANGUSTIAS *enter.*]

ADELA: I'm his. [*To* ANGUSTIAS.] Know that—and go out in the yard and tell him. He'll be master in this house.

ANGUSTIAS: My God!

BERNARDA: The gun! Where's the gun? [*She rushes out,* MARTIRIO *following.* AMELIA *enters and looks on frightened, leaning her head against the wall.*]

ADELA: No one can hold me back! [*She tries to go out.*]

ANGUSTIAS: [*Holding her.*] You're not getting out of here with your body's triumph! Thief! Disgrace of this house!

MAGDALENA: Let her go where we'll never see her again!

[*A shot is heard.*]

BERNARDA: [*Entering.*] Just try looking for him now!

MARTIRIO: [*Entering.*] That does away with Pepe el Romano.

ADELA: Pepe! My God! Pepe!

PONCIA: Did you kill him?

MARTIRIO: No. He raced away on his mare!

BERNARDA: It was my fault. A woman can't aim.

MAGDALENA: Then, why did you say . . . ?

MARTIRIO: For her! I'd like to pour a river of blood over her head!

PONCIA: Curse you!

MAGDALENA: Devil!

BERNARDA: Although it's better this way!

[*A thud is heard.*]

Adela! Adela!

PONCIA: [*At her door.*] Open this door!

BERNARDA: Open! Don't think the walls will hide your shame!

SERVANT: [*Entering.*] All the neighbors are up!

BERNARDA: [*In a low voice, but like a roar.*] Open! Or I'll knock the door down! [*Pause. Everything is silent.*]

Adela! [*She walks away from the door.*] A hammer!

[LA PONCIA *throws herself against the door. It opens and she goes in. As she enters, she screams and backs out.*]

What is it?

PONCIA: [*She puts her hands to her throat.*] May we never die like that!

[THE SISTERS *fall back.* THE SERVANT *crosses herself.* BERNARDA *screams and goes forward.*]

Don't go in!

BERNARDA: No, not I! Pepe, you're running now, alive, in the darkness, under the trees, but another day you'll fall. Cut her down! My daughter died a virgin. Take her to another room and dress her as though she were a virgin. No one will say anything about this! She died a virgin. Tell them, so that at dawn, the bells will ring twice.

MARTIRIO: A thousand times happy she, who had him.

BERNARDA: And I want no weeping. Death must be looked at face to face. Silence! [*To one daughter.*] Be still, I said! [*To another daughter.*] Tears when you're alone! We'll drown ourselves in a sea of mourning. She, the youngest daughter of Bernarda Alba, died a virgin. Did you hear me? Silence, silence, I said. Silence!

CURTAIN

JEAN GIRAUDOUX

DISSERTATION ON THE THEATER [1]

The problem of the theater and of spectacles, which has played
a leading and sometimes decisive role in the history of nations,
has lost none of its importance in an age when the eight or
seven-hour day has multiplied the time available to every citizen for leisure and amusement. The sole form of a nation's
moral or artistic education is theater. It provides, in the evening, the only worthwhile course in adult education; it is the
only way by which the most humble and least educated part of
the public can have personal contact with the loftiest conflicts
and can create for itself a secular religion—rites and saints,
sentiments and passions. Some nations dream, but for those
who do not there is theater. The intellectual clarity of the
French people does not in any way imply rejection of great
spiritual presences. The cult of the dead, this domineering
cult of heroes, really proves that the French love to see exalted
figures, close to them yet inaccessible, enact, in a higher, un-
limited region of nobleness, their own humble and limited
lives. . . .

The theater, the novel, and even literary criticism, instead
of being incidental to a superficial and tranquilly bourgeois
life, have again become, in our own age as in every full and
anguished age, greatly needed implements. That quartering of
literature into so many fragments, performed for the benefit of
salons and gala gatherings in a blissful century when novelists,
journalists, dramatists and philosophers were encouraged to
form so many independent and hostile brotherhoods, now no
longer has any reason to continue. The man of letters feels at
home in the theater, newspaper office and advertising agency:
he invades them. The heart of literature, the magnet that will
again pull so many scattered bits into one group, has again
been found; it is the writer, it is writing. Every great upheaval
in thought and manners diminishes the importance of literary
genres as such, but it heightens a hundredfold the function of
the writer by returning his universality to him. Our age does

[1] Jean Giraudoux, from "Dissertation on the Theater," *Littérature*
(Paris, 1941), pp. 198–9, 203–4. Copyright 1941. This selection trans-
lated by Martin Stanford. Reprinted by permission of Ninon Tallon
Karlweis and Jean-Pierre Giraudoux.

not ask the man of letters to produce more works—streets and alleys are filled with these unwanted effects—it craves from him above all a language. What it no longer expects is to have the writer, either as clown or happy monarch, enunciate his truths in tame, well-made plays and novels, in criticisms as contemptible as flattery. What the public of our age does expect of a writer is that he reveal truth as he sees it, that he disclose, so the public might organize its thought and feeling, the secret of which he alone is trustee—style. Our age also craves the same thing of theater. The protests of persons who do not wish to distinguish between dramatic works that have as their goal the formation of the public and those that aim only to fawn or to please are now no longer of any consequence; for the theater-going public does not experience, in hearing a dramatic work, what the semiliterate call boredom. A seat in the theater has for the public the extraterritoriality of an embassy in the kingdom of antiquity or of heroic ages, in the realm of the illogical and of the fantastic. And the public, while at the theater, intends to uphold the solemn character of this realm. The affection the public nourishes for verse drama lies in this very veneration of style and vocabulary. It likes the craftsmanship of well-turned verses, the care and scruple that this presupposes on the part of the poet. But when a writer reveals that prose is not slipshod, not coarse, not obscene, not indifferent, the public asks nothing more than to believe it. It is stirred to see actors and actresses suddenly exchanging, in place of that paper money that is the usual theatrical style, sentences which reveal that what a people possesses of greatest value, its language, is also a fund of gold.

JEAN GIRAUDOUX

Ondine

CHARACTERS

(IN ORDER OF APPEARANCE)

AUGUSTE.	MATHO.
EUGENIE.	SALAMMBO.
RITTER HANS.	A LORD.
ONDINE.	A LADY.
THE ONDINES.	THE ILLUSIONIST, *the old one.*
THE OLD ONE.	THE KING.
THE LORD CHAMBERLAIN.	A SERVANT.
THE SUPERINTENDENT OF THE THEATRE.	THE FIRST FISHERMAN.
THE TRAINER OF SEALS.	THE SECOND FISHERMAN, *the old one.*
BERTHA.	THE FIRST JUDGE.
BERTRAM.	THE SECOND JUDGE.
VIOLANTE.	THE EXECUTIONER.
ANGELIQUE.	THE KITCHEN MAID.
VENUS.	

ACT ONE: *A Fisherman's Cottage.*
ACT TWO: *A Hall in the King's Palace.*
ACT THREE: *The Courtyard in the Castle of the Wittenstein.*
TIME: *The Middle Ages.*

ACT ONE

A fisherman's hut near a lake in the forest. The living room has a fireplace, a door that leads into the kitchen, and a door that leads out into the forest. The windows are shuttered. There is a table near the fireplace, with a bench next to it and a heavy wooden chair next to the fire, which is blazing. It is night. A storm is raging.

Two old people, AUGUSTE *and* EUGENIE, *are in the room.* EUGENIE *is setting the table.* AUGUSTE *is at the window. He has opened the shutters and is peering out into the storm.*

AUGUSTE: What can she be doing out there at this hour?

EUGENIE: Don't worry about her. She can see in the dark.

AUGUSTE: In this storm!

EUGENIE: She's quite safe. The rain doesn't wet her.

AUGUSTE: She's singing. Is it she that's singing? You think that's her voice?

EUGENIE: Whose else? There is no other house within twenty leagues.

AUGUSTE: Now it comes from the top of the waterfall and now from the middle of the lake.

EUGENIE: Because now she's on top of the waterfall and now in the middle of the lake.

AUGUSTE: It's all so simple, isn't it? But did you, by any chance, ever amuse yourself by diving down the waterfalls in the nude when you were her age?

EUGENIE: Yes. Once. They fished me out by the feet. Every girl tries just once to do what Ondine does fifty times a day. I jumped into the whirlpool once, and I tried to catch the waterfall once in a bowl, and once I tried to walk on the water. It seems very long ago.

AUGUSTE: You've spoiled her, Eugenie. A girl of sixteen has no business running around in the forest in the dark in a storm. A well-brought-up girl does not insist on doing her sewing on the brink of a waterfall. She doesn't insist on saying her prayers under water. Where would we be today if you had been brought up like that?

EUGENIE: She's very helpful with the housework.

AUGUSTE: That brings up another question.

EUGENIE: Doesn't she wash the dishes? Doesn't she clean your boots?

AUGUSTE: I don't know. Does she?

EUGENIE: It's not clean, this dish?

AUGUSTE: That's not the point. Have you ever, in all her life, seen her cleaning or washing anything?

EUGENIE: What difference does it make whether or not I've seen her? She gets it done.

AUGUSTE: Yes. But explain this—three dishes or twelve, one shoe or eight, it takes her exactly the same time to do them. She takes them out; she's hardly gone a minute, and she's back. The dishcloth is dry. The shoe polish hasn't been used. But everything is clean, everything sparkles. And that affair of the golden plates on her birthday—did you ever get to the bottom of that? And her hands. Why are they never soiled, like anyone else's?

EUGENIE: Because she's not like anyone else. She's never been like anyone else.

AUGUSTE: Today she lifted the gate of the trout pond. All the trout are gone. All but the one I brought home for supper. Are you going to broil it? [*The windows spring open suddenly.*] Who did that?

EUGENIE: The wind, Auguste.

AUGUSTE: I hope she doesn't start that performance again with the lightning, and those horrible heads that peer in at the window out of the storm. The old man with the crown—oh!

EUGENIE: I love the woman with the pearls. Well, bar the window if you're afraid.

[AUGUSTE *crosses to close the window. There is a flash of lightning. The head of an old man with a crown and a streaming beard appears in the window frame.*]

THE HEAD: No use, Auguste. No lock so strong, no bar so stout will serve to keep the old one out!

[*He vanishes, laughing, in a clap of thunder.*]

AUGUSTE: I'll show you if it's too late, Ondine.

[*He closes the window. It immediately bursts open. There appears, in another lightning flash, a charming naiad's head with a necklace of pearls.*]

THE NAIAD: Good evening, Eugenie! [*It vanishes.*]

EUGENIE: Ondine, you're annoying your father. It's time to come in.

AUGUSTE: Ondine, I'm going to count up to three. If you're not inside when I finish, I'll bolt the door. And you can sleep out.

[*There is a roar of thunder.*]

EUGENIE: You're not serious?

AUGUSTE: You'll see if I'm serious. Ondine, one!

[*A roar of thunder.*]

EUGENIE: Stop it, Auguste. It's deafening.

AUGUSTE: Am I doing it?

EUGENIE: Well, then, hurry. We all know you can count up to three.

AUGUSTE: Ondine, two! [*Thunder. EUGENIE covers her ears.*]

EUGENIE: Really, Auguste, I don't see the use——

AUGUSTE: Ondine, three!

EUGENIE: [*Waiting for the thunder.*] Well, well, finish, Auguste, finish—

[*There is no thunder.*]

AUGUSTE: I've finished. [*He bolts the door.*] There. I'd like to see anyone come in now.

[*The door springs open. They turn in terror. A knight in full armor stands on the threshold. He holds his helmet under his arm.*]

RITTER HANS: [*Clicking his heels.*] Ritter Hans von Wittenstein zu Wittenstein.

AUGUSTE: [*Bows.*] My name is Auguste. I am a fisherman.

RITTER HANS: I took the liberty of putting my horse in your shed. The horse, as we know, is the most important part of the knight-errant. And the most sensitive.

AUGUSTE: I'll go and rub him down at once, my lord.

HANS: Thanks very much. I've already done it. I make it an invariable rule, away from home, to rub down my horse myself. In these parts, you rub horses down Swabian fashion, against the grain—the coat soon loses its luster. May I sit down?

AUGUSTE: The house is yours, my lord.

HANS: [*Sets down his helmet and puts by his sword.*] What a storm! The water has been running down my neck steadily since noon. Of course it doesn't stay. It runs out again through the blood gutters. But once it gets in, the damage is done. [*He sits down ponderously.*] That's what we fear most, we knights-errant, the rain. The water. And, of course, a flea. Once a flea gets in here—

AUGUSTE: Would you care to remove your armor, my lord?

HANS: My dear Auguste, have you ever watched a lobster shed his carapace? Then you know it's not the affair of a moment. I will rest first. You said your name was Auguste, I believe?

AUGUSTE: And my wife, Eugenie.

HANS: [*Bows to EUGENIE.*] Ah. Auguste and Eugenie. Charming names.

EUGENIE: Excuse them, my lord. They are not names for knights-errant.

HANS: Dear Eugenie, when a knight-errant has spent a month in the forest, searching in vain for Osmond and Pharamond, you cannot imagine his joy when he comes suddenly at dinner time upon Auguste and Eugenie.

EUGENIE: Thank you, my lord. It's ill-mannered, I know, to annoy a guest with questions, but perhaps you will forgive this one: are you hungry?

HANS: I am hungry. I am extremely hungry. It will give me great pleasure to share your meal.

EUGENIE: We have already supped, my lord. But there is a trout. Would you honor us by eating it?

HANS: With the greatest pleasure.

EUGENIE: Would you like it broiled or fried?

HANS: Poached, if you please.

[AUGUSTE *and* EUGENIE *make a gesture of fear.*]

EUGENIE: Poached? I really do them best *sautée, meunière,* with a little white butter. It's very good.

HANS: Since you ask my preference—

AUGUSTE: *Gratinée,* perhaps with fresh cream? Eugenie's specialty.

HANS: When we say poached—that's

when the fish is thrown into the boiling water alive?

EUGENIE: Yes. Alive.

HANS: So that the fish retains all its tenderness because the heat takes it by surprise?

AUGUSTE: Surprise is the word, my lord.

HANS: Then that's it. I'll have it poached.

EUGENIE: [*Walks slowly to the kitchen. She turns at the door.*] Broiled, they're very nice, with a slice of lemon—

HANS: Poached, if you please. [EUGENIE *goes into the kitchen.* HANS *makes himself comfortable in the chair by the fireside.*] I'm happy to see, Auguste, that knights-errant are not unwelcome in these parts . . . ?

AUGUSTE: Much more welcome than armies, my lord. When the winter is over, the robins come; when the wars are over, the knights. A knight-errant is a sign of peace.

HANS: I love war.

AUGUSTE: Each to his taste, my lord.

HANS: Don't misunderstand me. [*Expansively.*] If I love war, it's because by nature I'm a friendly person. I love company. Now in a war, you always have someone to talk to. If your comrades don't feel like chatting, there's always the enemy—you can always get yourself a prisoner. He shows you his wife's picture. You tell him about your sister. That's what I call living. But a knight-errant . . . ! Would you believe it, in all the time I've spent riding about this enchanted forest, I haven't so much as heard a human voice.

AUGUSTE: But isn't it true that knights-errant can understand the language of animals?

HANS: Ah, yes, that's true enough—they speak to us, the animals. And we understand them very well. But it's not quite what you think, the language of animals. For us every animal is a symbol, naturally, and its message is written indelibly on our souls. But that's it, you see, the animals write—they don't speak.

AUGUSTE: They don't speak?

HANS: They speak without speaking. What they say is important, of course. The stag speaks to us of nobility. The unicorn, of chastity. The lion, of courage. It's stimulating—but you don't call that a conversation.

AUGUSTE: But the birds . . . ?

HANS: To tell you the truth, Auguste,

I'm a little disappointed in the birds. They chatter incessantly. But they're not good listeners. They're always preaching.

AUGUSTE: That surprises me. Especially with the lark. I should have thought the lark would love to confide in one.

HANS: The knight's headgear does not permit him to converse with larks.

AUGUSTE: But what sent you, if I may ask, into the black forest?

HANS: What do you suppose? A woman.

AUGUSTE: I ask no more questions, my lord.

HANS: Please, Auguste! It's thirty days since I've said a word about her to a living soul. No, no, ask me questions. Ask me anything. Ask me her name.

AUGUSTE: My lord—I wouldn't dare.

HANS: Ask me. Ask me.

AUGUSTE: What is her name, my lord?

HANS: Bertha. Bertha! Tell me, fisherman, have you ever heard such a beautiful name? Bertha!

AUGUSTE: It's beautiful, my lord.

HANS: There are those who are called Angelique, Diane, Violante. Anybody can be called Angelique, Diane, Violante. But she alone deserves a name so solemn, vibrating, passionate: Bertha! [EUGENIE *comes in with a loaf of bread.*] And now, Eugenie, you will ask me is she beautiful?

EUGENIE: Is she beautiful?

AUGUSTE: We are speaking of Bertha, the Princess Bertha, Eugenie.

EUGENIE: Ah, yes, of course. And is she beautiful?

HANS: Eugenie, it is I who am entrusted with the purchase of horses for the king. You understand, then, my eye is sharp. No blemish, however slight, ever escapes me. The Angelique in question is not bad, but she has a ridge in her left thumbnail. Violante has a fleck of gold in her eye. Bertha is flawless.

AUGUSTE: That must be a lovely thing to see, a fleck of gold in a woman's eye.

EUGENIE: Stick to your fishing, Auguste.

HANS: A fleck of gold? Don't deceive yourself, my dear fellow. That might amuse you, a thing like that, for a day, two days at the most—

AUGUSTE: What is it like, exactly?

HANS: Well, it sparkles.

AUGUSTE: Like a grain of mica?

EUGENIE: Come, Auguste—you're getting on our nerves with your gold and your mica. Let the knight speak.

HANS: Yes, my dear Auguste, why this sudden partiality for Violante? Violante, when she joins with us in the hunt, crowns a white mare. And it's a pretty sight, a red-headed girl on a white mare, there's no denying it. And Violante, when she brings the queen the three-branched candlestick, always bears it high in both hands, like the celebrant approaching the altar. But Violante, when the old Duke takes her hand and tells her a spicy story, never laughs. She cries.

AUGUSTE: Violante cries?

HANS: I know. You are going to ask me what happens to these flecks of gold when they are drowned in tears—

EUGENIE: He's surely thinking of it, my lord. Once he gets his mind on anything . . . !

HANS: Yes, he will think of it till the day when he sees Bertha. For you shall certainly come to our wedding, both of you. You are invited. The condition Bertha made to our marriage was that I should come back alive after spending a month in the forest. And if I do come back, it will be thanks to you, my friends. And so, you shall see your Violante, fisherman, with her little red mouth and her pink ears and her little straight nose, you shall see what effect she makes next to my great dark angel! And now, fetch me my poached trout, Eugenie, or it will be overdone.

[*The door opens slowly.* ONDINE *appears on the threshold. She stands there motionless for a moment.*]

AUGUSTE: Ondine!

ONDINE: How beautiful he is!

AUGUSTE: What did she say?

ONDINE: I said, how beautiful he is!

AUGUSTE: It is our daughter, my lord. She has no manners.

ONDINE: It's thrilling to know that men are so beautiful. My heart is racing.

AUGUSTE: Will you keep still?

ONDINE: I'm trembling from head to foot.

AUGUSTE: She's only sixteen, my lord.

ONDINE: I knew there must be some reason for being a girl. The reason is that men are so beautiful.

AUGUSTE: You are embarrassing our guest, Ondine.

ONDINE: I'm not embarrassing him. He likes me. What's your name?

AUGUSTE: That's not the way to speak to a knight, my child.

ONDINE: [*Coming closer.*] Look at his ear,

Father. It's a perfect little shell. Do you expect me to treat it like a stranger? To whom do you belong, little shell? What is his name?

HANS: His name is Hans.

ONDINE: I should have guessed it. When people are happy and they open their mouths, they say Hans.

HANS: Hans von Wittenstein.

ONDINE: When there is sun in the morning, and the cloud of sadness lifts from your soul, when you sigh, you say Hans.

HANS: Hans von Wittenstein zu Wittenstein.

ONDINE: How lovely when a name makes its own echo! Why have you come, Hans? To take me away?

AUGUSTE: That will do, Ondine. Go to your room now.

ONDINE: Very well, take me. Take me with you.

[EUGENIE *comes in with the trout on a platter.*]

EUGENIE: Here is your trout, my lord.

ONDINE: His trout!

HANS: It looks magnificent.

ONDINE: You dared to poach a trout, Mother?

EUGENIE: Be quiet. In any case, it's done.

ONDINE: Oh, my poor darling trout! You who loved the cold water! What have they done to you?

AUGUSTE: You're not going to make a scene before our guest, Ondine?

ONDINE: They caught you—and they quenched your life in boiling water!

HANS: It was I, my girl, who asked them to.

ONDINE: You? I should have known. When one looks closely at your face, it all becomes clear. You're not very bright, are you? No. You are stupid.

EUGENIE: She doesn't know what she's saying, my lord.

ONDINE: That's chivalry! That's courage! You run about looking for giants who don't exist, and when you come upon a little joyous creature springing in the clear water, you boil it alive.

HANS: And I eat it. And I find it delicious.

ONDINE: You shall see how delicious it is! [*She snatches up the dish and throws it out of the window.*] Now eat it! [*She runs to the door.*]

AUGUSTE: Ondine!

EUGENIE: Where are you going, child?

ONDINE: There is someone out there who knows about men. So far I have refused to listen to him. Now that's over. I shall listen.

AUGUSTE: Ondine!

ONDINE: In a moment, I shall know. I shall know what they are, what they do, what they become. And so much the worse for you!

AUGUSTE: You're not going out. [*She springs aside.*]

ONDINE: I already know that they lie, that their beauty is ugliness, that their courage is cowardice. And I already know that I hate them.

HANS: And they already know that they love you.

ONDINE: [*Stops at the door, without turning.*] What did he say?

HANS: Nothing.

ONDINE: Say it once more, just to see.

HANS: They already know that they love you.

ONDINE: I hate them! [*She runs out into the darkness.*]

HANS: My compliments. You've brought her up well.

AUGUSTE: God knows I scold her often enough.

HANS: You should beat her.

EUGENIE: Beat her? Try and catch her.

HANS: You should send her to bed without supper.

AUGUSTE: What good would that do? She's never hungry.

HANS: I'm starved.

AUGUSTE: That was the last of the trout, my lord. But we have smoked a ham. Eugenie will go down and cut you some slices.

HANS: Then she permits you to kill her poor darling pigs?

AUGUSTE: She has no interest in pigs.

HANS: That's a mercy.

[EUGENIE *goes out for the ham.*]

AUGUSTE: You are annoyed with the girl, my lord.

HANS: I'm annoyed because I'm vain just as she said. When she said I was handsome, though I know I'm not handsome, I was pleased. And when she said I was a coward, though I know I'm no coward, I was hurt. I'm annoyed with myself.

AUGUSTE: You're very kind to take it so well.

HANS: Oh, I don't take it well at all. I'm furious.

[EUGENIE *comes in.*]

EUGENIE: Where is the ham, Auguste? I can't find it.

AUGUSTE: The ham? Why, the ham is hanging in the cellar. Excuse me, my lord, I'll go and get it. [*He goes out with* EUGENIE. HANS *turns to the fire and warms his hands.* ONDINE *comes in noiselessly and stands just behind him. He doesn't hear her till she speaks.*]

ONDINE: My name is Ondine.

HANS: [*Without turning.*] It's a pretty name.

ONDINE: Hans and Ondine. There are no more beautiful names in the world, are there?

HANS: Yes. Ondine and Hans.

ONDINE: Oh no. Hans first. He is the man. He commands. Ondine is the girl. She is always one step behind. She keeps quiet.

HANS: She keeps quiet? Now how the devil does she manage that?

ONDINE: Hans is always one step ahead. In the processions—before the king—before all the world, he goes first. He is the first to age. He is the first to die. It's terrible! But Ondine follows at once. She kills herself.

HANS: What are you talking about?

ONDINE: There is the little moment of agony to live through. The moment that comes after the death of Hans. But it is short.

HANS: At your age, luckily, it doesn't mean much to talk about death.

ONDINE: At my age? Is that what you think? Very well, try— [*She pulls his dagger from its sheath.*] Here, kill yourself. You'll see if I am not dead the next moment.

HANS: [*Takes the dagger from her hand.*] I never felt less like killing myself.

ONDINE: Say you don't love me. You'll see if I don't die.

HANS: Fifteen minutes ago, you didn't even know I existed. And now you want to kill yourself on my account. I thought we had quarreled on account of the trout.

ONDINE: Oh, I can't be bothered with the trout. They're not very clever, the trout. If they don't like to be caught, all they have to do is to keep away from men. It's different with me. I want to be caught.

HANS: In spite of your mysterious friend outside?

ONDINE: I learned nothing from him that I didn't already know.

HANS: Naturally not. You asked the questions. You gave the answers.

ONDINE: Don't joke. He's very near. And he's very dangerous.

HANS: Who?

ONDINE: The Old One.

HANS: The Old One?

ONDINE: The King of the Sea. I'm afraid, Hans.

HANS: [*Smiles.*] You're afraid of what?

ONDINE: I'm afraid you will deceive me. That's what he said. He also said you were not handsome. But you are!

HANS: Do you know that you're beautiful?

ONDINE: No, I don't know it yet. I would prefer to be beautiful. But I can be beautiful only if I love you.

HANS: You're a little liar. You were just as beautiful a moment ago when you hated me. Is that all he told you?

ONDINE: He said that if ever I kissed you, I would be lost. That was silly of him. I hadn't even thought of it till then.

HANS: And now you are thinking of it?

ONDINE: Very much.

HANS: Well, there is no harm in thinking.

ONDINE: Oh no. It's good to think about it. Of course, in the end I shall do it. But first we shall wait a long time, as long as possible. We shall wait an hour. Then in after years we shall have this hour always to remember. The hour before you kissed me.

HANS: My little Ondine—

ONDINE: The hour before you said you loved me. Hans, I can't wait an hour. There isn't time. Tell me now.

HANS: You think that's something one says—just like that?

ONDINE: No? Well, then speak, command. What must I do? What is the appropriate posture? Do I sit in your lap, is that it?

HANS: In my lap in full armor?

ONDINE: Oh. Take it off quickly.

HANS: Do you know what you're saying? It takes me fifteen minutes to unbolt the shoulder-plates alone.

ONDINE: I have a way of removing armor. [*The armor falls to the floor.*]

HANS: Well!

ONDINE: Sit down. [*He sits. She springs into his lap.*]

HANS: You're mad, Ondine!

ONDINE: Yes. That's what he said.

HANS: And my arms—do you think they open to the first comer?

ONDINE: I have a way of opening arms— [HANS *opens his arms, with an expression of surprise.*] And of closing them. [*He closes them. A woman's voice is heard outside the window.*]

THE VOICE: Ondine!

ONDINE: [*Turns furiously to the window.*] No! Go away. Nobody called you.

THE VOICE: Ondine! Be careful!

ONDINE: Do I meddle in your affairs? Did you consult me about your husband?

THE VOICE: Ondine!

ONDINE: A fine handsome husband you found yourself, wasn't it? A seal with nostrils like rabbit holes and no nose. He gave you a string of pearls and you were his. And not even matched pearls.

HANS: To whom are you speaking, Ondine?

ONDINE: Oh, one of the neighbors.

HANS: But I saw no other house in the forest. Do you have neighbors?

ONDINE: Thousands. And all jealous.

A SECOND VOICE: Ondine! Be careful!

ONDINE: Oh, you're a fine one to speak! You were careful, weren't you? A narwhal dazzled you with his jet of water, and you gave yourself to him without a word.

THE SECOND VOICE: Ondine!

HANS: Their voices are charming.

ONDINE: My name is charming, not their voices. Kiss me, Hans. Kiss me.

A MAN'S VOICE: Ondine!

ONDINE: It's too late, Old One. Let me alone.

HANS: Is that the friend?

ONDINE: I'm sitting in his lap. He loves me.

THE MAN'S VOICE: Ondine!

ONDINE: It's too late, I say. It's finished. I'm already his mistress. Yes, his mistress. You don't understand? That's another word they have for a wife.

[*There is a noise at the kitchen door.*]

HANS: [*Pushing* ONDINE *gently from his lap.*] That's your father, Ondine.

ONDINE: Oh. I didn't think I had taught you that?

HANS: What?

ONDINE: My way of opening arms.

[AUGUSTE *and* EUGENIE *come in.*]

EUGENIE: Your supper is almost ready, my lord.

AUGUSTE: I can't imagine who put the ham in the attic.

ONDINE: I did. So I could be alone with Hans.

AUGUSTE: Ondine! Have you no shame?

ONDINE: I've not wasted my time. He's going to marry me.

AUGUSTE: You might help your mother with the table instead of talking nonsense.

ONDINE: You're right. Give me the silver, Mother. From now on, it's I who will serve Hans.

AUGUSTE: I brought up a bottle of wine, my lord. If you permit, we shall drink a glass with you. The glasses, Ondine.

ONDINE: You will have to teach me everything, my lord Hans. From morning to night, I shall be your handmaid. In the morning, I shall wake you. . . .

HANS: You won't find that easy. I sleep very soundly.

ONDINE: [Sits down next to him and looks at him closely.] Tell me, what does one do to awaken you?

[EUGENIE comes out with a platter.]

EUGENIE: The glasses, Ondine.

ONDINE: Oh Mother, you set the table. Hans is teaching me how to awaken him. Let's see, Hans. Make believe you're asleep.

HANS: With this wonderful odor of cooking? Out of the question.

ONDINE: Wake up, little Hans. It's dawn. Take this kiss in your darkness and this in your day . . .

HANS: [Accepting a slice of ham.] Thank you.

AUGUSTE: Pay no attention to the child, my lord. She doesn't know what she's saying.

ONDINE: I love you.

EUGENIE: She's young. She becomes attached. It's nothing.

ONDINE: I love you, Hans.

HANS: [Eating.] This is what I call ham!

AUGUSTE: It's smoked with juniper.

HANS: Marvelous.

ONDINE: It was a mistake to awaken you, Hans. We should never awaken the man we love. In his sleep, he's ours completely. But the moment he opens his eyes, he escapes. Sleep again, little Hans—

HANS: [Accepting another slice.] Yes, thank you. Simply wonderful.

ONDINE: You don't want to be loved, you want to be stuffed.

HANS: Everything in its place, my dear.

EUGENIE: Ah, you'd make a fine wife, you would!

ONDINE: I?

AUGUSTE: Silence, Ondine. I want to say a word. [He lifts his glass.]

ONDINE: I shall certainly make a fine wife. You think you're a wife because you know how to cook a ham? That's not being a wife.

HANS: No? What else is it?

ONDINE: It's to be everything your husband is and everything he loves. It's to be the humblest part of him and the noblest. I shall be the shoes of your feet, my husband. I shall be the breath of your lungs. I shall be the hilt of your sword and the pommel of your saddle. I shall be your tears, your laughter and your dreams. What you are eating there, it's I.

HANS: It's seasoned to perfection.

ONDINE: Eat me, Hans. Eat me all. [AUGUSTE clears his throat.]

EUGENIE: Your father wishes to speak, Ondine. Quiet.

AUGUSTE: [Lifting his glass again.] Quiet! My lord, since you are doing us the honor of spending the night under our humble roof—

ONDINE: A hundred nights. A thousand nights—

AUGUSTE: Permit me to drink to the lady of your heart—

ONDINE: How nice of you, Father!

AUGUSTE: She who is even now trembling for your safety—

ONDINE: She's not trembling now. He's safe enough.

AUGUSTE: She whom you rightly call the most beautiful of women, although for my part, I am a little partial to Violante on account of—

EUGENIE: Yes, yes, we know. Go on.

AUGUSTE: I drink, then, to the most beautiful and noblest of women, to your dark angel, to your betrothed, the Princess Bertha.

ONDINE: [Rising to her feet.] What name did you say?

AUGUSTE: The name the knight told me.

ONDINE: Since when am I called Bertha?

EUGENIE: We were not speaking of you, dear.

AUGUSTE: The knight is going to marry the Princess Bertha, Ondine, as soon as he returns to court. Isn't that so, my lord?

ONDINE: It's not so at all!

HANS: My little Ondine—

ONDINE: Ah, he's emerging from the

ham at last, that one. Well, speak, since your mouth is no longer full—is there a Bertha? Yes or no?

HANS: Let me explain—

ONDINE: Is there a Bertha? Yes or no?

HANS: Yes. There is a Bertha. No. There was a Bertha.

ONDINE: So it's true, what he told me about men! They're all deceivers. They draw you to them with a thousand tricks, they seat you in their laps, they pass their hands all over your body and kiss you till you can't breathe—and all the time they are thinking of a dark angel called Bertha!

HANS: I did nothing like that to you, Ondine!

ONDINE: You did. Don't you dare deny it. And you hurt me, too. [*She bites her arm.*] Look at that, Father. See how he bit me? Let him deny it, if he dares!

HANS: You don't believe this nonsense, I hope?

ONDINE: I shall be the humblest part of you and the noblest, he said. I am your bare feet. I am the wine you drink. I am the bread you eat. Those were his words, Mother! And the things one has to do for him! One has to spend the whole morning waking him up. One has to kill oneself the moment he dies. Yes! And all the time, in their secret hearts, they are nursing the thought of a dark angel called Bertha!

HANS: Ondine, on my word—

ONDINE: I despise you! I detest you!

HANS: Nevertheless, you might listen to me—

ONDINE: I can see her from here, the dark angel, with her little shadowy mustache and her plucked eyebrows.

HANS: Now, Ondine, really . . . !

ONDINE: Don't come near me! Or I'll throw myself into the lake. [*She opens the door. It is raining heavily.*] So her name is Bertha!

HANS: I think there is no longer any Bertha, Ondine.

ONDINE: Leave this house at once, or I shall never enter it again! [*She turns suddenly.*] What did you say?

HANS: I said, I think there is no longer any Bertha, Ondine.

ONDINE: You lie! Farewell. [*She runs out into the rain.*]

HANS: Ondine! [*He runs to the door.*]

AUGUSTE: My lord, my lord—you'll get drenched! [*To* EUGENIE.] There's a pretty kettle of fish.

EUGENIE: Yes, there's a pretty kettle of fish.

AUGUSTE: I might as well tell him everything now.

EUGENIE: Yes, you might as well tell him everything now. [HANS *turns.*]

HANS: She's not your daughter, is she?

EUGENIE: No, my lord.

AUGUSTE: We had a daughter. She was stolen from the cradle.

HANS: Who left Ondine with you?

AUGUSTE: We found her at the edge of the lake the day our daughter disappeared.

HANS: These things happen only in fairy tales.

AUGUSTE: Yes, my lord. But it happened to us.

HANS: Then it is you who must be asked for her hand?

AUGUSTE: She calls us her parents, my lord.

HANS: Then, my friends, I have the honor of asking you for the hand of your daughter.

AUGUSTE: My lord, are you in your right mind?

HANS: Do you think that little wine of yours would turn my head?

AUGUSTE: The wine? Oh, never. It's a little Moselle, very modest, very reliable.

HANS: I assure you, I have never been more sober in my life. I ask you for the hand of Ondine with nothing in mind but the hand of Ondine. I want to hold this hand in mine. I want it to lead me to church, to war, and when the time comes, to death.

AUGUSTE: But, my lord, you already have a hand for that. This would be a hand too many.

HANS: A hand? Whose hand?

AUGUSTE: The lady Bertha.

HANS: Bertha? Do you know Bertha? I know her. I know her, that is, now that I know Ondine—

AUGUSTE: But is not a knight, above all, required to be loyal?

HANS: To his quest, yes. And I shall be loyal, above all, to my quest. Because, you know, up to now, we knights have been fools, all of us. We've been exploited; they take us for imbeciles. When we kill a monster, we're expected to vanish gracefully. When we find a treasure, we give it away. Well, that's finished. From now on I shall try to profit a little by my exploits. I have found a treasure and I shall keep it.

Whether or not I knew it, my quest was Ondine, and I have found Ondine, and I shall marry Ondine. And nobody else in this world.

EUGENIE: You are making a mistake, my lord.

HANS: Eugenie—there was once a knight and his quest was to find something wonderful. And one night in a forest on the edge of a lake, he found a girl called Ondine. In her hands, tin turned to gold and water to jewels. The rain did not wet her. Her eyes were full of joy and her manner was royal. And not only was she the most wonderful creature he had ever seen, but he knew also that she would bring him all the delight and tenderness and goodness he would ever know in this world. Whereupon he bowed to her and went off to marry a girl called Bertha. Tell me, Eugenie, what sort of knight was this?

AUGUSTE: You don't put the question properly, my lord.

HANS: I ask you what sort of knight this would be. You don't dare to answer, but you know as well as I do. He would be a sort of idiot, would he not?

EUGENIE: But, my lord, since you have given your word to another—

HANS: He would be an idiot!

EUGENIE: Speak, Auguste.

HANS: Yes, speak. If there is any reason why I should not have Ondine, tell it to me now.

AUGUSTE: My lord, you are asking us for the hand of Ondine. It's a great honor for us—but she's not ours to give.

HANS: You must have some idea who her parents may be?

AUGUSTE: With Ondine it's not a question of parents. If we had not adopted Ondine, she would have grown up just the same. Ondine is strange. You saw her tonight in the storm. You understand, my lord, it's not that she's in the storm. She is the storm. She's a beautiful child, my lord, there's no denying it. But there is more than beauty in Ondine. There is power.

HANS: It's because she's young.

EUGENIE: It's true, she's young—

AUGUSTE: When I first married you, my poor Eugenie, you too were young. But your youth had no effect on the lake. You were beautiful. But the lake remained what it had always been, selfish and rude. And the floods were brutal and senseless as always, and the storm was a beast of prey.

But since Ondine came to us, everything has changed. The water has become gentle.

HANS: It's because you're old.

AUGUSTE: It's true I'm no longer young. But a lake that counts into your net each day exactly the same twelve fish, a lake that never enters your boat, not even if it happens to have a hole in the bottom—I think you will agree that is a remarkably courteous lake.

HANS: Well, suppose it is. What do you suggest? That I apply to the lake for permission to marry?

AUGUSTE: I wouldn't joke about the lake. The lake has ears.

HANS: And what's it to me if the lake has ears? I have no designs on the lake.

AUGUSTE: We are speaking of Ondine, my lord. Ondine belongs to the lake. Ondine is the lake, my lord.

HANS: Then I shall gladly take the lake to my bosom, and with it all the water in the world. The rivers shall be my brothers, the sea my mother, and the ocean itself my father-in-law. I love the water.

AUGUSTE: Beware of the water, my lord!

HANS: But why, Auguste? Why?

AUGUSTE: That's all I know, my lord.

HANS: Give me Ondine, Auguste.

AUGUSTE: Give you Ondine! And who am I to give you Ondine? Where is she now, Ondine? Oh, I remember, naturally, having seen her once, the little Ondine. I remember her voice, her laughter, I remember she threw your trout out of the window, a twelve-inch trout, the only one I had left. But we shall never see her again, she will never again come to us except in tender little lightnings, in little storms; she will never again tell us she loves us except with the waves lapping at our feet, or the rain on our cheeks, or perhaps, suddenly one day with a great salt-water fish in my pike-weir. That wouldn't surprise me a bit.

EUGENIE: Auguste, you're tired. It's time you came to bed.

AUGUSTE: Do you remember the morning we found her, Eugenie?

EUGENIE: Permit us to retire, my lord.

AUGUSTE: There wasn't a mark on the sand, not a footprint—nothing—to show how the child got there. Only the wind and the sun and the lake staring at us fixedly with its eye—

EUGENIE: I will show you to your room.

HANS: Thank you. I shall sit here by the fire a little longer, if I may.

EUGENIE: Come, Auguste. Tomorrow we shall speak of Ondine.

AUGUSTE: If there is an Ondine. [*He shakes his head.*]

EUGENIE: Good night, my lord.

HANS: Good night. Good night.

[AUGUSTE *and* EUGENIE *go out.* HANS *sits down by the fire and closes his eyes for a moment. The wall of the hut slowly becomes transparent, and through it appear the lake and the forest. In the half-light there rises the figure of an* ONDINE, *blonde and nude.*]

THE ONDINE: Take me, handsome knight.

HANS: [*Looking up with a start.*] What?

THE ONDINE: Kiss me.

HANS: I beg pardon?

THE ONDINE: Take me. Kiss me.

HANS: What are you talking about?

THE ONDINE: Am I too bold, handsome knight? Do I frighten you?

HANS: Not in the least.

THE ONDINE: Would you rather I were clothed? Shall I put on a dress?

HANS: A dress? What for?

THE ONDINE: Come to me. Take me. I am yours.

[*She vanishes. Another* ONDINE *appears. She is dark and clothed.*]

THE SECOND ONDINE: Don't look at me, handsome knight.

HANS: Why not?

THE SECOND ONDINE: Don't come near me. I'm not that sort. If you touch me, I'll scream.

HANS: Don't worry.

THE SECOND ONDINE: If you touch my hair, if you touch my breasts, if you kiss my lips, I swear, I'll kill myself. I will not take off my dress!

HANS: As you please.

THE SECOND ONDINE: Don't come out, handsome knight. Don't come near me. I am not for you, handsome knight. [*She vanishes.* HANS *shrugs his shoulders. The* TWO ONDINES *appear together at opposite sides of the room.*]

FIRST ONDINE: Take me.

SECOND ONDINE: Don't touch me.

FIRST ONDINE: I am yours.

SECOND ONDINE: Keep your distance.

FIRST ONDINE: I want you.

SECOND ONDINE: You frighten me.

ONDINE: [*Appears suddenly.*] Oh how silly you look, both of you!

[*The* TWO ONDINES *vanish.*]

HANS: [*Takes* ONDINE *in his arms.*] Lit-

tle Ondine! What is this nonsense? Who are those women?

ONDINE: My friends. They don't want me to love you. They say anyone can have you for the asking. But they're wrong.

HANS: They're very nice, your friends. Are those the prettiest?

ONDINE: The cleverest. Kiss me, Hans.

FIRST ONDINE: [*Reappears.*] Kiss me, Hans—

ONDINE: Look at that fool! Oh, how silly a woman looks when she offers herself! Go away! Don't you know when you've lost? Hans—

SECOND ONDINE: [*Appears again next to the first.*] Hans—

ONDINE: Go away, I say! Hans—

A THIRD ONDINE: [*Appears next to the others.*] Hans—

ONDINE: It's not fair! No!

HANS: Let them speak, Ondine.

ONDINE: No. It's the Song of the Three Sisters. I'm afraid.

HANS: Afraid? Of them?

ONDINE: Cover your ears, Hans.

HANS: But I love music.

THE FIRST ONDINE: [*Sings.*]
Hans Wittenstein zu Wittenstein,
Without you life is but a fever.
Alles was ist mein ist dein,
Love me always, leave me never.

HANS: Bravo! That's charming.

ONDINE: In what way is that charming?

HANS: It's simple. It's direct. It's charming. The song of the sirens must have been about like that.

ONDINE: It was exactly like that. They copied it. They're going to sing again. Don't listen.

THE THREE ONDINES: [*Sing.*]
Heed no more the west wind's urging,
Slack your sail and rest your oar.
Drift upon the current surging
Powerfully toward our shore.

HANS: The tune is not bad.

ONDINE: Don't listen, Hans.

THE THREE ONDINES: [*Sing.*]
Sorrow once for all forsaking,
Take our laughter for your sighs.
These are yours but for the taking,
Tender breasts and wanton thighs.

ONDINE: If you think it's pleasant to hear others singing the things one feels and can't express. . . .

THE THREE ONDINES: [*Sing.*]
Come and take your fill of pleasure,
Taste delight and drink it deep.

We shall give you beyond measure
Joy and rest and love and sleep.

HANS: That's wonderful! Sing it again! Sing it again!

ONDINE: Don't you understand? They don't mean a word of it. They're just trying to take you away from me.

THE FIRST ONDINE: You've lost, Ondine, you've lost!

HANS: What have you lost?

ONDINE: Your song means nothing to him!

FIRST ONDINE: He holds you in his arms, Ondine, but he looks at me!

SECOND ONDINE: He speaks your name, Ondine, but he thinks of me!

THIRD ONDINE: He kisses your lips, Ondine, but he smiles at me!

THE THREE ONDINES: He deceives you! He deceives you! He deceives you!

HANS: What are they talking about?

ONDINE: He may look at you and smile at you and think of you as much as he pleases. He loves me. And I shall marry him.

THE FIRST ONDINE: Then you agree? You make the pact.

HANS: What pact?

ONDINE: Yes. I agree. I make the pact. [*The words are taken up mysteriously. They echo and re-echo from every quarter.*]

THE FIRST ONDINE: I am to tell them?

ONDINE: Yes. Tell them. Tell them all. Those who sit and those who swim, those who float in the sunlight and those who crawl in darkness on the ocean floor.

HANS: What the devil are you saying?

ONDINE: Tell them I said yes. [*The word "yes" is taken up by a thousand whispering voices.*]

THE FIRST ONDINE: And the Old One? Shall we tell him also?

ONDINE: Tell him I hate him! Tell him he lies!

THE FIRST ONDINE: Yes?

ONDINE: Yes! Yes! Yes!

[*Again the sound is taken up. The mysterious voices whisper through the darkness until the air is filled with echoes. There is a climax of sound, then silence.* THE ONDINES *vanish. The walls of the hut regain their solidity.*]

HANS: What a fuss! What a racket!

ONDINE: Naturally. It's the family. [HANS *sits in the armchair.* ONDINE *sits at his feet.*] You're caught, my little Hans?

HANS: Body and soul.

ONDINE: You don't wish to struggle a little more? Just a little more?

HANS: I'm too happy to struggle.

ONDINE: So it takes twenty minutes to catch a man. It takes longer to catch a bass.

HANS: Don't flatter yourself. It took thirty years to catch me. All my life. Ever since I was a child, I've felt something drawing me toward this forest and this lake. It was you?

ONDINE: Yes. And now after thirty years, would it be too much if you told me at last that you love me?

HANS: I love you.

ONDINE: You say it easily. You've said it before.

HANS: I've said something like it that meant something else.

ONDINE: You've said it often?

HANS: I've said it to every woman I didn't love. And now at last I know what it means.

ONDINE: Why didn't you love them? Were they ugly?

HANS: No. They were beautiful. But they no longer exist.

ONDINE: Oh, Hans, I meant to give you everything in the world, and I begin by taking everything away. Some day you will hate me for it.

HANS: Never, Ondine.

ONDINE: Shall I ever see them, these women you don't love?

HANS: Of course.

ONDINE: Where?

HANS: Everywhere. In their castles. In their gardens. At the court.

ONDINE: At the court? I?

HANS: Of course. We leave in the morning.

ONDINE: Oh, Hans, am I to leave my lake so soon?

HANS: I want to show the world the most perfect thing it possesses. Did you know you were the most perfect thing the world possessed?

ONDINE: I suspected it. But will the world have eyes to see it?

HANS: When the world sees you, it will know. It's really very nice, Ondine, the world.

ONDINE: Tell me, Hans. In this world of yours, do lovers live together always?

HANS: Together? Of course.

ONDINE: No. You don't understand. When a man and a woman love each other are they ever separate?

HANS: Separate? Of course.

ONDINE: No, you still don't understand. Take the dogfish, for instance. Not that I'm especially fond of dogfish, mind you. But, once the dogfish couples with its mate, he never leaves her, never as long as he lives, did you know that? Through storm and calm they swim together, thousands and thousands of miles, side by side, two fingers apart, as if an invisible link held them together. They are no longer two. They become one.

HANS: Well?

ONDINE: Do lovers live like that in your world?

HANS: It would be a little difficult for lovers to live like that in our world, Ondine. In our world, each has his own life, his own room, his own friends—

ONDINE: What a horrible word that is, each.

HANS: Each has his work—his play—

ONDINE: But the dogfish too have their work and their play. They have to hunt, you know, in order to live. And sometimes they come upon a school of herrings which scatter before them in a thousand flashes, and they have a thousand reasons to lose each other, to swerve one to the right, the other to the left. But they never do. As long as they live, not even a sardine can come between them.

HANS: In our world, Ondine, a whale can come between a husband and wife twenty times a day, no matter how much they love each other.

ONDINE: I was afraid of that.

HANS: The man looks to his affairs; the women to hers. They swim in different currents.

ONDINE: But the dogfish have to swim through different currents also. There are cold currents and warm currents. And sometimes the one likes the cold and the other the warm. And sometimes they swim into currents so powerful that they can divide a fleet, and yet they cannot divide these fish by the breadth of a nail.

HANS: That merely proves that men and fish are not the same.

ONDINE: And you and I, we are the same?

HANS: Oh yes, Ondine.

ONDINE: And you swear that you will never leave me, not even for a moment?

HANS: Yes, Ondine.

ONDINE: Because now that I love you,

two steps away from you my loneliness begins.

HANS: I will never leave you, Ondine.

ONDINE: Hans, listen to me seriously. I know someone who can join us forever, someone very powerful. And if I ask him, he will solder us together with a band of flesh so that nothing but death can separate us. Would you like me to call him?

HANS: No, Ondine.

ONDINE: But, Hans, the more I think of it, the more I see there is no other way to keep lovers together in your world.

HANS: And your dogfish? Do they need to be soldered like that?

ONDINE: It's true. But they don't live among men. Let me call him. You'll see. It's a very practical arrangement.

HANS: No. Let's try this way first. Later, we'll see.

ONDINE: I know what you're thinking. Of course, she's right, you're thinking, the little Ondine, and naturally I shall be with her always, but once in a while, for just a little moment perhaps I shall go and take a turn by myself, I shall go and visit my friend.

HANS: Or my horse.

ONDINE: Or your horse. When this angel falls asleep, you're thinking, this angel whom I shall never leave not even for a moment, then, at last, I shall have a chance to go and spend a good half hour with my horse.

HANS: As a matter of fact, I had better go and have a look at him now, don't you think? We're leaving at dawn, you know, and I ought to see if he's bedded properly. Besides I always tell him everything.

ONDINE: Ah yes. Well, tonight you shall tell him nothing.

HANS: But why, Ondine?

ONDINE: Because tonight you're going to sleep, my little Hans. [*And with a gesture, she throws sleep into his eyes.*] Good night, my love. [*He falls asleep.*]

THE FIRST ONDINE: [*Her voice seems very far away.*] Good-bye, Ondine.

ONDINE: Look after my lake!

THE SECOND ONDINE: Good-bye, Ondine.

ONDINE: Take care of my stream!

THE KING OF THE SEA: Ondine!

ONDINE: Farewell, Old One.

THE KING OF THE SEA: Don't leave us, Ondine.

ONDINE: I have left you, Old One.

THE KING OF THE SEA: The world of

men is not your world, Ondine. It will bring you sorrow.

ONDINE: It will bring me joy.

THE KING OF THE SEA: The man will deceive you. He will abandon you.

ONDINE: Never! Never!

THE KING OF THE SEA: And when he deceives you? When he abandons you? You will remember our pact?

ONDINE: I shall remember our pact.

THE KING OF THE SEA: [*His voice recedes.*] Remember, Ondine.

THE ONDINES: [*Their voices are like the murmur of water.*] Remember, Ondine.

HANS: [*Turning in his sleep.*] Remember, Ondine—

ONDINE: Oh dear, from this time on, how much I shall have to remember!

CURTAIN

ACT TWO

The hall of honor of the king's palace. It is a large vaulted loggia of Gothic design. The roof is supported by columns. The upstage side opens on the palace gardens, in which may be seen three jets of water playing in marble basins in the sunshine. To the left is a dais with the king's throne, and above the throne a mural depicting one of the labors of Hercules. There are arched doorways.

THE LORD CHAMBERLAIN *and* THE SUPERINTENDENT OF THE ROYAL THEATRES *are engaged in a conference. To one side stand respectfully* THE TRAINER OF THE SEALS *and* THE ILLUSIONIST.

THE CHAMBERLAIN: My dear Superintendent, this is a matter that will require all your skill, and all your inventiveness. The Knight of Wittenstein has at last been persuaded to present his bride at court. His Majesty has asked me to provide an amusing interlude with which to grace the occasion. But the reception is to take place immediately.

THE SUPERINTENDENT: The time is short, my Lord Chamberlain.

THE CHAMBERLAIN: It couldn't be shorter. Well? As Superintendent of the Royal Theatres, what do you propose?

THE SUPERINTENDENT: *Salammbo.*

[*At this word* MATHO *and* SALAMMBO *appear and begin at once to sing.*]

THE CHAMBERLAIN: [*Striking the floor with his staff for silence.*] But you played *Salammbo* only last night for the Margrave's birthday. Besides, *Salammbo* is sad.

THE SUPERINTENDENT: It's sad. But it's ready. [*He signs to his actors who burst at once into their duet.*]

THE CHAMBERLAIN: [*Stops them again.*] I don't see why it is any more ready than *Orpheus,* which has only one character. Or the *Interlude of Adam and Eve,* which requires no costumes.

THE SUPERINTENDENT: Excellency, my success in the theatre is based solely on the discovery that each particular stage has its likes and dislikes which it is useless to combat.

THE CHAMBERLAIN: Time presses, my good man.

THE SUPERINTENDENT: Each theatre, Excellency, is built for one play and one play only. The whole secret of management is to discover what play that is. It's not easy, especially when the play is not yet written. And so, a thousand disasters—until that happy day when the play for which it was intended comes to its proper theatre and gives it its life, its soul, and, if I may so, its sex.

THE CHAMBERLAIN: Superintendent—

THE SUPERINTENDENT: For years I managed a theatre which bumbled along miserably with the classics until suddenly one night it found its joy in a bawdy farce with sailors. It was a female theatre. I knew another which tolerated only *Othello.* It was male. Last year I was forced to close the Royal Ballet. Impossible to determine its sex.

THE CHAMBERLAIN: And you believe the Royal Auditorium—

THE SUPERINTENDENT: Exists only for *Salammbo,* yes, your Excellency. At the word *Salammbo,* the tightness of throat with which the royal chorus is normally afflicted suddenly relaxes, and the hall resounds with voices full of resonance and joy. [MATHO *and* SALAMMBO *begin singing, at first softly, crescendo to the end of the speech.*] I tell you, my Lord Chamberlain, sometimes when I play a German opera, I notice one of my singers, brimming with happiness, making magnificent gestures, sending out full-throated tones which fill the audience with such joy and comfort that it breaks into spontaneous applause— Why? Because among his fellow-actors, who are merely grinding out their parts by rote, this actor in the general confusion is blissfully singing his role in *Salammbo*.

THE CHAMBERLAIN: [*Silencing the singers.*] No. It would hardly do to entertain a newly married couple with a tragedy of unhappy love. *Salammbo* is out of the question. [THE SUPERINTENDENT *waves his singers away. They go reluctantly.* THE CHAMBERLAIN *turns to* THE TRAINER OF SEALS.] Who are you?

THE TRAINER: I am the Trainer of Seals, your Excellency.

THE CHAMBERLAIN: What do they do, your seals?

THE TRAINER: They don't sing *Salammbo*.

THE CHAMBERLAIN: That's a pity. A chorus of seals singing *Salammbo* would constitute a very appropriate entertainment. Besides, I am told that your head seal has a beard that makes him look like his Majesty's father-in-law. Is that true?

THE TRAINER: I could shave him, Excellency.

THE CHAMBERLAIN: By a regrettable coincidence, his Majesty's father-in-law shaved his beard only yesterday. We had best avoid even the shadow of a scandal. And who are you?

THE ILLUSIONIST: I am an illusionist, Excellency.

THE CHAMBERLAIN: Where is your apparatus?

THE ILLUSIONIST: I am an illusionist without apparatus.

THE CHAMBERLAIN: Now what do you take us for? You don't produce claps of thunder and lightning without apparatus.

THE ILLUSIONIST: Yes.

[*There is a clap of thunder and lightning.*]

THE CHAMBERLAIN: [*Cowering with fear.*] Nonsense. You can't produce sudden clouds of smoke which leave the stage covered with flowers without apparatus?

[*There is a sudden cloud of smoke, and flowers fall from the ceiling.*]

THE ILLUSIONIST: Yes.

THE CHAMBERLAIN: What stubbornness! You don't suddenly produce before the eyes of the Lord Chamberlain—

BERTRAM: [*Comes in.*] Your Excellency—

THE CHAMBERLAIN: Just a moment.— Venus completely nude—without apparatus.

THE ILLUSIONIST: Yes.

BERTRAM: Excellency—[*A nude* VENUS *appears.* BERTRAM *bows.*] Madame. [VENUS *disappears.*]

THE CHAMBERLAIN: I've always wondered who these Venuses are that magicians produce out of thin air? Relatives?

THE ILLUSIONIST: Or Venus herself. It depends on the magician.

BERTRAM: Excellency, his Majesty is unavoidably detained by the African envoy. The reception is postponed for an hour.

THE CHAMBERLAIN: Excellent. That gives us time to think of something. [*To the* SUPERINTENDENT.] Have you thought of something?

THE SUPERINTENDENT: Yes, Excellency.

THE CHAMBERLAIN: Ah. Splendid. What?

THE SUPERINTENDENT: *Salammbo*.

[*The two singers appear, only to be waved off peremptorily by* THE CHAMBERLAIN.]

THE CHAMBERLAIN: [*To* THE ILLUSIONIST.] And how do you propose to amuse his Majesty?

THE ILLUSIONIST: If your Excellency permits, I shall do what the occasion inspires.

THE CHAMBERLAIN: That's asking a great deal. After all, we have never seen your work.

THE ILLUSIONIST: I shall be happy, while we are waiting, to offer a little private entertainment by way of demonstration.

THE CHAMBERLAIN: Ah. Very good.

THE ILLUSIONIST: What would your Excellency like to see?

THE CHAMBERLAIN: I should very much like to see—

THE ILLUSIONIST: Splendid. I shall bring them together at once.

THE CHAMBERLAIN: You are also a mind-reader?

THE ILLUSIONIST: Yes. Excellency, I can, if you wish, bring together before your eyes a man and a woman who have been carefully avoiding each other for the past three months.

THE CHAMBERLAIN: Here? Now?

THE ILLUSIONIST: Here and now. If you will be so good as to conceal yourselves—

THE CHAMBERLAIN: But it's impossible, my dear fellow. Consider that the gentleman in question is at this very moment in the royal apartments supervising the last details of his wife's costume. A tornado could not draw him from her. The injured lady, on the other hand, is locked up in her room. She has sworn she will under no circumstances appear. These two cannot possibly meet.

THE ILLUSIONIST: Yes. But suppose that a dog were to steal the bride's glove and run out into the garden with it? And suppose that the lady's pet bullfinch should fly out of its cage and come to perch on the edge of the fountain?

THE CHAMBERLAIN: That will get you nowhere. It is the halberdier's high duty to divert all dogs from the royal apartments. And as for the bird—the king has just loosed a falcon in the garden. It is hovering over the bullfinch's cage.

THE ILLUSIONIST: Yes. But suppose that the halberdier slips on a banana peel? And suppose a gazelle distracts the falcon's attention?

THE CHAMBERLAIN: Bananas and gazelles are unknown in these parts.

THE ILLUSIONIST: Yes. But the African envoy peeled a banana while waiting for his morning audience. And among the gifts sent by his government, there was a gazelle which is at this moment feeding in the garden.

THE CHAMBERLAIN: Quite resourceful, you magicians.

THE ILLUSIONIST: Yes. Take your places. In a moment you shall see the Princess Bertha and the Knight of Wittenstein come together in this hall.

[VIOLANTE and ANGELIQUE come in from the garden. They hear the last words.]

VIOLANTE: Really?

ANGELIQUE: Really?

THE CHAMBERLAIN: [Beckoning to the ladies to join him behind a column.] Sh! Come here.

BERTRAM: But, Excellency, why are we doing this evil thing?

THE CHAMBERLAIN: Sooner or later it would have to happen. That's life.

BERTRAM: Then why not let life take its course?

THE CHAMBERLAIN: My dear Bertram, you are young and you are a poet. When you have reached my age, you will understand that life is a very poorly constructed play. As a rule, the curtain goes up in the wrong places, the climaxes don't come off, the denouement is interminably postponed, so that those who should die at once of a broken heart die instead of a kidney ailment at an advanced age. If this excellent illusionist can make us see a life unfold for once with the concision and logic that a good play requires—[To THE ILLUSIONIST.] Can you?

THE ILLUSIONIST: Perhaps.

THE CHAMBERLAIN: Just one little scene, then. Just one little scene.

BERTRAM: But, Excellency, the poor girl—

THE CHAMBERLAIN: The girl has caused a knight to be false to his word. She deserves to suffer.

BERTRAM: But why should we . . . ?

THE CHAMBERLAIN: Don't excite yourself, my boy. Six months from now, in the normal course of events, Hans and Bertha would meet. Six months after that, they would kiss. A year after that, beyond a shadow of a doubt, they would—it's inevitable. And if we spare ourselves these delays, and bring their hands together at once; and, ten minutes later, their lips; and five minutes after that, whatever else is necessary—will we be changing their story, really, in any way? We shall just be giving it a little pace, a little tempo— Magician!— What's that noise?

THE TRAINER: The halberdier. He slipped on a banana peel.

THE CHAMBERLAIN: Splendid.

BERTRAM: Excellency, I beg of you, let's carry this no further. It's a mischievous thing. Left to themselves, perhaps these two would never meet again. [There is a scream from the garden.] What's that scream?

THE SUPERINTENDENT: The gazelle. The falcon struck it.

THE CHAMBERLAIN: Perfect. You think you can bring off the whole thing at this pace, magician?

THE ILLUSIONIST: Perhaps.

[The bird appears, perched on the fountain.]

THE SUPERINTENDENT: The bird!

THE TRAINER: [Looking out into the garden.] The dog!

VIOLANTE: The knight!

[HANS *is seen running after the dog in the garden.*]

THE SUPERINTENDENT: The lady!

[BERTHA *runs in and catches the bird.*]

HANS: Ah! There you are, you rascal! At last I've caught you!

BERTHA: Ah! There you are, you rascal! At last I've found you!

[*Each goes off without seeing the other. The spectators poke their heads out of their hiding places. They hiss.*]

BERTRAM: [*Sighs with relief.*] Thank heaven!

THE CHAMBERLAIN: What's this, magician? Are you making fun of us?

THE ILLUSIONIST: Sorry, sir. A fault in direction.

THE CHAMBERLAIN: Are they going to meet or are they not?

THE ILLUSIONIST: They are going to meet. And this time there will be no mistake about it. I'll knock their heads together. [*The spectators hide once more.*] Now!

[*The dog runs across the garden, glove in mouth, with* HANS *in pursuit. The bird flies in and settles on the fountain.* BERTHA *runs in from the right and catches it.*]

BERTHA: Again! What a bad bird you are!

HANS: Again! What an obstinate beast! [*He enters the room with the glove in his hand, just as* BERTHA *runs up with the bird. They collide.* HANS *takes her hands to keep her from falling. They recognize each other.*] Oh! I beg your pardon, Bertha.

BERTHA: Oh! I'm sorry, Hans.

HANS: Did I hurt you?

BERTHA: Not a bit.

HANS: I'm a clumsy brute, Bertha.

BERTHA: Yes. You are. [*There is a moment of embarrassed silence. Then each turns and walks off slowly.* BERTHA *stops.*] Pleasant honeymoon?

HANS: Marvelous.

BERTHA: A blonde, I believe?

HANS: Blonde, like the sun.

BERTHA: Sunlit nights! I prefer the darkness.

HANS: Each to his taste.

BERTHA: It was dark that night under the oak tree. My poor Hans! You must have suffered!

HANS: Bertha!

BERTHA: I didn't suffer. I loved it.

HANS: Bertha, my wife is coming in at any moment.

BERTHA: I was happy that night in your arms. I thought it was for always.

HANS: And so it could have been, had you not insisted on sending me into the forest on a wild-goose chase. Why didn't you keep me with you, if you wanted me?

BERTHA: One takes off a ring sometimes to show to one's friends. Even an engagement ring.

HANS: I'm sorry. The ring didn't understand.

BERTHA: No. And so it rolled, as rings do, under the nearest bed.

HANS: I beg your pardon!

BERTHA: Forgive me. I shouldn't have mentioned a bed. Among peasants, you sleep in the straw, I believe? You pick it out of your hair the morning after. Is it fun?

HANS: One day you will see.

BERTHA: No, I don't think so. Black hair and straw don't go well together. That's for blondes.

HANS: You may be right. Although in love, these details don't seem to matter. But, of course, you've never had that experience.

BERTHA: You think?

HANS: When you're in love, you don't think of yourself so much. You think of the other. You will see one day. But when it happens to you, don't let your lover go.

BERTHA: No?

HANS: Don't send him into senseless danger and loneliness and boredom.

BERTHA: One would say you had a bad time in the Black Forest.

HANS: You are haughty. But when you meet the man you love, take my advice—pocket your pride, throw your arms around his neck and tell him, before all the world, that you love him.

BERTHA: [*She throws her arms around his neck.*] I love you. [*She kisses him, then tries to run off. But he holds her by the hands.*]

HANS: Bertha!

BERTHA: Let me go, Hans.

HANS: What game are you playing with me now, Bertha?

BERTHA: Be careful, Hans. I have a bird in my hand.

HANS: I love another woman, Bertha.

BERTHA: The bird!

HANS: You should have done that before, Bertha.

BERTHA: Hans, don't squeeze my hand so. You're going to kill it.

HANS: Let the bird go, Bertha.

BERTHA: No. Its little heart is beating with fear. And just now I need this little heart next to mine.

HANS: What is it you want of me, Bertha?

BERTHA: Hans— Oh! [*Opening her hand and showing the bird.*] There. You've killed it.

HANS: Oh, Bertha! [*Taking the bird.*] Forgive me, Bertha. Forgive me.

[BERTHA *looks at him a long moment. He is completely contrite.*]

BERTHA: Give it to me. I'll take the poor little thing away. [*She takes it from him.*]

HANS: Forgive me.

BERTHA: I want nothing of you now, Hans. But once, I wanted something for you, and that was my mistake. I wanted glory—for the man I loved. The man I had chosen when I was a little girl, and whom I led one night under the oak tree on which long ago I had carved his name. I thought it was a woman's glory to lead her lover not only to his table and his bed, but to whatever in the world is hardest to find and most difficult to conquer. I was wrong.

HANS: No, Bertha. No, Bertha.

BERTHA: I am dark. I thought that in the darkness of the forest this man would see my face in every shadow. I am dark, I trusted my love to the darkness. How could I have known that in these shadows, he would come one night upon a head of gold?

HANS: How could anyone have known it?

BERTHA: That was my error. I have confessed it. And that's the end of it. I shall carve no more initials in the bark of trees. A man alone in a dream of glory—that's already foolish. But a woman alone in a dream of glory is completely ridiculous. So much the worse for me.

HANS: Forgive me, Bertha?

BERTHA: Farewell, Hans.

[*She goes out, right. He goes out, left. The spectators appear, crying "Bravo!"*]

THE ILLUSIONIST: There it is, your Excellency. The scene that would have taken place, without my assistance, next winter. I have brought it about, as you see, here and now. It has happened.

BERTRAM: It is amply sufficient. We can stop here, can we not?

THE CHAMBERLAIN: No. No. No. No. I'm dying to see the next. The next, Magician, the next!

THE ILLUSIONIST: The next scene?

VIOLANTE: The next!

ANGELIQUE: The next!

THE ILLUSIONIST: At your service, ladies. Which one?

VIOLANTE: The one in which Hans unlaces the helmet of the knight he has killed and it is the Lady Bertha . . . ?

THE ILLUSIONIST: That scene is in another play, Mademoiselle.

THE SUPERINTENDENT: The scene in which the knight in the nick of time saves Bertha from the dragon . . . ?

THE TRAINER: The scene in which the knight, while twirling a ball on his nose—

THE ILLUSIONIST: Please!

THE CHAMBERLAIN: The scene in which Bertha and Hans first speak of Ondine.

THE ILLUSIONIST: Very well, Excellency. That takes place next spring.

THE CHAMBERLAIN: So much the better. I love the spring. [*He goes behind his column. The lights dim.* BERTHA *and* HANS *come in slowly from opposite directions.*]

HANS: [*Calls.*] Bertha.

BERTHA: [*Calls.*] Hans. [*They catch sight of each other.*] I was looking for you, Hans.

HANS: I was looking for you, Bertha.

[THE CHAMBERLAIN *comes out suddenly.*]

THE CHAMBERLAIN: Magician! What does this mean? What have you done to me?

THE ILLUSIONIST: It is one of the inconveniences of my system. You have grown an eight months' beard. You see, it is now next spring.

THE CHAMBERLAIN: Ah— [*He disappears. The scene continues.*]

BERTHA: Hans, must there be this awful cloud between us? Can't we be friends?

HANS: I wish we could be, Bertha. But—

BERTHA: I know. We can't be friends without Ondine. But it's your fault, Hans. You haven't let me see her since that awful day of the king's reception. And that's eight months ago, and quite forgotten. Send her to me this evening, Hans. I am illuminating a manuscript of the *Aeneid* for the king. Ondine can draw in the initials, and I shall teach her the secret of the gold leaf.

HANS: Thanks, Bertha. But I doubt very much—

BERTHA: Ondine doesn't letter?

HANS: Ondine doesn't write.

BERTHA: How lucky she is! When you write, it takes away half the pleasure of reading. She has a charming voice. I'm sure she reads aloud beautifully?

HANS: Ondine doesn't read.

BERTHA: How I envy her! How wonderful among all these pedants to be able to give oneself up to the luxury of not reading. But she dances, I know—

HANS: Never.

BERTHA: You're joking, Hans! You don't mean to say that she neither reads, nor writes, nor dances?

HANS: Yes. And she doesn't recite. And she doesn't play the rote. Nor the harp, nor the lute. And she won't go hunting. She can't bear to see things killed.

BERTHA: But what then does she do, in heaven's name?

HANS: Oh, she swims. Occasionally.

BERTHA: That's nice. Though it's not by swimming that a girl advances her husband's interests at court. And yet, let's be just, Hans. After all, these accomplishments mean nothing. A pretty woman has the right to be ignorant of everything, provided she knows when to keep still.

HANS: It is this point precisely, Bertha, that worries me the most. Ondine does not know when to keep still. Quite the contrary. She says whatever comes into her head—and the things that come into that girl's head! Bertha, you know, the jousting season opens this week. And the thought of the phrases which will issue from Ondine as she watches these tournaments in which every step and pass-at-arms has its appropriate term—it makes me shudder.

BERTHA: She can learn.

HANS: I spent the morning trying to teach her the rudiments. Each time I give her a new term, she thanks me with a kiss. Now in the first position of the horseman alone there are thirty-three points to identify—

BERTHA: Thirty-six.

HANS: God, that's true! What am I thinking of? I tell you, I'm losing my wits, Bertha!

BERTHA: Send her to me, Hans. I'll see that she learns what she needs to know.

HANS: Thanks. But, what she needs to know above all is the special signs and prerogatives of the Wittenstein. And those are a family secret.

BERTHA: You forget, Hans. I was almost one of the Wittenstein. Ask me a question.

HANS: If you can answer this, I shall owe you a forfeit. What device does a Wittenstein bear on his shield when he enters the lists?

BERTHA: On a field azure, a squirrel passant, gules.

HANS: Does he bear this device into combat?

BERTHA: Never. At the moment he lowers his visor, his squire hands him a shield on which are emblazoned three lions rampant or, on a field sable. That is his device of war.

HANS: Bertha! You're incredible! And how does a Wittenstein approach the barrier?

BERTHA: Lance squared, charger collected, slow trot.

HANS: Ah, Bertha, what a lucky man the knight will be who marries you! [He kisses her hand. She snatches it away. They go off in opposite directions.]

THE CHAMBERLAIN: [No beard.] Bravo! Bravo! Bravo! And how right he is! The Princess Bertha knows everything. She does everything. She is the ideal woman, beyond a doubt. You have us on pins and needles, Magician. The third scene! Quickly!

VIOLANTE: The scene in which Bertha sees Ondine dancing in the moonlight with her fairies.

THE ILLUSIONIST: You appear to be still a little confused, Mademoiselle.

THE CHAMBERLAIN: The first quarrel of Hans and Ondine.

BERTRAM: Couldn't we let that, at least, take care of itself?

THE CHAMBERLAIN: No, no. We'd never get to see it. Magician—

BERTRAM: But Excellency! His Majesty will be here in a moment.

THE CHAMBERLAIN: By heaven, that's true. I will just have time to give this young lady the customary words of advice before the reception begins. You're not planning to do anything more till I get back, Magician?

THE ILLUSIONIST: Just one tiny scene, perhaps.

THE CHAMBERLAIN: In connection with what?

THE ILLUSIONIST: In connection with nothing at all. Just a trifle to please an old fisherman whom I love. But your Excellency needn't leave.

THE CHAMBERLAIN: Oh no, I must. It

is the Lord Chamberlain's duty to instruct all those who are presented at court. And in this particular case—

THE ILLUSIONIST: If your Excellency wishes, I can save you the trouble of going. Take your place and you shall see yourself speaking to her.

THE CHAMBERLAIN: You can't do it!

THE ILLUSIONIST: Nothing simpler.

THE CHAMBERLAIN: [*He backs away in astonishment until he is lost from sight.*] What an extraordinary illusion!

THE ILLUSIONIST: Yes. But first, the Lady Violante. [VIOLANTE *steps forward.* AUGUSTE *walks in from the garden. He looks in bewilderment at* THE ILLUSIONIST.] The fleck of gold, Auguste.

AUGUSTE: [*He sees* VIOLANTE.] Are you the Lady Violante?

VIOLANTE: Yes. What do you wish?

AUGUSTE: [*Looking into her eyes.*] I was right! It's marvelous!

THE VOICE OF EUGENIE: Auguste! Stick to your fishing!

[AUGUSTE *makes a gesture of resignation, bows and goes.*]

THE ILLUSIONIST: Thank you, my lady. Here you come, your Excellency.

[VIOLANTE *goes behind the column.* THE CHAMBERLAIN *comes in leading* ONDINE *by the hand.*]

THE CHAMBERLAIN: Absolutely out of the question, dear lady!

ONDINE: But it would make me so happy—

THE CHAMBERLAIN: I regret deeply. To change the court reception, third class, into a water festival is entirely out of the question. The Minister of Finance would never hear of such a thing. Every time we turn the water into the pool, it costs us a fortune.

ONDINE: But this will cost you nothing.

THE CHAMBERLAIN: Please don't insist. There is absolutely no precedent for a court reception in the water.

ONDINE: But I am so much more at ease in the water.

THE CHAMBERLAIN: I am not.

ONDINE: You would be. You especially. Your palm is damp. In the water, it wouldn't show.

THE CHAMBERLAIN: I beg your pardon. My palm is not damp.

ONDINE: Oh, it is. Touch it and you will see.

THE CHAMBERLAIN: Madame, do you feel strong enough to listen for a moment to a word of advice which will help you to avoid a great deal of trouble in the future?

ONDINE: Oh yes.

THE CHAMBERLAIN: To listen without interrupting?

ONDINE: Oh, I shouldn't dream of interrupting.

THE CHAMBERLAIN: Splendid. Now, in the first place—the court is a sacred precinct—

ONDINE: Excuse me just one moment. [*She goes to the place where* BERTRAM *is hidden and fetches him out.*] What is your name? You?

BERTRAM: Bertram.

ONDINE: You are the poet, are you not?

BERTRAM: So they say.

ONDINE: You are not beautiful.

BERTRAM: They say that too. But usually they whisper it.

ONDINE: Writing doesn't improve the appearance?

BERTRAM: Oh yes. I used to be much uglier.

[ONDINE *laughs and goes back to* THE CHAMBERLAIN. BERTRAM *stands by.*]

ONDINE: Excuse me.

THE CHAMBERLAIN: [*Controlling himself.*] As I was saying. The court is a sacred precinct in which it is necessary for a man at all times to control—his face and his tongue. Here, when a man is afraid, he seems brave. When he lies, he seems frank. It is quite appropriate also, if by chance one is telling the truth, to appear to be lying. It inspires confidence.

ONDINE: I see.

THE CHAMBERLAIN: Let us take the example that you in your innocence bring up. It is true, my palm perspires. Ever since I was a child it has caused me infinite embarrassment. But damp as my hand is, my arm is long. It reaches to the throne. To displease me is to put oneself in jeopardy—and it does not please me to hear any mention of my physical shortcomings, to be precise, of my sole physical shortcoming. And now, lovely Ondine, tell me, as a sophisticated court lady, how is my hand, damp or dry?

ONDINE: Damp. Like your feet.

THE CHAMBERLAIN: What?

ONDINE: Just a moment. Do you mind?

THE CHAMBERLAIN: I mind very much!

[ONDINE *crosses once more to the poet, who comes this time to meet her.*]

ONDINE: What was the first poem you ever wrote?

BERTRAM: The most beautiful.

ONDINE: The most beautiful of your poems?

BERTRAM: The most beautiful of all poems. It so far surpassed the others as you, Ondine, surpass all women.

ONDINE: Tell it to me quickly.

BERTRAM: I don't remember it. It came to me in a dream. When I awoke, it was gone.

ONDINE: You should have written it down sooner.

BERTRAM: I did. Even a little too soon. I was still dreaming when I wrote it.

[ONDINE smiles and leaves him. She joins THE CHAMBERLAIN who is fuming.]

ONDINE: Yes, your Excellency?

THE CHAMBERLAIN: [With a prodigious effort.] My lady, let us admit that the Lord Chamberlain's palm is damp, and let's admit that he admits it. But tell me this—would you tell his Majesty that his hand was damp?

ONDINE: Oh no!

THE CHAMBERLAIN: Ah, bravo! And why not?

ONDINE: Because it's not.

THE CHAMBERLAIN: But I put you a case where it is! Look here, my girl, suppose his Majesty should question you about the wart on his nose. And his Majesty, believe me, has a wart on his nose. And for heaven's sake don't make me shout. It is death to mention it. No one ever has. Now—suppose he asked you what his wart resembled?

ONDINE: Is it usual for a monarch who meets a lady for the first time to ask her what his wart resembles?

THE CHAMBERLAIN: My dear girl, I am putting you a hypothetical case. In the event that you had a wart on your nose—

ONDINE: I shall never have a wart on my nose.

THE CHAMBERLAIN: The girl is impossible!

ONDINE: Warts come from touching frogs. Did you know that?

THE CHAMBERLAIN: No.

BERTRAM: [Coming forward.] Madame, the Lord Chamberlain is merely trying to tell you that it is inconsiderate to remind people of their ugliness.

ONDINE: It is inconsiderate of them to be ugly. Why should they be ugly?

THE CHAMBERLAIN: Courtesy is an investment, my dear girl. When you grow old, in your turn, people will tell you, out of courtesy, that you look distinguished. When you grow ugly, they will say that you look interesting. And all this in return for a tiny payment on your part now.

ONDINE: I don't need to make it. I shall never grow old.

THE CHAMBERLAIN: What a child you are!

ONDINE: Yes. Excuse me a moment. [She goes to BERTRAM.]

THE CHAMBERLAIN: [Exasperated.] Ondine!

ONDINE: I like you, Bertram.

BERTRAM: I'm delighted. But the Chamberlain is annoyed.

ONDINE: Oh dear. [She goes back to THE CHAMBERLAIN.] I'm sorry.

THE CHAMBERLAIN: [A bit stiffly.] There is just time now for me to instruct you on the question that his Majesty asks of every debutante at court. It has to do with the sixth labor of Hercules. Hercules, as you know, is his Majesty's name—he is Hercules the Sixth. Now listen carefully.

ONDINE: [Taking a little step toward BERTRAM.] If I could just—

THE CHAMBERLAIN: Madame, his Majesty is almost here. When he asks you about the sixth labor of Hercules— [A flourish of trumpets at some little distance.] Too late.

[HANS enters angrily.]

HANS: Excellency—

ONDINE: Don't interrupt, Hans. His Excellency is speaking.

HANS: What does this mean, Excellency? Have you put me below the Margrave of Salm?

THE CHAMBERLAIN: Yes, Knight.

HANS: I am entitled to the third rank below the king and the silver fork.

THE CHAMBERLAIN: You were. And even to the first, and even to the golden fork, if a certain project had materialized as we expected. But your present marriage assigns you to the fourteenth place and the pewter spoon.

HANS: The fourteenth place!

ONDINE: What difference does it make, Hans? I've been to the kitchen. I'm sure there's enough for all. [BERTRAM laughs.]

HANS: And why are you laughing, Bertram?

BERTRAM: I am laughing because my heart is gay.

ONDINE: You don't wish to stop him from laughing, Hans?

HANS: He's laughing at you.

ONDINE: He's laughing at me because he likes me.

BERTRAM: That's very true, Madame.

HANS: My wife must provoke no laughter of any description.

THE CHAMBERLAIN: Gentlemen! Gentlemen!

ONDINE: He won't laugh if you don't like it. He has no desire to displease me. Have you, Bertram?

BERTRAM: My only wish is to please you, Madame.

ONDINE: Don't be angry with my husband, Bertram. It's flattering that he should be so scrupulous on my account. Don't you think so?

BERTRAM: We all envy him the privilege.

HANS: [Belligerently.] Thanks very much.

ONDINE: Don't show your nervousness, Hans. Be like me. I'm trembling. But an earthquake could not shake this smile from my lips.

[Meanwhile people have streamed in from all sides. THE ILLUSIONIST comes up to ONDINE.]

THE ILLUSIONIST: Ondine—

ONDINE: What are you doing here?

THE ILLUSIONIST: I am furnishing the entertainment. Pardon the intrusion.

ONDINE: Yes. On one condition. Go away.

THE ILLUSIONIST: If you like. But in a little while, you will call me back, Ondine.

[He walks off. There is another flourish of trumpets near at hand. THE CHAMBERLAIN takes his place at the door. He strikes the floor with his staff three times.]

THE CHAMBERLAIN: His Majesty, the King!

[THE KING enters, bowing.]

THE KING: Hail, Knight von Wittenstein.

HANS: Your Majesty. [THE KING mounts his throne.]

THE CHAMBERLAIN: [Advancing with ONDINE.] Your Majesty, with your gracious permission, may I present the Lady von Wittenstein zu Wittenstein.

THE KING: Madame.

ONDINE: My name is Ondine.

[BERTHA takes her place on the lower step of the dais. ONDINE looks at no one else.]

THE CHAMBERLAIN: [Whispers.] Your curtsey, Madame.

[ONDINE curtseys, with her eyes still on BERTHA.]

THE KING: We receive you with pleasure, dear child, in this gallery which is called the Hall of Hercules. I love Hercules. Of all my many names, his is by far my favorite, and of course the one by which I am known. The resemblance between Hercules and myself has been noticed by everyone, ever since I was a little child, and I must confess that at work or at play I have tried to emulate him in everything. And speaking of work—you know, I presume, how many labors Hercules brought to a successful conclusion?

THE CHAMBERLAIN: [Whispers.] Twelve.

ONDINE: [Without taking her eyes from BERTHA'S face.] Twelve.

THE KING: Twelve. Exactly. The Lord Chamberlain prompts a little loudly, but your voice is delightful. It will be a little more difficult for him to whisper in your ear the complete description of the sixth labor, but he won't have to. If you lift your eyes, you will see it depicted on the wall. Look. Who is this woman who is trying to seduce Hercules, with a smile on her lips and a lie in her heart? Her name, my dear?

ONDINE: Bertha.

THE KING: I beg pardon?

ONDINE: [Taking a step toward BERTHA.] You shall never have him, Bertha!

BERTHA: What?

ONDINE: He will never be yours, Bertha. Never!

THE KING: Is the girl quite well?

THE CHAMBERLAIN: Madame, His Majesty is addressing you.

ONDINE: If you say a word to him, if you dare to touch him, I'll kill you!

HANS: Ondine!

BERTHA: The girl is mad!

ONDINE: Majesty, I'm frightened! I beg you, save us!

THE KING: Save you from what, my child?

HANS: Your Majesty, she's not used to the court.

ONDINE: You, be quiet. You don't see what's happening? Oh, King, isn't it a pity? You have a husband for whose sake you'd give up anything in the world. He's strong —he's brave—he's handsome—

HANS: Ondine, for heaven's sake!

ONDINE: I know what I'm saying. You're stupid, but you're handsome. It's no secret —all the women know it. And they say, what a lucky thing it is for us that being so handsome, he's so stupid! Because he's so handsome, how sweet it will be to take him in our arms. And how easy—since he's so stupid. Because he's so handsome, he will give us such joy as our husbands can never give us. And this, without the slightest danger to ourselves—since he's so stupid.

BERTRAM: Bravo!

ONDINE: I am right, am I not, Bertram?

HANS: Ondine, please! And you—what do you mean by saying, Bravo?

BERTRAM: When I say Bravo, Knight, I mean Bravo.

THE KING: That's quite enough, Count Bertram.

THE CHAMBERLAIN: [Intervening suavely.] Your Majesty, I had hoped to offer by way of interlude, a little diversion—

BERTHA: His Majesty is sufficiently diverted. His adopted daughter has been insulted before all the court by a peasant!

HANS: Majesty, permit us to take our leave. I have an adorable wife, but she is not like other women. She is very innocent, and she says whatever comes into her head. I humbly beg your forgiveness.

ONDINE: You see, King? You see what's happening?

THE KING: Bertha is the soul of sweetness. She wants only to be your friend—

ONDINE: You're entirely mistaken!

HANS: Ondine!

ONDINE: You think it's sweet to kill a bird!

THE KING: Bird? What bird? Why should Bertha kill a bird?

ONDINE: To trouble Hans. To bring him to his knees. To make him beg her pardon.

BERTHA: The bird was in my hand, Majesty. He pressed my hand so hard that the bird was killed.

ONDINE: He did not. A woman's hand, no matter how soft, becomes a shell of iron when it protects a living thing. If the bird were in my hand, Your Majesty, Hercules himself could press with all his strength and never hurt it. But Bertha knows men. These knights whom dragons cannot frighten grow faint at the death of a bird. The bird was alive in her hand. She killed it.

HANS: It was I who pressed her hand.

ONDINE: It was she who killed it.

THE KING: Ondine, my dear, I want you to be Bertha's friend.

ONDINE: If you wish. On condition she stops shouting.

HANS: But she hasn't said a word, Ondine.

THE KING: She really hasn't.

ONDINE: Are you deaf? Don't you hear? She says that a week of this foolishness will cost me my husband, and a month will cost me my life, that all she needs to do is to wait and I shall vanish. That's what your soul of sweetness is saying. Oh, Hans, take me in your arms, here, now, before her eyes, or we are lost forever!

HANS: You forget where you are, Ondine.

ONDINE: The bird is alive, Hans. I wouldn't let it die.

BERTHA: She is out of her mind. The bird is dead.

ONDINE: Go and see if you don't believe me. You killed it. I brought it to life. Which of us is out of her mind?

THE KING: You brought the bird back to life, you say?

ONDINE: Yes, King. Now do you see what a hypocrite she is?

THE KING: Bertha is no hypocrite, Ondine.

ONDINE: She is. She calculates her every word. She flatters you constantly.

THE KING: Nonsense, my dear.

ONDINE: Has she ever dared to speak to you about—

THE KING: About my descent from Hercules on the sinister side? Do you think that makes me blush?

ONDINE: No. About the wart on your nose.

THE KING: [Rises.] What? [General consternation. VIOLANTE faints and is carried out.] Leave us, all of you.

THE CHAMBERLAIN: Clear the room! Clear the room!

[All leave, with the exception of THE KING and ONDINE.]

THE KING: Ondine!

ONDINE: [Desperately.] If you ask me what it resembles, it resembles a flower, a mountain. It resembles a cathedral. Hercules had two in exactly the same place, one alongside of the other. They were called the Pillars of Hercules.

THE KING: Ondine!

ONDINE: He got them by touching the Hydra. He had to touch the Hydra, naturally, in order to strangle it. It was his fifth labor.

THE KING: [Sitting down again.] My little Ondine, I like you very much. It's a rare pleasure to hear a voice like yours at court, even when this voice insists on discussing my wart—which, incidentally, I do inherit from Hercules, precisely as you say. But, for your own sake—tell me the truth.

ONDINE: Yes. Yes, I shall tell you the truth.

THE KING: Who are you?

ONDINE: I belong to the water. I am an Ondine.

THE KING: How old are you?

ONDINE: Sixteen. But I was born many ages ago. And I shall never die.

THE KING: What are you doing here? Does our world attract you?

ONDINE: From the water it seems so beautiful.

THE KING: And from the land?

ONDINE: There are ways to have water before one's eyes always.

THE KING: It is in order to make the world seem beautiful that you are weeping?

ONDINE: No. It's because they wish to take Hans away from me.

THE KING: And suppose they do? Would that be so great a misfortune?

ONDINE: Oh yes. If he deceives me, he will die.

THE KING: Don't worry, my dear. Men have been known to survive under those conditions.

ONDINE: Not this one.

THE KING: And what makes you think that Hans will deceive you?

ONDINE: I don't know. But they knew it the moment they saw him. Isn't it strange? The lake had never known deceit, not even the sound of the word. Then one day there appeared on its banks a handsome man with a loyal face and an honest voice, and that very moment the word deceit thrilled through the depths.

THE KING: Poor Ondine!

ONDINE: It's because your world is inverted in ours. All the things that I trust in Hans—his straight look, his clear words—to the water they seem crooked and cunning. He said he would love me always—and the water said, he deceives you!

THE KING: The water speaks?

ONDINE: Everything in the universe speaks, even the fish. Each time I left the cottage that night, they spat the word at me. He is beautiful, I said. Yes, said the bass, he will deceive you. He is strong, I said. Yes, said the perch, he will deceive you. Are you fond of perch, by any chance?

THE KING: I have no particular feeling about them.

ONDINE: Spiteful little things! But I was proud of him. I decided to take the risk. I made the pact.

THE KING: The pact? What pact?

ONDINE: The king, my uncle, said to me, you agree that he shall die if he deceives you? What could I answer?

THE KING: But he hasn't deceived you—yet.

ONDINE: But he is a man. He will. And then he will die.

THE KING: A king's memory is short. Your uncle will forget.

ONDINE: No.

THE KING: But, after all, what power has your uncle over him? What danger is he in?

ONDINE: Whatever is wave or water is angry with him. If he goes near a well, the level rises. When it rains, the water drenches him to the skin. Wherever he goes, the water reaches after him.

THE KING: Will you take my advice, little Ondine?

ONDINE: Yes.

THE KING: Go away, my dear.

ONDINE: With Hans?

THE KING: Dive into the first river you come to, and vanish forever.

ONDINE: But he's so clumsy in the water.

THE KING: You have had three months of happiness with Hans. In our world, that is a lifetime. Go while there is time.

ONDINE: Without Hans?

THE KING: He's not for you. His soul is small.

ONDINE: I have no soul.

THE KING: Because you don't need one. You are a soul. But human souls are tiny. There is no man whose soul is great enough for you.

ONDINE: I wouldn't love him if there were. I have already seen men with great souls—they are completely wrapped up in them. No, the only men whom one can love are those who are just like other men, whose thoughts are the thoughts of other men, who are distinguished from other men only by being themselves and nothing more.

THE KING: You are describing Hans.

ONDINE: Yes. That is Hans.

THE KING: But don't you see, my dear, that Hans loves what is great in you only because he sees it small? You are the sunlight; he loves a blonde. You are grace itself; he loves a madcap. You are adventure; he loves an adventure. One day he will see his mistake—and at that moment, you will lose him.

ONDINE: He will never see it. If it were Bertram, he would see it. Not Hans.

THE KING: If you wish to save him, leave him.

ONDINE: But I cannot save him by leaving him. If I leave him, they will say he deceived me, and Hans will die. No, it's here that I must save him. Here.

THE KING: And how will you do that, my little Ondine?

ONDINE: I have the remedy. It came to me while I was quarreling with Bertha. Did you notice—each time I came between Hans and Bertha, I succeeded only in bringing them more closely together. The instant I said something against Bertha, he sprang to her defense. Very well, from now on I shall do exactly the opposite. I shall tell him twenty times a day how beautiful Bertha is, how right she is. Then she will be wrong. I shall manage so that they are always alone. Then they will no longer feel the slightest desire for each other. In that way, with Bertha always there, I shall have Hans completely to myself. Oh, how well I understand men! Don't I? [THE KING rises and kisses her.] Oh, Your Majesty! What are you doing?

THE KING: The king thanks you, my child.

ONDINE: Thanks me? For what?

THE KING: For a lesson in true love.

ONDINE: My idea is good?

THE KING: Stupendous.

[Enter THE CHAMBERLAIN.]

THE CHAMBERLAIN: Forgive me, Your Majesty. The court is in complete consternation. What is your will? Shall I tell them all to withdraw?

THE KING: By no means.

THE CHAMBERLAIN: The reception is to continue?

THE KING: Of course.

THE CHAMBERLAIN: And the interlude? You wish to see it?

THE KING: At once.

ONDINE: How wonderful! Now I shall be able to ask Bertha's pardon before everyone.

[THE CHAMBERLAIN goes to the door and waves his staff. THE COURT comes in from all sides. BERTHA takes her place, haughtily.]

THE KING: Princess Bertha, Ondine has something to say to you.

ONDINE: I ask your pardon, Bertha.

THE KING: Very nice, my child.

ONDINE: Yes. But she might answer me.

HANS: What?

ONDINE: I have asked her pardon, though I don't want to. She might at least answer me.

THE KING: Bertha, Ondine has acknowledged her error, whatever it was. I should like you to be friends.

BERTHA: Very well, Your Majesty. I pardon her.

ONDINE: Thank you, Bertha.

BERTHA: On condition that she admits publicly that I did not kill the bird.

ONDINE: I admit it publicly. She did not kill the bird. The bird is alive—you can hear it singing. But she tried to kill it.

BERTHA: You see, Your Majesty?

HANS: One doesn't speak like that to the royal princess, Ondine!

ONDINE: The royal princess? Would you like to know who she is, this royal princess? Shall I show you? Shall I?

HANS: Silence, Ondine.

ONDINE: I happen to know the father of this royal princess. He is not a king. He is a fisherman—

BERTHA: Hans!

HANS: Ondine. You've said enough. [He takes ONDINE by the wrist.] Come.

ONDINE: [Resisting.] Not yet, Hans!

HANS: Come, I say!

ONDINE: Old One! Old One! Help me!

[THE ILLUSIONIST appears. He is followed by THE CHAMBERLAIN.]

THE ILLUSIONIST: Your Majesty, the interlude.

THE KING: [As they seat themselves.] Yes, Ondine, you have gone too far. Everyone knows there was a golden crown on Bertha's pillow when she was found.

ONDINE: The crown was mine!

[The lights go out, and come up immediately on a little set on the garden level. It depicts the fisherman's cottage on the edge of the lake. TWO ONDINES are dancing in the waterfall. An ONDINE comes in with a child in its arms. The others join her as she puts the child into a basket which she covers with rich silks.]

THE ONDINE: [Sings.]
Wrap the child in silk and lace
So the princess of the sea
May be nurtured in her place

By Auguste and Eugenie.

[*At this moment the burly tenor dressed as* MATHO *and the robust soprano dressed as* SALAMMBO *advance to either side of the set and begin singing loudly.* THE ONDINES *stop in astonishment.*]

MATHO: [*Sings.*] I am a soldier, that is all.

SALAMMBO: [*Sings.*] And I the niece of Hannibal. [THE ILLUSIONIST *steps forward.*]

THE ILLUSIONIST: Who are these people, Excellency? They have nothing to do with my show.

MATHO: [*Sings.*] I am a common mercenary.

SALAMMBO: I stand at the other pole.

MATHO: But I love this sacred person.

SALAMMBO: I adore this humble soul.

THE ILLUSIONIST: Where did they come from? What are they singing?

THE CHAMBERLAIN: *Salammbo.*

THE ILLUSIONIST: But they're spoiling the illusion. Tell them to stop.

THE CHAMBERLAIN: Impossible. Once they begin, nothing can stop them.

SALAMMBO: [*Sings.*] Take me, take me, and Carthage too.

THE ILLUSIONIST: Enough! [*He makes a gesture. The two singers continue singing and posturing, but without a sound.* THE ONDINES *resume.*]

FIRST ONDINE: [*Sings.*]
Set the little creature down,
Whom we stole from Eugenie,
And beside her set the crown
Of the princess of the sea.

SECOND ONDINE: [*Sings.*]
Weep not, we shall not forsake you,
Helpless, human little thing,
Soon a knight will come and take you
To the palace of the king.

THIRD ONDINE: [*Sings.*]
But lest it ever be forgotten
Who she is and whence begotten,
On her skin I draw the sign
Of her father's hook and line.

[THE ONDINES *turn toward* BERTHA *and sing together.*]

THE ONDINES:
Bertha, Bertha, if you dare,
Show the world your shoulder bare!

[*The lights go on suddenly; the fisherman's cottage and* THE ONDINES *vanish. Hubbub.* BERTHA *is on her feet.*]

ONDINE: Well, Bertha?

BERTHA: It's a lie!

ONDINE: Is it? [*She tears the dress from* BERTHA's *shoulders. The sign is there.*] You see? [BERTHA *kneels before* THE KING.]

MATHO
SALAMMBO } : [*Suddenly audible, they walk off together, singing.*]
All is love beneath the stars,
Is love, is love, is love!

BERTHA: It's a lie! [*She kneels before* THE KING.] It's a lie, Your Majesty. [THE KING *glances at her shoulder on which the mark is visible.*]

THE KING: Is this true, Ondine?

ONDINE: Yes, King.

BERTHA: [*Desperately.*] Hans! [HANS *makes a protecting gesture.*]

ONDINE: Old One! Where are they? [THE ILLUSIONIST *lifts a hand.* AUGUSTE *and* EUGENIE *appear. They see* BERTHA.] Oh, my darlings!

THE KING: Bertha, it is your father. Have you no word to say to him, to your mother? [BERTHA *is silent.*] As you please . . . [AUGUSTE *and* EUGENIE *go.* THE KING *walks off. The court follows slowly.*] But—[*He stops.*]—until you have asked their pardon, I forbid you to show your face at court.

[*He goes off, followed by the court.* BERTHA *is left sobbing bitterly.*]

ONDINE: Forgive me, Bertha. [*There is no answer.*] You will see. The king will call you back in a moment. And they will all love you more than before. [BERTHA *says nothing.*] Ask her to come and stay with us, Hans.

HANS: Bertha. Come with us. [BERTHA *turns silently.*]

ONDINE: Oh, how difficult it is to live among you, where what has happened can never again not have happened! How terrible to live where a word can never be unspoken and a gesture can never be unmade! But I will undo it all. You will see.

HANS: Come with us, Bertha. My castle is large. You shall live with us always, in the wing that looks out on the lake.

ONDINE: A lake? Your castle has a lake, Hans?

HANS: It has a lake. The other side faces the Rhine.

ONDINE: The Rhine?

[THE CHAMBERLAIN *comes in.*]

THE CHAMBERLAIN: The king wishes to know whether the pardon has been asked.

ONDINE: It has been asked. From the heart.

THE CHAMBERLAIN: In that case, Princess—

ONDINE: Oh Hans, haven't you a castle in the plains, in the mountains far from the water?

THE CHAMBERLAIN: Princess Bertha, the king desires your presence. He forgives you.

ONDINE: You see?

HANS: Tell him we have asked you to come with us.

ONDINE: He already knows that.

[BERTHA and THE CHAMBERLAIN go out. HANS and ONDINE cross in the direction of the garden.]

HANS: [As they pass the fountain.] And why all this fear of the water? What is it that threatens you from the water?

ONDINE: Me? Nothing.

HANS: If I sit down at the edge of a brook, you drag me away. If I walk near a pond, you come between us. What is it you fear?

ONDINE: Nothing, Hans.

HANS: Yes, Ondine, my castle is surrounded by water. And in the mornings, I shall bathe under my waterfall, and at noon I shall fish in my lake, and in the evening I shall swim in the Rhine. You don't frighten me with these tales about water. What's water? Can it see? Can it hear?

[As he passes, the jets of water rise high and threatening over their basins. THE ILLUSIONIST appears.]

ONDINE: Yes, Hans.

[They go. THE CHAMBERLAIN comes out from behind his column, and, a moment later, THE SUPERINTENDENT,

THE TRAINER, BERTRAM and THE TWO LADIES come out of hiding.]

THE CHAMBERLAIN: Wonderful! Wonderful! [To THE ILLUSIONIST.] Very nice indeed.

THE SUPERINTENDENT: Wonderful!

VIOLANTE: But is all this really going to happen?

THE ILLUSIONIST: My dear, it has happened.

THE CHAMBERLAIN: And what happens next, Magician?

THE COURT: Yes. What next?

THE CHAMBERLAIN: Does he decide to marry Bertha?

THE COURT: Does he?

THE CHAMBERLAIN: Does he deceive Ondine?

THE COURT: Does he?

THE ILLUSIONIST: Naturally.

THE CHAMBERLAIN: When can we see that?

THE ILLUSIONIST: At once, if you like.

THE CHAMBERLAIN: Splendid. Let's see it. [He goes behind his column.] Go on.

BERTRAM: No, Excellency. No.

THE CHAMBERLAIN: Yes, yes. Go on. Go on. But what's this? What's happened? [He comes out.] I'm bald?

THE ILLUSIONIST: Five years have passed.

THE CHAMBERLAIN: My teeth are gone? I'm stuttering?

THE ILLUSIONIST: Shall I continue?

THE CHAMBERLAIN: No. No, for heaven's sake! An intermission! An intermission!

CURTAIN

ACT THREE

The courtyard of the castle of the Wittenstein. The yard is surrounded on three sides by the walls of the castle. Arched doorways lead into it. At one side there is a platform with a well.

It is the morning of the marriage of BERTHA and HANS. There is a sound of church bells from the chapel. HANS, splendidly dressed, is sitting on the platform steps with his head in his hands. A SERVANT enters.

THE SERVANT: My lord, the choir has filed into the chancel.

HANS: What did you say?

THE SERVANT: I refer to the choir which will sing at your wedding.

HANS: Do you have to use this pompous tone? Can't you talk like a human being?

[BERTHA comes in. She too is dressed for a wedding.]

THE SERVANT: Long life to the bride! To the Lady Bertha!

HANS: Oh. Go away!

BERTHA: But, Hans, why are you angry on the day of our wedding?

HANS: What? You too?

BERTHA: I had hoped that your face would be radiant with joy.

HANS: Stop it, stop it! Stop it!

BERTHA: Hans, really!

HANS: I'm lost, Bertha! I'm lost!

BERTHA: Hans, you frighten me. You're so strange today.

HANS: There is a tradition in our family, Bertha. Whenever misfortune threatens, the servants feel it before anyone else, and they begin to speak all at once in solemn language. On the day of misfortune, the kitchen maids are filled with grandeur. The swineherds see what they never saw before. They speak of the curve of the stream; the shape of the flower fills them with awe; they exclaim with wonder at the honeycomb. They speak of nature, of the soul of man. They become poets. That day, misfortune strikes.

BERTHA: But the man wasn't speaking in poetry, Hans. There were no rhymes.

HANS: When I hear him speak in rhymes, I shall know that death is at hand.

BERTHA: Oh Hans, that's superstitious!

HANS: You think?

BERTHA: This is not the day of your death, Hans. It is the day of your wedding.

HANS: [He calls.] Walter! [THE SERVANT enters.] Where is the swineherd?

THE SERVANT: Under a spreading oak—

HANS: Hold your tongue.

THE SERVANT: On a grassy bank he lies—

HANS: Go fetch him. Quickly.

[THE SERVANT goes out. BERTHA takes HANS in her arms.]

BERTHA: Oh Hans, my dear, I love you.

HANS: [Absently.] You're good to me, Bertha.

BERTHA: You are holding me in your arms, Hans, but you are not thinking of me. What are you thinking?

HANS: I was weak, Bertha. I should have made her confess. I should have made her suffer as she made me suffer.

BERTHA: Can't you put her out of your mind, Hans? Not even today?

HANS: Today less than any other. Oh, Bertha, you should have married a man full of joy and pride. And look at me! Oh, Bertha, how she lied to me, that woman!

BERTHA: She never lied to you, Hans. She was no woman. You married a creature of another world. You married an Ondine. You must forget her.

HANS: If she would only let me forget her! But that cry that awakened me the morning she left—"I have deceived you with Bertram!" Has it stopped echoing for even a moment? Does one hear anything else from the river, from the lake? Does the waterfall ever stop dinning it in my ears? Day and night, in the castle, in the city, from the fountains, from the wells—it's deafening! But why does she insist on proclaiming to the world that she deceived me with Bertram? [An echo comes from the well.]

THE ECHO: Deceived you with Bertram. [Another echo whispers from the right.] With Bertram. [From the left.] With Bertram.

HANS: You hear? You hear?

BERTHA: Let's be just, Hans. You had already deceived her with me. And of course she knew it. It was only in revenge that she deceived you with Bertram.

THE ECHOES: [Whisper back.] Deceived you with Bertram. With Bertram.

HANS: Where is she now, Bertha? What is she doing? In the six months since she left, every huntsman, every fisherman in the region has been trying to find her. You would say she had vanished. And yet she's not far off. This morning at dawn they found a wreath of starfish and sea urchins on the chapel door. She put it there, of course. You know that.

BERTHA: Oh, my darling, who would have thought that you of all men would have seen anything in a girl like Ondine? When I sent you into the forest, I thought, this man will surely come back. He will look carefully, right and left, but he will never find an enchanted lake, nor the cave of a dragon, he will never glimpse among the trees at twilight the white forehead of a unicorn. He has nothing to do in that world. He will follow the human path. He will not lose his way.

HANS: I lost it.

BERTHA: Yes, but you found it again. It was in the fifth year of your marriage, that night in the winter when you told me it was me you had always loved, and I ran away from you, and you followed my tracks in the snow. They were deep and wide. They spoke plainly of my distress. They were not the tracks of a spirit. They were human tracks, and you found them, and once more you found your way. You carried me back in your arms that night.

HANS: Yes. Like Bertram when he car-

ried away Ondine. [THE SERVANT enters.]
Where is the swineherd?

THE SERVANT: In the shadow of an oak, by the banks of a stream—

HANS: Well?

THE SERVANT: I called him, but he did not answer. He is gazing at the sky. He is looking at the clouds.

HANS: Never mind. Fetch me the kitchen maid.

THE SERVANT: There is a fisherman to see you, my lord.

HANS: Get me the kitchen maid at once, do you hear, no matter what she's gazing at.

THE SERVANT: Yes, my lord. The fisherman.

[THE SERVANT goes. THE FISHERMAN comes in.]

FIRST FISHERMAN: My lord! My lord!

HANS: Say it twice more and it's poetry.

FIRST FISHERMAN: We have her! She's caught.

HANS: Ondine?

FIRST FISHERMAN: Yes. Yes. An Ondine!

BERTHA: Are you sure?

HANS: Where did you catch her?

FIRST FISHERMAN: In the Rhine. In my net.

HANS: You're sure it's she?

FIRST FISHERMAN: Positive. Her hair was over her face, but her voice was marvelous, her skin like velvet. She's wonderfully formed, the little monster.

[THE SECOND FISHERMAN appears.]

SECOND FISHERMAN: Prepare yourself. The judges are coming.

BERTHA: Judges?

HANS: What judges?

SECOND FISHERMAN: The Imperial and Episcopal judges who have jurisdiction over the supernatural.

BERTHA: So soon?

SECOND FISHERMAN: They were already holding assizes below in the city.

FIRST FISHERMAN: They came from Bingen, you see, to hang a werewolf. Now they will try the Ondine.

BERTHA: But why must they try her here?

FIRST FISHERMAN: Because an Ondine must be tried on a rock.

SECOND FISHERMAN: And besides, you are the complainant.

HANS: That's true.

BERTHA: Don't they know what day this is? Couldn't they try her another time?

SECOND FISHERMAN: My lady, the trial must be now.

HANS: They're right, Bertha. The trial must be now.

BERTHA: Hans—don't see her again, I beg you.

HANS: I shall never see her again. You heard what he said—he caught an Ondine in the Rhine. What I shall see won't even know me.

BERTHA: Don't look at her, Hans.

THE SERVANT: [Comes in.] The judges, my lord.

HANS: Just a few minutes more, Bertha, and we shall be at peace.

THE FISHERMAN: The judges.

[The JUDGES come in, puffing a little. They are followed by an ANCIENT CLERK with a great book.]

FIRST JUDGE: Marvelous! The exact altitude. Just above the realm of the water. Just below the realm of the air. It couldn't be better. [He bows to BERTHA.] My lady. Our felicitations.

SECOND JUDGE: Our compliments, my lord.

BERTHA: I shall be within call, Hans, if you want me.

[BERTHA goes out.]

HANS: You come in the nick of time, gentlemen. But how did you know there was work for you here?

FIRST JUDGE: Our work gives us a degree of insight unknown to our colleagues in the civil and criminal law.

SECOND JUDGE: It is also more difficult.

[The SERVANTS arrange the court. THE CLERK sits down, opens his register and sharpens his quill.]

FIRST JUDGE: To determine the line that divides two vineyards is easy. But to fix the proper boundaries between humanity and the spirits, hoc opus, hic—excuse me—hic labor est.

SECOND JUDGE: But in the case at hand, our task appears to be easy.

FIRST JUDGE: It is the first time we have tried an Ondine who does not deny being an Ondine.

SECOND JUDGE: All the more reason to be careful.

FIRST JUDGE: Quite right, my dear colleague.

SECOND JUDGE: You have no idea of the subterfuges these creatures use to elude our investigations. The salamanders pretend to be Ondines. The Ondines pretend to be salamanders. [*He sits down.*]

FIRST JUDGE: Excuse me.

SECOND JUDGE: You remember, my dear colleague, that affair at Kreiznach, when we tried the pretended Dorothea, the alderman's cook? She gave us every reason to believe she was a salamander. But we didn't jump at conclusions. We put her to the torch to make sure. She burnt to a crisp.

FIRST JUDGE: [*Smiles reminiscently.*] She was no more salamander than I am. [*He sits down.*]

SECOND JUDGE: She was an Ondine.

FIRST JUDGE: We had a similar case last week, the matter of a certain Gertrude, a blonde barmaid of Tübingen. It was clearly established that in her presence the beer glasses filled by themselves and, what is even more miraculous, without heads of foam. You would have been certain she was an Ondine. We threw her into the water with her hands tied—

SECOND JUDGE: She immediately drowned.

FIRST JUDGE: [*He shrugs.*] A salamander.

HANS: Did you bring Ondine with you?

FIRST JUDGE: We have her in custody. But before we examine her, Knight, it would be extremely valuable for us to ascertain the exact nature of your complaint.

HANS: My complaint? My complaint is the complaint of all mankind. Is it so much after all that God has granted us, these few yards of air between hell and heaven? Is it so attractive, after all, this bit of life we have, with these hands that get dirty, these teeth that fall out, this hair that turns gray? Why must these creatures trespass on our little world? Gentlemen, on the morning of my marriage, I claim the right to be left in peace in a world that is free of these intrusions, these threats, these seductions, alone with myself, with my bride, alone at last.

FIRST JUDGE: That is a great deal to ask, Knight.

SECOND JUDGE: Yes. It may seem surprising that these creatures should derive all their satisfaction from staring at us while we wash our feet, kiss our wives, or beat our children. But that is the undeniable fact. Around each human gesture, the meanest, the noblest, a host of grotesque presences with tails and horns is constantly dancing its round. What's to be done? We must resign ourselves.

HANS: Has there never been an age when they did not infest us?

SECOND JUDGE: An age? To my knowledge, Knight, there has never been a moment.

FIRST JUDGE: Yes, once there was a moment. One only. It was late August, near Augsburg, in the harvest season when the peasants were dancing. I had stretched out under an apple tree. I looked up into the sky. And suddenly I felt that the whole world was free of these shadows that beset it. Above my head I saw a lark soaring in the heavens—without its usual twin, the raven. Our Swabia spread to the Alps, green and blue, without my seeing over it the Swabia of the air, peopled with blue angels, nor below it the Swabia of hell, teeming with green devils. On the road there trotted a horseman with a lance, unattended by the horseman with the scythe. By the river, in the sun, the mill wheel turned slowly, without dragging in its orbit that enormous shadowy wheel that grinds the souls of the damned. For that instant, the whole world was single-hearted, at work, at play, at peace—and yet I tasted for the first time a certain loneliness, the loneliness of humanity. But the next moment, the horseman was joined by Death, the clouds bristled as always with lances and brooms, and the customary fish-headed devils had joined the dancing couples. There they were, all back at their posts again just as before. Bring in the accused.

[ONDINE *is led in by* THE EXECUTIONER. *She is nude, but draped around her body is the net in which she was caught. She is made to stand on a little elevation opposite the* JUDGES. *A number of people come in to witness the trial.*]

SECOND JUDGE: [*Peering at her.*] Her hands are not webbed, apparently. She is wearing a ring.

HANS: Remove it.

ONDINE: No!

[THE EXECUTIONER *removes it by force and hands it to* HANS.]

HANS: It is my wedding ring. I shall need it presently.

FIRST JUDGE: Knight—

HANS: The necklace too. The locket has my picture in it.

ONDINE: No!

[THE EXECUTIONER *takes it off.*]

FIRST JUDGE: Knight, with all respect, I must ask you not to interfere with the conduct of this trial. Your anger is doubtless justified, but we must avoid even the semblance of confusion. We will proceed with the identification.

HANS: It is she.

FIRST JUDGE: Beyond a doubt. But we must follow the indicated procedure. Where is the fisherman who caught her? Summon the fishermen to the bar.

[*The* FIRST FISHERMAN *takes the stand.*]

FIRST FISHERMAN: It's the first time I ever caught one, your honor. This is my lucky day!

FIRST JUDGE: Congratulations. Now—what was she doing when you caught her?

FIRST FISHERMAN: I knew that some day I'd catch one. I have known it every morning for the last thirty years. How often have I said—today I'm going to catch one. But this morning, I was certain.

FIRST JUDGE: I asked you what she was doing.

FIRST FISHERMAN: And, mind you, I caught her alive. The one they caught at Regensburg, they bashed its head in with an oar. But I was careful. I just knocked her head against the side of the boat a few times to stun her. Then I dragged her in.

HANS: You ox. You hurt her head.

FIRST JUDGE: Answer my questions. Was she swimming when you caught her?

FIRST FISHERMAN: She was swimming. She was showing her breasts, her buttocks. She can stay under a full fifteen minutes. I timed her.

FIRST JUDGE: Was she singing?

FIRST FISHERMAN: She was making a little sound, like a moan. If it was a dog, you'd call it a yelp, a bark. I remember what she was barking. She was barking: I deceived you with Bertram.

FIRST JUDGE: You're talking nonsense. Since when can you understand a bark?

FIRST FISHERMAN: As a rule, I don't. To me a bark is a bark, as a rule. But this one I understood. And what it said was—

FIRST JUDGE: She had an odor of sulphur when you pulled her out?

FIRST FISHERMAN: She had an odor of algae, of pine.

SECOND JUDGE: That's not the same thing. Did she have an odor of algae or an odor of pine?

FIRST FISHERMAN: She had an odor of algae, of pine.

FIRST JUDGE: Never mind, my dear colleague.

FIRST FISHERMAN: She had an odor that said plainly: I deceived you with Bertram.

FIRST JUDGE: Since when do odors speak?

FIRST FISHERMAN: Odors don't speak. But this one said—

FIRST JUDGE: She struggled, I presume?

FIRST FISHERMAN: No. Not at all. You might say, she let herself be caught. But when I had her in the boat, she shuddered. It was a sort of movement of the shoulders that said, as clear as clear can be: I deceived you with—

HANS: Have you quite finished, you idiot?

FIRST JUDGE: You must excuse the man, Knight. These simple souls are always imagining things. That is the origin of folklore.

FIRST FISHERMAN: I swear by all that's holy that that's one of them. I'm sorry about the tail. She didn't have it when I caught her. There's a double reward for catching them alive?

FIRST JUDGE: You may collect it after the trial. Very well, Fisherman. That's all.

FIRST FISHERMAN: And what about my net? Can I have my net back?

FIRST JUDGE: Your net is in evidence. It will be returned to you in due course.

SECOND JUDGE: Out you go.

[THE FISHERMAN *goes out, grumbling.*]

FIRST JUDGE: Proceed with the examination.

[*The* SECOND JUDGE *extends a very long telescope and focuses it on* ONDINE.]

HANS: What are you doing?

SECOND JUDGE: I am going to examine the body of this girl—

HANS: No one is going to examine her body!

FIRST JUDGE: Calm your fears, Knight. My colleague is an experienced anatomist. It was he who personally established the physical integrity of the Electress Josepha in connection with the annulment of her marriage, and she commented especially on his tact.

HANS: I tell you, this is Ondine. That's enough.

SECOND JUDGE: Knight, I understand that it is painful for you to have me auscultate in public the body of someone who was once your wife. But I can, without touching her, study through the glass those parts which differentiate her species from the human race.

HANS: Never mind the glass. You can look at her from where you are.

SECOND JUDGE: To identify with the naked eye and from a distance the very subtle variations that distinguish an Ondine from a human being seems to me an extremely impractical operation. She could at least take off the net and walk a little. She could show us her legs?

HANS: She will do nothing of the sort.

FIRST JUDGE: It would perhaps be in better taste not to insist, my dear colleague. In any case, the evidence is sufficient. Is there anyone present who denies that this is an Ondine?

SECOND FISHERMAN: [*Without moving.*] I deny it.

FIRST JUDGE: Who said that? Remove that man.

THE SERVANT: Don't kill her, your honor. She was good to us.

SECOND JUDGE: [*Shrugs his shoulders.*] She was a good Ondine, that's all.

THE SERVANT: She loved us.

SECOND JUDGE: There are affectionate varieties even among turtles.

FIRST JUDGE: Since we hear no objection, we declare that the supernatural character of the accused has been established beyond a reasonable doubt. We proceed to the second part of the trial. Knight, do you accuse this creature, by reason of her illegal intrusion into our world, of having caused disorder and confusion in your domain?

HANS: I? Certainly not.

FIRST JUDGE: But you do accuse her of being a sorceress?

HANS: Ondine, a sorceress?

FIRST JUDGE: We are merely trying to define her crime, Knight.

SECOND FISHERMAN: [*Stepping forward.*] Ondine, a sorceress?

FIRST JUDGE: Who is this man?

SECOND FISHERMAN: I am a witness.

ONDINE: He's lying!

FIRST JUDGE: Ah. In that case, you may speak.

SECOND FISHERMAN: This Ondine is no longer an Ondine. She has renounced her race and betrayed its interests. She has become a woman.

FIRST JUDGE: A sorceress.

SECOND FISHERMAN: This woman could call upon the earth and the heavens to do her bidding. The Rhine is her servant. But she gave up her power in favor of such human specialties as hay fever, headaches

and cooking. Is that true, Knight, or is it false?

FIRST JUDGE: You accuse her, if I understand correctly, of having taken on a favorable appearance in order to ferret out the secrets of the human race?

HANS: Rubbish!

SECOND FISHERMAN: The human race has no secrets, your honor. It has only afflictions.

FIRST JUDGE: It also has treasures. Doubtless she stole your gold, Knight, your jewels?

HANS: She?

SECOND FISHERMAN: All the gold and the jewels of the world meant nothing to Ondine. Of the treasures of humanity, she preferred only the humblest—the stove, the kettle, the spoon. The elements loved Ondine, but she did not return their affection. She loved the fire because it was good for making omelettes, and the water because it made soup, and the wind because it dried the wash. Write this into your record, Judge —this Ondine was the most human being that ever lived. She was human by choice.

SECOND JUDGE: We are informed that the accused was in the habit of locking herself up for hours each day in order to practice her magic arts. What do you say to that?

SECOND FISHERMAN: It's true. And what was the result of her magic, you?

THE SERVANT: A meringue, your honor.

SECOND JUDGE: A meringue? What sort of meringue?

THE SERVANT: She worked for two months to discover the secret of a good meringue.

SECOND JUDGE: That is one of the deepest of human secrets. Did she succeed?

FIRST JUDGE: Fisherman, we thank you. We shall take account of these facts in considering our judgment. If these creatures envy us our pastry, our bric-a-brac, our ointments for eczema, it is hardly to be wondered at. It is only natural that they should recognize the pre-eminence of the human condition.

SECOND JUDGE: There's nothing in the world like a good meringue. You say she discovered the secret?

THE SERVANT: Her crust was pure magic, your honor.

SECOND JUDGE: [*To the FIRST JUDGE.*] You don't suppose that with a few turns on the rack we might perhaps induce her to—?

FIRST JUDGE: No, my dear colleague, no. [*He clears his throat.*] We come now to the heart of the matter. At last, Knight, I understand the full import of your complaint. Ondine, you are accused of having cheated this knight of the joys of marriage. In place of the loving companion to which every man is entitled, you foisted upon this knight a wearisome existence with a woman who cared for nothing but her kitchen. In this way—and this is the greatest of the crimes against the human spirit—you have robbed him of love. Naturally. An Ondine is incapable of love.

HANS: Ondine incapable of love?

FIRST JUDGE: Really, Knight, it is becoming a trifle difficult to follow you. Of what, precisely, do you accuse this woman?

HANS: I accuse this woman of adoring me beyond human endurance. I accuse her of thinking only of me, of dreaming only of me, of living only for me.

FIRST JUDGE: That is not a crime, exactly.

HANS: I was this woman's god, do you understand?

FIRST JUDGE: Now, now—

HANS: You don't believe me? Very well. Answer me, Ondine. Who was your god?

ONDINE: You.

HANS: You hear? She pushes love as far as blasphemy.

FIRST JUDGE: Oh, come, there's no need to complicate the issue. These creatures are not Christians. They cannot blaspheme. All she means is that she had a proper wifely reverence for you.

HANS: Who were your saints, Ondine?

ONDINE: You.

HANS: Who were your angels? Whose face did you see in the holy pictures in your Book of Hours?

ONDINE: Yours.

HANS: You see?

FIRST JUDGE: But where is all this leading us, Knight? We are here to try an Ondine, not to judge the nature of love.

HANS: Nevertheless, that is what you are required to judge. It is Love I am accusing. I accuse the highest love of being the foulest and the truest love of being the most false. This woman who lived only for me deceived me with Bertram.

FIRST JUDGE: You are heaping confusion on confusion, Knight. If what this woman says is true, she could not possibly have deceived you with anyone.

HANS: Answer, Ondine. Did you or did you not deceive me with Bertram?

ONDINE: With Bertram.

HANS: Swear it, then. Swear it before these judges.

ONDINE: [*Rises to her feet*]. I swear it before these judges.

FIRST JUDGE: If she deceived you, we shall see soon enough. My dear colleague, put the three canonical questions. The first?

SECOND JUDGE: Ondine, when you see this man running, what do you do?

ONDINE: I lose my breath.

FIRST JUDGE: Hm.

SECOND JUDGE: And when he snores in his sleep—excuse me, Knight—what do you hear?

ONDINE: I hear the sound of singing.

FIRST JUDGE: So far her answers are correct. The third question, if you please.

SECOND JUDGE: When he tells an amusing story for the twentieth time in your presence, how does it seem to you?

ONDINE: Twenty times funnier than before.

FIRST JUDGE: And nevertheless you deceived him with Bertram?

ONDINE: I deceived him with Bertram.

SECOND FISHERMAN: You needn't shout, Ondine. I heard you.

ONDINE: [*Whispers.*] I deceived him with Bertram.

HANS: There you have it.

FIRST JUDGE: Do you realize, young woman, what the punishment for adultery is? Do you realize that this is a crime that is never confessed, because the confession doubles the injury?

ONDINE: All the same—

SECOND FISHERMAN: You deceived him with Bertram?

ONDINE: Yes.

SECOND FISHERMAN: Answer me, now, Ondine. And see that you answer me truly. Where is Bertram now?

ONDINE: In Burgundy, where he is waiting for me to join him.

SECOND FISHERMAN: Where was it that you deceived your husband with Bertram?

ONDINE: In a forest.

SECOND FISHERMAN: In the morning? At noon?

ONDINE: At noon.

SECOND FISHERMAN: Was it cold? Was it warm?

ONDINE: It was icy. Bertram said: Our

love will keep us warm. One doesn't forget such words.

SECOND FISHERMAN: Very good. And now, if you please, summon Bertram to the bar.

FIRST JUDGE: Bertram has been gone these six months, Fisherman. He is beyond the power of the law.

SECOND FISHERMAN: Its power seems limited. Here he is.

[BERTRAM *comes in.*]

HANS: Bertram!

FIRST JUDGE: Just a moment, Knight. You are the Count Bertram?

BERTRAM: Yes.

FIRST JUDGE: This woman says she deceived her husband with you.

BERTRAM: What?

FIRST JUDGE: Is it true?

BERTRAM: If she says it, it is true.

FIRST JUDGE: Where did it happen?

BERTRAM: In her room. In this castle.

FIRST JUDGE: In the morning? At night?

BERTRAM: At midnight.

FIRST JUDGE: Was it cold? Was it warm?

BERTRAM: The logs were blazing on the hearth. Ondine said: How hot it is, the way to hell! One doesn't forget such words.

SECOND FISHERMAN: Perfect. And now everything is clear.

ONDINE: And why is it so clear? Why should we remember these trifles? When people really love each other do you think they know whether it is warm or cold or noon or midnight?

SECOND FISHERMAN: Count Bertram, take this woman in your arms and kiss her lips.

BERTRAM: I take my orders only from her.

SECOND FISHERMAN: Ask him to kiss you, Ondine.

ONDINE: Before all these people? Never.

SECOND JUDGE: And yet you expect us to believe that you gave yourself to him?

ONDINE: Kiss me, Bertram.

BERTRAM: You really wish it?

ONDINE: Yes. I wish you to kiss me. Just for a moment. Just to prove that we can. And if I should shudder a little when you take me in your arms, Bertram, it's only because it's cold.

SECOND JUDGE: We are waiting, Ondine.

ONDINE: Couldn't I have something to cover myself with, at least?

SECOND JUDGE: No. As you are.

ONDINE: Very well. So much the better. I love to feel Bertram's hands on my body

when he kisses me. Come, Bertram. But if I should scream a little, Bertram, when you take me in your arms, it's only because I'm frightened here before these people. Besides, I may not scream.

SECOND JUDGE: Make up your mind, Ondine.

ONDINE: Or if I should faint. But if I faint, Bertram, you may do whatever you please with me, whatever you please.

FIRST JUDGE: Well, Ondine?

ONDINE: Well, Bertram?

BERTRAM: Ondine! [*He takes her in his arms and kisses her.*]

ONDINE: Hans! Hans!

SECOND FISHERMAN: There's your proof, gentleman. [*The* JUDGES *put on their hats.*]

ONDINE: But you don't understand. If I say Hans when I kiss Bertram, it is only to deceive him the better. If I loved Bertram with no thought of Hans, would that be deceit? No, but every moment that I love Bertram, I think of Hans and I deceive him. With Bertram.

SECOND FISHERMAN: We understand. The trial is over. You may go, Count Bertram.

BERTRAM: Must I go, Ondine?

ONDINE: Farewell, Bertram.

BERTRAM: Farewell. [BERTRAM *goes.*]

FIRST JUDGE: The court will now deliver its judgment.

SECOND JUDGE: Oyez! Oyez!

FIRST JUDGE: It is the judgment of this court that this Ondine has transgressed the boundaries of nature. However the evidence indicates that in so doing she brought with her nothing but kindness and love.

SECOND JUDGE: And even a little too much kindness and love.

FIRST JUDGE: Why she wished to make us believe that she deceived you with Bertram when in fact she did not, is a question beyond the scope of our inquiry. As she has done no great harm, it is our judgment that she shall be spared the humiliation of a public execution. She shall have her throat cut without witnesses this day directly after sunset. Until that time, we place her in the custody of the public executioner. [*Church bells begin to ring again.*] What's that?

SECOND JUDGE: Wedding bells, my dear colleague. The Knight is about to be married.

FIRST JUDGE: Ah, of course. The nuptial procession is forming in front of the chapel. Knight, permit us to join you in the hour of your happiness. [THE KITCHEN MAID *walks up to* HANS.]

HANS: Who is this?

FIRST JUDGE: Who?

HANS: This woman who walks toward me like a creature from the other world?

SECOND JUDGE: We don't know her.

FIRST JUDGE: She seems to be of this world.

THE SERVANT: It's the kitchen maid, my lord. You asked me to fetch her.

HANS: How beautiful she is!

FIRST JUDGE: Beautiful?

HANS: How very beautiful!

SECOND JUDGE: We shall not contradict you. Will you precede us?

HANS: No, no. I have to hear first what she says. She alone knows the end of this story. Speak! Speak! We are listening.

SECOND JUDGE: Is he out of his mind?

FIRST JUDGE: He has every reason.

HANS: Speak! Speak!

THE KITCHEN MAID:
My face is plain, my nature sour,
But, oh, my soul is like a flower.

HANS: That rhymes?

FIRST JUDGE: Rhymes? Not at all.

THE KITCHEN MAID:
Had I been free to choose my lot,
My hands had never touched a pot.

HANS: You're going to tell me these verses don't rhyme?

SECOND JUDGE: Verses?

FIRST JUDGE: What verses?

THE KITCHEN MAID:
My clothes are poor, my face is plain,
And yet of high rank is my pain;
There is as much salt in my tears
As in those shed by emperors.
And when the butler vents his spleen,
It hurts as if I were a queen.
Oh, when we two come to your city,
And, kneeling, ask for grace and pity,
Both bearing on our brows the same
Affronts and thorns and marks of shame,
Will you know us one from the other,
My Lord, my savior and my brother?

HANS: That's a poem, is it not? Would you call that a poem?

FIRST JUDGE: A poem? All I heard was a scullion complaining that she had been falsely accused of stealing a spoon.

SECOND JUDGE: She said her corns have been aching since November.

HANS: Is that a scythe she bears in her hand?

FIRST JUDGE: A scythe? No, that's a spindle.

SECOND JUDGE: It's a broom.

HANS: I thank you, kitchen maid. When next you come, I shall be ready. Come, gentlemen.

[THE KITCHEN MAID *goes out.* THE SERVANT *crosses the stage solemnly. He turns.*]

THE SERVANT: Your bride is in the chapel, my lord. The priest is waiting.

HANS: Go and say that I am coming. [*The wedding bells begin to toll as for a funeral. They all go out, except* THE EXECUTIONER, THE SECOND FISHERMAN *and* ONDINE.]

THE EXECUTIONER: [*Taking hold of* ONDINE.] Now then, Mistress—

SECOND FISHERMAN: One moment, Executioner. [*With a gesture of his hand, he turns* THE EXECUTIONER *into an automaton and waves him off the stage.*] The end is near, Ondine.

ONDINE: Don't kill him, Old One.

SECOND FISHERMAN: You haven't forgotten our pact?

ONDINE: Don't judge men by our standards, Old One. Men don't deceive their wives unless they love them. When they love them most, they deceive them. It's a form of fidelity, their deceit.

SECOND FISHERMAN: Ah, Ondine, what a woman you are!

ONDINE: It's only because he wished to honor me that he deceived me. It was to show the world how pure I was, how true. I really don't see how else he could have done it.

SECOND FISHERMAN: You have always suffered from a lack of imagination.

ONDINE: When a man comes home in the evening with his eyes full of gratitude and his arms full of flowers, and he kisses our hands and calls us his savior and his angel—we all know what that means. It's scarcely an hour since he has deceived us. And is there anything more beautiful in marriage?

SECOND FISHERMAN: He has made you suffer, my little Ondine.

ONDINE: Yes. I have suffered. But remember we are speaking of humans. Among humans you are not unhappy when you suffer. On the contrary. To seek out in a world full of joy the one thing that is certain to give you pain, and to hug that to your bosom with all your strength—that's the greatest human happiness. People think you're strange if you don't do it. Save him, Old One.

SECOND FISHERMAN: He is going to die, Ondine.

ONDINE: Old One!

SECOND FISHERMAN: What does it matter to you, Ondine? You have only a few minutes left of human memory. Your sisters will call you three times, and you will forget everything.

ONDINE: Save him! Save him!

SECOND FISHERMAN: If you wish, I will let him die at the same moment that you forget him. That seems humane.

ONDINE: He is so young. So strong.

SECOND FISHERMAN: You have strained his heart, Ondine.

ONDINE: I? How could I?

SECOND FISHERMAN: Since you show such interest in dogfish, perhaps you remember a couple who broke their hearts one day while swimming together peacefully in a calm sea. They had crossed the entire width of the ocean side by side in winter, through a tempest, without the slightest difficulty. And then one day in a blue gulf, they swam against a little wave. All the steel of the sea was in that ripple of water, and the effort was too much for them. For a week their eyes grew pale, their lips drooped. But there was nothing wrong with them, they said . . . but they were dying. And so it is with men, Ondine. What breaks the woodsman's heart, or the knight's, is not the great oak, nor the battle with the dragon: It is a slender reed, it is a child who loves him.—He has only a few minutes left to live.

ONDINE: But he has everything to live for now. His life is in order.

SECOND FISHERMAN: His brain is full of the music of those who are dying. When the kitchen maid held forth just now on the price of eggs and cheese, you saw, it was all sheer poetry in his ears.

ONDINE: He has Bertha—

SECOND FISHERMAN: She is waiting for him in vain in the chapel. He is in the stable with his horse. His horse is speaking to him. Dear master, good-bye till we meet in the sky, his horse is saying. Today his horse has become a poet.

ONDINE: I can hear them singing in the chapel. He is being married.

SECOND FISHERMAN: What does this marriage mean to him now? The whole thing has slipped away from him like a ring too wide for the finger. He is wandering about by himself. He is talking to himself, he doesn't know what he's saying. It's a way men have of escaping when they come up suddenly against a reality. They become what is called mad. All at once they are logical. They don't compromise. They don't marry the woman they don't love. They reason simply and clearly like the plants and the water. Like us.

ONDINE: Listen to him. He is cursing me.

[HANS *is heard speaking offstage.*]

SECOND FISHERMAN: He loves you. He's mad. He's here. [*He goes.* HANS *comes in slowly and stands behind* ONDINE *for a moment.*]

HANS: My name is Hans.

ONDINE: It's a beautiful name.

HANS: Ondine and Hans. The most beautiful names in the world, are they not?

ONDINE: Yes. Hans and Ondine.

HANS: Oh, no. Ondine first. That's the title. Ondine. It will be called *Ondine,* this story in which I appear from time to time. And I don't play a very brilliant part in it, do I, because, as you said, once, I'm not very bright; I'm just the man in the story. I loved Ondine because she wanted me; I deceived her because I had to. I didn't count for much. I was born to live between the stable and the kennels—such was my fate, and I might have been happy there. But I strayed from the appointed path, and I was caught between nature and destiny. I was trapped.

ONDINE: Forgive me, Hans.

HANS: But why do you make this error, all of you? Was I the man for love? Lovers are of a different stamp—little threadbare professors full of fury, stockbrokers with heavy glasses; such men have the time and capacity for enjoyment and suffering. But you never choose such men, never. Instead you fall with all your weight on some poor general called Antony, or some poor knight called Hans, ordinary men of action for whom love is a torment and a poison. And then it's all up with them. Between the wars and the chase and the tourneys and the hospital, did I ever have a spare moment in my life? But you had to add also the poison in my veins, the flame in my eyes, the gall in my mouth! And then, oh God, how they shook me between them and bruised me, and flayed me between hell and heaven! It wasn't very just of you, Ondine.

ONDINE: Farewell, Hans.

HANS: And then, you see? One day they leave you. The day when suddenly everything becomes clear, the day you realize that you would die if they left you—that day they leave you. The day when you find them again, and with them, everything that gives life its meaning, that day, they look you in the eye with a limpid glance, and they say farewell.

ONDINE: I am going to forget everything, Hans.

HANS: And a real farewell, a farewell forever! Not like those lovers who part on the threshold of death, but are destined to meet again in another world, to jostle each other eternally in the same heaven. These part only in order never to part again—you don't call that a parting. But Ondine and I will never meet again. We part for eternity, we go to different worlds. We must do this properly, Ondine. It is the first real farewell that has ever been said in this world.

ONDINE: Live, Hans. You too will forget.

HANS: Live! It's easy to say. If at least I could work up a little interest in living— but I'm too tired to make the effort. Since you left me, Ondine, all the things my body once did by itself, it does now only by special order. The grass doesn't look green to my eyes unless I order them to see it green. And it's not very gay, you know, when the grass is black. It's an exhausting piece of management I've undertaken. I have to supervise five senses, two hundred bones, a thousand muscles. A single moment of inattention, and I forget to breathe. He died, they will say, because it was a nuisance to breathe . . . [He shakes his head.] He died of love. Why did you let the fisherman catch you, Ondine? What did you wish to tell me?

ONDINE: That an Ondine will mourn for you always.

HANS: No. No one will mourn for me. I am the last of my house. I shall leave no trace behind me. There will be only an Ondine, and she will have forgotten.

ONDINE: No, Hans. I have taken my precautions. You used to laugh at me because I always made the same movements in your house. You said I counted my steps. It was true. It was because I knew the day would come when I would have to go back. I was training myself. And now, in the depths of the Rhine or the ocean, without knowing why, I shall go on forever making the movements that I made when I lived with you. When I plunge to the bottom, I shall be going to the cellar—when I spring to the surface, I shall be going to the attic. I shall pass through doors in the water. I shall open windows. In this way I shall live a little with you always. Among the wild Ondines there will be one who will forever be your wife. Oh! What is it?

HANS: I forgot for a moment.

ONDINE: Forgot what?

HANS: To breathe. Go on, Ondine, go on.

ONDINE: Before I left, I took some of the things in our room. I threw them into the river. They seem strange to me in the water, these bits of wood and metal that speak to me of you, they float about aimlessly out of their element. It's because I'm not used to it yet: tomorrow they will seem as firm and stable as the currents in which they float. I shall not know what they mean, exactly, but I shall live among them, and it will be strange if I don't use them sometimes. I shall drink from your cup. I shall look into your mirror. Sometimes perhaps your clock will strike. Timeless, I shall not understand this sound but I shall hear it. And so, in my way, though death and the infinite come between us, I shall be true to you always.

HANS: Thank you, Ondine. And I—

THE FIRST VOICE: Ondine!

HANS: They are calling you, Ondine.

ONDINE: They will call me three times. I shall remember until the last. Hans, let us not waste these moments! Ask me something quickly. What is it, Hans? What is it? You're pale.

HANS: I too am being called, Ondine.

ONDINE: Speak! Question me!

HANS: What did you say, Ondine, when you came out of the storm, the first time I saw you?

ONDINE: I said: How beautiful he is!

HANS: And when you saw me eating the trout?

ONDINE: I said: How stupid he is!

HANS: And when I said: It does no harm to think?

ONDINE: I said: In after years we shall have this hour to remember. The hour before you kissed me.

HANS: I can't wait now, Ondine. Kiss me now.

THE SECOND VOICE: Ondine!

ONDINE: It's all whirling about in my head! Speak, Hans, speak!

HANS: I can't speak and kiss you at the same time.

ONDINE: I'll be quiet.

[*He kisses her.* THE KITCHEN MAID *comes in with her broom.*]

HANS: Look! Look! There she is!

ONDINE: Who?

HANS: Her face is plain, her nature sour. But oh, her soul is like a flower! [*He falls.*]

ONDINE: Help! Help!

HANS: Ondine—

THE THIRD VOICE: Ondine!

[HANS *dies.* ONDINE *looks about in surprise.*]

ONDINE: How did I get here? How strange! It's solid. It's empty. It's the earth?

[THE SECOND FISHERMAN *appears.*]

SECOND FISHERMAN: It is the earth, Ondine. It's no place for you.

ONDINE: No—

[THE ONDINES *are heard singing in the distance.*]

SECOND FISHERMAN: Come, little one, let us leave it.

ONDINE: Oh yes. Let us leave it. [*She takes a few steps, then stops before the body of* HANS *which is lying on the platform steps.*] Wait. Why is this handsome young man lying here? Who is he?

SECOND FISHERMAN: His name is Hans.

ONDINE: What a beautiful name! But why doesn't he move? Is there something wrong with him!

SECOND FISHERMAN: He is dead.

FIRST ONDINE: Come, Ondine.

ONDINE: Oh, I like him so much! Can you bring him back to life, Old One?

SECOND FISHERMAN: Impossible.

ONDINE: What a pity! How I should have loved him!

CURTAIN

BERTOLT BRECHT

THEATRE FOR PLEASURE OR THEATRE FOR INSTRUCTION

A few years back, anybody talking about the modern theatre meant the theatre in Moscow, New York and Berlin. He might have thrown in a mention of one of Jouvet's productions in Paris or Cochran's in London, or *The Dybbuk* as given by the Habima (which is to all intents and purposes part of the Russian theatre, since Vakhtangov was its director). But broadly speaking there were only three capitals so far as modern theatre was concerned.

Russian, American and German theatres differed widely from one another, but were alike in being modern, that is to say in introducing technical and artistic innovations. In a sense they even achieved a certain stylistic resemblance, probably because technology is international (not just that part which is directly applied to the stage but also that which influences it, the film for instance), and because large progressive cities in large industrial countries are involved. Among the older capitalist countries it is the Berlin theatre that seemed of late to be in the lead. For a period all that is common to the modern theatre received its strongest and (so far) maturest expression there.

The Berlin theatre's last phase was the so-called epic theatre, and it showed the modern theatre's trend of development in its purest form. Whatever was labelled *'Zeitstück'* or *'Piscatorbühne'* or *'Lehrstück'* belongs to the epic theatre.

THE EPIC THEATRE

Many people imagine that the term 'epic theatre' is self-contradictory, as the epic and dramatic ways of narrating a story are held, following Aristotle, to be basically distinct. The difference between the two forms was never thought simply to lie in the fact that the one is performed by living beings while the other operates via the written word; epic works such as those of Homer and the medieval singers were at the same time theatrical performances, while dramas like Goethe's *Faust* and Byron's *Manfred* are agreed to have been more effective as books. Thus even by Aristotle's definition the difference between the dramatic and epic forms was attributed to their different methods of construction, whose laws were dealt with by two different branches of aesthetics. The method of construction depended on the different way of presenting the work to the public, sometimes via the stage, sometimes through a book; and independently of that there was the 'dramatic element' in epic works and the 'epic element' in dramatic. The bourgeois novel in the last century developed much that was 'dramatic,' by which was meant the strong centralization of the story, a momentum that drew the separate parts into a common relationship. A particular passion of utterance, a certain emphasis on the clash of forces are hallmarks of the 'dramatic.' The epic writer Döblin provided an excellent criterion when he said that with an epic work, as opposed to a dramatic, one can as it were take a pair of scissors and cut it into individual pieces, which remain fully capable of life.

This is no place to explain how the opposition of epic and dramatic lost its rigidity after having long been held to be irreconcilable. Let us just point out that the technical advances alone were enough to permit the stage to incorporate an element of narrative in its dramatic productions. The possibility of projections, the greater adaptability of the stage due to mechanization, the film, all completed the theatre's equipment, and did so at a point where the most important transactions between people could no longer be shown simply by personifying the motive forces or subjecting the characters to invisible metaphysical powers.

To make these transactions intelligible the environment in which the people lived had to be brought to bear in a big and 'significant' way.

This environment had of course been shown in the existing drama, but only as seen from the central figure's point of view, and not as an independent element. It was defined by the hero's reactions to it. It was seen as a storm can be seen when one sees the ships on a sheet of water unfolding their sails, and the sails filling out. In the epic theatre it was to appear standing on its own.

The stage began to tell a story. The narrator was no longer missing, along with the fourth wall. Not only did the background adopt an attitude to the events on the stage—by big screens recalling other simultaneous events elsewhere, by projecting documents which confirmed or contradicted what the characters said, by concrete and intelligible figures to accompany abstract conversations, by figures and sentences to support mimed transactions whose sense was unclear—but the actors too refrained from going over wholly into their role, remaining detached from the character they were playing and clearly inviting criticism of him.

The spectator was no longer in any way allowed to submit to an experience uncritically (and without practical consequences) by means of simple empathy with the characters in a play. The production took the subject-matter and the incidents shown and put them through a process of alienation: the alienation that is necessary to all understanding. When something seems 'the most obvious thing in the world' it means that any attempt to understand the world has been given up.

What is 'natural' must have the force of what is startling. This is the only way to expose the laws of cause and effect. People's activity must simultaneously be so and be capable of being different.

It was all a great change.

The dramatic theatre's spectator says: Yes, I have felt like that too—Just like me—It's only natural—It'll never change—The sufferings of this man appal me, because they are inescapable—That's great art; it all seems the most obvious thing in the world—I weep when they weep, I laugh when they laugh.

The epic theatre's spectator says: I'd never have thought it—That's not the way—That's extraordinary, hardly believable—It's got to stop—The sufferings of this man appal me, because they are unnecessary—That's great art: nothing obvious in it—I laugh when they weep, I weep when they laugh.

THE INSTRUCTIVE THEATRE

The stage began to be instructive.

Oil, inflation, war, social struggles, the family, religion, wheat, the meat market, all became subjects for theatrical representation. Choruses enlightened the spectator about facts unknown to him. Films showed a montage of events from all over the world. Projections added statistical material. And as the 'background' came to the front of the stage so people's activity was subjected to criticism. Right and wrong courses of action were shown. People were shown who knew what they were doing, and others who did not. The theatre became an affair for philosophers, but only for such philosophers as wished not just to explain the world but also to change it. So we had philosophy, and we had instruction. And where was the amusement in all that? Were they sending us back to school, teaching us to read and write? Were we supposed to pass exams, work for diplomas?

Generally there is felt to be a very sharp distinction between learning and amusing oneself. The first may be useful, but only the second is pleasant. So we have to defend the epic theatre against the suspicion that it is a highly disagreeable, humourless, indeed strenuous affair.

Well: all that can be said is that the contrast between learning and amusing oneself is not laid down by divine rule; it is not one that has always been and must continue to be.

Undoubtedly there is much that is tedious about the kind of learning familiar to us from school, from our professional training, etc. But it must be remembered under what conditions and to what end that takes place.

It is really a commercial transaction. Knowledge is just a commodity. It is acquired in order to be resold. All those who have grown out of going to school have to do their learning virtually in secret, for anyone who admits that he still has something to learn devalues himself as a man whose knowledge is inadequate. Moreover the usefulness of learning is very much limited by factors outside the learner's control. There is unemployment, for instance, against which no knowledge can protect one. There is the division of labour, which makes generalized knowledge unnecessary and impossible. Learning is often among the concerns of those whom no amount of concern will get any forwarder. There is not much knowledge that leads to power, but plenty of knowledge to which only power can lead.

Learning has a very different function for different social strata. There are strata who cannot imagine any improvement in conditions: they find the conditions good enough for them. Whatever happens to oil they will benefit from it. And: they feel the years beginning to tell. There can't be all that many years more. What is the point of learning a lot now? They have said their final word: a grunt. But there are also strata 'waiting their turn' who are discontented with conditions, have a vast interest in the practical side of learning, want at all costs to find out where they stand, and know that they are lost without learning; these are the best and keenest learners. Similar differences apply to countries and peoples. Thus the pleasure of learning depends on all sorts of things; but none the less there is such a thing as pleasurable learning, cheerful and militant learning.

If there were not such amusement to be had from learning the theatre's whole structure would unfit it for teaching.

Theatre remains theatre even when it is instructive theatre, and in so far as it is good theatre it will amuse.

But what has knowledge got to do with art? We know that knowledge can be amusing, but not everything that is amusing belongs in the theatre.

I have often been told, when pointing out the invaluable services that modern knowledge and science, if properly applied, can perform for art and specially for the theatre, that art and knowledge are two estimable but wholly distinct fields of human activity. This is a fearful truism, of course, and it is as well to agree quickly that, like most truisms, it is perfectly true. Art and science work in quite different ways: agreed. But, bad as it may sound, I have to admit that I cannot get along as an artist without the use of one or two sciences. This may well arouse serious doubts as to my artistic capacities. People are used to seeing poets as unique and slightly unnatural beings who reveal with a truly godlike assurance things that other people can only recognize after much sweat and toil. It is naturally distasteful to have to admit that one does not belong to this select band. All the same, it must be admitted. It must at the same time be made clear that the scientific occupations just confessed to are not pardonable side interests, pursued on days off after a good week's work. We all know how Goethe was interested in natural history, Schiller in history: as a kind of hobby, it is charitable to assume. I have no wish promptly to accuse these two of having needed these sciences for their poetic activity; I am not trying to shelter behind them; but I must say that I do need the sciences. I have to admit, however, that I look askance at all sorts of people who I know do not operate on the level of scientific understanding: that is to say, who sing as the birds sing, or as people imagine the birds to sing. I don't mean by that that I would reject a charming poem about the taste of fried fish or the delights of a boating party just because the writer had not studied gastronomy or navigation. But in my view the great and complicated things that go on in the world cannot be adequately recognized by people who do not use every possible aid to understanding.

Let us suppose that great passions or great events have to be shown which influence the fate of nations. The lust for power is nowadays held to be such a passion. Given that a poet 'feels' this lust and wants to have someone strive for power, how is he to show the exceedingly complicated machinery within which the struggle for power nowadays takes place? If his hero is a politician, how do politics work? If he is a business man, how does business work? And yet there are writers who find business and politics nothing like so passionately interesting as the individual's lust for power. How are they to acquire the necessary knowledge? They are scarcely likely to learn enough by going round and keeping their eyes open, though even then it is more than they would get by just rolling their eyes in an exalted frenzy. The foundation of a paper like the *Völkischer Beobachter* or a business like Standard Oil is a pretty complicated affair, and such things cannot be conveyed just like that. One important field for the playwright is psychology. It is taken for granted that a poet, if not an ordinary man, must be able without further instruction to discover the motives that lead a man to commit murder; he must be able to give a picture of a murderer's mental state 'from within himself.' It is taken for granted that one only has to look inside oneself in such a case; and then there's always one's imagination. . . . There are various reasons why I can no longer surrender to this agreeable hope of getting a result quite so simply. I can no longer find in myself all those motives which the press or scientific reports show to have been observed in people. Like the average judge when pronouncing sentence, I cannot without further ado conjure up an adequate picture of a murderer's mental state. Modern psychology, from psychoanalysis to behaviourism, acquaints me with facts that lead me to judge the case quite differently, especially if I bear in mind the findings of sociology and do not overlook economics and history. You will say: but that's getting complicated. I have to answer that it *is* complicated. Even if you let yourself be convinced, and agree with me that a large slice of literature is exceedingly primitive, you may still ask with profound concern: won't an evening in such a theatre be a most alarming affair? The answer to that is: no.

Whatever knowledge is embodied in a piece of poetic writing has to be wholly transmuted into poetry. Its utilization fulfils the very pleasure that the poetic element provokes. If it does not at the same time fulfil that which is fulfilled by the scientific element, none the less in an age of great discoveries and inventions one must have a certain inclination to penetrate deeper into things—a desire to make the world controllable—if one is to be sure of enjoying its poetry.

IS THE EPIC THEATRE
SOME KIND OF 'MORAL INSTITUTION'?

According to Friedrich Schiller the theatre is supposed to be a moral institution. In making this demand it hardly occurred to Schiller that by moralizing from the stage he might drive the audience out of the theatre. Audiences had no objection to moralizing in his day. It was only later that Friedrich Nietzsche attacked him for blowing a moral trumpet. To Nietzsche any concern with morality was a depressing affair; to Schiller it seemed thoroughly enjoyable. He knew of nothing that could give greater amusement and satisfaction than the propagation of ideas. The bourgeoisie was setting about forming the ideas of the nation.

Putting one's house in order, patting oneself on the back, submitting one's account, is something highly agreeable. But describing the collapse of one's house, having pains in the back, paying one's account, is indeed a depressing affair, and that was how Friedrich Nietzsche saw things a century later. He was poorly disposed towards morality, and thus towards the previous Friedrich too.

The epic theatre was likewise often objected to as moralizing too much. Yet in the epic theatre moral arguments only took second place. Its aim was less to moralize than to observe. That is to say it observed, and then the thick end of the wedge followed: the story's moral. Of course we cannot pretend that we started our observations out of a pure passion for observing and without any more practical motive, only to be completely staggered by their results. Undoubtedly there were some painful discrepancies in our environment, circumstances that were barely tolerable, and this not merely on account of moral considerations. It is not only moral considerations that make hunger, cold and oppression hard to bear. Similarly the object of our inquiries was not just to arouse moral objections to such circumstances (even though they could easily be felt—though not by all the audience alike; such objections were seldom for instance felt by those who profited by the circumstances in question) but to discover means for their elimination. We were not in fact speaking in the name of morality but in that of the victims. These truly are two distinct matters, for the victims are often told that they ought to be contented with their lot, for moral reasons. Moralists of this sort see man as existing for morality, not morality for man. At least it should be possible to gather from the above to what degree and in what sense the epic theatre is a moral institution.

CAN EPIC THEATRE BE PLAYED ANYWHERE?

Stylistically speaking, there is nothing all that new about the epic theatre. Its expository character and its emphasis on virtuosity bring it close to the old Asiatic theatre. Didactic tendencies are to be found in the medieval mystery plays and the classical Spanish theatre, and also in the theatre of the Jesuits.

These theatrical forms corresponded to particular trends of their time, and vanished with them. Similarly the modern epic theatre is linked with certain trends. It cannot by any means be practised universally. Most of the great nations today are not disposed to use the theatre for ventilating their problems. London, Paris, Tokyo and Rome maintain their theatres for quite different purposes. Up to now favourable circumstances for an epic and didactic theatre have only been found in a few places and for a short period of time. In Berlin Fascism put a very definite stop to the development of such a theatre.

It demands not only a certain technological level but a powerful movement in society which is interested to see vital questions freely aired with a view to their solution, and can defend this interest against every contrary trend.

The epic theatre is the broadest and most far-reaching attempt at large-scale modern theatre, and it has all those immense difficulties to overcome that always confront the vital forces in the sphere of politics, philosophy, science and art.

BERTOLT BRECHT

The Caucasian Chalk Circle

REVISED ENGLISH VERSION BY ERIC BENTLEY

CHARACTERS

OLD MAN *on the right*
PEASANT WOMAN *on the right*
YOUNG PEASANT
A VERY YOUNG WORKER
OLD MAN *on the left*
PEASANT WOMAN *on the left*
AGRICULTURIST KATO
GIRL TRACTORIST
WOUNDED SOLDIER
THE DELEGATE *from the capital*
THE SINGER
GEORGI ABASHWILI, *the Governor*
NATELLA, *the Governor's wife*
MICHAEL, *their son*
SHALVA, *an adjutant*
ARSEN KAZBEKI, *a fat prince*
MESSENGER *from the capital*
NIKO MIKADZE *and* MIKA LOLADZE, *doctors*
SIMON SHASHAVA, *a soldier*
GRUSHA VASHNADZE, *a kitchen maid*
OLD PEASANT *with the milk*
CORPORAL *and* PRIVATE
PEASANT *and his wife*

LAVRENTI VASHNADZE, *Grusha's brother*
ANIKO, *his wife*
PEASANT WOMAN, *for a while Grusha's mother-in-law*
JUSSUP, *her son*
MONK
AZDAK, *village recorder*
SHAUWA, *a policeman*
GRAND DUKE
DOCTOR
INVALID
LIMPING MAN
BLACKMAILER
LUDOVICA
INNKEEPER, *her father-in-law*
STABLEBOY
POOR OLD PEASANT WOMAN
IRAKLI, *her brother-in-law, a bandit*
THREE WEALTHY FARMERS
ILLO SHUBOLADZE *and* SANDRO OBOLADZE, *lawyers*
OLD MARRIED COUPLE

Soldiers, Servants, Peasants, Beggars, Musicians, Merchants, Nobles, Architects

Bertolt Brecht, "The Caucasian Chalk Circle," revised English version by Eric Bentley (New York: Grove Press, 1966). © Copyright 1947, 1961, 1963 by Eric Bentley. Prologue © Copyright 1959 Eric Bentley. Introduction © Copyright 1965 by Eric Bentley. Originally published in PARABLES FOR THE THEATRE: TWO PLAYS BY BERTOLT BRECHT, University of Minnesota Press. Reprinted by permission of University of Minnesota Press.

The time and the place: After a prologue, set in 1945, we move back perhaps 1000 years.

The action of The Caucasian Chalk Circle *centers on Nuka (or Nukha), a town in Azerbaijan. However, the capital referred to in the prologue is not Baku (capital of Soviet Azerbaijan) but Tiflis (or Tbilisi), capital of Georgia. When Azdak, later, refers to "the capital" he means Nuka itself, though whether Nuka was ever capital of Georgia I do not know: in what reading I have done on the subject I have only found Nuka to be the capital of a Nuka Khanate.*

The word "Georgia" has not been used in this English version because of its American associations; instead, the alternative name "Grusinia" (in Russian, Gruziya) has been used.

The reasons for resettling the old Chinese story in Transcaucasia are not far to seek. The play was written when the Soviet chief of state, Joseph Stalin, was a Georgian, as was his favorite poet, cited in the Prologue, Mayakovsky. And surely there is a point in having this story acted out at the place where Europe and Asia meet, a place incomparably rich in legend and history. Here Jason found the Golden Fleece. Here Noah's Ark touched ground. Here the armies of both Genghis Khan and Tamerlane wrought havoc.

[E.B.]

PROLOGUE

Summer, 1945.

Among the ruins of a war-ravaged Caucasian village the members of two Kolkhoz villages, mostly women and older men, are sitting in a circle, smoking and drinking wine. With them is a DELEGATE *of the State Reconstruction Commission from Nuka.*

PEASANT WOMAN, *left*: [*Pointing.*] In those hills over there we stopped three Nazi tanks, but the apple orchard was already destroyed.

OLD MAN, *right*: Our beautiful dairy farm: a ruin.

GIRL TRACTORIST: I laid the fire, Comrade.

[*Pause.*]

DELEGATE: Nuka, Azerbaijan S.S.R. Delegation received from the goat-breeding Kolkhoz "Rosa Luxemburg." This is a collective farm which moved eastwards on orders from the authorities at the approach of Hitler's armies. They are now planning to return. Their delegates have looked at the village and the land and found a lot of destruction. [*Delegates on the right nod.*] But the neighboring fruit farm—Kolkhoz [*To the left.*] "Galinsk"—proposes to use the former grazing land of Kolkhoz "Rosa Luxemburg" for orchards and vineyards. This land lies in a valley where grass doesn't grow very well. As a delegate of the Reconstruction Commission in Nuka I request that the two Kolkhoz villages decide between themselves whether Kolkhoz "Rosa Luxemburg" shall return or not.

OLD MAN, *right*: First of all, I want to protest against the time limit on discussion. We of Kolkhoz "Rosa Luxemburg" have spent three days and three nights getting here. And now discussion is limited to half a day.

WOUNDED SOLDIER, *left*: Comrade, we haven't as many villages as we used to have. We haven't as many hands. We haven't as much time.

GIRL TRACTORIST: All pleasures have to be rationed. Tobacco is rationed, and wine. Discussion should be rationed.

OLD MAN, *right*: [*Sighing.*] Death to the fascists! But I will come to the point and explain why we want our valley back. There are a great many reasons, but I'll begin with one of the simplest. Makinä Abakidze, unpack the goat cheese. [*A peasant woman from right takes from a basket an enormous cheese wrapped in a cloth. Applause and laughter.*] Help yourselves, Comrades, start in!

OLD MAN, *left*: [*Suspiciously.*] Is this a way of influencing us?

OLD MAN, *right*: [*Amid laughter.*] How could it be a way of influencing you, Surab, you valley-thief? Everyone knows you'll take the cheese and the valley, too. [*Laughter.*] All I expect from you is an honest answer. Do you like the cheese?

OLD MAN, *left*: The answer is: yes.

OLD MAN, *right*: Really. [*Bitterly.*] I ought to have known you know nothing about cheese.

OLD MAN, *left*: Why not? When I tell you I like it?

OLD MAN, *right*: Because you can't like it. Because it's not what it was in the old days. And why not? Because our goats don't like the new grass as they did the old. Cheese is not cheese because grass is not grass, that's the thing. Please put that in your report.

OLD MAN, *left*: But your cheese is excellent.

OLD MAN, *right*: It isn't excellent. It's just passable. The new grazing land is no good, whatever the young people may say. One can't live there. It doesn't even smell of morning in the morning. [*Several people laugh.*]

DELEGATE: Don't mind their laughing: they understand you. Comrades, why does one love one's country? Because the bread tastes better there, the air smells better,

voices sound stronger, the sky is higher, the
ground is easier to walk on. Isn't that so?

OLD MAN, *right*: The valley has belonged
to us from all eternity.

SOLDIER, *left*: What does *that* mean—
from all eternity? Nothing belongs to anyone from all eternity. When you were
young you didn't even belong to yourself.
You belonged to the Kazbeki princes.

OLD MAN, *right*: Doesn't it make a difference, though, what kind of trees stand
next to the house you are born in? Or what
kind of neighbors you have? Doesn't that
make a difference? We want to go back just
to have you as our neighbors, valley-thieves!
Now you can all laugh again.

OLD MAN, *left*: [*Laughing.*] Then why
don't you listen to what your neighbor,
Kato Wachtang, our agriculturist, has to say
about the valley?

PEASANT WOMAN, *right*: We've not said
all we have to say about our valley. By no
means. Not all the houses are destroyed. As
for the dairy farm, at least the foundation
wall is still standing.

DELEGATE: You can claim State support
—here and there—you know that. I have
suggestions here in my pocket.

PEASANT WOMAN, *right*: Comrade Specialist, we haven't come here to haggle. I
can't take your cap and hand you another,
and say "This one's better." The other one
might *be* better, but you *like* yours better.

GIRL TRACTORIST: A piece of land is not
a cap—not in our country, Comrade.

DELEGATE: Don't get mad. It's true we
have to consider a piece of land as a tool to
produce something useful, but it's also true
that we must recognize love for a particular
piece of land. As far as I'm concerned, I'd
like to find out more exactly what you [*To
those on the left.*] want to do with the valley.

OTHERS: Yes, let Kato speak.

KATO: [*Rising; she's in military uniform.*]
Comrades, last winter, while we were fighting in these hills here as Partisans, we discussed how, once the Germans were expelled,
we could build up our fruit culture to ten
times its original size. I've prepared a plan
for an irrigation project. By means of a cof-
ferdam on our mountain lake, 300 hectares
of unfertile land can be irrigated. Our Kolkhoz could not only cultivate more fruit, but
also have vineyards. The project, however,
would pay only if the disputed valley of

Kolkhoz "Rosa Luxemburg" were also included. Here are the calculations. [*She
hands* DELEGATE *a briefcase.*]

OLD MAN, *right*: Write into the report
that our Kolkhoz plans to start a new stud
farm.

GIRL TRACTORIST: Comrades, the project
was conceived during days and nights when
we had to take cover in the mountains. We
were often without ammunition for our half-
dozen rifles. Even finding a pencil was difficult. [*Applause from both sides.*]

OLD MAN, *right*: Our thanks to the Comrades of Kolkhoz "Galinsk" and all those
who've defended our country! [*They shake
hands and embrace.*]

PEASANT WOMAN, *left*: In doing this our
thought was that our soldiers—both your
men and our men—should return to a still
more productive homeland.

GIRL TRACTORIST: As the poet Mayakovsky said: "The home of the Soviet people shall also be the home of Reason"!

[*The delegates excluding the* OLD MAN
have got up, and with the DELEGATE
*specified proceed to study the Agricul-
turist's drawings. Exclamations such as:*]
"Why is the altitude of fall 22 meters?"—
"This rock will have to be blown up"—
"Actually, all they need is cement and dyna-
mite"—"They force the water to come down
here, that's clever!"

A VERY YOUNG WORKER, *right*: [*To* OLD
MAN, *right.*] They're going to irrigate all the
fields between the hills, look at that, Aleko!

OLD MAN, *right*: I'm not going to look. I
knew the project would be good. I won't
have a pistol pointed at me!

DELEGATE: But they only want to point
a pencil at you!

[*Laughter.*]

OLD MAN, *right*: [*Gets up gloomily, and
walks over to look at the drawings.*] These
valley-thieves know only too well that we
in this country are suckers for machines and
projects.

PEASANT WOMAN, *right*: Aleko Beresh-
wili, you have a weakness for new projects.
That's well known.

DELEGATE: What about my report? May
I write that you will all support the cession
of your old valley in the interests of this
project when you get back to your Kolkhoz?

PEASANT WOMAN, *right*: I will. What
about you, Aleko?

OLD MAN, *right*: [*Bent over drawings.*] I suggest that you give us copies of the drawings to take along.

PEASANT WOMAN, *right*: Then we can sit down and eat. Once he has the drawings and he's ready to discuss them, the matter is settled. I know him. And it will be the same with the rest of us.

[*Delegates laughingly embrace again.*]

OLD MAN, *left*: Long live the Kolkhoz "Rosa Luxemburg" and much luck to your horse-breeding project!

PEASANT WOMAN, *left*: In honor of the visit of the delegates from Kolkhoz "Rosa Luxemburg" and of the Specialist, the plan is that we all hear a presentation of the Singer Arkadi Tscheidse.

[*Applause.* GIRL TRACTORIST *has gone off to bring the* SINGER.]

PEASANT WOMAN, *right*: Comrades, your entertainment had better be good. It's going to cost us a valley.

PEASANT WOMAN, *left*: Arkadi Tscheidse knows about our discussion. He's promised to perform something that has a bearing on the problem.

KATO: We wired Tiflis three times. The whole thing nearly fell through at the last minute because his driver had a cold.

PEASANT WOMAN, *left*: Arkadi Tscheidse knows 21,000 lines of verse.

OLD MAN, *left*: He's hard to get. You and the Planning Commission should persuade him to come north more often, Comrade.

DELEGATE: We are more interested in economics, I'm afraid.

OLD MAN, *left*: [*Smiling.*] You arrange the redistribution of vines and tractors, why not songs?

[*Enter the* SINGER *Arkadi Tscheidse, led by* GIRL TRACTORIST. *He is a well-built man of simple manners, accompanied by* FOUR MUSICIANS *with their instruments. The artists are greeted with applause.*]

GIRL TRACTORIST: This is the Comrade Specialist, Arkadi.

[*The* SINGER *greets them all.*]

DELEGATE: Honored to make your acquaintance. I heard about your songs when I was a boy at school. Will it be one of the old legends?

SINGER: A very old one. It's called "The Chalk Circle" and comes from the Chinese. But we'll do it, of course, in a changed version. Comrades, it's an honor for me to entertain you after a difficult debate. We hope you will find that the voice of the old poet also sounds well in the shadow of Soviet tractors. It may be a mistake to mix different wines, but old and new wisdom mix admirably. Now I hope we'll get something to eat before the performance begins —it would certainly help.

VOICES: Surely. Everyone into the Club House!

[*While everyone begins to move,* DELEGATE *turns to* GIRL TRACTORIST.]

DELEGATE: I hope it won't take long. I've got to get back tonight.

GIRL TRACTORIST: How long will it last, Arkadi? The Comrade Specialist must get back to Tiflis tonight.

SINGER: [*Casually.*] It's actually two stories. An hour or two.

GIRL TRACTORIST: [*Confidentially.*] Couldn't you make it shorter?

SINGER: No.

VOICE: Arkadi Tscheidse's performance will take place here in the square after the meal.

[*And they all go happily to eat.*]

1

THE NOBLE CHILD

As the lights go up, the SINGER *is seen sitting on the floor, a black sheepskin cloak round his shoulders, and a little, well-thumbed notebook in his hand. A small group of listeners—the chorus—sits with him. The manner of his recitation makes it clear that he has told his story over and over again. He mechanically fingers the pages, seldom looking at them. With appropriate gestures, he gives the signal for each scene to begin.*

SINGER:
>   In olden times, in a bloody time,
>   There ruled in a Caucasian city—
>   Men called it City of the Damned—
>   A Governor.
>   His name was Georgi Abashwili.
>   He was rich as Croesus
>   He had a beautiful wife
>   He had a healthy baby.
>   No other governor in Grusinia
>   Had so many horses in his stable
>   So many beggars on his doorstep
>   So many soldiers in his service
>   So many petitioners in his courtyard.
>   Georgi Abashwili—how shall I describe
>   him to you?
>   He enjoyed his life.
>   On the morning of Easter Sunday
>   The Governor and his family went to
>   church.

[*At the left a large doorway, at the right an even larger gateway.* BEGGARS *and* PETITIONERS *pour from the gateway, holding up thin* CHILDREN, *crutches, and petitions. They are followed by* IRONSHIRTS, *and then, expensively dressed, the* GOVERNOR'S FAMILY.]

BEGGARS AND PETITIONERS:
—Mercy! Mercy, Your Grace! The taxes are too high.
—I lost my leg in the Persian War, where can I get . . .
—My brother is innocent, Your Grace, a misunderstanding . . .
—The child is starving in my arms!
—Our petition is for our son's discharge from the army, our last remaining son!
—Please, Your Grace, the water inspector takes bribes.

[*One servant collects the petitions. Another distributes coins from a purse. Soldiers push the crowd back, lashing at them with thick leather whips.*]

SOLDIER: Get back! Clear the church door!

[*Behind the* GOVERNOR, *his* WIFE, *and the* ADJUTANT, *the* GOVERNOR'S CHILD *is brought through the gateway in an ornate carriage.*]

CROWD:
—The baby!
—I can't see it, don't shove so hard!
—God bless the child, Your Grace!

SINGER: [*While the crowd is driven back with whips.*]

For the first time on that Easter Sunday, the people saw the Governor's heir.
Two doctors never moved from the noble child, apple of the Governor's eye.
Even the mighty Prince Kazbeki bows before him at the church door.

[*The* FAT PRINCE *steps forwards and greets the* FAMILY.]

FAT PRINCE: Happy Easter, Natella Abashwili! What a day! When it was raining last night, I thought to myself, gloomy holidays! But this morning the sky was gay. I love a gay sky, a simple heart, Natella Abashwili. And little Michael is a governor from head to foot! Tititi! [*He tickles the* CHILD.]

GOVERNOR'S WIFE: What do you think, Arsen, at last Georgi has decided to start building the east wing. All those wretched slums are to be torn down to make room for the garden.

FAT PRINCE: Good news after so much bad! What's the latest on the war, Brother Georgi? [*The* GOVERNOR *indicates a lack of interest.*] Strategical retreat, I hear. Well, minor reverses are to be expected. Sometimes things go well, sometimes not. Such is war. Doesn't mean a thing, does it?

GOVERNOR'S WIFE: He's coughing. Georgi, did you hear? [*She speaks sharply to the* DOCTORS, *two dignified men standing close to the little carriage.*] He's coughing!

FIRST DOCTOR: [*To the* SECOND.] May I remind you, Niko Mikadze, that I was against the lukewarm bath? [*To the* GOVERNOR'S WIFE.] There's been a little error over warming the bath water, Your Grace.

SECOND DOCTOR: [*Equally polite.*] Mika Loladze, I'm afraid I can't agree with you. The temperature of the bath water was exactly what our great, beloved Mishiko Oboladze prescribed. More likely a slight draft during the night, Your Grace.

GOVERNOR'S WIFE: But do pay more attention to him. He looks feverish, Georgi.

FIRST DOCTOR: [*Bending over the* CHILD.] No cause for alarm, Your Grace. The bath water will be warmer. It won't occur again.

SECOND DOCTOR: [*With a venomous glance at the* FIRST.] I won't forget that, my dear Mika Loladze. No cause for concern, Your Grace.

FAT PRINCE: Well, well, well! I always say: "A pain in my liver? Then the doctor gets fifty strokes on the soles of his feet." We live in a decadent age. In the old days one said: "Off with his head!"

GOVERNOR'S WIFE: Let's go into church. Very likely it's the draft here.

[*The procession of* FAMILY *and* SERVANTS *turns into the doorway. The* FAT PRINCE *follows, but the* GOVERNOR *is kept back by the* ADJUTANT, *a handsome young man. When the crowd of* PETITIONERS *has been driven off, a young dust-stained* RIDER, *his arm in a sling, remains behind.*]

ADJUTANT: [*Pointing at the* RIDER, *who steps forward.*] Won't you hear the messenger from the capital, Your Excellency? He arrived this morning. With confidential papers.

GOVERNOR: Not before Service, Shalva. But did you hear Brother Kazbeki wish me a happy Easter? Which is all very well, but I don't believe it did rain last night.

ADJUTANT: [*Nodding.*] We must investigate.

GOVERNOR: Yes, at once. Tomorrow.

[*They pass through the doorway. The* RIDER, *who has waited in vain for an audience, turns sharply round and, muttering a curse, goes off. Only one of the palace guards—*SIMON SHASHAVA*— remains at the door.*]

SINGER:
The city is still.
Pigeons strut in the church square.
A soldier of the Palace Guard
Is joking with a kitchen maid
As she comes up from the river with a bundle.

[*A girl—*GRUSHA VASHNADZE*—comes through the gateway with a bundle made of large green leaves under her arm.*]

SIMON: What, the young lady is not in church? Shirking?

GRUSHA: I was dressed to go. But they needed another goose for the banquet. And they asked me to get it. I know about geese.

SIMON: A goose? [*He feigns suspicion.*] I'd like to see that goose. [GRUSHA *does not understand.*] One must be on one's guard with women. "I only went for a fish," they tell you, but it turns out to be something else.

GRUSHA: [*Walking resolutely toward him and showing him the goose.*] There! If it isn't a fifteen-pound goose stuffed full of corn, I'll eat the feathers.

SIMON: A queen of a goose! The Governor himself will eat it. So the young lady has been down to the river again?

GRUSHA: Yes, at the poultry farm.

SIMON: Really? At the poultry farm, down by the river . . . not higher up maybe? Near those willows?

GRUSHA: I only go to the willows to wash the linen.

SIMON: [*Insinuatingly.*] Exactly.

GRUSHA: Exactly what?

SIMON: [*Winking.*] Exactly that.

GRUSHA: Why shouldn't I wash the linen by the willows?

SIMON: [*With exaggerated laughter.*] "Why shouldn't I wash the linen by the willows!" That's good, really good!

GRUSHA: I don't understand the soldier. What's so good about it?

SIMON: [*Slyly.*] "If something I know someone learns, she'll grow hot and cold by turns!"

GRUSHA: I don't know what I could learn about those willows.

SIMON: Not even if there was a bush opposite? That one could see everything from? Everything that goes on there when a certain person is—"washing linen"?

GRUSHA: What does go on? Won't the soldier say what he means and have done?

SIMON: Something goes on. Something can be seen.

GRUSHA: Could the soldier mean I dip my toes in the water when it's hot? There's nothing else.

SIMON: There's more. Your toes. And more.

GRUSHA: More what? At most my foot?

SIMON: Your foot. And a little more. [*He laughs heartily.*]

GRUSHA: [*Angrily.*] Simon Shashava, you ought to be ashamed of yourself! To sit in a bush on a hot day and wait till a girl comes and dips her legs in the river! And I bet you bring a friend along too! [*She runs off.*]

SIMON: [*Shouting after her.*] I didn't bring any friend along!

[*As the* SINGER *resumes his tale, the* SOLDIER *steps into the doorway as though to listen to the service.*]

SINGER:
The city lies still
But why are there armed men?
The Governor's palace is at peace
But why is it a fortress?
And the Governor returned to his palace

And the fortress was a trap
And the goose was plucked and roasted
But the goose was not eaten this time
And noon was no longer the hour to
    eat:
Noon was the hour to die.
[*From the doorway at the left the* FAT
PRINCE *quickly appears, stands still,
looks around. Before the gateway at the
right two* IRONSHIRTS *are squatting and
playing dice. The* FAT PRINCE *sees
them, walks slowly past, making a sign
to them. They rise: one goes through
the gateway, the other goes off at the
right. Muffled voices are heard from
various directions in the rear:* "To your
posts!" *The palace is surrounded. The*
FAT PRINCE *quickly goes off. Church
bells in the distance. Enter, through
the doorway, the Governor's family and
procession, returning from church.*]
GOVERNOR'S WIFE: [*Passing the* ADJU-
TANT.] It's impossible to live in such a slum.
But Georgi, of course, will only build for
his little Michael. Never for me! Michael is
all! All for Michael!
    [*The procession turns into the gateway.
    Again the* ADJUTANT *lingers behind.
    He waits. Enter the wounded* RIDER
    from the doorway. Two IRONSHIRTS *of
    the Palace Guard have taken up posi-
    tions by the gateway.*]
ADJUTANT: [*To the* RIDER.] The Governor does not wish to receive military news
before dinner—especially if it's depressing,
as I assume. In the afternoon His Excellency will confer with prominent architects.
They're coming to dinner too. And here
they are! [*Enter three gentlemen through
the doorway.*] Go to the kitchen and eat,
my friend. [*As the* RIDER *goes, the* ADJU-
TANT *greets the* ARCHITECTS.] Gentlemen,
His Excellency expects you at dinner. He
will devote all his time to you and your
great new plans. Come!
ONE OF THE ARCHITECTS: We marvel that
His Excellency intends to build. There are
disquieting rumors that the war in Persia
has taken a turn for the worse.
ADJUTANT: All the more reason to build!
There's nothing to those rumors anyway.
Persia is a long way off, and the garrison
here would let itself be hacked to bits for
its Governor. [*Noise from the palace. The
shrill scream of a woman. Someone is shouting orders. Dumbfounded, the* ADJUTANT

moves toward the gateway. An IRONSHIRT
steps out, points his lance at him.] What's
this? Put down that lance, you dog.
ONE OF THE ARCHITECTS: It's the Princes!
Don't you know the Princes met last night
in the capital? And they're against the
Grand Duke and his Governors? Gentlemen,
we'd better make ourselves scarce. [*They
rush off. The* ADJUTANT *remains helplessly
behind.*]
ADJUTANT: [*Furiously to the Palace
Guard.*] Down with those lances! Don't you
see the Governor's life is threatened?
    [*The* IRONSHIRTS *of the Palace Guard
    refuse to obey. They stare coldly and
    indifferently at the* ADJUTANT *and fol-
    low the next events without interest.*]
SINGER:
    O blindness of the great!
    They go their way like gods,
    Great over bent backs,
    Sure of hired fists,
    Trusting in the power
    Which has lasted so long.
    But long is not forever.
    O Change from age to age!
    Thou hope of the people!
[*Enter the* GOVERNOR, *through the
gateway, between two* SOLDIERS *armed
to the teeth. He is in chains. His face
is gray.*]
    Up, great sir, deign to walk upright!
    From your palace the eyes of many foes
        follow you!
    And now you don't need an architect,
        a carpenter will do.
    You won't be moving into a new palace
    But into a little hole in the ground.
    Look about you once more, blind man!
    [*The arrested man looks round.*]
    Does all you have please you?
    Between the Easter Mass and the Easter
        meal
    You are walking to a place whence no
        one returns.
[*The* GOVERNOR *is led off. A horn
sounds an alarm. Noise behind the
gateway.*]
    When the house of a great one col-
        lapses
    Many little ones are slain.
    Those who had no share in the *good*
        fortunes of the mighty
    Often have a share in their *mis*fortunes.
    The plunging wagon
    Drags the sweating oxen down with it

Into the abyss.

[*The* SERVANTS *come rushing through the gateway in panic.*]

SERVANTS: [*Among themselves.*]

—The baskets!

—Take them all into the third courtyard! Food for five days!

—The mistress has fainted! Someone must carry her down.

—She must get away.

—What about us? We'll be slaughtered like chickens, as always.

—Goodness, what'll happen? There's bloodshed already in the city, they say.

—Nonsense, the Governor has just been asked to appear at a Princes' meeting. All very correct. Everything'll be ironed out. I heard this on the best authority . . .

[*The two* DOCTORS *rush into the courtyard.*]

FIRST DOCTOR: [*Trying to restrain the other.*] Niko Mikadze, it is your duty as a doctor to attend Natella Abashwili.

SECOND DOCTOR: My duty! It's yours!

FIRST DOCTOR: Whose turn is it to look after the child today, Niko Mikadze, yours or mine?

SECOND DOCTOR: Do you really think, Mika Loladze, I'm going to stay a minute longer in this accursed house on that little brat's account? [*They start fighting. All one hears is:* "You neglect your duty!" *and* "Duty, my foot!" *Then the* SECOND DOCTOR *knocks the* FIRST *down.*] Go to hell! [*Exit.*]

[*Enter the soldier,* SIMON SHASHAVA. *He searches in the crowd for* GRUSHA.]

SIMON: Grusha! There you are at last! What are you going to do?

GRUSHA: Nothing. If worst comes to worst, I've a brother in the mountains. How about you?

SIMON: Forget about me. [*Formally again.*] Grusha Vashnadze, your wish to know my plans fills me with satisfaction. I've been ordered to accompany Madam Abashwili as her guard.

GRUSHA: But hasn't the Palace Guard mutinied?

SIMON: [*Seriously.*] That's a fact.

GRUSHA: Isn't it dangerous to go with her?

SIMON: In Tiflis, they say: Isn't the stabbing dangerous for the knife?

GRUSHA: You're not a knife, you're a man, Simon Shashava, what has that woman to do with you?

SIMON: That woman has nothing to do with me. I have my orders, and I go.

GRUSHA: The soldier is pigheaded: he is running into danger for nothing—nothing at all. I must get into the third courtyard, I'm in a hurry.

SIMON: Since we're both in a hurry we shouldn't quarrel. You need time for a good quarrel. May I ask if the young lady still has parents?

GRUSHA: No, just a brother.

SIMON: As time is short—my second question is this: Is the young lady as healthy as a fish in water?

GRUSHA: I may have a pain in the right shoulder once in a while. Otherwise I'm strong enough for my job. No one has complained. So far.

SIMON: That's well known. When it's Easter Sunday, and the question arises who'll run for the goose all the same, she'll be the one. My third question is this: Is the young lady impatient? Does she want apples in winter?

GRUSHA: Impatient? No. But if a man goes to war without any reason and then no message comes—that's bad.

SIMON: A message will come. And now my final question . . .

GRUSHA: Simon Shashava, I must get to the third courtyard at once. My answer is yes.

SIMON: [*Very embarrassed.*] Haste, they say, is the wind that blows down the scaffolding. But they also say: The rich don't know what haste is. I'm from . . .

GRUSHA: Kutsk . . .

SIMON: The young lady has been inquiring about me? I'm healthy, I have no dependents, I make ten piasters a month, as paymaster twenty piasters, and I'm asking—very sincerely—for your hand.

GRUSHA: Simon Shashava, it suits me well.

SIMON: [*Taking from his neck a thin chain with a little cross on it.*] My mother gave me this cross, Grusha Vashnadze. The chain is silver. Please wear it.

GRUSHA: Many thanks, Simon.

SIMON: [*Hangs it round her neck.*] It would be better to go to the third courtyard now. Or there'll be difficulties. Anyway, I must harness the horses. The young lady will understand?

GRUSHA: Yes, Simon.

[*They stand undecided.*]

SIMON: I'll just take the mistress to the troops that have stayed loyal. When the war's over, I'll be back. In two weeks. Or three. I hope my intended won't get tired, awaiting my return.

GRUSHA:

Simon Shashava, I shall wait for you.
Go calmly into battle, soldier
The bloody battle, the bitter battle
From which not everyone returns:
When you return I shall be there.
I shall be waiting for you under the green elm
I shall be waiting for you under the bare elm
I shall wait until the last soldier has returned
And longer
When you come back from the battle
No boots will stand at my door
The pillow beside mine will be empty
And my mouth will be unkissed.
When you return, when you return
You will be able to say: It is just as it was.

SIMON: I thank you, Grusha Vashnadze. And good-bye!

[*He bows low before her. She does the same before him. Then she runs quickly off without looking round. Enter the* ADJUTANT *from the gateway.*]

ADJUTANT: [*Harshly.*] Harness the horses to the carriage! Don't stand there doing nothing, scum!

[SIMON SHASHAVA *stands to attention and goes off. Two* SERVANTS *crowd from the gateway, bent low under huge trunks. Behind them, supported by her women, stumbles* NATELLA ABASHWILI. *she is followed by a* WOMAN *carrying the* CHILD.]

GOVERNOR'S WIFE: I hardly know if my head's still on. Where's Michael? Don't hold him so clumsily. Pile the trunks onto the carriage. No news from the city, Shalva?

ADJUTANT: None. All's quiet so far, but there's not a minute to lose. No room for all those trunks in the carriage. Pick out what you need. [*Exit quickly.*]

GOVERNOR'S WIFE: Only essentials! Quick, open the trunks! I'll tell you what I need. [*The trunks are lowered and opened. She points at some brocade dresses.*] The green one! And, of course, the one with the fur trimming. Where are Niko Mikadze and Mika Loladze? I've suddenly got the most

terrible migraine again. It always starts in the temples. [*Enter* GRUSHA.] Taking your time, eh? Go and get the hot water bottles this minute! [GRUSHA *runs off, returns later with hot water bottles; the* GOVERNOR'S WIFE *orders her about by signs.*] Don't tear the sleeves.

A YOUNG WOMAN: Pardon, madam, no harm has come to the dress.

GOVERNOR'S WIFE: Because I stopped you. I've been watching you for a long time. Nothing in your head but making eyes at Shalva Tzereteli. I'll kill you, you bitch! [*She beats the* YOUNG WOMAN.]

ADJUTANT: [*Appearing in the gateway.*] Please make haste, Natella Abashwili. Firing has broken out in the city. [*Exit.*]

GOVERNOR'S WIFE: [*Letting go of the* YOUNG WOMAN.] Oh dear, do you think they'll lay hands on us? Why should they? Why? [*She herself begins to rummage in the trunks.*] How's Michael? Asleep?

WOMAN WITH THE CHILD: Yes, madam.

GOVERNOR'S WIFE: Then put him down a moment and get my little saffron-colored boots from the bedroom. I need them for the green dress. [*The* WOMAN *puts down the* CHILD *and goes off.*] Just look how these things have been packed! No love! No understanding! If you don't give them every order yourself . . . At such moments you realize what kind of servants you have! They gorge themselves at your expense, and never a word of gratitude! I'll remember this.

ADJUTANT: [*Entering, very excited.*] Natella, you must leave at once!

GOVERNOR'S WIFE: Why? I've got to take this silver dress—it cost a thousand piasters. And that one there, and where's the wine-colored one?

ADJUTANT: [*Trying to pull her away.*] Riots have broken out! We must leave at once. Where's the baby?

GOVERNOR'S WIFE: [*Calling to the* YOUNG WOMAN *who was holding the baby.*] Maro, get the baby ready! Where on earth are you?

ADJUTANT: [*Leaving.*] We'll probably have to leave the carriage behind and go ahead on horseback.

[*The* GOVERNOR'S WIFE *rummages again among her dresses, throws some onto the heap of chosen clothes, then takes them off again. Noises, drums are heard. The* YOUNG WOMAN *who was beaten creeps away. The sky begins to grow red.*]

GOVERNOR'S WIFE: [*Rummaging desperately.*] I simply cannot find the wine-colored dress. Take the whole pile to the carriage. Where's Asja? And why hasn't Maro come back? Have you all gone crazy?

ADJUTANT: [*Returning.*] Quick! Quick!

GOVERNOR'S WIFE: [*To the* FIRST WOMAN.] Run! Just throw them into the carriage!

ADJUTANT: We're not taking the carriage. And if you don't come now, I'll ride off on my own.

GOVERNOR'S WIFE: [*As the* FIRST WOMAN *can't carry everything.*] Where's that bitch Asja? [*The* ADJUTANT *pulls her away.*] Maro, bring the baby! [*To the* FIRST WOMAN.] Go and look for Masha. No, first take the dresses to the carriage. Such nonsense! I wouldn't dream of going on horseback!

[*Turning round, she sees the red sky, and starts back rigid. The fire burns. She is pulled out by the* ADJUTANT. *Shaking, the* FIRST WOMAN *follows with the dresses.*]

MARO: [*From the doorway with the boots.*] Madam! [*She sees the trunks and dresses and runs toward the* CHILD, *picks it up, and holds it a moment.*] They left it behind, the beasts. [*She hands it to* GRUSHA.] Hold it a moment. [*She runs off, following the* GOVERNOR'S WIFE.]

[*Enter* SERVANTS *from the gateway.*]

COOK: Well, so they've actually gone. Without the food wagons, and not a minute too early. It's time for us to clear out.

GROOM: This'll be an unhealthy neighborhood for quite a while. [*To one of the* WOMEN.] Suliko, take a few blankets and wait for me in the foal stables.

GRUSHA: What have they done with the Governor?

GROOM: [*Gesturing throat cutting.*] Fffft.

A FAT WOMAN: [*Seeing the gesture and becoming hysterical.*] Oh dear, oh dear, oh dear, oh dear! Our master Georgi Abashwili! A picture of health he was, at the morning Mass—and now! Oh, take me away, we're all lost, we must die in sin like our master, Georgi Abashwili!

OTHER WOMAN: [*Soothing her.*] Calm down, Nina! You'll be taken to safety. You've never hurt a fly.

FAT WOMAN: [*Being led out.*] Oh dear, oh dear, oh dear! Quick! Let's all get out before they come, before they come!

A YOUNG WOMAN: Nina takes it more to heart than the mistress, that's a fact. They even have to have their weeping done for them.

COOK: We'd better get out, all of us.

ANOTHER WOMAN: [*Glancing back.*] That must be the East Gate burning.

YOUNG WOMAN: [*Seeing the* CHILD *in* GRUSHA's *arms.*] The baby! What are you doing with it?

GRUSHA: It got left behind.

YOUNG WOMAN: She simply left it there. Michael, who was kept out of all the drafts!

[*The* SERVANTS *gather round the* CHILD.]

GRUSHA: He's waking up.

GROOM: Better put him down, I tell you. I'd rather not think what'd happen to anybody who was found with that baby.

COOK: That's right. Once they get started, they'll kill each other off, whole families at a time. Let's go.

[*Exeunt all but* GRUSHA, *with the* CHILD *on her arm, and* TWO WOMEN.]

TWO WOMEN: Didn't you hear? Better put him down.

GRUSHA: The nurse asked me to hold him a moment.

OLDER WOMAN: She's not coming back, you simpleton.

YOUNGER WOMAN: Keep your hands off it.

OLDER WOMAN: [*Amiably.*] Grusha, you're a good soul, but you're not very bright, and you know it. I tell you, if he had the plague he couldn't be more dangerous.

GRUSHA: [*Stubbornly.*] He hasn't got the plague. He looks at me! He's human!

OLDER WOMAN: Don't look at *him*. You're a fool—the kind that always gets put upon. A person need only say, "Run for the salad, you have the longest legs," and you run. My husband has an ox cart—you can come with us if you hurry! Lord, by now the whole neighborhood must be in flames.

[*Both women leave, sighing. After some hesitation,* GRUSHA *puts the sleeping* CHILD *down, looks at it for a moment, then takes a brocade blanket from the heap of clothes and covers it. Then both women return, dragging bundles.* GRUSHA *starts guiltily away from the* CHILD *and walks a few steps to one side.*]

YOUNGER WOMAN: Haven't you packed

anything yet? There isn't much time, you know. The Ironshirts will be here from the barracks.

GRUSHA: Coming!

[She runs through the doorway. Both women go to the gateway and wait. The sound of horses is heard. They flee, screaming. Enter the FAT PRINCE with drunken IRONSHIRTS. One of them carries the Governor's head on a lance.]

FAT PRINCE: Here! In the middle! [One soldier climbs into the other's back, takes the head, holds it tentatively over the door.] That's not the middle. Farther to the right. That's it. What I do, my friends, I do well. [While with hammer and nail, the soldier fastens the head to the wall by its hair.] This morning at the church door I said to Georgi Abashwili: "I love a gay sky." Actually, I prefer the lightning that comes out of a gay sky. Yes, indeed. It's a pity they took the brat along, though, I need him, urgently.

[Exit with IRONSHIRTS through the gateway. Trampling of horses again. Enter GRUSHA through the doorway looking cautiously about her. Clearly she has waited for the IRONSHIRTS to go. Carrying a bundle, she walks toward the gateway. At the last moment, she turns to see if the CHILD is still there. Catching sight of the head over the doorway, she screams. Horrified, she picks up her bundle again, and is about to leave when the SINGER starts to speak. She stands rooted to the spot.]

SINGER:

As she was standing between courtyard and gate,
She heard or she thought she heard a low voice calling.
The child called to her,
Not whining, but calling quite sensibly,
Or so it seemed to her.
"Woman," it said, "help me."
And it went on, not whining, but saying quite sensibly:

"Know, woman, he who hears not a cry for help
But passes by with troubled ears will never hear
The gentle call of a lover nor the blackbird at dawn
Nor the happy sighs of the tired grapepicker as the Angelus rings."

[She walks a few steps toward the CHILD and bends over it.]

Hearing this she went back for one more look at the child:
Only to sit with him for a moment or two,
Only till someone should come,
His mother, or anyone.

[Leaning on a trunk, she sits facing the CHILD.]

Only till she would have to leave, for the danger was too great,
The city was full of flame and crying.

[The light grows dimmer, as though evening and night were coming on.]

Fearful is the seductive power of goodness!

[GRUSHA now settles down to watch over the CHILD through the night. Once, she lights a small lamp to look at it. Once, she tucks it in with a coat. From time to time she listens and looks to see whether someone is coming.]

And she sat with the child a long time,
Till evening came, till night came, till dawn came.
She sat too long, too long she saw
The soft breathing, the small clenched fists,
Till toward morning the seduction was complete
And she rose, and bent down and, sighing, took the child
And carried it away.

[She does what the SINGER says as he describes it.]

As if it was stolen goods she picked it up.
As if she was a thief she crept away.

2

THE FLIGHT INTO THE
NORTHERN MOUNTAINS

SINGER:
> When Grusha Vashnadze left the city
> On the Grusinian highway
> On the way to the Northern Moun-
> tains
> She sang a song, she bought some milk.

CHORUS:
> How will this human child escape
> The bloodhounds, the trap-setters?
> Into the deserted mountains she jour-
> neyed
> Along the Grusinian highway she
> journeyed
> She sang a song, she bought some milk.

[GRUSHA VASHNADZE *walks on. On her
back she carries the* CHILD *in a sack, in
one hand is a large stick, in the other
a bundle. She sings.*]

THE SONG OF THE FOUR GENERALS
> Four generals
> Set out for Iran.
> With the first one, war did not agree.
> The second never won a victory.
> For the third the weather never was
> right.
> For the fourth the men would never
> fight.
> Four generals
> And not a single man!
> Sosso Robakidse
> Went marching to Iran
> With him the war did so agree
> He soon had won a victory.
> For him the weather was always right.
> For him the men would always fight.
> Sosso Robakidse,
> He is our man!

[*A peasant's cottage appears.*]

GRUSHA: [*To the* CHILD.] Noontime is
meal time. Now we'll sit hopefully in the
grass, while the good Grusha goes and buys
a little pitcher of milk. [*She lays the* CHILD
down and knocks at the cottage door. An
OLD MAN *opens it.*] Grandfather, could I
have a little pitcher of milk? And a corn
cake, maybe?

OLD MAN: Milk? We have no milk. The

soldiers from the city have our goats. Go
to the soldiers if you want milk.

GRUSHA: But grandfather, you must have
a little pitcher of milk for a baby?

OLD MAN: And for a God-bless-you, eh?

GRUSHA: Who said anything about a God-
bless-you? [*She shows her purse.*] We'll pay
like princes. "Head in the clouds, backside
in the water." [*The peasant goes off, grumbling, for milk.*] How much for the milk?

OLD MAN: Three piasters. Milk has gone
up.

GRUSHA: Three piasters for this little
drop? [*Without a word the* OLD MAN *shuts
the door in her face.*] Michael, did you hear
that? Three piasters! We can't afford it!
[*She goes back, sits down again, and gives
the* CHILD *her breast.*] Suck. Think of the
three piasters. There's nothing there, but
you *think* you're drinking, and that's something. [*Shaking her head, she sees that the*
CHILD *isn't sucking any more. She gets up,
walks back to the door, and knocks again.*]
Open, grandfather, we'll pay. [*Softly.*] May
lightning strike you! [*When the* OLD MAN
appears.] I thought it would be half a
piaster. But the baby must be fed. How
about one piaster for that little drop?

OLD MAN: Two.

GRUSHA: Don't shut the door again. [*She
fishes a long time in her bag.*] Here are two
piasters. The milk better be good. I still
have two days' journey ahead of me. It's a
murderous business you have here—and sinful, too!

OLD MAN: Kill the soldiers if you want
milk.

GRUSHA: [*Giving the* CHILD *some milk.*]
This is an expensive joke. Take a sip,
Michael, it's a week's pay. Around here they
think we earned our money just sitting on
our behinds. Oh, Michael, Michael, you're
a nice little load for a girl to take on! [*Uneasy, she gets up, puts the* CHILD *on her
back, and walks on. The* OLD MAN, *grumbling, picks up the pitcher and looks after
her unmoved.*]

SINGER:

As Grusha Vashnadze went northward
The Princes' Ironshirts went after her.

CHORUS:

How will the barefoot girl escape the
    Ironshirts,
The bloodhounds, the trap-setters?
They hunt even by night.
Pursuers never tire.
Butchers sleep little.

[*Two* IRONSHIRTS *are trudging along
the highway.*]

CORPORAL: You'll never amount to anything, blockhead, your heart's not in it.
Your senior officer sees this in little things.
Yesterday, when I made the fat gal, yes, you
grabbed her husband as I commanded, and
you did kick him in the belly, at my request,
but did you *enjoy* it, like a loyal Private,
or were you just doing your duty? I've kept
an eye on you blockhead, you're a hollow
reed and a tinkling cymbal, you won't get
promoted. [*They walk a while in silence.*]
Don't think I've forgotten how insubordinate
you are, either. Stop limping! I forbid you
to limp! You limp because I sold the horses,
and I sold the horses because I'd never have
got that price again. You limp to show me
you don't like marching. I know you. It
won't help. You wait. Sing!

TWO IRONSHIRTS: [*Singing.*]

Sadly to war I went my way
Leaving my loved one at her door.
My friends will keep her honor safe
Till from the war I'm back once more.

CORPORAL: Louder!

TWO IRONSHIRTS: [*Singing.*]

When 'neath a headstone I shall be
My love a little earth will bring:
"Here rest the feet that oft would run
    to me
And here the arms that oft to me would
    cling."

[*They begin to walk again in silence.*]

CORPORAL: A good soldier has his heart
and soul in it. When he receives an order,
he gets a hard-on, and when he drives his
lance into the enemy's guts, he comes. [*He
shouts for joy.*] He lets himself be torn to
bits for his superior officer, and as he lies
dying he takes note that his corporal is nodding approval, and that is reward enough,
it's his dearest wish. *You* won't get any nod
of approval, but you'll croak all right. Christ,
how'm I to get my hands on the Governor's
bastard with the help of a fool like you!

[*They stay on stage behind.*]

SINGER:

When Grusha Vashnadze came to the
    River Sirra
Flight grew too much for her, the
    helpless child too heavy.
In the cornfields the rosy dawn
Is cold to the sleepless one, only cold.
The gay clatter of the milk cans in the
    farmyard where the smoke rises
Is only a threat to the fugitive.
She who carries the child feels its
    weight and little more.

[GRUSHA *stops in front of a farm. A fat*
PEASANT WOMAN *is carrying a milk can
through the door.* GRUSHA *waits until
she has gone in, then approaches the
house cautiously.*]

GRUSHA: [*To the* CHILD.] Now you've
wet yourself again, and you know I've no
linen. Michael, this is where we part company. It's far enough from the city. They
wouldn't want you so much that they'd
follow you all *this* way, little good-for-
nothing. The peasant woman is kind, and
can't you just smell the milk? [*She bends
down to lay the* CHILD *on the threshold.*]
So farewell, Michael, I'll forget how you
kicked me in the back all night to make
me walk faster. And you can forget the
meager fare—it was meant well. I'd like to
have kept you—your nose is so tiny—but I
can't be. I'd have shown you your first
rabbit, I'd have trained you to keep dry, but
now I must turn around. My sweetheart the
soldier might be back soon, and suppose he
didn't find me? You can't ask that, can you?
[*She creeps up to the door and lays the*
CHILD *on the threshold. Then, hiding behind a tree, she waits until the* PEASANT
WOMAN *opens the door and sees the bundle.*]

PEASANT WOMAN: Good heavens, what's
this? Husband!

PEASANT: What is it? Let me finish my
soup.

PEASANT WOMAN: [*To the* CHILD.]
Where's your mother then? Haven't you got
one? It's a boy. Fine linen. He's from a good
family, you can see that. And they just leave
him on our doorstep. Oh, these are times!

PEASANT: If they think we're going to
feed it, they're wrong. You can take it to
the priest in the village. That's the best we
can do.

PEASANT WOMAN: What'll the priest do

with him? He needs a mother. There, he's waking up. Don't you think we could keep him, though?

PEASANT: [*Shouting.*] No!

PEASANT WOMAN: I could lay him in the corner by the armchair. All I need is a crib. I can take him into the fields with me. See him laughing? Husband, we have a roof over our heads. We can do it. Not another word out of you!

[*She carries the* CHILD *into the house. The* PEASANT *follows protesting.* GRUSHA *steps out from behind the tree, laughs, and hurries off in the opposite direction.*]

SINGER:
Why so cheerful, making for home?

CHORUS:
Because the child has won new parents with a laugh,
Because I'm rid of the little one, I'm cheerful.

SINGER:
And why so sad?

CHORUS:
Because I'm single and free, I'm sad
Like someone who's been robbed
Someone who's newly poor.

[*She walks for a short while, then meets the two* IRONSHIRTS *who point their lances at her.*]

CORPORAL: Lady, you are running straight into the arms of the Armed Forces. Where are you coming from? And when? Are you having illicit relations with the enemy? Where is he hiding? What movements is he making in your rear? How about the hills? How about the valleys? How are your stockings held in position? [GRUSHA *stands there frightened.*] Don't be scared, we always withdraw, if necessary . . . what, blockhead? I always withdraw. In that respect at least, I can be relied on. Why are you staring like that at my lance? In the field no soldier drops his lance, that's a rule. Learn it by heart, blockhead. Now, lady, where are you headed?

GRUSHA: To meet my intended, one Simon Shashava, of the Palace Guard in Nuka.

CORPORAL: Simon Shashava? Sure, I know him. He gave me the key so I could look you up once in a while. Blockhead, we are getting to be unpopular. We must make her realize we have honorable intentions. Lady, behind apparent frivolity I conceal a

serious nature, so let me tell you officially: I want a child from you. [GRUSHA *utters a little scream.*] Blockhead, she understands me. Uh-huh, isn't it a sweet shock? "Then first I must take the noodles out of the oven, Officer. Then first I must change my torn shirt, Colonel." But away with jokes, away with my lance! We are looking for a baby. A baby from a good family. Have you heard of such a baby, from the city, dressed in fine linen, and suddenly turning up here?

GRUSHA: No, I haven't heard a thing. [*Suddenly she turns round and runs back, panic-stricken. The* IRONSHIRTS *glance at each other, then follow her, cursing.*]

SINGER:
Run, kind girl! The killers are coming!
Help the helpless babe, helpless girl!
And so she runs!

CHORUS:
In the bloodiest times
There are kind people.

[*As* GRUSHA *rushes into the cottage, the* PEASANT WOMAN *is bending over the* CHILD's *crib.*]

GRUSHA: Hide him. Quick! The Ironshirts are coming! I laid him on your doorstep. But he isn't mine. He's from a good family.

PEASANT WOMAN: Who's coming? What Ironshirts?

GRUSHA: Don't ask questions. The Ironshirts that are looking for it.

PEASANT WOMAN: They've no business in my house. But I must have a little talk with you, it seems.

GRUSHA: Take off the fine linen. It'll give us away.

PEASANT WOMAN: Linen, my foot! In this house I make the decisions! "*You* can't vomit in *my* room!" Why did you abandon it? It's a sin.

GRUSHA: [*Looking out of the window.*] Look, they're coming out from behind those trees! I shouldn't have run away, it made them angry. Oh, what shall I do?

PEASANT WOMAN: [*Looking out of the window and suddenly starting with fear.*] Gracious! Ironshirts!

GRUSHA: They're after the baby.

PEASANT WOMAN: Suppose they come in!

GRUSHA: You mustn't give him to them. Say he's yours.

PEASANT WOMAN: Yes.

GRUSHA: They'll run him through if you hand him over.

PEASANT WOMAN: But suppose they ask for it? The silver for the harvest is in the house.

GRUSHA: If you let them have him, they'll run him through, right here in this room! You've got to say he's yours!

PEASANT WOMAN: Yes. But what if they don't believe me?

GRUSHA: You must be firm.

PEASANT WOMAN: They'll burn the roof over our heads.

GRUSHA: That's why you must say he's yours. His name's Michael. But I shouldn't have told you. [The PEASANT WOMAN nods.] Don't nod like that. And don't tremble —they'll notice.

PEASANT WOMAN: Yes.

GRUSHA: And stop saying yes, I can't stand it. [She shakes the WOMAN.] Don't you have any children?

PEASANT WOMAN: [Muttering.] He's in the war.

GRUSHA: Then maybe he's an Ironshirt? Do you want him to run children through with a lance? You'd bawl him out. "No fooling with lances in my house!" you'd shout, "is that what I've reared you for? Wash your neck before you speak to your mother!"

PEASANT WOMAN: That's true, he couldn't get away with anything around here!

GRUSHA: So you'll say he's yours?

PEASANT WOMAN: Yes.

GRUSHA: Look! They're coming!

[There is a knocking at the door. The women don't answer. Enter IRONSHIRTS. The PEASANT WOMAN bows low.]

CORPORAL: Well, here she is. What did I tell you? What a nose I have! I smelt her. Lady, I have a question for you. Why did you run away? What did you think I would do to you? I'll bet it was something unchaste. Confess!

GRUSHA: [While the PEASANT WOMAN bows again and again.] I'd left some milk on the stove, and I suddenly remembered it.

CORPORAL: Or maybe you imagined I looked at you unchastely? Like there could be something between us? A carnal glance, know what I mean?

GRUSHA: I didn't see it.

CORPORAL: But it's possible, huh? You admit that much. After all, I might be a pig. I'll be frank with you: I could think of all sorts of things if we were alone. [To the

PEASANT WOMAN.] Shouldn't you be busy in the yard? Feeding the hens?

PEASANT WOMAN: [Falling suddenly to her knees.] Soldier, I didn't know a thing about it. Please don't burn the roof over our heads.

CORPORAL: What are you talking about?

PEASANT WOMAN: I had nothing to do with it. She left it on my doorstep, I swear it!

CORPORAL: [Suddenly seeing the CHILD and whistling.] Ah, so there's a little something in the crib! Blockhead, I smell a thousand piasters. Take the old girl outside and hold on to her. It looks like I have a little cross-examining to do. [The PEASANT WOMAN lets herself be led out by the PRIVATE, without a word.] So, you've got the child I wanted from you! [He walks toward the crib.]

GRUSHA: Officer, he's mine. He's not the one you're after.

CORPORAL: I'll just take a look. [He bends over the crib.]

[GRUSHA looks round in despair.]

GRUSHA: He's mine! He's mine!

CORPORAL: Fine linen!

[GRUSHA dashes at him to pull him away. He throws her off and again bends over the crib. Again looking round in despair, she sees a log of wood, seizes it, and hits the CORPORAL over the head from behind. The CORPORAL collapses. She quickly picks up the CHILD and rushes off.]

SINGER:

And in her flight from the Ironshirts
After twenty-two days of journeying
At the foot of the Janga-Tau Glacier
Grusha Vashnadze decided to adopt the child.

CHORUS:

The helpless girl adopted the helpless child.

[GRUSHA squats over a half-frozen stream to get the CHILD water in the hollow of her hand.]

GRUSHA:

Since no one else will take you, son,
I must take you.
Since no one else will take you, son,
You must take me.
O black day in a lean, lean year,
The trip was long, the milk was dear,
My legs are tired, my feet are sore:

But I wouldn't be without you any
more.
I'll throw your silken shirt away
And wrap you in rags and tatters.
I'll wash you, son, and christen you in
glacier water.
We'll see it through together.
[*She had taken off the child's fine
linen and wrapped it in a rag.*]
SINGER:
When Grusha Vashnadze
Pursued by the Ironshirts
Came to the bridge on the glacier
Leading to the villages of the Eastern
Slope
She sang the Song of the Rotten Bridge
And risked two lives.
[*A wind has risen. The bridge on the
glacier is visible in the dark. One rope
is broken and half the bridge is hang-
ing down the abyss.* MERCHANTS, *two
men and a woman, stand undecided
before the bridge as* GRUSHA *and the*
CHILD *arrive. One man is trying to
catch the hanging rope with a stick.*]
FIRST MAN: Take your time, young woman. You won't get across here anyway.
GRUSHA: But I *have* to get the baby to the
east side. To my brother's place.
MERCHANT WOMAN: Have to? How d'you
mean, "have to"? I have to get there, too—
because I have to buy carpets in Atum—
carpets a woman had to sell because her
husband had to die. But can *I* do what I
have to? Can she? Andrei's been fishing
for that rope for hours. And I ask you, how
are we going to fasten it, even if he gets
it up?
FIRST MAN: [*Listening.*] Hush, I think I
hear something.
GRUSHA: The bridge isn't quite rotted
through. I think I'll try it.
MERCHANT WOMAN: I wouldn't—if the
devil himself were after me. It's suicide.
FIRST MAN: [*Shouting.*] Hi!
GRUSHA: Don't shout. [*To the* MERCHANT
WOMAN.] Tell him not to shout.
FIRST MAN: But there's someone down
there calling. Maybe they've lost their way.
MERCHANT WOMAN: Why shouldn't he
shout? Is there something funny about you?
Are they after you?
GRUSHA: All right, I'll tell. The Ironshirts
are after me. I knocked one down.
SECOND MAN: Hide our merchandise!

[*The* WOMAN *hides a sack behind a
rock.*]
FIRST MAN: Why didn't you say so right
away? [*To the others.*] If they catch her
they'll make mincemeat out of her!
GRUSHA: Get out of my way. I've got to
cross that bridge.
SECOND MAN: You can't. The precipice is
two thousand feet deep.
FIRST MAN: Even with the rope it'd be
no use. We could hold it up with our
hands. But then we'd have to do the same
for the Ironshirts.
GRUSHA: Go away.
[*There are calls from the distance:*
"Hi, up there!"]
MERCHANT WOMAN: They're getting near.
But you can't take the child on that bridge.
It's sure to break. And look!
[GRUSHA *looks down into the abyss.
The* IRONSHIRTS *are heard calling again
from below.*]
SECOND MAN: Two thousand feet!
GRUSHA: But those men are worse.
FIRST MAN: You can't do it. Think of the
baby. Risk your life but not a child's.
SECOND MAN: With the child she's that
much heavier!
MERCHANT WOMAN: Maybe she's *really*
got to get across. Give *me* the baby. I'll hide
it. Cross the bridge alone!
GRUSHA: I won't. We belong together.
[*To the* CHILD.] "Live together, die to-
gether." [*She sings.*]
THE SONG OF THE ROTTEN
BRIDGE
Deep is the abyss, son,
I see the weak bridge sway
But it's not for us, son,
To choose the way.
The way I know
Is the one you must tread,
And all you will eat
Is my bit of bread.
Of every four pieces
You shall have three.
Would that I knew
How big they will be!
Get out of my way, I'll try it without the
rope.
MERCHANT WOMAN: You are tempting
God!
[*There are shouts from below.*]
GRUSHA: Please, throw that stick away,
or they'll get the rope and follow me. [*Press-*

ing the CHILD to her, she steps onto the swaying bridge. The MERCHANT WOMAN screams when it looks as though the bridge is about to collapse. But GRUSHA walks on and reaches the far side.]

FIRST MAN: She made it!

MERCHANT WOMAN: [Who has fallen on her knees and begun to pray, angrily.] I still think it was a sin.

[The IRONSHIRTS appear; the CORPORAL's head is bandaged.]

CORPORAL: Seen a woman with a child?

FIRST MAN: [While the SECOND MAN throws the stick into the abyss.] Yes, there! But the bridge won't carry you!

CORPORAL: You'll pay for this, blockhead!

[GRUSHA, from the far bank, laughs and shows the CHILD to the IRONSHIRTS. She walks on. The wind blows.]

GRUSHA: [Turning to the CHILD.] You musn't be afraid of the wind. He's a poor thing too. He has to push the clouds along and he gets quite cold doing it. [Snow starts falling.] And the snow isn't so bad, either, Michael. It covers the little fir trees so they won't die in winter. Let me sing you a little song. [She sings.]

THE SONG OF THE CHILD
Your father is a bandit
A harlot the mother who bore you.
Yet honorable men
Shall kneel down before you.
Food to the baby horses
The tiger's son will take.
The mothers will get milk
From the son of the snake.

3

IN THE NORTHERN MOUNTAINS

SINGER:
Seven days the sister, Grusha Vashnadze,
Journeyed across the glacier
And down the slopes she journeyed.
"When I enter my brother's house,"
she thought,
"He will rise and embrace me."
"Is that you, sister?" he will say,
"I have long expected you.
This is my dear wife,
And this is my farm, come to me by marriage,
With eleven horses and thirty-one cows.
Sit down.
Sit down with your child at our table and eat."
The brother's house was in a lovely valley.
When the sister came to the brother,
She was ill from walking.
The brother rose from the table.

[A fat peasant couple rise from the table. LAVRENTI VASHNADZE still has a napkin round his neck, as GRUSHA, pale and supported by a SERVANT, enters with the CHILD.]

LAVRENTI: Where've you come from, Grusha?

GRUSHA: [Feebly.] Across the Janga-Tu Pass, Lavrenti.

SERVANT: I found her in front of the hay barn. She has a baby with her.

SISTER-IN-LAW: Go and groom the mare. [Exit the SERVANT.]

LAVRENTI: This is my wife Aniko.

SISTER-IN-LAW: I thought you were in service in Nuka.

GRUSHA: [Barely able to stand.] Yes, I was.

SISTER-IN-LAW: Wasn't it a good job? We were told it was.

GRUSHA: The Governor got killed.

LAVRENTI: Yes, we heard there were riots. Your aunt told us. Remember, Aniko?

SISTER-IN-LAW: Here with us, it's very quiet. City people always want something going on. [She walks toward the door, calling.] Sosso, Sosso, don't take the cake out of the oven yet, d'you hear? Where on earth are you? [Exit, calling.]

LAVRENTI: [Quietly, quickly.] Is there a father? [As she shakes her head.] I thought not. We must think up something. She's religious.

SISTER-IN-LAW: [Returning.] Those servants! [To GRUSHA.] You have a child.

GRUSHA: It's mine. [She collapses. LAVRENTI rushes to her assistance.]

SISTER-IN-LAW: Heavens, she's ill—what are we going to do?

LAVRENTI: [Escorting her to a bench near

the stove.] Sit down, sit. I think it's just weakness, Aniko.

SISTER-IN-LAW: As long as it's not scarlet fever!

LAVRENTI: She'd have spots if it was. It's only weakness. Don't worry, Aniko. [*To* GRUSHA.] Better, sitting down?

SISTER-IN-LAW: Is the child hers?

GRUSHA: Yes, mine.

LAVRENTI: She's on her way to her husband.

SISTER-IN-LAW: I see. Your meat's getting cold. [LAVRENTI *sits down and begins to eat.*] Cold food's not good for you, the fat mustn't get cold, you know your stomach's your weak spot. [*To* GRUSHA.] If your husband's not in the city, where is he?

LAVRENTI: She got married on the other side of the mountain, she says.

SISTER-IN-LAW: On the other side of the mountain. I see. [*She also sits down to eat.*]

GRUSHA: I think I should lie down somewhere, Lavrenti.

SISTER-IN-LAW: If it's consumption we'll all get it. [*She goes on cross-examining her.*] Has your husband got a farm?

GRUSHA: He's a soldier.

LAVRENTI: But he's coming into a farm— a small one—from his father.

SISTER-IN-LAW: Isn't he in the war? Why not?

GRUSHA: [*With effort.*] Yes, he's in the war.

SISTER-IN-LAW: Then why d'you want to go to the farm?

LAVRENTI: When he comes back from the war, he'll return to his farm.

SISTER-IN-LAW: But you're going there now?

LAVRENTI: Yes, to wait for him.

SISTER-IN-LAW: [*Calling shrilly.*] Sosso, the cake!

GRUSHA: [*Murmuring feverishly.*] A farm —a soldier—waiting—sit down, eat.

SISTER-IN-LAW: It's scarlet fever.

GRUSHA: [*Starting up.*] Yes, he's got a farm!

LAVRENTI: I think it's just weakness, Aniko. Would you look after the cake yourself, dear?

SISTER-IN-LAW: But when will he come back if war's broken out again as people say? [*She waddles off, shouting.*] Sosso! Where on earth are you? Sosso!

LAVRENTI: [*Getting up quickly and going to* GRUSHA.] You'll get a bed in a min-ute. She has a good heart. But wait till after supper.

GRUSHA: [*Holding out the* CHILD *to him.*] Take him.

LAVRENTI: [*Taking it and looking around.*] But you can't stay here long with the child. She's religious, you see.

[GRUSHA *collapses.* LAVRENTI *catches her.*]

SINGER:
The sister was so ill,
The cowardly brother had to give her shelter.
Summer departed, winter came.
The winter was long, the winter was short.
People mustn't know anything.
Rats mustn't bite.
Spring mustn't come.

[GRUSHA *sits over the weaving loom in a workroom. She and the* CHILD, *who is squatting on the floor, are wrapped in blankets. She sings.*]

THE SONG OF THE CENTER
And the lover started to leave
And his betrothed ran pleading after him
Pleading and weeping, weeping and teaching:
"Dearest mine, dearest mine
When you go to war as now you do
When you fight the foe as soon you will
Don't lead with the front line
And don't push with the rear line
At the front is red fire
In the rear is red smoke
Stay in the war's center
Stay near the standard bearer
The first always die
The last are also hit
Those in the center come home."

Michael, we must be clever. If we make our-selves as small as cockroaches, the sister-in-law will forget we're in the house, and then we can stay till the snow melts.

[*Enter* LAVRENTI. *He sit down beside his sister.*]

LAVRENTI: Why are you sitting there muffled up like coachmen, you two? Is it too cold in the room?

GRUSHA: [*Hastily removing one shawl.*] It's not too cold, Lavrenti.

LAVRENTI: If it's too cold, you shouldn't be sitting here with the child. Aniko would never forgive herself! [*Pause.*] I hope our priest didn't question you about the child?

GRUSHA: He did, but I didn't tell him anything.

LAVRENTI: That's good. I wanted to speak to you about Aniko. She has a good heart but she's very, very sensitive. People need only mention our farm and she's worried. She takes everything hard, you see. One time our milkmaid went to church with a hole in her stocking. Ever since, Aniko has worn two pairs of stockings in church. It's the old family in her. [He listens.] Are you sure there are no rats around? If there are rats, you couldn't live here. [There are sounds as of dripping from the roof.] What's that, dripping?

GRUSHA: It must be a barrel leaking.

LAVRENTI: Yes, it must be a barrel. You've been here six months, haven't you? Was I talking about Aniko? [They listen again to the snow melting.] You can't imagine how worried she gets about your soldier-husband. "Suppose he comes back and can't find her!" she says and lies awake. "He can't come before the spring," I tell her. The dear woman! [The drops begin to fall faster.] When d'you think he'll come? What do you think? [GRUSHA is silent.] Not before the spring, you agree? [GRUSHA is silent.] You don't believe he'll come at all? [GRUSHA is silent.] But when the spring comes and the snow melts here and on the passes, you can't stay on. They may come and look for you. There's already talk of an illegitimate child. [The "glockenspiel" of the falling drops has grown faster and steadier.] Grusha, the snow is melting on the roof. Spring is here.

GRUSHA: Yes.

LAVRENTI: [Eagerly.] I'll tell you what we'll do. You need a place to go, and, because of the child [He sighs.], you have to have a husband, so people won't talk. Now I've made cautious inquiries to see if we can find you a husband. Grusha, I have one. I talked to a peasant woman who has a son. Just the other side of the mountain. A small farm. And she's willing.

GRUSHA: But I can't marry! I must wait for Simon Shashava.

LAVRENTI: Of course. That's all been taken care of. You don't need a man in bed —you need a man on paper. And I've found you one. The son of this peasant woman is going to die. Isn't that wonderful? He's at his last gasp. And all in line with our story —a husband from the other side of the moun-tain! And when you met him he was at the last gasp. So you're a widow. What do you say?

GRUSHA: It's true. I could use a document with stamps on it for Michael.

LAVRENTI: Stamps make all the difference. Without something in writing the Shah couldn't prove he's a Shah. And you'll have a place to live.

GRUSHA: How much does the peasant woman want?

LAVRENTI: Four hundred piasters.

GRUSHA: Where will you find it?

LAVRENTI: [Guilty.] Aniko's milk money.

GRUSHA: No one would know us there. I'll do it.

LAVRENTI: [Getting up.] I'll let the peasant woman know.

[Quick exit.]

GRUSHA: Michael, you make a lot of work. I came by you as the pear tree comes by sparrows. And because a Christian bends down and picks up a crust of bread so nothing will go to waste. Michael, it would have been better had I walked quickly away on that Easter Sunday in Nuka in the second courtyard. Now I am a fool.

SINGER:

The bridegroom was on his deathbed when the bride arrived.

The bridegroom's mother was waiting at the door, telling her to hurry.

The bride brought a child along.

The witness hid it during the wedding.

[On one side the bed. Under the mosquito net lies a very sick man. GRUSHA is pulled in at a run by her future mother-in-law. They are followed by LAVRENTI and the CHILD.]

MOTHER-IN-LAW: Quick! Quick! Or he'll die on us before the wedding. [To LAVRENTI.] I was never told she had a child already.

LAVRENTI: What difference does it make? [Pointing toward the dying man.] It can't matter to him—in his condition.

MOTHER-IN-LAW: To him? But I'll never survive the shame! We are honest people. [She begins to weep.] My Jussup doesn't have to marry a girl with a child!

LAVRENTI: All right, make it another two hundred piasters. You'll have it in writing that the farm will go to you: but she'll have the right to live here for two years.

MOTHER-IN-LAW: [Drying her tears.] It'll hardly cover the funeral expenses. I hope she'll really lend a hand with the work. And what's happened to the monk? He must have slipped out through the kitchen window. We'll have the whole village on our necks when they hear Jussup's end is come! Oh dear! I'll go get the monk. But he mustn't see the child!

LAVRENTI: I'll take care he doesn't. But why only a monk? Why not a priest?

MOTHER-IN-LAW: Oh, he's just as good. I only made one mistake: I paid half his fee in advance. Enough to send him to the tavern. I only hope . . . [She runs off.]

LAVRENTI: She saved on the priest, the wretch! Hired a cheap monk.

GRUSHA: You will send Simon Shashava to see me if he turns up after all?

LAVRENTI: Yes. [Pointing at the SICK PEASANT.] Won't you take a look at him? [GRUSHA, taking MICHAEL to her, shakes her head.] He's not moving an eyelid. I hope we aren't too late.

[They listen. On the opposite side enter neighbors who look around and take up positions against the walls, thus forming another wall near the bed, yet leaving an opening so that the bed can be seen. They start murmuring prayers. Enter the MOTHER-IN-LAW with a MONK. Showing some annoyance and surprise, she bows to the guests.]

MOTHER-IN-LAW: I hope you won't mind waiting a few moments? My son's bride has just arrived from the city. An emergency wedding is about to be celebrated. [To the MONK in the bedroom.] I might have known you couldn't keep your trap shut. [To GRUSHA.] The wedding can take place at once. Here's the license. Me and the bride's brother [LAVRENTI tries to hide in the background, after having quietly taken MICHAEL back from GRUSHA. The MOTHER-IN-LAW waves him away.] are the witnesses.

[GRUSHA has bowed to the MONK. They go to the bed. The MOTHER-IN-LAW lifts the mosquito net. The MONK starts reeling off the marriage ceremony in Latin. Meanwhile the MOTHER-IN-LAW beckons to LAVRENTI to get rid of the CHILD, but fearing that it will cry he draws its attention to the ceremony, GRUSHA glances once at the CHILD, and LAVRENTI waves the CHILD's hand in a greeting.]

MONK: Are you prepared to be a faithful, obedient, and good wife to this man, and to cleave to him until death you do part?

GRUSHA: [Looking at the CHILD.] I am.

MONK: [To the SICK PEASANT.] Are you prepared to be a good and loving husband to your wife until death you do part? [As the SICK PEASANT does not answer, the MONK looks inquiringly around.]

MOTHER-IN-LAW: Of course he is! Didn't you hear him say yes?

MONK: All right. We declare the marriage contracted! How about extreme unction?

MOTHER-IN-LAW: Nothing doing! The wedding cost quite enough. Now I must take care of the mourners. [To LAVRENTI.] Did we say seven hundred?

LAVRENTI: Six hundred. [He pays.] Now I don't want to sit with the guests and get to know people. So farewell, Grusha, and if my widowed sister comes to visit me, she'll get a welcome from my wife, or I'll show my teeth. [Nods, gives the CHILD to GRUSHA, and leaves. The mourners glance after him without interest.]

MONK: May one ask where this child comes from?

MOTHER-IN-LAW: Is there a child? I don't see a child. And you don't see a child either —you understand? Or it may turn out I saw all sorts of things in the tavern! Now come on.

[After GRUSHA has put the CHILD down and told him to be quiet, they move over left, GRUSHA is introduced to the neighbors.]

This is my daughter-in-law. She arrived just in time to find dear Jussup still alive.

ONE WOMAN: He's been ill now a whole year, hasn't he? When our Vassili was drafted he was there to say good-bye.

ANOTHER WOMAN: Such things are terrible for a farm. The corn all ripe and the farmer in bed! It'll really be a blessing if he doesn't suffer too long, I say.

FIRST WOMAN: [Confidentially.] You know why we thought he'd taken to his bed? Because of the draft! And now his end is come!

MOTHER-IN-LAW: Sit yourselves down, please! And have some cakes!

[She beckons to GRUSHA and both women go into the bedroom, where they pick up the cake pans off the floor. The guests, among them the MONK, sit on the floor and begin conversing in subdued voices.]

ONE PEASANT: [*To whom the* MONK *has handed the bottle which he has taken from his soutane.*] There's a child, you say! How can that have happened to Jussup?

A WOMAN: She was certainly lucky to get herself married, with him so sick!

MOTHER-IN-LAW: They're gossiping already. And wolfing down the funeral cakes at the same time! If he doesn't die today, I'll have to bake some more tomorrow!

GRUSHA: I'll bake them for you.

MOTHER-IN-LAW: Yesterday some horsemen rode by, and I went out to see who it was. When I came in again he was lying there like a corpse! So I sent for you. It can't take much longer. [*She listens.*]

MONK: Dear wedding and funeral guests! Deeply touched, we stand before a bed of death and marriage. The bride gets a veil; the groom, a shroud: how varied, my children, are the fates of men! Alas! One man dies and has a roof over his head, and the other is married and the flesh turns to dust from which it was made. Amen.

MOTHER-IN-LAW: He's getting his own back. I shouldn't have hired such a cheap one. It's what you'd expect. A more expensive monk would behave himself. In Sura there's one with a real air of sanctity about him, but of course he charges a fortune. A fifty piaster monk like that has no dignity, and as for piety, just fifty piasters' worth and no more! When I came to get him in the tavern he'd just made a speech, and he was shouting: "The war is over, beware of the peace!" We must go in.

GRUSHA: [*Giving* MICHAEL *a cake.*] Eat this cake, and keep nice and still, Michael. [*The two women offer cakes to the guests. The dying man sits up in bed. He puts his head out from under the mosquito net, stares at the two women, then sinks back again. The* MONK *takes two bottles from his soutane and offers them to the peasant beside him. Enter three* MUSICIANS *who are greeted with a sly wink by the* MONK.]

MOTHER-IN-LAW: [*To the* MUSICIANS.] What are you doing here? With instruments?

ONE MUSICIAN: Brother Anastasius here [*Pointing at the* MONK.] told us there was a wedding on.

MOTHER-IN-LAW: What? You brought them? Three more on my neck! Don't you know there's a dying man in the next room?

MONK: A very tempting assignment for a musician: something that could be either a subdued Wedding March or a spirited Funeral Dance.

MOTHER-IN-LAW: Well, you might as well play. Nobody can stop you eating in any case.

[*The musicians play a potpourri. The women serve cakes.*]

MONK: The trumpet sounds like a whining baby. And you, little drum, what have you got to tell the world?

DRUNKEN PEASANT: [*Beside the* MONK, *sings.*]

There was a young woman who said:
I thought I'd be happier, wed.
But my husband is old
And remarkably cold
So I sleep with a candle instead.

[*The* MOTHER-IN-LAW *throws the* DRUNKEN PEASANT *out. The music stops. The guests are embarrassed.*]

GUESTS: [*Loudly.*]
—Have you heard? The Grand Duke is back! But the Princes are against him.
—They say the Shah of Persia has lent him a great army to restore order in Grusinia.
—But how is that possible? The Shah of Persia is the enemy . . .
—The enemy of Grusinia, you donkey, not the enemy of the Grand Duke!
—In any case, the war's over, so our soldiers are coming back.

[GRUSHA *drops a cake pan.* GUESTS *help her pick up the cake.*]

AN OLD WOMAN: [*To* GRUSHA.] Are you feeling bad? It's just excitement about dear Jussup. Sit down and rest a while, my dear. [GRUSHA *staggers.*]

GUESTS: Now everything'll be the way it was. Only the taxes'll go up because now we'll have to pay for the war.

GRUSHA: [*Weakly.*] Did someone say the soldiers are back?

A MAN: I did.

GRUSHA: It can't be true.

FIRST MAN: [*To a woman.*] Show her the shawl. We bought it from a soldier. It's from Persia.

GRUSHA: [*Looking at the shawl.*] They are here. [*She gets up, takes a step, kneels down in prayer, takes the silver cross and chain out of her blouse, and kisses it.*]

MOTHER-IN-LAW: [*While the guests si-*

lently watch GRUSHA.] What's the matter with you? Aren't you going to look after our guests? What's all this city nonsense got to do with us?

GUESTS: [Resuming conversation while GRUSHA remains in prayer.]
—You can buy Persian saddles from the soldiers too. Though many want crutches in exchange for them.
—The leaders on one side can win a war, the soldiers on both sides lose it.
—Anyway, the war's over. It's something they can't draft you any more.

[The dying man sits bolt upright in bed. He listens.]
—What we need is two weeks of good weather.
—Our pear trees are hardly bearing a thing this year.

MOTHER-IN-LAW: [Offering cakes.] Have some more cakes and welcome! There are more!

[The MOTHER-IN-LAW goes to the bedroom with the empty cake pans. Unaware of the dying man, she is bending down to pick up another tray when he begins to talk in a hoarse voice.]

PEASANT: How many more cakes are you going to stuff down their throats? D'you think I can shit money?

[The MOTHER-IN-LAW starts, stares at him aghast, while he climbs out from behind the mosquito net.]

FIRST WOMAN: [Talking kindly to GRUSHA in the next room.] Has the young wife got someone at the front?

A MAN: It's good news that they're on their way home, huh?

PEASANT: Don't stare at me like that! Where's this wife you've saddled me with?

[Receiving no answer, he climbs out of bed and in his nightshirt staggers into the other room. Trembling, she follows him with the cake pan.]

GUESTS: [Seeing him and shrieking.] Good God! Jussup!

[Everyone leaps in alarm. The women rush to the door. GRUSHA, still on her knees, turns round and stares at the man.]

PEASANT: A funeral supper! You'd enjoy that, wouldn't you? Get out before I throw you out! [As the guests stampede from the house, gloomily to GRUSHA.] I've upset the apple cart, huh? [Receiving no answer, he

turns round and takes a cake from the pan which his mother is holding.]

SINGER:
O confusion! The wife discovers she has a husband.
By day there's the child, by night there's the husband.
The lover is on his way both day and night.
Husband and wife look at each other.
The bedroom is small.

[Near the bed the PEASANT is sitting in a high wooden bathtub, naked, the MOTHER-IN-LAW is pouring water from a pitcher. Opposite GRUSHA cowers with MICHAEL, who is playing at mending straw mats.]

PEASANT: [To his mother.] That's her work, not yours. Where's she hiding out now?

MOTHER-IN-LAW: [Calling.] Grusha! The peasant wants you!

GRUSHA: [To MICHAEL.] There are still two holes to mend.

PEASANT: [When GRUSHA approaches.] Scrub my back!

GRUSHA: Can't the peasant do it himself?

PEASANT: "Can't the peasant do it himself?" Get the brush! To hell with you! Are you the wife here? Or are you a visitor? [To the MOTHER-IN-LAW.] It's too cold!

MOTHER-IN-LAW: I'll run for hot water.

GRUSHA: Let me go.

PEASANT: You stay here. [The MOTHER-IN-LAW exits.] Rub harder. And no shirking. You've seen a naked fellow before. That child didn't come out of thin air.

GRUSHA: The child was not conceived in joy, if that's what the peasant means.

PEASANT: [Turning and grinning.] You don't look the type. [GRUSHA stops scrubbing him, starts back. Enter the MOTHER-IN-LAW.]

PEASANT: A nice thing you've saddled me with! A simpleton for a wife!

MOTHER-IN-LAW: She just isn't cooperative.

PEASANT: Pour—but go easy! Ow! Go easy, I said. [To GRUSHA.] Maybe you did something wrong in the city . . . I wouldn't be surprised. Why else should you be here? But I won't talk about that. I've not said a word about the illegitimate object you brought into my house either. But my patience has limits! It's against nature. [To the MOTHER-IN-LAW.] More! [To GRUSHA.]

And even if your soldier does come back, you're married.

GRUSHA: Yes.

PEASANT: But your soldier won't come back. Don't you believe it.

GRUSHA: No.

PEASANT: You're cheating me. You're my wife and you're not my wife. Where you lie, nothing lies, and yet no other woman can lie there. When I go to work in the morning I'm tired—when I lie down at night I'm awake as the devil. God has given you sex—and what d'you do? I don't have ten piasters to buy myself a woman in the city. Besides, it's a long way. Woman weeds the fields and opens up her legs, that's what our calendar says. D'you hear?

GRUSHA: [Quietly.] Yes. I didn't mean to cheat you out of it.

PEASANT: She didn't mean to cheat me out of it! Pour some more water! [The MOTHER-IN-LAW pours.] Ow!

SINGER:
As she sat by the stream to wash the linen
She saw his image in the water
And his face grew dimmer with the passing moons.
As she raised herself to wring the linen
She heard his voice from the murmuring maple
And his voice grew fainter with the passing moons.
Evasions and sighs grew more numerous,
Tears and sweat flowed.
With the passing moons the child grew up.

[GRUSHA sits by a stream, dipping linen into the water. In the rear, a few children are standing.]

GRUSHA: [To MICHAEL.] You can play with them, Michael, but don't let them boss you around just because you're the littlest. [MICHAEL nods and joins the children. They start playing.]

BIGGEST BOY: Today it's the Heads-Off Game. [To a FAT BOY.] You're the Prince and you laugh. [To MICHAEL.] You're the Governor. [To a GIRL.] You're the Governor's wife and you cry when his head's cut off. And I do the cutting. [He shows his wooden sword.] With this. First, they lead the Governor into the yard. The Prince walks in front. The Governor's wife comes last.

[They form a procession. The FAT BOY is first and laughs. Then comes MICHAEL, then the BIGGEST BOY, and then the GIRL, who weeps.]

MICHAEL: [Standing still.] Me cut off head!

BIGGEST BOY: That's my job. You're the littlest. The Governor's the easy part. All you do is kneel down and get your head cut off—simple.

MICHAEL: Me want sword!

BIGGEST BOY: It's mine! [He gives MICHAEL a kick.]

GIRL: [Shouting to GRUSHA.] He won't play his part!

GRUSHA: [Laughing.] Even the little duck is a swimmer, they say.

BIGGEST BOY: You can be the Prince if you can laugh. [MICHAEL shakes his head.]

FAT BOY: I laugh best. Let him cut off the head just once. Then you do it, then me.

[Reluctantly, the BIGGEST BOY hands MICHAEL the wooden sword and kneels down. The FAT BOY sits down, slaps his thigh, and laughs with all his might. The GIRL weeps loudly. MICHAEL swings the big sword and "cuts off" the head. In doing so, he topples over.]

BIGGEST BOY: Hey! I'll show you how to cut heads off!

[MICHAEL runs away. The children run after him. GRUSHA laughs, following them with her eyes. On looking back, she sees SIMON SHASHAVA standing on the opposite bank. He wears a shabby uniform.]

GRUSHA: Simon!

SIMON: Is that Grusha Vashnadze?

GRUSHA: Simon!

SIMON: [Formally.] A good morning to the young lady. I hope she is well.

GRUSHA: [Getting up gaily and bowing low.] A good morning to the soldier. God be thanked he has returned in good health.

SIMON: They found better fish, so they didn't eat me, said the haddock.

GRUSHA: Courage, said the kitchen boy. Good luck, said the hero.

SIMON: How are things here? Was the winter bearable? The neighbor considerate?

GRUSHA: The winter was a trifle rough, the neighbor as usual, Simon.

SIMON: May one ask if a certain person still dips her toes in the water when rinsing the linen?

GRUSHA: The answer is no. Because of the eyes in the bushes.

SIMON: The young lady is speaking of soldiers. Here stands a paymaster.

GRUSHA: A job worth twenty piasters?

SIMON: And lodgings.

GRUSHA: [*With tears in her eyes.*] Behind the barracks under the date trees.

SIMON: Yes, there. A certain person has kept her eyes open.

GRUSHA: She has, Simon.

SIMON: And has not forgotten? [GRUSHA *shakes her head.*] So the door is still on its hinges as they say? [GRUSHA *looks at him in silence and shakes her head again.*] What's this? Is anything not as it should be?

GRUSHA: Simon Shashava, I can never return to Nuka. Something has happened.

SIMON: What can have happened?

GRUSHA: For one thing, I knocked an Ironshirt down.

SIMON: Grusha Vashnadze must have had her reasons for that.

GRUSHA: Simon Shashava, I am no longer called what I used to be called.

SIMON: [*After a pause.*] I do not understand.

GRUSHA: When do women change their names, Simon? Let me explain. Nothing stands between us. Everything is just as it was. You must believe that.

SIMON: Nothing stands between us and yet there's something?

GRUSHA: How can I explain it so fast and with the stream between us? Couldn't you cross the bridge there?

SIMON: Maybe it's no longer necessary.

GRUSHA: It is very necessary. Come over on this side, Simon, quick!

SIMON: Does the young lady wish to say someone has come too late?

[GRUSHA *looks up at him in despair, her face streaming with tears.* SIMON *stares before him. He picks up a piece of wood and starts cutting it.*]

SINGERS
So many words are said, so many left unsaid.
The soldier has come.
Where he comes from, he does not say.
Hear what he thought and did not say:
"The battle began, gray at dawn, grew bloody at noon.
The first man fell in front of me, the second behind me, the third at my side.

I trod on the first, left the second behind, the third was run through by the captain.
One of my brothers died by steel, the other by smoke.
My neck caught fire, my hands froze in my gloves, my toes in my socks.
I fed on aspen buds, I drank maple juice, I slept on stone, in water."

SIMON: I see a cap in the grass. Is there a little one already?

GRUSHA: There is, Simon. There's no keeping *that* from you. But please don't worry, it is not mine.

SIMON: When the wind once starts to blow, they say, it blows through every cranny. The wife need say no more. [GRUSHA *looks into her lap and is silent.*]

SINGER:
There was yearning but there was no waiting.
The oath is broken. Neither could say why.
Hear what she thought but did not say:
"While you fought in the battle, soldier,
The bloody battle, the bitter battle
I found a helpless infant
I had not the heart to destroy him
I had to care for a creature that was lost
I had to stoop for breadcrumbs on the floor
I had to break myself for that which was not mine
That which was other people's.
Someone must help!
For the little tree needs water
The lamb loses its way when the shepherd is asleep
And its cry is unheard!"

SIMON: Give me back the cross I gave you. Better still, throw it in the stream. [*He turns to go.*]

GRUSHA: [*Getting up.*] Simon Shashava, don't go away! He isn't mine! He isn't mine! [*She hears the children calling.*] What's the matter, children?

VOICES: Soldiers! And they're taking Michael away!

[GRUSHA *stands aghast as two* IRONSHIRTS, *with* MICHAEL *between them, come toward her.*]

ONE OF THE IRONSHIRTS: Are you Grusha? [*She nods.*] Is this your child?

GRUSHA: Yes. [SIMON *goes.*] Simon!

IRONSHIRT: We have orders, in the name of the law, to take this child, found in your custody, back to the city. It is suspected that the child is Michael Abashwili, son and heir of the late Governor Georgi Abashwili, and his wife, Natella Abashwili. Here is the document and the seal. [*They lead the* CHILD *away.*]

GRUSHA: [*Running after them, shouting.*] Leave him here. Please! He's mine!

SINGER:
> The Ironshirts took the child, the beloved child.
> The unhappy girl followed them to the city, the dreaded city.

> She who had borne him demanded the child.
> She who had raised him faced trial.
> Who will decide the case?
> To whom will the child be assigned?
> Who will the judge be? A good judge? A bad?
> The city was in flames.
> In the judge's seat sat Azdak:*

* The name Azdak should be accented on the second syllable.—E. B.

4

THE STORY OF THE JUDGE

SINGER:
> Hear the story of the judge
> How he turned judge, how he passed judgment, what kind of judge he was.
> On that Easter Sunday of the great revolt, when the Grand Duke was overthrown
> And his Governor Abashwili, father of our child, lost his head
> The Village Scrivener Azdak found a fugitive in the woods and hid him in his hut.

[AZDAK, *in rags and slightly drunk, helping an old beggar into his cottage.*]

AZDAK: Stop snorting, you're not a horse. And it won't do you any good with the police to run like a snotty nose in April. Stand still, I say. [*He catches the* OLD MAN, *who has marched into the cottage as if he'd like to go through the walls.*] Sit down. Feed. Here's a hunk of cheese. [*From under some rags, in a chest, he fishes out some cheese, and the* OLD MAN *greedily begins to eat.*] Haven't eaten in a long time, huh? [*The* OLD MAN *growls.*] Why were you running like that, asshole? The cop wouldn't even have seen you.

OLD MAN: Had to! Had to!

AZDAK: Blue funk? [*The* OLD MAN *stares, uncomprehending.*] Cold feet? Panic? Don't lick your chops like a Grand Duke. Or an old sow. I can't stand it. We have to accept respectable stinkers as God made them, but not you! I once heard of a senior judge who farted at a public dinner to show an independent spirit! Watching you eat like that gives me the most awful ideas. Why don't you say something? [*Sharply.*] Show me your hand. Can't you hear? [*The* OLD MAN *slowly puts out his hand.*] White! So you're not a beggar at all! A fraud, a walking swindle! And I'm hiding you from the cops like you were an honest man! Why were you running like that if you're a landowner? For that's what you are. Don't deny it! I see it in your guilty face! [*He gets up.*] Get out! [*The* OLD MAN *looks at him uncertainly.*] What are you waiting for, peasant-flogger?

OLD MAN: Pursued. Need undivided attention. Make proposition . . .

AZDAK: Make what? A proposition? Well, if that isn't the height of insolence. He's making me a proposition! The bitten man scratches his fingers bloody, and the leech that's biting him makes him a proposition! Get out, I tell you!

OLD MAN: Understand point of view! Persuasion! Pay hundred thousand piasters one night! Yes?

AZDAK: What, you think you can buy me? For a hundred thousand piasters? Let's say a hundred and fifty thousand. Where are they?

OLD MAN: Have not them here. Of course. Will be sent. Hope do not doubt.

AZDAK: Doubt very much. Get out!

[The OLD MAN gets up, waddles to the door. A VOICE is heard offstage.]

VOICE: Azdak!

[The OLD MAN turns, waddles to the opposite corner, stands still.]

AZDAK: [Calling out.] I'm not in! [He walks to door.] So you're sniffing around here again, Shauwa?

SHAUWA: [Reproachfully.] You caught another rabbit, Azdak. And you'd promised me it wouldn't happen again!

AZDAK: [Severely.] Shauwa, don't talk about things you don't understand. The rabbit is a dangerous and destructive beast. It feeds on plants, especially on the species of plants known as weeds. It must therefore be exterminated.

SHAUWA: Azdak, don't be so hard on me. I'll lose my job if I don't arrest you. I know you have a good heart.

AZDAK: I do not have a good heart! How often must I tell you I'm a man of intellect?

SHAUWA: [Slyly.] I know, Azdak. You're a superior person. You say so yourself. I'm just a Christian and an ignoramus. So I ask you: When one of the Prince's rabbits is stolen, and I'm a policeman, what should I do with the offending party?

ADZAK: Shauwa, Shauwa, shame on you. You stand and ask me a question, than which nothing could be more seductive. It's like you were a woman—let's say that bad girl Nunowna, and you showed me your thigh—Nunowna's thigh, that would be—and asked me: "What shall I do with my thigh, it itches?" Is she as innocent as she pretends? Of course not. I catch a rabbit, but you catch a man. Man is made in God's image. Not so a rabbit, you know that. I'm a rabbit-eater, but you're a man-eater, Shauwa. And God will pass judgment on you. Shauwa, go home and repent. No, stop, there's something . . . [He looks at the OLD MAN who stands trembling in the corner.] No, it's nothing. Go home and repent. [He slams the door behind SHAUWA.] Now

you're surprised, huh? Surprised I didn't hand you over? I couldn't hand over a bedbug to that animal. It goes against the grain. Now don't tremble because of a cop! So old and still so scared? Finish your cheese, but eat it like a poor man, or else they'll still catch you. Must I even explain how a poor man behaves? [He pushes him down, and then gives him back the cheese.] That box is the table. Lay your elbows on the table. Now, encircle the cheese on the plate like it might be snatched from you at any moment—what right have you to be safe, huh?—now, hold your knife like an undersized sickle, and give your cheese a troubled look because, like all beautiful things, it's already fading away. [AZDAK watches him.] They're after you, which speaks in your favor, but how can we be sure they're not mistaken about you? In Tiflis one time they hanged a landowner, a Turk, who could prove he quartered his peasants instead of merely cutting them in half, as is the custom, and he squeezed twice the usual amount of taxes out of them, his zeal was above suspicion. And yet they hanged him like a common criminal—because he was a Turk—a thing he couldn't do much about. What injustice! He got onto the gallows by a sheer fluke. In short, I don't trust you.

SINGER:
Thus Azdak gave the old beggar a bed,
And learned that old beggar was the old butcher, the Grand Duke himself,
And was ashamed.
He denounced himself and ordered the policeman to take him to Nuka, to court, to be judged.

[In the court of justice three IRON-SHIRTS sit drinking. From a beam hangs a man in judge's robes. Enter AZDAK, in chains, dragging SHAUWA behind him.]

AZDAK: [Shouting.] I've helped the Grand Duke, the Grand Thief, the Grand Butcher, to escape! In the name of justice I ask to be severely judged in public trial!

FIRST IRONSHIRT: Who's this queer bird?

SHAUWA: That's our Village Scrivener, Azdak.

AZDAK: I am contemptible! I am a traitor! A branded criminal! Tell them, flatfoot, how I insisted on being tied up and brought to the capital. Because I sheltered the Grand Duke, the Grand Swindler, by mistake. And how I found out afterwards. See the marked man denounce himself! Tell them how I forced you to walk half the night with me to clear the whole thing up.

SHAUWA: And all by threats. That wasn't nice of you, Azdak.

AZDAK: Shut your mouth, Shauwa. You don't understand. A new age is upon us! It'll go thundering over you. You're finished. The police will be wiped out—poof! Everything will be gone into, everything will be brought into the open. The guilty will give themselves up. Why? They couldn't escape the people in any case. [To SHAUWA.] Tell them how I shouted all along Shoemaker Street [With big gestures, looking at the IRONSHIRTS.] "In my ignorance I let the Grand Swindler escape! So tear me to pieces, brothers!" I wanted to get it in first.

FIRST IRONSHIRT: And what did your brothers answer?

SHAUWA: They comforted him in Butcher Street, and they laughed themselves sick in Shoemaker Street. That's all.

AZDAK: But with you it's different. I can see you're men of iron. Brothers, where's the judge? I must be tried.

FIRST IRONSHIRT: [Pointing at the hanged MAN.] There's the judge. And please stop "brothering" us. It's rather a sore spot this evening.

AZDAK: "There's the judge." An answer never heard in Grusinia before. Townsman, where's His Excellency the Governor? [Pointing to the ground.] There's His Excellency, stranger. Where's the Chief Tax Collector? Where's the official Recruiting Officer? The Patriarch? The Chief of Police? There, there, there—all there. Brothers, I expected no less of you.

SECOND IRONSHIRT: What? What was it you expected, funny man?

AZDAK: What happened in Persia, brother, what happened in Persia?

SECOND IRONSHIRT: What did happen in Persia?

AZDAK: Everybody was hanged. Viziers, tax collectors. Everybody. Forty years ago now. My grandfather, a remarkable man by the way, saw it all. For three whole days. Everywhere.

SECOND IRONSHIRT: And who ruled when the Vizier was hanged?

AZDAK: A peasant ruled when the Vizier was hanged.

SECOND IRONSHIRT: And who commanded the army?

AZDAK: A soldier, a soldier.

SECOND IRONSHIRT: And who paid the wages?

AZDAK: A dyer. A dyer paid the wages.

SECOND IRONSHIRT: And why did all this happen, Persian?

AZDAK: Why did all this happen? Must there be a special reason? Why do you scratch yourself, brother? War! Too long a war! And no justice! My grandfather brought back a song that tells how it was. I will sing it for you. With my friend the policeman. [To SHAUWA.] And hold the rope tight. It's very suitable. [He sings, with SHAUWA holding the rope tight around him.]

THE SONG OF INJUSTICE IN PERSIA

Why don't our sons bleed any more?
   Why don't our daughters weep?
Why do only the slaughterhouse cattle
   have blood in their veins?
Why do only the willows shed tears
   on Lake Urmia?
The king must have a new province,
   the peasant must give up his savings.
That the roof of the world might be
   conquered, the roof of the cottage is
   torn down.
Our men are carried to the ends of the
   earth, so that great ones can eat at
   home.
The soldiers kill each other, the mar-
   shals salute each other.
They bite the widow's tax money to
   see if it's good, their swords break.
The battle was lost, the helmets were
   paid for.
Refrain: Is it so? Is it so?

SHAUWA: [Refrain.] Yes, yes, yes, yes, yes it's so.

AZDAK: Want to hear the rest of it? [The FIRST IRONSHIRT nods.]

SECOND IRONSHIRT: [To SHAUWA.] Did he teach you that song?

SHAUWA: Yes, only my voice isn't very good.

SECOND IRONSHIRT: No. [To AZDAK.] Go on singing.

AZDAK: The second verse is about the peace. [He sings.]

The officers are packed, the streets
   overflow with officials.
The rivers jump their banks and rav-
   age the fields.
Those who cannot let down their own
   trousers rule countries.

They can't count up to four, but they
    devour eight courses.
The corn farmers, looking round for
    buyers, see only the starving.
The weavers go home from their looms
    in rags.
Refrain: Is it so? Is it so?
SHAUWA: [*Refrain.*] Yes, yes, yes, yes, yes
it's so.
AZDAK:
That's why our sons don't bleed any
    more, that's why our daughters don't
    weep.
That's why only the slaughterhouse
    cattle have blood in their veins.
And only the willows shed tears by
    Lake Urmia toward morning.
FIRST IRONSHIRT: Are you going to sing
that song here in town?
AZDAK: Sure. What's wrong with it?
FIRST IRONSHIRT: Have you noticed that
the sky's getting red? [*Turning round,* AZDAK
sees the sky red with fire.] It's the people's
quarters on the outskirts of town. The carpet weavers have caught the "Persian Sickness," too. And they've been asking if Prince
Kazbeki isn't eating too many courses. This
morning they strung up the city judge. As
for us we beat them to pulp. We were paid
one hundred piasters per man, you understand?
AZDAK: [*After a pause.*] I understand.
[*He glaces shyly round and, creeping away,
sits down in a corner, his head in his hands.*]
IRONSHIRTS: [*To each other.*] If there
ever was a troublemaker it's him.
—He must've come to the capital to fish in
the troubled waters.
SHAUWA: Oh, I don't think he's a really
bad character, gentlemen. Steals a few chickens here and there. And maybe a rabbit.
SECOND IRONSHIRT: [*Approaching* AZDAK.]
Came to fish in the troubled waters, huh?
AZDAK: [*Looking up.*] I don't know why
I came.
SECOND IRONSHIRT: Are you in with the
carpet weavers maybe? [AZDAK *shakes his
head.*] How about that song?
AZDAK: From my grandfather. A silly and
ignorant man.
SECOND IRONSHIRT: Right. And how
about the dyer who paid the wages?
AZDAK: [*Muttering.*] That was in Persia.
FIRST IRONSHIRT: And this denouncing
of yourself? Because you didn't hang the
Grand Duke with your own hands?

AZDAK: Didn't I tell you I let him run?
[*He creeps farther away and sits on the
floor.*]
SHAUWA: I can swear to that: he let him
run.
[*The* IRONSHIRTS *burst out laughing
and slap* SHAUWA *on the back.* AZDAK
laughs loudest. They slap AZDAK *too,
and unchain him. They all start drinking as the* FAT PRINCE *enters with a
young man.*]
FIRST IRONSHIRT: [*To* AZDAK, *pointing at
the* FAT PRINCE.] There's your "new age"
for you! [*More laughter.*]
FAT PRINCE: Well, my friends, what is
there to laugh about? Permit me a serious
word. Yesterday morning the Princes of
Grusinia overthrew the warmongering government of the Grand Duke and did away
with his Governors. Unfortunately the
Grand Duke himself escaped. In this fateful
hour our carpet weavers, those eternal trou-
blemakers, had the effrontery to stir up a
rebellion and hang the univerally loved city
judge, our dear Illo Orbeliani. Ts—ts—ts.
My friends, we need peace, peace, peace
in Grusinia! And justice! So I've brought
along my dear nephew Bizergan Kazbeki.
He'll be the new judge, hm? A very gifted
fellow. What do you say? I want your opinion. Let the people decide!
SECOND IRONSHIRT: Does this mean *we*
elect the judge?
FAT PRINCE: Precisely. Let the people
propose some very gifted fellow! Confer
among yourselves, my friends. [*The* IRON-
SHIRTS *confer.*] Don't worry, my little fox.
The job's yours. And when we catch the
Grand Duke we won't have to kiss this
rabble's ass any longer.
IRONSHIRTS: [*Among themselves.*]
—Very funny: they're wetting their pants
because they haven't caught the Grand
Duke.
—When the outlook isn't so bright, they say:
"My friends!" and "Let the people decide!"
—Now he even wants justice for Grusinia!
But fun is fun as long as it lasts! [*Pointing
at* AZDAK.] He knows all about justice. Hey,
rascal, would you like this nephew fellow
to be the judge?
AZDAK: Are you asking me? You're not
asking *me*?!
FIRST IRONSHIRT: Why not? Anything
for a laugh!
AZDAK: You'd like to test him to the

marrow, correct? Have you a criminal on hand? An experienced one? So the candidate can show what he knows?

SECOND IRONSHIRT: Let's see. We do have a couple of doctors downstairs. Let's use them.

AZDAK: Oh, no, that's no good, we can't take real criminals till we're sure the judge will be appointed. He may be dumb, but he must be appointed, or the law is violated. And the law is a sensitive organ. It's like the spleen, you mustn't hit it—that would be fatal. Of course you can hang those two without violating the law, because there was no judge in the vicinity. But judgment, when pronounced, must be pronounced with absolute gravity—it's all such nonsense. Suppose, for instance, a judge jails a woman— let's say she's stolen a corn cake to feed her child—and this judge isn't wearing his robes—or maybe he's scratching himself while passing sentence and half his body is uncovered—a man's thigh *will* itch once in a while—the sentence this judge passes is a disgrace and the law is violated. In short it would be easier for a judge's robe and a judge's hat to pass judgment than for a man with no robe and no hat. If you don't treat it with respect, the law just disappears on you. Now you don't try out a bottle of wine by offering it to a dog; you'd only lose your wine.

FIRST IRONSHIRT: Then what do you suggest, hairsplitter?

AZDAK: I'll be the defendant.

FIRST IRONSHIRT: You? [*He bursts out laughing.*]

FAT PRINCE: What have you decided?

FIRST IRONSHIRT: We've decided to stage a rehearsal. Our friend here will be the defendant. Let the candidate be the judge and sit there.

FAT PRINCE: It isn't customary, but why not? [*To the* NEPHEW:] A mere formality, my little fox. What have I taught you? Who got there first—the slow runner or the fast?

NEPHEW: The silent runner, Uncle Arsen.

[*The* NEPHEW *takes the chair. The* IRONSHIRTS *and the* FAT PRINCE *sit on the steps. Enter* AZDAK, *mimicking the gait of the Grand Duke.*]

AZDAK: [*In the Grand Duke's accent.*] Is any here knows me? Am Grand Duke.

IRONSHIRTS:

—*What* is he?

—The Grand Duke. He knows him, too.

—Fine. So get on with the trial.

AZDAK: Listen! Am accused instigating war? Ridiculous! Am saying ridiculous! That enough? If not, have brought lawyers. Believe five hundred. [*He points behind him, pretending to be surrounded by lawyers.*] Requisition all available seats for lawyers! [*The* IRONSHIRTS *laugh; the* FAT PRINCE *joins in.*]

NEPHEW: [*To the* IRONSHIRTS.] You really wish me to try this case? I find it rather unusual. From the taste angle, I mean.

FIRST IRONSHIRT: Let's go!

FAT PRINCE: [*Smiling.*] Let him have it, my little fox!

NEPHEW: All right. People of Grusinia versus Grand Duke. Defendant, what have you got to say for yourself?

AZDAK: Plenty. Naturally, have read war lost. Only started on the advice of patriots. Like Uncle Arsen Kazbeki. Call Uncle Arsen as witness.

FAT PRINCE: [*To the* IRONSHIRTS, *delightedly.*] What a madcap!

NEPHEW: Motion rejected. One cannot be arraigned for declaring a war, which every ruler has to do once in a while, but only for running a war badly.

AZDAK: Rubbish! Did not run it at all! Had it run! Had it run by Princes! Naturally, they messed it up.

NEPHEW: Do you by any chance deny having been commander-in-chief?

AZDAK: Not at all! Always *was* commander-in-chief. At birth shouted at wet nurse. Was trained drop turds in toilet, grew accustomed to command. Always commanded officials rob my cash box. Officers flog soldiers only on command. Landowners sleep with peasants' wives only on strictest command. Uncle Arsen here grew belly at *my* command!

IRONSHIRTS: [*Clapping.*] He's good! Long live the Grand Duke!

FAT PRINCE: Answer him, my little fox: I'm with you.

NEPHEW: I shall answer him according to the dignity of the law. Defendant, preserve the dignity of the law!

AZDAK: Agreed. Command you proceed with trial!

NEPHEW: It is not your place to command me. You claim that the Princes forced you to declare war. How can you claim, then, that they—er—"messed it up"?

AZDAK: Did not send enough people. Embezzled funds. Sent sick horses. During attack, drinking in whorehouse. Call Uncle Arsen as witness.

NEPHEW: Are you making the outrageous suggestion that the Princes of this country did not fight?

AZDAK: No. Princes fought. Fought for war contracts.

FAT PRINCE: [Jumping up.] That's too much! This man talks like a carpet weaver!

AZDAK: Really? Told nothing but truth.

FAT PRINCE: Hang him! Hang him!

FIRST IRONSHIRT: [Pulling the PRINCE down.] Keep quiet! Go on, Excellency!

NEPHEW: Quiet! I now render a verdict: You must be hanged! By the neck! Having lost war!

AZDAK: Young man, seriously advise not fall publicly into jerky clipped speech. Cannot be watchdog if howl like wolf. Got it? If people realize Princes speak same language as Grand Duke, may hang Grand Duke and Princes, huh? By the way, must overrule verdict. Reason? War lost, but not for Princes. Princes won their war. Got 3,863,000 piasters for horses not delivered, 8,240,000 piasters for food supplies not produced. Are therefore victors. War lost only for Grusinia, which is not present in this court.

FAT PRINCE: I think that will do, my friends. [To AZDAK.] You can withdraw, funny man. [To the IRONSHIRTS.] You may now ratify the new judge's appointment, my friends.

FIRST IRONSHIRT: Yes, we can. Take down the judge's gown. [One IRONSHIRT climbs on the back of the other, pulls the gown off the hanged man.] [To the NEPHEW.] Now you run away so the right ass can get on the right chair. [To AZDAK.] Step foward! Go to the judge's seat! Now sit in! [AZDAK steps up, bows and sits down.] The judge was always a rascal! Now the rascal shall be a judge! [The judge's gown is placed round his shoulders, the hat on his head.] And what a judge!

SINGER:
And there was civil war in the land.
The mighty were not safe.
And Azdak was made a judge by the Ironshirts.
And Azdak remained a judge for two years.

SINGER AND CHORUS:
When the towns were set afire

And rivers of blood rose higher and higher,
Cockroaches crawled out of every crack.
And the court was full of schemers
And the church of foul blasphemers.
In the judge's cassock sat Azdak.

[AZDAK sits in the judge's chair, peeling an apple, SHAUWA is sweeping out the hall. On one side an INVALID in a wheelchair. Opposite, a young man accused of blackmail. An IRONSHIRT stands guard, holding the Ironshirts' banner.]

AZDAK: In consideration of the large number of cases, the Court today will hear two cases at a time. Before I open the proceedings, a short announcement—I accept. [He stretches out his hand. The BLACKMAILER is the only one to produce any money. He hands it to AZDAK.] I reserve the right to punish one of the parties for contempt of court. [He glances at the INVALID.] You [To the DOCTOR.] are a doctor, and you [To the INVALID.] are bringing a complaint against him. Is the doctor responsible for your condition?

INVALID: Yes. I had a stroke on his account.

AZDAK: That would be professional negligence.

INVALID: Worse than negligence. I gave this man money for his studies. So far, he hasn't paid me back a cent. It was when I heard he was treating a patient free that I had my stroke.

AZDAK: Rightly. [To a LIMPING MAN.] And what are you doing here?

LIMPING MAN: I'm the patient, Your Honor.

AZDAK: He treated your leg for nothing?

LIMPING MAN: The wrong leg! My rheumatism was in the left leg, he operated on the right. That's why I limp.

AZDAK: And you were treated free?

INVALID: A five-hundred-piaster operation free! For nothing! For a God-bless-you! And I paid for this man's studies! [To the DOCTOR.] Did they teach you to operate free?

DOCTOR: Your Honor, it is the custom to demand the fee before the operation, as the patient is more willing to pay before an operation than after. Which is only human. In the case in question I was convinced, when I started the operation, that my servant had already received the fee. In this I was mistaken.

INVALID: He was mistaken! A good doctor doesn't make mistakes! He examines before he operates!

AZDAK: That's right. [To SHAUWA.] Public Prosecutor, what's the other case about?

SHAUWA: [Busily sweeping.] Blackmail.

BLACKMAILER: High Court of Justice, I'm innocent. I only wanted to find out from the landowner concerned if he really had raped his niece. He informed me very politely that this was not the case, and gave me the money only so I could pay for my uncle's studies.

AZDAK: [To the DOCTOR.] You, on the other hand, can cite no extenuating circumstances for your offense, huh?

DOCTOR: Except that to err is human.

AZDAK: And you are aware that in money matters a good doctor is a highly responsible person? I once heard of a doctor who got a thousand piasters for a sprained finger by remarking that sprains have something to do with blood circulation, which after all a less good doctor might have overlooked, and who, on another occasion made a real gold mine out of a somewhat disordered gall bladder, he treated it with such loving care. You have no excuse, Doctor. The corn merchant Uxu had his son study medicine to get some knowledge of trade, our medical schools are so good. [To the BLACKMAILER.] What's the landowner's name?

SHAUWA: He doesn't want it mentioned.

AZDAK: In that case I will pass judgment. The Court considers the blackmail proved. And you [To the INVALID.] are sentenced to a fine of one thousand piasters. If you have a second stroke, the doctor will have to treat you free. Even if he has to amputate. [To the LIMPING MAN.] As compensation, you will receive a bottle of rubbing alcohol. [To the BLACKMAILER.] You are sentenced to hand over half the proceeds of your deal to the Public Prosecutor to keep the landowner's name secret. You are advised, moreover, to study medicine—you seem well suited to that calling. [To the DOCTOR.] You have perpetrated an unpardonable error in the practice of your profession: you are acquitted. Next cases!

SINGER AND CHORUS:
Men won't do much for a shilling.
For a pound they may be willing.
For twenty pounds the verdict's in the sack.
As for the many, all too many,

Those who've only got a penny—
They've one single, sole recourse: Azdak.

[Enter AZDAK from the caravansary on the highroad, followed by an old bearded INNKEEPER. The judge's chair is carried by a stableman and SHAUWA. An IRONSHIRT, with a banner, takes up his position.]

AZDAK: Put me down. Then we'll get some air. maybe even a good stiff breeze from the lemon grove there. It does justice good to be done in the open: the wind blows her skirts up and you can see what she's got. Shauwa, we've been eating too much. These official journeys are exhausting. [To the INNKEEPER.] It's a question of your daughter-in-law?

INNKEEPER: Your Worship, it's a question of the family honor. I wish to bring an action on behalf of my son, who's away on business on the other side the mountain. This is the offending stableman, and here's my daughter-in-law.

[Enter the DAUGHTER-IN-LAW, a voluptuous wench. She is veiled.]

AZDAK: [Sitting down.] I accept. [Sighing, the INNKEEPER hands him some money.] Good. Now the formalities are disposed of. This is a case of rape?

INNKEEPER: Your Honor, I caught the fellow in the act. Ludovica was in the straw on the stable floor.

AZDAK: Quite right, the stable. Lovely horses; I specially liked the little roan.

INNKEEPER: The first thing I did, of course, was to question Ludovica. On my son's behalf.

AZDAK: [Seriously.] I said I specially liked the little roan.

INNKEEPER: [Coldly.] Really? Ludovica confessed the stableman took her against her will.

AZDAK: Take your veil off, Ludovica. [She does so.] Ludovica, you please the Court. Tell us how it happened.

LUDOVICA: [Well schooled.] When I entered the stable to see the new foal the stableman said to me on his own accord: "It's hot today!" and laid his hand on my left breast. I said to him: "Don't do that!" But he continued to handle me indecently, which provoked my anger. Before I realized his sinful intentions, he got much closer. It was all over when my father-in-law entered and accidentally trod on me.

INNKEEPER: [*Explaining.*] On my son's behalf.

AZDAK: [*To the* STABLEMAN.] You admit you started it?

STABLEMAN: Yes.

AZDAK: Ludovica, you like to eat sweet things?

LUDOVICA: Yes, sunflower seeds!

AZDAK: You like to lie a long time in the bathtub?

LUDOVICA: Half an hour or so.

AZDAK: Public Prosecutor, drop your knife —there on the ground. [SHAUWA *does so.*] Ludovica, pick up that knife. [LUDOVICA, *swaying her hips, does so.*] See that? [*He points at her.*] The way it moves? The rape is now proven. By eating too much—sweet things, especially—by lying too long in warm water, by laziness and too soft a skin, you have raped that unfortunate man. Think you can run around with a behind like that and get away with it in court? This is a case of intentional assault with a dangerous weapon! You are sentenced to hand over to the Court the little roan which your father liked to ride "on his son's behalf." And now, come with me to the stables, so the Court can inspect the scene of the crime, Ludovica.

SINGER AND CHORUS:
When the sharks the sharks devour
Little fishes have their hour.
For a while the load is off their back.
On Grusinia's highways faring
Fixed-up scales of justice bearing
Strode the poor man's magistrate: Azdak.
And he gave to the forsaken
All that from the rich he'd taken.
And a bodyguard of roughnecks was Azdak's.
And our good and evil man, he
Smiled upon Grusinia's Granny.
His emblem was a tear in sealing wax.
All mankind should love each other
But when visiting your brother
Take an ax along and hold it fast.
Not in theory but in practice
Miracles are wrought with axes
And the age of miracles is not past.

[AZDAK'S *judge's chair is in a tavern. Three rich* FARMERS *stand before* AZDAK. SHAUWA *brings him wine. In a corner stands an* OLD PEASANT WOMAN. *In the open doorway, and outside, stand villagers looking on. An* IRONSHIRT *stands guard with a banner.*]

AZDAK: The Public Prosecutor has the floor.

SHAUWA: It concerns a cow. For five weeks, the defendant has had a cow in her stable, the property of the farmer Suru. She was also found to be in possession of a stolen ham, and a number of cows belonging to Shutoff were killed after he asked the defendant to pay the rent on a piece of land.

FARMERS:
—It's a matter of my ham, Your Honor.
—It's a matter of my cow, Your Honor.
—It's a matter of my land, Your Honor.

AZDAK: Well, Granny, what have *you* got to say to all this?

OLD WOMAN: Your Honor, one night toward morning, five weeks ago, there was a knock at my door, and outside stood a bearded man with a cow. "My dear woman," he said, "I am the miracle-working Saint Banditus and because your son has been killed in the war, I bring you this cow as a souvenir. Take good care of it."

FARMERS:
—The robber, Irakli, Your Honor!
—Her brother-in-law, Your Honor!
—The cow-thief!
—The incendiary!
—He must be beheaded!

[*Outside, a woman screams. The crowd grows restless, retreats. Enter the* BANDIT *Irakli with a huge ax.*]

BANDIT: A very good evening, dear friends! A glass of vodka!

FARMERS: [*Crossing themselves.*] Irakli!

AZDAK: Public Prosecutor, a glass of vodka for our guest. And who are you?

BANDIT: I'm a wandering hermit. Your Honor. Thanks for the gracious gift. [*He empties the glass which* SHAUWA *has brought.*] Another!

AZDAK: I am Azdak. [*He gets up and bows. The* BANDIT *also bows.*] The Court welcomes the foreign hermit. Go on with your story, Granny.

OLD WOMAN: Your Honor, that first night I didn't yet know Saint Banditus could work miracles, it was only the cow. But one night, a few days later, the farmer's servants came to take the cow away again. Then they turned round in front of my door and went off without the cow. And bumps as big as a fist sprouted on their heads. So I knew that Saint Banditus had changed their hearts and turned them into friendly people.

[*The* BANDIT *roars with laughter.*]

FIRST FARMER: I know what changed them.

AZDAK: That's fine. You can tell us later. Continue.

OLD WOMAN: Your Honor, the next one to become a good man was the farmer Shut-off—a devil, as everyone knows. But Saint Banditus arranged it so he let me off the rent on the little piece of land.

SECOND FARMER: Because my cows were killed in the field.

[*The* BANDIT *laughs.*]

OLD WOMAN: [*Answering* AZDAK's *sign to continue.*] Then one morning the ham came flying in at my window. It hit me in the small of the back. I'm still lame, Your Honor, look. [*She limps a few steps. The* BANDIT *laughs.*] Your Honor, was there ever a time when a poor old woman could get a ham *without* a miracle?

[*The* BANDIT *starts sobbing.*]

AZDAK: [*Rising from his chair.*] Granny, that's a question that strikes straight at the Court's heart. Be so kind as to sit here. [*The* OLD WOMAN, *hesitating, sits in the judge's chair.*]

AZDAK: [*Sits on the floor, glass in hand, reciting.*]

Granny
We could almost call you Granny Grusinia
The Woebegone
The Bereaved Mother
Whose sons have gone to war.
Receiving the present of a cow
She bursts out crying.
When she is beaten
She remains hopeful.
When she's not beaten
She's surprised.
On us
Who are already damned
May you render a merciful verdict
Granny Grusinia!

[*Bellows at the* FARMERS.] Admit you don't believe in miracles, you atheists! Each of you is sentenced to pay five hundred piasters! For godlessness! Get out! [*The* FARMERS *slink out.*] And you Granny, and you [*To the* BANDIT.] pious man, empty a pitcher of wine with the Public Prosecutor and Azdak!

SINGER AND CHORUS:
And he broke the rules to save them.
Broken law like bread he gave them,

Brought them to shore upon his crooked back.
At long last the poor and lowly
Had someone who was not too holy
To be bribed by empty hands: Azdak.
For two years it was his pleasure
To give the beasts of prey short measure:
He became a wolf to fight the pack.
From All Hallows to All Hallows
On his chair beside the gallows
Dispensing justice in his fashion sat Azdak.

SINGER:
But the era of disorder came to an end.
The Grand Duke returned.
The Governor's wife returned.
A trial was held.
Many died.
The people's quarters burned anew.
And fear seized Azdak.

[AZDAK's *judge's chair stands again in the court of justice.* AZDAK *sits on the floor, shaving and talking to* SHAUWA. *Noises outside. In the rear the* FAT PRINCE's *head is carried by on a lance.*]

AZDAK: Shauwa, the days of your slavery are numbered, maybe even the minutes. For a long time now I have held you in the iron curb of reason, and it has torn your mouth till it bleeds. I have lashed you with reasonable arguments, I have manhandled you with logic. You are by nature a weak man, and if one slyly throws an argument in your path, you *have* to snap it up, you can't resist. It is your nature to lick the hand of some superior being. But superior beings can be of very different kinds. And now, with your liberation, you will soon be able to follow your natural inclinations, which are low. You will be able to follow your infallible instinct, which teaches you to plant your fat heel on the faces of men. Gone is the era of confusion and disorder, which I find described in the Song of Chaos. Let us now sing that song together in memory of those terrible days. Sit down and don't do violence to the music. Don't be afraid. It sounds all right. And it has a fine refrain. [*He sings.*]

THE SONG OF CHAOS

Sister, hide your face! Brother, take your knife!
The times are out of joint!
Big men are full of complaint
And small men full of joy.

The city says:
"Let us drive the mighty from our midst!"
Offices are raided. Lists of serfs are destroyed.
They have set Master's nose to the grindstone.
They who lived in the dark have seen the light.
The ebony poor box is broken.
Sesnem* wood is sawed up for beds.
Who had no bread have full barns.
Who begged for alms of corn now mete it out.

SHAUWA: [Refrain.] Oh, oh, oh, oh.
AZDAK: [Refrain.]
Where are you, General, where are you?
Please, please, please, restore order!
The nobleman's son can no longer be recognized;
The lady's child becomes the son of her slave-girl
The councilors meet in a shed.
Once, this man was barely allowed to sleep on the wall;
Now, he stretches his limbs in a bed.
Once, this man rowed a boat; now, he owns ships.
Their owner looks for them, but they're his no longer.
Five men are sent on a journey by their master.
"Go yourself," they say, "we have arrived."

SHAUWA: [Refrain.] Oh, oh, oh, oh.
AZDAK: [Refrain.]
Where are you, General, where are you?

---

* I do not know what kind of wood this is, so I have left the word exactly as it stands in the German original. The song is based on an Egyptian papyrus which Brecht cites as such in his essay, "Five Difficulties in the Writing of the Truth." I should think he must have come across it in Adolf Erman's *Die Literatur der Aegypter*, 1923, p. 130 ff. Erman too gives the word as Sesnem. The same papyrus is quoted in Karl Jaspers' *Man in the Modern Age* (Anchor edition, pp. 18-19) but without the sentence about the Sesnem wood.—E.B.

Please, please, please, restore order!
Yes, so it might have been, had order been neglected much longer. But now the Grand Duke has returned to the capital, and the Persians have lent him an army to restore order with. The people's quarters are already aflame. Go and get me the big book I always sit on. [SHAUWA *brings the big book from the judge's chair.* AZDAK *opens it.*] This is the Statute Book and I've always used it, as you can testify. Now I'd better look in this book and see what they can do to me. I've let the down-and-outs get away with murder, and I'll have to pay for it. I helped poverty onto its skinny legs, so they'll hang me for drunkenness. I peeped into the rich man's pocket, which is bad taste. And I can't hide anywhere—everybody knows me because I've helped everybody.

SHAUWA: Someone's coming!
AZDAK: [In panic, he walks trembling to the chair.] It's the end. And now they'd enjoy seeing what a Great Man I am. I'll deprive them of that pleasure. I'll beg on my knees for mercy. Spittle will slobber down my chin. The fear of death is in me.

[Enter Natella Abashwili, the GOVERNOR'S WIFE, followed by the ADJUTANT and an IRONSHIRT.]

GOVERNOR'S WIFE: What sort of a creature is that, Shalva?
AZDAK: A willing one, Your Highness, a man ready to oblige.
ADJUTANT: Natella Abashwili, wife of the late Governor, has just returned. She is looking for her two-year-old son, Michael. She has been informed that the child was carried off to the mountains by a former servant.
AZDAK: The child will be brought back, Your Highness, at your service.
ADJUTANT: They say that the person in question is passing it off as her own.
AZDAK: She will be beheaded, Your Highness, at your service.
ADJUTANT: That is all.
GOVERNOR'S WIFE: [Leaving.] I don't like that man.
AZDAK: [Following her to door, bowing.] At your service, Your Highness, it will all be arranged.

5

THE CHALK CIRCLE

SINGER:
Hear now the story of the trial
Concerning Governor Abashwili's child
And the determination of the true
    mother
By the famous test of the Chalk Circle.
[*Law court in Nuka.* IRONSHIRTS *lead*
MICHAEL *across stage and out at the
back.* IRONSHIRTS *hold* GRUSHA *back
with their lances under the gateway
until the child has been led through.
Then she is admitted. She is accom-
panied by the former Governor's* COOK.
Distant noises and a fire-red sky.]
GRUSHA: [*Trying to hide.*] He's brave, he
can wash himself now.
COOK: You're lucky. It's not a real judge.
It's Azdak, a drunk who doesn't know what
he's doing. The biggest thieves have got by
through him. Because he gets everything
mixed up and the rich never offer him big
enough bribes, the like of us sometimes do
pretty well.
GRUSHA: I *need* luck right now.
COOK: Touch wood. [*She crosses herself.*]
I'd better offer up another prayer that the
judge may be drunk. [*She prays with motionless lips, while* GRUSHA *looks around, in
vain, for the child.*] Why must you hold on
to it at any price if it isn't yours? In days
like these?
GRUSHA: He's mine. I brought him up.
COOK: Have you never thought what'd
happen when she came back?
GRUSHA: At first I thought I'd give him
to her. Then I thought she wouldn't come
back.
COOK: And even a borrowed coat keeps a
man warm, hm? [GRUSHA *nods.*] I'll swear
to anything for you. You're a decent girl.
[*She sees the soldier* SIMON SHASHAVA *approaching.*] You've done wrong by Simon,
though. I've been talking with him. He just
can't understand.
GRUSHA: [*Unaware of* SIMON'S *presence.*]
Right now I can't be bothered whether he
understands or not!
COOK: He knows the child isn't yours, but
you married and not free "till death you do
part"—he can't understand *that.*
[GRUSHA *sees* SIMON *and greets him.*]
SIMON: [*Gloomily.*] I wish the lady to

know I will swear I am the father of the
child.
GRUSHA: [*Low.*] Thank you, Simon.
SIMON: At the same time I wish the lady
to know my hands are not tied—nor are hers.
COOK: You needn't have said that. You
know she's married.
SIMON: And it needs no rubbing in.
[*Enter an* IRONSHIRT.]
IRONSHIRT: Where's the judge? Has any-
one seen the judge?
ANOTHER IRONSHIRT: [*Stepping forward.*]
The judge isn't here yet. Nothing but a bed
and a pitcher in the whole house!
[*Exeunt* IRONSHIRTS.]
COOK: I hope nothing has happened to
him. With any other judge you'd have as
much chance as a chicken has teeth.
GRUSHA: [*Who has turned away and cov-
ered her face.*] Stand in front of me. I
shouldn't have come to Nuka. If I run into
the Ironshirt, the one I hit over the head . . .
[*She screams. An* IRONSHIRT *had
stopped and, turning his back, had
been listening to her. He now wheels
around. It is the* CORPORAL, *and he has
a huge scar across his face.*]
IRONSHIRT: [*In the gateway.*] What's the
matter, Shotta? Do you know her?
CORPORAL: [*After staring for some time.*]
No.
IRONSHIRT: She's the one who stole the
Abashwili child, or so they say. If you know
anything about it you can make some money,
Shotta.
[*Exit the* CORPORAL, *cursing.*]
COOK: Was it him? [GRUSHA *nods.*] I
think he'll keep his mouth shut, or he'd be
admitting he was after the child.
GRUSHA: I'd almost forgotten him.
[*Enter the* GOVERNOR'S WIFE, *followed
by the* ADJUTANT *and two* LAWYERS.]
GOVERNOR'S WIFE: At least there are no
common people here, thank God. I can't
stand their smell. It always gives me migraine.
FIRST LAWYER: Madam, I must ask you
to be careful what you say until we have
another judge.
GOVERNOR'S WIFE: But I didn't say anything, Illo Shuboladze. I love the people
with their simple straightforward minds. It's

only that their smell brings on my migraine.

SECOND LAWYER: There won't be many spectators. The whole population is sitting at home behind locked doors because of the riots in the people's quarters.

GOVERNOR'S WIFE: [Looking at GRUSHA.] Is that the creature?

FIRST LAWYER: Please, most gracious Natella Abashwili, abstain from invective until it is certain the Grand Duke has appointed a new judge and we're rid of the present one, who's about the lowest fellow ever seen in judge's gown. Things are all set to move, you see.

[Enter IRONSHIRTS from the courtyard.]

COOK: Her Grace would pull your hair out on the spot if she didn't know Azdak is for the poor. He goes by the face.

[IRONSHIRTS begin fastening a rope to a beam. AZDAK, in chains, is led in, followed by SHAUWA, also in chains. The three FARMERS bring up the rear.]

AN IRONSHIRT: Trying to run away, were you? [He strikes AZDAK.]

ONE FARMER: Off with his judge's gown before we string him up!

[IRONSHIRTS and FARMERS tear off Azdak's gown. His torn underwear is visible. Then someone kicks him.]

AN IRONSHIRT: [Pushing him into someone else.] Want a load of justice? Here it is!

[Accompanied by shouts of "You take it!" and "Let me have him, Brother!" they throw AZDAK back and forth until he collapses. Then he is lifted up and dragged under the noose.]

GOVERNOR'S WIFE: [Who, during this "ballgame," has clapped her hands hysterically.] I disliked that man from the moment I first saw him.

AZDAK: [Covered with blood, panting.] I can't see. Give me a rag.

AN IRONSHIRT: What is it you want to see?

AZDAK: You, you dogs! [He wipes the blood out of his eyes with his shirt.] Good morning, dogs! How goes it, dogs! How's the dog world? Does it smell good? Got another boot for me to lick? Are you back at each other's throats, dogs?

[Accompanied by a CORPORAL, a dust-covered RIDER enters. He takes some documents from a leather case, looks at them, then interrupts.]

RIDER: Stop! I bring a dispatch from the Grand Duke, containing the latest appointments.

CORPORAL: [Bellowing.] Atten—shun!

RIDER: Of the new judge it says: "We appoint a man whom we have to thank for saving a life indispensable to the country's walfare—a certain Azdak of Nuka." Which is he?

SHAUWA: [Pointing.] That's him, Your Excellency.

CORPORAL: [Bellowing.] What's going on here?

AN IRONSHIRT: I beg to report that His Honor Azdak was already His Honor Azdak, but on these farmers' denunciation was pronounced the Grand Duke's enemy.

CORPORAL: [Pointing at the FARMERS.] March them off! [They are marched off. They bow all the time.] See to it that His Honor Azdak is exposed to no more violence.

[Exeunt RIDER and CORPORAL.]

COOK: [To SHAUWA.] She clapped her hands! I hope he saw it!

FIRST LAWYER: It's a catastrophe.

[AZDAK has fainted. Coming to, he is dressed again in judge's robes. He walks, swaying, toward the IRONSHIRTS.]

AN IRONSHIRT: What does Your Honor desire?

AZDAK: Nothing, fellow dogs, or just an occasional boot to lick. [To SHAUWA.] I pardon you. [He is unchained.] Get me some red wine, the sweet kind. [SHAUWA stumbles off.] Get out of here, I've got to judge a case. [Exeunt IRONSHIRTS. SHAUWA returns with a pitcher of wine. AZDAK gulps it down.] Something for my backside. [SHAUWA brings the Statute Book, puts it on the judge's chair. AZDAK sits on it.] I accept.

[The Prosecutors, among whom a worried council has been held, smile with relief. They whisper.]

COOK: Oh dear!

SIMON: A well can't be filled with dew, they say.

LAWYERS: [Approaching AZDAK, who stands up, expectantly.] A quite ridiculous case, Your Honor. The accused has abducted a child and refuses to hand it over.

AZDAK: [Stretching out his hand, glancing at GRUSHA.] A most attractive person. [He fingers the money, then sits down, satisfied.] I declare the proceedings open and demand the whole truth. [To GRUSHA.] Especially from you.

FIRST LAWYER: High Court of Justice! Blood, as the popular saying goes, is thicker than water. This old adage . . .

AZDAK: [*Interrupting.*] The Court wants to know the lawyers' fee.

FIRST LAWYER: [*Surprised.*] I beg your pardon? [AZDAK, *smiling, rubs his thumb and index finger.*] Oh, I see. Five hundred piasters, Your Honor, to answer the Court's somewhat unusual question.

AZDAK: Did you hear? The question is unusual. I ask it because I listen in quite a different way when I know you're good.

FIRST LAWYER: [*Bowing.*] Thank you, Your Honor. High Court of Justice, of all ties the ties of blood are strongest. Mother and child—is there a more intimate relationship? Can one tear a child from its mother? High Court of Justice, she has conceived it in the holy ecstasies of love. She has carried it in her womb. She has fed it with her blood. She has borne it with pain. High Court of Justice, it has been observed that the wild tigress, robbed of her young, roams restless through the mountains, shrunk to a shadow. Nature herself . . .

AZDAK: [*Interrupting, to* GRUSHA.] What's your answer to all this and anything else that lawyer might have to say?

GRUSHA: He's mine.

AZDAK: Is that all? I hope you can prove it. Why should I assign the child to you in any case?

GRUSHA: I brought him up like the priest says "according to my best knowledge and conscience." I always found him something to eat. Most of the time he had a roof over his head. And I went to such trouble for him. I had expenses too. I didn't look out for my own comfort. I brought the child up to be friendly with everyone, and from the beginning taught him to work. As well as he could, that is. He's still very little.

FIRST LAWYER: Your Honor, it is significant that the girl herself doesn't claim any tie of blood between her and the child.

AZDAK: The Court takes note of that.

FIRST LAWYER: Thank you, Your Honor. And now permit a woman bowed in sorrow —who has already lost her husband and now has also to fear the loss of her child—to address a few words to you. The gracious Natella Abashwili is . . .

GOVERNOR'S WIFE: [*Quietly.*] A most cruel fate, sir, forces me to describe to you the tortures of a bereaved mother's soul, the anxiety, the sleepless nights, the . . .

SECOND LAWYER: [*Bursting out.*] It's outrageous the way this woman is being treated!

Her husband's palace is closed to her! The revenue of her estates is blocked, and she is cold-bloodedly told that it's tied to the heir. She can't do a thing without that child. She can't even pay her lawyers! ! [*To the* FIRST LAWYER, *who, desperate about this outburst, makes frantic gestures to keep him from speaking.*] Dear Illo Shuboladze, surely it can be divulged now that the Abashwili estates are at stake?

FIRST LAWYER: Please, Honored Sandro Oboladze! We agreed . . . [*To* AZDAK.] Of course it is correct that the trial will also decide if our noble client can take over the Abashwili estates, which are rather extensive. I say "also" advisedly, for in the foreground stands the human tragedy of a mother, as Natella Abashwili very properly explained in the first words of her moving statement. Even if Michael Abashwili were not heir to the estates, he would still be the dearly beloved child of my client.

AZDAK: Stop! The Court is touched by the mention of estates. It's a proof of human feeling.

SECOND LAWYER: Thanks, Your Honor. Dear Illo Shuboladze, we can prove in any case that the woman who took the child is not the child's mother. Permit me to lay before the Court the bare facts. High Court of Justice, by an unfortunate chain of circumstances, Michael Abashwili was left behind on that Easter Sunday while his mother was making her escape. Grusha, a palace kitchen maid, was seen with the baby . . .

COOK: All her mistress was thinking of was what dresses she'd take along!

SECOND LAWYER: [*Unnoticed.*] Nearly a year later Grusha turned up in a mountain village with a baby and there entered into the state of matrimony with . . .

AZDAK: How'd you get to that mountain village?

GRUSHA: On foot, Your Honor. And he was mine.

SIMON: I'm the father, Your Honor.

COOK: I used to look after it for them, Your Honor. For five piasters.

SECOND LAWYER: This man is engaged to Grusha, High Court of Justice: his testimony is suspect.

AZDAK: Are you the man she married in the mountain village?

AZDAK: [*To* GRUSHA.] Why? [*Pointing at* SIMON.] Is he no good in bed? Tell the truth.

GRUSHA: We didn't get that far. I married because of the baby. So he'd have a roof over his head. [*Pointing at* SIMON.] He was in the war, Your Honor.

AZDAK: And now he wants you back again, huh?

SIMON: I wish to state in evidence . . .

GRÚSHA: [*Angrily.*] I am no longer free, Your Honor.

AZDAK: And the child, you claim, comes from whoring? [GRUSHA *doesn't answer.*] I'm going to ask you a question: What kind of child is he? A ragged little bastard? Or from a good family?

GRUSHA: [*Angrily.*] He's an ordinary child.

AZDAK: I mean—did he have refined features from the beginning?

GRUSHA: He had a nose on his face.

AZDAK: A very significant comment! It has been said of me that I went out one time and sniffed at a rosebush before rendering a verdict—tricks like that are needed nowadays. Well, I'll make it short, and not listen to any more lies. [*To* GRUSHA.] Especially not yours. [*To all the accused.*] I can imagine what you've cooked up to cheat me! I know you people. You're swindlers.

GRUSHA: [*Suddenly.*] I can understand your wanting to cut it short, now I've seen what you accepted!

AZDAK: Shut up! Did I accept anything from you?

GRUSHA: [*While the* COOK *tries to restrain her.*] I haven't got anything.

AZDAK: True. Quite true. From starvelings I never get a thing. I might just as well starve, myself. You want justice, but do you want to pay for it, hm? When you go to a butcher you know you have to pay, but you people go to a judge as if you were off to a funeral supper.

SIMON: [*Loudly.*] When the horse was shod, the horsefly held out its leg, as the saying is.

AZDAK: [*Eagerly accepting the challenge.*] Better a treasure in manure than a stone in a mountain stream.

SIMON: A fine day. Let's go fishing, said the angler to the worm.

AZDAK: I'm my own master, said the servant, and cut off his foot.

SIMON: I love you as a father, said the Czar to the peasants, and had the Czarevitch's head chopped off.

AZDAK: A fool's worst enemy is himself.

SIMON: However, a fart has no nose.

AZDAK: Fined ten piasters for indecent language in court! That'll teach you what justice is.

GRUSHA: [*Furiously.*] A fine kind of justice! You play fast and loose with us because we don't talk as refined as that crowd with their lawyers.

AZDAK: That's true. You people are too dumb. It's only right you should get it in the neck.

GRUSHA: You want to hand the child over to her, and she wouldn't even know how to keep it dry, she's so "refined"! You know about as much about justice as I do!

AZDAK: There's something in that. I'm an ignorant man. Haven't even a decent pair of pants on under this gown. Look! With me, everything goes on food and drink—I was educated in a convent. Incidentally, I'll fine you ten piasters for contempt of court. And you're a very silly girl, to turn me against you, instead of making eyes at me and wiggling your backside a little to keep me in a good temper. Twenty piasters!

GRUSHA: Even if it was thirty, I'd tell you what I think of your justice, you drunken onion! [*Incoherently.*] How dare you talk to me like the cracked Isaiah on the church window? As if you were somebody? For you weren't born to this. You weren't born to rap your own mother on the knuckles if she swipes a little bowl of salt someplace. Aren't you ashamed of yourself when you see how I tremble before you? You've made yourself their servant so no one will take their houses from them—houses they had stolen! Since when have houses belonged to the bedbugs? But you're on the watch, or they couldn't drag our men into their wars! You bribetaker!

[AZDAK *half gets up, starts beaming. With his little hammer he halfheartedly knocks on the table as if to get silence. As* GRUSHA's *scolding continues, he only beats time with his hammer.*] I've no respect for you. No more than for a thief or a bandit with a knife! You can do what you want. You can take the child away from me, a hundred against one, but I tell you one thing: only extortioners should be chosen for a profession like yours, and men who rape children! As punishment! Yes, let *them* sit in judgment on their fellow creatures. It is worse than to hang from the gallows.

AZDAK: [*Sitting down.*] Now it'll be thirty!

And I won't go on squabbling with you—we're not in a tavern. What'd happen to my dignity as a judge? Anyway, I've lost interest in your case. Where's the couple who wanted a divorce? [*To* SHAUWA.] Bring 'em in. This case is adjourned for fifteen minutes.

FIRST LAWYER: [*To the* GOVERNOR'S WIFE.] Even without using the rest of the evidence, Madam, we have the verdict in the bag.

COOK: [*To* GRUSHA.] You've gone and spoiled your chances with him. You won't get the child now.

GOVERNOR'S WIFE: Shalva, my smelling salts!

[*Enter a very old couple.*]

AZDAK: I accept. [*The old couple don't understand.*] I hear you want to be divorced. How long have you been together?

OLD WOMAN: Forty years, Your Honor.

AZDAK: And why do you want a divorce?

OLD MAN: We don't like each other, Your Honor.

AZDAK: Since when?

OLD WOMAN: Oh, from the very beginning, Your Honor.

AZDAK: I'll think about your request and render my verdict when I'm through with the other case. [SHAUWA *leads them back.*] I need the child. [*He beckons* GRUSHA *to him and bends not unkindly toward her.*] I've noticed you have a soft spot for justice. I don't believe he's your child, but if he *were* yours, woman, wouldn't you want him to be rich? You'd only have to say he wasn't yours, and he'd have a palace and many horses in his stable and many beggars on his doorstep and many soldiers in his service and many petitioners in his courtyard, wouldn't he? What do you say—don't you want him to be rich?

[GRUSHA *is silent.*]

SINGER:
Hear now what the angry girl thought
    but did not say:
Had he golden shoes to wear
He'd be cruel as a bear
Evil would his life disgrace.
He'd laugh in my face.
Carrying a heart of flint
Is too troublesome a stint.
Being powerful and bad
Is hard on a lad.
Then let hunger be his foe!
Hungry men and women, no.
Let him fear the darksome night

But not daylight!

AZDAK: I think I understand you, woman.

GRUSHA: [*Suddenly and loudly.*] I won't give him up. I've raised him, and he knows me.

[*Enter* SHAUWA *with the* CHILD.]

GOVERNOR'S WIFE: He's in rags!

GRUSHA: That's not true. But I wasn't given time to put his good shirt on.

GOVERNOR'S WIFE: He must have been in a pigsty.

GRUSHA: [*Furiously.*] I'm not a pig, but there are some who are! Where did you leave your baby?

GOVERNOR'S WIFE: I'll show you, you vulgar creature! [*She is about to throw herself on* GRUSHA, *but is restrained by her lawyers.*] She's a criminal, she must be whipped. Immediately!

SECOND LAWYER: [*Holding his hand over her mouth.*] Natella Abashwili, you promised . . . Your Honor, the plaintiff's nerves . . .

AZDAK: Plaintiff and defendant! The Court has listened to your case, and has come to no decision as to who the real mother is; therefore, I, the judge, am obliged to *choose* a mother for the child. I'll make a test. Shauwa, get a piece of chalk and draw a circle on the floor. [SHAUWA *does so.*] Now place the child in the center. [SHAUWA *puts* MICHAEL, *who smiles at* GRUSHA, *in the center of the circle.*] Stand near the circle, both of you. [*The* GOVERNOR'S WIFE *and* GRUSHA *step up to the circle.*] Now each of you take the child by one hand. [*They do so.*] The true mother is she who can pull the child out of the circle.

SECOND LAWYER: [*Quickly.*] High Court of Justice, I object! The fate of the great Abashwili estates, which are tied to the child, as the heir, should not be made dependent on such a doubtful duel. In addition, my client does not command the strength of this person, who is accustomed to physical work.

AZDAK: She looks pretty well fed to me. Pull! [*The* GOVERNOR'S WIFE *pulls the* CHILD *out of the circle on her side;* GRUSHA *has let go and stands aghast.*] What's the matter with you? You didn't pull.

GRUSHA: I didn't hold on to him.

FIRST LAWYER: [*Congratulating the* GOVERNOR'S WIFE.] What did I say! The ties of blood!

GRUSHA: [*Running to* AZDAK.] Your Honor, I take back everything I said against you. I ask your forgiveness. But could I keep him till he can speak all the words? He knows a few.

AZDAK: Don't influence the Court. I bet you only know about twenty words yourself. All right, I'll make the test once more, just to be certain. [*The two women take up their positions again.*] Pull! [*Again* GRUSHA *lets go of the* CHILD.]

GRUSHA: [*In despair.*] I brought him up! Shall I also tear him to bits? I can't!

AZDAK: [*Rising.*] And in this manner the Court has determined the true mother. [*To* GRUSHA.] Take your child and be off. I advise you not to stay in the city with him. [*To the* GOVERNOR'S WIFE.] And you disappear before I fine you for fraud. Your estates fall to the city. They'll be converted into a playground for the children. They need one, and I've decided it'll be called after me: Azdak's Garden.

[*The* GOVERNOR'S WIFE *has fainted and is carried out by the* LAWYERS *and the* ADJUTANT. GRUSHA *stands motionless.* SHAUWA *leads the* CHILD *toward her.*] Now I'll take off this judge's gown—it's got too hot for me. I'm not cut out for a hero. In token of farewell I invite you all to a little dance in the meadow outside. Oh, I'd almost forgotten something in my excitement . . . to sign the divorce decree. [*Using the judge's chair as a table, he writes something on a piece of paper, and prepares to leave. Dance music has started.*]

SHAUWA: [*Having read what is on the paper.*] But that's not right. You've not divorced the old people. You've divorced Grusha!

AZDAK: Divorced the wrong couple? What a pity! And I never retract! If I did, how could we keep order in the land? [*To the old couple.*] I'll invite you to my party in-

stead. You don't mind dancing with each other, do you? [*To* GRUSHA *and* SIMON.] I've got forty piasters coming from you.

SIMON: [*Pulling out his purse.*] Cheap at the price, Your Honor. And many thanks.

AZDAK: [*Pocketing the cash.*] I'll be needing this.

GRUSHA: [*To* MICHAEL.] So we'd better leave the city tonight, Michael? [*To* SIMON.] You like him?

SIMON: With my respects, I like him.

GRUSHA: Now I can tell you. I took him because on that Easter Sunday I got engaged to you. So he's a child of love. Michael, let's dance.

[*She dances with* MICHAEL, SIMON *dances with the* COOK, *the old couple with each other.* AZDAK *stands lost in thought. The dancers soon hide him from view. Occasionally he is seen, but less and less as more couples join the dance.*]

SINGER:
And after that evening Azdak vanished and was never seen again.
The people of Grusinia did not forget him but long remembered
The period of his judging as a brief golden age,
Almost an age of justice.

[*All the couples dance off.* AZDAK *has disappeared.*]

But you, you who have listened to the Story of the Chalk Circle.
Take note what men of old concluded:
That what there is shall go to those who are good for it,
Children to the motherly, that they prosper,
Carts to good drivers, that they be driven well,
The valley to the waterers, that it yield fruit.

GEORGE BERNARD SHAW

THE TECHNICAL NOVELTY IN IBSEN'S PLAYS [1]

It is a striking and melancholy example of the preoccupation of
critics with phrases and formulas to which they have given life
by taking them into the tissue of their own living minds, and
which therefore seem and feel vital and important to them
whilst they are to everybody else the deadest and dreariest
rubbish (this is the great secret of academic dryasdust), that
to this day they remain blind to a new technical factor in the
art of popular stage-play making which every considerable
playwright has been thrusting under their noses night after
night for a whole generation. This technical factor in the play
is the discussion. Formerly you had in what was called a well
made play an exposition in the first act, a situation in the second, and unravelling in the third. Now you have exposition,
situation, and discussion; and the discussion is the test of the
playwright. The critics protest in vain. They declare that dis-
cussions are not dramatic, and that art should not be didactic.
Neither the playwrights nor the public take the smallest notice
of them. The discussion conquered Europe in Ibsen's Doll's
House; and now the serious playwright recognizes in the discussion not only the main test of his highest powers, but also
the real centre of his play's interest. Sometimes he even takes
every possible step to assure the public beforehand that his play
will be fitted with that newest improvement. . . .

Now an interesting play cannot in the nature of things mean
anything but a play in which problems of conduct and character of personal importance to the audience are raised and
suggestively discussed. People have a thrifty sense of taking
away something from such plays: they not only have had something for their money, but they retain that something as a permanent possession. Consequently none of the commonplaces of
the box office hold good of such plays. In vain does the experienced acting manager declare that people want to be amused
and not preached at in the theatre; that they will not stand
long speeches; that a play must not contain more than 18,000

[1] George Bernard Shaw, from "The Technical Novelty in Ibsen's Plays,"
The Quintessence of Ibsenism (New York, 1925), pp. 213–4, 221–2.
Copyright 1913 by George Bernard Shaw. Reprinted by permission
of the Society of Authors and the Public Trustee.

words; that it must not begin before nine nor last beyond eleven; that there must be no politics and no religion in it; that breach of these golden rules will drive people to the variety theatres; that there must be a woman of bad character, played by a very attractive actress, in the piece; and so on and so forth. All these counsels are valid for plays in which there is nothing to discuss. They may be disregarded by the playwright who is a moralist and a debater as well as a dramatist. From him, within the inevitable limits set by the clock and by the physical endurance of the human frame, people will stand anything as soon as they are matured enough and cultivated enough to be susceptible to the appeal of his particular form of art. The difficulty at present is that mature and cultivated people do not go to the theatre, just as they do not read penny novelets; and when an attempt is made to cater for them they do not respond to it in time, partly because they have not the habit of play-going, and partly because it takes too long for them to find out that the new theatre is not like all the other theatres. But when they do at last find their way there, the attraction is not the firing of blank cartridges at one another by actors, nor the pretence of falling down dead that ends the stage combat, nor the simulation of erotic thrills by a pair of stage lovers, nor any of the other tomfooleries called action, but the exhibition and discussion of the character and conduct of stage figures who are made to appear real by the art of the playwright and the performers. . . .

In the new plays, the drama arises through a conflict of unsettled ideals rather than through vulgar attachments, rapacities, generosities, resentments, ambitions, misunderstandings, oddities and so forth as to which no moral question is raised. The conflict is not between clear right and wrong: the villain is as conscientious as the hero, if not more so: in fact, the question which makes the play interesting (when it is interesting) is which is the villain and which the hero. Or, to put it another way, there are no villains and no heroes. This strikes the critics mainly as a departure from dramatic art; but it is really the inevitable return to nature which ends all the merely technical fashions. Now the natural is mainly the everyday; and its climaxes must be, if not everyday, at least everylife, if they are to have any importance for the spectator. Crimes, fights, big legacies, fires, shipwrecks, battles, and thunderbolts are mistakes in a play, even when they can be effectively simulated. No doubt they may acquire dramatic interest by putting a character through the test of an emergency; but the test is likely to be too obviously theatrical, because, as the playwright cannot in the nature of things have much experience of such catastrophes, he is forced to substitute a set of conventions or conjectures for the feelings they really produce. . . .

. . . Dick Dudgeon, the devil's disciple, is a Puritan of the Puritans. He is brought up in a household where the Puritan religion has died, and become, in its corruption, an excuse for his mother's master passion of hatred in all its phases of cruelty and envy. This corruption has already been dramatized for us by Charles Dickens in his picture of the Clennam household in Little Dorrit: Mrs Dudgeon being a replica of Mrs Clennam with certain circumstantial variations, and perhaps a touch of the same author's Mrs Gargery in Great Expectations. In such a home the young Puritan finds himself starved of religion, which is the most clamorous need of his nature. With all his mother's indomitable selffulness, but with Pity instead of Hatred as his master passion, he pities the devil; takes his side: and champions him, like a true Covenanter, against the world. He thus becomes, like all genuinely religious men, a reprobate and an outcast. Once this is understood, the play becomes straightforwardly simple.

The Diabolonian position is new to the London playgoer of today, but not to lovers of serious literature. From Prometheus to the Wagnerian Siegfried, some enemy of the gods, unterrified champion of those oppressed by them, has always towered among the heroes of the loftiest poetry. Our newest idol, the Superman, celebrating the death of godhead, may be younger than the hills; but he is as old as the shepherds. Two and a half centuries ago our greatest English dramatizer of life, John Bunyan, ended one of his stories with the remark that there is a way to hell even from the gates of heaven, and so led us to the equally true proposition that there is a way to heaven even from the gates of hell. A century ago William Blake was, like Dick Dudgeon, an avowed Diabolonian: he called his angels devils and his devils angels. His devil is a Redeemer. Let those who have praised my originality in conceiving Dick Dudgeon's strange religion read Blake's Marriage of Heaven and Hell, and I shall be fortunate if they do not rail at me for a plagiarist. But they need not go back to Blake and Bunyan. Have they not heard the recent fuss about Nietzsche and his Good and Evil Turned Inside Out? Mr Robert Buchanan has actually written a long poem of which the Devil is the merciful hero, which poem was in my hands before a word of The Devil's Disciple was written. There never was a play more certain to be written than The Devil's Disciple at the end of the nineteenth century. The age was visibly pregnant with it.

[2] George Bernard Shaw, from "On Diabolonian Ethics," *Three Plays for Puritans* (London, 1931), pp. xxiv–xxvii. Copyright 1900 by George Bernard Shaw. Reprinted by permission of the Society of Authors and the Public Trustee.

I grieve to have to add that my old friends and colleagues the London critics for the most part showed no sort of connoisseurship either in Puritanism or in Diabolonianism when the play was performed for a few weeks at a suburban theatre (Kennington) in October 1899 by Mr Murray Carson. They took Mrs Dudgeon at her own valuation as a religious woman because she was detestably disagreeable. And they took Dick as a blackguard, on her authority, because he was neither detestable nor disagreeable. But they presently found themselves in a dilemma. Why should a blackguard save another man's life, and that man no friend of his, at the risk of his own? Clearly, said the critic, because he is redeemed by love. All wicked heroes are, on the stage: that is the romantic metaphysic. Unfortunately for this explanation (which I do not profess to understand) it turned out in the third act that Dick was a Puritan in this respect also: a man impassioned only for saving grace, and not to be led or turned by wife or mother, Church or State, pride of life or lust of the flesh. In the lovely home of the courageous, affectionate, practical minister who marries a pretty wife twenty years younger than himself, and turns soldier in an instant to save the man who has saved him, Dick looks round and understands the charm and the peace and the sanctity, but knows that such material comforts are not for him. When the woman nursed in that atmosphere falls in love with him and concludes (like the critics, who somehow always agree with my sentimental heroines) that he risked his life for her sake, he tells her the obvious truth that he would have done as much for any stranger—that the law of his own nature, and no interest nor lust whatsoever, forbad him to cry out that the hangman's noose should be taken off his neck only to be put on another man's.

But then, said the critics, where is the motive? *Why* did Dick save Anderson? On the stage, it appears, people do things for reasons. Off the stage they don't: that is why your penny-in-the-slot heroes, who only work when you drop a motive into them, are so oppressively automatic and uninteresting. The saving of life at the risk of the saver's own is not a common thing: but modern populations are so vast that even the most uncommon things are recorded once a week or oftener. Not one of my critics but has seen a hundred times in his paper how some policeman or fireman or nursemaid has received a medal, or the compliments of a magistrate, or perhaps a public funeral, for risking his or her life to save another's. Has he ever seen it added that the saved was the husband of the woman the saver loved, or was that woman herself, or was even known to the saver as much as by sight? Never. When we want to read of the deeds that are done for love, whither do we turn? To the murder column; and there we are rarely disappointed.

Need I repeat that the theatre critic's professional routine so discourages any association between real life and the stage, that he soon loses the natural habit of referring to the one to explain the other? The critic who discovered a romantic motive for Dick's sacrifice was no mere literary dreamer, but a clever barrister. He pointed out that Dick Dudgeon clearly did adore Mrs Anderson; that it was for her sake that he offered his life to save her beloved husband; and that his explicit denial of his passion was the splendid mendacity of a gentleman whose respect for a married woman, and duty to her absent husband, sealed his passion-palpitating lips. From the moment that this fatally plausible explanation was launched, my play became my critic's play, not mine. Thenceforth Dick Dudgeon every night confirmed the critic by stealing behind Judith, and mutely attesting his passion by surreptitiously imprinting a heartbroken kiss on a stray lock of her hair whilst he uttered the barren denial. As for me, I was just then wandering about the streets of Constantinople, unaware of all these doings. When I returned all was over. My personal relations with the critic and the actor forbad me to curse them. I had not even a chance of publicly forgiving them. They meant well by me; but if they ever write a play, may I be there to explain!

GEORGE BERNARD SHAW

The Devil's Disciple

CHARACTERS

RICHARD DUDGEON.

MRS ANNIE DUDGEON.

CHRISTOPHER DUDGEON.

LAWYER HAWKINS.

GENERAL BURGOYNE.

JUDITH ANDERSON.

ANTHONY ANDERSON.

ESSIE.

MAJOR SWINDON.

A SERGEANT.

UNCLE WILLIAM DUDGEON.

UNCLE TITUS DUDGEON.

George Bernard Shaw, "The Devil's Disciple," *Three Plays for Puritans* (London, 1931). Copyright 1900 by George Bernard Shaw. Reprinted with the permission of the Society of Authors and the Public Trustee.

ACT I

At the most wretched hour between a black night and a wintry morning in the year 1777, MRS DUDGEON, of New Hampshire, is sitting up in the kitchen and general dwelling room of her farm house on the outskirts of the town of Websterbridge. She is not a prepossessing woman. No woman looks her best after sitting up all night; and MRS DUDGEON'S face, even at its best, is grimly trenched by the channels into which the barren forms and observances of a dead Puritanism can pen a bitter temper and a fierce pride. She is an elderly matron who has worked hard and got nothing by it except dominion and detestation in her sordid home, and an unquestioned reputation for piety and respectability among her neighbors, to whom drink and debauchery are still so much more tempting than religion and rectitude, that they conceive goodness simply as self-denial. This conception is easily extended to others-denial, and finally generalized as covering anything disagreeable. So MRS DUDGEON, being exceedingly disagreeable, is held to be exceedingly good. Short of flat felony, she enjoys complete license except for amiable weaknesses of any sort, and is consequently, without knowing it, the most licentious woman in the parish on the strength of never having broken the seventh commandment or missed a Sunday at the Presbyterian church.

The year 1777 is the one in which the passions roused by the breaking-off of the American colonies from England, more by their own weight than by their own will, boiled up to shooting point, the shooting being idealized to the English mind as suppression of rebellion and maintenance of British dominion, and to the American as defence of liberty, resistance to tyranny, and self-sacrifice on the altar of the Rights of Man. Into the merits of these idealizations it is not here necessary to inquire: suffice it to say, without prejudice, that they have convinced both Americans and English that the most high-minded course for them to pursue is to kill as many of one another as possible, and that military operations to that end are in full swing, morally supported by confident requests from the clergy of both sides for the blessing of God on their arms.

Under such circumstances many other women besides this disagreeable MRS DUDGEON find themselves sitting up all night waiting for news. Like her, too, they fall asleep towards morning at the risk of nodding themselves into the kitchen fire. MRS DUDGEON sleeps with a shawl over her head, and her feet on a broad fender of iron laths, the step of the domestic altar of the fireplace, with its huge hobs and boiler, and its hinged arm above the smoky mantelshelf for roasting. The plain kitchen table is opposite the fire, at her elbow, with a candle on it in a tin sconce. Her chair, like all the others in the room, is uncushioned and unpainted; but as it has a round railed back and a seat conventionally moulded to the sitter's curves, it is comparatively a chair of state. The room has three doors, one on the same side as the fireplace, near the corner, leading to the best bedroom; one, at the opposite end of the oppo-

site wall, leading to the scullery and washhouse; and the house-door, with its latch, heavy lock, and clumsy wooden bar, in the front wall, between the window in its middle and the corner next the bedroom door. Between the door and the window a rack of pegs suggests to the deductive observer that the men of the house are all away, as there are no hats or coats on them. On the other side of the window the clock hangs on a nail, with its white wooden dial, black iron weights, and brass pendulum. Between the clock and the corner, a big cupboard, locked, stands on a dwarf dresser full of common crockery.

On the side opposite the fireplace, between the door and the corner, a shamelessly ugly black horsehair sofa stands against the wall. An inspection of its stridulous surface shews that MRS DUDGEON *is not alone. A girl of sixteen or seventeen has fallen asleep on it. She is a wild, timid looking creature with black hair and tanned skin. Her frock, a scanty garment, is rent, weather-stained, berrystained, and by no means scrupulously clean. It hangs on her with a freedom which, taken with her brown legs and bare feet, suggests no great stock of underclothing.*

Suddenly there comes a tapping at the door, not loud enough to wake the sleepers. Then knocking, which disturbs MRS DUDGEON *a little. Finally the latch is tried, whereupon she springs up at once.*

MRS DUDGEON: [*Threateningly.*] Well, why dont you open the door? [*She sees that the girl is asleep, and immediately raises a clamour of heartfelt vexation.*] Well, dear, dear me! Now this is— [*Shaking her.*] wake up, wake up: do you hear?

THE GIRL: [*Sitting up.*] What is it?

MRS DUDGEON: Wake up; and be ashamed of yourself, you unfeeling sinful girl, falling asleep like that, and your father hardly cold in his grave.

THE GIRL: [*Half asleep still.*] I didnt mean to. I dropped off—

MRS DUDGEON: [*Cutting her short.*] Oh yes, youve plenty of excuses, I daresay. Dropped off! [*Fiercely, as the knocking recommences.*] Why dont you get up and let your uncle in? after me waiting up all night for him! [*She pushes her rudely off the sofa.*] There: I'll open the door: much good you are to wait up. Go and mend that fire a bit.

[*The girl, cowed and wretched, goes to the fire and puts a log on.* MRS DUDGEON *unbars the door and opens it, letting into the stuffy kitchen a little of the freshness and a great deal of the chill of the dawn, also her second son* CHRISTY, *a fattish, stupid, fair-haired, roundfaced man of about 22, muffled in a plaid shawl and grey overcoat. He hurries, shivering, to the fire, leaving* MRS DUDGEON *to shut the door.*]

CHRISTY: [*At the fire.*] F—f—f! but it is cold. [*Seeing the girl, and staring lumpishly at her.*] Why, who are you?

THE GIRL: [*Shyly.*] Essie.

MRS DUDGEON: Oh, you may well ask. [*To* ESSIE.] Go to your room, child, and lie down, since you havnt feeling enough to keep you awake. Your history isnt fit for your own ears to hear.

ESSIE: I—

MRS DUDGEON: [*Peremptorily.*] Dont answer me, Miss; but shew your obedience by doing what I tell you. [ESSIE, *almost in tears, crosses the room to the door near the sofa.*] And dont forget your prayers. [ESSIE *goes out.*] She'd have gone to bed last night just as if nothing had happened if I'd let her.

CHRISTY: [*Phlegmatically.*] Well, she cant be expected to feel Uncle Peter's death like one of the family.

MRS DUDGEON: What are you talking about, child? Isnt she his daughter—the punishment of his wickedness and shame? [*She assaults her chair by sitting down.*]

CHRISTY: [*Staring.*] Uncle Peter's daughter!

MRS DUDGEON: Why else should she be here? D'ye think Ive not had enough trouble and care put upon me bringing up my own girls, let alone you and your good-for-nothing brother, without having your uncle's bastards—

CHRISTY: [*Interrupting her with an ap-*

prehensive glance at the door by which ESSIE *went out.*] Sh! She may hear you.

MRS DUDGEON: [*Raising her voice.*] Let her hear me. People who fear God dont fear to give the devil's work its right name. [CHRISTY, *soullessly indifferent to the strife of Good and Evil, stares at the fire, warming himself.*] Well, how long are you going to stare there like a stuck pig? What news have you for me?

CHRISTY: [*Taking off his hat and shawl and going to the rack to hang them up.*] The minister is to break the news to you. He'll be here presently.

MRS DUDGEON: Break what news?

CHRISTY: [*Standing on tiptoe, from boyish habit, to hang his hat up, though he is quite tall enough to reach the peg, and speaking with callous placidity, considering the nature of the announcement.*] Father's dead too.

MRS DUDGEON: [*Stupent.*] Your father!

CHRISTY: [*Sulkily, coming back to the fire and warming himself again, attending much more to the fire than to his mother.*] Well, it's not my fault. When we got to Nevinstown we found him ill in bed. He didnt know us at first. The minister sat up with him and sent me away. He died in the night.

MRS DUDGEON: [*Bursting into dry angry tears.*] Well, I do think this is hard on me —very hard on me. His brother, that was a disgrace to us all his life, gets hanged on the public gallows as a rebel; and your father, instead of staying at home where his duty was, with his own family, goes after him and dies, leaving everything on my shoulders. After sending this girl to me to take care of, too! [*She plucks her shawl vexedly over her ears.*] It's sinful, so it is: downright sinful.

CHRISTY: [*With a slow, bovine cheerfulness, after a pause.*] I think it's going to be a fine morning, after all.

MRS DUDGEON: [*Railing at him.*] A fine morning! And your father newly dead! Wheres your feelings, child?

CHRISTY: [*Obstinately.*] Well, I didnt mean any harm. I suppose a man may make a remark about the weather even if his father's dead.

MRS DUDGEON: [*Bitterly.*] A nice comfort my children are to me! One son a fool, and the other a lost sinner thats left his home to live with smugglers and gypsies and villains, the scum of the earth!

[*Someone knocks.*]

CHRISTY: [*Without moving.*] Thats the minister.

MRS DUDGEON: [*Sharply.*] Well, arnt you going to let Mr Anderson in?

[CHRISTY *goes sheepishly to the door.* MRS DUDGEON *buries her face in her hands, as it is her duty as a widow to be overcome with grief.* CHRISTY *opens the door, and admits the minister,* ANTHONY ANDERSON, *a shrewd, genial, ready Presbyterian divine of about 50, with something of the authority of his profession in his bearing. But it is an altogether secular authority, sweetened by a conciliatory, sensible manner not at all suggestive of a quite thoroughgoing other-worldliness. He is a strong, healthy man too, with a thick sanguine neck; and his keen, cheerful mouth cuts into somewhat fleshy corners. No doubt an excellent parson, but still a man capable of making the most of this world, and perhaps a little apologetically conscious of getting on better with it than a sound Presbyterian ought.*]

ANDERSON: [*To* CHRISTY, *at the door, looking at* MRS DUDGEON *whilst he takes off his cloak.*] Have you told her?

CHRISTY: She made me. [*He shuts the door; yawns; and loafs across to the sofa, where he sits down and presently drops off to sleep.*]

[ANDERSON *looks compassionately at* MRS DUDGEON. *Then he hangs his cloak and hat on the rack.* MRS DUDGEON *dries her eyes and looks up at him.*]

ANDERSON: Sister: the Lord has laid his hand very heavily upon you.

MRS DUDGEON: [*With intensely recalcitrant resignation.*] It's His will, I suppose; and I must bow to it. But I do think it hard. What call had Timothy to go to Springtown, and remind everybody that he belonged to a man that was being hanged? —and [*Spitefully.*] that deserved it, if ever a man did.

ANDERSON: [*Gently.*] They were brothers, Mrs Dudgeon.

MRS DUDGEON: Timothy never acknowledged him as his brother after we were married: he had too much respect for me to insult me with such a brother. Would such a selfish wretch as Peter have come thirty miles to see Timothy hanged, do you think? Not thirty yards, not he. However, I must bear my cross as best I may: least said is soonest mended.

ANDERSON: [*Very grave, coming down to the fire to stand with his back to it.*] Your eldest son was present at the execution, Mrs Dudgeon.

MRS DUDGEON: [*Disagreeably surprised.*] Richard?

ANDERSON: [*Nodding.*] Yes.

MRS DUDGEON: [*Vindictively.*] Let it be a warning to him. He may end that way himself, the wicked, dissolute, godless—[*She suddenly stops; her voice fails; and she asks, with evident dread.*] Did Timothy see him?

ANDERSON: Yes.

MRS DUDGEON: [*Holding her breath.*] Well?

ANDERSON: He only saw him in the crowd: they did not speak. [MRS DUDGEON, *greatly relieved, exhales the pent up breath and sits at her ease again.*] Your husband was greatly touched and impressed by his brother's awful death. [MRS DUDGEON *sneers.* ANDERSON *breaks off to demand with some indignation.*] Well, wasnt it only natural, Mrs Dudgeon? He softened towards his prodigal son in that moment. He sent for him to come to see him.

MRS DUDGEON: [*Her alarm renewed.*] Sent for Richard!

ANDERSON: Yes; but Richard would not come. He sent his father a message; but I'm sorry to say it was a wicked message—an awful message.

MRS DUDGEON: What was it?

ANDERSON: That he would stand by his wicked uncle and stand against his good parents, in this world and the next.

MRS DUDGEON: [*Implacably.*] He will be punished for it. He will be punished for it—in both worlds.

ANDERSON: That is not in our hands, Mrs Dudgeon.

MRS DUDGEON: Did I say it was, Mr Anderson? We are told that the wicked shall be punished. Why should we do our duty and keep God's law if there is to be no difference made between us and those who follow their own likings and dislikings, and make a jest of us and of their Maker's word?

ANDERSON: Well, Richard's earthly father has been merciful to him; and his heavenly judge is the father of us all.

MRS DUDGEON: [*Forgetting herself.*] Richard's earthly father was a softheaded—

ANDERSON: [*Shocked.*] Oh!

MRS DUDGEON: [*With a touch of shame.*] Well, I am Richard's mother. If I am against him who has any right to be for him? [*Trying to conciliate him.*] Wont you sit down, Mr Anderson? I should have asked you before; but I'm so troubled.

ANDERSON: Thank you. [*He takes a chair from beside the fireplace, and turns it so that he can sit comfortably at the fire. When he is seated he adds, in the tone of a man who knows that he is opening a difficult subject.*] Has Christy told you about the new will?

MRS DUDGEON: [*All her fears returning.*] The new will! Did Timothy—? [*She breaks off, gasping, unable to complete the question.*]

ANDERSON: Yes. In his last hours he changed his mind.

MRS DUDGEON: [*White with intense rage.*] And you let him rob me?

ANDERSON: I had no power to prevent him giving what was his to his own son.

MRS DUDGEON: He had nothing of his own. His money was the money I brought him as my marriage portion. It was for me to deal with my own money and my own son. He dare not have done it if I had been with him; and well he knew it. That was why he stole away like a thief to take advantage of the law to rob me by making a new will behind my back. The more shame on you, Mr Anderson,—you, a minister of the gospel—to act as his accomplice in such a crime.

ANDERSON: [*Rising.*] I will take no offence at what you say in the first bitterness of your grief.

MRS DUDGEON: [*Contemptuously.*] Grief!

ANDERSON: Well, of your disappointment, if you can find it in your heart to think that the better word.

MRS DUDGEON: My heart! My heart! And since when, pray, have you begun to hold up our hearts as trustworthy guides for us?

ANDERSON: [*Rather guiltily.*] I—er—

MRS DUDGEON: [*Vehemently.*] Don't lie, Mr Anderson. We are told that the heart of man is deceitful above all things, and desperately wicked. My heart belonged, not to Timothy, but to that poor wretched brother of his that has just ended his days with a rope round his neck—aye, to Peter

Dudgeon. You know it: old Eli Hawkins, the man to whose pulpit you succeeded, though you are not worthy to loose his shoe latchet, told it you when he gave over our souls into your charge. He warned me and strengthened me against my heart, and made me marry a Godfearing man—as he thought. What else but that discipline has made me the woman I am? And you, you, who followed your heart in your marriage, you talk to me of what I find in my heart. Go home to your pretty wife, man; and leave me to my prayers. [*She turns from him and leans with her elbows on the table, brooding over her wrongs and taking no further notice of him.*]

ANDERSON: [*Willing enough to escape.*] The Lord forbid that I should come between you and the source of all comfort! [*He goes to the rack for his coat and hat.*]

MRS DUDGEON: [*Without looking at him.*] The Lord will know what to forbid and what to allow without your help.

ANDERSON: And whom to forgive, I hope —Eli Hawkins and myself, if we have ever set up our preaching against His law. [*He fastens his cloak, and is now ready to go.*] Just one word—on necessary business, Mrs Dudgeon. There is the reading of the will to be gone through; and Richard has a right to be present. He is in the town; but he has the grace to say that he does not want to force himself in here.

MRS DUDGEON: He shall come here. Does he expect us to leave his father's house for his convenience? Let them all come, and come quickly, and go quickly. They shall not make the will an excuse to shirk half their day's work. I shall be ready, never fear.

ANDERSON: [*Coming back a step or two.*] Mrs Dudgeon: I used to have some little influence with you. When did I lose it?

MRS DUDGEON: [*Still without turning to him.*] When you married for love. Now youre answered.

ANDERSON: Yes: I am answered. [*He goes out, musing.*]

MRS DUDGEON: [*To herself, thinking of her husband.*] Thief! Thief! [*She shakes herself angrily out of her chair; throws back the shawl from her head; and sets to work to prepare the room for the reading of the will, beginning by replacing ANDERSON's chair against the wall and pushing back her own to the window. Then she calls, in her hard, driving, wrathful way.*]

Christy. [*No answer: he is fast asleep.*] Christy. [*She shakes him roughly.*] Get up out of that; and be ashamed of yourself— sleeping, and your father dead! [*She returns to the table; puts the candle on the mantelshelf; and takes from the table drawer a red table cloth which she spreads.*]

CHRISTY: [*Rising reluctantly.*] Well, do you suppose we are never going to sleep until we are out of mourning?

MRS DUDGEON: I want none of your sulks. Here: help me to set this table. [*They place the table in the middle of the room, with CHRISTY's end towards the fireplace and MRS DUDGEON's towards the sofa. CHRISTY drops the table as soon as possible, and goes to the fire, leaving his mother to make the final adjustment of its position.*] We shall have the minister back here with the lawyer and all the family to read the will before you have done toasting yourself. Go and wake that girl; and then light the stove in the shed: you cant have your breakfast here. And mind you wash yourself, and make yourself fit to receive the company. [*She punctuates these orders by going to the cupboard; unlocking it; and producing a decanter of wine, which has no doubt stood there untouched since the last state occasion in the family, and some glasses, which she sets on the table. Also two green ware plates, on one of which she puts a barn-brack with a knife beside it. On the other she shakes some biscuits out of a tin, putting back one or two, and counting the rest.*] Now mind: there are ten biscuits there: let there be ten there when I come back after dressing myself. And keep your fingers off the raisins in that cake. And tell Essie the same. I suppose I can trust you to bring in the case of stuffed birds without breaking the glass? [*She replaces the tin in the cupboard, which she locks, pocketing the key carefully.*]

CHRISTY: [*Lingering at the fire.*] Youd better put the inkstand instead, for the lawyer.

MRS DUDGEON: Thats no answer to make to me, sir. Go and do as youre told. [CHRISTY turns sullenly to obey.] Stop: take down that shutter before you go, and let the daylight in: you cant expect me to do all the heavy work of the house with a great lout like you idling about.

[CHRISTY takes the window bar out of its clamps, and puts it aside; then opens the shutter, shewing the grey *morning.* MRS DUDGEON *takes the sconce from the mantelshelf; blows out the candle; extinguishes the snuff by pinching it with her fingers, first licking them for the purpose; and replaces the sconce on the shelf.*]

CHRISTY: [*Looking through the window.*] Heres the minister's wife.

MRS DUDGEON: [*Displeased.*] What! Is she coming here?

CHRISTY: Yes.

MRS DUDGEON: What does she want troubling me at this hour, before I am properly dressed to receive people?

CHRISTY: Youd better ask her.

MRS DUDGEON: [*Threateningly.*] Youd better keep a civil tongue in your head. [*He goes sulkily towards the door. She comes after him, plying him with instructions.*] Tell that girl to come to me as soon as she's had her breakfast. And tell her to make herself fit to be seen before the people.* [CHRISTY *goes out and slams the door in her face.*] Nice manners, that! [*Someone knocks at the house door: she turns and cries inhospitably.*] Come in. [JUDITH ANDERSON, *the minister's wife, comes in.* JUDITH *is more than twenty years younger than her husband, though she will never be as young as he in vitality. She is pretty and proper and ladylike, and has been admired and petted into an opinion of herself sufficiently favorable to give her a self-assurance which serves her instead of strength. She has a pretty taste in dress, and in her face the pretty lines of a sentimental character formed by dreams. Even her little self-complacency is pretty, like a child's vanity. Rather a pathetic creature to any sympathetic observer who knows how rough a place the world is. One feels, on the whole, that* ANDERSON *might have chosen worse, and that she, needing protection, could not have chosen better.*] Oh, it's you, is it, Mrs Anderson?

JUDITH: [*Very politely—almost patronizingly.*] Yes. Can I do anything for you, Mrs Dudgeon? Can I help to get the place ready before they come to read the will?

MRS DUDGEON: [*Stiffly.*] Thank you, Mrs Anderson, my house is always ready for anyone to come into.

MRS ANDERSON: [*With complacent amiability.*] Yes, indeed it is. Perhaps you had rather I did not intrude on you just now.

MRS DUDGEON: Oh, one more or less will make no difference this morning, Mrs Anderson. Now that youre here, youd better stay. If you wouldnt mind shutting the door! [JUDITH *smiles, implying "How stupid of me!" and shuts it with an exasperating air of doing something pretty and becoming.*] Thats better. I must go and tidy myself a bit. I suppose you dont mind stopping here to receive anyone that comes until I'm ready.

JUDITH: [*Graciously giving her leave.*] Oh yes, certainly. Leave that to me, Mrs Dudgeon; and take your time. [*She hangs her cloak and bonnet on the rack.*]

MRS DUDGEON: [*Half sneering.*] I thought that would be more in your way than getting the house ready. [ESSIE *comes back.*] Oh, here you are! [*Severely.*] Come here: let me see you. [ESSIE *timidly goes to her.* MRS DUDGEON *takes her roughly by the arm and pulls her round to inspect the results of her attempt to clean and tidy herself—results which shew little practice and less conviction.*] Mm! Thats what you call doing your hair properly, I suppose. It's easy to see what you are, and how you were brought up. [*She throws her arm away, and goes on, peremptorily.*] Now you listen to me and do as youre told. You sit down there in the corner by the fire; and when the company comes dont dare to speak until youre spoken to. [ESSIE *creeps away to the fireplace.*] Your father's people had better see you and know youre there: theyre as much bound to keep you from starvation as I am. At any rate they might help. But let me have no chattering and making free with them, as if you were their equal. Do you hear?

ESSIE: Yes.

MRS DUDGEON: Well, then go and do as youre told. [ESSIE *sits down miserably on the corner of the fender furthest from the door.*] Never mind her, Mrs Anderson: you know who she is and what she is. If she gives you any trouble, just tell me; and I'll settle accounts with her. [MRS DUDGEON *goes into the bedroom, shutting the door sharply behind her as if even it had to be made do its duty with a ruthless hand.*]

JUDITH: [*Patronizing* ESSIE, *and arranging the cake and wine on the table more becomingly.*] You must not mind if your aunt is strict with you. She is a very good woman, and desires your good too.

ESSIE: [*In listless misery.*] Yes.

JUDITH: [*Annoyed with* ESSIE *for her*

failure to be consoled and edified, and to appreciate the kindly condescension of the remark.] You are not going to be sullen, I hope, Essie.

ESSIE: No.

JUDITH: Thats a good girl! [She places a couple of chairs at the table with their backs to the window, with a pleasant sense of being a more thoughtful housekeeper than MRS DUDGEON.] Do you know any of your father's relatives?

ESSIE: No. They wouldnt have anything to do with him: they were too religious. Father used to talk about Dick Dudgeon; but I never saw him.

JUDITH: [Ostentatiously shocked.] Dick Dudgeon! Essie: do you wish to be a really respectable and grateful girl, and to make a place for yourself here by steady good conduct?

ESSIE: [Very half-heartedly.] Yes.

JUDITH: Then you must never mention the name of Richard Dudgeon—never even think about him. He is a bad man.

ESSIE: What has he done?

JUDITH: You must not ask questions about him, Essie. You are too young to know what it is to be a bad man. But he is a smuggler; and he lives with gypsies; and he has no love for his mother and his family; and he wrestles and plays games on Sunday instead of going to church. Never let him into your presence, if you can help it, Essie; and try to keep yourself and all womanhood unspotted by contact with such men.

ESSIE: Yes.

JUDITH: [Again displeased.] I am afraid you say Yes and No without thinking very deeply.

ESSIE: Yes. At least I mean—

JUDITH: [Severely.] What do you mean?

ESSIE: [Almost crying.] Only—my father was a smuggler; and— [Someone knocks.]

JUDITH: They are beginning to come. Now remember your aunt's directions, Essie; and be a good girl. [CHRISTY comes back with the stand of stuffed birds under a glass case, and an inkstand, which he places on the table.] Good morning, Mr Dudgeon. Will you open the door, please: the people have come.

CHRISTY: Good morning. [He opens the house door.]

[The morning is now fairly bright and warm; and ANDERSON, who is the first to enter, has left his cloak at home. He is accompanied by LAWYER HAWKINS, a brisk, middleaged man in brown riding gaiters and yellow breeches, looking as much squire as solicitor. He and ANDERSON are allowed precedence as representing the learned professions. After them comes the family, headed by the senior uncle, WILLIAM DUDGEON, a large, shapeless man, bottle-nosed and evidently no ascetic at table. His clothes are not the clothes, nor his anxious wife the wife, of a prosperous man. The junior uncle, TITUS DUDGEON, is a wiry little terrier of a man, with an immense and visibly purseproud wife, both free from the cares of the WILLIAM household.]

[HAWKINS at once goes briskly to the table and takes the chair nearest the sofa, CHRISTY having left the inkstand there. He puts his hat on the floor beside him, and produces the will. UNCLE WILLIAM comes to the fire and stands on the hearth warming his coat tails, leaving MRS WILLIAM derelict near the door. UNCLE TITUS, who is the lady's man of the family, rescues her by giving her his disengaged arm and bringing her to the sofa, where he sits warmly between his own lady and his brother's. ANDERSON hangs up his hat and waits for a word with JUDITH.]

JUDITH: She will be here in a moment. Ask them to wait. [She taps at the bedroom door. Receiving an answer from within, she opens it and passes through.]

ANDERSON: [Taking his place at the table at the opposite end to HAWKINS.] Our poor afflicted sister will be with us in a moment. Are we all here?

CHRISTY: [At the house door, which he has just shut.] All except Dick.

[The callousness with which CHRISTY names the reprobate jars on the moral sense of the family. UNCLE WILLIAM shakes his head slowly and repeatedly. MRS TITUS catches her breath convulsively through her nose. Her husband speaks.]

UNCLE TITUS: Well, I hope he will have the grace not to come. I hope so.

[The DUDGEONS all murmur assent, except CHRISTY, who goes to the window and posts himself there, looking out. HAWKINS smiles secretively as if he *knew something that would change their tune if they knew it.* ANDERSON *is uneasy: the love of solemn family councils, especially funeral ones, is not in his nature.* JUDITH *appears at the bedroom door.*]

JUDITH: [*With gentle impressiveness.*] Friends, Mrs Dudgeon. [*She takes the chair from beside the fireplace; and places it for* MRS DUDGEON, *who comes from the bedroom in black, with a clean handkerchief to her eyes. All rise, except* ESSIE. MRS TITUS *and* MRS WILLIAM *produce equally clean handkerchiefs and weep. It is an affecting moment.*]

UNCLE WILLIAM: Would it comfort you, sister, if we were to offer up a prayer?

UNCLE TITUS: Or sing a hymn?

ANDERSON: [*Rather hastily.*] I have been with our sister this morning already, friends. In our hearts we ask a blessing.

ALL: [*Except* ESSIE.] Amen.

[*They all sit down, except* JUDITH, *who stands behind* MRS DUDGEON'S *chair.*]

JUDITH: [*To* ESSIE.] Essie: did you say Amen?

ESSIE: [*Scaredly.*] No.

JUDITH: Then say it, like a good girl.

ESSIE: Amen.

UNCLE WILLIAM: [*Encouragingly.*] Thats right: thats right. We know who you are; but we are willing to be kind to you if you are a good girl and deserve it. We are all equal before the Throne.

[*This republican sentiment does not please the women, who are convinced that the Throne is precisely the place where their superiority, often questioned in this world, will be recognized and rewarded.*]

CHRISTY: [*At the window.*] Heres Dick.

[ANDERSON *and* HAWKINS *look round sociably.* ESSIE, *with a gleam of interest breaking through her misery, looks up.* CHRISTY *grins and gapes expectantly at the door. The rest are petrified with the intensity of their sense of Virtue menaced with outrage by the approach of flaunting Vice. The reprobate appears in the doorway, graced beyond his alleged merits by the morning sunlight. He is certainly the best looking member of the family; but his expression is reckless and sardonic, his manner defiant and satirical, his dress picturesquely*

careless. Only, his forehead and mouth betray an extraordinary steadfastness; and his eyes are the eyes of a fanatic.]

RICHARD: [*On the threshold, taking off his hat.*] Ladies and gentlemen: your servant, your very humble servant. [*With this comprehensive insult, he throws his hat to* CHRISTY *with a suddenness that makes him jump like a negligent wicket keeper, and comes into the middle of the room, where he turns and deliberately surveys the company.*] How happy you all look! how glad to see me! [*He turns towards* MRS DUDGEON'S *chair; and his lip rolls up horribly from his dog tooth as he meets her look of undisguised hatred.*] Well, mother: keeping up appearances as usual? thats right, thats right. [JUDITH *pointedly moves away from his neighborhood to the other side of the kitchen, holding her skirt instinctively as if to save it from contamination.* UNCLE TITUS *promptly marks his approval of her action by rising from the sofa, and placing a chair for her to sit down upon.*] What! Uncle William! I havnt seen you since you gave up drinking. [*Poor* UNCLE WILLIAM, *shamed, would protest; but* RICHARD *claps him heartily on his shoulder, adding.*] you have given it up, havnt you? [*Releasing him with a playful push.*] of course you have: quite right too: you overdid it. [*He turns away from* UNCLE WILLIAM *and makes for the sofa.*] And now, where is that upright horsedealer Uncle Titus? Uncle Titus: come forth. [*He comes upon him holding the chair as* JUDITH *sits down.*] As usual, looking after the ladies!

UNCLE TITUS: [*Indignantly.*] Be ashamed of yourself, sir—

RICHARD: [*Interrupting him and shaking his hand in spite of him.*] I am: I am; but I am proud of my uncle—proud of all my relatives—[*Again surveying them.*] who could look at them and not be proud and joyful? [UNCLE TITUS, *overborne, resumes his seat on the sofa.* RICHARD *turns to the table.*] Ah, Mr Anderson, still at the good work, still shepherding them. Keep them up to the mark, minister, keep them up to the mark. Come! [*With a spring he seats himself on the table and takes up the decanter.*] clink a glass with me, Pastor, for the sake of old times.

ANDERSON: You know, I think, Mr Dudgeon, that I do not drink before dinner.

RICHARD: You will, some day, Pastor; Uncle William used to drink before breakfast. Come: it will give your sermons unction. [*He smells the wine and makes a wry face.*] But do not begin on my mother's company sherry. I stole some when I was six years old; and I have been a temperate man ever since. [*He puts the decanter down and changes the subject.*] So I hear you are married, Pastor, and that your wife has a most ungodly allowance of good looks.

ANDERSON: [*Quietly indicating* JUDITH.] Sir: you are in the presence of my wife. [JUDITH *rises, and stands with stony propriety.*]

RICHARD: [*Quickly slipping down from the table with instinctive good manners.*] Your servant, madam: no offence. [*He looks at her earnestly.*] You deserve your reputation; but I'm sorry to see by your expression that youre a good woman. [*She looks shocked, and sits down amid a murmur of indignant sympathy from his relatives.* ANDERSON, *sensible enough to know that these demonstrations can only gratify and encourage a man who is deliberately trying to provoke them, remains perfectly good-humored.*] All the same, Pastor, I respect you more than I did before. By the way, did I hear, or did I not, that our late lamented Uncle Peter, though unmarried, was a father?

UNCLE TITUS: He had only one irregular child, sir.

RICHARD: Only one! He thinks one a mere trifle! I blush for you, Uncle Titus.

ANDERSON: Mr Dudgeon: you are in the presence of your mother and her grief.

RICHARD: It touches me profoundly, Pastor. By the way, what has become of the irregular child?

ANDERSON: [*Pointing to* ESSIE.] There, sir, listening to you.

RICHARD: [*Shocked into sincerity.*] What! Why the devil didnt you tell me that before? Children suffer enough in this house without—[*He hurries remorsefully to* ESSIE.] Come, little cousin! never mind me: it was not meant to hurt you. [*She looks up gratefully at him. Her tearstained face affects him violently; and he bursts out, in a transport of wrath.*] Who has been making her cry? Who has been ill-treating her? By God—

MRS DUDGEON: [*Rising and confronting him.*] Silence your blasphemous tongue. I will bear no more of this. Leave my house.

RICHARD: How do you know it's your house until the will is read? [*They look at one another for a moment with intense hatred; and then she sinks, checkmated, into her chair.* RICHARD *goes boldly up past* ANDERSON *to the window, where he takes the railed chair in his hand.*] Ladies and gentlemen: as the eldest son of my late father, and the unworthy head of this household, I bid you welcome. By your leave, Minister Anderson: by your leave, Lawyer Hawkins. The head of the table for the head of the family. [*He places the chair at the table between the minister and the attorney; sits down between them; and addresses the assembly with a presidential air.*] We meet on a melancholy occasion: a father dead! an uncle actually hanged, and probably damned. [*He shakes his head deploringly. The relatives freeze with horror.*] Thats right: pull your longest faces [*His voice suddenly sweetens gravely as his glance lights on* ESSIE.] provided only there is hope in the eyes of the child. [*Briskly.*] Now then, Lawyer Hawkins: business, business. Get on with the will, man.

TITUS: Do not let yourself be ordered or hurried, Mr Hawkins.

HAWKINS: [*Very politely and willingly.*] Mr Dudgeon means no offence, I feel sure. I will not keep you one second, Mr Dudgeon. Just while I get my glasses—[*He fumbles for them.* THE DUDGEONS *look at one another with misgiving.*]

RICHARD: Aha! They notice your civility, Mr Hawkins. They are prepared for the worst. A glass of wine to clear your voice before you begin. [*He pours out one for him and hands it; then pours one for himself.*]

HAWKINS: Thank you, Mr Dudgeon. Your good health, sir.

RICHARD: Yours, sir. [*With the glass half way to his lips, he checks himself, giving a dubious glance at the wine, and adds, with quaint intensity.*] Will anyone oblige me with a glass of water?

[ESSIE, *who has been hanging on his every word and movement, rises stealthily and slips out behind* MRS DUDGEON *through the bedroom door, returning presently with a jug and going out of the house as quietly as possible.*]

HAWKINS: The will is not exactly in proper legal phraseology.

RICHARD: No: my father died without the consolations of the law.

HAWKINS: Good again, Mr Dudgeon, good again. [Preparing to read.] Are you ready, sir?

RICHARD: Ready, aye ready. For what we are about to receive, may the Lord make us truly thankful. Go ahead.

HAWKINS: [Reading.] "This is the last will and testament of me Timothy Dudgeon on my deathbed at Nevinstown on the road from Springtown to Websterbridge on this twenty-fourth day of September, one thousand seven hundred and seventy seven. I hereby revoke all former wills made by me and declare that I am of sound mind and know well what I am doing and that this is my real will according to my own wish and affections."

RICHARD: [Glancing at his mother.] Aha!

HAWKINS: [Shaking his head.] Bad phraseology, sir, wrong phraseology. "I give and bequeath a hundred pounds to my younger son Christopher Dudgeon, fifty pounds to be paid to him on the day of his marriage to Sarah Wilkins if she will have him, and ten pounds on the birth of each of his children up to the number of five."

RICHARD: How if she wont have him?

CHRISTY: She will if I have fifty pounds.

RICHARD: Good, my brother. Proceed.

HAWKINS: "I give and bequeath to my wife Annie Dudgeon, born Annie Primrose"—you see he did not know the law, Mr Dudgeon: your mother was not born Annie: she was christened so—"an annuity of fifty-two pounds a year for life [MRS DUDGEON, with all eyes on her, holds herself convulsively rigid.] to be paid out of the interest on her own money"—there's a way to put it, Mr Dudgeon! Her own money!

MRS DUDGEON: A very good way to put God's truth. It was every penny my own. Fifty-two pounds a year!

HAWKINS: "And I recommend her for her goodness and piety to the forgiving care of her children, having stood between them and her as far as I could to the best of my ability."

MRS DUDGEON: And this is my reward! [Raging inwardly.] You know what I think, Mr Anderson: you know the word I gave to it.

ANDERSON: It cannot be helped, Mrs Dudgeon. We must take what comes to us. [To HAWKINS.] Go on, sir.

HAWKINS: "I give and bequeath my house at Websterbridge with the land belonging to it and all the rest of my property soever to my eldest son and heir, Richard Dudgeon."

RICHARD: Oho! The fatted calf, Minister, the fatted calf.

HAWKINS: "On these conditions—"

RICHARD: The devil! Are there conditions?

HAWKINS: "To wit: first, that he shall not let my brother Peter's natural child starve or be driven by want to an evil life."

RICHARD: [Emphatically, striking his fist on the table.] Agreed.

[MRS DUDGEON, turning to look malignantly at ESSIE, misses her and looks quickly round to see where she has moved to; then, seeing that she has left the room without leave, closes her lips vengefully.]

HAWKINS: "Second, that he shall be a good friend to my old horse Jim"—[Again shaking his head.] he should have written James, sir.

RICHARD: James shall live in clover. Go on.

HAWKINS: —"and keep my deaf farm labourer Prodger Feston in his service."

RICHARD: Prodger Feston shall get drunk every Saturday.

HAWKINS: "Third, that he make Christy a present on his marriage out of the ornaments in the best room."

RICHARD: [Holding up the stuffed birds.] Here you are, Christy.

CHRISTY: [Disappointed.] I'd rather have the china peacocks.

RICHARD: You shall have both. [CHRISTY is greatly pleased.] Go on.

HAWKINS: "Fourthly and lastly, that he try to live at peace with his mother as far as she will consent to it."

RICHARD: [Dubiously.] Hm! Anything more, Mr Hawkins?

HAWKINS: [Solemnly.] "Finally I give and bequeath my soul into my Maker's hands, humbly asking forgiveness for all my sins and mistakes, and hoping that He will so guide my son that it may not be said that I have done wrong in trusting to him rather than to others in the perplexity of my last hour in this strange place."

ANDERSON: Amen.

THE UNCLES AND AUNTS: Amen.

RICHARD: My mother does not say Amen.

MRS DUDGEON: [*Rising, unable to give up her property without a struggle.*] Mr Hawkins: is that a proper will? Remember, I have his rightful, legal will, drawn up by yourself, leaving all to me.

HAWKINS: This is a very wrongly and irregularly worded will, Mrs Dudgeon: though [*Turning politely to* RICHARD.] it contains in my judgment an excellent disposal of his property.

ANDERSON: [*Interposing before* MRS DUDGEON *can retort.*] That is not what you are asked, Mr Hawkins. Is it a legal will?

HAWKINS: The courts will sustain it against the other.

ANDERSON: But why, if the other is more lawfully worded?

HAWKINS: Because, sir, the courts sustain the claim of a man—and that man the eldest son—against any woman, if they can. I warned you, Mrs Dudgeon, when you got me to draw that other will, that it was not a wise will, and that though you might make him sign it, he would never be easy until he revoked it. But you wouldnt take advice; and now Mr Richard is cock of the walk. [*He takes his hat from the floor; rises; and begins pocketing his papers and spectacles.*]

[*This is the signal for the breaking-up of the party.* ANDERSON *takes his hat from the rack and joins* UNCLE WILLIAM *at the fire.* TITUS *fetches* JUDITH *her things from the rack. The three on the sofa rise and chat with* HAWKINS. MRS DUDGEON, *now an intruder in her own house, stands inert, crushed by the weight of the law on women, accepting it, as she has been trained to accept all monstrous calamities, as proofs of the greatness of the power that inflicts them, and of her own wormlike insignificance. For at this time, remember, Mary Wollstonecraft is as yet only a girl of eighteen, and her Vindication of the Rights of Women is still fourteen years off.* MRS DUDGEON *is rescued from her apathy by* ESSIE, *who comes back with the jug full of water. She is taking it to* RICHARD *when* MRS DUDGEON *stops her.*]

MRS DUDGEON: [*Threatening her.*] Where have you been? [ESSIE, *appalled,*

tries to answer, but cannot.] How dare you go out by yourself after the orders I gave you?

ESSIE: He asked for a drink—[*She stops, her tongue cleaving to her palate with terror.*]

JUDITH: [*With gentler severity.*] Who asked for a drink? [ESSIE, *speechless, points to* RICHARD.]

RICHARD: What! I!

JUDITH: [*Shocked.*] Oh Essie, Essie!

RICHARD: I believe I did. [*He takes a glass and holds it to* ESSIE *to be filled. Her hand shakes.*] What! afraid of me?

ESSIE: [*Quickly.*] No. I—[*She pours out the water.*]

RICHARD: [*Tasting it.*] Ah, youve been up the street to the market gate spring to get that. [*He takes a draught.*] Delicious! Thank you. [*Unfortunately, at this moment he chances to catch sight of* JUDITH's *face, which expresses the most prudish disapproval of his evident attraction for* ESSIE, *who is devouring him with her grateful eyes. His mocking expression returns instantly. He puts down the glass; deliberately winds his arm round* ESSIE's *shoulders; and brings her into the middle of the company.* MRS DUDGEON *being in* ESSIE's *way as they come past the table, he says.*] By your leave, mother [*And compels her to make way for them.*] What do they call you? Bessie?

ESSIE: Essie.

RICHARD: Essie, to be sure. Are you a good girl, Essie?

ESSIE: [*Greatly disappointed that he, of all people, should begin at her in this way.*] Yes. [*She looks doubtfully at* JUDITH.] I think so. I mean I—I hope so.

RICHARD: Essie: did you ever hear of a person called the devil?

ANDERSON: [*Revolted.*] Shame on you, sir, with a mere child—

RICHARD: By your leave, Minister: I do not interfere with your sermons: do not you interrupt mine. [*To* ESSIE.] Do you know what they call me, Essie?

ESSIE: Dick.

RICHARD: [*Amused: patting her on the shoulder.*] Yes, Dick; but something else too. They call me the Devil's Disciple.

ESSIE: Why do you let them?

RICHARD: [*Seriously.*] Because it's true. I was brought up in the other service; but I knew from the first that the Devil was my natural master and captain and friend. I saw that he was in the right, and that the world cringed to his conqueror only through fear. I prayed secretly to him; and he comforted me, and saved me from having my spirit broken in this house of children's tears. I promised him my soul, and swore an oath that I would stand up for him in this world and stand by him in the next. [*Solemnly.*] That promise and that oath made a man of me. From this day this house is his home; and no child shall cry in it: this hearth is his altar; and no soul shall ever cower over it in the dark evenings and be afraid. Now [*Turning forcibly on the rest.*] which of you good men will take this child and rescue her from the house of the devil?

JUDITH: [*Coming to* ESSIE *and throwing a protecting arm about her.*] I will. You should be burnt alive.

ESSIE:But I don't want to. [*She shrinks back, leaving* RICHARD *and* JUDITH *face to face.*]

RICHARD: [*To* JUDITH.] Actually doesnt want to, most virtuous lady!

UNCLE TITUS: Have a care, Richard Dudgeon. The law—

RICHARD: [*Turning threateningly on him.*] Have a care, you. In an hour from this there will be no law here but martial law. I passed the soldiers within six miles on my way here: before noon Major Swindon's gallows for rebels will be up in the market place.

ANDERSON: [*Calmly.*] What have we to fear from that, sir?

RICHARD: More than you think. He hanged the wrong man at Springtown: he thought Uncle Peter was respectable, because the Dudgeons had a good name. But his next example will be the best man in the town to whom he can bring home a rebellious word. Well, we're all rebels; and you know it.

ALL THE MEN: [*Except* ANDERSON.] No, no, no!

RICHARD: Yes, you are. You havnt damned King George up hill and down dale as I have; but youve prayed for his defeat; and you, Anthony Anderson, have conducted the service, and sold your family bible to buy a pair of pistols. They maynt hang me, perhaps; because the moral effect of the Devil's Disciple dancing on nothing wouldnt help them. But a minister! [JUDITH, *dismayed, clings to* ANDERSON.] or a lawyer! [HAWKINS *smiles like a man able to take care of himself.*] or an upright horsedealer! [UNCLE TITUS *snarls at him in rage and terror.*] or a reformed drunkard! [UNCLE WILLIAM, *utterly unnerved, moans and wobbles with fear.*] eh? Would that shew that King George meant business—ha?

ANDERSON: [*Perfectly self-possessed.*] Come, my dear: he is only trying to frighten you. There is no danger. [*He takes her out of the house. The rest crowd to the door to follow him, except* ESSIE, *who remains near* RICHARD.]

RICHARD: [*Boisterously derisive.*] Now then: how many of you will stay with me; run up the American flag on the devil's house; and make a fight for freedom? [*They scramble out,* CHRISTY *among them, hustling one another in their haste.*] Ha ha! Long live the devil! [*To* MRS DUDGEON, *who is following them.*] What, mother! Are you off too?

MRS DUDGEON: [*Deadly pale, with her hand on her heart as if she had received a deathblow.*] My curse on you! My dying curse! [*She goes out.*]

RICHARD: [*Calling after her.*] It will bring me luck. Ha ha ha!

ESSIE: [*Anxiously.*] Maynt I stay?

RICHARD: [*Turning to her.*] What! Have they forgotten to save your soul in their anxiety about their own bodies? Oh yes: you may stay. [*He turns excitedly away again and shakes his fist after them. His left fist, also clenched, hangs down.* ESSIE *seizes it and kisses it, her tears falling on it. He starts and looks at it.*] Tears! The devil's baptism! [*She falls on her knees, sobbing. He stoops good-naturedly to raise her, saying.*] Oh yes, you may cry that way, Essie, if you like.

ACT II

MINISTER ANDERSON's *house is in the main street of Webster-*
bridge, not far from the town hall. To the eye of the eighteenth
century New Englander, it is much grander than the plain farm-
house of the DUDGEONS; *but it is so plain itself that a modern house*
agent would let both at about the same rent. The chief dwelling
room has the same sort of kitchen fireplace, with boiler, toaster
hanging on the bars, movable iron griddle socketed to the hob,
hook above for roasting, and broad fender, on which stand a kettle
and a plate of buttered toast. The door, between the fireplace and
the corner, has neither panels, fingerplates nor handles: it is made
of plain boards, and fastens with a latch. The table is a kitchen
table, with a treacle colored cover of American cloth, chapped at
the corners by draping. The tea service on it consists of two thick
cups and saucers of the plainest ware, with milk jug and bowl to
match, each large enough to contain nearly a quart, on a black
japanned tray, and, in the middle of the table, a wooden trencher
with a big loaf upon it, and a square half pound block of butter
in a crock. The big oak press facing the fire from the opposite side
of the room, is for use and storage, not for ornament; and the
minister's house coat hangs on a peg from its door, shewing that he
is out; for when he is in, it is his best coat that hangs there. His
big riding boots stand beside the press, evidently in their usual
place, and rather proud of themselves. In fact, the evolution of
the minister's kitchen, dining room and drawing room into three
separate apartments has not yet taken place; and so, from the point
of view of our pampered period, he is no better off than the
DUDGEONS.

But there is a difference, for all that. To begin with, MRS ANDER-
SON *is a pleasanter person to live with than* MRS DUDGEON. *To*
which MRS DUDGEON *would at once reply, with reason, that* MRS
ANDERSON *has no children to look after; no poultry, pigs, nor cattle;*
a steady and sufficient income not directly dependent on harvests
and prices at fairs; an affectionate husband who is a tower of
strength to her: in short, that life is as easy at the minister's house
as it is hard at the farm. This is true; but to explain a fact is not
to alter it; and however little credit MRS ANDERSON *may deserve for*
making her home happier, she has certainly succeeded in doing it.
The outward and visible signs of her superior social pretensions
are, a drugget on the floor, a plaster ceiling between the timbers,
and chairs which, though not upholstered, are stained and pol-
ished. The fine arts are represented by a mezzotint portrait of
some Presbyterian divine, a copperplate of Raphael's St Paul
preaching at Athens, a rococo presentation clock on the mantel-
shelf, flanked by a couple of miniatures, a pair of crockery dogs
with baskets in their mouths, and, at the corners, two large cowrie
shells. A pretty feature of the room is the low wide latticed win-
dow, nearly its whole width, with little red curtains running on a
rod half way up it to serve as a blind. There is no sofa; but one of
the seats, standing near the press, has a railed back and is long
enough to accommodate two people easily. On the whole, it is
rather the sort of room that the nineteenth century has ended in
struggling to get back to under the leadership of Mr Philip Webb

*and his disciples in domestic architecture, though no genteel clergy-
man would have tolerated it fifty years ago.*

*The evening has closed in; and the room is dark except for the
cosy firelight and the dim oil lamps seen through the window in
the wet street, where there is a quiet, steady, warm, windless down-
pour of rain. As the town clock strikes the quarter,* JUDITH *comes in
with a couple of candles in earthenware candlesticks, and sets them
on the table. Her self-conscious airs of the morning are gone: she
is anxious and frightened. She goes to the window and peers into
the street. The first thing she sees there is her husband, hurrying
home through the rain. She gives a little gasp of relief, not very
far removed from a sob, and turns to the door.* ANDERSON *comes in,
wrapped in a very wet cloak.*

JUDITH: [*Running to him.*] Oh, here you are at last, at last! [*She attempts to embrace him.*]

ANDERSON: [*Keeping her off.*] Take care, my love: I'm wet. Wait till I get my cloak off. [*He places a chair with its back to the fire; hangs his cloak on it to dry; shakes the rain from his hat and puts it on the fender; and at last turns with his hands outstretched to* JUDITH.] Now! [*She flies into his arms.*] I am not late, am I? The town clock struck the quarter as I came in at the front door. And the town clock is always fast.

JUDITH: I'm sure it's slow this evening. I'm so glad youre back.

ANDERSON: [*Taking her more closely in his arms.*] Anxious, my dear?

JUDITH: A little.

ANDERSON: Why, youve been crying.

JUDITH: Only a little. Never mind: it's all over now. [*A bugle call is heard in the distance. She starts in terror and retreats to the long seat, listening.*] What's that?

ANDERSON: [*Following her tenderly to the seat and making her sit down with him.*] Only King George, my dear. He's returning to barracks, or having his roll called, or getting ready for tea, or booting or saddling or something. Soldiers dont ring the bell or call over the banisters when they want anything: they send a boy out with a bugle to disturb the whole town.

JUDITH: Do you think there is really any danger?

ANDERSON: Not the least in the world.

JUDITH: You say that to comfort me, not because you believe it.

ANDERSON: My dear: in this world there is always danger for those who are afraid of it. Theres a danger that the house will catch fire in the night; but we shant sleep any the less soundly for that.

JUDITH: Yes, I know what you always say, and youre quite right. Oh, quite right: I know it. But—I suppose I'm not brave: thats all. My heart shrinks every time I think of the soldiers.

ANDERSON: Never mind that, dear: bravery is none the worse for costing a little pain.

JUDITH: Yes, I suppose so. [*Embracing him again.*] Oh how brave you are, my dear! [*With tears in her eyes.*] Well, I'll be brave too: you shant be ashamed of your wife.

ANDERSON: Thats right. Now you make me happy. Well, well! [*He rises and goes cheerily to the fire to dry his shoes.*] I called on Richard Dudgeon on my way back; but he wasnt in.

JUDITH: [*Rising in consternation.*] You called on that man!

ANDERSON: [*Reassuring her.*] Oh, nothing happened, dearie. He was out.

JUDITH: [*Almost in tears, as if the visit were a personal humiliation to her.*] But why did you go there?

ANDERSON: [*Gravely.*] Well, it is all the talk that Major Swindon is going to do what he did in Springtown—make an example of some notorious rebel, as he calls us. He pounced on Peter Dudgeon as the worst character there; and it is the general belief that he will pounce on Richard as the worst here.

JUDITH: But Richard said—

ANDERSON: [*Goodhumoredly cutting her short.*] Pooh! Richard said! He said what he thought would frighten you and frighten me, my dear. He said what perhaps (God forgive him!) he would like to believe. It's a terrible thing to think of what death must mean for a man like that. I felt that I must warn him. I left a message for him.

JUDITH: [*Querulously.*] What message?

ANDERSON: Only that I should be glad to

see him for a moment on a matter of importance to himself, and that if he would look in here when he was passing he would be welcome.

JUDITH: [Aghast.] You asked that man to come here!

ANDERSON: I did.

JUDITH: [Sinking on the seat and clasping her hands.] I hope he wont come! Oh, I pray that he may not come!

ANDERSON: Why? Dont you want him to be warned?

JUDITH: He must know his danger. Oh, Tony, is it wrong to hate a blasphemer and a villain? I do hate him. I cant get him out of my mind: I know he will bring harm with him. He insulted you: he insulted me: he insulted his mother.

ANDERSON: [Quaintly.] Well, dear, lets forgive him; and then it wont matter.

JUDITH: Oh, I know it's wrong to hate anybody; but—

ANDERSON: [Going over to her with humorous tenderness.] Come, dear, youre not so wicked as you think. The worst sin towards our fellow creatures is not to hate them, but to be indifferent to them; thats the essence of inhumanity. After all, my dear, if you watch people carefully, youll be surprised to find how like hate is to love. [She starts, strangely touched—even appalled. He is amused at her.] Yes: I'm quite in earnest. Think of how some of our married friends worry one another, tax one another, are jealous of one another, cant bear to let one another out of sight for a day, are more like jailers and slave-owners than lovers. Think of those very same people with their enemies, scrupulous, lofty, self-respecting, determined to be independent of one another, careful of how they speak of one another—pooh! havnt you often thought that if they only knew it, they were better friends to their enemies than to their own husbands and wives? Come: depend on it, my dear, you are really fonder of Richard than you are of me, if you only knew it. Eh!

JUDITH: Oh, dont say that: dont say that, Tony, even in jest. You dont know what a horrible feeling it gives me.

ANDERSON: [Laughing.] Well, well: never mind, pet. He's a bad man; and you hate him as he deserves. And youre going to make the tea, arnt you?

JUDITH: [Remorsefully.] Oh yes, I forgot. I've been keeping you waiting all this time. [She goes to the fire and puts on the kettle.]

ANDERSON: [Going to the press and taking his coat off.] Have you stitched up the shoulder of my old coat?

JUDITH: Yes, dear. [She goes to the table, and sets about putting the tea into the teapot from the caddy.]

ANDERSON: [As he changes his coat for the older one hanging on the press, and replaces it by the one he has just taken off.] Did anyone call when I was out?

JUDITH: No, only—[Someone knocks at the door. With a start which betrays her intense nervousness, she retreats to the further end of the table with the tea caddy and spoon in her hands, exclaiming.] Who's that?

ANDERSON: [Going to her and patting her encouragingly on the shoulder.] All right, pet, all right. He wont eat you, whoever he is. [She tries to smile, and nearly makes herself cry. He goes to the door and opens it. RICHARD is there, without overcoat or cloak.] You might have raised the latch and come in, Mr Dudgeon. Nobody stands on much ceremony with us. [Hospitably.] Come in. [RICHARD comes in carelessly and stands at the table, looking round the room with a slight pucker of his nose at the mezzotinted divine on the wall. JUDITH keeps her eyes on the tea caddy.] Is it still raining? [He shuts the door.]

RICHARD: Raining like the very [His eye catches JUDITH's as she looks quickly and haughtily up.]—I beg your pardon; but [Shewing that his coat is wet.] you see—!

ANDERSON: Take it off, sir; and let it hang before the fire a while: my wife will excuse your shirtsleeves. Judith: put in another spoonful of tea for Mr Dudgeon.

RICHARD: [Eyeing him cynically.] The magic of property, Pastor! Are even you civil to me now that I have succeeded to my father's estate?

[JUDITH throws down the spoon indignantly.]

ANDERSON: [Quite unruffled, and helping RICHARD off with his coat.] I think, sir, that since you accept my hospitality, you cannot have so bad an opinion of it. Sit down. [With the coat in his hand, he points to the railed seat. RICHARD, in his shirtsleeves, looks at him half quarrelsomely for a moment; then, with a nod, acknowledges that the minister has got the better of him, and sits down on the seat. ANDERSON pushes *his cloak into a heap on the seat of the chair at the fire, and hangs* RICHARD'S *coat on the back in its place.*]

RICHARD: I come, sir, on your own invitation. You left word you had something important to tell me.

ANDERSON: I have a warning which it is my duty to give you.

RICHARD: [*Quickly rising.*] You want to preach to me. Excuse me: I prefer a walk in the rain. [*He makes for his coat.*]

ANDERSON: [*Stopping him.*] Dont be alarmed, sir: I am no great preacher. You are quite safe. [RICHARD *smiles in spite of himself. His glance softens: he even makes a gesture of excuse.* ANDERSON, *seeing that he has tamed him, now addresses him earnestly.*] Mr Dudgeon: you are in danger in this town.

RICHARD: What danger?

ANDERSON: Your uncle's danger. Major Swindon's gallows.

RICHARD: It is you who are in danger. I warned you—

ANDERSON: [*Interrupting him goodhumoredly but authoritatively.*] Yes, yes, Mr Dudgeon; but they do not think so in the town. And even if I were in danger, I have duties here which I must not forsake. But you are a free man. Why should you run any risk?

RICHARD: Do you think I should be any great loss, Minister?

ANDERSON: I think that a man's life is worth saving, whoever it belongs to. [RICHARD *makes him an ironical bow.* ANDERSON *returns the bow humorously.*] Come: youll have a cup of tea, to prevent you catching cold?

RICHARD: I observe that Mrs Anderson is not quite so pressing as you are, Pastor.

JUDITH: [*Almost stifled with resentment, which she has been expecting her husband to share and express for her at every insult of* RICHARD'S.] You are welcome for my husband's sake. [*She brings the teapot to the fireplace and sets it on the hob.*]

RICHARD: I know I am not welcome for my own, madam. [*He rises.*] But I think I will not break bread here, Minister.

ANDERSON: [*Cheerily.*] Give me a good reason for that.

RICHARD: Because there is something in you that I respect, and that makes me desire to have you for my enemy.

ANDERSON: Thats well said. On those terms, sir, I will accept your enmity or any

man's. Judith: Mr Dudgeon will stay to tea. Sit down: it will take a few minutes to draw by the fire. [RICHARD *glances at him with a troubled face; then sits down with his head bent, to hide a convulsive swelling of his throat.*] I was just saying to my wife, Mr Dudgeon, that enmity— [*She grasps his hand and looks imploringly at him, doing both with an intensity that checks him at once.*] Well, well, I mustnt tell you, I see; but it was nothing that need leave us worse friend—enemies, I mean. Judith is a great enemy of yours.

RICHARD: If all my enemies were like Mrs Anderson, I should be the best Christian in America.

ANDERSON: [*Gratified, patting her hand.*] You hear that, Judith? Mr Dudgeon knows how to turn a compliment.

[*The latch is lifted from without.*]

JUDITH: [*Starting.*] Who is that?

[CHRISTY *comes in.*]

CHRISTY: [*Stopping and staring at* RICHARD.] Oh, are you here?

RICHARD: Yes. Begone, you fool: Mrs Anderson doesnt want the whole family to tea at once.

CHRISTY: [*Coming further in.*] Mother's very ill.

RICHARD: Well, does she want to see me?

CHRISTY: No.

RICHARD: I thought not.

CHRISTY: She wants to see the minister— at once.

JUDITH: [*To* ANDERSON.] Oh, not before youve had some tea.

ANDERSON: I shall enjoy it more when I come back, dear. [*He is about to take up his cloak.*]

CHRISTY: The rain's over.

ANDERSON: [*Dropping the cloak and picking up his hat from the fender.*] Where is your mother, Christy?

CHRISTY: At Uncle Titus's.

ANDERSON: Have you fetched the doctor?

CHRISTY: No: she didnt tell me to.

ANDERSON: Go on there at once: I'll overtake you on his doorstep. [CHRISTY *turns to go.*] Wait a moment. Your brother must be anxious to know the particulars.

RICHARD: Psha! not I: he doesnt know; and I dont care. [*Violently.*] Be off, you oaf. [CHRISTY *runs out.* RICHARD *adds, a little shamefacedly.*] We shall know soon enough.

ANDERSON: Well, perhaps you will let me bring you the news myself. Judith: will you give Mr Dudgeon his tea, and keep him here until I return.

JUDITH: [*White and trembling.*] Must I—

ANDERSON: [*Taking her hands and interrupting her to cover her agitation.*] My dear: I can depend on you?

JUDITH: [*With a piteous effort to be worthy of his trust.*] Yes.

ANDERSON: [*Pressing her hand against his cheek.*] You will not mind two old people like us, Mr Dudgeon. [*Going.*] I shall not say good evening: you will be here when I come back. [*He goes out.*]

[*They watch him pass the window, and then look at each other dumbly, quite disconcerted.* RICHARD, *noting the quiver of her lips, is the first to pull himself together.*]

RICHARD: Mrs Anderson: I am perfectly aware of the nature of your sentiments towards me. I shall not intrude on you. Good evening. [*Again he starts for the fireplace to get his coat.*]

JUDITH: [*Getting between him and the coat.*] No, no. Dont go: please dont go.

RICHARD: [*Roughly.*] Why? You dont want me here.

JUDITH: Yes, I— [*Wringing her hands in despair.*] Oh, if I tell you the truth, you will use it to torment me.

RICHARD: [*Indignantly.*] Torment! What right have you to say that? Do you expect me to stay after that?

JUDITH: I want you to stay; but [*Suddenly raging at him like an angry child.*] it is not because I like you.

RICHARD: Indeed!

JUDITH: Yes: I had rather you did go than mistake me about that. I hate and dread you; and my husband knows it. If you are not here when he comes back, he will believe that I disobeyed him and drove you away.

RICHARD: [*Ironically.*] Whereas, of course, you have really been so kind and hospitable and charming to me that I only want to go away out of mere contrariness, eh?

[JUDITH, *unable to bear it, sinks on the chair and bursts into tears.*]

RICHARD: Stop, stop, stop, I tell you. Dont do that. [*Putting his hand to his breast as if to a wound.*] He wrung my heart by being a man. Need you tear it by being a woman? Has he not raised you above my insults, like himself? [*She stops crying, and recovers herself somewhat, looking at him with a scared curiosity.*] There: thats right. [*Sympathetically.*] Youre better now, arnt you? [*He puts his hand encouragingly on her shoulder. She instantly rises haughtily, and stares at him defiantly. He at once drops into his usual sardonic tone.*] Ah, thats better. You are yourself again: so is Richard. Well, shall we go to tea like a quiet respectable couple, and wait for your husband's return?

JUDITH: [*Rather ashamed of herself.*] If you please. I—I am sorry to have been so foolish. [*She stoops to take up the plate of toast from the fender.*]

RICHARD: I am sorry, for your sake, that I am—what I am. Allow me. [*He takes the plate from her and goes with it to the table.*]

JUDITH: [*Following with the teapot.*] Will you sit down? [*He sits down at the end of the table nearest the press. There is a plate and knife laid there. The other plate is laid near it: but* JUDITH *stays at the opposite end of the table, next the fire, and takes her place there, drawing the tray towards her.*] Do you take sugar?

RICHARD: No: but plenty of milk. Let me give you some toast. [*He puts some on the second plate, and hands it to her, with the knife. The action shews quickly how well he knows that she has avoided her usual place so as to be as far from him as possible.*]

JUDITH: [*Consciously.*] Thanks. [*She gives him his tea.*] Wont you help yourself?

RICHARD: Thanks. [*He puts a piece of toast on his own plate; and she pours out tea for herself.*]

JUDITH: [*Observing that he tastes nothing.*] Dont you like it? You are not eating anything.

RICHARD: Neither are you.

JUDITH: [*Nervously.*] I never care much for my tea. Please dont mind me.

RICHARD: [*Looking dreamily round.*] I am thinking. It is all so strange to me. I can see the beauty and peace of this home: I think I have never been more at rest in my life than at this moment; and yet I know quite well I could never live here. It's not in my nature, I suppose, to be domesticated. But it's very beautiful: it's almost holy. [*He muses a moment, and then laughs softly.*]

JUDITH: [*Quickly.*] Why do you laugh?

RICHARD: I was thinking that if any

stranger came in here now, he would take us for man and wife.

JUDITH: [*Taking offence.*] You mean, I suppose, that you are more my age than he is.

RICHARD: [*Staring at this unexpected turn.*] I never thought of such a thing. [*Sardonic again.*] I see there is another side to domestic joy.

JUDITH: [*Angrily.*] I would rather have a husband whom everybody respects than—than—

RICHARD: Than the devil's disciple. You are right; but I daresay your love helps him to be a good man, just as your hate helps me to be a bad one.

JUDITH: My husband has been very good to you. He has forgiven you for insulting him, and is trying to save you. Can you not forgive him for being so much better than you are? How dare you belittle him by putting yourself in his place?

RICHARD: Did I?

JUDITH: Yes, you did. You said that if anybody came in they would take us for man and— [*She stops, terror-stricken, as a squad of soldiers tramps past the window.*] The English soldiers! Oh, what do they—

RICHARD: [*Listening.*] Sh!

A VOICE: [*Outside.*] Halt! Four outside: two in with me.

[*Judith half rises, listening and looking with dilated eyes at RICHARD, who takes up his cup prosaically, and is drinking his tea when the latch goes up with a sharp click, and an English sergeant walks into the room with two privates, who post themselves at the door. He comes promptly to the table between them.*]

THE SERGEANT: Sorry to disturb you, mum. Duty! Anthony Anderson: I arrest you in King George's name as a rebel.

JUDITH: [*Pointing at RICHARD.*] But that is not— [*He looks up quickly at her, with a face of iron. She stops her mouth hastily with the hand she has raised to indicate him, and stands staring affrightedly.*]

THE SERGEANT: Come, parson: put your coat on and come along.

RICHARD: Yes: I'll come. [*He rises and takes a step towards his own coat; then recollects himself, and, with his back to the sergeant, moves his gaze slowly round the room without turning his head until he sees ANDERSON's black coat hanging up on the press. He goes composedly to it; takes it*

down; and puts it on. The idea of himself as a parson tickles him: he looks down at the black sleeve on his arm, and then smiles slyly at JUDITH, whose white face shews him that what she is painfully struggling to grasp is not the humor of the situation but its horror. He turns to the sergeant, who is approaching him with a pair of handcuffs hidden behind him, and says lightly.*] Did you ever arrest a man of my cloth before, Sergeant?

THE SERGEANT: [*Instinctively respectful, half to the black coat, and to RICHARD's good breeding.*] Well, no sir. At least, only an army chaplain. [*Shewing the handcuffs.*] I'm sorry sir; but duty—

RICHARD: Just so, Sergeant. Well, I'm not ashamed of them: thank you kindly for the apology. [*He holds out his hands.*]

SERGEANT: [*Not availing himself of the offer.*] One gentleman to another, sir. Wouldnt you like to say a word to your missis, sir, before you go?

RICHARD: [*Smiling.*] Oh, we shall meet again before—eh? [*Meaning "before you hang me."*]

SERGEANT: [*Loudly, with ostentatious cheerfulness.*] Oh, of course, of course. No call for the lady to distress herself. Still— [*In a lower voice, intended for RICHARD alone.*] your last chance, sir.

[*They look at one another significantly for a moment. Then RICHARD exhales a deep breath and turns towards JUDITH.*]

RICHARD: [*Very distinctly.*] My love. [*She looks at him, pitiably pale, and tries to answer, but cannot—tries also to come to him, but cannot trust herself to stand without the support of the table.*] This gallant gentleman is good enough to allow us a moment of leavetaking. [*The sergeant retires delicately and joins his men near the door.*] He is trying to spare you the truth; but you had better know it. Are you listening to me? [*She signifies assent.*] Do you understand that I am going to my death? [*She signifies that she understands.*] Remember, you must find our friend who was with us just now. Do you understand? [*She signifies yes.*] See that you get him safely out of harm's way. Dont for your life let him know of my danger; but if he finds it out, tell him that he cannot save me: they would hang him; and they would not spare me. And tell him that I am steadfast in my religion as he is in his, and that he may depend on me to the death. [*He turns to go, and meets the eyes of the sergeant, who looks a little suspicious. He considers a moment, and then, turning roguishly to* JUDITH *with something of a smile breaking through his earnestness, says.*] And now, my dear, I am afraid the sergeant will not believe that you love me like a wife unless you give one kiss before I go.

[*He approaches her and holds out his arms. She quits the table and almost falls into them.*]

JUDITH: [*The words choking her.*] I ought to—it's murder—

RICHARD: No: only a kiss [*Softly to her.*] for his sake.

JUDITH: I cant. You must—

RICHARD: [*Folding her in his arms with an impulse of compassion for her distress.*] My poor girl!

[JUDITH, *with a sudden effort, throws her arms round him; kisses him; and swoons away, dropping from his arms to the ground as if the kiss had killed her.*]

RICHARD: [*Going quickly to the sergeant.*] Now, Sergeant: quick, before she comes to. The handcuffs. [*He puts out his hands.*]

SERGEANT: [*Pocketing them.*] Never mind, sir: I'll trust you. Youre a game one. You ought to a bin a soldier, sir. Between them two, please. [*The soldiers place themselves one before* RICHARD *and one behind him. The sergeant opens the door.*]

RICHARD: [*Taking a last look round him.*] Goodbye, wife: goodbye, home. Muffle the drums, and quick march!

[*The sergeant signs to the leading soldier to march. They file out quickly.* ***************When ANDERSON *returns from* MRS DUDGEON'S, *he is astonished to find the room apparently empty and almost in darkness except for the glow from the fire; for one of the candles has burnt out, and the other is at its last flicker.*]

ANDERSON: Why, what on earth—? [*Calling.*] Judith, Judith! [*He listens: there is no answer.*] Hm! [*He goes to the cupboard; takes a candle from the drawer; lights it at the flicker of the expiring one on the table; and looks wonderingly at the untasted meal by its light. Then he sticks it in the candlestick; takes off his hat; and scratches his head, much puzzled. This action causes him to look at the floor for the first time; and there he see* JUDITH *lying motionless with her eyes closed. He runs to her and stoops beside her, lifting her head.*] Judith.

JUDITH: [*Waking; for her swoon has passed into the sleep of exhaustion after suffering.*] Yes. Did you call? Whats the matter?

ANDERSON: Ive just come in and found you lying here with the candles burnt out and the tea poured out and cold. What has happened?

JUDITH: [*Still astray.*] I dont know. Have I been asleep? I suppose— [*She stops blankly.*] I dont know.

ANDERSON: [*Groaning.*] Heaven forgive me, I left you alone with that scoundrel. [JUDITH *remembers. With an agonized cry, she clutches his shoulders and drags herself to her feet as he rises with her. He clasps her tenderly in his arms.*] My poor pet!

JUDITH: [*Frantically clinging to him.*] What shall I do? Oh my God, what shall I do?

ANDERSON: Never mind, never mind, my dearest dear: it was my fault. Come: youre safe now; and youre not hurt, are you? [*He takes his arms from her to see whether she can stand.*] There: thats right, thats right. If only you are not hurt, nothing else matters.

JUDITH: No, no, no: I'm not hurt.

ANDERSON: Thank Heaven for that! Come now: [*Leading her to the railed seat and making her sit down beside him.*] sit down and rest: you can tell me about it tomorrow. Or [*Misunderstanding her distress.*] you shall not tell me at all if it worries you. There, there! [*Cheerfully.*] I'll make you some fresh tea: that will set you up again. [*He goes to the table, and empties the teapot into the slop bowl.*]

JUDITH: [*In a strained tone.*] Tony.

ANDERSON: Yes, dear?

JUDITH: Do you think we are only in a dream now?

ANDERSON: [*Glancing round at her for a moment with a pang of anxiety, though he goes on steadily and cheerfully putting fresh tea into the pot.*] Perhaps so, pet. But you may as well dream a cup of tea when youre about it.

JUDITH: Oh stop, stop. You don't know— [*Distracted she buries her face in her knotted hands.*]

ANDERSON: [*Breaking down and coming to her.*] My dear, what is it? I cant bear it any longer: you must tell me. It was all my fault: I was mad to trust him.

JUDITH: No: dont say that. You mustnt say that. He—oh no, no: I cant. Tony: dont speak to me. Take my hands—both my hands. [*He takes them, wondering.*] Make me think of you, not of him. Theres danger, frightful danger; but it is your danger; and I cant keep thinking of it: I cant, I cant: my mind goes back to his danger. He must be saved—no: you must be saved: you, you, you. [*She springs up as if to do something or go somewhere, exclaiming.*] Oh, Heaven help me!

ANDERSON: [*Keeping his seat and holding her hands with resolute composure.*] Calmly, calmly, my pet. Youre quite distracted.

JUDITH: I may well be. I dont know what to do. I dont know what to do. [*Tearing her hands away.*] I must save him. [ANDERSON *rises in alarm as she runs wildly to the door. It is opened in her face by* ESSIE, *who hurries in full of anxiety. The surprise is so disagreeable to* JUDITH *that it brings her to her senses. Her tone is sharp and angry as she demands.*] What do you want?

ESSIE: I was to come to you.

ANDERSON: Who told you to?

ESSIE: [*Staring at him, as if his presence astonished her.*] Are you here?

JUDITH: Of course. Dont be foolish, child.

ANDERSON: Gently, dearest: youll frighten her. [*Going between them.*] Come here, Essie. [*She comes to him.*] Who sent you?

ESSIE: Dick. He sent me word by a soldier. I was to come here at once and do whatever Mrs Anderson told me.

ANDERSON: [*Enlightened.*] A soldier! Ah, I see it all now! They have arrested Richard. [JUDITH *makes a gesture of despair.*]

ESSIE: No. I asked the soldier. Dick's safe. But the soldier said you had been taken.

ANDERSON: I! [*Bewildered, he turns to* JUDITH *for an explanation.*]

JUDITH: [*Coaxingly.*] All right, dear: I understand. [*To* ESSIE.] Thank you, Essie, for coming: but I dont need you now. You may go home.

ESSIE: [*Suspicious.*] Are you sure Dick has not been touched? Perhaps he told the soldier to say it was the minister. [*Anxiously.*] Mrs Anderson: do you think it can have been that?

ANDERSON: Tell her the truth if it is so, Judith. She will learn it from the first neighbor she meets in the street. [JUDITH *turns away and covers her eyes with her hands.*]

ESSIE: [*Wailing.*] But what will they do to him? Oh, what will they do to him? Will they hang him? [JUDITH *shudders convulsively, and throws herself into the chair in which* RICHARD *sat at the tea table.*]

ANDERSON: [*Patting* ESSIE'S *shoulder and trying to comfort her.*] I hope not. I hope not. Perhaps if youre very quiet and patient, we may be able to help him in some way.

ESSIE: Yes—help him—yes, yes, yes. I'll be good.

ANDERSON: I must go to him at once, Judith.

JUDITH: [*Springing up.*] Oh no. You must go away—far away, to some place of safety.

ANDERSON: Pooh!

JUDITH: [*Passionately.*] Do you want to kill me? Do you think I can bear to live for days and days with every knock at the door —every footstep—giving me a spasm of terror? to lie awake for nights and nights in an agony of dread, listening for them to come and arrest you?

ANDERSON: Do you think it would be better to know that I had run away from my post at the first sign of danger?

JUDITH: [*Bitterly.*] Oh, you wont go. I know it. Youll stay; and I shall go mad.

ANDERSON: My dear, your duty—

JUDITH: [*Fiercely.*] What do I care about my duty?

ANDERSON: [*Shocked.*] Judith!

JUDITH: I am doing my duty. I am clinging to my duty. My duty is to get you away, to save you, to leave him to his fate. [ESSIE *utters a cry of distress and sinks on the chair at the fire, sobbing silently.*] My instinct is the same as hers—to save him above all things, though it would be so much better for him to die! so much greater! But I know you will take your own way as he took it. I have no power. [*She sits down sullenly on the railed seat.*] I'm only a woman: I can do nothing but sit here and suffer. Only, tell him I tried to save you—that I did my best to save you.

ANDERSON: My dear, I am afraid he will be thinking more of his own danger than of mine.

JUDITH: Stop; or I shall hate you.

ANDERSON: [*Remonstrating.*] Come, come, come! How am I to leave you if you talk like this? You are quite out of your senses. [*He turns to* ESSIE.] Essie.

ESSIE: [*Eagerly rising and drying her eyes.*] Yes?

ANDERSON: Just wait outside a moment, like a good girl: Mrs Anderson is not well. [ESSIE *looks doubtful.*] Never fear: I'll come to you presently; and I'll go to Dick.

ESSIE: You are sure you will go to him? [*Whispering.*] You wont let her prevent you?

ANDERSON: [*Smiling.*] No, no: it's all right. All right. [*She goes.*] Thats a good girl. [*He closes the door, and returns to* JUDITH.]

JUDITH: [*Seated—rigid.*] You are going to your death.

ANDERSON: [*Quaintly.*] Then I shall go in my best coat, dear. [*He turns to the press, beginning to take off his coat.*] Where—? [*He stares at the empty nail for a moment; then looks quickly round to the fire; strides across to it; and lifts* RICHARD's *coat.*] Why, my dear, it seems that he has gone in my best coat.

JUDITH: [*Still motionless.*] Yes.

ANDERSON: Did the soldiers make a mistake?

JUDITH: Yes: they made a mistake.

ANDERSON: He might have told them. Poor fellow, he was too upset, I suppose.

JUDITH: Yes: he might have told them. So might I.

ANDERSON: Well, it's all very puzzling—almost funny. It's curious how these little things strike us even in the most— [*He breaks off and begins putting on* RICHARD's *coat.*] I'd better take him his own coat. I know what he'll say— [*Imitating* RICHARD's *sardonic manner.*] "Anxious about my soul, Pastor, and also about your best coat." Eh?

JUDITH: Yes, that is just what he will say to you. [*Vacantly.*] It doesnt matter: I shall never see either of you again.

ANDERSON: [*Rallying her.*] Oh pooh, pooh, pooh! [*He sits down beside her.*] Is this how to keep your promise that I shant be ashamed of my brave wife?

JUDITH: No: this is how I break it. I cannot keep my promises to him: why should I keep my promises to you?

ANDERSON: Dont speak so strangely, my love. It sounds insincere to me. [*She looks unutterable reproach at him.*] Yes, dear, nonsense is always insincere; and my dearest is talking nonsense. Just nonsense. [*Her face darkens into dumb obstinacy. She*

stares straight before her, and does not look at him again, absorbed in RICHARD's fate. He scans her face; sees that his rallying has produced no effect; and gives it up, making no further effort to conceal his anxiety.] I wish I knew what has frightened you so. Was there a struggle? Did he fight?

JUDITH: No. He smiled.

ANDERSON: Did he realize his danger, do you think?

JUDITH: He realized yours.

ANDERSON: Mine!

JUDITH: [*Monotonously.*] He said "See that you get him safely out of harm's way." I promised: I cant keep my promise. He said, "Dont for your life let him know of my danger." Ive told you of it. He said that if you found it out, you could not save him —that they will hang him and not spare you.

ANDERSON: [*Rising in generous indignation.*] And you think that I will let a man with that much good in him die like a dog, when a few words might make him die like a Christian. I'm ashamed of you, Judith.

JUDITH: He will be steadfast in his religion as you are in yours; and you may depend on him to the death. He said so.

ANDERSON: God forgive him! What else did he say?

JUDITH: He said goodbye.

ANDERSON: [*Fidgeting nervously to and fro in great concern.*] Poor fellow, poor fellow! You said goodbye to him in all kindness and charity, Judith, I hope.

JUDITH: I kissed him.

ANDERSON: What! Judith!

JUDITH: Are you angry?

ANDERSON: No, no. You were right: you were right. Poor fellow, poor fellow! [*Greatly distressed.*] To be hanged like that at his age! And then did they take him away?

JUDITH: [*Wearily.*] Then you were here: thats the next thing I remember. I suppose I fainted. Now bid me goodbye, Tony. Perhaps I shall faint again. I wish I could die.

ANDERSON: No, no, my dear: you must pull yourself together and be sensible. I am in no danger—not the least in the world.

JUDITH: [*Solemnly.*] You are going to your death, Tony—your sure death, if God will let innocent men be murdered. They will not let you see him: they will arrest you the moment you give your name. It was for you the soldiers came.

ANDERSON: [*Thunderstruck.*] For me! ! !

[*His fists clinch; his neck thickens; his face reddens; the fleshy purses under his eyes become injected with hot blood; the man of peace vanishes, transfigured into a choleric and formidable man of war. Still, she does not come out of her absorption to look at him: her eyes are steadfast with a mechanical reflection of* RICHARD'S *steadfastness.*]

JUDITH: He took your place: he is dying to save you. That is why he went in your coat. That is why I kissed him.

ANDERSON: [*Exploding.*] Blood an' owns! [*His voice is rough and dominant, his gesture full of brute energy.*] Here! Essie, Essie!

ESSIE: [*Running in.*] Yes.

ANDERSON: [*Impetuously.*] Off with you as hard as you can run, to the inn. Tell them to saddle the fastest and strongest horse they have [JUDITH *rises breathless, and stares at him incredulously.*]—the chestnut mare, if she's fresh—without a moment's delay. Go into the stable yard and tell the black man there that I'll give him a silver dollar if the horse is waiting for me when I come, and that I am close on your heels. Away with you. [*His energy sends* ESSIE *flying from the room. He pounces on his riding boots; rushes with them to the chair at the fire; and begins pulling them on.*]

JUDITH: [*Unable to believe such a thing of him.*] You are not going to him!

ANDERSON: [*Busy with the boots.*] Going to him! What good would that do? [*Growling to himself as he gets the first boot on with a wrench.*] I'll go to them, so I will. [*To* JUDITH *peremptorily.*] Get me the pistols: I want them. And money, money: I want money—all the money in the house. [*He stoops over the other boot, grumbling.*] A great satisfaction it would be to him to have my company on the gallows. [*He pulls on the boot.*]

JUDITH: You are deserting him, then?

ANDERSON: Hold your tongue, woman; and get me the pistols. [*She goes to the press and takes from it a leather belt with two pistols, a powder horn, and a bag of bullets attached to it. She throws it on the table. Then she unlocks a drawer in the press and takes out a purse.* ANDERSON *grabs the belt and buckles it on, saying.*] If they took him for me in my coat, perhaps they'll take me for him in his. [*Hitching the belt into its place.*] Do I look like him?

JUDITH: [*Turning with the purse in her hand.*] Horribly unlike him.

ANDERSON: [*Snatching the purse from her and emptying it on the table.*] Hm! We shall see.

JUDITH: [*Sitting down helplessly.*] Is it of any use to pray, do you think, Tony?

ANDERSON: [*Counting the money.*] Pray! Can we pray Swindon's rope off Richard's neck?

JUDITH: God may soften Major Swindon's heart.

ANDERSON: [*Contemptuously—pocketing a handful of money.*] Let him, then. I am not God; and I must go to work another way. [JUDITH *gasps at the blasphemy. He throws the purse on the table.*] Keep that. Ive taken 25 dollars.

JUDITH: Have you forgotten even that you are a minister?

ANDERSON: Minister be—faugh! My hat: wheres my hat? [*He snatches up hat and cloak, and puts both on in hot haste.*] Now listen, you. If you can get a word with him by pretending youre his wife, tell him to hold his tongue until morning: that will give me all the start I need.

JUDITH: [*Solemnly.*] You may depend on him to the death.

ANDERSON: Youre a fool, a fool, Judith. [*For a moment checking the torrent of his haste, and speaking with something of his old quiet and impressive conviction.*] You dont know the man youre married to. [ESSIE *returns. He swoops at her at once.*] Well: is the horse ready?

ESSIE: [*Breathless.*] It will be ready when you come.

ANDERSON: Good. [*He makes for the door.*]

JUDITH: [*Rising and stretching out her arms after him involuntarily.*] Wont you say goodbye?

ANDERSON: And waste another half minute! Psha! [*He rushes out like an avalanche.*]

ESSIE: [*Hurrying to* JUDITH.] He has gone to save Richard, hasnt he?

JUDITH: To save Richard! No: Richard has saved him. He has gone to save himself. Richard must die.

[ESSIE *screams with terror and falls on her knees, hiding her face.* JUDITH, *without heeding her, looks rigidly straight in front of her, at the vision of* RICHARD, *dying.*]

ACT III

Early next morning the sergeant, at the British headquarters in the Town Hall, unlocks the door of a little empty panelled waiting room, and invites JUDITH *to enter. She has had a bad night, probably a rather delirious one; for even in the reality of the raw morning, her fixed gaze comes back at moments when her attention is not strongly held.*

The SERGEANT *considers that her feelings do her credit, and is sympathetic in an encouraging military way. Being a fine figure of a man, vain of his uniform and of his rank, he feels specially qualified, in a respectful way, to console her.*

SERGEANT: You can have a quiet word with him here, mum.

JUDITH: Shall I have long to wait?

SERGEANT: No, mum, not a minute. We kep him in the Bridewell for the night; and he's just been brought over here for the court martial. Dont fret, mum: he slep like a child, and has made a rare good breakfast.

JUDITH: [*Incredulously.*] He is in good spirits!

SERGEANT: Tip top, mum. The chaplain looked in to see him last night; and he won seventeen shillings off him at spoil five. He spent it among us like the gentleman he is. Duty's duty, mum, of course; but youre among friends here. [*The tramp of a couple of soldiers is heard approaching.*] There: I think he's coming. [RICHARD *comes in, without a sign of care or captivity in his bearing. The sergeant nods to the two soldiers, and shews them the key of the room in his hand. They withdraw.*] Your good lady, sir.

RICHARD: [*Going to her.*] What! My wife. My adored one. [*He takes her hand and kisses it with a perverse, raffish gallantry.*] How long do you allow a broken-hearted husband for leave-taking, Sergeant?

SERGEANT: As long as we can, sir. We shall not disturb you till the court sits.

RICHARD: But it has struck the hour.

SERGEANT: So it has, sir; but theres a delay. General Burgoyne's just arrived— Gentlemanly Johnny we call him, sir—and he wont have done finding fault with everything this side of half past. I know him, sir: I served with him in Portugal. You may count on twenty minutes, sir; and by your leave I wont waste any more of them. [*He goes out, locking the door.* RICHARD *imme-diately drops his raffish manner and turns to* JUDITH *with considerate sincerity.*]

RICHARD: Mrs Anderson: this visit is very kind of you. And how are you after last night? I had to leave you before you recovered; but I sent word to Essie to go and look after you. Did she understand the message?

JUDITH: [*Breathless and urgent.*] Oh, dont think of me: I havnt come here to talk about myself. Are they going to—to— [*Meaning "to hang you."*]?

RICHARD: [*Whimsically.*] At noon, punctually. At least, that was when they disposed of Uncle Peter. [*She shudders.*] Is your husband safe? Is he on the wing?

JUDITH: He is no longer my husband.

RICHARD: [*Opening his eyes wide.*] Eh?

JUDITH: I disobeyed you. I told him everything. I expected him to come here and save you. I wanted him to come here and save you. He ran away instead.

RICHARD: Well, thats what I meant him to do. What good would his staying have done? Theyd only have hanged us both.

JUDITH: [*With reproachful earnestness.*] Richard Dudgeon: on your honor, what would you have done in his place?

RICHARD: Exactly what he has done, of course.

JUDITH: Oh, why will you not be simple with me—honest and straightforward? If you are so selfish as that, why did you let them take you last night?

RICHARD: [*Gaily.*] Upon my life, Mrs Anderson, I dont know. Ive been asking myself that question ever since; and I can find no manner of reason for acting as I did.

JUDITH: You know you did it for his sake, believing he was a more worthy man than yourself.

RICHARD: [Laughing.] Oho! No: thats a very pretty reason, I must say; but I'm not so modest as that. No: it wasnt for his sake.

JUDITH: [After a pause, during which she looks shamefacedly at him, blushing painfully.] Was it for my sake?

RICHARD: [Gallantly.] Well, you had a hand in it. It must have been a little for your sake. You let them take me, at all events.

JUDITH: Oh, do you think I have not been telling myself that all night? Your death will be at my door. [Impulsively, she gives him her hand, and adds, with intense earnestness.] If I could save you as you saved him, I would do it, no matter how cruel the death was.

RICHARD: [Holding her hand and smiling, but keeping her almost at arms length.] I am very sure I shouldnt let you.

JUDITH: Dont you see that I can save you?

RICHARD: How? by changing clothes with me, eh?

JUDITH: [Disengaging her hand to touch his lips with it.] Dont [Meaning "Dont jest."] No: by telling the Court who you really are.

RICHARD: [Frowning.] No use: they wouldnt spare me; and it would spoil half his chance of escaping. They are determined to cow us by making an example of somebody on that gallows today. Well, let us cow them by showing that we can stand by one another to the death. That is the only force that can send Burgoyne back across the Atlantic and make America a nation.

JUDITH: [Impatiently.] Oh, what does all that matter?

RICHARD: [Laughing.] True: what does it matter? what does anything matter? You see, men have these strange notions, Mrs Anderson; and women see the folly of them.

JUDITH: Women have to lose those they love through them.

RICHARD: They can easily get fresh lovers.

JUDITH: [Revolted.] Oh! [Vehemently.] Do you realize that you are going to kill yourself?

RICHARD: The only man I have any right to kill, Mrs Anderson. Dont be concerned: no woman will lose her lover through my death. [Smiling.] Bless you, nobody cares for me. Have you heard that my mother is dead?

JUDITH: Dead!

RICHARD: Of heart disease—in the night. Her last word to me was her curse: I dont think I could have borne her blessing. My other relatives will not grieve much on my account. Essie will cry for a day or two; but I have provided for her: I made my own will last night.

JUDITH: [Stonily, after a moment's silence.] And I!

RICHARD: [Surprised.] You?

JUDITH: Yes, I. Am I not to care at all?

RICHARD: [Gaily and bluntly.] Not a scrap. Oh, you expressed your feelings towards me very frankly yesterday. What happened may have softened you for the moment; but believe me, Mrs Anderson, you dont like a bone in my skin or a hair on my head. I shall be as good a riddance at 12 today as I should have been at 12 yesterday.

JUDITH: [Her voice trembling.] What can I do to shew you that you are mistaken.

RICHARD: Dont trouble. I'll give you credit for liking me a little better than you did. All I say is that my death will not break your heart.

JUDITH: [Almost in a whisper.] How do you know? [She puts her hands on his shoulders and looks intently at him.]

RICHARD: [Amazed—divining the truth.] Mrs Anderson! [The bell of the town clock strikes the quarter. He collects himself, and removes her hands, saying rather coldly.] Excuse me: they will be here for me presently. It is too late.

JUDITH: It is not too late. Call me as witness: they will never kill you when they know how heroically you have acted.

RICHARD: [With some scorn.] Indeed! But if I dont go through with it, where will the heroism be? I shall simply have tricked them; and theyll hang me for that like a dog. Serve me right too!

JUDITH: [Wildly.] Oh, I believe you want to die.

RICHARD: [Obstinately.] No I dont.

JUDITH: Then why not try to save yourself? I implore you—listen. You said just now that you saved him for my sake—yes [Clutching him as he recoils with a gesture of denial.] a little for my sake. Well, save yourself for my sake. And I will go with you to the end of the world.

RICHARD: [Taking her by the wrists and holding her a little way from him, looking steadily at her.] Judith.

JUDITH: [*Breathless—delighted at the name.*] Yes.

RICHARD: If I said—to please you—that I did what I did ever so little for your sake, I lied as men always lie to women. You know how much I have lived with worthless men —aye, and worthless women too. Well, they could all rise to some sort of goodness and kindness when they were in love. [*The word love comes from him with true Puritan scorn.*] That has taught me to set very little store by the goodness that only comes out red hot. What I did last night, I did in cold blood, caring not half so much for your husband, or [*Ruthlessly.*] for you [*She droops, stricken.*] as I do for myself. I had no motive and no interest: all I can tell you is that when it came to the point whether I would take my neck out of the noose and put another man's into it, I could not do it. I dont know why not: I see myself as a fool for my pains; but I could not and I cannot. I have been brought up standing by the law of my own nature; and I may not go against it, gallows or no gallows. [*She has slowly raised her head and is now looking full at him.*] I should have done the same for any other man in the town, or any other man's wife. [*Releasing her.*] Do you understand that?

JUDITH: Yes: you mean that you do not love me.

RICHARD: [*Revolted—with fierce contempt.*] Is that all it means to you?

JUDITH: What more—what worse—can it mean to me? [*The sergeant knocks. The blow on the door jars on her heart.*] Oh, one moment more. [*She throws herself on her knees.*] I pray to you—

RICHARD: Hush! [*Calling.*] Come in. [*The sergeant unlocks the door and opens it. The guard is with him.*]

SERGEANT: [*Coming in.*] Time's up, sir.

RICHARD: Quite ready, Sergeant. Now, my dear. [*He attempts to raise her.*]

JUDITH: [*Clinging to him.*] Only one thing more—I entreat, I implore you. Let me be present in the court. I have seen Major Swindon: he said I should be allowed if you asked it. You will ask it. It is my last request: I shall never ask you anything again. [*She clasps his knee.*] I beg and pray it of you.

RICHARD: If I do, will you be silent?

JUDITH: Yes.

RICHARD: You will keep faith?

JUDITH: I will keep—[*She breaks down, sobbing.*]

RICHARD: [*Taking her arm to lift her.*] Just—her other arm, Sergeant.

[*They go out, she sobbing convulsively, supported by the two men.*]

[*Meanwhile, the Council Chamber is ready for the court martial. It is a large, lofty room, with a chair of state in the middle under a tall canopy with a gilt crown, and maroon curtains with the royal monogram G.R. In front of the chair is a table, also draped in maroon, with a bell, a heavy inkstand, and writing materials on it. Several chairs are set at the table. The door is at the right hand of the occupant of the chair of state when it has an occupant: at present it is empty.*]

MAJOR SWINDON, *a pale, sandy-haired, very conscientious looking man of about 45, sits at the end of the table with his back to the door, writing. He is alone until the sergeant announces the* GENERAL *in a subdued manner which suggests that* GENTLEMANLY JOHNNY *has been making his presence felt rather heavily.*]

SERGEANT: The General, sir.

[SWINDON *rises hastily. The general comes in: the sergeant goes out.* GENERAL BURGOYNE *is 55, and very well preserved. He is a man of fashion, gallant enough to have made a distinguished marriage by an elopement, witty enough to write successful comedies, aristocratically-connected enough to have had opportunities of high military distinction. His eyes, large, brilliant, apprehensive, and intelligent, are his most remarkable feature: without them his fine nose and small mouth would suggest rather more fastidiousness and less force than go to the making of a first rate general. Just now the eyes are angry and tragic, and the mouth and nostrils tense.*]

BURGOYNE: Major Swindon, I presume.

SWINDON: Yes. General Burgoyne, if I mistake not. [*They bow to one another ceremoniously.*] I am glad to have the support of your presence this morning. It is not particularly lively business, hanging this poor devil of a minister.

BURGOYNE: [*Throwing himself into* SWINDON'S *chair.*] No, sir, it is not. It is making too much of the fellow to execute him: what more could you have done if he had been a member of the Church of England? Martyrdom, sir, is what these people like: it is the only way in which a man can become famous without ability. However, you have committed us to hanging him; and the sooner he is hanged the better.

SWINDON: We have arranged it for 12 o'clock. Nothing remains to be done except to try him.

BURGOYNE: [*Looking at him with suppressed anger.*] Nothing—except to save your own necks, perhaps. Have you heard the news from Springtown?

SWINDON: Nothing special. The latest reports are satisfactory.

BURGOYNE: [*Rising in amazement.*] Satisfactory, sir! Satisfactory!! [*He stares at him for a moment, and then adds, with grim intensity.*] I am glad you take that view of them.

SWINDON: [*Puzzled.*] Do I understand that in your opinion—

BURGOYNE: I do not express my opinion. I never stoop to that habit of profane language which unfortunately coarsens our profession. If I did, sir, perhaps I should be able to express my opinion of the news from Springtown—the news which you [*Severely.*] have apparently not heard. How soon do you get news from your supports here?—in the course of a month, eh?

SWINDON: [*Turning sulkily.*] I suppose the reports have been taken to you, sir, instead of to me. Is there anything serious?

BURGOYNE: [*Taking a report from his pocket and holding it up.*] Springtown's in the hands of the rebels. [*He throws the report on the table.*]

SWINDON: [*Aghast.*] Since yesterday!

BURGOYNE: Since two o'clock this morning. Perhaps we shall be in their hands before two o'clock tomorrow morning. Have you thought of that?

SWINDON: [*Confidently.*] As to that, General, the British soldier will give a good account of himself.

BURGOYNE: [*Bitterly.*] And therefore, I suppose, sir, the British officer need not know his business: the British soldier will get him out of all his blunders with the bayonet. In future, sir, I must ask you to be a little less generous with the blood of your men, and a little more generous with your own brains.

SWINDON: I am sorry I cannot pretend to your intellectual eminence, sir. I can only do my best, and rely on the devotion of my countrymen.

BURGOYNE: [*Suddenly becoming suavely sarcastic.*] May I ask are you writing a melodrama, Major Swindon?

SWINDON: [*Flushing.*] No, sir.

BURGOYNE: What a pity! What a pity! [*Dropping his sarcastic tone and facing him suddenly and seriously.*] Do you at all realize, sir, that we have nothing standing between us and destruction but our own bluff and the sheepishness of these colonists? They are men of the same English stock as ourselves: six to one of us [*Repeating it emphatically.*] six to one, sir; and nearly half our troops are Hessians, Brunswickers, German dragoons, and Indians with scalping knives. These are the countrymen on whose devotion you rely! Suppose the colonists find a leader! Suppose the news from Springtown should turn out to mean that they have already found a leader! What shall we do then? Eh?

SWINDON: [*Sullenly.*] Our duty, sir, I presume.

BURGOYNE: [*Again sarcastic—giving him up as a fool.*] Quite so, quite so. Thank you, Major Swindon, thank you. Now youve settled the question, sir—thrown a flood of light on the situation. What a comfort to me to feel that I have at my side so devoted and able an officer to support me in this emergency! I think, sir, it will probably relieve both our feelings if we proceed to hang this dissenter without further delay [*He strikes the bell.*] especially as I am debarred by my principles from the customary military vent for my feelings. [*The sergeant appears.*] Bring your man in.

SERGEANT: Yes, sir.

BURGOYNE: And mention to any officer you may meet that the court cannot wait any longer for him.

SWINDON: [*Keeping his temper with difficulty.*] The staff is perfectly ready, sir. They have been waiting your convenience for fully half an hour. Perfectly ready, sir.

BURGOYNE: [*Blandly.*] So am I. [*Several officers come in and take their seats. One of them sits at the end of the table furthest from the door, and acts throughout as clerk of the court, making notes of the proceedings. The uniforms are those of the 9th, 20th, 21st, 24th, 47th, 53rd, and 62nd British Infantry. One officer is a Major General of the Royal Artillery. There are also German officers of the Hessian Rifles, and of German dragoon and Brunswicker regiments.*] Oh, good morning, gentlemen. Sorry to disturb you, I am sure. Very good of you to spare us a few moments.

SWINDON: Will you preside, sir?

BURGOYNE: [*Becoming additionally polished, lofty, sarcastic, and urbane now that he is in public.*] No, sir: I feel my own deficiencies too keenly to presume so far. If you will kindly allow me, I will sit at the feet of Gamaliel. [*He takes the chair at the end of the table next the door, and motions* SWINDON *to the chair of state, waiting for him to be seated before sitting down himself.*]

SWINDON: [*Greatly annoyed.*] As you please, sir, I am only trying to do my duty under excessively trying circumstances. [*He takes his place in the chair of state.*]

[BURGOYNE, *relaxing his studied demeanor for the moment, sits down and begins to read the report with knitted brows and careworn looks, reflecting on his desperate situation and* SWINDON's *uselessness.* RICHARD *is brought in.* JUDITH *walks beside him. Two soldiers precede and two follow him, with the sergeant in command. They cross the room to the wall opposite the door; but when* RICHARD *has just passed before the chair of state the sergeant stops him with a touch on the arm, and posts himself behind him, at his elbow.* JUDITH *stands timidly at the wall. The four soldiers place themselves in a squad near her.*]

BURGOYNE: [*Looking up and seeing* JUDITH.] Who is that woman?

SEAGEANT: Prisoner's wife, sir.

SWINDON: [*Nervously.*] She begged me to allow her to be present; and I thought—

BURGOYNE: [*Completing the sentence for him ironically.*] You thought it would be a pleasure for her. Quite so, quite so. [*Blandly.*] Give the lady a chair; and make her thoroughly comfortable.

[*The sergeant fetches a chair and places it near* RICHARD.]

JUDITH: Thank you, sir. [*She sits down after an awe-stricken curtsy to* BURGOYNE, *which he acknowledges by a dignified bend of his head.*]

SWINDON: [*To* RICHARD, *sharply.*] Your name; sir?

RICHARD: [*Affable, but obstinate.*] Come: you dont mean to say that youve brought me here without knowing who I am?

SWINDON: As a matter of form, sir, give your name.

RICHARD: As a matter of form then, my name is Anthony Anderson, Presbyterian minister in this town.

BURGOYNE: [*Interested.*] Indeed! Pray, Mr Anderson, what do you gentlemen believe?

RICHARD: I shall be happy to explain if time is allowed me. I cannot undertake to complete your conversion in less than a fortnight.

SWINDON: [*Snubbing him.*] We are not here to discuss your views.

BURGOYNE: [*With an elaborate bow to the unfortunate* SWINDON.] I stand rebuked.

SWINDON: [*Embarrassed.*] Oh, not you, I as—

BURGOYNE: Don't mention it. [*To* RICHARD, *very politely.*] Any political views, Mr Anderson?

RICHARD: I understand that that is just what we are here to find out.

SWINDON: [*Severely.*] Do you mean to deny that you are a rebel?

RICHARD: I am an American, sir.

SWINDON: What do you expect me to think of that speech, Mr Anderson?

RICHARD: I never expect a soldier to think, sir.

[BURGOYNE *is boundlessly delighted by this retort, which almost reconciles him to the loss of America.*]

SWINDON: [*Whitening with anger.*] I advise you not to be insolent, prisoner.

RICHARD: You cant help yourself, General. When you make up your mind to hang a man, you put yourself at a disadvantage with him. Why should I be civil to you? I may as well be hanged for a sheep as a lamb.

SWINDON: You have no right to assume that the court has made up its mind without a fair trial. And you will please not address me as General. I am Major Swindon.

RICHARD: A thousand pardons. I thought I had the honor of addressing Gentlemanly Johnny.

[*Sensation among the officers. The sergeant has a narrow escape from a guffaw.*]

BURGOYNE: [*With extreme suavity.*] I believe I am Gentlemanly Johnny, sir, at your service. My more intimate friends call me General Burgoyne. [RICHARD *bows with perfect politeness.*] You will understand, sir, I hope, since you seem to be a gentleman and a man of some spirit in spite of your calling, that if we should have the misfortune to hang you, we shall do so as a mere matter of political necessity and military duty, without any personal ill-feeling.

RICHARD: Oh, quite so. That makes all the difference in the world, of course.

[*They all smile in spite of themselves; and some of the younger officers burst out laughing.*]

JUDITH: [*Her dread and horror deepening at every one of these jests and compliments.*] How can you?

RICHARD: You promised to be silent.

BURGOYNE: [*To* JUDITH, *with studied courtesy.*] Believe me, Madam, your husband is placing us under the greatest obligation by taking this very disagreeable business so thoroughly in the spirit of a gentleman. Sergeant: give Mr Anderson a chair. [*The sergeant does so.* RICHARD *sits down.*] Now, Major Swindon: we are waiting for you.

SWINDON: You are aware, I presume, Mr Anderson, of your obligations as a subject of His Majesty King George the Third.

RICHARD: I am aware, sir, that His Majesty King George the Third is about to hang me because I object to Lord North's robbing me.

SWINDON: That is a treasonable speech, sir.

RICHARD: [*Briefly.*] Yes. I meant it to be.

BURGOYNE: [*Strongly deprecating this line of defence, but still polite.*] Don't you think, Mr Anderson, that this is rather—if you will excuse the word—a vulgar line to take? Why should you cry out robbery because of a stamp duty and a tea duty and so forth? After all, it is the essence of your position as a gentleman that you pay with a good grace.

RICHARD: It is not the money, General. But to be swindled by a pig-headed lunatic like King George—

SWINDON: [*Scandalized.*] Chut, sir—silence!

SEARGENT: [*In stentorian tones, greatly shocked.*] Silence!

BURGOYNE: [*Unruffled.*] Ah, that is another point of view. My position does not allow of my going into that, except in private. But [*Shrugging his shoulders.*] of course, Mr Anderson, if you are determined to be hanged [JUDITH *flinches.*] theres

nothing more to be said. An unusual taste! however [*With a final shrug.*]—!

SWINDON: [*To* BURGOYNE.] Shall we call witnesses?

RICHARD: What need is there of witnesses? If the townspeople here had listened to me, you would have found the streets barricaded, the houses loopholed, and the people in arms to hold the town against you to the last man. But you arrived, unfortunately, before we had got out of the talking stage; and then it was too late.

SWINDON: [*Severely.*] Well, sir, we shall teach you and your townspeople a lesson they will not forget. Have you anything more to say?

RICHARD: I think you might have the decency to treat me as a prisoner of war, and shoot me like a man instead of hanging me like a dog.

BURGOYNE: [*Sympathetically.*] Now there, Mr Anderson, you talk like a civilian, if you will excuse my saying so. Have you any idea of the average marksmanship of the army of His Majesty King George the Third? If we make you up a firing party, what will happen? Half of them will miss you: the rest will make a mess of the business and leave you to the provo-marshal's pistol. Whereas we can hang you in a perfectly workmanlike and agreeable way. [*Kindly.*] Let me persuade you to be hanged, Mr Anderson?

JUDITH: [*Sick with horror.*] My God!

RICHARD: [*To* JUDITH]. Your promise! [*To* BURGOYNE.] Thank you, General: that view of the case did not occur to me before. To oblige you, I withdraw my objection to the rope. Hang me, by all means.

BURGOYNE: [*Smoothly.*] Will 12 o'clock suit you, Mr Anderson?

RICHARD: I shall be at your disposal then, General.

BURGOYNE: [*Rising.*] Nothing more to be said, gentlemen. [*They all rise.*]

JUDITH: [*Rushing to the table.*] Oh, you are not going to murder a man like that, without a proper trial—without thinking of what you are doing—without—[*She cannot find words.*]

RICHARD: Is this how you keep your promise?

JUDITH: If I am not to speak, you must. Defend yourself: save yourself: tell them the truth.

RICHARD: [*Worriedly.*] I have told them truth enough to hang me ten times over.

If you say another word you will risk other lives; but you will not save mine.

BURGOYNE: My good lady, our only desire is to save unpleasantness. What satisfaction would it give you to have a solemn fuss made, with my friend Swindon in a black cap and so forth? I am sure we are greatly indebted to the admirable tact and gentlemanly feeling shewn by your husband.

JUDITH: [*Throwing the words in his face.*] Oh, you are mad. Is it nothing to you what wicked thing you do if only you do it like a gentleman? Is it nothing to you whether you are a murderer or not, if only you murder in a red coat? [*Desperately.*] You shall not hang him: that man is not my husband.

[*The officers look at one another, and whisper: some of the Germans asking their neighbors to explain what the woman had said.* BURGOYNE, *who has been visibly shaken by* JUDITH's *reproach, recovers himself promptly at this new development.* RICHARD *meanwhile raises his voice above the buzz.*]

RICHARD: I appeal to you, gentlemen, to put an end to this. She will not believe that she cannot save me. Break up the court.

BURGOYNE: [*In a voice so quiet and firm that it restores silence at once.*] One moment, Mr Anderson. One moment, gentlemen. [*He resumes his seat.* SWINDON *and the officers follow his example.*] Let me understand you clearly, madam. Do you mean that this gentleman is not your husband, or merely—I wish to put this with all delicacy—that you are not his wife?

JUDITH: I dont know what you mean. I say that he is not my husband—that my husband has escaped. This man took his place to save him. Ask anyone in the town—send out into the street for the first person you find there, and bring him in as a witness. He will tell you that the prisoner is not Anthony Anderson.

BURGOYNE: [*Quietly, as before.*] Sergeant.

SERGEANT: Yes, sir.

BURGOYNE: Go out into the street and bring in the first townsman you see there.

SERGEANT: [*Making for the door.*] Yes, sir.

BURGOYNE: [*As the sergeant passes.*] The first clean, sober townsman you see.

SERGEANT: Yes, sir. [*He goes out.*]

BURGOYNE: Sit down, Mr Anderson—if I may call you so for the present. [RICHARD *sits down.*] Sit down, madam, whilst we wait. Give the lady a newspaper.

RICHARD: [*Indignantly.*] Shame!

BURGOYNE: [*Keenly, with a half smile.*] If you are not her husband, sir, the case is not a serious one—for her. [RICHARD *bites his lip, silenced.*]

JUDITH: [*To* RICHARD, *as she returns to her seat.*] I couldnt help it. [*He shakes his head. She sits down.*]

BURGOYNE: You will understand, of course, Mr Anderson, that you must not build on this little incident. We are bound to make an example of somebody.

RICHARD: I quite understand. I suppose theres no use in my explaining.

BURGOYNE: I think we should prefer independent testimony, if you dont mind.

[*The sergeant, with a packet of papers in his hand, returns conducting* CHRISTY, *who is much scared.*]

SERGEANT: [*Giving* BURGOYNE *the packet.*] Dispatches, sir. Delivered by a corporal of the 33rd. Dead beat with hard riding, sir.

[BURGOYNE *opens the dispatches, and presently becomes absorbed in them. They are so serious as to take his attention completely from the court martial.*]

THE SERGEANT: [*To* CHRISTY.] Now then. Attention; and take your hat off. [*He posts himself in charge of* CHRISTY, *who stands on* BURGOYNE's *side of the court.*]

RICHARD: [*In his usual bullying tone to* CHRISTY.] Don't be frightened, you fool: youre only wanted as a witness. Theyre not going to hang you.

SWINDON: Whats your name?

CHRISTY: Christy.

RICHARD: [*Impatiently.*] Christopher Dudgeon, you blatant idiot. Give your full name.

SWINDON: Be silent, prisoner. You must not prompt the witness.

RICHARD: Very well. But I warn you youll get nothing out of him unless you shake it out of him. He has been too well brought up by a pious mother to have any sense or manhood left in him.

BURGOYNE: [*Springing up and speaking to the sergeant in a startling voice.*] Where is the man who brought these?

SERGEANT: In the guard-room, sir.

[BURGOYNE *goes out with a haste that sets the officers exchanging looks.*]

SWINDON: [*To* CHRISTY.] Do you know

Anthony Anderson, the Presbyterian minister?

CHRISTY: Of course I do. [*Implying that* SWINDON *must be an ass not to know it.*]

SWINDON: Is he here?

CHRISTY: [*Staring round.*] I dont know.

SWINDON: Do you see him?

CHRISTY: No.

SWINDON: You seem to know the prisoner?

CHRISTY: Do you mean Dick?

SWINDON: Which is Dick?

CHRISTY: [*Pointing to* RICHARD.] Him.

SWINDON: What is his name?

CHRISTY: Dick.

RICHARD: Answer properly, you jumping jackass. What do they know about Dick?

CHRISTY: Well, you are Dick, aint you? What am I to say?

SWINDON: Address me, sir; and do you, prisoner, be silent. Tell us who the prisoner is.

CHRISTY: He's my brother Dick—Richard —Richard Dudgeon.

SWINDON: Your brother!

CHRISTY: Yes.

SWINDON: You are sure he is not Anderson.

CHRISTY: Who?

RICHARD: [*Exasperatedly.*] Me, me, me, you—

SWINDON: Silence, sir.

SERGEANT: [*Shouting.*] Silence.

RICHARD: [*Impatiently.*] Yah! [*To* Christy.] He wants to know am I Minister Anderson. Tell him, and stop grinning like a zany.

CHRISTY: [*Grinning more than ever.*] You Pastor Anderson! [*To* SWINDON.] Why, Mr Anderson's a minister—a very good man; and Dick's a bad character: the respectable people wont speak to him. He's the bad brother: I'm the good one. [*The officers laugh outright. The soldiers grin.*]

SWINDON: Who arrested this man?

SERGEANT: I did, sir. I found him in the minister's house, sitting at tea with the lady with his coat off, quite at home. If he isnt married to her, he ought to be.

SWINDON: Did he answer to the minister's name?

SERGEANT: Yes, sir, but not to a minister's nature. You ask the chaplain, sir.

SWINDON: [*To* RICHARD, *threateningly.*] So, sir, you have attempted to cheat us. And your name is Richard Dudgeon?

RICHARD: Youve found it out at last, have you?

SWINDON: Dudgeon is a name well known to us, eh?

RICHARD: Yes: Peter Dudgeon, whom you murdered, was my uncle.

SWINDON: Hm! [*He compresses his lips, and looks at* RICHARD *with vindictive gravity.*]

CHRISTY: Are they going to hang you, Dick?

RICHARD: Yes. Get out: theyve done with you.

CHRISTY: And I may keep the china peacocks?

RICHARD: [*Jumping up.*] Get out. Get out, you blithering baboon, you. [CHRISTY *flies, panicstricken.*]

SWINDON: [*Rising—all rise.*] Since you have taken the minister's place, Richard Dudgeon, you shall go through with it. The execution will take place at 12 o'clock as arranged; and unless Anderson surrenders before then, you shall take his place on the gallows. Sergeant: take your man out.

JUDITH: [*Distracted.*] No, no—

SWINDON: [*Fiercely dreading a renewal of her entreaties.*] Take that woman away.

RICHARD: [*Springing across the table with a tiger-like bound ,and seizing* SWINDON *by the throat.*] You infernal scoundrel—

[*The sergeant rushes to the rescue from one side, the soldiers from the other. They seize* RICHARD *and drag him back to his place.* SWINDON, *who has been thrown supine on the table, rises, arranging his stock. He is about to speak, when he is anticipated by* BURGOYNE, *who has just appeared at the door with two papers in his hand: a white letter and a blue dispatch.*]

BURGOYNE: [*Advancing to the table, elaborately cool.*] What is this? Whats happening? Mr Anderson: I'm astonished at you.

RICHARD: I am sorry I disturbed you, General. I merely wanted to strangle your understrapper there. [*Breaking out violently at* SWINDON.] Why do you raise the devil in me by bullying the woman like that? You oatmeal faced dog, I'd twist your cursed head off with the greatest satisfaction. [*He puts out his hands to the sergeant.*] Here: handcuff me, will you; or I'll not undertake to keep my fingers off him.

[*The sergeant takes out a pair of*

handcuffs and looks to BURGOYNE *for instructions.*]

BURGOYNE: Have you addressed profane language to the lady, Major Swindon?

SWINDON: [*Very angry.*] No, sir, certainly not. That question should not have been put to me. I ordered the woman to be removed, as she was disorderly; and the fellow sprang at me. Put away those handcuffs. I am perfectly able to take care of myself.

RICHARD: Now you talk like a man, I have no quarrel with you.

BURGOYNE: Mr Anderson—

SWINDON: His name is Dudgeon, sir, Richard Dudgeon. He is an imposter.

BURGOYNE: [*Brusquely.*] Nonsense, sir: you hanged Dudgeon at Springtown.

RICHARD: It was my uncle, General.

BURGOYNE: Oh, your uncle. [*To* SWINDON, *handsomely.*] I beg your pardon, Major Swindon. [SWINDON *acknowledges the apology stiffly.* BURGOYNE *turns to* RICHARD.] We are somewhat unfortunate in our relations with your family. Well, Mr. Dudgeon, what I wanted to ask you is this. Who is [*Reading the name from the letter.*] William Maindeck Parshotter?

RICHARD: He is the Mayor of Springtown.

BURGOYNE: Is William—Maindeck and so on—a man of his word?

RICHARD: Is he selling you anything?

BURGOYNE: No.

RICHARD: Then you may depend on him.

BURGOYNE: Thank you, Mr—'m Dudgeon. By the way, since you are not Mr Anderson, do we still—eh, Major Swindon? [*Meaning "do we still hang him?".*]

RICHARD: The arrangements are unaltered, General.

BURGOYNE: Ah, indeed. I am sorry. Good morning, Mr Dudgeon. Good morning, madam.

RICHARD: [*Interrupting* JUDITH *almost fiercely as she is about to make some wild appeal, and taking her arm resolutely.*] Not one word more. Come.

[*She looks imploringly at him, but is overborne by his determination. They are marched out by the four soldiers: the sergeant very sulky, walking between* SWINDON *and* RICHARD, *whom he watches as if he were a dangerous animal.*]

BURGOYNE: Gentlemen: we need not detain you. Major Swindon: a word with you. [*The officers go out.* BURGOYNE *waits with unruffled serenity until the last of them disappears. Then he becomes very grave, and addresses* SWINDON *for the first time without his title.*] Swindon: do you know what this is [*Shewing him the letter.*]?

SWINDON: What?

BURGOYNE: A demand for a safe-conduct for an officer of their militia to come here and arrange terms with us.

SWINDON: Oh, they are giving in.

BURGOYNE: They add that they are sending the man who raised Springtown last night and drove us out; so that we may know that we are dealing with an officer of importance.

SWINDON: Pooh!

BURGOYNE: He will be fully empowered to arrange the terms of—guess what.

SWINDON: Their surrender, I hope.

BURGOYNE: No: our evacuation of the town. They offer us just six hours to clear out.

SWINDON: What monstrous impudence!

BURGOYNE: What shall we do, eh?

SWINDON: March on Springtown and strike a decisive blow at once.

BURGOYNE: [*Quietly.*] Hm! [*Turning to the door.*] Come to the adjutant's office.

SWINDON: What for?

BURGOYNE: To write out that safe-conduct. [*He puts his hand to the door knob to open it.*]

SWINDON: [*Who has not budged.*] General Burgoyne.

BURGOYNE: [*Returning.*] Sir?

SWINDON: It is my duty to tell you, sir, that I do not consider the threats of a mob of rebellious tradesmen a sufficient reason for our giving way.

BURGOYNE: [*Imperturbable.*] Suppose I resign my command to you, what will you do?

SWINDON: I will undertake to do what we have marched south from Quebec to do, and what General Howe has marched north from New York to do: effect a junction at Albany and wipe out the rebel army with our united forces.

BURGOYNE: [*Enigmatically.*] And will you wipe out our enemies in London, too?

SWINDON: In London! What enemies?

BURGOYNE: [*Forcibly.*] Jobbery and snobbery, incompetence and Red Tape. [*He holds up the dispatch and adds, with despair in his face and voice.*] I have just learnt, sir, that General Howe is still in New York.

SWINDON: [*Thunderstruck.*] Good God! He has disobeyed orders!

BURGOYNE: [*With sardonic calm.*] He has received no orders, sir. Some gentleman in London forgot to dispatch them: he was leaving town for his holiday, I believe. To avoid upsetting his arrangements, England will lose her American colonies; and in a few days you and I will be at Saratoga with 5,000 men to face 18,000 rebels in an impregnable position.

SWINDON: [*Appalled.*] Impossible!

BURGOYNE: [*Coldly.*] I beg your pardon?

SWINDON: I cant believe it! What will History say?

BURGOYNE: History, sir, will tell lies, as usual. Come: we must send the safe-conduct. [*He goes out.*]

SWINDON: [*Following distractedly.*] My God, my God! We shall be wiped out.

[*As noon approaches there is excitement in the market place. The gallows which hangs there permanently for the terror of evildoers, with such minor advertizers and examples of crime as the pillory, the whipping post, and the stocks, has a new rope attached, with the noose hitched up to one of the uprights, out of reach of the boys. Its ladder, too, has been brought out and placed in position by the town beadle, who stands by to guard it from unauthorized climbing. The Websterbridge townsfolk are present in force, and in high spirits; for the news has spread that it is the devil's disciple and not the minister that King George and his terrible general are about to hang: consequently the execution can be enjoyed without any misgiving as to its righteousness, or to the cowardice of allowing it to take place without a struggle. There is even some fear of a disappointment as midday approaches and the arrival of the beadle with the ladder remains the only sign of preparation. But at last reassuring shouts of Here they come: Here they are, are heard; and a company of soldiers with fixed bayonets, half British infantry, half Hessians, tramp quickly into the middle of the market place, driving the crowd to the sides.*]

THE SERGEANT: Halt. Front. Dress. [*The soldiers change their column into a square*] *enclosing the gallows, their petty officers, energetically led by the sergeant, hustling the persons who find themselves inside the square out at the corners.*] Now then! Out of it with you: out of it. Some o youll get strung up yourselves presently. Form that square there, will you, you damned Hoosians. No use talkin German to them: talk to their toes with the butt ends of your muskets: theyll understand that. Get out of it, will you. [*He comes upon* JUDITH, *standing near the gallows.*] Now then: youve no call here.

JUDITH: May I not stay? What harm am I doing?

SERGEANT: I want none of your argufying. You ought to be ashamed of yourself, running to see a man hanged thats not your husband. And he's no better than yourself. I told my major he was a gentleman; and then he goes and tries to strangle him, and calls his blessed Majesty a lunatic. So out of it with you, double quick.

JUDITH: Will you take these two silver dollars and let me stay?

[*The sergeant, without an instant's hesitation, looks quickly and furtively round as he shoots the money dexterously into his pocket. Then he raises his voice in virtuous indignation.*]

THE SERGEANT: Me take money in the execution of my duty! Certainly not. Now I'll tell you what I'll do, to teach you to corrupt the King's officer. I'll put you under arrest until the execution's over. You just stand there; and dont let me see you as much as move from that spot until youre let. [*With a swift wink at her he points to the corner of the square behind the gallows on his right, and turns noisily away, shouting.*] Now then, dress up and keep em back, will you.

[*Cries of Hush and Silence are heard among the townsfolk; and the sound of a military band, playing the Dead March from Saul, is heard. The crowd becomes quiet at once; and the sergeant and petty officers, hurrying to the back of the square, with a few whispered orders and some stealthy hustling cause it to open and admit the funeral procession, which is protected from the crowd by a double file of soldiers. First come* BURGOYNE *and* SWINDON, *who, on entering the square, glance with distaste at the gallows, and avoid passing under it by wheeling a*

*little to the right and stationing them-
selves on that side. Then* MR. BRUD-
ENELL, *the chaplain, in his surplice,
with his prayer book open in his hand,
walking beside* RICHARD, *who is moody
and disorderly. He walks doggedly
through the gallows framework, and
posts himself a little in front of it.
Behind him comes the executioner, a
stalwart soldier in his shirtsleeves. Following him, two soldiers haul a light
military waggon. Finally comes the
band, which posts itself at the back of
the square, and finishes the Dead
March.* JUDITH, *watching* RICHARD
*painfully, steals down to the gallows;
and stands leaning against its right
post. During the conversation which
follows, the two soldiers place the
cart under the gallows, and stand by
the shafts, which point backwards.
The executioner takes a set of steps
from the cart and places it ready for
the prisoner to mount. Then he climbs
the tall ladder which stands against the
gallows, and cuts the string by which
the rope is hitched up; so that the
noose drops dangling over the cart,
into which he steps as he descends.*]

RICHARD: [*With suppressed impatience,
to* BRUDENELL.] Look here, sir: this is no
place for a man of your profession. Hadnt
you better go away?

SWINDON: I appeal to you, prisoner, if
you have any sense of decency left, to listen
to the ministrations of the chaplain, and pay
due heed to the solemnity of the occasion.

THE CHAPLAIN: [*Gently reproving* RICH-
ARD.] Try to control yourself, and submit to
the divine will. [*He lifts his book to proceed
with the service.*]

RICHARD: Answer for your own will, sir,
and those of your accomplices here [*Indicating* BURGOYNE *and* SWINDON.]: I see little
divinity about them or you. You talk to me
of Christianity when you are in the act of
hanging your enemies. Was there ever such
blasphemous nonsense! [*To* SWINDON, *more
rudely.*] Youve got up the solemnity of the
occasion, as you call it, to impress the people
with your own dignity—Handel's music and
a clergyman to make murder look like piety!
Do you suppose *I* am going to help you?
Youve asked me to choose the rope because
you don't know your own trade well enough
to shoot me properly. Well, hang away and
have done with it.

SWINDON: [*To the chaplain.*] Can you do
nothing with him, Mr Brudenell?

CHAPLAIN: I will try, sir. [*Beginning to
read.*] Man that is born of woman hath—

RICHARD: [*Fixing his eyes on him.*]
"Thou shalt not kill."
[*The book drops in* BRUDENELL's
hands].

CHAPLAIN: [*Confessing his embarrassment.*] What am I to say, Mr Dudgeon?

RICHARD: Let me alone, man, cant you?

BURGOYNE: [*With extreme urbanity.*] I
think Mr Brudenell, that as the usual professional observations seem to strike Mr
Dudgeon as incongruous under the circumstances, you had better omit them until—er
—until Mr Dudgeon can no longer be in-
convenienced by them. [BRUDENELL, *with a
shrug, shuts his book and retires behind the
gallows.*] You seem in a hurry, Mr Dudgeon.

RICHARD: [*With the horror of death upon
him.*] Do you think this is a pleasant sort of
thing to be kept waiting for? Youve made
up your mind to commit murder: well, do
it and have done with it.

BURGOYNE: Mr Dudgeon: we are only
doing this—

RICHARD: Because youre paid to do it.

SWINDON: You insolent—[*He swallows
his rage.*]

BURGOYNE: [*With much charm of manner.*] Ah, I am really sorry that you should
think that, Mr Dudgeon. If you knew what
my commission cost me, and what my pay
is, you would think better of me. I should
be glad to part from you on friendly terms.

RICHARD: Hark ye, General Burgoyne. If
you think that I like being hanged, youre
mistaken. I dont like it; and I dont mean to
pretend that I do. And if you think I'm
obliged to you for hanging me in a gentlemanly way, youre wrong there too. I take
the whole business in devilish bad part; and
the only satisfaction I have in it is that
youll feel a good deal meaner than I'll look
when it's over. [*He turns away, and is
striding to the cart when* JUDITH *advances
and interposes with her arms stretched out
to him.* RICHARD, *feeling that a very little
will upset his self-possession, shrinks from
her, crying.*] What are you doing here? This
is no place for you. [*She makes a gesture as
if to touch him. He recoils impatiently.*] No:
go away, go away: youll unnerve me. Take
her away, will you.

JUDITH: Wont you bid me goodbye?

RICHARD: [*Allowing her to take his hand.*] Oh goodbye, goodbye. Now go—go —quickly. [*She clings to his hand—will not be put off with so cold a last farewell—at last, as he tries to disengage himself, throws herself on his breast in agony.*]

SWINDON: [*Angrily to the sergeant, who, alarmed at* JUDITH's *movement, has come from the back of the square to pull her back, and stopped irresolutely on finding that he is too late.*] How is this? Why is she inside the lines?

SERGEANT: [*Guiltily.*] I dunno, sir. She's that artful—cant keep her away.

BURGOYNE: You were bribed.

SERGEANT: [*Protesting.*] No, sir—

SWINDON: [*Severely.*] Fall back. [*He obeys.*]

RICHARD: [*Imploringly to those around him, and finally to* BURGOYNE, *as the least stolid of them.*] Take her away. Do you think I want a woman near me now?

BURGOYNE: [*Going to* JUDITH *and taking her hand.*] Here, madam: you had better keep inside the lines; but stand here behind us; and dont look.

[RICHARD, *with a great sobbing sigh of relief as she releases him and turns to* BURGOYNE, *flies for refuge to the cart and mounts into it. The executioner takes off his coat and pinions him.*]

JUDITH: [*Resisting* BURGOYNE *quietly and drawing her hand away.*] No: I must stay. I wont look. [*She goes to the right of the gallows. She tries to look at* RICHARD, *but turns away with a frightful shudder, and falls on her knees in prayer.* BRUDENELL *comes towards her from the back of the square.*]

BURGOYNE: [*Nodding approvingly as she kneels.*] Ah, quite so. Do not disturb her, Mr Brudenell: that will do very nicely. [BRUDENELL *nods also, and withdraws a little, watching her sympathetically.* BURGOYNE *resumes his former position, and takes out a handsome gold chronometer.*] Now then, are those preparations made? We must not detain Mr Dudgeon.

[*By this time* RICHARD's *hands are bound behind him; and the noose is round his neck. The two soldiers take the shafts of the waggon, ready to pull it away. The executioner, standing in the cart behind* RICHARD, *makes a sign to the sergeant.*]

SERGEANT: [*To* BURGOYNE.] Ready, sir.

BURGOYNE: Have you anything more to say, Mr Dudgeon? It wants two minutes of twelve still.

RICHARD: [*In the strong voice of a man who has conquered the bitterness of death.*] Your watch is two minutes slow by the town clock, which I can see from here, General. [*The town clock strikes the first stroke of twelve. Involuntarily the people flinch at the sound, and a subdued groan breaks from them.*] Amen! my life for the world's future!

ANDERSON: [*Shouting as he rushes into the market place.*] Amen; and stop the execution. [*He bursts through the line of soldiers opposite* BURGOYNE, *and rushes, panting, to the gallows.*] I am Anthony Anderson, the man you want.

[*The crowd, intensely excited, listens with all its ears.* JUDITH, *half rising; stares at him; then lifts her hands like one whose dearest prayer has been granted.*]

SWINDON: Indeed. Then you are just in time to take your place on the gallows. Arrest him.

[*At a sign from the sergeant, two soldiers come forward to seize* ANDERSON.]

ANDERSON: [*Thrusting a paper under* SWINDON's *nose.*] Theres my safe-conduct, sir.

SWINDON: [*Taken aback.*] Safe-conduct! Are you—!

ANDERSON: [*Emphatically.*] I am. [*The two soldiers take him by the elbows.*] Tell these men to take their hands off me.

SWINDON: [*To the men.*] Let him go.

SERGEANT: Fall back.

[*The two men return to their places. The townsfolk raise a cheer; and begin to exchange exultant looks, with a presentiment of triumph as they see their Pastor speaking with their enemies in the gate.*]

ANDERSON: [*Exhaling a deep breath of relief, and dabbing his perspiring brow with his handkerchief.*] Thank God, I was in time!

BURGOYNE: [*Calm as ever, and still watch in hand.*] Ample time, sir. Plenty of time. I should never dream of hanging any gentleman by an American clock. [*He puts up his watch.*]

ANDERSON: Yes: we are some minutes ahead of you already, General. Now tell them to take the rope from the neck of that American citizen.

BURGOYNE: [*To the executioner in the cart—very politely.*] Kindly undo Mr Dudgeon.

[*The executioner takes the rope from* RICHARD'S *neck, unties his hands, and helps him on with his coat.*]

JUDITH: [*Stealing timidly to* ANDERSON.] Tony.

ANDERSON: [*Putting his arm round her shoulders and bantering her affectionately.*] Well, what do you think of your husband now, eh?—eh?—eh? ? ?

JUDITH: I am ashamed—[*She hides her face against his breast.*]

BURGOYNE: [*To* SWINDON.] You look disappointed, Major Swindon.

SWINDON: You look defeated, General Burgoyne.

BURGOYNE: I am, sir; and I am humane enough to be glad of it. [RICHARD *jumps down from the cart,* BRUDENELL *offering his hand to help him, and runs to* ANDERSON, *whose left hand he shakes heartily, the right being occupied by* JUDITH.] By the way, Mr Anderson, I do not quite understand. The safe-conduct was for a commander of the militia. I understand you are a—[*He looks as pointedly as his good manners permit at the riding boots, the pistols, and* RICHARD'S *coat, and adds.*]—a clergyman.

ANDERSON: [*Between* JUDITH *and* RICHARD.] Sir: it is in the hour of trial that a man finds his true profession. This foolish young man [*Placing his hand on* RICHARD'S *shoulder.*] boasted himself the Devil's Disciple; but when the hour of trial came to him, he found that it was his destiny to suffer and be faithful to the death. I thought myself a decent minister of the gospel of peace; but when the hour of trial came to me, I found that it was my destiny to be a man of action, and that my place was amid the thunder of the captains and the shouting. So I am starting life at fifty as Captain Anthony Anderson of the Springtown militia; and the Devil's Disciple here will start presently as the Reverend Richard Dudgeon, and wag his pow in my old pulpit, and give good advice to this silly sentimental little wife of mine. [*Putting his other hand on her shoulder. She steals a glance at* RICHARD *to see how the prospect pleases him*]. Your mother told me, Richard, that I should never have chosen Judith if I'd been born for the ministry. I am afraid she was right; so, by your leave, you may keep my coat and I'll keep yours.

RICHARD: Minister—I should say Captain. I have behaved like a fool.

JUDITH: Like a hero.

RICHARD: Much the same thing, perhaps. [*With some bitterness towards himself.*] But no: if I had been any good, I should have done for you what you did for me, instead of making a vain sacrifice.

ANDERSON: Not vain, my boy. It takes all sorts to make a world—saints as well as soldiers. [*Turning to* BURGOYNE.] And now, General, time presses; and America is in a hurry. Have you realized that though you may occupy towns and win battles, you cannot conquer a nation?

BURGOYNE: My good sir, without a Conquest you cannot have an aristocracy. Come and settle the matter at my quarters.

ANDERSON: At your service, sir. [*To* RICHARD.] See Judith home for me, will you, my boy. [*He hands her over to him.*] Now, General. [*He goes busily up the market place towards the Town Hall, leaving* JUDITH *and* RICHARD *together.* BURGOYNE *follows him a step or two; then checks himself and turns to* RICHARD.]

BURGOYNE: Oh, by the way, Mr. Dudgeon, I shall be glad to see you at lunch at half-past one. [*He pauses a moment, and adds, with politely veiled slyness.*] Bring Mrs Anderson, if she will be so good. [*To* SWINDON, *who is fuming.*] Take it quietly, Major Swindon: your friend the British soldier can stand up to anything except the British War Office. [*He follows* ANDERSON.]

SERGEANT: [*To* SWINDON.] What orders, sir?

SWINDON: [*Savagely.*] Orders! What use are orders now! Theres no army. Back to quarters; and be d— [*He turns on his heel and goes.*]

SERGEANT: [*Pugnacious and patriotic, repudiating the idea of defeat.*] 'Tention. Now then: cock up your chins, and shew em you dont care a damn for em. Slope arms! Fours! Wheel! Quick march!

[*The drums mark time with a tremendous bang; the band strikes up British Grenadiers; and the* SERGEANT, BRUDENELL, *and the English troops march off defiantly to their quarters. The townsfolk press in behind, and follow them up the market, jeering at them; and the town band, a very primitive affair, brings up the rear, playing Yankee Doodle.* ESSIE, *who comes in with them, runs to* RICHARD.]

ESSIE: Oh, Dick!

RICHARD: [*Good-humoredly, but wilfully.*] Now, now: come, come! I don't mind being hanged: but I will not be cried over.

ESSIE: No, I promise. I'll be good. [*She trys to restrain her tears, but cannot.*] I—I want to see where the soldiers are going to. [*She goes a little way up the market, pretending to look after the crowd.*]

JUDITH: Promise me you will never tell him.

RICHARD: Dont be afraid.

[*They shake hands on it.*]

ESSIE: [*Calling to them.*] Theyre coming back. They want you.

[*Jubilation in the market. The townsfolk surge back again in wild enthusiasm with their band, and hoist* RICHARD *on their shoulders, cheering him.*]

GEORGE BERNARD SHAW

NOTES TO *The Devil's Disciple* [3]

BURGOYNE

GENERAL JOHN BURGOYNE, who is presented in this play for the first time (as far as I am aware) on the English stage, is not a conventional stage soldier, but as faithful a portrait as it is in the nature of stage portraits to be. His objection to profane swearing is not borrowed from Mr Gilbert's H.M.S. Pinafore: it is taken from the Code of Instructions drawn up by himself for his officers when he introduced Light Horse into the English Army. His opinion that English soldiers should be treated as thinking beings was no doubt as unwelcome to the military authorities of his time, when nothing was thought of ordering a soldier a thousand lashes, as it will be to those modern victims of the flagellation neurosis who are so anxious to revive that discredited sport. His military reports are very clever as criticisms, and are humane and enlightened within certain aristocratic limits, best illustrated perhaps by his declaration, which now sounds so curious, that he should blush to ask for promotion on any other ground than that of family influence. As a parliamentary candidate, Burgoyne took our common expression "fighting an election" so very literally that he led his supporters to the poll at Preston in 1768 with a loaded pistol in each hand, and won the seat, though he was fined £1000, and denounced by Junius, for the pistols.

It is only within quite recent years that any general recognition has become possible for the feeling that led Burgoyne, a professed enemy of oppression in India and elsewhere, to accept his American command when so many other officers threw up their commissions rather than serve in a civil war against the Colonies. His biographer De Fonblanque, writing in 1876, evidently regarded his position as indefensible. Nowadays, it is sufficient to say that Burgoyne was an Imperialist. He sympathized with the colonists; but when they proposed as a remedy the disruption of the Empire, he regarded that as a

---

[3] George Bernard Shaw, "Notes to *The Devil's Disciple*," *Three Plays for Puritans* (London, 1931), pp. 76–82. Copyright 1900 by George Bernard Shaw. Reprinted by permission of the Society of Authors and the Public Trustee.

step backward in civilization. As he put it to the House of Commons, "while we remember that we are contending against brothers and fellow subjects, we must also remember that we are contending in this crisis for the fate of the British Empire." Eightyfour years after his defeat, his republican conquerors themselves engaged in a civil war for the integrity of their Union. In 1885 the Whigs who represented the anti-Burgoyne tradition of American Independence in English politics, abandoned Gladstone and made common cause with their political opponents in defence of the Union between England and Ireland. Only the other day England sent 200,000 men into the field south of the equator to fight out the question whether South Africa should develop as a Federation of British Colonies or as an independent Afrikander United States. In all these cases the Unionists who were detached from their parties were called renegades, as Burgoyne was. That, of course, is only one of the unfortunate consequences of the fact that mankind, being for the most part incapable of politics, accepts vituperation as an easy and congenial substitute. Whether Burgoyne or Washington, Lincoln or Davis, Gladstone or Bright, Mr Chamberlain or Mr Leonard Courtney was in the right will never be settled, because it will never be possible to prove that the government of the victor has been better for mankind than the government of the vanquished would have been. It is true that the victors have no doubt on the point; but to the dramatist, that certainty of theirs is only part of the human comedy. The American Unionist is often a Separatist as to Ireland; the English Unionist often sympathizes with the Polish Home Ruler; and both English and American Unionists are apt to be Disruptionists as regards that Imperial Ancient of Days, the Empire of China. Both are Unionists concerning Canada, but with a difference as to the precise application to it of the Monroe doctrine. As for me, the dramatist, I smile, and lead the conversation back to Burgoyne.

Burgoyne's surrender at Saratoga made him that occasionally necessary part of our British system, a scapegoat. The explanation of his defeat given in the play (p. 73) is founded on a passage quoted by De Fonblanque from Fitzmaurice's Life of Lord Shelburne, as follows: "Lord George Germain, having among other peculiarities a particular dislike to be put out of his way on any occasion, had arranged to call at his office on his way to the country to sign the dispatches; but as those addressed to Howe had not been fair-copied, and he was not disposed to be balked of his projected visit to Kent, they were not signed then and were forgotten on his return home." These were the dispatches instructing Sir William Howe, who was in New York, to effect a junction at Albany with Burgoyne, who had marched from Quebec for that purpose. Burgoyne got as far as Saratoga, where, failing the expected reinforcement, he was hopelessly outnumbered, and his officers picked off, Boer fashion, by the American farmer-sharpshooters. His own collar was pierced by a bullet. The publicity of his defeat, however, was more than compensated at home by the fact that Lord George's trip to Kent had not been interfered with, and that nobody knew about the oversight of the dispatch. The policy of the English Government and Court for the next two years was simply concealment of Germain's neglect. Burgoyne's demand for an inquiry was defeated in the House of Commons by the court party; and when he at last obtained a committee, the king got rid of it by a prorogation. When Burgoyne realized what had happened about the instructions to Howe (the scene in which I have represented him as learning it before Saratoga is not historical: the truth did not dawn on him until many months afterwards) the king actually took advantage of his being a prisoner of war in England on parole, and ordered him to return to America into captivity. Burgoyne immediately resigned all his appointments; and this practically closed his military career, though he was afterwards made Commander of the Forces in Ireland for the purpose of banishing him from parliament.

The episode illustrates the curious perversion of the English sense of honor when the privileges and prestige of the aristocracy are at stake. Mr Frank Harris said, after the disastrous battle of Modder River, that the English, having lost America a century ago because they preferred George III, were quite prepared to lose South Africa today because they preferred aristocratic commanders to successful ones. Horace Walpole, when the parliamentary recess came at a critical period of the War of Independence, said that the Lords could not be expected to lose their pheasant shooting for the sake of America. In the working class, which, like all classes, has its own official aristocracy, there is the same reluctance to discredit an institution or to "do a man out of his job." At bottom, of course, this apparently shameless sacrifice of great public interests to petty personal ones, is simply the preference of the ordinary man for the things he can feel and understand to the things that are beyond his capacity. It is stupidity, not dishonesty.

Burgoyne fell a victim to this stupidity in two ways. Not only was he thrown over, in spite of his high character and distinguished services, to screen a court favorite who had actually been cashiered for cowardice and misconduct in the field fifteen years before; but his peculiar critical temperament and talent, artistic, satirical, rather histrionic, and his fastidious delicacy of sentiment, his fine spirit and humanity, were just the qualities to make him disliked by stupid people because of their dread of ironic criticism. Long after his death, Thackeray, who had an intense sense of human character, but was typically stupid in valuing and interpreting it, instinctively sneered at him and exulted in his defeat. That sneer represents the common English attitude towards the Burgoyne type. Every instance in which the critical genius is defeated and the stupid genius (for both temperaments have their genius) "muddles through all right," is popular in England. But Burgoyne's failure was not the work of his own temperament, but of the stupid temperament. What man could do under the circumstances he did, and did handsomely and loftily. He fell, and his ideal empire was dismembered, not through his own misconduct, but because Lord George Germain overestimated the importance of his Kentish holiday, and underestimated the difficulty of conquering those remote and inferior creatures, the colonists. And King George and the rest of the nation agreed, on the whole, with Germain. It is a signficant point that in America, where Burgoyne was an enemy and an invader, he was admired and praised. The climate there is no doubt more favorable to intellectual vivacity.

I have described Burgoyne's temperament as rather histrionic; and the reader will have observed that the Burgoyne of the Devil's Disciple is a man who plays his part in life, and makes all its points, in the manner of a born high comedian. If he had been killed at Saratoga, with all his comedies unwritten, and his plan for turning As You Like It into a Beggar's Opera unconceived, I should still have painted the same picture of him on the strength of his reply to the articles of capitulation proposed to him by the victorious Gates (an Englishman). Here they are:

PROPOSITION.	ANSWER.
1. General Burgoyne's army being reduced by repeated defeats, by desertion, sickness, etc., their provisions exhausted, their military horses, tents and baggage taken or destroyed, their retreat cut off, and their camp invested, they can only be allowed to surrender as prisoners of war.	Lieut-General Burgoyne's army, however reduced, will never admit that their retreat is cut off while they have arms in their hands.
2. The officers and soldiers may keep the baggage belonging to them. The Generals of the United States never permit individuals to be pillaged.	Noted.
3. The troops under his Excellencey General Burgoyne will be conducted by the most convenient route to New England, marching by easy marches, and sufficiently provided for by the way.	Agreed.

PROPOSITION.	ANSWER.
4. The officers will be admitted on parole and will be treated with the liberality customary in such cases, so long as they, by proper behaviour, continue to deserve it; but those who are apprehended having broke their parole, as some British officers have done, must expect to be close confined.	There being no officer in this army under, or capable of being under, the description of breaking parole, this article needs no answer.
5. All public stores, artillery, arms, ammunition, carriages, horses, etc., etc., must be delivered to commissaries appointed to receive them.	All public stores may be delivered, arms excepted.
6. These terms being agreed to and signed, the troops under his Excellency's, General Burgoyne's command, may be drawn up in their encampments, where they will be ordered to ground their arms, and may thereupon be marched to the riverside on their way to Bennington.	This article is inadmissible in any extremity. Sooner than this army will consent to ground their arms in their encampments, they will rush on the enemy determined to take no quarter.

And, later on, "If General Gates does not mean to recede from the 6th article, the treaty ends at once: the army will to a man proceed to any act of desperation sooner than submit to that article."

Here you have the man at his Burgoynest. Need I add that he had his own way; and that when the actual ceremony of surrender came, he would have played poor General Gates off the stage, had not that commander risen to the occasion by handing him back his sword.

In connection with the reference to Indians with scalping knives, who, with the troops hired from Germany, made up about half Burgoyne's force, I may cite the case of Jane McCrea, betrothed to one of Burgoyne's officers. A Wyandotte chief attached to Burgoyne's force was bringing her to the British camp as a prisoner of war, when another party of Indians, sent by her betrothed, claimed her. The Wyandotte settled the dispute by killing her and bringing her scalp to Burgoyne. Burgoyne let the deed pass. Possibly he feared that a massacre of whites on the Canadian border by the Wyandottes would follow any attempt at punishment. But his own proclamations had threatened just what the savage chief executed.

BRUDENELL

Brudenell is also a real person. At least, an artillery chaplain of that name distinguished himself at Saratoga by reading the burial service over Major Fraser under fire, and by a quite

274

readable adventure, chronicled, with exaggerations, by Burgoyne, concerning Lady Harriet Acland. Others have narrated how Lady Harriet's husband killed himself in a duel, by falling with his head against a pebble; and how Lady Harriet then married the warrior chaplain. All this, however, is a tissue of romantic lies, though it has been repeated in print as authentic history from generation to generation, even to the first edition of this book. As a matter of fact, Major Acland died in his bed of a cold shortly after his return to England; and Lady Harriet remained a widow until her death in 1815.

The rest of the Devil's Disciple may have actually occurred, like most stories invented by dramatists; but I cannot produce any documents. Major Swindon's name is invented; but the man, of course, is real. There are dozens of him extant to this day.

SEAN O'CASEY

THE GREEN GODDESS OF REALISM[1]

In the theater of today, realism is the totem pole of the dramatic critics.

Matter-of-fact plays, true-to-life arrangement, and real, live characters are the three gods the critics adore and saturate with the incense of their commonplace praise once a day and twice on Sundays in their trimly-dressed little articles. What the dramatic critics mean by the various terms they use for Realism is the yearly ton of rubbish that falls on the English stage and is swiftly swept away into the dustbins. The critics give a cordial welcome to the trivial plays because, in my opinion, they are, oh, so easy to understand, and gorge the critics with the ease of an easy explanation. It is very dangerous for a dramatist to be superior to the critics, to be a greater dramatist than the critic is a critic. They don't like it, and so most of them do all they can to discourage any attempt in the theater towards an imagination fancy-free, or an attempt to look on life and mold it into a form fit for the higher feeling and intelligence of the stage. They are those who compare Beaumont and Fletcher's *Philaster* with *Charley's Aunt*, and in their heart of hearts vote for the farce and shove the poetic play out of their way (a few split the preference in our face, as Archer did). Charley's Aunt is loved by Charley's uncles. They have grown fat and lazy on triviality, so fat and lazy that they are hardly able to move. The curse is that these critics do their best to prevent anyone else from moving either. They will have simply to be roughly shunted out of the way, and these few words are one of the first sharp prods to get them to buzz off and do their sleeping somewhere else. Realism, or what the critics childishly believe to be Realism, has had its day, and has earned a rest. It began on a sunny autumn evening in 1886, or thereabouts, as the lawyers say, at the first production of *Ours* by Robertson, when the miracle took place. "In reading the play today," says William Archer, the world-famous drama critic, "we recognize in Robertson—just what the stage wanted in its progress towards verisimilitude—the genius of the commonplace. The first act of *Ours* was, in intention at any rate, steeped in an atmosphere quite new to the theater. The scene was an avenue in Shendryn Park which Robertson describes in the abhorrent prompt-book jargon of the time. But one line had, I venture to say, as yet appeared in no prompt-book in the world: *'Throughout the act the autumn leaves fall from the trees.'* How this effect was produced and whether it was successful, I cannot say. Nor can I discuss the question whether it was a desirable effect, or a mere trick of mechanical realism which the true artist would despise." Now the falling of the leaves from the trees was and could have been nothing but "a mere trick of mechanical realism," because the trees couldn't have been true-to-life trees, and, even if they were, the autumnal leaves couldn't have fallen with the regularity and rhythm required to create the desirable effect. And no true artist of the theater would despise "a mere trick of mechanical realism" by which to get a scenic or an emotional effect out of his play and over to his audience. We remember the fine effect that the first sound of the first fall of rain had as it fell in the first act of Obey's *Noah*; and this fall of rain was a mere trick of mechanical realism as it was also the opening of the floodgates of Heaven, swelling into a flood that destroyed all life that was in the world save only those who found safe shelter in the faith of Noah; or the sudden change in the wind in *Saint Joan* that set the pennon streaming eastward, and sent Dunois and Saint Joan hurrying out to make for the flash of the guns, and drive the English out of France. You see the artist in the theater never despises a mere trick of mechanical realism; but he knows how to keep it in its proper place. Let Archer open his mouth again: "Then as the act proceeds, *The patter of rain is heard upon the leaves*, and again, *The rain comes down more heavily and the stage darkens*." The stage darkens, mind you, not the sky. "This effect of the rain falling and the stage darkening would," Archer tells us, "have been absolutely impossible in a candle-lit scene." Well, we have our floodlights, our spotlights, our baby-spots, our amber, blue, and pink footlights, but rarely do we get in our great progress towards verisimilitude the thunder, the lightning, and the rain that flashed and roared and fell on the heath scene in Shakespeare's *Macbeth*. Archer speaks again: "Then enter the sentimental hero and heroine, caught in the rain; and—conceive the daring novelty!—*Blanche carries the skirt of her dress over her head*. In the center of the stage was a large tree with a bench around it, and to get the best shelter possible, the hero and the heroine stand on the bench. Meanwhile Sir Alexander and Lady Shendryn, a middle-aged couple, hop in and sit down on the stump of a tree under another shelter. Unaware of each other's presence, the two couples talk in a sort of counterpoint, the romantic dialogue of the youthful pair contrasting with the weary snappiness of the elderly couple." And this is called an exact imitation of real life. Two couples, unknown to each other, carry on a counterpoint conversation on the same stage in the same scene at the same time, and Archer calls this "an exact imitation at any rate of the surfaces of life." Here's a bit of the dialogue:

> Angus: What was the song you sang at the Sylvesters'?
> Blanche: Oh!
> Angus: I wish you'd hum it now.
> Blanche: Without music?
> Angus: It won't be without music.

—and Blanche croons over Offenbach's exquisite *Chanson de Fortunio,* and then we are told that we may search the Restoration and eighteenth-century comedy in vain for a piece of subtle truth like this. Where the subtle truth is in a girl under the rain holding her skirt over her head, standing on a bench, crooning Offenbach's *Chanson de Fortunio* or murmuring to her young man, "Cousin, do you know, I rather like to see you getting wet," only Archer or some other present-day critic-guardian angel of the theater could tell us. This arch-critical prate about verisimilitude, exact imitation of real life, and the unmistakable originality of the conception of this scene in Robertson's *Ours,* is an example of the commonplace genius of dramatic criticism. The incident of two couples taking their set times to say their say on the same stage in the same scene at the same time in full view of the audience is as true to life, is about as exact an imitation of real life, as the incident of Malvolio's soliloquy in full view of his tormentors and his audience. But the autumn leaves falling one by one and two by two, the sound of the rain pattering on the leaves, and the stage getting darker and darker and the rain getting heavier and heavier as the act proceeds, is all so sweet and all so simple to see and feel and follow that Archer and his fellow-follows-on hail this exact imitation of real life on the stage as a great and glorious godsend to them and their wives and children. They are so easy to manage in a weekly article; no beating about the bush, no humiliating strain on the mind or the emotions, no danger of giving a stupid judgment, for autumn leaves are autumn leaves, rain is rain, and the darkening night means the end of the day. And so we find that stuff like *Call It a Day* gets a rosy welcome from our regimental sergeant-major critics, while a work like *Strange Interlude* is pooh-bahed off the stage. And how quietly clever and exact this realism, or naturalism, or exact imitation of life has made the critics! Commenting on *Espionage,* Mr. Agate tells us that "the First Act is a corker, and readers will note my wideawakeness in the perception that whereas the draught in the railway carriage fritters the blinds, the passengers are able to put their heads out of window without a hair stirring." I'm sure all the readers felt an exaltation in the conscientiousness of criticism when they got sufficiently soaked in that wonderful bit of information. It gave them something to look forward to when they went to see the play. Not a hair stirring! Fancy that now. Strange that the same wideawakeness which saw a corker in *Espionage,* saw nothing, or very little, in O'Neill's *Strange Interlude.* But then O'Neill's great plays are "morbid masterpieces which have to be seen under the penalty of remaining mum in Bloomsbury," or, if the truth be told, of remaining mum in any civilized place where the drama is honored more in the observance than in the breach. . . .

This headlong search or quiet scrutiny for realism, exact imitation of life in the drama, has outwitted the critics into being puzzled over everything in a play that doesn't fit calmly into their poor spirit level and timid thumb rule. The dramatist is told that he must see life steadily and see it whole; and a critic-at-arms (there are barons, knights, esquires, men-at-arms, and grooms among the critics) writing in the *Evening Standard* complained that a play he saw wasn't "a study of the whole seething brew of life"! He wasn't asking for much. The whole world, parallels of longitude and meridians of latitude and all, popped on to the stage in a flood of limelight, and the critics tossing it about like kids playing with a balloon. This critic-at-arms didn't (and doesn't still, I'm sure) realize that no one can view or understand the brew of life encased in an acorn cup; or holding this little miracle in the palm of the hand, no human pair of eyes can at any time see it steadily and see it whole. So the complaint about a play failing to show the whole seething brew of life is the complaint of a dodo critic.

Although the bone of realism in the theater has been picked pretty clean, the critics keep gnawing away at it, so that if a playwright as much as gets a character to blow his nose (preferably when "the autumn leaves are falling from the trees"), the critics delightedly nod to each other, and murmur, "An exact imitation of life, brothers." Commenting on *Call It a Day,* a play in which everything is attempted and nothing done, Mr. Agate tells us that "Miss Dodie Smith is never concerned whether 'it' is a play or not, but whether she has assembled on her stage characters so real that she might have gone into the street and compelled them into the theater," though these characters that might have been pulled in off the street are as tender and delicate and true as the tenderest and most delicate characters wistfully wandering about in the most wistful Barrie play. J. G. B., commenting on *Love From a Stranger,* tells us that "it is written with brilliant matter-of-

279

factness, and is a real play about real people." Here our noses are shoved up against the image of realism in the theater. A real play about real people: here's a sentence that apparently punches home; but look well into it, and you'll find it empty of any real meaning. Week in and week out these commonplace plays are reducing the poor critics into more and more vague and vapid expressions that would give a sparkle to the mouth of a politician trying to cod his constituents—and very often succeeding. A real play about real people—what does it mean? This is something of a triumph—a real play with real people in a real theater before a real audience. But every play is a real play whether it be good or bad, just as a real lion is a real lion and a real mouse is a real mouse, and both are animals. But the real mouse isn't a real lion, nor is the real lion a real mouse, though both are animals. I wonder do the critics get this? There is a big difference between a lion and a mouse, though both are animals, and there is a bigger difference between a good and a bad play, though both are plays just the same. What is a "real play"? Answer, according to J. G. B., *Love From a Stranger* is a real play, therefore the nearer we get to this praised play, the nearer we get to a real play. Now is *The Dream Play* by Strindberg a real play? It certainly bears no resemblance to *Love From a Stranger,* but the imagination can handle *The Dream Play* just as well and with far fuller satisfaction. Apparently the critics think that a play to be a real play must have real people in it, though they never take breath to tell us what they mean by real people. Take people off the street or carry them out of a drawing-room, plonk them on the stage and make them speak as they speak in real, real life, and you will have the dullest thing imaginable. I suppose the critics will be shocked to hear that no real character can be put in a play unless some of the reality is taken out of him through the heightening, widening, and deepening of the character by the dramatist who creates him. Would the dramatic critics call the characters in *Hamlet* real people, or only the creations out of the mind of a poet, and isn't *Hamlet* all the better for its want of reality? . . .

As a matter-of-factness no one, least of all a playwright, can go out into the streets and lanes of the city and compel the people to come on to the stage, for the people on the stage must be of the stage and not of the streets and lanes of the city or of the highways and hedges of the country. The most realistic characters in the most realistic play cannot be true to life. Perhaps the most real character in any play we know of is the character of Falstaff done by Shakespeare. Here is realism as large as life; but it is realism larger, and a lot larger, than life. Falstaff was never pulled off the streets into the theater by Shakespeare. God never created Falstaff—he sprang from Shakespeare's brain. God, if you like, created Shakespeare, but Shakespeare created Falstaff. Falstaff is no more real, there is no more matter-of-factness in the character of Falstaff, than there is in Caliban or Puck or Ariel. He is a bigger creation than any of these three, and that is all. A play, says Dryden, ought to be a just image of human nature, and this is true of *Hamlet*, of *John Bull's Other Island*, of *Strange Interlude*, of *Six Characters in Search of an Author*, of *Peer Gynt*, of *The Dream Play*; but it is not true of the trivial tomtit-realism in the thousand and one entertainment plays patted and praised by the dramatic critics. Why, even the sawdust characters of the Moor, Petroushka, and the Ballerina are a more just image of human nature than the characters in the matter-of-fact, exact-imitation-of-life plays that flit about on the English stage.

As it is with the play, so it is with the dressed-up stage—the critics want to be doped into the belief that the scene on the stage is as real as life itself. The stirring of the hair is more to them than the stirring of the heart. But things as real as life itself on the stage they can never have; a room can never be a room, a tree a tree, or a death a death. These must take the nature of a child's toys and a child's play. Let me quote from Allardyce Nicoll's *British Drama*: "Illusion for the ordinary spectator is only partial at the best, and nearly all of us are aware, even at the moment of highest tension or of most hilarious laughter, that the battlements are not of Elsinore and the trees are not of Arden forest. The scene-painter's art allied to that of the electrician can now obtain effects undreamt of before. Our drawing-rooms can look like drawing-rooms now, our woods can look like woods, and our seas like seas. Those, too, who have witnessed some recent productions in which the new German lighting effects were employed will agree that it would be hard to tell the fictional clouds that flit over the painted sky from real clouds, or the fictional sunrise from real sunrise. The question is, however, not whether the semblance of actuality can be obtained, but whether it is precisely that which we desire. Would we not rather have the real drawing-room of Mrs. So-and-so, the real Epping Forest, the real Atlantic, rather than these feigned copies of them? Would we not choose to watch those beautiful clouds from an open moorland rather than from our seats in gallery or in stalls? It is precisely the same problem that arises in the consideration of drama itself. We do not want merely an excerpt from reality; it is the imaginative transformation of reality, as it is seen through the eyes of the poet, that we desire. The great art of the theater is to suggest, not to tell openly; to dilate the mind by symbols, not by actual things; to express in Lear a world's sorrow, and in Hamlet the grief of humanity. Many of our modern producers are striving in this direction, although it must be confessed that England here is well in the background." And what is the greatest obstacle the progressive producers have to face? In my opinion, the dramatic critics who prefer the stirring of the hair to the stirring of the heart; the death-or-drivel boys gunning with their gab from their pill-boxes in the theater those who take a step forward to enthrone imagination in the theater and make it more of a temple and less of a den of thieves.

This rage for real, real life on the stage has taken all the life out of the drama. If everything on the stage is to be a fake exact imitation (for fake realism it can only be), where is the chance for the original and imaginative artist? Less chance for him than there was for Jonah in the whale's belly. The beauty, fire, and poetry of drama have perished in the storm of fake realism. Let real birds fly through the air (not like Basil Dean's butterflies in *Midsummer Night's Dream*, fluttering over the stage and pinning themselves to trees), real animals roam through the jungle, real fish swim in the sea; but let us have the make-believe of the artist and the child in the theater. Less of what the critics call "life," and more of symbolism; for even in the most commonplace of realistic plays the symbol can never be absent. A house on a stage can never be a house, and that which represents it must always be a symbol. A room in a realistic play must always be a symbol for a room. There can never be any important actuality on the stage, except an actuality that is unnecessary and out of place. An actor representing a cavalier may come on the stage mounted on a real horse, but the horse will always look only a little less ridiculous than the "cavalier." The horse can have nothing to do with the drama. I remember a play written round Mr. Pepys, and in this play was used "the identical snuff-box used by him when he was head of the Admiralty in the reign of Charles the Second." So much was said about the snuff-box that I expected it to be carried in on a cushion preceded by a brass band, and hawked around for all to admire before the play began. Now this snuff-box added nothing to the play, and because of this commonplace spirit in the play, the play added nothing to the drama. It seems that the closer we move to actual life, the further we move away from the drama. Drama purely imitative of life isn't drama at all. . . .

SEAN O'CASEY

Juno and the Paycock

CHARACTERS

"CAPTAIN" JACK BOYLE.
JUNO BOYLE, *his wife.*
JOHNNY BOYLE. ⎱ *their children*
MARY BOYLE. ⎰
JERRY DEVINE.
CHARLIE BENTHAM, *a school teacher.*
AN IRREGULAR MOBILIZER.
TWO IRREGULARS.

"JOXER" DALY.
MRS. MAISIE MADIGAN.
"NEEDLE" NUGENT, *a tailor.*   *residents in the tenement*
MRS. TANCRED.
A COAL-BLOCK VENDOR.
A SEWING MACHINE MAN.
TWO FURNITURE REMOVAL MEN.
TWO NEIGHBOURS.

SCENE

ACT I: *The living apartment of a two-roomed tenancy of the Boyle family, in a tenement house in Dublin.*

ACT II: *The same.*

ACT III: *The same.*
A few days elapse between Acts I and II, and two months between Acts II and III.

During Act III the curtain is lowered for a few minutes to denote the lapse of one hour.

Period of the play: 1922

ACT I

The living room of a two-room tenancy occupied by the BOYLE *family in a tenement house in Dublin. Left, a door leading to another part of the house; left of door a window looking into the street; at back a dresser; farther to right at back, a window looking into the back of the house. Between the window and the dresser is a picture of the Virgin; below the picture, on a bracket, is a crimson bowl in which a floating votive light is burning. Farther to the right is a small bed partly concealed by cretonne hangings strung on a twine. To the right is the fireplace; near the fireplace is a door leading to the other room. Beside the fireplace is a box containing coal. On the mantelshelf is an alarm clock lying on its face. In a corner near the window looking into the back is a galvanized bath. A table and some chairs. On the table are breakfast things for one. A teapot is on the hob and a frying-pan stands inside the fender. There are a few books on the dresser and one on the table. Leaning against the dresser is a long-handled shovel—the kind invariably used by labourers when turning concrete or mixing mortar.* JOHNNY BOYLE *is sitting crouched beside the fire.* MARY *with her jumper off—it is lying on the back of a chair—is arranging her hair before a tiny mirror perched on the table. Beside the mirror is stretched out the morning paper, which she looks at when she isn't gazing into the mirror. She is a well-made and good-looking girl of twenty-two. Two forces are working in her mind—one, through the circumstances of her life, pulling her back; the other, through the influence of books she has read, pushing her forward. The opposing forces are apparent in her speech and her manners, both of which are degraded by her environment, and improved by her acquaintance—slight though it be—with literature. The time is early forenoon.*

MARY: [*Looking at the paper.*] On a little bye-road, out beyant Finglas, he was found.

[MRS. BOYLE *enters by door on right; she has been shopping and carries a small parcel in her hand. She is forty-five years of age, and twenty years ago she must have been a pretty woman; but her face has now assumed that look which ultimately settles down upon the faces of the women of the working-class; a look of listless monotony and harassed anxiety, blending with an expression of mechanical resistance. Were circumstances favourable, she would probably be a handsome, active and clever woman.*]

MRS. BOYLE: Isn't he come in yet?

MARY: No, mother.

MRS. BOYLE: Oh, he'll come in when he likes; struttin' about the town like a pay-cock with Joxer, I suppose. I hear all about Mrs. Tancred's son is in this mornin's paper.

MARY: The full details are in it this mornin'; seven wounds he had—one entherin' the neck, with an exit wound beneath the left shoulder-blade; another in the left breast penethratin' the heart, an' . . .

JOHNNY: [*Springing up from the fire.*] Oh, quit that readin', for God's sake! Are yous losin' all your feelin's? It'll soon be that none of yous'll read anythin' that's not about butcherin'! [*He goes quickly into the room on left.*]

MARY: He's gettin' very sensitive, all of a sudden!

MRS. BOYLE: I'll read it myself, Mary, by an' by, when I come home. Everybody's sayin' that he was a die-hard—thanks be to God that Johnny had nothin' to do with him this long time. . . . [*Opening the parcel and taking out some sausages, which she places on a plate.*] Ah, then, if that father o' yours doesn't come in soon for his breakfast, he may go without any; I'll not wait much longer for him.

MARY: Can't you let him get it himself when he comes in?

MRS. BOYLE: Yes, an' let him bring in Joxer Daly along with him? Ay, that's what he'd like, an' that's what he's waitin' for—till he thinks I'm gone to work, an' then sail in with the boul' Joxer, to burn all the coal an' dhrink all the tea in the place, to show them what a good Samaritan he is! But I'll stop here till he comes in, if I have to wait till to-morrow mornin'.

VOICE OF JOHNNY: [*Inside.*] Mother!

MRS. BOYLE: Yis?

VOICE OF JOHNNY: Bring us in a dhrink o' wather.

MRS. BOYLE: Bring in that fella a dhrink o' wather, for God's sake, Mary.

MARY: Isn't he big an' able enough to come out an' get it himself?

MRS. BOYLE: If you weren't well yourself you'd like somebody to bring you in a dhrink o' wather. [*She brings in drink and returns.*]

MRS. BOYLE: Isn't it terrible to have to be waitin' this way! You'd think he was bringin' twenty poun's a week into the house the way he's goin' on. He wore out the Health Insurance long ago, he's afther wearin' out the unemployment dole, an', now, he's thryin' to wear out me! An' constantly singin', no less, when he ought always to be on his knees offerin' up a Novena for a job!

MARY: [*Tying a ribbon, fillet-wise around her head.*] I don't like this ribbon, ma; I think I'll wear the green—it looks betther than the blue.

MRS. BOYLE: Ah, wear whatever ribbon you like, girl, only don't be botherin' me. I don't know what a girl on strike wants to be wearin' a ribbon round her head for or silk stockin's on her legs either; it's wearin' them things that make the employers think they're givin' yous too much money.

MARY: The hour is past now when we'll ask the employers' permission to wear what we like.

MRS. BOYLE: I don't know why you wanted to walk out for Jennie Claffey; up to this you never had a good word for her.

MARY: What's the use of belongin' to a Trades Union if you won't stand up for your principles? Why did they sack her? It was a clear case of victimization. We couldn't let her walk the streets, could we?

MRS. BOYLE: No, of course yous couldn't—yous wanted to keep her company. Wan victim wasn't enough. When the employers sacrifice wan victim, the Trades Unions go wan betther be sacrificin' a hundred.

MARY: It doesn't matther what you say, ma—a principle's a principle.

MRS. BOYLE: Yis; an' when I go into oul' Murphy's to-morrow, an' he gets to know that, instead o' payin' all, I'm goin' to borry more, what'll he say when I tell him a principle's a principle? What'll we do if he refuses to give us any more on tick?

MARY: He daren't refuse—if he does, can't you tell him he's paid?

MRS. BOYLE: It's lookin' as if he was paid, whether he refuses or no.

[JOHNNY *appears at the door on left. He can be plainly seen now; he is a thin delicate fellow, something younger than* MARY. *He has evidently gone through a rough time. His face is pale and drawn; there is a tremulous look of indefinite fear in his eyes. The left sleeve of his coat is empty, and he walks with a slight halt.*]

JOHNNY: I was lyin' down; I thought yous were gone. Oul' Simon Mackay is thrampin' about like a horse over me head, an' I can't sleep with him—they're like thunder-claps in me brain! The curse o'—God forgive me for goin' to curse!

MRS. BOYLE: There, now; go back an' lie down again, an' I'll bring you in a nice cup o' tay.

JOHNNY: Tay, tay, tay! You're always thinkin' o' tay. If a man was dyin', you'd thry to make him swally a cup o' tay! [*He goes back.*]

MRS. BOYLE: I don't know what's goin' to be done with him. The bullet he got in the hip in Easter Week was bad enough, but the bomb that shatthered his arm in the fight in O'Connell Street put the finishin' touch on him. I knew he was makin' a fool of himself. God knows I went down on me bended knees to him not to go agen the Free State.

MARY: He stuck to his principles, an', no matther how you may argue, ma, a principle's a principle.

VOICE OF JOHNNY: Is Mary goin' to stay here?

MARY: No, I'm not goin' to stay here; you

can't expect me to be always at your beck an' call, can you?

VOICE OF JOHNNY: I won't stop here be meself!

MRS. BOYLE: Amn't I nicely handicapped with the whole o' yous! I don't know what any o' yous ud do without your ma. [*To* JOHNNY.] Your father'll be here in a minute, an' if you want anythin', he'll get it for you.

JOHNNY: I hate assin' him for anythin'. . . . He hates to be assed to stir. . . . Is the light lightin' before the picture o' the Virgin?

MRS. BOYLE: Yis, yis! The wan inside to St. Anthony isn't enough, but he must have another wan to the Virgin here!

[*JERRY* DEVINE *enters hastily. He is about twenty-five, well set, active and earnest. He is a type, becoming very common now in the Labour Movement, of a mind knowing enough to make the mass of his associates, who know less, a power, and too little to broaden that power for the benefit of all.* MARY *seizes her jumper and runs hastily into room left.*]

JERRY: [*Breathless.*] Where's the Captain, Mrs. Boyle; where's the Captain?

MRS. BOYLE: You may well ass a body that: he's wherever Joxer Daly is—dhrinkin' in some snug or another.

JERRY: Father Farrell is just afther stoppin' to tell me to run up an' get him to go to the new job that's goin' on in Rathmines; his cousin is foreman o' the job, an' Father Farrell was speakin' to him about poor Johnny an' his father bein' idle so long, an' the foreman told Father Farrell to send the Captain up an' he'd give him a start—I wondher where I'd find him?

MRS. BOYLE: You'll find he's ayther in Ryan's or Foley's.

JERRY: I'll run round to Ryan's—I know it's a great house o' Joxer's. [*He rushes out.*]

MRS. BOYLE: [*Piteously.*] There now, he'll miss that job, or I know for what! If he gets win' o' the word, he'll not come back till evenin', so that it'll be too late. There'll never be any good got out o' him so long as he goes with that shouldher-shruggin' Joxer. I killin' meself workin', an' he shruttin' about from mornin' till night like a paycock!

[*The steps of two persons are heard coming up a flight of stairs. They are* the footsteps of CAPTAIN BOYLE *and* JOXER. CAPTAIN BOYLE *is singing in a deep, sonorous, self-honouring voice.*]

THE CAPTAIN: Sweet Spirit, hear me prayer! Hear . . . oh . . . hear . . . me prayer . . . hear, oh, hear . . . Oh, he . . . ar . . . oh, he . . . ar . . . me . . . pray . . . er!

JOXER: [*Outside.*] Ah, that's a darlin' song, a daaarlin' song!

MRS. BOYLE: [*Viciously.*] Sweet spirit hear his prayer! Oh, then, I'll take me solemn affeydavey, it's not for a job he's prayin'!

[*She sits down on the bed so that the cretonne hangings hide her from the view of those entering.*]

[THE CAPTAIN *comes slowly in. He is a man of about sixty; stout, grey-haired and stocky. His neck is short, and his head looks like a stone ball that one sometimes sees on top of a gatepost. His cheeks, reddish-purple, are puffed out, as if he were always repressing an almost irrepressible ejaculation. On his upper lip is a crisp, tightly cropped moustache; he carries himself with the upper part of his body slightly thrown back, and his stomach slightly thrust forward. His walk is a slow, consequential strut. His clothes are dingy, and he wears a faded seaman's cap with a glazed peak.*]

BOYLE: [*To* JOXER, *who is still outside.*] Come on, come on in, Joxer; she's gone out long ago, man. If there's nothing else to be got, we'll furrage out a cup o' tay, anyway. It's the only bit I get in comfort when she's away. 'Tisn't Juno should be her pet name at all, but Deirdre of the Sorras, for she's always grousin'.

[*JOXER steps cautiously into the room. He may be younger than* THE CAPTAIN *but he looks a lot older. His face is like a bundle of crinkled paper; his eyes have a cunning twinkle; he is spare and loosely built; he has a habit of constantly shrugging his shoulders with a peculiar twitching movement, meant to be ingratiating. His face is invariably ornamented with a grin.*]

JOXER: It's a terrible thing to be tied to a woman that's always grousin'. I don't know how you stick it—it ud put years on me. It's a good job she has to be so ofen away, for [*With a shrug.*] when the cat's away, the mice can play!

BOYLE: [*With a commanding and complacent gesture.*] Pull over to the fire, Joxer, an' we'll have a cup o' tay in a minute.

JOXER: Ah, a cup o' tay's a darlin' thing, a daaarlin' thing—the cup that cheers but doesn't . . .

[JOXER's *rhapsody is cut short by the sight of* JUNO *coming forward and confronting the two cronies. Both are stupefied.*]

MRS. BOYLE: [*With sweet irony—poking the fire, and turning her head to glare at* JOXER.] Pull over to the fire, Joxer Daly, an' we'll have a cup o' tay in a minute! Are you sure now, you wouldn't like an egg?

JOXER: I can't stop, Mrs. Boyle; I'm in a desperate hurry, a desperate hurry.

MRS. BOYLE: Pull over to the fire, Joxer Daly; people is always far more comfortabler here than they are in their own place.

[JOXER *makes hastily for the door.* BOYLE *stirs to follow him; thinks of something to relieve the situation—stops, and says suddenly*]:

Joxer!

JOXER: [*At door ready to bolt.*] Yis?

BOYLE: You know the foreman o' that job that's goin' on down in Killesther, don't you, Joxer?

JOXER: [*Puzzled.*] Foreman—Killesther?

BOYLE: [*With a meaning look.*] He's a butty o' yours, isn't he?

JOXER: [*The truth dawning on him.*] The foreman at Killesther—oh, yis, yis. He's an oul' butty o' mine—oh, he's a darlin' man, a daaarlin' man.

BOYLE: Oh, then, it's a sure thing. It's a pity we didn't go down at breakfast first thing this mornin'—we might ha' been working now; but you didn't know it then.

JOXER: [*With a shrug.*] It's betther late than never.

BOYLE: It's nearly time we got a start, anyhow; I'm fed up knockin' round, doin' nothin'. He promised you—gave you the straight tip?

JOXER: Yis. "Come down on the blow o' dinner," says he, "an' I'll start you, an' any friend you like to brin' with you." Ah, says I, you're a darlin' man, a daaarlin' man.

BOYLE: Well, it couldn't come at a betther time—we're a long time waitin' for it.

JOXER: Indeed we were; but it's a long lane that has no turnin'.

BOYLE: The blow up for dinner is at one —wait till I see what time it 'tis. [*He goes over to the mantelpiece, and gingerly lifts the clock.*]

MRS. BOYLE: Min' now, how you go on fiddlin' with that clock—you know the least little thing sets it asthray.

BOYLE: The job couldn't come at a betther time; I'm feelin' in great fettle, Joxer, I'd hardly believe I ever had a pain in me legs, an' last week I was nearly crippled with them.

JOXER: That's betther and betther; ah, God never shut wan door but he opened another!

BOYLE: It's only eleven o'clock; we've lashins o' time. I'll slip on me oul' moleskins afther breakfast, an' we can saunter down at our ayse. [*Putting his hand on the shovel.*] I think, Joxer, we'd betther bring our shovels?

JOXER: Yis, Captain, yis; it's betther to go fully prepared, an' ready for all eventualities. You bring your long-tailed shovel, an' I'll bring me navvy. We mighten' want them, an', then agen, we might: for want of a nail the shoe was lost, for want of a shoe the horse was lost, an' for want of a horse the man was lost—aw, that's a darlin' proverb, a daaarlin' . . .

[*As* JOXER *is finishing his sentence,* MRS. BOYLE *approaches the door and* JOXER *retreats hurriedly. She shuts the door with a bang.*]

BOYLE: [*Suggestively.*] We won't be long pullin' ourselves together agen when I'm working for a few weeks.

[MRS. BOYLE *takes no notice.*]

BOYLE: The foreman on the job is an oul' butty o' Joxer's; I have an idea that I know him meself. [*Silence.*] . . . There's a button off the back o' me moleskin trousers. . . . If you leave out a needle an' thread I'll sew it on meself. . . . Thanks be to God, the pains in me legs is gone, anyhow!

MRS. BOYLE: [*With a burst.*] Look here, Mr. Jacky Boyle, them yarns won't go down with Juno. I know you an' Joxer Daly of an oul' date, an', if you think you're able to come it over me with them fairy tales, you're in the wrong shop.

BOYLE: [*Coughing subduedly to relieve the tenseness of the situation.*] U-u-u-ugh.

MRS. BOYLE: Butty o' Joxer's! Oh, you'll do a lot o' good as long as you continue to be a butty o' Joxer's!

BOYLE: U-u-u-ugh.

MRS. BOYLE: Shovel! Ah, then, me boyo, you'd do far more work with a knife an' fork than ever you'll do with a shovel! If there was e'er a genuine job goin' you'd be dh'other way about—not able to lift your arms with the pains in your legs! Your poor wife slavin' to keep the bit in your mouth, an' you gallivantin' about all the day like a paycock!

BOYLE: It ud be betther for a man to be dead, bretther for a man to be dead.

MRS. BOYLE: [*Ignoring the interruption.*] Everybody callin' you "Captain," an' you only wanst on the wather, in an oul' collier from here to Liverpool, when anybody, to listen or look at you, ud take you for a second Christo For Columbus!

BOYLE: Are you never goin' to give us a rest?

MRS. BOYLE: Oh, you're never tired o' lookin' for a rest.

BOYLE: D'ye want to dhrive me out o' the house?

MRS. BOYLE: It ud be easier to dhrive you out o' the house than to dhrive you into a job. Here, sit down an' take your breakfast—it may be the last you'll get, for I don't know where the next is goin' to come from.

BOYLE: If I get this job we'll be all right.

MRS. BOYLE: Did ye see Jerry Devine?

BOYLE: [*Testily.*] No, I didn't see him.

MRS. BOYLE: No, but you seen Joxer. Well, he was here lookin' for you.

BOYLE: Well, let him look!

MRS. BOYLE: Oh, indeed, he may well look, for it ud be hard for him to see you, an' you stuck in Ryan's snug.

BOYLE: I wasn't in Ryan's snug—I don't go into Ryan's.

MRS. BOYLE: Oh, is there a mad dog there? Well, if you weren't in Ryan's you were in Foley's.

BOYLE: I'm telling you for the last three weeks I haven't tasted a dhrop of intoxicatin' liquor. I wasn't in ayther wan snug or dh'other—I could swear that on a prayer-book—I'm as innocent as the child unborn!

MRS. BOYLE: Well, if you'd been in for your breakfast you'd ha' seen him.

BOYLE: [*Suspiciously.*] What does he want me for?

MRS. BOYLE: He'll be back any minute an' then you'll soon know.

BOYLE: I'll dhrop out an' see if I can meet him.

MRS. BOYLE: You'll sit down an' take your breakfast, an' let me go to me work,

for I'm an hour late already waitin' for you.

BOYLE: You needn't ha' waited, for I'll take no breakfast—I've a little spirit left in me still!

MRS. BOYLE: Are you goin' to have your breakfast—yes or no?

BOYLE: [*Too proud to yield.*] I'll have no breakfast—yous can keep your breakfast. [*Plaintively.*] I'll knock out a bit somewhere, never fear.

MRS. BOYLE: Nobody's goin' to coax you —don't think that. [*She vigorously replaces the pan and the sausages in the press.*]

BOYLE: I've a little spirit left in me still.

[JERRY DEVINE *enters hastily.*]

JERRY: Oh, here you are at last! I've been searchin' for you everywhere. The foreman in Foley's told me you hadn't left the snug with Joxer ten minutes before I went in.

MRS. BOYLE: An' he swearin' on the holy prayer-book that he wasn't in no snug!

BOYLE: [*To* JERRY.] What business is it o' yours whether I was in a snug or no? What do you want to be gallopin' about afther me for? Is a man not to be allowed to leave his house for a minute without havin' a pack o' spies, pimps an' informers cantherin' at his heels?

JERRY: Oh, you're takin' a wrong view of it, Mr. Boyle; I simply was anxious to do you a good turn. I have a message for you from Father Farrell: he says that if you go to the job that's on in Rathmines, an' ask for Foreman Mangan, you'll get a start.

BOYLE: That's all right, but I don't want the motions of me body to be watched the way an asthronomer ud watch a star. If you're folleyin' Mary aself, you've no pereeogative to be folleyin' me. [*Suddenly catching his thigh.*] U-ugh, I'm afther gettin' a terrible twinge in me right leg!

MRS. BOYLE: Oh, it won't be very long now till it travels into your left wan. It's miraculous that whenever he scents a job in front of him, his legs begin to fail him! Then, me bucko, if you lose this chance, you may go an' furrage for yourself!

JERRY: This job'll last for some time, too, Captain, an' as soon as the foundations are in, it'll be cushy enough.

BOYLE: Won't it be a climbin' job? How d'ye expect me to be able to go up a ladder with these legs? An', if I get up aself, how am I goin' to get down agen?

MRS. BOYLE: [*Viciously.*] Get wan o' the

labourers to carry you down in a hod! You can't climb a laddher, but you can skip like a goat into a snug!

JERRY: I wouldn't let meself be let down that easy, Mr. Boyle; a little exercise, now, might do you all the good in the world.

BOYLE: It's a docthor you should have been, Devine—maybe you know more about the pains in me legs than meself that has them?

JERRY: [Irritated.] Oh, I know nothin' about the pains in your legs; I've brought the message that Father Farrell gave me, an' that's all I can do.

MRS. BOYLE: Here, sit down an' take your breakfast, an' go an' get ready; an' don't be actin' as if you couldn't pull a wing out of a dead bee.

BOYLE: I want no breakfast, I tell you; it ud choke me afther all that's been said. I've a little spirit left in me still.

MRS. BOYLE: Well, let's see your spirit, then, an' go in at wanst an' put on your moleskin trousers!

BOYLE: [Moving towards the door on left.] It ud be betther for a man to be dead! U-ugh! There's another twinge in me other leg! Nobody but meself knows the sufferin' I'm goin' through with the pains in these legs o' mine! [He goes into the room on left as MARY comes out with her hat in her hand.]

MRS. BOYLE: I'll have to push off now, for I'm terrible late already, but I was determined to stay an' hunt that Joxer this time. [She goes off.]

JERRY: Are you going out, Mary?

MARY: It looks like it when I'm putting on my hat, doesn't it?

JERRY: The bitther word agen, Mary.

MARY: You won't allow me to be friendly with you; if I thry, you deliberately misundherstand it.

JERRY: I didn't always misundherstand it; you were ofen delighted to have the arms of Jerry around you.

MARY: If you go on talkin' like this, Jerry Devine, you'll make me hate you!

JERRY: Well, let it be either a weddin' or a wake! Listen, Mary, I'm standin' for the Secretaryship of our Union. There's only one opposin' me; I'm popular with all the men, an' a good speaker—all are sayin' that I'll get elected.

MARY: Well?

JERRY: The job's worth three hundred an' fifty pounds a year, Mary. You an' I could live nice an' cosily on that; it would lift you out o' this place an' . . .

MARY: I haven't time to listen to you now—I have to go. [She is going out when JERRY bars the way.]

JERRY: [Appealingly.] Mary, what's come over you with me for the last few weeks? You hardly speak to me, an' then only a word with a face o' bitherness on it. Have you forgotten, Mary, all the happy evenin's that were as sweet as the scented hawthorn that sheltered the sides o' the road as we saunthered through the country?

MARY: That's all over now. When you get your new job, Jerry, you won't be long findin' a girl far betther than I am for your sweetheart.

JERRY: Never, never, Mary! No matther what happens you'll always be the same to me.

MARY: I must be off; please let me go, Jerry.

JERRY: I'll go a bit o' the way with you.

MARY: You needn't, thanks; I want to be by meself.

JERRY: [Catching her arm.] You're goin' to meet another fella; you've clicked with some one else, me lady!

MARY: That's no concern o' yours, Jerry Devine; let me go!

JERRY: I saw yous comin' out o' the Cornflower Dance Class, an' you hangin' on his arm—a thin, lanky strip of a Micky Dazzler, with a walkin'-stick an' gloves!

VOICE OF JOHNNY: [Loudly.] What are you doin' there—pullin' about everything!

VOICE OF BOYLE: [Loudly and viciously.] I'm puttin' on me moleskin trousers!

MARY: You're hurtin' me arm! Let me go, or I'll scream, an' then you'll have the oul' fella out on top of us!

JERRY: Don't be so hard on a fella, Mary, don't be so hard.

BOYLE: [Appearing at the door.] What's the meanin' of all this hillabaloo?

MARY: Let me go, let me go!

BOYLE: D'ye hear me—what's all this hillabaloo about?

JERRY: [Plaintively.] Will you not give us one kind word, one kind word, Mary?

BOYLE: D'ye hear me talkin' to yous? What's all this hillabaloo for?

JERRY: Let me kiss your hand, your little, tiny, white hand!

BOYLE: Your little, tiny, white hand—are you takin' leave o' your senses, man?

[MARY *breaks away and rushes out.*]

BOYLE: This is nice goin's on in front of her father!

JERRY: Ah, dhry up, for God's sake! [*He follows* MARY.]

BOYLE: Chiselurs don't care a damn now about their parents, they're bringin' their fathers' grey hairs down with sorra to the grave, an' laughin' at it, laughin' at it. Ah, I suppose it's just the same everywhere—the whole worl's in a state o' chassis! [*He sits by the fire.*] Breakfast! Well, they can keep their breakfast for me. Not if they went down on their bended knees would I take it—I'll show them I've a little spirit left in me still! [*He goes over to the press, takes out a plate and looks at it.*] Sassige! Well, let her keep her sassige. [*He returns to the fire, takes up the teapot and gives it a gentle shake.*] The tay's wet right enough. [*A pause; he rises, goes to the press, takes out the sausage, puts it on the pan, and puts both on the fire. He attends the sausage with a fork.*]

BOYLE: [*Singing.*]
When the robins nest agen,
And the flowers are in bloom,
When the Springtime's sunny smile seems to banish all sorrow an' gloom;
Then me bonny blue-ey'd lad, if me heart be true till then—
He's promised he'll come back to me,
When the robins nest agen!
[*He lifts his head at the high note, and then drops his eyes to the pan.*]

BOYLE: [*Singing.*]
When the . . .
[*Steps are heard approaching; he whips the pan off the fire and puts it under the bed, then sits down at the fire. The door opens and a bearded man looking in says.*]
You don't happen to want a sewin' machine?

BOYLE: [*Furiously.*] No, I don't want e'er a sewin' machine! [*He returns the pan to the fire, and commences to sing again.*]

BOYLE: [*Singing.*]
When the robins nest agen,
And the flowers they are in bloom,
He's . . .
[*A thundering knock is heard at the street door.*]

BOYLE: There's a terrible tatheraraa—that's a stranger—that's nobody belongin' to the house. [*Another loud knock.*]

JOXER: [*Sticking his head in at the door.*] Did ye hear them tatherarahs?

BOYLE: Well, Joxer, I'm not deaf.

JOHNNY: [*Appearing in his shirt and trousers at the door on left; his face is anxious and his voice is tremulous.*] Who's that at the door; who's that at the door? Who gave that knock—d'ye yous hear me—are yous deaf or dhrunk or what?

BOYLE: [*To* JOHNNY.] How the hell do I know who 'tis? Joxer, stick your head out o' the window an' see.

JOXER: An' mebbe get a bullet in the kisser? Ah, none o' them thricks for Joxer! It's betther to be a coward than a corpse!

BOYLE: [*Looking cautiously out of the window.*] It's a fella in a thrench coat.

JOHNNY: Holy Mary, Mother o' God, I . . .

BOYLE: He's goin' away—he must ha' got tired knockin'.
[JOHNNY *returns to the room on left.*]

BOYLE: Sit down an' have a cup o' tay, Joxer.

JOXER: I'm afraid the missus ud pop in on us agen before we'd know where we are. Somethin's tellin' me to go at wanst.

BOYLE: Don't be superstitious, man; we're Dublin men, an' not boyos that's only afther comin' up from the bog o' Allen—though if she did come in, right enough, we'd be caught like rats in a thrap.

JOXER: An' you know the sort she is—she wouldn't listen to reason—an' wanse bitten twice shy.

BOYLE: [*Going over to the window at back.*] If the worst came to the worst, you could dart out here, Joxer; it's only a dhrop of a few feet to the roof of the return room, an' the first minute she goes into dh'other room, I'll give you the bend, an' you can slip in an' away.

JOXER: [*Yielding to the temptation.*] Ah, I won't stop very long anyhow. [*Picking up a book from the table.*] Whose is the buk?

BOYLE: Aw, one o' Mary's; she's always readin' lately—nothin' but thrash, too. There's one I was lookin' at dh'other day: three stories, The Doll's House, Ghosts, an' The Wild Duck—buks only fit for chiselurs!

JOXER: Didja ever rade *Elizabeth, or Th' Exile o' Sibayria* . . . ah, it's a darlin' story, a daarlin' story!

BOYLE: You eat your sassige, an' never min' Th' Exile o' Sibayria.

[*Both sit down;* BOYLE *fills out tea, pours gravy on* JOXER'S *plate, and keeps the sausage for himself.*]

JOXER: What are you wearin' your moleskin trousers for?

BOYLE: I have to go to a job, Joxer. Just afther you'd gone, Devine kem runnin' in to tell us that Father Farrell said if I went down to the job that's goin' on in Rathmines I'd get a start.

JOXER: Be the holy, that's good news!

BOYLE: How is it good news? I wondher if you were in my condition, would you call it good news?

JOXER: I thought . . .

BOYLE: You thought! You think too sudden sometimes, Joxer. D'ye know, I'm hardly able to crawl with the pains in me legs!

JOXER: Yis, yis; I forgot the pains in your legs. I know you can do nothin' while they're at you.

BOYLE: You forgot; I don't think any of yous realize the state I'm in with the pains in me legs. What ud happen if I had to carry a bag o' cement?

JOXER: Ah, any man havin' the like of them pains id be down an' out, down an' out.

BOYLE: I wouldn't mind if he had said it to meself; but, no, oh no, he rushes in an' shouts it out in front o' Juno, an' you know what Juno is, Joxer. We all know Devine knows a little more than the rest of us, but he doesn't act as if he did; he's a good boy, sober, able to talk an' all that, but still . . .

JOXER: Oh ay; able to argufy, but still . . .

BOYLE: If he's runnin' afther Mary, aself, he's not goin' to be runnin' afther me. Captain Boyle's able to take care of himself. Afther all, I'm not gettin' brought up on Virol. I never heard him usin' a curse; I don't believe he was ever dhrunk in his life—sure he's not like a Christian at all!

JOXER: You're afther takin' the word out o' me mouth—afther all, a Christian's natural, but he's unnatural.

BOYLE: His oul' fella was just the same— a Wicklow man.

JOXER: A Wicklow man! That explains the whole thing. I've met many a Wicklow man in me time, but I never met wan that was any good.

BOYLE: "Father Farrell," says he, "sent me down to tell you." Father Farrell! . . .

D'ye know, Joxer, I never like to be beholden to any o' the clergy.

JOXER: It's dangerous, right enough.

BOYLE: If they do anything for you, they'd want you to be livin' in the Chapel. . . . I'm goin' to tell you somethin', Joxer, that I wouldn't tell to anybody else—the clergy always had too much power over the people in this unfortunate country.

JOXER: You could sing that if you had an air to it!

BOYLE: [*Becoming enthusiastic.*] Didn't they prevent the people in '47 from seizin' the corn, an' they starvin'; didn't they down Parnell; didn't they say that hell wasn't hot enough nor eternity long enough to punish the Fenians? We don't forget, we don't forget them things, Joxer. If they've taken everything else from us, Joxer, they've left us our memory.

JOXER: [*Emotionally.*] For mem'ry's the only friend that grief can call its own, that grief . . . can . . . call . . . its own!

BOYLE: Father Farrell's beginnin' to take a great intherest in Captain Boyle; because of what Johnny did for his country, says he to me wan day. It's a curious way to reward Johnny be makin' his poor oul' father work. But, that's what the clergy want, Joxer—work, work, work for me an' you; havin' us mulin' from mornin' till night, so that they may be in betther fettle when they come hoppin' round for their dues! Job! Well, let him give his job to wan of his hymn-singin', prayer-spoutin', crawthumpin' Confraternity men!

[*The voice of a coal-block vendor is heard chanting in the street.*]

VOICE OF COAL VENDOR: Blocks . . . coal-blocks! Blocks . . . coal-blocks!

JOXER: God be with the young days when you were steppin' the deck of a manly ship, with the win' blowin' a hurricane through the masts, an' the only sound you'd hear was, "Port your helm!" an' the only answer, "Port it is, sir!"

BOYLE: Them was days, Joxer, them was days. Nothin' was too hot or too heavy for me then. Sailin' from the Gulf o' Mexico to the Antarctic Ocean. I seen things, I seen things, Joxer, that no mortal man should speak about that knows his Catechism. Ofen, an' ofen, when I was fixed to the wheel with a marlin-spike, an' the win's blowin' fierce an' the waves lashin' an' lashin', till you'd think every minute was goin' to be your last, an' it blowed, an' blowed—blew is the right word, Joxer, but blowed is what the sailors use. . . .

JOXER: Aw, it's a darlin' word, a daarlin' word.

BOYLE: An', as it blowed an' blowed, I ofen looked up at the sky an' assed meself the question—what is the stars, what is the stars?

VOICE OF COAL VENDOR: Any blocks, coal-blocks; blocks, coal-blocks!

JOXER: Ah, that's the question, that's the question—what is the stars?

BOYLE: An' then, I'd have another look, an' I'd ass meself—what is the moon?

JOXER: Ah, that's the question—what is the moon, what is the moon?

[Rapid steps are heard coming towards the door. BOYLE makes desperate efforts to hide everything; JOXER rushes to the window in a frantic effort to get out; BOYLE begins to innocently lilt—"Oh, me darlin' Jennie, I will be thrue to thee," when the door is opened, and the black face of the COAL VENDOR appears.]

THE COAL VENDOR: D'yes want any blocks?

BOYLE: [With a roar.] No, we don't want any blocks!

JOXER: [Coming back with a sigh of relief.] That's affther puttin' the heart across me—I could ha' sworn it was Juno. I'd better be goin', Captain; you couldn't tell the minute Juno'd hop in on us.

BOYLE: Let her hop in; we may as well have it out first as at last. I've made up me mind—I'm not goin' to do only what she damn well likes.

JOXER: Them sentiments does you credit, Captain; I don't like to say anything as between man an' wife, but I say as a butty, as a butty, Captain, that you've stuck it too long, an' that it's about time you showed a little spunk.

How can a man die better than
        facin' fearful odds,
For th' ashes of his fathers an' the
        temples of his gods.

BOYLE: She has her rights—there's no one denyin' it, but haven't I me rights too?

JOXER: Of course you have—the sacred rights o' man!

BOYLE: To-day, Joxer, there's goin' to be issued a proclamation be me, establishin' an independent Republic, an' Juno'll have to take an oath of allegiance.

JOXER: Be firm, be firm, Captain; the

first few minutes'll be the worst:—if you gently touch a nettle it'll sting you for your pains; grasp it like a lad of mettle, an's as soft as silk remains!

VOICE OF JUNO: [Outside.] Can't stop, Mrs. Madigan—I haven't a minute!

JOXER: [Flying out of the window.] Holy God, here she is!

BOYLE: [Packing the things away with a rush in the press.] I knew that fella ud stop till she was in on top of us! [He sits down by the fire.]

[JUNO enters hastily; she is flurried and excited.]

JUNO: Oh, you're in—you must have been only affther comin' in?

BOYLE: No, I never went out.

JUNO: It's curious, then, you never heard the knockin'. [She puts her coat and hat on bed.]

BOYLE: Knockin'? Of course I heard the knockin'.

JUNO: An' why didn't you open the door, then? I suppose you were so busy with Joxer that you hadn't time.

BOYLE: I haven't seen Joxer since I seen him before. Joxer! What ud bring Joxer here?

JUNO: D'ye mean to tell me that the pair of yous wasn't collogin' together here when me back was turned?

BOYLE: What ud we be collogin' together about? I have somethin' else to think of besides collogin' with Joxer. I can swear on all the holy prayer-books . . .

MRS. BOYLE: That you weren't in no snug! Go on in at wanst now, an' take aff that moleskin trousers o' yours, an' put on a collar an' tie to smarten yourself up a bit. There's a visitor comin' with Mary in a minute, an' he has great news for you.

BOYLE: A job, I suppose; let us get wan first before we start lookin' for another.

MRS. BOYLE: That's the thing that's able to put the win' up you. Well, it's no job, but news that'll give you the chance o' your life.

BOYLE: What's all the mystery about?

MRS. BOYLE: G'win an' take off the moleskin trousers when you're told!

[BOYLE goes into room on left. MRS. BOYLE tidies up the room, puts the shovel under the bed, and goes to the press.]

MRS. BOYLE: Oh, God bless us, looka the way everythin's thrun about! Oh, Joxer was here, Joxer was here!

[MARY *enters with* CHARLIE BENTHAM; *he is a young man of twenty-five, tall, good-looking, with a very high opinion of himself generally. He is dressed in a brown coat, brown knee-breeches, grey stockings, a brown sweater, with a deep blue tie; he carries gloves and a walking-stick.*]

MRS. BOYLE: [*Fussing round.*] Come in, Mr. Bentham; sit down, Mr. Bentham, in this chair; it's more comfortabler than that, Mr. Bentham. Himself'll be here in a minute; he's just takin' off his trousers.

MARY: Mother!

BENTHAM: Please don't put yourself to any trouble, Mrs. Boyle—I'm quite all right here, thank you.

MRS. BOYLE: An' to think of you knowin' Mary, an' she knowin' the news you had for us, an' wouldn't let on; but it's all the more welcomer now, for we were on our last lap!

VOICE OF JOHNNY: [*Inside.*] What are you kickin' up all the racket for?

BOYLE: [*Roughly.*] I'm takin' off me moleskin trousers!

JOHNNY: Can't you do it, then, without lettin' th' whole house know you're takin' off your trousers? What d'ye want puttin' them on an' takin' them off again?

BOYLE: Will you let me alone, will you let me alone? Am I never goin' to be done thryin' to please th' whole o' yous?

MRS. BOYLE: [*To* BENTHAM.] You must excuse th' state o' th' place, Mr. Bentham; th' minute I turn me back that man o' mine always makes a litther o' th' place, a litther o' th' place.

BENTHAM: Don't worry, Mrs. Boyle; it's all right, I assure . . .

BOYLE: [*Inside.*] Where's me braces; where in th' name o' God did I leave me braces. . . . Ay, did you see where I put me braces?

JOHNNY: [*Inside, calling out.*] Ma, will you come in here an' take da away ou' o' this or he'll dhrive me mad.

MRS. BOYLE: [*Going towards door.*] Dear, dear, dear, that man'll be lookin' for somethin' on th' day o' Judgment. [*Looking into room and calling to* BOYLE.] Look at your braces, man, hangin' round your neck!

BOYLE: [*Inside.*] Aw, Holy God!

MRS. BOYLE: [*Calling.*] Johnny, Johnny, come out here for a minute.

JOHNNY: Oh, leave Johnny alone, an' don't be annoyin' him!

MRS. BOYLE: Come on, Johnny, till I inthroduce you to Mr. Bentham. [*To* BENTHAM.] Me son, Mr. Bentham; he's afther goin' through the mill. He was only a chiselur of a Boy Scout in Easter Week, when he got hit in the hip; and his arm was blew off in the fight in O'Connell Street. [JOHNNY *comes in.*] Here he is, Mr. Bentham; Mr. Bentham, Johnny. None can deny he done his bit for Irelan', if that's going to do him any good.

JOHNNY: [*Boastfully.*] I'd do it agen, ma, I'd do it agen; for a principle's a principle.

MRS. BOYLE: Ah, you lost your best principle, me boy, when you lost your arm; them's the only sort o' principles that's any good to a workin' man.

JOHNNY: Ireland only half free'll never be at peace while she has a son left to pull a trigger.

MRS. BOYLE: To be sure, to be sure—no bread's a lot betther than half a loaf. [*Calling loudly in to* BOYLE.] Will you hurry up there?

[BOYLE *enters in his best trousers, which aren't too good, and looks very uncomfortable in his collar and tie.*]

MRS. BOYLE: This is me husband; Mr. Boyle, Mr. Bentham.

BENTHAM: Ah, very glad to know you, Mr. Boyle. How are you?

BOYLE: Ah, I'm not too well at all; I suffer terrible with pains in me legs. Juno can tell you there what . . .

MRS. BOYLE: You won't have many pains in your legs when you hear what Mr. Bentham has to tell you.

BENTHAM: Juno! What an interesting name! It reminds one of Homer's glorious story of ancient gods and heroes.

BOYLE: Yis, doesn't it? You see, Juno was born an' christened in June, I met her in June; we were married in June, an' Johnny was born in June, so wan day I says to her, "You should ha' been called Juno," an' the name stuck to her ever since.

MRS. BOYLE: Here, we can talk o' them things agen; let Mr. Bentham say what he has to say now.

BENTHAM: Well, Mr. Boyle, I suppose you'll remember a Mr. Ellison of Santry—he's a relative of yours, I think.

BOYLE: [*Viciously.*] Is it that prognosticator an' procrastinator! Of course I remember him.

BENTHAM: Well, he's dead, Mr. Boyle . . .

BOYLE: Sorra many'll go into mournin' for him.

MRS. BOYLE: Wait till you hear what Mr. Bentham has to say, an' then, maybe, you'll change your opinion.

BENTHAM: A week before he died he sent for me to write his will for him. He told me that there were two only that he wished to leave his property to: his second cousin Michael Finnegan of Santry, and John Boyle, his first cousin of Dublin.

BOYLE: [Excitedly.] Me, is it me, me?

BENTHAM: You, Mr. Boyle; I'll read a copy of the will that I have here with me, which has been duly filed in the Court of Probate. [He takes a paper from his pocket and reads.]

6th February 1922.
This is the last Will and Testament of William Ellison, of Santry, in the County of Dublin. I hereby order and wish my property to be sold and divided as follows:—

£20 to the St. Vincent De Paul Society.

£60 for Masses for the repose of my soul (5s. for Each Mass).

The rest of my property to be divided between my first and second cousins.

I hereby appoint Timothy Buckly, of Santry, and Hugh Brierly, of Coolock, to be my Executors.

[Signed]
WILLIAM ELLISON.
HUGH BRIERLY.
TIMOTHY BUCKLY.
CHARLES BENTHAM, N.T.

BOYLE: [Eagerly.] An' how much'll be comin' out of it, Mr. Bentham?

BENTHAM: The Executors told me that half of the property would be anything between £1500 and £2000.

MARY: A fortune, father, a fortune!

JOHNNY: We'll be able to get out o' this place now, an' go somewhere we're not known.

MRS. BOYLE: You won't have to trouble about a job for a while, Jack.

BOYLE: [Fervently.] I'll never doubt the goodness o' God agen.

BENTHAM: I congratulate you, Mr. Boyle. [They shake hands.]

BOYLE: An' now, Mr. Bentham, you'll have to have a wet.

BENTHAM: A wet?

BOYLE: A wet—a jar—a boul!

MRS. BOYLE: Jack, you're speakin' to Mr. Bentham, an' not to Joxer.

BOYLE: [Solemnly.] Juno . . . Mary . . . Johnny . . . we'll have to go into mournin' at wanst. . . . I never expected that poor Bill ud die so sudden. . . . Well, we all have to die some day . . . you, Juno, to-day . . . an' me, maybe, to-morrow. . . . It's sad, but it can't be helped. . . . Requiescat in pace . . . or, usin' our oul' tongue like St. Patrick or St. Briget, Guh sayeree jeea ayera!

MARY: Oh, father, that's not Rest in Peace; that's God save Ireland.

BOYLE: U-u-ugh, it's all the same—isn't it a prayer? . . . Juno, I'm done with Joxer; he's nothin' but a prognosticator an' a . . .

JOXER: [Climbing angrily through the window and bounding into the room.] You're done with Joxer, are you? Maybe you thought I'd stop on the roof all the night for you! Joxer out on the roof with the win' blowin' through him was nothin' to you an' your friend with the collar an' tie!

MRS. BOYLE: What in the name o' God brought you out on the roof; what were you doin' there?

JOXER: [Ironically.] I was dhreamin' I was standin' on the bridge of a ship, an' she sailin' the Antarctic Ocean, an' it blowed, an' blowed, an' I lookin' up at the sky an' sayin', what is the stars, what is the stars?

MRS. BOYLE: [Opening the door and standing at it.] Here, get ou' o' this, Joxer Daly; I was always thinkin' you had a slate off.

JOXER: [Moving to the door.] I have to laugh every time I look at the deep sea sailor; an' a row on a river ud make him sea-sick!

BOYLE: Get ou' o' this before I take the law into me own hands!

JOXER: [Going out.] Say aw rewaeawr, but not good-bye. Lookin' for work, an' prayin' to God he won't get it! [He goes.]

MRS. BOYLE: I'm tired tellin' you what Joxer was; maybe now you see yourself the kind he is.

BOYLE: He'll never blow the froth off a pint o' mine agen, that's a sure thing. Johnny . . . Mary . . . you're to keep yourselves to yourselves for the future. Juno, I'm done with Joxer. . . . I'm a

new man from this out. . . . [*Clasping* JUNO'S *hand, and singing emotionally.*]:
Oh, me darlin' Juno, I will be thrue
to thee;

Me own, me darlin' Juno, you're all
the world to me.

CURTAIN

ACT II

SCENE. *The same, but the furniture is more plentiful, and of a vulgar nature. A glaringly upholstered arm-chair and lounge; cheap pictures and photos everywhere. Every available spot is ornamented with huge vases filled with artificial flowers. Crossed festoons of coloured paper chains stretch from end to end of ceiling. On the table is an old attaché case. It is about six in the evening, and two days after the First Act.* BOYLE, *in his shirt sleeves, is voluptuously stretched on the sofa; he is smoking a clay pipe. He is half asleep. A lamp is lighting on the table. After a few moments' pause the voice of* JOXER *is heard singing softly outside at the door—"Me pipe I'll smoke, as I dhrive me moke—are you there, Mor . . . ee . . . ar . . . i . . . teee!"*

BOYLE: [*Leaping up, takes a pen in his hand and busies himself with papers.*] Come along, Joxer, me son, come along.

JOXER: [*Putting his head in.*] Are you be yourself?

BOYLE: Come on, come on; that doesn't matther; I'm masther now, an' I'm goin' to remain masther.

[JOXER *comes in.*]

JOXER: How d'ye feel now, as a man o' money?

BOYLE: [*Solemnly.*] It's a responsibility, Joxer, a great responsibility.

JOXER: I suppose 'tis now, though you wouldn't think it.

BOYLE: Joxer, han' me over that attackey case on the table there. [JOXER *hands the case.*] Ever since the Will was passed I've run hundhreds o' dockyments through me han's—I tell you, you have to keep your wits about you. [*He busies himself with papers.*]

JOXER: Well, I won't disturb you; I'll dhrop in when . . .

BOYLE: [*Hastily.*] It's all right, Joxer, this is the last one to be signed today. [*He signs a paper, puts it into the case, which he shuts with a snap, and sits back pompously in the chair.*] Now, Joxer, you want to see me; I'm at your service—what can I do for you, me man?

JOXER: I've just dhropped in with the £3 : 5s. that Mrs. Madigan riz on the blankets an' table for you, and she says you're to be in no hurry payin' it back.

BOYLE: She won't be long without it; I expect the first cheque for a couple o' hundhred any day. There's the five bob for yourself—go on, take it, man; it'll not be the last you'll get from the Captain. Now an' agen we have our differ, but we're there together all the time.

JOXER: Me for you, an' you for me, like the two Musketeers.

BOYLE: Father Farrell stopped me to-day an' tole me how glad he was I fell in for the money.

JOXER: He'll be stoppin' you often enough now; I suppose it was "Mr." Boyle with him?

BOYLE: He shuk me be the han'. . . .

JOXER: [*Ironically.*] I met with Napper Tandy, an' he shuk me be the han'!

BOYLE: You're seldom asthray, Joxer, but you're wrong shipped this time. What you're sayin' of Father Farrell is very near to blasfeemey. I don't like any one to talk disrespectful of Father Farrell.

JOXER: You're takin' me up wrong, Captain; I wouldn't let a word be said agen Father Farrell—the heart o' the rowl, that's what he is; I always said he was a darlin' man, a daarlin' man.

BOYLE: Comin' up the stairs who did I meet but that bummer, Nugent. "I seen you talkin' to Father Farrell," says he, with a grin on him. "He'll be folleyin' you," says he, "like a Guardian Angel from this out"—all the time the oul' grin on him, Joxer.

JOXER: I never seen him yet but he had that oul' grin on him!

BOYLE: "Mr. Nugent," says I, "Father Farrell is a man o' the people, an', as far as I know the History o' me country, the priests was always in the van of the fight for Irelan's freedom."

JOXER: [Fervently.]

Who was it led the van, Soggart Aroon?
Since the fight first began, Soggart Aroon?

BOYLE: "Who are you tellin'?" says he. "Didn't they let down the Fenians, an' didn't they do in Parnell? An' now . . ." "You ought to be ashamed o' yourself," says I, interruptin' him, "not to know the History o' your country." An' I left him gawkin' where he was.

JOXER: Where ignorance 's bliss 'tis folly to be wise; I wondher did he ever read the Story o' Irelan'.

BOYLE: Be J. L. Sullivan? Don't you know he didn't?

JOXER: Ah, it's a darlin' buk, a daarlin' buk!

BOYLE: You'd betther be goin', now, Joxer, his Majesty, Bentham, 'll be here any minute, now.

JOXER: Be the way things is lookin', it'll be a match between him an' Mary. She's thrun over Jerry altogether. Well, I hope it will, for he's a darlin' man.

BOYLE: I'm glad you think so—I don't. [Irritably.] What's darlin' about him?

JOXER: [Nonplussed.] I only seen him twiced; if you want to know me, come an' live with me.

BOYLE: He's too ignified for me—to hear him talk you'd think he knew as much as a Boney's Oraculum. He's given up his job as teacher, an' is goin' to become a solicitor in Dublin—he's been studyin' law. I suppose he thinks I'll set him up, but he's wrong shipped. An' th' other fella—Jerry's as bad. The two o' them ud give you a pain in your face, listenin' to them; Jerry believin' in nothin', an' Bentham believin' in everythin'. One that says all is God an' no man; an' th' other that says all is man an' no God!

JOXER: Well, I'll be off now.

BOYLE: Don't forget to dhrop down afther a while; we'll have a quiet jar, an' a song or two.

JOXER: Never fear.

BOYLE: An' tell Mrs. Madigan that I hope we'll have the pleasure of her organization at our little enthertainment.

JOXER: Righto; we'll come down together. [He goes out.]

[JOHNNY comes from room on left, and sits down moodily at the fire. BOYLE looks at him for a few moments, and shakes his head. He fills his pipe.]

VOICE OF JUNO AT THE DOOR: Open the door, Jack; this thing has me nearly kilt with the weight.

[BOYLE opens the door. JUNO enters carrying the box of a gramophone, followed by MARY carrying the horn, and some parcels. JUNO leaves the box on the table and flops into a chair.]

JUNO: Carryin' that from Henry Street was no joke.

BOYLE: U-u-ugh, that's a grand lookin' insthrument—how much was it?

JUNO: Pound down, an' five to be paid at two shillin's a week.

BOYLE: That's reasonable enough.

JUNO: I'm afraid we're runnin' into too much debt; first the furniture, an' now this.

BOYLE: The whole lot won't be much out of £2000.

MARY: I don't know what you wanted a gramophone for—I know Charlie hates them; he says they're destructive of real music.

BOYLE: Desthructive of music—that fella ud give you a pain in your face. All a gramophone wants is to be properly played; its thrue wondher is only felt when everythin's quiet—what a gramophone wants is dead silence!

MARY: But, father, Jerry says the same; afther all, you can only appreciate music when your ear is properly trained.

BOYLE: That's another fella ud give you a pain in your face. Properly thrained! I suppose you couldn't appreciate football unless your fut was properly thrained.

MRS. BOYLE: [To MARY.] Go on in ower that an' dress, or Charlie 'll be in on you, an' tay nor nothin' 'll be ready.

[MARY goes into room left.]

MRS. BOYLE: [Arranging table for tea.] You didn't look at our new gramophone, Johnny?

JOHNNY: 'Tisn't gramophones I'm thinking of.

MRS. BOYLE: An' what is it you're thinkin' of, allanna?

JOHNNY: Nothin', nothin', nothin'.

MRS. BOYLE: Sure, you must be thinkin' of somethin'; it's yourself that has yourself the way y'are; sleepin' wan night in me sisther's, an' the nex' in your father's brother's—you'll get no rest goin' on that way.

JOHNNY: I can rest nowhere, nowhere, nowhere.

MRS. BOYLE: Sure, you're not thryin' to rest anywhere.

JOHNNY: Let me alone, let me alone, let me alone, for God's sake.

[A knock at street door.]

MRS. BOYLE: [In a flutter.] Here he is; here's Mr. Bentham!

BOYLE: Well, there's room for him; it's a pity there's not a brass band to play him in.

MRS. BOYLE: We'll han' the tay round, an' not be clusthered round the table, as if we never seen nothin'.

[Steps are heard approaching, and JUNO, opening the door, allows BENTHAM to enter.]

JUNO: Give your hat an' stick to Jack, there . . . sit down, Mr. Bentham . . . no, not there . . . in th' easy chair be the fire . . . there, that's betther. Mary'll be out to you in a minute.

BOYLE: [Solemnly.] I seen be the paper this mornin' that Consols was down half per cent. That's serious, min' you, an' shows the whole counthry's in a state o' chassis.

MRS. BOYLE: What's Consols, Jack?

BOYLE: Consols? Oh, Consols is—oh, there's no use tellin' women what Consols is—th' wouldn't undherstand.

BENTHAM: It's just as you were saying, Mr. Boyle . . .

[MARY enters charmingly dressed.]

BENTHAM: Oh, good evening, Mary; how pretty you're looking!

MARY: [Archly.] Am I?

BOYLE: We were just talkin' when you kem in, Mary, I was tellin' Mr. Bentham that the whole counthry's in a state o' chassis.

MARY: [To BENTHAM.] Would you prefer the green or the blue ribbon round me hair, Charlie?

MRS. BOYLE: Mary, your father's speakin'.

BOYLE: [Rapidly.] I was jus' tellin' Mr. Bentham that the whole counthry's in a state o' chassis.

MARY: I'm sure you're frettin', da, whether it is or no.

MRS. BOYLE: With all our churches an' religions, the worl's not a bit the betther.

BOYLE: [With a commanding gesture.] Tay!

[MARY and MRS. BOYLE dispense the tea.]

MRS. BOYLE: An' Irelan's takin' a leaf out o' the worl's buk; when we got the makin' of our own laws I thought we'd never stop to look behind us, but instead of that we never stopped to look before us! If the people ud folley up their religion betther there'd be a betther chance for us—what do you think, Mr. Bentham?

BENTHAM: I'm afraid I can't venture to express an opinion on that point, Mrs. Boyle; dogma has no attraction for me.

MRS. BOYLE: I forgot you didn't hold with us: what's this you said you were?

BENTHAM: A Theosophist, Mrs. Boyle.

MRS. BOYLE: An' what in the name o' God's a Theosophist?

BOYLE: A Theosophist, Juno, 's a—tell her, Mr. Bentham, tell her.

BENTHAM: It's hard to explain in a few words: Theosophy's founded on The Vedas, the religious books of the East. Its central theme is the existence of an all-pervading Spirit—the Life-Breath. Nothing really exists but this one Universal Life-Breath. And whatever even seems to exist separately from this Life-Breath, doesn't really exist at all. It is all vital force in man, in all animals, and in all vegetation. This Life-Breath is called the Prawna.

MRS. BOYLE: The Prawna! What a comical name!

BOYLE: Prawna; yis, the Prawna. [Blowing gently through his lips.] That's the Prawna!

MRS. BOYLE: Whist, whist, Jack.

BENTHAM: The happiness of man depends upon his sympathy with this Spirit. Men who have reached a high state of excellence are called Yogi. Some men become Yogi in a short time, it may take others millions of years.

BOYLE: Yogi! I seen hundhreds of them in the streets o' San Francisco.

BENTHAM: It is said by these Yogi that if we practise certain mental exercises that we would have powers denied to others—for instance, the faculty of seeing things that happen miles and miles away.

MRS. BOYLE: I wouldn't care to meddle with that sort o' belief; it's a very curious religion, altogether.

BOYLE: What's curious about it? Isn't all religions curious? If they weren't, you wouldn't get any one to believe them. But religions is passin' away—they've had their day like everything else. Take the real Dublin people, f'rinstance: they know more about Charlie Chaplin an' Tommy Mix than they do about SS. Peter an' Paul!

MRS. BOYLE: You don't believe in ghosts, Mr. Bentham?

MARY: Don't you know he doesn't, mother?

BENTHAM: I don't know that, Mary. Scientists are beginning to think that what we call ghosts are sometimes seen by persons of a certain nature. They say that sensational actions, such as the killing of a person, demand great energy, and that that energy lingers in the place where the action occurred. People may live in the place and see nothing, when some one may come along whose personality has some peculiar connection with the energy of the place, and, in a flash, the person sees the whole affair.

JOHNNY: [Rising swiftly, pale and affected.] What sort o' talk is this to be goin' on with? Is there nothin' betther to be talkin' about but the killin' o' people? My God, isn't it bad enough for these things to happen without talkin' about them! [He hurriedly goes into the room on left.]

BENTHAM: Oh, I'm very sorry, Mrs. Boyle; I never thought . . .

MRS. BOYLE: [Apologetically.] Never mind, Mr. Bentham, he's very touchy. [A frightened scream is heard from JOHNNY inside.]

MRS. BOYLE: Mother of God? What's that?

[He rushes out again, his face pale, his lips twitching, his limbs trembling.]

JOHNNY: Shut the door, shut the door, quick, for God's sake! Great God, have mercy on me! Blessed Mother o' God, shelter me, shelter your son!

MRS. BOYLE: [Catching him in her arms.] What's wrong with you? What ails you? Sit down, sit down, here, on the bed . . . there now . . . there now.

MARY: Johnny, Johnny, what ails you?

JOHNNY: I seen him, I seen him . . . kneelin' in front o' the statue . . . merciful Jesus, have pity on me!

MRS. BOYLE: [To BOYLE.] Get him a glass o' whisky . . . quick, man, an' don't stand gawkin'.

[BOYLE gets the whisky.]

JOHNNY: Sit here, sit here, mother . . . between me an' the door.

MRS. BOYLE: I'll sit beside you as long as you like, only tell me what was it came across you at all?

JOHNNY: [After taking some drink.] I seen him. . . . I seen Robbie Tancred kneelin' down before the statue . . . an' the red light shinin' on him . . . an' when I went in . . . he turned an' looked at me . . . an' I seen the woun's bleedin' in his breast. . . . Oh, why did he look at me like that . . . it wasn't my fault that he was done in. . . . Mother o' God, keep him away from me!

MRS. BOYLE: There, there, child, you've imagined it all. There was nothin' there at all—it was the red light you seen, an' the talk we had put all the rest into your head. Here, dhrink more o' this—it'll do you good. . . . An', now, stretch yourself down on the bed for a little. [To BOYLE.] Go in, Jack, an' show him it was only in his own head it was.

BOYLE: [Making no move.] E-e-e-e-eh; it's all nonsense; it was only a shadda he saw.

MARY: Mother o' God, he made me heart lep!

BENTHAM: It was simply due to an overwrought imagination—we all get that way at times.

MRS. BOYLE: There, dear, lie down in the bed, an' I'll put the quilt across you . . . e-e-e-eh, that's it . . . you'll be as right as the mail in a few minutes.

JOHNNY: Mother, go into the room an' see if the light's lightin' before the statue.

MRS. BOYLE: [To BOYLE.] Jack, run in, an' see if the light's lightin' before the statue.

BOYLE: [To MARY.] Mary, slip in an' see if the light's lightin' before the statue.

[MARY hesitates to go in.]

BENTHAM: It's all right; Mary, I'll go. [He goes into the room; remains a few moments, and returns.]

BENTHAM: Everything's just as it was—the light burning bravely before the statue.

BOYLE: Of course; I knew it was all nonsense.

[A knock at the door.]

BOYLE: [Going to open the door.] E-e-e-e-eh. [He opens it, and JOXER, followed by MRS. MADIGAN, enters. MRS. MADIGAN is a strong, dapper little woman of about forty-five; her face is almost al-

ways a widespread smile of complacency. She is a woman who, in manner at least, can mourn with them that mourn, and rejoice with them that do rejoice. When she is feeling comfortable, she is inclined to be reminiscent; when others say anything, or following a statement made by herself, she has a habit of putting her head a little to one side, and nodding it rapidly several times in succession, like a bird pecking at a hard berry. Indeed, she has a good deal of the bird in her, but the bird instinct is by no means a melodious one. She is ignorant, vulgar and forward, but her heart is generous withal. For instance, she would help a neighbour's sick child; she would probably kill the child, but her intentions would be to cure it; she would be more at home helping a drayman to lift a fallen horse. She is dressed in a rather soiled grey dress and a vivid purple blouse; in her hair is a huge comb, ornamented with huge coloured beads. She enters with a gliding step, beaming smile and nodding head. BOYLE *receives them effusively.*]

BOYLE: Come on in, Mrs. Madigan; come on in; I was afraid you weren't comin'. . . . [*Slyly.*] There's some people able to dhress, ay, Joxer?

JOXER: Fair as the blossoms that bloom in the May, an' sweet as the scent of the new mown hay. . . . Ah, well she may wear them.

MRS. MADIGAN: [*Looking at* MARY.] I know some as are as sweet as the blossoms that bloom in the May—oh, no names, no pack dhrill!

BOYLE: An', now, I'll inthroduce the pair o' yous to Mary's intended: Mr. Bentham, this is Mrs. Madigan, an oul' back-parlour neighbour, that, if she could help it at all, ud never see a body shuk!

BENTHAM: [*Rising, and tentatively shaking the hand of* MRS. MADIGAN.] I'm sure, it's a great pleasure to know you, Mrs. Madigan.

MRS. MADIGAN: An' I'm goin' to tell you, Mr. Bentham, you're goin' to get as nice a bit o' skirt in Mary, there, as ever you seen in your puff. Not like some of the dhressed up dolls that's knockin' about lookin' for men when it's a skelpin' they want. I remember as well as I remember yesterday, the day she was born—of a Tuesday, the 25th o' June, in the year 1901, at thirty-three minutes past wan

in the day be Foley's clock, the pub at the corner o' the street. A cowld day it was too, for the season o' the year, an' I remember sayin' to Joxer, there, who I met comin' up th' stairs, that the new arrival in Boyle's ud grow up a hardy chiselur if it lived, an' that she'd be somethin' one o' these days that nobody suspected, an' so signs on it, here she is to-day, goin' to be married to a young man lookin' as if he'd be fit to commensurate in any position in life it ud please God to call him!

BOYLE: [*Effusively.*] Sit down, Mrs. Madigan, sit down, me oul' sport. [*To* BENTHAM.] This is Joxer Daly, Past Chief Ranger of the Dear Little Shamrock Branch of the Irish National Foresters, an oul' front-top neighbour, that never despaired, even in the darkest days of Ireland's sorra.

JOXER: Nil desperandum, Captain, nil desperandum.

BOYLE: Sit down, Joxer, sit down. The two of us was ofen in a tight corner.

MRS. BOYLE: Ay, in Foley's snug!

JOXER: An' we kem out of it flyin', we kem out of it flyin', Captain.

BOYLE: An', now, for a dhrink—I know yous won't refuse an oul' friend.

MRS. MADIGAN: [*To* JUNO.] Is Johnny not well, Mrs. . . .

MRS. BOYLE: [*Warningly.*] S-s-s-sh.

MRS. MADIGAN: Oh, the poor darlin'.

BOYLE: Well, Mrs. Madigan, is it tay or what?

MRS. MADIGAN: Well, speakin' for meself, I jus' had me tea a minute ago, an' I'm afraid to dhrink any more—I'm never the same when I dhrink too much tay. Thanks, all the same, Mr. Boyle.

BOYLE: Well, what about a bottle o' stout or a dhrop o' whisky?

MRS. MADIGAN: A bottle o' stout ud be a little too heavy for me stummock afther me tay. . . . A-a-ah, I'll thry the ball o' malt.

[BOYLE *prepares the whisky.*]

MRS. MADIGAN: There's nothin' like a ball o' malt occasional like—too much of it isn't good. [*To* BOYLE, *who is adding water.*] Ah, God, Johnny, don't put too much wather on it! [*She drinks.*] I suppose yous'll be lavin' this place.

BOYLE: I'm looking for a place near the sea; I'd like the place that you might say was me cradle, to be me grave as well. The sea is always callin' me.

JOXER: She is callin', callin', callin', in the win' an' on the sea.

BOYLE: Another dhrop o' whisky, Mrs. Madigan?

MRS. MADIGAN: Well, now, it ud be hard to refuse seein' the suspicious times that's in it.

BOYLE: [With a commanding gesture.] Song! . . . Juno . . . Mary . . . "Home to Our Mount'ins"!

MRS. MADIGAN: [Enthusiastically.] Hear, hear!

JOXER: Oh, tha's a darlin' song, a daarlin' song!

MARY: [Bashfully.] Ah, no, da; I'm not in a singin' humour.

MRS. MADIGAN: Gawn with you, child, an' you only goin' to be marrid; I remember as well as I remember yesterday,—it was on a lovely August evenin', exactly, accordin' to date, fifteen years ago, come the Tuesday folleyin' the nex' that's comin' on, when me own man (the Lord be good to him) an' me was sittin' shy together in a doty little nook on a counthry road, adjacent to The Stiles. "That'll scratch your lovely, little white neck," says he, ketchin' hould of a danglin' bramble branch, holdin' clusters of the loveliest flowers you ever seen, an' breakin' it off, so that his arm fell, accidental like, roun' me waist, an' as I felt it tightenin', an' tightenin', an' tightenin', I thought me buzzum was every minute goin' to burst out into a roystherin' song about

> The little green leaves that were shakin' on the threes,
> The gallivantin' buttherflies, an' buzz-in' o' the bees!

BOYLE: Ordher for the song!

JUNO: Come on, Mary—we'll do our best. [JUNO and MARY stand up, and choosing a suitable position, sing simply "Home to Our Mountains."]

[They bow to company, and return to their places.]

BOYLE: [Emotionally, at the end of the song.] Lull . . . me . . . to . . . rest!

JOXER: [Clapping his hands.] Bravo, bravo! Darlin' girulls, darlin' girulls!

MRS. MADIGAN: Juno, I never seen you in bether form.

BENTHAM: Very nicely rendered indeed.

MRS. MADIGAN: A noble call, a noble call!

MRS. BOYLE: What about yourself, Mrs.

Madigan? [After some coaxing, MRS. MADIGAN rises, and in a quavering voice sings the following verse.]

> If I were a blackbird I'd whistle and sing;
> I'd follow the ship that my thrue love was in;
> An' on the top riggin', I'd there build me nest,
> An' at night I would sleep on me Willie's white breast!

[Becoming husky, amid applause, she sits down.]

MRS. MADIGAN: Ah, me voice is too husky now, Juno; though I remember the time when Maisie Madigan could sing like a nightin-gale at matin' time. I remember as well as I remember yesterday, at a party given to celebrate the comin' of the first chiselur to Annie an' Benny Jimeson—who was the barber, yous may remember, in Henri-etta Street, that, after Easter Week, hung out a green, white an' orange pole, an', then, when the Tans started their Jazz dancin', whipped it in agen, an' stuck out a red, white an' blue wan instead, given as an excuse that a barber's pole was strictly non-political—singin' "An' You'll Remember Me," with the top notes quiverin' in a dead hush of pethrified attention, folleyed by a clappin' o' han's that shuk the tumblers on the table, an' capped be Jimeson, the barber, sayin' that it was the best rendherin' of "You'll Remember Me" he ever heard in his natural!

BOYLE: [Peremptorily.] Ordher for Joxer's song!

JOXER: Ah, no, I couldn't; don't ass me, Captain.

BOYLE: Joxer's song, Joxer's song—give us wan of your shut-eyed wans. [JOXER settles himself in his chair; takes a drink; clears his throat; solemnly closes his eyes, and begins to sing in a very querulous voice.]

> She is far from the lan' where her young hero sleeps,
> An' lovers around her are sighing [He hesitates.]
> An' lovers around her are sighin' . . . sighin' . . . sighin' . . . [A pause.]

BOYLE: [Imitating JOXER.]

And lovers around her are sighing!

What's the use of you thryin' to sing the song if you don't know it?

MARY: Thry another one, Mr. Daly— maybe you'd be more fortunate.

MRS. MADIGAN: Gawn, Joxer, thry another wan.

JOXER: [Starting again.]

> I have heard the mavis singin' his love song to the morn;
> I have seen the dew-dhrop clingin' to the rose jus' newly born;
> but . . . but . . . [Frantically.] to the rose jus' newly born
> . . . newly born . . . born.

JOHNNY: Mother, put on the gramophone, for God's sake, an' stop Joxer's bawlin'.

BOYLE: [Commandingly.] Gramophone! . . . I hate to see fellas thryin' to do what they're not able to do. [BOYLE arranges the gramophone, and is about to start it, when voices are heard of persons descending the stairs.]

MRS. BOYLE: [Warningly.] Whisht, Jack, don't put it on, don't put it on yet; this must be poor Mrs. Tancred comin' down to go to the hospital—I forgot all about them bringin' the body to the church to-night. Open the door, Mary, an' give them a bit o' light.

> [MARY opens the door, and MRS. TANCRED—a very old woman, obviously shaken by the death of her son —appears, accompanied by several neighbours. The first few phrases are spoken before they appear.]

FIRST NEIGHBOUR: It's a sad journey we're goin' on, but God's good, an' the Republicans won't be always down.

MRS. TANCRED: Ah, what good is that to me now? Whether they're up or down— it won't bring me darlin' boy from the grave.

MRS. BOYLE: Come in an' have a hot cup o' tay, Mrs. Tancred, before you go.

MRS. TANCRED: Ah, I can take nothin' now, Mrs. Boyle—I won't be long afther him.

FIRST NEIGHBOUR: Still an' all, he died a noble death, an' we'll bury him like a king.

MRS. TANCRED: An' I'll go on livin' like a pauper. Ah, what's the pains I suffered bringin' him into the world to carry him to his cradle, to the pains I'm sufferin' now, carryin' him out o' the world to bring him to his grave!

MARY: It would be better for you not to go at all, Mrs. Tancred, but to stay at home beside the fire with some o' the neighbours.

MRS. TANCRED: I seen the first of him, an' I'll see the last of him.

MRS. BOYLE: You'd want a shawl, Mrs. Tancred; it's a cowld night, an' the win's blowin' sharp.

MRS. MADIGAN: [Rushing out.] I've a shawl above.

MRS. TANCRED: Me home is gone, now; he was me only child, an' to think that he was lyin' for a whole night stretched out on the side of a lonely counthry lane, with his head, his darlin' head, that I ofen kissed an' fondled, half hidden in the wather of a runnin' brook. An' I'm told he was the leadher of the ambush where me nex' door neighbour, Mrs. Mannin', lost her Free State soldier son. An' now here's the two of us oul' women, standin' one on each side of a scales o' sorra, balanced be the bodies of our two dead darlin' sons. [MRS. MADIGAN returns, and wraps a shawl around her.] God bless you, Mrs. Madigan. . . . [She moves slowly towards the door.] Mother o' God, Mother o' God, have pity on the pair of us! . . . O Blessed Virgin, where were you when me darlin' son was riddled with bullets, when me darlin' son was riddled with bullets! . . . Sacred Heart of the Crucified Jesus, take away our hearts o' stone . . . an' give us hearts o' flesh! . . . Take away this murdherin' hate . . . an' give us Thine own eternal love! [They pass out of the room.]

MRS. BOYLE: [Explanatorily to BENTHAM.] That was Mrs. Tancred of the two-pair back; her son was found, e'er yesterday, lyin' out beyant Finglas riddled with bullets. A die-hard he was, be all accounts. He was a nice quiet boy, but latherly he went to hell, with his Republic first, an' Republic last an' Republic over all. He ofen took tea with us here, in the oul' days, an' Johnny, there, an' him used to be always together.

JOHNNY: Am I always to be havin' to tell you that he was no friend o' mine? I never cared for him, an' he could never stick me. It's not because he was Commandant of the Battalion that I was Quarther-Masther of, that we were friends.

MRS. BOYLE: He's gone, now—the Lord be good to him! God help his poor oul' creature of a mother, for no matther whose friend or enemy he was, he was her poor son.

BENTHAM: The whole thing is terrible, Mrs. Boyle; but the only way to deal with a mad dog is to destroy him.

MRS. BOYLE: An' to think of me forgettin' about him bein' brought to the church to-night, an' we singin' an' all, but it was well we hadn't the gramophone goin', anyhow.

BOYLE: Even if we had aself. We've nothin' to do with these things, one way or t'other. That's the Government's business, an' let them do what we're payin' them for doin'.

MRS. BOYLE: I'd like to know how a body's not to mind these things; look at the way they're afther leavin' the people in this very house. Hasn't the whole house, nearly, been massacreed? There's young Mrs. Dougherty's husband with his leg off; Mrs. Travers that had her son blew up be a mine in Inchegeela, in Co. Cork; Mrs. Mannin' that lost wan of her sons in an ambush a few weeks ago, an' now, poor Mrs. Tancred's only child gone West with his body made a collandher of. Sure, if it's not our business, I don't know whose business it is.

BOYLE: Here, there, that's enough about them things; they don't affect us, an' we needn't give a damn. If they want a wake, well, let them have a wake. When I was a sailor, I was always resigned to meet with a wathery grave; an', if they want to be soldiers, well, there's no use o' them squealin' when they meet a soldier's fate.

JOXER: Let me like a soldier fall—me breast expandin' to th' ball!

MRS. BOYLE: In wan way, she deserves all she got; for lately, she let th' die-hards make an open house of th' place; an' for th' last couple of months, either when th' sun was risin', or when th' sun was settin', you had C.I.D. men burstin' into your rooms, assin' you where were you born, where were you christened, where were you married, an' where would you be buried!

JOHNNY: For God's sake, let us have no more o' this talk.

MRS. MADIGAN: What about Mr. Boyle's song before we start th' gramophone?

MARY: [Getting her hat, and putting it on.] Mother, Charlie and I am goin' out for a little sthroll.

MRS. BOYLE: All right, darlin'.

BENTHAM: [Going out with MARY.] We won't be long away, Mrs. Boyle.

MRS. MADIGAN: Gwan, Captain, gwan.

BOYLE: E-e-e-e-eh, I'd want to have a few more jars in me, before I'd be in fettle for singin'.

JOXER: Give us that poem you writ t'other day. [To the rest.] Aw, it's a darlin' poem, a daarlin' poem.

MRS. BOYLE: God bless us, is he startin' to write poetry!

BOYLE: [Rising to his feet.] E-e-e-e-eh. [He recites in an emotional, consequential manner the following verses]:

Shawn an' I were friends, sir, to me he was all in all.
His work was very heavy and his wages were very small.
None betther on th' beach as Docker, I'll go bail,
'Tis now I'm feelin' lonely, for to-day he lies in jail.
He was not what some call pious— seldom at church or prayer;
For the greatest scoundrels I know, sir, goes every Sunday there.
Fond of his pint—well, rather, but hated the Boss by creed
But never refused a copper to comfort a pal in need.

E-e-e-e-eh. [He sits down.]

MRS. MADIGAN: Grand, grand; you should folley that up, you should folley that up.

JOXER: It's a daarlin' poem!

BOYLE: [Delightedly.] E-e-e-e-eh.

JOHNNY: Are yous goin' to put on th' gramophone to-night, or are yous not?

MRS. BOYLE: Gwan, Jack, put on a record.

MRS. MADIGAN: Gwan, Captain, gwan.

BOYLE: Well, yous'll want to keep a dead silence. [He sets a record, starts the machine, and it begins to play "If you're Irish, come into the Parlour." As the tune is in full blare, the door is suddenly opened by a brisk, little bald-headed man, dressed circumspectly in a black suit; he glares fiercely at all in the room; he is "NEEDLE NUGENT," a tailor. He carries his hat in his hands.]

NUGENT: [Loudly, above the noise of the gramophone.] Are yous goin' to have that thing bawlin' an' the funeral of Mrs. Tancred's son passin' the house? Have none of yous any respect for the Irish people's National regard for the dead?

[BOYLE *stops the gramophone.*]

MRS. BOYLE: Maybe, Needle Nugent, it's nearly time we had a little less respect for the dead, an' a little more regard for the livin'.

MRS. MADIGAN: We don't want you, Mr. Nugent, to teach us what we learned at our mother's knee. You don't look yourself as if you were dyin' of grief; if y'ass Maisie Madigan anything, I'd call you a real thrue die-hard an' live-soft Republican, attendin' Republican funerals in the day, an' stoppin' up half the night makin' suits for the Civic Guards! [*Persons are heard running down to the street, some saying, "Here it is, here it is."* NUGENT *withdraws, and the rest, except* JOHNNY, *go to the window looking into the street, and look out. Sounds of a crowd coming nearer are heard; portion are singing.*]

To Jesus' Heart all burning
With fervent love for men,
My heart with fondest yearning
Shall raise its joyful strain.
While ages course along,
Blest be with loudest song,
The Sacred Heart of Jesus
By every heart and tongue.

MRS. BOYLE: Here's the hearse, here's the hearse!

BOYLE: There's t'oul' mother, walkin' behin' the coffin.

MRS. MADIGAN: You can hardly see the coffin with the wreaths.

JOXER: Oh, it's a darlin' funeral, a daarlin' funeral!

MRS. MADIGAN: We'd have a betther view from the street.

BOYLE: Yes—this place ud give you a crick in your neck. [*They leave the room, and go down.* JOHNNY *sits moodily by the fire.*]

[*A young man enters; he looks at* JOHNNY *for a moment.*]

THE YOUNG MAN: Quarther-Masther Boyle.

JOHNNY: [*With a start.*] The Mobilizer!

THE YOUNG MAN: You're not at the funeral?

JOHNNY: I'm not well.

THE YOUNG MAN: I'm glad I've found you; you were stoppin' at your aunt's; I called there but you'd gone. I've to give you an ordher to attend a Battalion Staff meetin' the night afther to-morrow.

JOHNNY: Where?

THE YOUNG MAN: I don't know; you're to meet me at the Pillar at eight o'clock; then we're to go to a place I'll be told of to-night; there we'll meet a mothor that'll bring us to the meeting. They think you might be able to know somethin' about them that gave the bend where Commandant Tancred was shelterin'.

JOHNNY: I'm not goin', then. I know nothing about Tancred.

THE YOUNG MAN: [*At the door.*] You'd betther come for your own sake—remember your oath.

JOHNNY: [*Passionately.*] I won't go! Haven't I done enough for Ireland! I've lost me arm, an' me hip's desthroyed so that I'll never be able to walk right agen! Good God, haven't I done enough for Ireland?

THE YOUNG MAN: Boyle, no man can do enough for Ireland! [*He goes.*]

[*Faintly in the distance the crowd is heard saying.*]

Hail, Mary, full of grace, the Lord is with Thee;
Blessed art Thou amongst women, and blessed, etc.

CURTAIN

ACT III

SCENE. *The same as Act Two. It is about half-past six on a November evening; a bright fire is burning in the grate;* MARY, *dressed to go out, is sitting on a chair by the fire, leaning forward, her hands under her chin, her elbows on her knees. A look of dejection, mingled with uncertain anxiety, is on her face. A lamp, turned low, is lighting on the table. The votive light under the picture of the Virgin, gleams more redly than ever.* MRS. BOYLE *is putting on her hat and coat. It is two months later.*

MRS. BOYLE: An' has Bentham never even written to you since—not one line for the past month?

MARY: [*Tonelessly.*] Not even a line, mother.

MRS. BOYLE: That's very curious. . . . What came between the two of yous at all? To leave you so sudden, an' yous so great together. . . . To go away t' England, an' not to even leave you his address. . . . The way he was always bringin' you to dances, I thought he was mad afther you. Are you sure you said nothin' to him?

MARY: No, mother—at least nothing that could possibly explain his givin' me up.

MRS. BOYLE: You know you're a bit hasty at times, Mary, an' say things you shouldn't say.

MARY: I never said to him what I shouldn't say, I'm sure of that.

MRS. BOYLE: How are you sure of it?

MARY: Because I love him with all my heart and soul, mother. Why, I don't know; I often thought to myself that he wasn't the man poor Jerry was, but I couldn't help loving him, all the same.

MRS. BOYLE: But you shouldn't be frettin' the way you are; when a woman loses a man, she never knows what she's afther losin', to be sure, but, then, she never knows what she's afther gainin', either. You're not the one girl of a month ago—you look like one pinin' away. It's long ago I had a right to bring you to the doctor, instead of waitin' till to-night.

MARY: There's no necessity, really, mother, to go to the doctor; nothing serious is wrong with me—I'm run down and disappointed, that's all.

MRS. BOYLE: I'll not wait another minute; I don't like the look of you at all. . . . I'm afraid we made a mistake in throwin' over poor Jerry. . . . He'd have been better for you than that Bentham.

MARY: Mother, the best man for a woman is the one for whom she has the most love, and Charlie had it all.

MRS. BOYLE: Well, there's one thing to be said for him—he couldn't have been thinkin' of the money, or he wouldn't ha' left you . . . it must ha' been somethin' else.

MARY: [*Wearily.*] I don't know . . . I don't know, mother . . . only I think . . .

MRS. BOYLE: What d'ye think?

MARY: I imagine . . . he thought . . . we weren't . . . good enough for him.

MRS. BOYLE: An' what was he himself, only a school teacher? Though I don't blame him for fightin' shy of people like that Joxer fella an' that oul' Madigan wan—nice sort o' people for your father to inthroduce to a man like Mr. Bentham. You might have told me all about this before now, Mary; I don't know why you had to hide everything from your mother; you knew Bentham, an' I'd ha' known nothin' about it if it hadn't bin for the Will; an' it was only to-day, afther long coaxin', that you let out that he'd left you.

MARY: It would have been useless to tell you—you wouldn't understand.

MRS. BOYLE: [*Hurt.*] Maybe not. . . . Maybe I wouldn't understand. . . . Well, we'll be off now. [*She goes over to the door left, and speaks to* BOYLE *inside.*]

MRS. BOYLE: We're goin' now to the doctor's. Are you goin' to get up this evenin'?

BOYLE: [*From inside.*] The pains in me legs is terrible! It's me should be poppin' off to the doctor instead o' Mary, the way I feel.

MRS. BOYLE: Sorra mend you! A nice way you were in last night—carried in a frog's march, dead to the world. If that's the way you'll go on when you get the money it'll be the grave for you, an asylum for me and the Poorhouse for Johnny.

BOYLE: I thought you were goin'?

MRS. BOYLE: That's what has you as you are—you can't bear to be spoken to. Knowin' the way we are, up to our ears in debt, it's a wondher you wouldn't ha' got up to go to th' solicitor's an' see if we could ha' gettin' a little o' the money even.

BOYLE: [Shouting.] I can't be goin' up there night, noon an' mornin', can I? He can't give the money till he gets it, can he? I can't get blood out of a turnip, can I?

MRS. BOYLE: It's nearly two months since we heard of the Will, an' the money seems as far off as ever. . . . I suppose you know we owe twenty poun's to oul' Murphy?

BOYLE: I've a faint recollection of you tellin' me that before.

MRS. BOYLE: Well, you'll go over to the shop yourself for the things in future—I'll face him no more.

BOYLE: I thought you said you were goin'?

MRS. BOYLE: I'm goin' now; come on, Mary.

BOYLE: Ey, Juno, ey!

MRS. BOYLE: Well, what d'ye want now?

BOYLE: Is there e'er a bottle o' stout left?

MRS. BOYLE: There's two o' them here still.

BOYLE: Show us in one o' them an' leave t'other there till I get up. An' throw us in the paper that's on the table, an' the bottle o' Sloan's Liniment that's in th' drawer.

MRS. BOYLE: [Getting the liniment and the stout.] What paper is it you want—the Messenger?

BOYLE: Messenger! The News o' the World!

[MRS. BOYLE brings in the things asked for and comes out again.]

MRS. BOYLE: [At door.] Mind the candle, now, an' don't burn the house over our heads. I left t'other bottle o' stout on the table. [She puts bottle of stout on table. She goes out with MARY. A cork is heard popping inside.]

[A pause; then outside the door is heard the voice of JOXER lilting softly: "Me pipe I'll smoke, as I dhrive me

moke . . . are you . . . there . . . More . . . aar . . . i . . . tee!" A gentle knock is heard and, after a pause, the door opens, and JOXER, followed by NUGENT, enters.]

JOXER: Be God, they must all be out; I was thinkin' there was somethin' up when he didn't answer the signal. We seen Juno an' Mary goin', but I didn't see him, an' it's very seldom he escapes me.

NUGENT: He's not goin' to escape me—he's not goin' to be let go to the fair altogether.

JOXER: Sure, the house couldn't hould them lately; an' he goin' about like a mastherpiece of the Free State counthry; forgettin' their friends; forgettin' God—wouldn't even lift his hat passin' a chapel! Sure they were bound to get a dhrop! An' you really think there's no money comin' to him afther all?

NUGENT: Not as much as a red rex, man; I've been a bit anxious this long time over me money, an' I went up to the solicitor's to find out all I could—ah, man, they were goin' to throw me down the stairs. They toul' me that the oul' cock himself had the stairs worn away comin' up afther it, an' they black in the face tellin' him he'd get nothin'. Some way or another that the Will is writ he won't be entitled to get as much as a make!

JOXER: Ah, I thought there was somethin' curious about the whole thing; I've bin havin' sthrange dreams for the last couple o' weeks. An' I notice that that Bentham fella doesn't be comin' here now—there must be somethin' on the mat there too. Anyhow, who, in the name o' God, ud leave anythin' to that oul' bummer? Sure it ud be unnatural. An' the way Juno an' him's been throwin' their weight about for the last few months! Ah, him that goes a borrowin' goes a sorrowin'!

NUGENT: Well, he's not goin' to throw his weight about in the suit I made for him much longer. I'm tellin' you seven poun's aren't to be found growin' on the bushes these days.

JOXER: An' there isn't hardly a neighbour in the whole street that hasn't lent him money on the strength of what he was goin' to get, but they're after backing the wrong horse. Wasn't it a mercy o' God that I'd nothin' to give him! The softy I am, you know, I'd ha' lent him me last juice! I must have had somebody's good prayers.

Ah, afther all, an honest man's the noblest work o' God!

[BOYLE *coughs inside*.]

JOXER: Whisht, damn it, he must be inside in bed.

NUGENT: Inside o' bed or outside of it he's goin' to pay me for that suit, or give it back—he'll not climb up my back as easily as he thinks.

JOXER: Gwan in at wanst, man, an' get it off him, an' don't be a fool.

NUGENT: [*Going to the door left, opening it and looking in.*] Ah, don't disturb yourself, Mr. Boyle; I hope you're not sick?

BOYLE: Th' oul' legs, Mr. Nugent, the oul' legs.

NUGENT: I just called over to see if you could let me have anything off the suit?

BOYLE: E-e-e-eh, how much is this it is?

NUGENT: It's the same as it was at the start—seven poun's.

BOYLE: I'm glad you kem, Mr. Nugent; I want a good heavy top-coat—Irish frieze, if you have it. How much would a top-coat like that be now?

NUGENT: About six poun's.

BOYLE: Six poun's—six an' seven, six an' seven is thirteen—that'll be thirteen poun's I'll owe you.

[JOXER *slips the bottle of stout that is on the table into his pocket.* NUGENT *rushes into the room, and returns with the suit on his arm; he pauses at the door.*]

NUGENT: You'll owe me no thirteen poun's. Maybe you think you're bether able to owe it than pay it!

BOYLE: [*Frantically.*] Here, come back to hell ower that—where're you goin' with them clothes o' mine?

NUGENT: Where am I goin' with them clothes o' yours? Well, I like your damn cheek!

BOYLE: Here, what am I going to dhress meself in when I'm goin' out?

NUGENT: What do I care what you dhress yourself in? You can put yourself in a bolsther cover, if you like. [*He goes toward the other door, followed by* JOXER.]

JOXER: What'll he dhress himself in! Gentleman Jack an' his frieze coat!

[*They go out.*]

BOYLE: [*Inside.*] Ey, Nugent, ey, Mr. Nugent, Mr. Nugent! [*After a pause* BOYLE *enters hastily, buttoning the braces of his moleskin trousers; his coat and vest are on his arms; he throws these on a chair and hurries to the door on right.*]

BOYLE: Ey, Mr. Nugent, Mr. Nugent!

JOXER: [*Meeting him at the door.*] What's up, what's wrong, Captain?

BOYLE: Nugent's been here an' took away me suit—the only things I had to go out in!

JOXER: Tuk your suit—for God's sake! An' what were you doin' while he was takin' them?

BOYLE: I was in bed when he stole in like a thief in the night, an' before I knew even what he was thinkin' of, he whipped them from the chair, an' was off like a redshank!

JOXER: An' what, in the name o' God, did he do that for?

BOYLE: What did he do it for? How the hell do I know what he done it for? Jealousy an' spite, I suppose.

JOXER: Did he not say what he done it for?

BOYLE: Amn't I afther tellin' you that he had them whipped up an' was gone before I could open me mouth?

JOXER: That was a very sudden thing to do; there mus' be somethin' behin' it. Did he hear anythin', I wondher?

BOYLE: Did he hear anythin'?—you talk very queer, Joxer—what could he hear?

JOXER: About you not gettin' the money, in some way or t'other?

BOYLE: An' what ud prevent me from gettin' th' money?

JOXER: That's jus' what I was thinkin' —what ud prevent you from gettin' the money—nothin', as far as I can see.

BOYLE: [*Looking round for bottle of stout with an exclamation.*] Aw, holy God!

JOXER: What's up, Jack?

BOYLE: He must have afther lifted the bottle o' stout that Juno left on the table!

JOXER: [*Horrified.*] Ah, no, ah, no! He wouldn't be afther doin' that, now.

BOYLE: An' who done it then? Juno left a bottle o' stout here, an' it's gone— it didn't walk, did it?

JOXER: Oh, that's shockin'; ah, man's inhumanity to man makes countless thousands mourn!

MRS. MADIGAN: [*Appearing at the door.*] I hope I'm not disturbin' you in any discussion on your forthcomin' legacy—if I may use the word—an' that you'll let me have a barny for a minute or two with you, Mr. Boyle.

BOYLE: [*Uneasily.*] To be sure, Mrs. Madigan—an oul' friend's always welcome.

JOXER: Come in the evenin', come in th' mornin'; come when you're assed, or come without warnin', Mrs. Madigan.

BOYLE: Sit down, Mrs. Madigan.

MRS. MADIGAN: [*Ominously.*] Th' few words I have to say can be said standin'. Puttin' aside all formularies, I suppose you remember me lendin' you some time ago three poun's that I raised on blankets an' furniture in me uncle's?

BOYLE: I remember it well. I have it recorded in me book—three poun's five shillin's from Maisie Madigan, raised on articles pawned; an', item: fourpence, given to make up the price of a pint, on th' principle that no bird ever flew on wan wing; all to be repaid at par, when the ship comes home.

MRS. MADIGAN: Well, ever since I shoved in the blankets I've been perishing with th' cowld, an' I've decided, if I'll be too hot in th' nex' world aself, I'm not goin' to be too cowld in this wan; an' consequently, I want me three poun's, if you please.

BOYLE: This is a very sudden demand, Mrs. Madigan, an' can't be met; but I'm willin' to give you a receipt in full, in full.

MRS. MADIGAN: Come on, out with th' money, an' don't be jack-actin'.

BOYLE: You can't get blood out of a turnip, can you?

MRS. MADIGAN: [*Rushing over and shaking him.*] Gimme me money, y'oul' reprobate, or I'll shake the worth of it out of you!

BOYLE: Ey, houl' on, there; houl' on, there! You'll wait for your money now, me lassie!

MRS. MADIGAN: [*Looking around the room and seeing the gramophone.*] I'll wait for it, will I? Well, I'll not wait long; if I can't get th' cash, I'll get th' worth of it. [*She catches up the gramophone.*]

BOYLE: Ey, ey, there, wher'r you goin' with that?

MRS. MADIGAN: I'm goin' to th' pawn to get me three quid five shillin's; I'll bring you th' ticket, an' then you can do what you like, me bucko.

BOYLE: You can't touch that, you can't touch that! It's not my property, an' it's not ped for yet!

MRS. MADIGAN: So much th' bether. It'll be an ayse to me conscience, for I'm takin' what doesn't belong to you. You're not goin' to be swankin' it like a paycock with Maisie Madigan's money—I'll pull some o' the gorgeous feathers out o' your tail! [*She goes off with the gramophone.*]

BOYLE: What's th' world comin' to at all? I ass you, Joxer Daly, is there any morality left anywhere?

JOXER: I wouldn't ha' believed it, only I seen it with me own two eyes. I didn't think Maisie Madigan was that sort of a woman; she has either a sup taken, or she's heard somethin'.

BOYLE: Heard somethin'—about what, if it's not any harm to ass you?

JOXER: She must ha' heard some rumour or other that you weren't goin' to get th' money.

BOYLE: Who says I'm not goin' to get th' money?

JOXER: Sure, I know—I was only sayin'.

BOYLE: Only sayin' what?

JOXER: Nothin'.

BOYLE: You were goin' to say somethin', don't be a twisther.

JOXER: [*Angrily.*] Who's a twisther?

BOYLE: Why don't you speak your mind, then?

JOXER: You never twisted yourself—no, you wouldn't know how!

BOYLE: Did you ever know me to twist; did you ever know me to twist?

JOXER: [*Fiercely.*] Did you ever do anythin' else! Sure, you can't believe a word that comes out o' your mouth.

BOYLE: Here, get out, ower o' this; I always knew you were a prognosticator an' a procrastinator!

JOXER: [*Going out as* JOHNNY *comes in.*] The anchor's weighed, farewell, re . . . mem . . . ber . . . me. Jacky Boyle, Esquire, infernal rogue an' damned liar!

JOHNNY: Joxer an' you at it agen?—when are you goin' to have a little respect for yourself, an' not be always makin' a show of us all?

BOYLE: Are you goin' to lecture me now?

JOHNNY: Is mother back from the doctor yet, with Mary?

[MRS. BOYLE *enters; it is apparent from the serious look on her face that something has happened. She takes off her hat and coat without a word and puts them by. She then sits down near the fire, and there is a few moments' pause.*]

BOYLE: Well, what did the doctor say about Mary?

MRS. BOYLE: [*In an earnest manner and with suppressed agitation.*] Sit down here, Jack; I've something to say to you . . . about Mary.

BOYLE: [*Awed by her manner.*] About . . . Mary?

MRS. BOYLE: Close that door there and sit down here.

BOYLE: [*Closing the door.*] More throuble in our native land, is it? [*He sits down.*] Well, what is it?

MRS. BOYLE: It's about Mary.

BOYLE: Well, what about Mary—there's nothin' wrong with her, is there?

MRS. BOYLE: I'm sorry to say there's a gradle wrong with her.

BOYLE: A gradle wrong with her! [*Peevishly.*] First Johnny an' now Mary; is the whole house goin' to become an hospital! It's not consumption, is it?

MRS. BOYLE: No . . . it's not consumption . . . it's worse.

JOHNNY: Worse! Well, we'll have to get her into some place ower this, there's no one here to mind her.

MRS. BOYLE: We'll all have to mind her now. You might as well know now, Johnny, as another time. [*To* BOYLE.] D'ye know what the doctor said to me about her, Jack?

BOYLE: How ud I know—I wasn't there, was I?

MRS. BOYLE: He told me to get her married at wanst.

BOYLE: Married at wanst! An' why did he say the like o' that?

MRS. BOYLE: Because Mary's goin' to have a baby in a short time.

BOYLE: Goin' to have a baby!—my God, what'll Bentham say when he hears that?

MRS. BOYLE: Are you blind, man, that you can't see that it was Bentham that has done this wrong to her?

BOYLE: [*Passionately.*] Then he'll marry her, he'll have to marry her!

MRS. BOYLE: You know he's gone to England, an' God knows where he is now.

BOYLE: I'll folley him, I'll folley him, an' bring him back, an' make him do her justice. The scoundrel, I might ha' known what he was, with his yogees an' his prawna!

MRS. BOYLE: We'll have to keep it quiet till we see what we can do.

BOYLE: Oh, isn't this a nice thing to come on top o' me, an' the state I'm in! A pretty show I'll be to Joxer, an' to that oul' wan, Madigan! Amn't I afther goin' through enough without havin' to go through this!

MRS. BOYLE: What you an' I'll have to go through'll be nothin' to what poor Mary'll have to go through; for you an' me is middlin' old, an' most of our years is spent; but Mary'll have maybe forty years to face an' handle, an' every wan of them'll be tainted with a bitther memory.

BOYLE: Where is she? Where is she till I tell her off? I'm tellin' you when I'm done with her she'll be a sorry girl!

MRS. BOYLE: I left her in me sisther's till I came to speak to you. You'll say nothin' to her, Jack; ever since she left school she's earned her livin', an' your fatherly care never throubled the poor girl.

BOYLE: Gwan, take her part agen her father! But I'll let you see whether I'll say nothin' to her or no! Her an' her readin'! That's more o' th' blasted nonsense that has the house fallin' down on top of us! What did th' likes of her, born in a tenement house, want with readin'? Her readin's afther bringin' her to a nice pass —oh, it's madnin', madnin', madnin'!

MRS. BOYLE: When she comes back say nothin' to her, Jack or she'll leave this place.

BOYLE: Leave this place! Ay, she'll leave this place, an' quick too!

MRS. BOYLE: If Mary goes, I'll go with her.

BOYLE: Well, go with her! Well, go, th' pair o' yous! I lived before I seen yous, an' I can live when yous are gone. Isn't this a nice thing to come rollin' in on top o' me afther all your prayin' to St. Anthony an' The Little Flower. An' she's a child o' Mary, too—I wonder what'll the nuns think of her now? An' it'll be bellows'd all over th' disthrict before you could say Jack Robinson; an' whenever I'm seen they'll whisper, "That's th' father of Mary Boyle that had th' kid be th' swank she used to go with; d'ye know, d'ye know?" To be sure they'll know—more about it than I will meself!

JOHNNY: She should be dhriven out o' th' house she's brought disgrace on!

MRS. BOYLE: Hush, you, Johnny. We needn't let it be bellows'd all over the place; all we've got to do is to leave this place quietly an' go somewhere where we're not known, an' nobody'll be the wiser.

BOYLE: You're talkin' like a two-year-oul', woman. Where'll we get a place ou' o' this? —places aren't that easily got.

MRS. BOYLE: But, Jack, when we get the money . . .

BOYLE: Money—what money?

MRS. BOYLE: Why, oul' Ellison's money, of course.

BOYLE: There's no money comin' from oul' Ellison, or any one else. Since you heard of wan throuble, you might as well hear of another. There's no money comin' to us at all—the Will's a wash out!

MRS. BOYLE: What are you sayin', man —no money?

JOHNNY: How could it be a wash out?

BOYLE: The boyo that's afther doin' it to Mary done it to me as well. The thick made out the Will wrong; he said in th' Will, only first cousin an' second cousin, instead of mentionin' our names, an' now any one that thinks he's a first cousin or second cousin t'oul' Ellison can claim the money as well as me, an' they're springin' up in hundreds, an' comin' from America an' Australia, thinkin' to get their whack out of it, while all the time the lawyers is gobblin' it up, till there's not as much as ud buy a stockin' for your lovely daughter's baby!

MRS. BOYLE: I don't believe it, I don't believe it, I don't believe it!

JOHNNY: Why did you say nothin' about this before?

MRS. BOYLE: You're not serious, Jack; you're not serious!

BOYLE: I'm tellin' you the scholar, Bentham, made a banjax o' th' Will; instead o' sayin', "th' rest o' me property to be divided between me first cousin, Jack Boyle, an' me second cousin, Mick Finnegan, o' Santhry," he writ down only, "me first an' second cousins," an' the world an' his wife are afther th' property now.

MRS. BOYLE: Now, I know why Bentham left poor Mary in th' lurch; I can see it all now—oh, is there not even a middlin' honest man left in th' world?

JOHNNY: [To BOYLE.] An' you let us run into debt, an' you borreyed money from everybody to fill yourself with beer! An' now, you tell us the whole thing's a wash out! Oh, if it's thrue, I'm done with you, for you're worse than me sisther Mary!

BOYLE: You hole your tongue, d'ye hear? I'll not take any lip from you. Go an' get Bentham if you want satisfaction for all that's afther happenin' us.

JOHNNY: I won't hole me tongue, I won't hole me tongue! I'll tell you what I think of you, father an' all as you are . . . you . . .

MRS. BOYLE: Johnny, Johnny, Johnny, for God's sake, be quiet!

JOHNNY: I'll not be quiet, I'll not be quiet; he's a nice father, isn't he? Is it any wondher Mary went asthray, when . . .

MRS. BOYLE: Johnny, Johnny, for my sake be quiet—for your mother's sake!

BOYLE: I'm going out now to have a few dhrinks with th' last few makes I have, an' tell that lassie o' yours not to be here when I come back; for if I lay me eyes on her, I'll lay me han's on her, an' if I lay me han's on her, I won't be accountable for me actions!

JOHNNY: Take care somebody doesn't lay his han's on you—y'oul' . . .

MRS. BOYLE: Johnny, Johnny!

BOYLE: [At door, about to go out.] Oh, a nice son, an' a nicer daughter, I have. [Calling loudly upstairs.] Joxer, Joxer, are you there?

JOXER: [From a distance.] I'm here, More . . . ee . . . aar . . . i . . . tee!

BOYLE: I'm goin' down to Foley's—are you comin'?

JOXER: Come with you? With that sweet call me heart is stirred; I'm only waiting for the word, an' I'll be with you, like a bird!

[BOYLE and JOXER pass the door going out.]

JOHNNY: [Throwing himself on the bed.] I've a nice sisther, an' a nice father, there's no bettin' on it. I wish to God a bullet or a bomb had whipped me ou' o' this long ago! Not one o' yous, not one o' yous, have any thought for me!

MRS. BOYLE: [With passionate remonstrance.] If you don't whisht, Johnny, you'll drive me mad. Who has kep' th' home together for the past few years—only me. An' who'll have to bear th' biggest part o' this throuble but me—but whinin' an' whingin' isn't going to do any good.

JOHNNY: You're to blame yourself for a gradle of it—givin' him his own way in everything, an' never assin' to check him, no matther what he done. Why didn't you look afther th' money? why . . .

[*There is a knock at the door;* MRS. BOYLE *opens it;* JOHNNY *rises on his elbow to look and listen; two men enter.*]

FIRST MAN: We've been sent up be th' Manager of the Hibernian Furnishing Co., Mrs. Boyle, to take back the furniture that was got a while ago.

MRS. BOYLE: Yous'll touch nothin' here —how do I know who yous are?

FIRST MAN: [*Showing a paper.*] There's the ordher, ma'am. [*Reading.*] A chest o' drawers, a table, wan easy an' two ordinary chairs; wan mirror; wan chestherfield divan, an' a wardrobe an' two vases. [*To his comrade.*] Come on, Bill, it's afther knockin' off time already.

JOHNNY: For God's sake, mother, run down to Foley's an' bring father back, or we'll be left without a stick.

[*The men carry out the table.*]

MRS. BOYLE: What good would it be? You heard what he said before he went out.

JOHNNY: Can't you thry? He ought to be here, an' the like of this goin' on.

[MRS. BOYLE *puts a shawl around her, as* MARY *enters.*]

MARY: What's up, mother? I met men carryin' away the table, an' everybody's talking about us not gettin' the money after all.

MRS. BOYLE: Everythin's gone wrong, Mary, everythin'. We're not gettin' a penny out o' the Will, not a penny—I'll tell you all when I come back; I'm goin' for your father. [*She runs out.*]

JOHNNY: [*To* MARY, *who has sat down by the fire.*] It's a wondher you're not ashamed to show your face here, afther what has happened.

[JERRY *enters slowly; there is a look of earnest hope on his face. He looks at* MARY *for a few moments.*]

JERRY: [*Softly.*] Mary!

[MARY *does not answer.*]

JERRY: Mary, I want to speak to you for a few moments, may I?

[MARY *remains silent;* JOHNNY *goes slowly into room on left.*]

JERRY: Your mother has told me everything, Mary, and I have come to you . . . I have come to tell you, Mary, that my love for you is greater and deeper than ever. . . .

MARY: [*With a sob.*] Oh, Jerry, Jerry, say no more; all that is over now; anything like that is impossible now!

JERRY: Impossible? Why do you talk like that, Mary?

MARY: After all that has happened.

JERRY: What does it matter what has happened? We are young enough to be able to forget all those things. [*He catches her hand.*] Mary, Mary, I am pleading for your love. With Labour, Mary, humanity is above everything; we are the Leaders in the fight for a new life. I want to forget Bentham, I want to forget that you left me—even for a while.

MARY: Oh, Jerry, Jerry, you haven't the bitter word of scorn for me after all.

JERRY: [*Passionately.*] Scorn! I love you, love you, Mary!

MARY: [*Rising, and looking him in the eyes.*] Even though . . .

JERRY: Even though you threw me over for another man; even though you gave me many a bitter word!

MARY: Yes, yes, I know; but you love me, even though . . . even though . . . I'm . . . goin' . . . goin' . . . [*He looks at her questioningly, and fear gathers in his eyes.*] Ah, I was thinkin' so. . . . You don't know everything!

JERRY: [*Poignantly.*] Surely to God, Mary, you don't mean that . . . that . . . that . . .

MARY: Now you know all, Jerry; now you know all!

JERRY: My God, Mary, have you fallen as low as that?

MARY: Yes, Jerry, as you say, I have fallen as low as that.

JERRY: I didn't mean it that way, Mary . . . it came on me so sudden, that I didn't mind what I was sayin'. . . . I never expected this—your mother never told me. . . . I'm sorry . . . God knows, I'm sorry for you, Mary.

MARY: Let us say no more, Jerry; I don't blame you for thinkin' it's terrible. . . . I suppose it is. . . . Everybody'll think the same. . . . It's only as I expected—your humanity is just as narrow as the humanity of the others.

JERRY: I'm sorry, all the same. . . . I shouldn't have troubled you. . . . I wouldn't if I'd known . . . if I can do anything for you . . . Mary . . . I will. [*He turns to go, and halts at the door.*]

MARY: Do you remember, Jerry, the verses you read when you gave the lecture in the Socialist Rooms some time ago, on Humanity's Strife with Nature?

JERRY: The verses—no; I don't remember them.

MARY: I do. They're runnin' in me head now—

> An' we felt the power that fashion'd
> All the lovely things we saw,
> That created all the murmur
> Of an everlasting law,
> Was a hand of force an' beauty,
> With an eagle's tearin' claw.
>
> Then we saw our globe of beauty
> Was an ugly thing as well,
> A hymn divine whose chorus
> Was an agonizin' yell;
> Like the story of a demon,
> That an angel had to tell.
>
> Like a glowin' picture by a
> Hand unsteady, brought to ruin;
> Like her craters, if their deadness
> Could give life unto the moon;
> Like the agonizing horror
> Of a violin out of tune.

[*There is a pause, and* DEVINE *goes slowly out.*]

JOHNNY: [*Returning.*] Is he gone?

MARY: Yes.

[*The two men re-enter.*]

FIRST MAN: We can't wait any longer for t'oul' fella—sorry, Miss, but we have to live as well as th' nex' man.

[*They carry out some things.*]

JOHNNY: Oh, isn't this terrible! . . . I suppose you told him everything . . . couldn't you have waited for a few days . . . he'd have stopped th' takin' of the things, if you'd kep' your mouth shut. Are you burnin' to tell every one of the shame you've brought on us?

MARY: [*Snatching up her hat and coat.*] Oh, this is unbearable! [*She rushes out.*]

FIRST MAN: [*Re-entering.*] We'll take the chest o' drawers next—it's the heaviest.

[*The votive light flickers for a moment, and goes out.*]

JOHNNY: [*In a cry of fear.*] Mother o' God, the light's after goin' out!

FIRST MAN: You put the win' up me the way you bawled that time. The oil's all gone, that's all.

JOHNNY: [*With an agonizing cry.*] Mother o' God, there's a shot I'm after gettin'!

FIRST MAN: What's wrong with you, man? Is it a fit you're takin'?

JOHNNY: I'm after feelin' a pain in me breast, like the tearin' by of a bullet!

FIRST MAN: He's goin' mad—it's a wondher they'd leave a chap like that here be himself.

[TWO IRREGULARS *enter swiftly; they carry revolvers; one goes over to* JOHNNY; *the other covers the two furniture men.*]

FIRST IRREGULAR: [*To the men, quietly and incisively.*] Who are you—what are yous doin' here—quick!

FIRST MAN: Removin' furniture that's not paid for.

FIRST IRREGULAR: Get over to the other end of the room an' turn your faces to the wall—quick.

[*The two men turn their faces to the wall, with their hands up.*]

SECOND IRREGULAR: [*To* JOHNNY.] Come on, Sean Boyle, you're wanted; some of us have a word to say to you.

JOHNNY: I'm sick, I can't—what do you want with me?

SECOND IRREGULAR: Come on, come on; we've a distance to go, an' haven't much time—come on.

JOHNNY: I'm an oul' comrade—yous wouldn't shoot an oul' comrade.

SECOND IRREGULAR: Poor Tancred was an oul' comrade o' yours, but you didn't think o' that when you gave him away to the gang that sent him to his grave. But we've no time to waste; come on—here, Dermot, ketch his arm. [*To Johnny.*] Have you your beads?

JOHNNY: Me beads! Why do you ass me that, why do you ass me that?

SECOND IRREGULAR: Go on, go on, march!

JOHNNY: Are yous goin' to do in a comrade—look at me arm, I lost it for Ireland.

SECOND IRREGULAR: Commandant Tancred lost his life for Ireland.

JOHNNY: Sacred Heart of Jesus, have mercy on me! Mother o' God, pray for me—be with me now in the agonies o' death! . . . Hail, Mary, full o' grace . . . the Lord is . . . with Thee.

[*They drag out* JOHNNY BOYLE, *and the curtain falls. When it rises again most of the furniture is gone.* MARY *and* MRS. BOYLE, *one on each side, are sitting in a darkened room, by the fire; it is an hour later.*]

MRS. BOYLE: I'll not wait much longer

. . . what did they bring him away in the mothor for? Nugent says he thinks they had guns . . . is me throubles never goin' to be over? . . . If anything ud happen to poor Johnny, I think I'd lost me mind . . . I'll go to the Police Station, surely they ought to be able to do somethin'.

[*Below is heard the sound of voices.*]

MRS. BOYLE: Whisht, is that something? Maybe, it's your father, though when I left him in Foley's he was hardly able to lift his head. Whisht!

[*A knock at the door, and the voice of* MRS. MADIGAN, *speaking very softly.*] Mrs. Boyle, Mrs. Boyle. [MRS. BOYLE *opens the door.*]

MRS. MADIGAN: Oh, Mrs. Boyle, God an' His Blessed Mother be with you this night!

MRS. BOYLE: [*Calmly.*] What is it, Mrs. Madigan? It's Johnny—something about Johnny.

MRS. MADIGAN: God send it's not. God send it's not Johnny!

MRS. BOYLE: Don't keep me waitin', Mrs. Madigan; I've gone through so much lately that I feel able for anything.

MRS. MADIGAN: Two polismen below wantin' you.

MRS. BOYLE: Wantin' me; an' why do they want me?

MRS. MADIGAN: Some poor fella's been found, an' they think it's, it's . . .

MRS. BOYLE: Johnny, Johnny!

MARY: [*With her arms round her mother.*] Oh, mother, mother, me poor, darlin' mother.

MRS. BOYLE: Hush, hush, darlin'; you'll shortly have you own throuble to bear. [*To* MRS. MADIGAN.] An' why do the polis think it's Johnny, Mrs. Madigan?

MRS. MADIGAN: Because one o' the doctors knew him when he was attendin' with his poor arm.

MRS. BOYLE: Oh, it's thrue, then; it's Johnny, it's me son, me own son!

MARY: Oh, it's thrue, it's thrue what Jerry Devine says—there isn't a God, there isn't a God; if there was He wouldn't let these things happen!

MRS. BOYLE: Mary, Mary, you mustn't say them things. We'll want all the help we can get from God an' His Blessed Mother now! These things have nothin' to do with the Will o' God. Ah, what can God do agen the stupidity o' men!

MRS. MADIGAN: The polis want you to go with them to the hospital to see the poor body—they're waitin' below.

MRS. BOYLE: We'll go. Come, Mary, an' we'll never come back here agen. Let your father furrage for himself now; I've done all I could an' it was all no use—he'll be hopeless till the end of his days. I've got a little room in me sisther's where we'll stop till your throuble is over, an' then we'll work together for the sake of the baby.

MARY: My poor little child that'll have no father!

MRS. BOYLE: It'll have what's far better —it'll have two mothers.

[*A rough voice shouting from below.*] Are yous goin' to keep us waitin' for yous all night?

MRS. MADIGAN: [*Going to the door, and shouting down.*] Take your hour, there, take your hour! If yous are in such a hurry, skip off, then, for nobody wants you here— if they did yous wouldn't be found. For you're the same as you were undher the British Government—never where yous are wanted! As far as I can see, the Polis as Polis, in this city, is Null an' Void!

MRS. BOYLE: We'll go, Mary, we'll go; you to see your poor dead brother, an' me to see me poor dead son!

MARY: I dhread it, mother, I dhread it!

MRS. BOYLE: I forgot, Mary, I forgot; your poor oul' selfish mother was only thinkin' of herself. No, no, you mustn't come—it wouldn't be good for you. You go on to me sisther's an' I'll face th' ordeal meself. Maybe I didn't feel sorry enough for Mrs. Tancred when her poor son was found as Johnny's been found now—because he was a Die-hard! Ah, why didn't I remember that then he wasn't a Die-hard or a Stater, but only a poor dead son! It's well I remember all that she said—an' it's my turn to say it now: What was the pain I suffered, Johnny, bringin' you into the world to carry you to your cradle to the pains I'll suffer carryin' you out o' the world to bring you to your grave! Mother o' God, Mother o' God, have pity on us all! Blessed Virgin, where were you when me darlin' son was riddled with bullets, when me darlin' son was riddled with bullets? Sacred Heart o' Jesus, take away our hearts o' stone, and give us hearts o' flesh! Take away this murdherin' hate, an' give us Thine own eternal love!

[*They all go slowly out.*]

[*There is a pause; then a sound of shuffling steps on the stairs outside. The door opens and* BOYLE *and* JOXER, *both of them very drunk, enter.*]

BOYLE: I'm able to go no farther. . . . Two polis, ey . . . what were they doin' here, I wondher? . . . Up to no good, anyhow . . . an' Juno an' that lovely daughter o' mine with them. [*Taking a sixpence from his pocket and looking at it.*] Wan single, solitary tanner left out of all I borreyed. . . . [*He lets it fall.*] The last o' the Mohicans. . . . The blinds is down, Joxer, the blinds is down!

JOXER: [*Walking unsteadily across the room, and anchoring at the bed.*] Put all . . . your throubles . . . in your oul' kit bag . . . an' smile . . . smile . . . smile!

BOYLE: The counthry'll have to steady itself . . . it's goin' . . . to hell. . . . Where'r all . . . the chairs . . . gone to . . . steady itself, Joxer. . . . Chairs'll have to . . . steady themselves. . . . No matther . . . what any one may . . . say . . . Irelan's sober . . . is Irelan' . . . free.

JOXER: [*Stretching himself on the bed.*] Chains . . . an' . . . slaveree . . . that's a darlin' motto . . . a daaarlin' . . . motto!

BOYLE: If th' worst comes . . . to th' worse . . . I can join a . . . flyin' . . . column. . . . I done . . . me bit . . . in Easther Week . . . had no business . . . to . . . be . . . there . . . but Captain Boyle's Captain Boyle!

JOXER: Breathes there a man with soul . . . so . . . de . . . ad . . . this . . . me . . . o . . . wn, me nat . . . ive l . . . an'!

BOYLE: [*Subsiding into a sitting posture on the floor.*] Commandant Kelly died . . . in them . . . arms . . . Joxer. . . . Tell me Volunteer Butties . . . says he . . . that . . . I died for . . . Irelan'!

JOXER: D'jever rade Willie . . . Reilly . . . an' his . . . own . . . Colleen . . . Bawn? It's a darlin' story, a daarlin' story!

BOYLE: I'm telling you . . . Joxer . . . th' whole worl's . . . in a terr . . . ible state o' . . . chassis!

CURTAIN

CLIFFORD ODETS

HOW *The Country Girl* CAME ABOUT[1] by Armand Aulicino

BROOKS ATKINSON *in the New York Times,* . . . : "Odets has never written with so profound a knowledge of people as he does in *The Country Girl.*"

CLIFFORD ODETS *on how it began:* "Very simply, I have dozens of ideas in my files; eight or ten plays outlined at a time. The important thing is what impels me to work on any one of them before the others. In the case of *The Country Girl* the idea wasn't worked out very much. I happened to see Charles Coburn in New York and he mentioned he wanted to do a play. I looked in my files and got this idea and began to write. I soon realized that Coburn was too old for the romantic triangle of the two men and the woman. Practically speaking, however, if Coburn hadn't mentioned wanting to do a play, I might not have started *The Country Girl.*

"I wrote at least two or three versions of the play before showing it to anyone. No one saw it before the fourth draft. The differences in the versions were mainly rewriting of certain scenes pertaining to the dramatic structure. I didn't know until the second draft, for example, that Georgie wasn't a destructive, emasculative woman. She really was in the first drafts. She had cancer too, and discovers in the middle of the play she hasn't much time. I wrote that out, however— How God-like. You give someone cancer, then take it away. Maybe playwrights should cure cancer, instead of doctors. Put a sheet of paper into the typewriter, take it out and cancer is cured."

BROOKS ATKINSON'S *review said:* "At least for the time being, Mr. Odets has set the ailing cosmos to one side and written a plain, human story."

ODETS: "I never wrote a play that didn't tell a story. The only thing is that I usually verbalized the implications. In *The Country Girl* I didn't verbalize or comment on them—things

[1] Armand Aulicino, from "How *The Country Girl* Came About," *Theatre Arts Magazine,* XXXVI (May 1952), 54–57. Rewritten in part by Clifford Odets with slight revisions by Lee Strasberg. Reprinted by permission of *Theatre Arts Magazine.*

314

like what makes a man like Frank Elgin a drunkard, for instance.

"Usually when I start to write, I have only a general idea of the play. It expands, as I write, out of a general mood. In *The Country Girl* my 'mood' was held in abeyance because I wanted to accomplish something particular. As a technical exercise, I wanted to take simple elements and make something sharp and theatrical out of them, steadily keeping them aloft, clear and simple. I stated a fact, the story of these people, rather than speculating about the fact.

"Someone who writes or works creatively doesn't function on all fronts at once. I can always write a good theatre piece. I ought to be able to do that. I'm forty-five and I've spent twenty-seven of those years in the theatre. But it's not my interest to write just a theatrical piece. Every so often I want to correct certain technical problems that bother me: It's like writing myself a lesson. I write fluently; but how to combine a certain linear drive of story with psychological depth is the *real* problem. I don't know anyone who can do it, who ever did it, excepting Shakespeare; and even he has more misses than hits to his credit.

"Theatre must appeal to man's immediate perception. Writing plays isn't like doing a painting. You can't say if they don't get it now, then they'll get it forty years later; the play doesn't usually survive that long. I'm a popular writer and I don't want to write for the library."

LEE STRASBERG, *co-producer of* The Country Girl, *says:* "In the first draft he showed me Georgie was not already a positive and sensitive character. I had a feeling at the time that Odets was aware of the destructiveness in people. It's not a psychological play since he couldn't have changed the role of the wife the way he did if it were. Odets in this play is like most intelligent people in the theatre today. They find that the ideas they cherish come over too personally so they seek to be impersonal or theatrical. I feel *The Country Girl* has the straightforwardness of his earlier plays such as *Waiting for Lefty,* the quality of taking the directness of life and using it. This is evidenced by the way he uses the theatre background in *The Country Girl.* The scenes don't have the propaganda of *Lefty,* but they do have the same directness in making their point. He tried to follow through with the theme of the story and not allow himself to tell the audience his own feelings."

BORIS ARONSON, *who designed the sets:* "If you're familiar with Odets' work, you know everything he writes is written personally. He was trying to get *inside* of the people because the story, like that of every great play or movie, when told in three sentences seems like nothing has happened. But when you *see* it, the *inside* has so much to it; so much humanity, and it's so deeply felt that the conventional story becomes something you identify yourself with."

Clifford Odets set The Country Girl *in a theatrical background.*
ODETS: "I might have set it that way because I missed the theatre, but of course there were other reasons."

LEE STRASBERG: "Odets first described the play to me as beginning in an empty theatre while rehearsals are going on."

BORIS ARONSON: "There is nothing more glamorous and more sad than backstage in the theatre. There is something about the very *nakedness* of a rehearsal which is dramatic because it is stripped of all the superficiality that's added later."

[Odets directed the original production of *The Country Girl.*]

LEE STRASBERG: "This was his first important show on his own. I felt it was an important thing for him to do. Anything that brought him closer to the theatre was good. As a director, he works from the character's point of view."

FORREST C. HARING, *company manager, on Odets' direction:* "His approach is different with each actor. He works nicely with them—takes them aside and talks quietly about what the people are like in his plays. He talks about the characters, rather than tries to demonstrate what the actors should do. He never reads lines for an experienced actor."

LEE STRASBERG: "Odets works logically. He explains what's supposed to be happening. He's very concerned about character behavior."

ODETS *on directing:* "The technical requirements of this play are such that each scene must be played as structurally written —there isn't much room for personal interpretation by the director of the performer.

"To my mind there are three ways to direct a play. First, *critically.* That is, to analyze each scene and moment for the actors. Secondly, to direct it *synthetically,* to take the material of the play and create something new out of it by enlarging or changing it. Thirdly, and the best way, is a combination of both. From the years I've spent in the theatre, I almost feel that it is better not to have the actors know too much of the 'meaning' of a play. The wedding of the actor to the actual part is far more important. I'm against this business of profound nonsense where an actor with three lines wants to know what his 'inner motivation' is to say 'Hello' to the lead during a minor moment."

BORIS ARONSON *on his settings for the production:* "My entire approach was based on the conception of Odets' trying to get *inside* his characters. The play is mostly about two people on stage. I felt there should be a feeling of great emptiness of the stage during the rehearsal scene as contrasted with the very limited, condensed and tiny place where they live, with everything cluttered up. I wanted to create the feeling you get with so many actors, that if they walked out, you'd feel they had never lived there at all. Then, there's the dressing room. I attempted to dramatize different things. The Boston one was very depressing: The beams overhead, the steam pipes showing and the walls broken down. That's because the play at that time is at its lowest point. Frank is drunk, he is failing, etc. Finally, the most attractive setting, comparatively speaking, in color, proportion and design, was the last scene. This is where there's hope, where they succeed and can look forward to life confidently." . . .

LEE STRASBERG: "Odets has a romantic attitude of life. Not quite in the sense that 'Love conquers all,' but that in the feeling people have for each other there is a great deal of life force. He's concerned with the misunderstandings people have of each other and their cruelty. Not in the political or economic sense, but in a purely human sense."

In Odets' mind, Georgie was the leading character, but Boris Aronson leaned heavily toward Frank Elgin, the actor.

ARONSON: "That's because he's extremely important: Of course his wife's important too—but he's a combination: He has real glamor although he's a lot of trouble to his wife. That's why she stays with him. A real play is when two people are both right. No drama exists when one is a villain and the other pure gold. Georgie is very right and you understand her. And Frank, on the other hand, is an artist; he is sensitive and things go wrong and he takes to drink.

"The reason I lean toward Frank in terms of the environment of the play is because Georgie didn't have a chance to create a permanent home. So I couldn't dramatize it. She couldn't do it on the empty stage, in the little room—or in the Boston dressing room. That's why the only scene that was pleasant was the last one in New York. I couldn't dramatize her world of living because she's fighting it all the time. She doesn't have the chance to do anything about where they are."

The last scene of The Country Girl *is the dressing room in New York during Frank's opening night in the play within the play.*

ODETS: "As it is now written, the action is resolved by Georgie sticking with Frank and Bernie going off alone. But the real interpretation of what will happen later to these people is for the reader or the audience. The last scene, incidentally, was not in the play until four or five nights before the New York opening."

Odets knew he had a problem with the last scene but wanted to wait until the play went into rehearsal to take advantage of things he could visualize once the actors had assumed their roles.

ODETS: "The last scene is the best technical job I ever did. It had to take place on opening night in New York. Next, what woman would leave her husband that night but a real positive horror of a gal? So Georgie had to stay with Frank, but with psychological and theatrical truth. The audience wants, too, to know about the wife and the director: Will she perhaps leave with him? And what will be Bernie's response to her decision? Will Frank be a hit, will he go for the bottle again, etc.? And all this is covered in only nine typed pages of script. I had more fun in rewriting the last scene than anything I've ever done. But I was worried. I wanted to stay out another week, but it all worked out fine."

LEE STRASBERG: "I'm proud of his last scene, too. It was real 'reworking.' It was done by *working;* it didn't just happen. It was an actual problem that had to be dealt with, and he tackled it. This was an achievement for him!"

BROOKS ATKINSON: "Clifford Odets has really got down to work. *The Country Girl* is the best play he has written for years, perhaps the best play of his career."

A REVIEW of *The Country Girl* [2] by Brooks Atkinson

At last Clifford Odets has really got down to work. *The Country Girl,* which opened at the Lyceum last evening, is the best play he has written for years, and perhaps the best of his career. Freed from a lot of fixations and mannerisms he has gone straight to the heart of three characters in a vivid and stinging play about theatre people, and written about them with pitiless integrity.

He has always been a pungently theatrical writer with an actor's special knowledge of stage expression. In *The Country Girl* that is a gift that has brought us a memorable reward. For Paul Kelly, Uta Hagen and Steven Hill are extraordinary actors and they are filling the Lyceum Theatre with some of the most exciting acting of the year.

Don't look for anything extraordinary in the way of story. For *The Country Girl* is only an account of how a rather phlegmatic and taciturn wife and an arrogant director reclaim an old star from drunkenness and put him back in the theatre. At least for the time being, Mr. Odets has set the ailing old cosmos to one side and written a plain, human story.

[2] Brooks Atkinson, "A Review of *The Country Girl,*" *The New York Times,* C (November 11, 1950), 10. Reprinted by permission of *The New York Times.*

Even in his bad plays he cannot write without distinction. In his good plays every line has tension and every scene is full of power. And the impact of *The Country Girl* derives, not from the story, but from the cruel penetration into the secret corners of some human hearts—the twists of temperament, the agony of failure, the desperation with which people hang together, the quicksilver of personalities in conflict and confusion. Since Mr. Odets is a man with a highly wrought personality, he understands the pain and the wounding uncertainties with which similar people blunder through their affairs. In *The Country Girl* he has expressed it with strength, brilliance and candor.

Serving as his own director, he has found a group of interesting actors who can bring his episodic play into a kind of life that practically burns a hole right through the theatre. Boris Aronson in his most appreciative mood has designed an inviting sequence of shabby backstage scenes and lighted them —especially the opening scene—with loveliness and wonder. As in the case of *Detective Story*, Mr. Aronson has given dingy materials the mood and luster of art.

Mr. Kelly plays the part of the derelict actor who fights his way out of alcoholism back to sanity through a series of exhausting crises. Miss Hagen is the wife who understands him and has no illusions. Mr. Hill is the megalomaniac who makes diagnoses that are terribly wrong and wounds everyone who gets in his way.

There are some other parts that are happily cast and pleasantly acted—Phyllis Love as an ingenue, Peter Kass, Louis Veda Quince, Joseph Sullivan and Tony Albert as various theatre people involved in the blasting ordeal of a new production.

But according to the structure of the play, Mr. Kelly, Miss Hagen and Mr. Hill carry the burden of the performance with a drive and an intensity that are overwhelming in the big scenes. Mr. Kelly's lean and muscular honesty, Miss Hagen's womanly strength and disillusioned detachment, Mr. Hill's shrill violence are all tangled and interwoven into a headlong performance.

Since the play is basically theatrical, the fury of the performance is valid. None of the effects is gaudy or meretricious. For Mr. Odets is master of the medium and the big strokes become him. In the past he has written on some more portentous subjects. But he has never written with so profound a knowledge of people as he discloses in *The Country Girl*.

A REVIEW of *The Country Girl* [3] by Wolcott Gibbs

The corrosive effect of drunkenness on talent has always had a strong attraction for writers, who are, generally speaking, suckers for romantic ruins, and Clifford Odets, usually preoccupied with more cosmic matters, has brought the subject up again in *The Country Girl,* at the Lyceum. To judge by the ecstatic tone of the majority of the reviews and the fervent applause on opening night, this is destined to be a successful enterprise, but my own enthusiasm for it is, I'm sorry to say, only temperate. For one thing, the piece is so crowded with the special terminology of the theatre and the unique problems of those employed in it that it is hard to believe it will be wholly comprehensible or entirely fascinating to the untutored audiences that will attend it later in the run. For another, I can't help feeling that Mr. Odets' dialogue is less an actual rendering of human speech than a stylized and somewhat overemotional approximation of it, full of compassion for the damned, appreciation of the tragic irony that so often dilutes genius with alcohol, indignation at a system that places the gifted at the mercy of the solvent, mournful recognition of the fact that few men can face life alone, and, indeed, practically every high-class literary stencil in the book. For still another, the nature of the play is such that almost every character in it is tormented by something or other from beginning to end, and the result is a steady level of desperate conversation, of pleas, denunciations, threats, and confessions, that defeats itself by its very violence, achieving, in fact, only a sort of angry monotone. And, finally, the plot is so profuse in dramatic cliches and so predictable in nearly all its developments that it seems scarcely worth discussing. The reader, however, has a right to a certain amount of information, and so we will discuss the darn thing, but we will do it as briefly as possible.

The structure is the familiar one of a play within a play. When the curtain rises, rehearsals are in progress on a work having something to do with a corrupt and ruthless old politician and his fight to prevent his granddaughter's marriage. For some reason, possibly as a form of criticism, the actor originally hired for the part has withdrawn from the cast, and the producer and the director, an earnest young man called Dodd, are confronted with the problem of replacing him.

[3] Wolcott Gibbs, "A Review of *The Country Girl,*" *The New Yorker,* XXVI (November 18, 1950), 77–79. © 1950 *The New Yorker Magazine,* Inc. Reprinted by permission of *The New Yorker Magazine,* Inc.

The director's choice, vehemently opposed by his colleague, is a performer named Frank Elgin, who was once a star but now, because of some basic insecurity, is apparently a hopeless slave to drink. After a good deal of argument, this man is employed, and the producer's misgivings are borne out in the course of the Boston tryout, when Elgin gets blind drunk on the night before the opening. The director, proficient at his trade but rather innocent in the ways of the world, is convinced that his star's downfall can be laid to his wife, who he thinks is jealous of her husband's career and determined to destroy it, an idea he got from Elgin's habit of transposing his own past to her—of describing her, that is, as an ex-alcoholic, whose picturesque behavior has been largely responsible for the wrecking of both their lives. Under this delusion, the young man orders her back to New York but discovers at the last moment not only that she has been the one saving force in her husband's career but also that he, Dodd, loves her himself, though she loyally refuses to love him back. In a manner perhaps not entirely clear, this straightens everything out. The actor is retained in his part; the play moves on to New York, where, of course, its star scores a triumph said to resemble that of the late Laurette Taylor in *The Glass Menagerie;* and the producer is repaid for his villainous reluctance to employ a notorious souse in the leading role of his play by being obliged to take off his hat and apologize.

The action also involves a young playwright, who possesses the unusual knack of being able to operate a typewriter on his lap; a stage manager, who nobly refuses to allow the producer to berate Elgin for being drunk; and a pretty little ingenue, who dislikes getting beaten up on the stage, even in the interest of a great performance. These, and the producer, are only supernumeraries, however. *The Country Girl* is concerned almost exclusively with its three leading characters, Elgin and his wife and the director. Of them, I thought that Uta Hagen was really superb, playing throughout with a fine, restrained intensity and rising in one scene to an emotional crescendo as effective as anything I have seen for a long while. Paul Kelly, as Elgin, has a difficult assignment in that he is asked to make the audience believe simultaneously in a weak, petulant, and rather stupid man and an artist of considerable imagination and stature, but I think on the whole he manages it very successfully. Young Steven Hill, as Dodd, has another hard part, a peculiar combination of personal hysteria and professional competence, and though I suspected from time to time that he was a little beyond his depth, his work was satisfactory enough. Peter Kass, Louis

Veda Quince, Joseph Sullivan, Phyllis Love, and Tony Albert are spirited in their subsidiary activities, and Boris Aronson's sets—two dressing rooms, a bare stage, and what appears to be a cold-water flat—do everything but smell of greasepaint, alcohol, and cabbage.

CLIFFORD ODETS

The Country Girl

BERNIE DODD.

LARRY.

PHIL COOK.

PAUL UNGER.

NANCY STODDARD.

FRANK ELGIN.

GEORGIE ELGIN.

RALPH.

SYNOPSIS OF SCENES

The action is contemporary

ACT I

SCENE 1. *The stage of a New York theater.*

SCENE 2. *A furnished room, later the same day.*

SCENE 3. *The stage, ten days later.*

SCENE 4. *The furnished room, a week later.*

SCENE 5. *A dressing room in a Boston theater, after midnight, a week later.*

ACT II

SCENE 1. *The Boston dressing room, a few nights later.*

SCENE 2. *The same, the next day.*

SCENE 3. *A dressing room in a New York theater, evening, some weeks later.*

ACT ONE

Scene One

TIME: *The Present*

PLACE: *A New York theater*

In a muted gloomy atmosphere three men are seated or standing on a bare stage which is disposed for a rehearsal; chairs are strewn about in an order which indicates the demarcation of a set. A pilot light and a strip make the illumination.

Soft radio music, a popular Mexican song handled by a lamenting but insinuating tenor, comes from one side. BERNIE DODD, *the director, is softly whistling with the song.* PAUL UNGER, *the play-wright, has straddled a chair with his back to us. The producer,* PHIL COOK, *is gravely and thoughtfully smoking a cigarette. It is very evident that the men have something on their minds. Looking intently at* COOK, BERNIE DODD *finally stops whistling and asks no one in particular:*

BERNIE DODD: Where's that music coming from . . .? [*No one answers;* BERNIE *pauses before sauntering down to* COOK.] Well, what about it . . .? [COOK's *face tightens and he won't answer.* LARRY, *the stage manager, comes in from* R., *respectfully addresses* BERNIE.]

LARRY: Do you want me to hold the company, Bernie? They're waiting.

BERNIE: Dismiss them—no. But tell them to stand by for a possible seven o'clock call tonight.

LARRY: [*Starts out, stops when* BERNIE *says.*]

BERNIE: Elgin, I want Elgin to wait.

LARRY: Frank Elgin?

BERNIE: Yes, have him wait. Where's that music coming from?

LARRY: Prop man's room.

BERNIE: Oh . . . [LARRY *leaves.* BERNIE *asks* COOK *again.*]

BERNIE: Well, what's the verdict?

COOK: [*In a low voice.*] I wish I could lay myself away in a safety-deposit box for a few months! [BERNIE *snorts not impolitely;* UNGER *turns, represses a yawn.* COOK *looks painfully and resentfully at* BERNIE.]

COOK: Bernie, you get the damnedest damn ideas of any man I ever met!

BERNIE: [*Quietly.*] I'm as annoyed as you are, Phil, but a little realism is of the essence, to quote one of your favorite lines.

COOK: But what the heck's realistic about giving Elgin a reading? Am I dumb? Why not let the doorman read for the part?

[NANCY, *a young ingenue, enters very timidly from* R.]

BERNIE: [*Sternly.*] Don't come in here, Nancy—we're busy.

NANCY: I'm awfully sorry, Mr. Dodd . . . I left my part on the chair. May I? [BERNIE *nods impatiently, watches* NANCY *as she takes her part and leaves, saying,* "Please excuse me, everyone." *Meanwhile.*]

COOK: [*Fumingly.*] Damn it, Bernie, I don't follow you and that's the truth!

BERNIE: [*Coldly.*] What don't you follow? We've been in rehearsal four days. [*Sarcastically.*] Due to a technical fluke with the contract—not your fault, of course —Mr. Billy Hertz, our leading man, is on his way to Hollywood and a flowery two-picture deal. As of today, here and now, we are minus a leading man. Since we are booked into Boston on the 28th we are in trouble!

COOK: [*Impatiently.*] I know all of this . . .

BERNIE: Then let me read Elgin for the part. Twelve years ago I saw him give two performances that made my hair stand up. [*Abruptly calling off.*] Close that door and keep it closed! [*Back to* COOK, *angrily.*] Cookie, don't you understand? All I'm saying is let me read him for the part!

PAUL UNGER: [*Quietly.*] That's right,

Phil. It doesn't do any harm to give the man a reading.

COOK: [*Pausing, shrugging.*] All right, read him, read him—I don't say don't read him. [BERNIE *is annoyed and prowling.*]

BERNIE: But don't make any cracks when I call him in.

COOK: But I happen to remember you looked this Elgin up five weeks ago for the part. He didn't do then and he won't do now.

BERNIE: But I gave him the general understudy, didn't I?

COOK: Proving what?

BERNIE: Proving I didn't think his whole future was behind him. [COOK *muttering something.*] What?

COOK: Nothing . . . [BERNIE *looks at him, then abruptly swings off to R., calling.*]

BERNIE: Larry . . . Larry! [LARRY *appears R.*] Ask Frank Elgin to come in, kid. [*Disgusted,* COOK *grinding his cigarette underfoot; he is always gloomy, with a certain heavy pout about him, always dependent and uncertain of himself, but never wanting to admit it.* UNGER *is thirty, tenderhearted, open, simple in a good sense.* BERNIE DODD *can be very direct; he is small but with lots of wiry and graceful physical energy. At thirty-five he is very successful, somewhat fretful and prowling when in rehearsal. Normally, however, his manner is friendly if a little watchful. From former excess of feeling about any and all things he has become saturnine and impassive in the face; there is a gloomy, thoughtful overtone about him. This gives him an air of unwillingness, as if he no longer wanted to be personally involved with persons or things; actually it is a form of protective distrust, expressing itself in what seems a main quality of being objective and impersonal, as if one were working with a screwdriver on a cold piece of machinery. But, of course, this mask of impersonality is not the truth. Just now* BERNIE *is typically prowling.* LARRY *returns with* FRANK ELGIN, *an actor of fifty, whose present seediness does not hide a certain distinction of personality. He is nervous but nevertheless deports himself like the important actor he used to be. He stands there awkwardly, quite aware that three pairs of eyes are searching him.*]

FRANK ELGIN: You want me, Mr. Dodd?

BERNIE: Yeah, Frank, sit down a minute. [*To* LARRY.] Company dismissed?

LARRY: Yes, sir.

BERNIE: Frank, I want you to do something for me. Not so much for me as for our producer and Mr. Unger, the author. Read the part of Judge Murray for them.

FRANK: Billy Hertz *is* out for good, huh?

BERNIE: [*Ignoring his remark.*] Not that I can promise anything.

FRANK: Why do you want *me* to read?

COOK: [*Darkly.*] Why does someone want you to read a part? [FRANK *is puzzled, nervous.* BERNIE *abruptly calls off.*]

BERNIE: Hey, "Props"! Shut off that radio or close the door! [*Gently, back to* FRANK.] Read the part, Frank . . .

FRANK: Sure . . . all right . . . [*He stands, but his attitude seems so slow and reluctant that it annoys* COOK. *Music stops.*]

COOK: Of course, you wouldn't take the part if we offered it to you, would you?

FRANK: [*Humbly.*] I'm not fighting, Mr. Cook. If you want me to read for you . . .

BERNIE: [*To* LARRY.] The disclosure scene, end of act two. Find the place for him and wait outside, kid.

COOK: Everyone in the theater is slightly bats-in-the-belfry!

LARRY: Don't you want me to cue him in? [LARRY *has picked up script and now hands* FRANK *the part.* BERNIE, *annoyed with* COOK, *takes script from* LARRY.]

BERNIE: No, I'll do it. [LARRY *finds place, hands part back to* FRANK *and goes. Part in hand,* FRANK *seems momentarily helpless as he crosses and elaborately drops cigarette into a pail.*]

BERNIE: Take it easy, Frank. I'm not looking for a performance. Sit, walk, anything you want . . . Got the place? [FRANK *turns, hefting the part in his hand, attempting humor.*]

FRANK: Yes. Feels like the *Sunday Times.*

BERNIE: We can cut down to—Bert is already in—the Judge's line: "I didn't ask you to sit down . . ." [*Trying to hide his agitation,* FRANK *paces, looking upward for best light by which to read.*]

FRANK: "I didn't ask you to sit down . . . because I don't want a louse on my furniture." That it?

BERNIE: Yes. [*Continuing in the play.*] "I don't think this furniture will be yours much longer, Judge Murray!"

FRANK: "And I think I'll have to ask for

an explanation of this big-mouth attitude. You damn Reform Party kids come and go like a ten-cent piece of ice. Now get out before I kick you out! You only got in here because you know Ellen!"

BERNIE: "I resent that!"

FRANK: "Not as much as I—" [*Nervously moving under lights.*] What is that? I can't make it out. [*Then.*] Oh! "Not as much as I resent you, you little Wop bastard!"

BERNIE: "I'm not letting you put this discussion on any personal plane! There's too much at stake!"

FRANK: [*As* BERNIE *begins to read same line.*] "I represent the collective will of thousands of our best . . ."

BERNIE: No, that's my line, Frank.

FRANK: [*Lamely.*] Well, it's in this part. I can't see what I'm reading. I mean the light, I mean . . . Hertz is got the whole part pencilled up.

BERNIE: [*Urgently.*] Go on, don't stop.

FRANK: I can't. I'm sorry. I'm saying "hands, behave!", but they're shaking like a leaf.

BERNIE: Start right from where you left off. [FRANK *looks at* BERNIE *and* COOK *from under his eyebrows, not lifting his head; then drops his eyes and slowly shakes head.*]

BERNIE: What's the matter?

FRANK: It won't do, Mr. Dodd. I always was a dead bunny when it came to sight-reading. Thanks for the chance, but it won't do. [*Walks to a table with bitter dignity, puts part down.* COOK *enjoys this part of the scene;* BERNIE *is annoyed, saying to* UNGER.]

BERNIE: Give him a clean script, Paul.

FRANK: [*Unhappily.*] What's the use? You've been very nice, Dodd—you looked me up before—gave me the general understudy—I appreciate what you did, but— [BERNIE *abruptly calls off:* "Dammit, I want that door shut and stay shut!" *Then throws script to table, turns.*]

BERNIE: I can't be that wrong, Frank—I know an actor when I see one! Let's forget the damn script! Let's improvise the scene! Just the situation—not the author's scene!

FRANK: How do you mean?

BERNIE: Ad-lib, just ad-lib it—improvise it. Look at me! I'm a fresh kid—I wanna marry your grandchild and you don't want me to! That's the situation . . . [BERNIE *begins to pace, waving others aside. Soon he is pacing around* FRANK, *like a bull-*

fighter around a helpless animal, which is the impression FRANK *gives for the moment.*]

BERNIE: [*Angrily.*] I don't leave this house until I get your answer. Don't call in any servants or I'll knock them all on their ears!

FRANK: [*Slowly.*] What . . . do you want!

BERNIE: I want to marry your grandchild and you don't want me to!

FRANK: Why should I let you marry my grandchild? [*Anxiously.*] Right? [*Then.*] Who the hell are you to come busting in this house like a hurricane?

BERNIE: You don't answer phones, so I'm here in person! [*They are gradually slipping into a really dramatic scene,* FRANK *standing stock-still until, in a moment, he begins to follow* BERNIE *wherever he moves; shortly they begin banging table.*]

FRANK: I usually make up my own mind when and when not to answer the phone. As far as Ellen's concerned, as far as she's concerned—you can go to hell!

BERNIE: You won't talk to me that way again!

FRANK: I'll talk to you that way again and again and again! Is that what you want? [*Suddenly choleric.*] Now get out before I open your head with a poker!

BERNIE: We have to have a talk, a long talk, Frank.

FRANK: [*Dropping his voice.*] I'll talk, I'll talk to you, son. Let's see what's really on your mind.

BERNIE: [*Tauntingly.*] I don't think you can stop me, Frank!

FRANK: [*Scornfully.*] Oh, I'll stop you! I'll stop you, Dodd, if it's the last thing I do! Don't underestimate me. I haven't begun to fight yet. And—

BERNIE: I'm sorry for you—by next week you'll be front-page news!

FRANK: [*Angrily.*] Wait a minute, wait a minute! What the devil are you talking about? Explain this thing to me!

BERNIE: I'm head of the Citizens' Non-Partisan Committee, too. [FRANK, *really acting now, looks at him increduously, then abruptly bursts into laughter. Then, breaking that up with a fit of coughing.*]

FRANK: Did you ever tell that to Ellen?

BERNIE: I'm telling her tonight.

FRANK: [*Chortling.*] Well, boy, that's just what I want you to do! God almighty, I want you to tell her your plans! I want to be behind a door when you tell her your plans!

BERNIE: [*Quickly.*] That's it, Frank! Now change the color. You've lost everything. Where is Ellen? You haven't seen her for two days—she's deserted you.

FRANK: [*Changing to a pensive thoughtfulness.*] Ellen? Where's Ellen . . .? Haven't seen her for two days . . . [*He has seated himself, but now he slowly stands, shakes his head, shows worry and nervousness for first time.*] Is . . . my daughter in the house . . . ? [*Turning, moving about like an old man.*] I have the greatest confidence in her! [*Scornfully.*] Now I think I asked you to get out of here about a long moment ago! [*The two men are standing, facing each other in the scene. Now, after long pause, BERNIE drops out of scene and says admiringly.*]

BERNIE: That's it, Frank . . . that's the way you used to go! [*But FRANK, as BERNIE glances triumphantly at COOK and UNGER, continues scene with strength and bitterness, flinging his overcoat in BERNIE's face.*]

FRANK: Now get out of here! Don't look at me that way. Nobody wants your pity or your help! It's no satisfaction in a cold world to have your colder pity! Werba was a great man in his day—that's what all the loafers are saying. Werba made his millions, but the boy wonder is living with his in-laws now, they say! And now you come here and tell me, "Mr. Werba, you're going to prison within the month. Well, let me tell you—Werba won't give up his name and take a number—Werba is still a great man! He tore an empire out of the world before he was thirty and he'll live to do it again! And when that time comes—you listen to this!—I won't forget my enemies or my friends. I will never forget those who dragged me down! [*FRANK has been talking directly front to BERNIE, who has seated himself at table, back to the theater. FRANK sighs deeply, breaking a strange spell of majesty.*]

BERNIE: That was the last speech of "Werba's Millions," wasn't it?

FRANK: Yes . . . [*Standing, rubs his hands, shakes head, as though dizzy. Gives impression of slowly waking into a colder, shabbier world.*] It came back to me . . . [*Glancing briefly at others, BERNIE says gently to FRANK.*]

BERNIE: Frank, would you wait outside

for me? Two minutes, in one of the dressing-rooms, please.

FRANK: Yes, I'll wait . . . [*Stands and goes off R. BERNIE joins others, repressing satisfaction.*]

BERNIE: Well, what did you see?

UNGER: If you're asking me, something I wouldn't have believed. Where was that seedy guy hiding all that power and majesty?

COOK: We've done three shows together —Bernie, I know you well. You're a man of violent preconceptions.

BERNIE: Didn't that scene speak for itself?

COOK: What did it speak? Does five minutes of ad-lib prove he can memorize and play eighty sides? Just bear in mind this is for a potent seventy thousand bucks! He's been laying in pickle for a good ten years!

BERNIE: [*Quietly.*] Someone took a chance one day with an actress named Laurette Taylor . . . and look what she did in her last few years.

COOK: But, darling, that man's a bleary bum!

BERNIE: I don't want him to hear you— don't raise your voice. [*Then, waiting.*] Well, what about him?

COOK: Look, you own twenty percent of this show *yourself!* [*To UNGER.*] You're the playwright—doesn't this worry *you?*

UNGER: [*Promptly.*] Not if it doesn't worry Bernie. [*Momentarily stymied, COOK hesitates before turning and quickly saying.*]

COOK: What about Ray Newton? He's still available.

BERNIE: [*Sharply.*] I don't want Ray Newton! He's my idea of nothing, just nothing!

COOK: Well, what do you think you can get out of *him?*

BERNIE: [*Flatly.*] I don't know.

COOK: [*Aghast.*] You don't know?!

BERNIE: How the hell should I know? [*Making a mark in the air.*] He's a big dark X! [*Prowling again.*] Do you think I underestimate the job if I use this lush?

UNGER: [*Smiling to himself.*] Don't raise your voice.

BERNIE: We open in Boston in three weeks and two days. I'll have to manipulate and out-think him every inch of the way. [*Snorting.*] Big comfort—my father was a lush—I have some background for the job.

[*Turning to* UNGER.] But if this comes off you're apt to get something that happens once in twenty years!

UNGER: [*Impressed.*] I believe you if you say so . . .

COOK: And he's apt to have an ulcerated sponge for a brain, too.

BERNIE: We can stay out till he's letter-perfect. The season's young.

COOK: But I'm not!

BERNIE: Then what do you want to do? Postpone? [*Answering his own question.*] Postpone!

COOK: [*Dismayed.*] How can we postpone? We're in for a twenty-thousand dollar bite already. The scenery's ordered, the guarantees on the house—

BERNIE: [*Swiftly.*] *Then what do you want to do?!*

COOK: [*Pausing.*] Could we . . . look around for someone else while he's rehearsing?

BERNIE: [*Firmly.*] No, I won't do that. Once we start we don't let him go without real cause. A binge is real cause. Or if he can't retain lines. And, hold your hat, I wanna give him a run-of-the-play contract, not a two weeks' deal. [*Quickly.*] Because I'd need his complete confidence, Cookie. Give him a two weeks' deal and he knows we can let him out any time.

COOK: [*Indignantly.*] No, sir! No run-of-the-play contract for Mr. Elgin. I'd rather go back to Dallas and—[*Starting out, but* BERNIE *takes him by an arm and turns him.*]

BERNIE: [*Quietly.*] Okay, Phil—two weeks' deal.

COOK: [*Disturbed, pausing.*] What do we pay him?

BERNIE: A few hundred a week. [*Pause.* COOK *agrees by not answering. Prop-man must have opened his door, for music begins again.*]

BERNIE: [*Warningly.*] But I mean it, Phil—I don't let him out without real cause.

COOK: Umm . . .

BERNIE: [*Turning.*] Agreed with you, Paul?

UNGER: Umm . . . [*Poised, as if a dancer,* BERNIE's *eyes and manner begin to sparkle; his attitude is tense but quietly expressive.*]

BERNIE: I'm one of those fools who saw Laurette Taylor in *The Glass Menagerie* eight times. Now . . . maybe something here . . . I'm not saying what . . . but it needs your real cooperation. [*Walking over, calling.*] Frank! Frank Elgin! Oh, Frank!

[LARRY *enters from* R. *as* BERNIE *begins prowling expectantly.*]

LARRY: You want Mr. Elgin?

BERNIE: [*Walking back.*] Yes, send him in.

LARRY: He's gone—he left.

BERNIE: What do you mean he left?

LARRY: He left about five minutes ago.

BERNIE: [*Impatiently.*] Where? Coffee? What?

LARRY: He just walked out, Bernie. He didn't say. [BERNIE's *face grows grim; behind him* COOK *smirks.*]

BERNIE: I see I'll have to go and get him. [*Pausing, glowering,* BERNIE *turns abruptly, hurries out.*]

COOK: [*Bitterly.*] He's going to go and get him! In what Eighth Avenue bar . . . ? [*Wagging his head,* COOK *starts out,* UNGER *following.*]

CURTAIN

Scene Two

TIME: *A little later*
PLACE: FRANK's *furnished room in mid-Manhattan, west of Eighth Avenue*

The shabby room is lighted by a lamp and a small window; it is not possible to tell that it is high noon outside. Loud music is coming out of small radio. FRANK's *wife,* GEORGIE ELGIN, *is obviously doing two things—suffering a toothache and packing a suitcase. She turns at a knock at the door.*

GEORGIE ELGIN: Yes, yes, I'll turn it down . . . [*Turns off radio completely. Numb and listless, she returns to pick up* and examine a dress on a hanger. She is surprised when knocking starts again; stands, thinks and finally asks, "Who is it . . . ?"]

BERNIE'S VOICE: Is Mr. Elgin in?

GEORGIE: Just a minute. [*Stuffs dress into suitcase, closes it hastily, pushes it under bed; smooths out top of bed; walks warily to door, opens it, revealing* BERNIE.]

GEORGIE: Yes . . . ?

BERNIE: Is Mr. Elgin in?

GEORGIE: No. I don't know when he'll be back.

BERNIE: Are you Mrs. Elgin? [*She nods.*] I wanted to talk to Frank.

GEORGIE: I don't know when he'll be back—he's rehearsing—in a show, you know.

BERNIE: [*Briskly.*] I'll wait—it's important. [BERNIE *has pushed past her and is inside, looking at room; she looks at him rather stupidly; only when he looks at her does she seem to come to with a start, saying.*]

GEORGIE: I was just going to make some coffee . . . [*Vaguely beginning this business, looking back, wondering who* BERNIE *is, she says, to make talk.*]

GEORGIE: Is it raining hard outside?

BERNIE: It isn't raining.

GEORGIE: Isn't . . . ? Felt as if it were. It's cold out . . . the summer collapsed so abruptly, didn't it? You could fall asleep here and not wake up till they called you for the Judgment Day.

BERNIE: [*Who has been making notes in a small book.*] What do I smell, incense?

GEORGIE: It cuts the restaurant odors from down below.

BERNIE: I think I'd rather have the restaurant.

GEORGIE: It always comes in such spooky flavors, Sandalwood, Wisteria . . . this one's called Cobra.

BERNIE: I guess it's supposed to kill you. [*He snorts and she smiles, but abruptly winces.*]

GEORGIE: Does my face look swollen?

BERNIE: No . . .

GEORGIE: I have a bad toothache. All of autumn's in this tooth . . . [*Coming closer.*] You don't look like one of Frank's friends.

BERNIE: I'm the director of the play he's working in.

GEORGIE: Oh! . . . you're what's-his-name?

BERNIE: Bernie Dodd.

GEORGIE: [*Staring at him.*] Dodd . . . [*Then.*] You're even younger than I thought, from what I've read and heard.

BERNIE: [*Archly.*] In this spot most people would put in a flattering word.

GEORGIE: I amuse you, don't I?

BERNIE: No, but you act like an old lady, and you're not. [*Seeing him looking impatiently at his watch, she crosses, picks up a clock, asking.*]

GEORGIE: What time is it?

BERNIE: Twenty minutes to twelve.

GEORGIE: Three clocks, a radio . . . and never know the time. [*Turning.*] Twenty after twelve? [BERNIE, *crossing to look at a framed photo, corrects her; she sets clock, puts it down.*]

BERNIE: That's a good photograph of Frank. Recent?

GEORGIE: No, that's a very long time ago —the year we were married. We went out to Hollywood that year.

BERNIE: [*Surprised.*] Was Frank ever in pictures?

GEORGIE: For a year or two, but it was spooky. People were endlessly kind, but it never worked out, and we came back. [*Of another photo, sarcastically.*] That's my father. I come from Hartford. No, I won't, thanks. [*She has refused one of* BERNIE's *cigarettes. Crossing, she picks up small bottle of hand lotion and rubs lotion into her hands.*] Isn't it strange—I thought it was raining . . . My hands are numb . . .

BERNIE: Does Frank usually come right home?

GEORGIE: Unless he sits out on the brownstone stoop. [*Abruptly.*] Is something wrong?

BERNIE: Does Frank still drink?

GEORGIE: [*With sudden alert evasion.*] Just like us . . . one mouth and five fingers on every hand. [*Seeing his arch look.*] What did you think I'd answer, Mr. Dodd?

BERNIE: Touché. That means . . .

GEORGIE: [*Cutting him off.*] Oh, come, everyone knows what *touché* means.

BERNIE: [*Faintly annoyed.*] What are we doing here, jockeying for position? [*Jabbing a finger at them.*] Who reads these books?

GEORGIE: [*Coldly.*] I borrow them on a library card.

BERNIE: Balzac, Dreiser, Jane Austen . . . [*Smiling.*] I'm afraid to ask you if you enjoy them—you'll bite my head off.

GEORGIE: [*Intently.*] I enjoy them . . . But I'd like to know what you're doing here. You're making me very nervous and I don't like it. What is this about Frank? [*She stands.* FRANK *walks in, stops when he sees* BERNIE; *a very direct man and a very indirect man are looking at each other.*]

BERNIE: What happened to you?

FRANK: I decided to walk . . .

BERNIE: I asked you to wait.

FRANK: [*Pausing.*] Any coffee, Georgie? Make some coffee . . . [GEORGIE *crosses to cooking coffee pot, keeping eyes on* FRANK.]

BERNIE: I'm a busy man, Frank.

FRANK: [*Uneasily.*] What do you want me to do?

BERNIE: Make up your mind—I want you to play that part.

GEORGIE: [*Turning.*] I'm an innocent by-stander. Don't shoot me—just tell me what this is all about.

FRANK: Mr. Dodd says he wants me to play the lead in his play . . .

BERNIE: [*Briskly annoyed.*] It's a starring part that needs an actor who can stay sober and learn lines. Are you that actor, or not?

FRANK: [*With flare.*] Well, I'm not one of those goddam microphone actors, like Billy Hertz! I'm an actor!

BERNIE: [*Waiting.*] That's what I used to think . . .

FRANK: [*Evasively.*] What about the producer? If looks would kill, I was dead.

BERNIE: He's afraid you're a drinker.

FRANK: [*Sullenly.*] I don't drink on a show.

BERNIE: [*Sharply.*] Not according to Gilbert. I checked with him—you worked with him in '44? What happened? [FRANK *looks at* GEORGIE *before answering.*]

FRANK: We lost our little daughter . . . that year. [*Silence.* FRANK *sits on bed.* GEORGIE *pours coffee.*]

BERNIE: [*Quietly.*] Can you stay on the wagon now?

FRANK: [*Pausing.*] Look, son, I think we oughta forget it. . . .

BERNIE: Don't call me son! You've played bigger parts—you used to be a star!

FRANK: [*Gloomily.*] Yeah, I used to drink a glass of money for breakfast, too.

BERNIE: [*Angrily.*] What's the matter with you?

GEORGIE: [*As if waking up.*] You don't listen, Mr. Dodd. Don't you see he's afraid of the responsibility?

BERNIE: But I'm willing to take a chance—the gamble's all on *my* side. [FRANK *expostulates uneasily.*]

FRANK: Why kid around? They open in Boston the 28th. I couldn't even learn the lines in that time! [*Then, lapsing, to* BERNIE.] That part needs a Bennett or a Blinn—

BERNIE: [*Sardonically.*] Bad enough to go to Hollywood to cast—now you suggest I go to heaven! [BERNIE *stares at them coldly; about to walk out, turns, says earnestly.*]

BERNIE: Listen, Frank, you don't know me. But I was a kid when I saw you give two great performances in mediocre plays—*Proud People* and *Werba's Millions*. I can get the same show out of you right now . . . if you lay off the liquor! I have more confidence in you than you have in yourself!

GEORGIE: [*Sitting back, watching.*] Why . . . ?

BERNIE: Because I saw him as a kid—I was a hat-check boy in the Shubert Theaters. [*To* FRANK.] You and Lunt and Walter Huston—you were my heroes. I know everything you did.

FRANK: Hear that, Georgie . . . ? [GEORGIE *speaks with quiet thoughtfulness.*]

GEORGIE: Naturally, Mr. Dodd, you exaggerate the sentiment to make your point. [BERNIE *turns, looks at her very carefully.*]

BERNIE: We killed the cat with sentiment? Okay, we'll bring him back to life with some antiseptic truth. I come from realistic people—I'm Italian. [*Pausing.*] I'm not blind to Frank's condition—he's a bum! But I'm tough, not one of those nice "humane" people: they hand you a drink and a buck and that's exactly where they stop. [*To* FRANK.] I won't hand you a buck . . . but I'll think about you, if you take this job. I'll commit myself to you—we'll work and worry together—it's a marriage! And I'll make you work, if you take this job: *I'll be your will!* [*Pausing.*] But if you do me dirt—only once!—no pity, Frank! Not a drop of pity! Joke ending, kid . . .

[GEORGIE *looks more carefully at* BERNIE. *We can almost see her come to life as she stands and comes in closer.*]

GEORGIE: You'll be his "will" . . . I like that. That's what he needs, a will. And "no pity," I like that, too. I like the "antiseptic truth." But what kind of contract do you offer?

BERNIE: [*Promptly.*] Standard two-week contract.

GEORGIE: Not run-of-the-play?

BERNIE: No.

GEORGIE: Doesn't that mean you could let Frank out any time with two weeks' notice?

BERNIE: [*Impatiently.*] That's what it means.

GEORGIE: But suppose he takes the part and opens the show? He gets you over the top of the hill. How does he know you won't replace him?

BERNIE: [*With flat indignation.*] No run-of-the-play contract. Suppose we have to drop him? For drinking or for not retaining his lines? What do you want? Drop him, replace him and *still* pay his salary for the run of the show?

GEORGIE: [*Pausing.*] I don't think he should take it. He needs confidence. He won't have it with that two weeks' clause over his head. Would *you*? [*She has spiked* BERNIE's *guns by presenting him the same case he previously presented to* COOK. *Finally, pausing, looking from one to the other,* BERNIE *says.*]

BERNIE: I have nothing in my mind except for Frank to play this part!

GEORGIE: [*As sharply.*] That's sentiment again!

BERNIE: [*Heatedly.*] I can't believe my ears! I came up here with the best intentions in the world—now I find I'm victimizing you!

FRANK: [*Nervously.*] May I get a word in edgewise?

BERNIE: What the hell did I do? Bring you a basket of snakes?

GEORGIE: [*Coldly.*] Noblesse oblige, Mr. Dodd. Stop whirling like a dervish.

FRANK: Nobody wants to get your goat, Mr. Dodd. I . . . what I mean, Mr. Dodd, it's only a matter of not wanting to bite off more than I can chew . . . [*Pausing,* BERNIE *says coldly.*]

BERNIE: You have the offer. We're booked into Boston for two weeks, but the season's young—we can stay out till you're letter-perfect.

FRANK: [*Eagerly.*] And . . . would you do that?

BERNIE: [*Promptly.*] Do it? I *insist* upon it! Do I look green? [*Then, looking at* GEORGIE.] I'll take that back—I *am* green! [*Then, to* FRANK.] Call me at the office by three o'clock. That means not later. [BERNIE *starts out, stops.*]

BERNIE: You need a twenty-dollar bill? You need it . . . [*Puts bill on radio and goes. Silence.* FRANK *does not move.*]

GEORGIE: Is that boy as talented as he throws himself around?

FRANK: [*Moodily.*] Best average in both the leagues . . .

GEORGIE: He's wilful, but he meant what he said.

FRANK: [*Turned aside.*] I can't do it, can I?

GEORGIE: Doesn't it seem strange for you to ask me that?

FRANK: [*Unhappily.*] You're my wife . . .

GEORGIE: [*Quietly.*] Frank, we've been through all this before, many times before . . . [*Then.*] I'm tired, Frank . . . [*Brooding, not looking at her,* FRANK *murmurs.*]

FRANK: What happened? Where did I get so bolloxed up? I was the best young leading man in this business, not a slouch!

GEORGIE: Scripts didn't come . . .

FRANK: I knew it then—on the coast—I lost my nerve! And then, when we lost the money, in '39, after those lousy Federal Theater jobs—! [*Pausing, shaking head.*] This is the face that once turned down radio work. [*Pacing.*] What ever the hell I did, I don't know what! [*Abruptly defiant, stopping behind her.*] But I'm good! I'm still good, baby, because I see what *they think* is good! [*He waits, but she is silent.*] Don't you think I'm good? *I* think I'm good!

GEORGIE: [*Quietly.*] Then take the part. Make it your own responsibility, not mine . . . take the part. [*He looks at her, it is plain that the idea frightens him.*]

GEORGIE: Don't wiggle and caper, Frank. [*Suddenly.*] Can't you admit to yourself you're a failure? You'd die to save your face, not to fail in public—but I'm your wife; you have no face. Try to be clear about this offer—think.

FRANK: I didn't hear him say he'd star me.

GEORGIE: [*With dry weariness.*] I have a message for you, Frank: take the part!

FRANK: Yes, but what will *you* do if I—?

GEORGIE: [*Firmly.*] Leave me out. Take the part and do your level best. [*Slowly moves a hand against her aching jaw.*]

FRANK: [*Uneasily.*] But what about that two weeks' clause? You yourself tried—

GEORGIE: All I tried was to get a better deal. But you won't get perfect terms.

FRANK: You certainly gave him a scrap . . . [*Abruptly excited and cunning.*] Georgie, I'll tell you! That two weeks' clause—they can give me notice any time, but *I* can give *them* notice, too!

GEORGIE: ? ? ?

FRANK: Don't you see? They can let me out, but *I* can walk out any time I want! If I feel I'm breaking my neck—

GEORGIE: You can quit?

FRANK: Yeah, that's sort of what I mean, yeah. [*Bright, shrewd.*] You see? Get it?

GEORGIE: [*Dubious, waiting.*] Yes . . .

FRANK: [*Cunningly grand.*] Why, with this two weeks' clause I don't even have to come into New York, do I? [GEORGIE *murmurs a "No" as* FRANK *chortlingly seats himself.*] That's the thing, that's it—two can play the same game! [*Delighted at this discovery,* GEORGIE *much less so,* FRANK *abruptly snaps his fingers, lights up even more.*] Wait a minute! Quarter to seven this morning I had a dream! I laughed so hard it woke me up! That's a sign, Georgie, a hunch!

GEORGIE: [*Puzzled.*] A dream . . . ?

FRANK: [*Seeing it.*] A big sign—now get this—a big banner was stretched across the street: "Frank Elgin in—" . . . I couldn't make out in what. Mayor La Guardia was in the dream—lots of people laughing and feeling good. I'm going to take that part, Georgie! You don't have to tell me not to drink—haven't I been a good boy all summer? [*Wagging around.*] This morning I

got up early—that funny laughing dream. And I was thinking about our lives . . . everything . . . and now this chance! Don't you see that all those people in the dream, they wish me luck. I won't fail this time! Because that's what counts—if the world is with you—and your wife! [*Looks at her, earnest, boyish and questioning, appealing for her support. Finally, she says with reluctance.*]

GEORGIE: I don't have any appointments . . . all winter . . .

FRANK: [*Excitedly.*] That's what counts! I can't fail this time—I feel like Jack-A-Million! I'll let Dodd know—I'll go up to the office in person. [*Taking twenty-dollar bill.*] But my first stop is the barber shop—I want the tonsorial works. Anything you want me to bring *you* back?

GEORGIE: No . . .

FRANK: Catch that, dear! [*He throws her an extravagant kiss, really excited, and she catches the gift with an open hand. Alone, thinking, we see how unhappy* GEORGIE *is. Then she remembers her suitcase; she takes it from under bed, opens it and unhappily looks down at its contents. Then, murmuring, "My God, my God, my God . . . ," she takes out dress and goes back to wardrobe to replace it on a hanger.*]

CURTAIN

Scene Three

TIME: *Ten days later*
PLACE: *The rehearsal stage*

BERNIE, *back to audience, is sitting to one side, watching* FRANK *and* NANCY *play a scene.* LARRY, *at working table, is only other person in the theater. It is late night and the outer world has stopped for these working people; they have the quality of functioning fully, unaware of anything else.*

NANCY *is seventeen and virginal, which is to say untried and initiatory; but she has real if unfocussed talent.* FRANK *is working well, old muscles slowly coming to life; but he is worried about an inability to memorize his lines, although he will not say so. His part is rolled up in his hand.* NANCY *is letter-perfect.*

FRANK: [*In the play, with an Irish flavor.*] "You know me, Ellen. You call me Granddad, but I'm all your parents rolled into one. Consequently, I have to talk to

you as father and mother, too. Now why do you like that boy?"

NANCY: "I don't know. Maybe because he likes me."

FRANK: "That's a human enough reason. How long do you know the lad?"

BERNIE: Play him suspicious, Frank, suspicious—you don't trust her!

FRANK: "No, you told me—four months. That ain't very long, as time goes, is it?"

NANCY: "Why, four months can be eternity, Granddad! Didn't you know that?"

FRANK: "I guess I knew it, Ellen, but forgot it." [Pausing.] "Now, what about that boy?"

NANCY: "Oh, you mustn't worry about him—he's only one of a dozen! I'm very popular, you know."

FRANK: [Pausing.] That's me! Throw me the line, Larry . . .

LARRY: [Doing so.] "Yes, you're a grown-up lady now . . ."

FRANK: [Back in the play.] "Yes, you're a grown-up lady now . . ." [Stopping again.] Now what? [NANCY answers automatically, before LARRY can.]

NANCY: "But I can easily call to mind when you were this high."

LARRY: That's right. [FRANK stops, looks grumpily at NANCY.]

FRANK: Never usurp the stage manager's position, dear. Older actors don't like it.

NANCY: [Overwhelmed.] I beg your pardon—I'm very sorry, Mr. Elgin.

BERNIE: [Impatiently.] Let's go, let's go . . . [FRANK resumes the play, a headache building up in him.]

FRANK: "But I can easily call to mind when you were . . . this high. You had a funny habit. You said when you'd grow big I'd grow small. Children have that delusion, don't they?" [Turning.] That's tricky there, Bernie, a real mouthful.

BERNIE: That's true.

FRANK: [Hesitating.] What does he mean? . . .

BERNIE: [Moving in.] First, a real psychological fact about kids. But the theatrical meaning is more important. Show that he's trying to win her over to his side.

FRANK: But he isn't the kind who would openly ask for sympathy.

BERNIE: Normally, no, but this is his only grandchild—his defenses are down. [FRANK thinks about this somberly.]

NANCY: [Timidly.] Do I know that he wants sympathy?

BERNIE: [Looking at his watch.] No, Ellen doesn't understand the situation yet. Now, it's almost eleven o'clock! [LARRY comes in with typical tact and deference.]

LARRY: I was just about to call your attention to that.

BERNIE: Tell you what . . . let's send Nancy home. Our little ingenue needs her beauty rest.

NANCY: [Earnestly.] I'm not tired at all, truly I'm not!

BERNIE: Don't rush, child—life is long. [Scene breaks up with the quality of "seventh inning stretch."]

NANCY: Well, will you want me at ten tomorrow then?

BERNIE: [Ogling her.] Why?

NANCY: [Flustered.] Well, I mean I'm available whenever you want me, night or day. [The men are laughing.] Oh, I didn't mean that! I can't bear it! I mean I wanted to get my hair washed tomorrow and—

BERNIE: [Grinning.] All right, come in at eleven. And beat a hasty retreat right now, before I forget I'm a parent myself! I eat little girls like you, without salt!

LARRY: Button up your coat and don't look so flustered—we all adore you.

NANCY: [Simpering.] You're very nasty, all of you, tonight! [Then, laughing.] Good-night, everyone. Happy dreams!

ALL: Good-night, etc. etc. [NANCY goes, happy and self-conscious, full of young excitement.]

FRANK: Off in a flurry of tender jingle bells—that's the age.

LARRY: Baby.

BERNIE: Larryola, you don't have to hang around.

LARRY: Want me to put out the pilot light? [Abstracted, leafing through his script, BERNIE murmurs, "Yeah, sure . . ." LARRY will drag out the pilot light and shut off a strip of border lights while FRANK sits at BERNIE's table. The feeling of the scene, out of which the above joshing came, is late and tired.]

FRANK: Did I hear you say you were a parent?

BERNIE: I have a little girl of four.

FRANK: There's nothing quite like a little girl. Funny, I never got the impression you were married.

BERNIE: Neither did my wife. Five months ago she invented a phrase, "the perennial bachelor," and went to Reno to patent the invention! [Of the script.] What about this damn hospital scene? You tired? [Yawning.] Wanna stop?

FRANK: Well, I have a touch of headache—

BERNIE: Let's stop—

FRANK: [*Troubled.*] No, let's go on . . . Judge Murray's character escapes me.

BERNIE: Well, let's chase him.

FRANK: Who's he like in real life? Hague, Hines—?

BERNIE: Any of those big political bosses. [*Turns to* LARRY. *who is leaving.*] What's tomorrow morning's call?

LARRY: Whole company at eleven. Except Mabel Beck—she's got that radio shot.

BERNIE: Scan the horizon, Larry. Come back if that little man is still outside. [LARRY *nods sympathetically, and goes.* BERNIE *pauses pensively.*] In my old age I'm ducking a man with a summons. Money—my wife wants money.

FRANK: [*Sympathetically.*] Oh, no . . . [*Real loneliness shows itself in* BERNIE, *but now he briskly pulls himself together, saying, as he crosses to* FRANK.]

BERNIE: Let's talk about the character. How do *you* feel the Judge?

FRANK: Can I go wild? [*Then intently, seeing and feeling something inwardly.*] A fox . . . that's the image. Nimble. Quiet. On the alert, but nothing shows—a rigid face. A concrete slab for a face . . .

BERNIE: That's power . . .

FRANK: [*Turning inwardly.*] That's power . . . and pride.

BERNIE: Pride's a big color to work for.

FRANK: Yes, he can't be wrong. Got everything he wants. Above the battle—withdrawn. [*Face narrow with thought,* FRANK, *standing, has begun to illustrate his words; a ridiculous and cagey strut comes into his walk. He murmurs, in the role.*]

FRANK: I'm illiterate—why?

BERNIE: Because he's narrow, prejudiced, intolerant—

FRANK: But that's his strength.

BERNIE: [*Agreeing.*] That's his strength —he goes narrow but deep—his own man.

FRANK: [*Excitedly, staying in the mask.*] I can do that—sure! Now I know how this boy-o walks and talks! That's in his way . . . [FRANK, *without change of expression, sends the chair scuttling across the stage with one powerful vicious kick. Imperturbably struts back to* BERNIE, *drops back to himself.*]

FRANK: Isn't that it?

BERNIE: [*Admiringly.*] That's it.

FRANK: [*Eagerly.*] But I have to like him, Bernie, even when he puts his wife away. Otherwise I can't get inside him.

BERNIE: [*Admiringly.*] Where do you get these kind of feelings from?

FRANK: I don't know . . . [*Circling a hand around his chest.*] But when I get it here, inside . . . you can't get it technically.

BERNIE: No, you're not a technical actor.

FRANK: [*Sighing.*] Not many directors understood that about me.

BERNIE: Smoke? [*Silence. Moodiness. Both men light up, smoke cigarettes while putting on their coats.* FRANK *looks at his part.*]

FRANK: I'm worried about the lines . . .

BERNIE: Don't answer if you don't want to . . . how did a man with your talents go so haywire?

FRANK: [*Evasively.*] That's a bow-wow with a very long tail . . .

BERNIE: What kind of woman is your wife? Just for chatter's sake. . . .

FRANK: Georgie's got a very good mind.

BERNIE: Then why didn't she want you to play this part?

FRANK: Was that your impression?

BERNIE: A yard wide!

FRANK: [*Evasively.*] I don't know . . . she's on a hairspring, Georgie. Always has been . . . a hairspring. [*Leafing nervously through his part.*] Sorry I don't know the words yet, Bernie. I wanted to surprise you tonight, but non compos mentis.

BERNIE: The sooner you get that second act out of your hands, the better. Why on a hairspring?

FRANK: [*Uneasily.*] It's like the hospital scene in the play. Where they tell the Judge his wife is . . . psychotic? What's the exact meaning of the word?

BERNIE: Insane. . . . [FRANK *pauses, looking at part, his voice low.*]

FRANK: [*Pausing.*] The Judge, you see . . . isn't glad to get rid of his wife, the way the author says. It's very complicated. . . . [*Clearing throat.*] You tell an unhappily married man his wife is insane. He may feel relief, but at the same time he hopes it isn't true. . . .

BERNIE: [*Watching him keenly.*] That makes a richer scene. . . .

FRANK: You can even say it's tender when he gets the news. There's so much to remember of living together . . . all the winters and summers, the times they were poor. . . . [*Voice trembling.*] And the fights, snarling and yipping—settling blue murder with an hour in the bed. . . .

BERNIE: [*Keenly.*] Yes, if you played the scene that way. . . .

FRANK: I'm not talking about the scene.

BERNIE: You're not?

FRANK: [*Fingering his part.*] Georgie . . . was "Miss America" in the late 30s, the year I met her. She gave up a big career to marry me.

BERNIE: [*Delicately.*] Is that according to Luke or Mark? You or her?

FRANK: [*Turning.*] Don't you believe me . . . ?

BERNIE: Sure, but what the hell is "Miss America" past twenty-five or thirty? What career? Marriage doesn't suit them anymore—they don't want a home: the only piece of furniture they'll touch is the psychoanalyst's couch!

FRANK: [*Solemnly.*] It cost me thousands. . . .

BERNIE: [*Bitterly.*] I had it for five years with the former Mrs. Dodd.

FRANK: I bought a fourteen-room house down in Great Neck the year we married. Never knew a better life. Swimming, boating, tennis, dinner at six—at seven she'd kiss me goodbye and I'd drive into town for my show. On matinee days she'd come in and we'd stay out late. Little spats and things, but it looked like a dream life to me. And then one night, from way out left field— don't know what hit me—I find her dead drunk across a bed—a kid who never took a real drink in her life! I didn't catch on that year—who could figure *that?* Career versus career—she didn't want me to play! Bernie, she was a hopeless drunkard inside a year. Then we had a child. . . . [*Moved, pausing.*] After that . . . every part I play, it's just like I ran off with another woman. I begin to drink myself. Don't ask me where the money went. She cuts her wrists, sets fire to a hotel suite—any time I'm on the stage she needs a nurse to watch her. And then, finally, we lost the child. You don't say, "Go to hell, goodbye!", do you? By 1940, '41—well, when you're in that situation you beat a bottle hard! [*Hushed pause; BERNIE pulls at an ear.*]

BERNIE: Does she still drink?

FRANK: [*Smiling ruefully, standing.*] She stopped when I began. . . . But I know how to handle her now—backwards, like a crab. About this part—to give you an instance—I had to make believe I didn't want this part. That leaves it open for *her* to convince me, her idea, not mine, see?

[*Both men are standing, BERNIE, with a soft exclamation, gathering up his things on table.*]

BERNIE: I guess you have to bring her up to Boston. I'm not against it. *My* wife was so twisted, "I hope your next play's a big flop!"' she says. "So the whole world can see I love you even if you're a failure!" [*Turning.*] As far as the work's concerned, I'm very pleased.

FRANK: [*Eagerly.*] You are . . . ?

BERNIE: You're a born actor, Frank . . . and this can mean the world to you.

FRANK: [*Solemnly.*] I appreciate it, son. . . .

BERNIE: [*Grinning.*] And don't call me son again—I don't like it! [*They are about to leave.*]

BERNIE: Can your wife louse you up in this show?

FRANK: Don't worry, I can handle her. You know, you're a hot, gifted guy who got somewhere in a hurry. But you might be surprised in another ten years what you'll do for a little companionship.

BERNIE: [*Flatly.*] No one now living, under or over the earth, will ever again put me out on a tether! I go wild when— [*Stops abruptly, looking over FRANK's shoulder. FRANK turns around.. GEORGIE has just entered. From her reserved but pleasant manner neither man can tell what she has heard.*]

FRANK: [*Quickly.*] Georgie, what are you doing here? Where you coming from?

GEORGIE: From the movie show. Passing by . . . I thought you might be through.

FRANK: We were just breaking up.

BERNIE: [*Quietly.*] Your timing was perfect—good evening, Mrs. Elgin.

GEORGIE: [*Smiling.*] Yes, I have a knack that way. Good evening, Mr. Dodd. How is my husband doing?

BERNIE: In my less than humble opinion, he's what they call a natural.

GEORGIE: Did I intrude?

[*Both men together.*]

FRANK: Not at all, we were going to—

BERNIE: No, we were just closing—

[*Both men stop dead.*]

GEORGIE: I don't like to make myself obtrusive when Frank is working. Unless he needs my help, of course. Am I in the way?

BERNIE: [*Taking her measure.*] No, we were just closing up shop and giving it back to the theater ghosts.

[*Smiling vaguely,* GEORGIE *steps down to footlights, looks out at the house. Stands there, unconscious of a kind of oriental posturing, consisting of a listening attitude and a faint smile, both polite and deprecating; she is her own aristocratic personage, unaware that a certain air of breeding never leaves her.*]

GEORGIE: [*Softly.*] Nothing is quite so mysterious and silent as a dark theater. . . . A night without a start. . . .

[FRANK *and* BERNIE *look at each other.*]

BERNIE: Why don't we go out for some coffee?

FRANK: Georgie? She makes all the decisions in our family.

BERNIE: [*Very politely.*] Is that true, Mrs. Elgin?

GEORGIE: [*Archly.*] To the extent that Frank's brought out the mother in me, yes. I'd like some coffee. And I'd like to get to know Mr. Dodd better.

BERNIE: And I'd like to get to know you better.

GEORGIE: [*Looking out again.*] The theater is mysterious. . . .

BERNIE: That's true. . . .

[*She smiles at him, goes off* R., *followed by* FRANK. BERNIE, *looking reflectively after them, drops his cigarette, steps on it, starts off.*]

SLOW CURTAIN

Scene Four

TIME: *One week later*
PLACE: FRANK'S *room, as before*

It is early morning, bed disarranged. FRANK, *suspenders hanging, is finishing shaving. Ebullient, in rare form, he keeps dressing through the scene.* GEORGIE, *wearing a wrap, is pouring coffee at a little folding table.*

FRANK: Gonna get me some real expensive shaving lotion any minute now! Little things like that . . . the spice of life. . . .

GEORGIE: What?

FRANK: [*Raising voice.*] Shaving lotion, toots! I want some luxuries out of life!

GEORGIE: You talk like a courtesan, Frank.

FRANK: Then put me smack-dab in the middle of the courtesans if they like luxuries, too! Boyo, I'll be glad to get away from this Chinese laundry! [*Shaking out a shirt.*] The way they do shirts—it's a crime and a shame! Look at this . . . and they don't even give away free nuts any more!

GEORGIE: Let's see . . . where would I be if I were a pair of glasses . . . ?

FRANK: Right in my paws! [*Picks up glasses, hands them to her. She is very near-sighted, it seems.*]

FRANK: [*Chortling.*] See? you couldn't get along without me, Georgiana!

GEORGIE: [*Smiling.*] Someone's feeling mighty good today. [*She stops, having*

kicked over two empty beer bottles on floor. Looks up seriously at FRANK.]

FRANK: [*Appealingly.*] Put down that tomahawk. Didn't hide them, did I? Those two bottles of beer gave me a good night's sleep.

GEORGIE: When did you get them?

FRANK: After you fell asleep. I walked to the corner—got a *News* and a *Mirror*, the *Tribune* for you. [*She is looking at him thoughtfully, but he refuses to take her seriously.*] Now, come on, Georgie, have a heart: I didn't hide the bottles and I got a good night's sleep.

GEORGIE: Are you worried about anything . . . ?

FRANK: [*Readily, with broad Italian accent.*] Nothing is-a-worry me, except-a the lines. Poppa Hubbard, he's-a go to the cupboard and is-a bare!

GEORGIE: [*Quietly.*] Don't start drinking beer, Frank. I'll get you some sleeping pills today. One a night can't hurt. [*She sips coffee as he goes to mirror to make his tie.*]

FRANK: Gosh, I'm getting baggy under

the eyes. Sometimes I ask myself if it's me. [*Into the mirror.*] Hey, is that you, Frank? [*A basso profundo answer.*] Yes. . . . [*Then.*] Need a few ties, too, don't I?

GEORGIE: Wouldn't know where to start, you need so many things. Wait and see what happens.

FRANK: Yeah, we'll soon know . . . oh, those critics! Momma mia, those critics!

GEORGIE: [*Sipping coffee.*] How are they up in Boston?

FRANK: Leave it to Poppa—he can charm a bird off a branch. No, ma'am, I'm not worried, not a thing. I'm taking it all in my stride! [*Throws a towel aside and goes to coffee.*] Oh, my, when I think of those great big fluffy bath towels in a good hotel! We're gonna have fun, baby—you know that, don't you? Wait'll I lock you in that hotel room!

GEORGIE: Drink your coffee, rooster.

FRANK: Yes, sir, everything is good and solid! It's autumn again—I'm rehearsing a show—hear that? Let the wind blow down the street—the oysters and lobsters are delicious! [*Of the coffee.*] Hey, that's been near the fire!

GEORGIE: Look before you leap, silly.

FRANK: [*Grimacing.*] My tie straight?

GEORGIE: Straight. Your shoes are being soled and heeled, the black ones. What else?

FRANK: [*Appealingly.*] Blow on Frank's coffee for him . . . ? [*She smiles. He sips coffee carefully, looking at his paper.*] Who could dream it—to blow a double-header! How do you like it—I'll miss the whole series up in Boston!

GEORGIE: [*Pausing.*] Frank, does Bernie Dodd like me?

FRANK: [*Over-casually careful.*] Why . . . shouldn't the boy like you?

GEORGIE: [*Sincerely.*] I don't know. Seems to be a chip on his shoulder. Does he like women?

FRANK: [*Innocently.*] He's been married, divorced, has a child. . . .

GEORGIE: I don't mind him not liking me, but shouldn't we face it realistically if it's true?

FRANK: [*Lightly.*] See how it goes? Leave you alone for a few days and you get morbid.

GEORGIE: [*Patiently quiet.*] Seriously, for your own sake, Frank. There's too much at stake. I don't want to be in your way.

FRANK: [*Abruptly, with edge.*] Georgie, I'm winging like a lark—a million bucks couldn't compensate for this feeling of being back in harness!

GEORGIE: [*Agreeing.*] I haven't seen you with such zip in ten years. . . .

FRANK: Then why make trouble, dear? When we get up to Boston I'm going—

GEORGIE: [*Quietly.*] I'm not going up to Boston. My fine, womanly intuition tells me that Mr. Dodd doesn't want me there.

FRANK: [*Angrily.*] Yes, but *I* want you up in Boston! [*Wagging around.*] That's all I need in this day and age—to leave my wife alone here, in a city full of wolves!

GEORGIE: [*Soberly.*] Are you jealous?

FRANK: What the hell are you talking about? Would I take this job without you? I *need* you up in Boston!

GEORGIE: [*Pausing, simply.*] If you need me up in Boston . . . that's most likely where I'll be. [*Stopping him.*] That's enough, Frank—we've said enough. [*Crossing to kitchenette.*] You'll be late. [*Then, smiling.*] You have a real conviction of woman's perfidy, don't you?

FRANK: [*Sullenly.*] I thought we'd said enough. . . . [GEORGIE *has come up to wardrobe for his coat; presently she brings it down, beckoning him over while she holds it for him to slip into.*]

GEORGIE: I haven't felt like a woman in ten years.

FRANK: [*Sullenly.*] I suppose that's my fault?

GEORGIE: [*Lightly.*] Summer dies, autumn comes, a fact of nature—nobody's fault.

FRANK: Didn't you sew on this loose button? [*She crosses to a drawer for needle and thread, looking back archly.*]

GEORGIE: Spoiling for a fight, aren't you? [*He refuses to answer. She sits meanwhile and, sewing on button deftly, speaks with serious lightness.*]

GEORGIE: You mystify me, Frank, your sense of guilt and insecurity. Take a lesson from my father, the late Delaney the Great. He didn't care what people thought of him, no matter what he did. Played every vaudeville house in the world. Didn't show up at home but twice a year . . . and those two times he was down in the cellar perfecting new magic tricks.

FRANK: Oh, sure, you'd love that—seeing me only twice a year!

GEORGIE: [*Whimsically.*] My mother

didn't mind it as much as I did—it orphaned me. Might not have married you if I'd had a father. But he *believed* in himself, I mean—*you* don't. That's cost you plenty . . . it's cost me as much. . . . [*She has bitten off thread and is holding up coat for him again. Simmering, he slips into it.*]

FRANK: You want me to beg you, don't you?

GEORGIE: [*Puzzled.*] Beg me what?

FRANK: To come up to Boston.

GEORGIE: I thought we'd settled that. . . . [*Disgruntled, he is looking at coat.*]

GEORGIE: I pressed it last night.

FRANK: Where's that lousy part?

GEORGIE: In your right-hand pocket. [*Feeling sheepish, laughing a little,* FRANK *brings out part and small address book.*]

FRANK: See, you can't live without me. But I don't know why you talk that way —winter, summer—you're still a kid.

GEORGIE: [*With a moue.*] Oh, sure, of course, why not? [FRANK *holds up address book, needling her.*]

FRANK: Well, it's a small world. Took her address—she's living up in Boston now. Susie Lewis from Saratoga Springs. Our playwright's aunt, no less!—he brought her around last night: haven't seen her in eighteen years!

GEORGIE: Attractive?

FRANK: Widowed and sitting on a mint. [GEORGIE *is putting handkerchief in his upper pocket.*]

GEORGIE: [*Smiling.*] I'd investigate if I were you. . . .

FRANK: Sue? She'd have me in a minute! [*Then, all dressed.*] Well, am I decent?

GEORGIE: [*Nodding.*] Say good morning to Bernardo the Great for me.

FRANK: [*Getting his overcoat.*] You can bet your sweet Fanny Maloney I won't tell him what you're calling him! Don't you go tangling with him at the run-through tomorrow night! [GEORGIE *stops him at door by asking,* "Run-through . . . ?" *He is caught.*]

FRANK: Now, don't tell me I didn't tell you about it. I didn't tell you yesterday . . . ?

GEORGIE: Maybe you told Susie Peppermint or whatever her name is. Don't you want me to come tomorrow night? [*Slightly, irked by his hesitant manner.*] Oh, come on, Frank, tell me what you want me to do. I won't love you less.

FRANK: [*Uneasily.*] Don't feel offended, dear . . . I'd feel better if you didn't come. This isn't a dress rehearsal—just a run-through with a few props. [*Wryly.*] They want the backers to see what they're getting for their dough.

GEORGIE: [*Easily.*] Then I'll see it in Boston with the sets and the costumes.

FRANK: [*Fondly.*] 'At's my girl! [*Starting out.*] My only real worry is the lines—they won't stick in the dome!

GEORGIE: We'll drill some more—I'll cue you. Frank . . . don't get secretive. If I go on the road with you . . . tell me straight out anything that's on your mind. Don't shuffle—I don't often talk this way any more. We're both of us miles behind. Don't try to catch up all at once. We both know what's happened in the past. We'll have to live one day at a time, without resentments and evasions. We're at the bottom—

FRANK: [*Stoutly.*] But we'll be at the top!

GEORGIE: [*Correcting him.*] But . . . one rung at a time, separated by quiet, healthy sleep.

FRANK: [*Squirming.*] Yeah, you're right, dear, you're right. . . .

GEORGIE: He's young, but he's a good man, that Dodd. Talk out all your worries with him. [*She looks at him keenly; he drops his eyes.*]

FRANK: I love you, Georgie. [*Then he goes to door and turns from there, about to throw her a defiant kiss.*] Catch this one —it's a lulu! No, really get it. [*He returns, holds and kisses her, then turns and goes. She smiles faintly to herself. After a moment she goes to table and, whistling softly to herself, takes some of coffee things to sink. Returning, the rhythm of her whistling slows down as she sees beer bottles. She picks them up, looks at them with a thought; then places them under sink. Whistles again as she starts for little table once more.*]

CURTAIN

Scene Five

TIME: *A week later, midnight*
PLACE: FRANK's *dressing-room in a Boston theater*

*A first dress rehearsal has just ended out on stage. A murmur of
voices heard outside door of the empty, disarrayed room. In a
moment* LARRY, *the stage-manager, looks in; seeing room is
empty he is about to leave but heads, instead, for makeup shelf
where he helps himself impatiently to cigarette and match. A
fretful* UNGER *looks in, script under one arm.*

UNGER: Frank . . . ? Where's Frank?

LARRY: Looking for him myself. [*The two men meet in middle of room.*]

UNGER: I have a few more cuts in scene four.

LARRY: I'll take them later, if you don't mind. I'm trying to find out what happened in scene six. They keep blowing in the same spot.

[*Next lines take both men out of the room.*]

UNGER: Six? I think the girl's throwing the wrong cue. Watch her when she walks down to the table. . . .

LARRY: I don't know . . . maybe . . . Frank cuts in there a moment too soon and . . .

[*Stage is empty again; outside, voices of stagehands are heard. A moment later* GEORGIE *enters, surprised to find room empty. She is chewing gum and wearing eyeglasses. She wipes her nose with a tissue; next begins to tidy up the room, chiefly picking up garments and brushing a coat.* BERNIE *enters.*]

BERNIE: Where's Frank?

GEORGIE: Isn't he out on stage?

BERNIE: No. [*Sniffing.*] Cobra?

GEORGIE: [*Smiling.*] Wisteria.

BERNIE: [*About to exit, returns.*] Keeping in mind that it was a damn rough first dress rehearsal—the first time they've played in the sets—what did you think of the show?

GEORGIE: Oh, I didn't judge—just sat and listened to the words. But Frank looks wonderful, doesn't he? Chewed the flavor out of this two hours ago. [*Removes her chewing gum. Each is trying to get on a good footing with the other.* BERNIE *lights cigarette.*]

BERNIE: Smoke . . . ?

GEORGIE: Never use them.

BERNIE: There's a whole pack since eight o'clock. These are really bad ones, these dress rehearsal nights. Knock on wood—not one real case of nerves yet. The show's new to you, isn't it? What did you think of friend Frank?

GEORGIE: He was very tense, poor chick. [BERNIE *crosses to makeup shelf, throwing away crumpled cigarette pack.*]

GEORGIE: I'm fairly level-headed, making allowances for my sex, but I'd be in a blizzard, too, if my show were this ragged just before opening night.

BERNIE: But that's what two more dress rehearsals are for.

GEORGIE: You're as tense as a bug in June, aren't you?

BERNIE: [*Laughing.*] Shh—not so loud. My cast thinks I'm made of steel. Everyone looks for poppa on an opening week, and I'm it.

GEORGIE: Frank thinks the sun rises and sets in you, Mr. Dodd.

BERNIE: [*Carefully.*] You'd make me very happy by being careful with Frank. You're his wife—he's probably all focussed on your reaction.

GEORGIE: Is his performance pleasing you?

BERNIE: What do *you* think?

GEORGIE: Don't ask me. I had one long old-fashioned cry out there. Just a country girl. [*She sits, having hung up all of* FRANK's *clothes.*]

BERNIE: Give him another week or two. He'll be very good.

GEORGIE: [*Thinking.*] But the show opens Wednesday night. . . .

BERNIE: [*Reassuringly.*] They'll get a show up here, but not what they'll get in New York.

GEORGIE: But what about Frank's notices here, on Thursday morning? You can't tell the Boston critics he'll be wonderful in *New York.*

BERNIE: That's the chance we take. Out of town try-outs mean education in public. You think Frank's that bad?

GEORGIE: I think he's wonderful! [*Hesitantly.*] But . . . I do wish I could follow the shape of what he's doing.

BERNIE: Too much detail, you mean. . . .

GEORGIE: [*Carefully.*] Yes, since you put it that way. . . .

[*Abruptly* BERNIE *crosses to her and speaks with a consciously used air of candor, like a politician.*]

BERNIE: I think I can trust your intelligence, Mrs. Elgin. Most actors don't need four weeks' rehearsing. They repeat the same glib, superficial patterns they found the first or second week. The usual actor gives himself small aims—or the director does it for him. In a couple of weeks they're fulfilled . . . and it all fits into a small, dull peanut shell.

GEORGIE: And you think Frank—?

BERNIE: [*Humorously.*] No peanut shell, he. His talent—the quality of it is improvisatory. That's his blessing and his burden —he never knows what he's going to do next.

GEORGIE: [*Thoughtfully.*] That's very keen of you to notice that. Many of his personal problems come from that.

BERNIE: He explores and discovers, as an actor, opening up the part very slowly. And my problem is to keep him going—overflowing. The longer I keep him fluid and open, the more gold we mine.

GEORGIE: You shut his talent off if you rein him in?

BERNIE: [*Nodding.*] That's why I want him fluid for another week or two. Let him flounder—in *his* case it's healthy. New York's five long weeks away. [*Going to door.*] Don't mention any of this to Frank.

GEORGIE: [*Stoutly.*] I won't be that foolish, Mr. Dodd.

BERNIE: I know you won't. Tell him I'll be right back. [*He looks at her carefully, with a polite charm, masking a certain scorn. Despite her awareness of his good sense, he knows* GEORGIE *is somewhere disturbed by him. Thinking, she turns on a small radio.* FRANK *enters as she looks up; he begins undressing, but with his attitude questioning. He is an imposing and somewhat romantic figure, in evening clothes, a portly political boss with gray hair and moustache.*

Nervous and tired, he has slammed his part down on makeup shelf.]

FRANK: I was upstairs, running lines with the kid. I blew like a bat all night. I hope this doesn't happen Wednesday, when we open. Well, what's the verdict . . .? [*She looks at him, very moved, momentarily not knowing how to grapple with his mood. He is afraid to hear what she will say.*]

GEORGIE: Frank . . . you look wonderful. I scarcely recognized you out there.

FRANK: Was it bad . . . ?

GEORGIE: [*Gently.*] Nothing was bad, dear. It was a bad rehearsal, of course.

FRANK: [*Disappointed and glum.*] Yeah, I floundered like a fish, didn't I? What else did you see? I won't faint—you can tell me if I'm bad!

GEORGIE: [*Quietly.*] I think you'll be astonishing in the part.

FRANK: Maybe my eye is jaundiced— you don't look astonished to me!

GEORGIE: Maybe I'm a little choked up, Frank. . . . [*He looks at her with suspicion, not trusting her, irritably throwing his collar against mirror.*]

GEORGIE: You're keyed up and nervous. Be as unreasonable as you like.

FRANK: [*Outraged.*] Didn't you just see me age for the first time in seven years? Say hello, goodbye or kiss my foot! But don't stand there like Minne-ha-ha! [*Sulking,* FRANK *pulls off his shirt and begins removing a stomach padding; she hangs his coat, trying to josh him out of his mood.*]

GEORGIE: I *thought* you were a little thick in the middle. . . .

FRANK: [*Turned away, muttering.*] I need the portliness. If I ever learn these lines, I'll call it Columbus Day! [*He cocks another suspicious eye at her, lights cigarette, puts on robe and sits at mirror to begin removing makeup.*]

GEORGIE: Frank, I don't . . . *you're magnificent in this part!* And the play— I'm deeply surprised that that quiet, smiling boy has so much talent!

FRANK: Shut the radio off. . . .

[*She crosses, does so. He sniffs loudly, blowing his nose, clears his throat.*]

GEORGIE: Are you catching a cold?

FRANK: [*Morosely.*] That's all I need this week, a cold—I'd be a dead bunny for sure! You need more than a haircut to play this part . . . that's what *I* know!

[*She crosses, offers him aspirins; he rejects her testily.*]

GEORGIE: Aspirins . . . ?

FRANK: Give me a minute, dear! [*He has bent down and is about to unlace shoes in the same hurried rhythm which has blown him into the room; stops abruptly, dropping his foot to the floor,* GEORGIE *asking, "What's the matter?"*] Look at me going zip, zip, zip! I can't even catch my breath! Why don't they get me a dresser? Don't I deserve it? How can I make those fast changes by myself?

GEORGIE: Do you want me to speak to Mr. Cook about it?

FRANK: [*Not looking at her.*] Speak to Cook about it, Cook or Bernie. They can afford it, with the salary I'm getting. [*Turning abruptly.*] Do you know Mabel Beck gets more than I do? Five hundred a week and she stinks up every scene!

GEORGIE: [*Quietly.*] She isn't bad in the part. . . .

FRANK: That's right—stand up for everybody else! And look at that Nancy kid! Don't they learn stage deportment any more? Upstaged me twice tonight! [*Acting it out.*] Once I didn't even know where in the hell she was! [*She laughs soothingly as he begins to clean up.*]

GEORGIE: Now, Frank, come on, take it easy. You'll have yourself believing all this nonsense before the week's out. First things first. Work well—that's your only concern.

FRANK: [*Promptly.*] How'm I supposed to work with that damn understudy snooping around in the wings? Is that nonsense, too?

GEORGIE: Speak to Mr. Dodd about it.

FRANK: You speak to him about it. Tell him to keep the guy out front.

GEORGIE: What're you looking for? Aspirins? They're right under your nose.

FRANK: Yeah, but where's my nose? [*He laughs sheepishly, ashamed of his bad humor; this breaks tension between them. While he is swallowing aspirins and water, a knock sounds at door.* FRANK *calls "Come!"* UNGER *enters,* COOK *behind him.* FRANK'S *manner changes immediately. Jovial, self-deprecating humor is the note, a protective masking, with nothing seeming to bother him.*] Welcome, gentry! Don't tell me about the show! I know—stank on rye bread!

UNGER: [*Sincerely.*] Not to me. That hospital scene put a fine prickle on my skin.

FRANK: Don't kid the ugly man! [*But pleased.*] Hear that, Georgie? The boy must like me.

UNGER: I like a good actor.

COOK: [*Gloomily, sitting, to say something.*] Me, too. . . .

[BERNIE *pushes in jauntily at door.*]

BERNIE: Why's everyone so depressed?

FRANK: [*Jauntily.*] Not me, I'm not depressed.

UNGER: Neither am I. I think the show's in swell shape.

COOK: Me, too, but it wasn't a very good dress rehearsal, was it?

BERNIE: [*Laughing heartily.*] The worst damn dress rehearsal I've ever seen!

COOK: Then I fail to see the humor. I may be dense. Am I dense?

UNGER: I, if I may be excused, I have a date with my typewriter and a pocket full of notes.

BERNIE: Call you in the morning, Paul.

UNGER: [*Going.*] Fine. Good-night, all you keepers of my integrity.

FRANK: Nice boy, one in a million. Not a speck of ego in him.

[LARRY *taps discreetly at open door.*]

LARRY: Excuse me, Frank . . . I have all the last scene people on stage. I'd like to run the spot where everyone blew—we can't locate what happened.

FRANK: [*Protestingly.*] But I just ran it with the kid.

LARRY: [*Politely.*] I'd be very obliged, Frank, if you'd run it again for me and the rest of the cast . . . ? [FRANK *gets up with a mock groan, executing a half dance step.*]

FRANK: Oi, gentry, oi! Duty calls, but I'll be back. [*Towel in hand, he goes with* LARRY.]

BERNIE: Frank's in high good humor.

GEORGIE: [*Quietly.*] Yes, he is. . . .

COOK: [*Glumly.*] Me, too, but don't ask me why. If he spoke one line of the author's script tonight, it never reached my ears.

BERNIE: Cookie, why do they open shows out of town?

COOK: Bernie, I'll never know. . . . [*Then.*] Will he know his lines for opening night?

BERNIE: [*Annoyed.*] A little grey matter, Phil. He tripped on a rug he'd never seen before tonight! He couldn't find his slippers —his specs were in a drawer that wouldn't open! What do you want, miracles? Of course he dropped his lines!

COOK: I'm not worried. Like the author —me, too—I beg to be excused. The crew is still out there on double time. [GEORGIE *stops him as he sulkily starts for door.*]

GEORGIE: Mr. Cook . . . do you think Frank needs a dresser?

COOK: [*Holding back exasperation.*] No, I don't. But I suppose you do?

BERNIE: [*Helping her.*] What does Frank think?

GEORGIE: Those two quick changes . . . it's a very large part, after all. . . . [BERNIE *makes a signal of assent behind* GEORGIE'S *back.*]

COOK: I know, Bernie— you think I eat shredded fifty-dollar bills for salad. [*Shakes head dolefully, walks out.*]

BERNIE: Don't worry, we'll get him a dresser. . . .

GEORGIE: Mr. Cook is almost what the bad fairy promised Frank at his cradle.

BERNIE: He's not that bad.

GEORGIE: I'm glad *we're* getting along, Mr. Dodd.

BERNIE: [*Archly.*] Did you think we wouldn't?

GEORGIE: You smoke too much. [*Then.*] Who is that tall gloomy man that lurks around backstage? Lucas? Is that the name?

BERNIE: [*Agreeable but wary.*] Yes. General understudy. Not much personality, but competent.

GEORGIE: Excuse me for saying this— must he stay backstage? It seems to bother Frank.

BERNIE: I'll watch that. But is Frank that insecure? He's working well, in good humor all the time—

GEORGIE: [*With a little friendly laugh.*] Golly, don't you know he hides behind that humor? He's not a simple man, Mr. Dodd. That's why I offer myself as a sort of liaison officer between you both.

BERNIE: Is that what you're doing . . . ?

GEORGIE: [*Braking.*] I hope you don't misunderstand—

BERNIE: No, I think I understand. . . .

GEORGIE: [*Pausing.*] Certain kinds of men, you know, are very strange. Business couldn't be better, wife and kiddies are fine . . . the next day you read he's hung himself from the chandelier. He can be the biggest kidder, too, it doesn't matter.

BERNIE: [*Solemnly.*] Is that a picture of Frank?

GEORGIE: [*Carefully, a little afraid.*] Yes, and no. . . . [*Then.*] He doesn't like to make the slightest remark that might lose him people's regard or affection. I've sim-

ply grown into the habit of doing it for him. [BERNIE *pauses, looking at her with polite, regretful air.*]

BERNIE: I'm really sorry to say so, Mrs. Elgin, but I hired an actor, a *good* actor. I may want him without his sisters and his cousins and his aunts. [GEORGIE, *withdrawn, doesn't know what to say, watching and testing her,* BERNIE *sits.*] What, for instance, bothers him now?

GEORGIE: [*Pausing, then plunging.*] Mr. Cook. His attitude. The ever-present understudy. The fact that he can't retain the lines. He thinks he's not regarded highly enough to deserve a dresser. Salary, for another.

BERNIE: Why salary?

GEORGIE: [*Shrugging.*] He's learned that Mabel Beck is earning more. In fairness to him, the figure is low for the part.

BERNIE: [*Archly.*] The figure's fair. Not great, but fair.

GEORGIE: Granted, but not to him. [BERNIE *pauses; both are beginning to tighten.*]

BERNIE: What was his last salary? And what year was it earned?

GEORGIE: If you thought enough of Frank to give him the part—and you did!— isn't that a very silly remark?

BERNIE: [*Coldly.*] I happen to have other plans for Frank's financial participation in the show. If he works out—if the show runs —I make him a five percent partner, as a gift.

GEORGIE: [*Hesitantly.*] Would . . . you give him that in writing?

BERNIE: [*Angrily jumping up.*] No, I won't give you that in writing.

GEORGIE: [*Pallidly.*] It would help him if you did. Tomorrow—this week, staring probable bad reviews in the face.

BERNIE: [*Eyeing her.*] You're clever . . . don't overplay your hand. Let's face it, Frank may go anywhere from here, even to a wealthy movie career. Or he may go right back to the gutter, and you right with him!

GEORGIE: [*Pausing.*] Do you think that was called for . . . ?

BERNIE: Just like you, I don't always say and do what's "called for."

GEORGIE: [*Puzzled, hurt, wary, trying to understand.*] I don't mind you being angry . . . if I know why. . . .

BERNIE: [*Flaring.*] I have no problems with Frank—don't you make them where they don't exist! [*Then, swinging away.*] I could almost love a woman like you: my motto is "No pity!", too!

GEORGIE: I wonder if you'd be kind enough to give me the code: what're you talking about? [*She has turned, careful and restricted. Invited, as it were, he comes down from door, stands behind her, almost enjoying this moment.*]

BERNIE: Here's the code. I'm ambitious —I wanna get *my* picture on a green postage stamp, too. There's a difference between us, of course. Way up on the twenty-fourth floor is where I live. And sometimes, late at night, I look out way over the sleeping city and think how I'd like to change the history of the world. I know I won't—the idea is talented but phoney. I admit I'm a gifted mountebank. What are you? Do you know? Do you admit it, even to yourself?

GEORGIE: What am I . . . ?

BERNIE: Lady, you ride that man like a broom: you're a bitch!

[GEORGIE *takes this with a slight gasp and roll; it is a long moment before she says.*]

GEORGIE: You have a very lyric and lurid opinion of me. . . .

BERNIE: [*Rapidly, dropping voice.*] Now, be careful, Mrs. E. It's a bitter mess for me if Frank fails. But I can hire other actors. I doubt if Frank can hire another director.

GEORGIE: I had no idea you were this tense tonight.

BERNIE: I'd tell you these same things any other night.

GEORGIE: [*Stronger.*] Yes, you would . . . you have the bloody eye of a man who smokes too much. Tobacco's a drug— it warps your judgment. I'll have to remember that.

BERNIE: [*Sardonically.*] I have to go stroke some more of my tender chicks. [GEORGIE *stands in proud, helpless silence, deeply hurt.* BERNIE *walks to door.* FRANK, *in an exuberant mood, opens it, bumps into* BERNIE.]

FRANK: Shut my mouth, the traffic's bad tonight! Well, that spot's all cleaned up! Bernie, that line mixup—it was the kid's fault all the time!

BERNIE: Be back in two minutes—have to give Mabel Beck some notes. By the way, Frank, does it bother you to have the understudy hanging around?

FRANK: [*Heartily.*] Me? Why in hell would a Lucas bother an Elgin? Never heard of the watch! Ha-ha-ha! [*Cocking a quick smart eye at* GEORGIE, BERNIE *goes.* FRANK *ripples on like a happy river, washing and dressing quickly.*] Georgie, that line mixup—it was the kid's fault all the time! We'll get a load of fresh air in our lungs— I'll be dressed in a jiffy. How about a walk right across the Common? [*Humming his happy snatch of tune,* FRANK *does not see, as we do, that* GEORGIE, *who has withdrawn to trunk across room, is trying to hold back imperious tears.* FRANK *dresses, chatters on happily.*] Guess what I'm in the mood for? One of those one-dozen oyster stews, half and half—just what the doctor ordered! Oh, boy, what that'll do for my stomach! What did that Gloomy Gus say, that Cook, after I left? [*Unable to speak,* GEORGIE *merely shakes her head;* FRANK *half turns.*] What? Huh?

GEORGIE: You're getting a dresser next week. . . . [*She, unturned, is restraining tears;* FRANK *is practically exultant.*]

FRANK: Really? Georgie, you beat the band! Can't live without me! I'll betcha Bernie was on my side!

GEORGIE: Yes . . .

FRANK: Look at me, just look at me— I'm winging like a lark!

GEORGE: [*Half turning.*] Frank . . . I wonder if I shouldn't go back to New York soon. You're getting a dresser now . . . and I think I'll be in the way. They resent me here and—

FRANK: What are you talking about? Are you kidding? Who resents you . . . ? [*He starts towards her; the lark is grounded now. Turned away,* GEORGIE *abruptly bursts into tears.* FRANK *stops dead, baffled and frightened. Only slowly does he move in to her with the shuffling gait of guilt.*] Why, darling . . . what's the matter? What is it, dear? Come on now, tell Poppa . . . what is it? [*He has turned her and has her in his arms, but it is a moment before she can say.*]

GEORGIE: I really must . . . get these teeth fixed . . . [*Relieved,* FRANK *says with fond and rough sympathy.*]

FRANK: Honey, why don't you tell me when something's on your mind . . . ? We'll get you a good dentist in the morning. Here, take some aspirin.

GEORGIE: [*Stopping him.*] No, I took a few.

[*He comes back again, all sympathy, about to kiss and embrace her.*]

FRANK: Darling . . . don't you know

this is gonna be a honeymoon, up here in Boston . . . ?

[*She can not help a bite of bitterness as she pulls away from him and sits.*]

GEORGIE: Yes, we all love each other, don't we?

FRANK: [*Stopped.*] Boy, I'll never understand your moods, and that's the truth! A man can't be right, can he? Two strikes against him before he opens his mouth!

[*Sullen and offended, he goes back to his dressing; she sits, stiff, cold and wordless.*] Now my stomach's all in a whirl again. That's what you wanted, isn't it? [*He sits at makeup shelf; there is silence and distance between them.*]

GEORGIE: One day soon . . . we'll see what I want. . . .

CURTAIN

ACT TWO

Scene One

TIME: *Several nights later*
PLACE: FRANK'S *dressing-room, as before*

Past one o'clock in the morning, a cold depressing time. They are taking photographs of production on stage.

GEORGIE *and* PAUL UNGER *are sitting in the room, she knitting and he pecking away on a portable typewriter.* GEORGIE, *wearing coat over her shoulders, is tired and depressed but is covering it with a certain brightness and an excess of interest in what actually does not interest her.*

Radio playing softly. After a time GEORGIE, *chewing gum, looks up from her knitting.*

GEORGIE: I wish they'd get finished out there. . . .

UNGER: [*Hiding yawn.*] I've seen them take all night to photograph a show.

GEORGIE: Uhh! I've dropped a stitch. . . . [*Carefully.*] Stitch, stitch. . . . Makes me think of Hood's poem, *The Song of the Shirt.*

UNGER: You're very well-read. I've noticed that before.

GEORGIE: [*Smiling.*] What else could I do? My father was always away on tour, my mother was off with gardening and hobbies. [*Sighing.*] I do wish they'd get finished out there.

UNGER: I've seen them take all night to photograph a show. Didn't I just say that? Groggy! [UNGER *usually talks with a certain wry drollery and exaggeration, because he is shy. Now he suppresses a yawn,* GEORGIE *doing likewise as she looks at a watch.*]

GEORGIE: Well, it's twenty after one. . . . [*Then, musingly.*] When you think about it . . . so many plays and books, so much reading in the stillness of the night

. . . and for all of it, what? [UNGER *stops his typing, looks over at her quizzically.*] ·

UNGER: The moment I saw you, Mrs. Elgin—the day I met you—I was touched.

GEORGIE: [*Turning, with a moue.*] Golly, you mean I'm touching?

UNGER: Tell me . . . why did Frank begin to drink . . . ?

GEORGIE: There's no one reason a man becomes a drinker. You should know that —you're a writer, Mr. Unger. Looking back . . . I'd say bad judgment started him off. He had some money once, but you don't know my Frank—he wanted to be his own producer—eighty thousand went in fifteen months, most of it on two bad shows. I didn't know a thing about it—he was afraid to tell me. A year later we lost our child . . . it was awesome how he went for the bottle . . . he just didn't stop after that. You know what the theater is . . . give a dog a bad name. . . .

UNGER: [*Quickly, as she turns.*] Excuse me, I didn't mean to yawn.

GEORGIE: [*Smiling.*] Let's make a pact,

Mr. Unger—let's both yawn right out loud. [*Then, impatiently.*] Bernardo wasn't back tonight, was he?

UNGER: You don't like Bernie, do you?

GEORGIE: What's wrong with him? His wife?

UNGER: Among other things. But don't let that bluster fool you—he's actually a very innocent kid.

GEORGIE: [*Scoffingly.*] Oh, sure, of course, why not?

UNGER: No, I mean it. Despite the talent, he's a dumb innocent kid in more ways than one. He's in love with art, for instance, and would make it a felony that you are not. But, as I say, there's more than popcorn in that head. Does my typing bother you?

GEORGIE: No. Does the music? [*He shakes head, deciding to pack his belongings and go. She meanwhile has restlessly crossed room and sips coffee from container.*] Frank should be in bed with his cold. What did *you* think of the opening last night? Were Frank's bad write-ups justified?

UNGER: Man is to man as the wolf—they were not!

GEORGIE: [*Hesitantly.*] Would you tell that to Frank? Make him feel good—he's low tonight.

UNGER: Sure I will. [GEORGIE *looks out of doorway.* UNGER *massages a kink.*]

GEORGIE: Why do you work in a dressing-room?

UNGER: Frank's anxious about the new scene. And hotel rooms are very lonely.

GEORGIE: [*Turning.*] You're young to have found that out.

UNGER: [*Grinning*] As a friend, Mrs. Elgin, that's a conceit with you—to talk like a veteran of all the wars. Actually, you're a young, very attractive woman.

[GEORGIE *crosses to makeup shelf.*]

UNGER: As for me, I'll talk big. This is my third play. Loneliness is the badge of the writer's profession. It's ruined more good writers than every other reason combined.

GEORGIE: Am I as attractive as your aunt?

UNGER: Sue? She's almost as old as Frank. Very decent. My uncle left her cash, much cash.

GEORGIE: [*Delicately.*] You could do something else for Frank. Ask her to have him out to lunch—it's a depressing week for him.

UNGER: Can do. . . .

[FRANK *hurries in. He has a bad head cold and is hiding a gnawing, nervous anxiety with affability and bluffness.*]

FRANK: How's that new scene going, sonny boy?

UNGER: I'll write you out of the play if that's all the respect I get!

FRANK: Well, two more scenes to photograph and we can walk. [*Moving around room, he stops at makeup shelf.*] Where's that cough syrup?

GEORGIE: It would bite you if it had teeth.

[*Bottle is right under his hand; he takes a quick swig, looks around, as if bewildered.*]

FRANK: Lemme see . . . what in hell do I wear next?

GEORGIE: Just the smoking jacket. [*She crosses, gets it for him.*]

FRANK: Bernie hasn't been around yet? [*Quickly.*] How *about* the new scene?

UNGER: I won't get to bed till it's finished. Bernie wants to put it in tomorrow.

[*Dressing,* FRANK *thinks about this; then bends and picks up a newspaper clipping with a snort and chuckle.*]

FRANK: Yum yum! Did you see this notice! He claims I should have stayed retired!

UNGER: Forget those notices, Frank—they don't mean a damn! [FRANK *drops cigarette he was about to light.*] How's your cold?

FRANK: [*Grimacing.*] Tutti-fruity! Are we losing you?

GEORGIE: I wish they'd get through out there.

UNGER: Intuition tells me to get back to the hotel—it's very close back here. [*Hefting typewriter case.*] It is generally supposed that I own this machine, but *it* owns *me*, body and soul—a form of depravity! Goodnight. . . . [*He drifts out wearily,* GEORGIE *murmuring good-night.*]

FRANK: Goodnight, baby. I like that boy. Nice boy—not a speck of ego in him. I have to have a cigarette, Georgie. I'm nervous. . . .

[GEORGIE *says nothing.* FRANK *lights cigarette and gulps more from the syrup bottle; his nerves and anxiety show through now.*]

GEORGIE: [*Quietly.*] I don't like that cough mixture you bought yourself.

FRANK: Why? It's a buck a bottle.

GEORGIE: A "buck a bottle" is a jim-dandy slogan, but you can read labels as well as the next one. Twenty-two percent alcohol.

FRANK: Just leave it to me, dear. You know, Poppa—walks like a mountain goat —never slips.

GEORGIE: Let me straighten your tie, mountain goat. [*He comes to her dutifully, holding up his chin.*] You're naughty, Frank.

FRANK: You get some more sleeping pills?

GEORGIE: Yes. Don't twist. . . .

FRANK: Red, or yellow?

GEORGIE: Red, but all you get is one.

FRANK: How about the blue ones? I hear they *really* knock you down.

GEORGIE: Why don't we have a party some night? We'll start with the red ones in chicken broth. Then . . . [*Laughing lightly, she steps back, the tie fixed. But he abruptly takes her arms with a frightening intensity.*]

FRANK: Come here, Georgie. . . . [*Then.*] You're tired, too. Poppa's little helper. Go back to the hotel—we might be here another hour.

GEORGIE: I've waited this long. . . . [*She watches him as he goes, looks at himself in mirror.*]

FRANK: Look at that class, willya? Anything fits me! [*Then.*] Cook didn't come back, did he?

GEORGIE: No. [*Then.*] Frank . . . ? What's the matter?

FRANK: [*Flaring.*] Why in hell didn't Bernie come back tonight?

GEORGIE: [*Minimizingly.*] Does he have to run back after every show to hold your hand?

FRANK: This is only the second night, that's all! What're you saying every show? [*She watches him carefully as he turns away.* FRANK *says slowly.*] They wouldn't spend all that money taking photos, would they, if they were considering cast changes? [*Then, defiantly.*] But I'm glad I got that two weeks' clause. And that's the truth—!

GEORGIE: The pluperfect truth—?

FRANK: [*Bitterly.*] The pluperfect truth! I'll hand in my notice! Why should I care —do they? Producer and director don't come back the second night of a show?!

GEORGIE: [*Quietly.*] God is just where He was before. . . .

FRANK: [*Whirling around.*] How do I know if I'm good? Can't you understand how I feel?

GEORGIE: Yes, I can. I think you're really agonized. But one thing is gospel, Frank: if you walk off *this* show, too, you'll never see me again.

FRANK: Yes, ma'm, take their part— never mind what I'm feeling—take their part!

GEORGIE: [*With quiet incisiveness.*] This year I'm taking my own part. . . . [*Her tone seems to frighten him; he stops and goes to mirror, daubs at his face with a puff. Finally he makes a morose attempt at humor.*]

FRANK: Why'd you ever marry me . . . ?

GEORGIE: That's easy: you always had a box of chiclets in your pocket. [*He snorts morosely, picks up several letters, reading one.*]

FRANK: How do you like it? Fan mail— three of them—all jail bait. "Have always wanted to be in the theater. Am seventeen and think I have the talent." Jealous? [*She smiles. He tears up mail, throws it in basket.*] No, it wouldn't matter to you, would it, if I took out a gal? [*She smiles inscrutably. She knows* FRANK *wants to recoup position, that actually he is trying to taunt her into a response of jealousy, affection and regard.*] Well, would it? Would you care if I didn't show up some night?

GEORGIE: I'm not exactly taking sealed bids, Frank. [FRANK *answers a knock at door with "Yes?"* LARRY *looks in.*]

LARRY: We're ready, Frank, whenever you are.

FRANK: I'll be right there, Larry. [LARRY *nods and goes.* FRANK, *sheepishly, doesn't quite know what to say to* GEORGIE. *He slips bottle into his smoking jacket pocket.*] Wanna come out watch them take a few of these archive specials?

GEORGIE: No, it's cold out there.

FRANK: [*Contritely, crossing to her.*] Mad at Poppa? [*She is shaking her head.*] Not even if we go back to the same life, same room . . . ?

GEORGIE: People don't go back to the same life, Frank. They go above it or below it, but they don't go back.

FRANK: But do I still have the country girl?

GEORGIE: Here I am. . . .

FRANK: I appreciate you, dear. Don't wanna lose you. But I hope you know that if not for me, you'd still be on the vine, in Hartford. . . . [*He is starting out. She nods, crossing.*]

GEORGIE: A toadstool in the woods. Here, take these tissues—you'll need them. [*They meet in middle of room, each holding on to an end of tissues.*]

FRANK: Thanks.

GEORGIE: And, Frank, leave the bottle here.

FRANK: I need it, dear.

GEORGIE: [*Quietly.*] Over thirty years of know-how? Leave the bottle here.

FRANK: Georgie, I need it. [*Abruptly fierce but hushed.*] I need it! [*He jerks tissues out of her hand, walks out. Alone,* GEORGIE *shows she is tired; she stands shy, inward for the moment, head turned to one side, something very sad and lonely about her. Backstage hubbub is heard outside door.* NANCY, *the flurried virgin, enters. Life is a long, delicious time to* NANCY.]

NANCY: Mrs. Elgin, may I use your pier-glass a sec?

GEORGIE: Pier-glass? Haven't heard that phrase since I was a girl. [*Nancy postures at glass;* GEORGIE *smiles.*]

NANCY: Don't all people call this a pier-glass?

GEORGIE: Only old ladies like me. Why, I go so far back I call rhubarb a "pie-plant."

NANCY: But you don't! I can't bear it!

GEORGIE: I do. . . .

[NANCY *giggles as she examines her beautiful self.*]

NANCY: It's a beautiful dress, isn't it? My mother'll have kittens when she sees how low it's cut. [*Sighing, but examining still.*] Oh, Mrs. Elgin, do you think I'll ever grow up? *Really* grow up?

GEORGIE: I know someone who wishes she hadn't. . . .

NANCY: But you have no idea of what it means to be called "sweet child" or "Nancy-kins" by everyone and his brother!

GEORGIE: [*Dryly.*] Yes, that can hurt.

NANCY: May I be forward? How old are you?

GEORGIE: [*Smiling.*] On the dim, mysterious other side of thirty.

NANCY: That's old, isn't it? But look at you—we could be sisters! [NANCY *has taken* GEORGIE *by hand; arms around each other's waists, they look in mirror.*]

GEORGIE: [*Sadly, pausing.*] Cherish your puppy fat, dear. It's a passport to the best of life.

LARRY'S VOICE: Nancy Stoddard!

NANCY: [*Calling.*] Here!

LARRY: [*Looking in.*] Hey, you're wanted on stage, Nancykins.

NANCY: See what I mean? I can't bear it! Now you see why I'm so introvert! [*Despairing, she rushes off in a flurry.* GEORGIE *remains standing at mirror; takes off her glasses, looks at herself; something poignant reaches out from image to reality. The radio has begun playing a waltz.* GEORGIE *begins to sway in its rhythm and, in another moment, she is waltzing alone, almost as if it were possible to waltz herself back to a better time. What she is murmuring to herself we can not hear. Then she stops abruptly, routed: a sardonic* BERNIE *stands in doorway.*]

BERNIE: Excuse me, the both of you. [*He steps into the room. She crosses to make-up shelf.*]

GEORGIE: Some aspirin . . . a headache. [*He wordlessly extends an aspirin tin taken from a pocket.*]

BERNIE: It's the Age of Aspirin, they say.

[*She puts on her glasses, swallows some water. Finally turns.*]

GEORGIE: A splitting headache . . . too much stuffy dressing-room. . . .

BERNIE: Where's Frank?

GEORGIE: On stage. [*He starts out; she stops him, now in balance.*] His cold is getting worse, Mr. Dodd. He shouldn't be kept up this late. It's more than flesh and blood can stand.

BERNIE: Them's melodramatic words. We need production pictures, don't we? How's his spirit?

GEORGIE: Low.

BERNIE: The show's in fair shape—why?

GEORGIE: Ask the Boston critics. Everyone doesn't have your confidence.

BERNIE: [*Promptly.*] That's true.

GEORGIE: And while I'm on the subject, that confidence makes you push. That makes you a bit of a bully.

BERNIE: [*Even more promptly.*] That's true, too.

GEORGIE: Don't minimize what I say by agreeing with me—it's *really* true. [*Tired, he looks at her with the typical curl of smile and sits, almost as if to bait her, a way of releasing his own present tensions.*]

BERNIE: What else is bothering friend Frank . . . ?

GEORGIE: You didn't come back after the show tonight. Neither did Mr. Cook.

BERNIE: This last month I've spent from

ten to fifteen hours a day with Frank. Nothing ever bothers him except through your mouth. Why?

GEORGIE: We've been through all of that before. . . . [*Then, abruptly, closing door, stopping radio.*] He thinks it's a crime to lack a sense of humor. He doesn't want to be disliked. He hides when he's nervous. Either he jigs and jabbers away . . . or he sits in silence and rots away inside. But either way, for your edification, he's headed for a bender!

BERNIE: [*Mockingly.*] Women always think they understand their men, don't they?

GEORGIE: [*Deliberately dimming her electricity.*] I won't fight with you, Mr. Dodd. He expected you backstage tonight. Your absence was a reprimand. If you care at all for his sense of security—

BERNIE: Follow your advice . . . ? [GEORGIE *stops, looks at him as one wrestler looks at another.*]

GEORGIE: Do you know anything about drinkers?

BERNIE: Something. . . .

GEORGIE: If you're not careful, you'll have him full of whiskey before he goes to bed tonight. He's got a bad cold. That's a respectable surface reason for any drinker to jump down the well.

BERNIE: Why work so hard at this marriage? Why not take a rest? You wear your husband down! You make him tense, uneasy—you don't stop "handling" him. You try to "handle" me, too.

GEORGIE: [*In a flash.*] And don't think I can't, after handling a cunning drunkard for ten years!

BERNIE: [*Quickly up on his feet.*] Who the hell do you think you are? Secretary of State?

GEORGIE: [*Defiantly.*] I'm a drunkard's wife.

BERNIE: [*Snorting.*] Girlie, I have to give you credit, but—!

GEORGIE: [*Quickly.*] No compliments, Mr. Dodd!

BERNIE: But I'm going to fight you as hard as I can for this man!

GEORGIE: [*Smiling faintly.*] Not too hard . . . I may let you have him.

BERNIE: No, you want him wholly dependent! Now let's not waste words. I—

GEORGIE: Oh, it's much too late for that.

BERNIE: I was married to one like you. Roughly, half my weight—ninety-seven pounds. It took her two years—she sewed me up!

GEORGIE: [*Dryly.*] Love is hell. . . .

BERNIE: We'll leave it at that . . . joke ending. [*He jaunts to door, but turns.*] What a bitter pity you don't realize the size of your husband's talent!

GEORGIE: What have *you* given up for that talent?

BERNIE: [*Coming back.*] Then why do you stay?

GEORGIE: Because he's helpless!

BERNIE: I'll help him!

GEORGIE: *You!* You wouldn't know where to begin. Life with him is three-quarters the avoidance of painful scenes. He's taught me to be a fish, to swim in any direction, including up, down and sideways. Now, disregarding facts, you happen to think I wheedle his life away. You're very—

BERNIE: [*Unable to contain himself.*] Look, look, look! Half the world's shamed by sentiment. Say "mother" or "babe," "sacrifice," and they drip like axle grease! But you've ruined this man—don't explain it away by sentiment!

GEORGIE: [*Incredulously.*] How did I so over-rate your intellect? You're a boy!

BERNIE: Man or boy, I'm putting on a show—it has to work! We can discuss universals some other day! To be frank, you are slightly grotesque to me, Mrs. Elgin!

GEORGIE: [*Bitterly.*] And what about yourself? Look at you, fearful of failure, effective and hard-hitting—a machine, without manners or style—self-driven, curt, wary and worried—pretending to a humanity you never practice!

BERNIE: [*Contemptuously.*] You called your own husband a cunning drunkard!

GEORGIE: [*Flatly.*] It is necessary for you to know it! [*Pause; they are murdering each other with their eyes.*] This is getting stupid. Now tell me, in God's name, exactly what you want me to do for Frank. [*She turns and sits at make-up shelf. He steps in, throws a pointed finger at her.*]

BERNIE: That's fair! I'll believe everything you say; prove it!

GEORGIE: How?

BERNIE: Get out of town! [*Pausing.*] I've just had a bad fight in the box-office with Cook. He's got a first-class replacement for Frank and seventy thousand dollars to protect! Frank will improve every day—I think he will—Cook thinks he won't. Well, he won't, unless *you get out of town!*

[GEORGIE *thinks, stops, looks and listens.*]

GEORGIE: Umm . . . I'll do it. I'll go back to New York. [*Stopping him from leaving.*] But only on one condition: let *me* carefully tell Frank, in my own way, at my own time.

BERNIE: As long as you're on the train by tomorrow night, understand?

GEORGIE: [*Nodding.*] Life is earnest, life is real, and so are investments—I understand. But you may be sorry.

BERNIE: You're as phoney to me as an opera soprano!

[GEORGIE *abruptly slashes him across face with her open hand.*]

GEORGIE: [*Fiercely.*] Did I forget to tell you I'm proud? Someone has to stop you from calling me any name that pops into your little head!

BERNIE: [*Frigidly.*] Maybe I deserved that. Maybe not. Time alone will tell.

GEORGIE: It brings all things, they say. [*Holding back tears.*] Thank God for *that* inevitability. . . .

[FRANK *opens door before* BERNIE *reaches it.*]

FRANK: [*Jovially.*] Bernie, old boy, where you been all night? Every time I come in here—you and my wife—what gives?

BERNIE: [*Turned away.*] How they doing out there?

FRANK: [*Chortling.*] We're through! Georgie, we're through—called it a day! [*To* BERNIE, *cautiously.*] But, baby, did you see the show tonight? [BERNIE *nodding.*] Well, give!

BERNIE: I'll tell you what a Harvard professor said—which is why I got back this late: "That man's extraordinary!"

[FRANK *begins to change to street clothes, putting cough syrup on shelf.*]

FRANK: Hear that, dear? We're in the colleges now!

BERNIE: What happened there in act two again?

FRANK: Bernie, it's that same damn thing, that same fast cue. Unger says it's all right to fix.

BERNIE: I don't see why not. . . . [*Making note.*] I'd like to put the new scene in tomorrow. You tired?

FRANK: [*Scoffingly.*] Who? Elgin, the actor who likes to be compared?

BERNIE: Your energy was low again tonight.

FRANK: Sure, it's this goddam cold.

[BERNIE *begins to search* FRANK. *He is not stupid, and there may be a modicum of truth in what* GEORGIE *has said. She is on other side of room, bracing herself, ready to have the truth at any cost.*]

BERNIE: Not nerves? [*Warningly.*] We're gonna begin bearing down now. How *is* the cold?

FRANK: Under control. . . .

GEORGIE: Why don't you tell him what's bothering you?

FRANK: [*Rolling his eyes.*] What's bothering me?

GEORGIE: Cook and the notices, for instance. . . .

FRANK: [*Innocently, to Bernie.*] I just wondered why he didn't come back, that's all. Is he mad? I mean, let's face it, they weren't exactly money notices.

[*But* GEORGIE *is not to be shaken off this time, despite* FRANK's *tacit warning that she keep quiet. She steps in.* BERNIE *watches carefully.*]

GEORGIE: Frank, Mr. Dodd believes in you. I can't help you if you're worried—he can.

FRANK: [*Very firmly.*] But I'm not worried. He's got his own headaches, dear.

[BERNIE *steps in, testing situation.*]

BERNIE: Frank . . . you're a talent—I expect to pay for that. I don't expect you to be easy and convenient—I'm no fool. Now, does anything seriously bother you?

FRANK: Wouldn't I tell you if it did?

BERNIE: I think you would. . . . [*But* BERNIE *still watches and probes.* GEORGIE *steps in sharply between the men.*]

GEORGIE: Did you or did you not tell me, ten minutes ago, right in this room, that you wanted to hand in your notice?

FRANK: [*Exploding.*] Well, for crying out loud! if a man can't say anything in a gag—! Have to watch my step—can't open my mouth no more! [*Throws* BERNIE *a long-suffering look. Stopped,* GEORGIE *purses her lips.* BERNIE *deliberately throws another chemical into the brew.*]

BERNIE: Your wife says she's thinking of returning to New York.

GEORGIE: I told you nothing of the sort! [FRANK *turns, alarmed and anxious, syrup bottle in one hand.*]

FRANK: What do you mean, New York?

GEORGIE: [*Deciding to take a new tack.*] Yes . . . I might go back to New York. . . .

[*Puzzled, worried, wary and off balance,* FRANK *is about to take a swig of the syrup.* GEORGIE *lifts bottle out of his hand and bangs it down on shelf behind her. Then crosses to her purse.* BERNIE *starts to leave, but turns abruptly, picks up bottle.*]

BERNIE: What is this?

FRANK: [*Minimizingly.*] Cough syrup. Pine, tar, cherries—a whole bush in a bottle!

BERNIE: Do you know it's laced with twenty-two percent alcohol?

FRANK: Alcohol . . . ? [*Very surprised, pretending puzzlement,* FRANK *glances at label, saying glibly.*] Yeah, there's alcohol in it, all right. I asked Georgie to get me some stuff to loosen me up in the chest and this is what she brought me back.

BERNIE: [*Sternly, but emotionalized.*] What do you think you're doing, Frank. My father was a drinker—he ended up under subway wheels. I know what these little appetizers can do!

FRANK: Didn't even occur to me, Bernie. [*Chidingly, to* GEORGIE.] Gee, dear, you wanna watch yourself on a thing like that.

[BERNIE *looks away from* FRANK *to* GEORGIE; *she is tired but undaunted.*]

GEORGIE: Get dressed, Frank. I want to go home. I'll be waiting outside. [*She walks out, taking purse, closing door.*]

BERNIE: Frank, my problem is the show. She's jealous of the show and jealous of me. [*He has taken bottle and is pouring its contents down sink.*] This is how far she'd go—far enough to kick you off the wagon!

[FRANK *watches furtively and uneasily.*]

FRANK: Bernie, I know she's high-strung and difficult, but I can't believe she'd—

[BERNIE *stops him by clatteringly slamming bottle into metal waste-basket; he speaks harshly.*]

BERNIE: I want her back in New York! We have hard work ahead! [*Stopping.*] Frank, I wouldn't relish having to tell you. . . . [*Then.*] Go back to the hotel—get a good night's sleep. I want you fresh and clear—I'm putting the new scene in at one o'clock.

FRANK: [*Warily.*] Yah. . . . [BERNIE *opens door, curtly calls, "Mrs. Elgin!" This makes* FRANK *very uneasy.* GEORGIE *returns. Door open,* BERNIE *says tiredly.*]

BERNIE: Frank knows exactly how I feel. See you at one tomorrow, Frank.

FRANK: Good-night. . . . [BERNIE *goes,*

closing door. GEORGIE *is silent.* FRANK, *full of childish guilt, doesn't know where to look. He chooses to begin by taking his make-up off, but can't look* GEORGIE *in the face. She is tired, worn thin, doesn't need much to make her break through.*] Where's my cigarette . . . ? He can be very arrogant and insulting, can't he? [*Waiting.*] Must be cold out. . . .

GEORGIE: Clean up, Frank. I'm beat out and in no mood to socialize.

FRANK: He had no right to talk to you that way.

GEORGIE: [*With some bitterness.*] Did you tell him so?

FRANK: Georgie . . . he . . . I'm ashamed of myself. . . . [*He stands up, wiping his face quickly.*] Give me two more minutes, dear. . . .

[*She sits stiffly on edge of a chair, not looking at him. He is working swiftly, changing trousers. Slowly she looks up, turning her head this way and that.*]

GEORGIE: Frank . . . [*He turns innocently; she is eyeing him cannily.*]

FRANK: Yes . . . ?

GEORGIE: Where's the other bottle?

FRANK: What bottle?

GEORGIE: I'm tired, Frank—don't play peek-a-boo. Do you have another bottle of that syrup?

FRANK: No, I don't.

GEORGIE: [*Standing.*] Give it to me. . . .

FRANK: But I didn't buy another bottle, dear. . . . [*A twisted, punished child, he stands there while her eyes roam from his face to corners of room. She crosses abruptly, pulling down a hatbox; finding nothing in box, she goes through pockets of a garment.*] Wish you'd take my word for something for, a change. . . . [*She ignores his hushed protesting as she goes down to trunk, pulls out two drawers in her search.*]

GEORGIE: What a night, what a night . . . ! And all the time there's been a clanging in my head . . . I don't know who's punishing who any more!

FRANK: I wish you'd take my word for a change. . . .

GEORGIE: [*Abruptly.*] Never mind! I give up—I'm not going to look! Where's my knitting? [*She looks around, trying to locate both knitting and herself. When she finds knitting bag under his clothes on cot she brings it down to her purse on a chair. He is confused and humble, abject.*]

FRANK: Georgie, I wanna apologize, Georgie. He had no right to take that attitude.

GEORGIE: Didn't he? He has the right to take *any* attitude—in ten years he's the only friend you've had!

FRANK: Excepting you, dear! And that's what I want, dear, the chance to show you how much I love you!

[*She is having difficulty putting on her coat—one sleeve is turned inside out, and this only increases her frustration and anger.*]

GEORGIE: How much you *need* me, you mean! [FRANK *is now revealed in all his naked helplessness and agony.*]

FRANK: Please, Georgie, don't be mad at me. I know I'm no damn good, but I'm worried to death—!

GEORGIE: Tell that to Bernardo!

FRANK: Think of what it means to me to walk out on that stage every night—the whole responsibility of the show is on my head!

GEORGIE: *Tell that to Bernardo!*

FRANK: Baby, I don't know where to hide—I'm ashamed! Don't know the old lines and tomorrow I get a big new scene—! And now you say you're going back to New York—I can't do this if you don't help me! Did I ask them for this part! Didn't they come to me? Weren't you there when he came to me? They don't appreciate what I'm doing for them! They don't—

[*She cuts him off intensely, changing his direction to one of heated indignation.*]

GEORGIE: Stop putting on a front!

FRANK: Who's putting on a front?

GEORGIE: You're putting on a front! And you lie, you lie—!

FRANK: [*Flaring.*] What can I do, whine and complain? You want me to make them hate me?

GEORGIE: [*Bitterly.*] They'll adore you when you go off on a bender!

FRANK: Who says on a bender?

GEORGIE: Old waffle-iron says! The mop behind the door. . . . [*Pausing, eyes flooding despite herself.*] This is how it ends, that *laughing* dream . . . you had a laughing dream, five weeks ago. . . . [*She takes handkerchief from her purse and uses it on her nose. He turns away, dressing and muttering to himself.*]

FRANK: I don't know anybody up here in Boston. . . . The whole company—none

of them like me, not even Bernie. How do I know he's keeping me on? Did he act like a friend tonight . . . ? [*Turning to her.*] Are you going back to New York?

GEORGIE: I don't know why not. . . .

FRANK: You wanna leave me, don't you?

GEORGIE: It's late, Frank—I have to wash some stockings—

FRANK: [*Stepping it.*] Tell me! You do, don't you?

GEORGIE: I want to go to bed—I may have a happy dream!

FRANK: Who's in New York?

GEORGIE: [*Turning.*] ? ? ?

FRANK: [*Harshly.*] What pair of pants are you looking for?

GEORGIE: [*Outraged.*] Frank, I warn you —I'll hit you with the first thing I pick up! [*Face to face, they eye each other for a moment,* FRANK *finally moving away to clothes hooks but not dropping his voice.*]

FRANK: They all want me to fail! And you want me to fail, too! You don't love me!

GEORGIE: [*Wearily.*] Come on, Frank. . . .

FRANK: All I've got is two hands!

GEORGIE: Well, use them—it's two a.m. —you have a one o'clock call.

FRANK: If you're in such a big hurry, there's the door! I, as a matter of fact, may take myself a walk. Get myself a baked apple and some milk.

GEORGIE: Your cold is getting worse—

FRANK: Let *them* worry about it! And I told you what *you* can do!

GEORGIE: [*Everything hurting.*] You want me to go? Is that what you want?

FRANK: If you're in such a hurry. . . . [*She looks at him and her face tightens; she picks up her purse and knitting bag angrily.*]

GEORGIE: Oh, the hell with it! Just the hell with it! I'm going back to the hotel—do what you want! Sometimes I think you're plain out of your head! [*She exits without more ado, slamming door hard.* FRANK *whirls around; he glowers bitterly, snorting and mimicking her tone, walking in circles before he snatches his tie off a hook.*]

FRANK: Out of your mind! Do what you want—plain out of your mind! Your cold is getting worse! That's right—walk out on me! Typical! Typical! [*He is down at pier-glass now, angrily snapping tie into a knot, muttering to himself.*] Forget I'm alive. Take their part and forget I'm alive! Helpmate, real helpmate. . . . [*He dribbles off, attitude abruptly changing. Stops, then tip-toes to closed door and listens. Then goes down to trunk and from bottom section brings out a full bottle of cough syrup. Un-caps it, takes a swig and throws cap away over one shoulder. The bottle plopped down* *on trunk in front of him, he continues with tie and collar. His tone is less intense but as bitter as he says.]* Helpmate! Sweetheart! Country Girl! . . .

CURTAIN

Scene Two

TIME: *Twelve hours later*
PLACE: *As the last scene*

It is early afternoon. The dressing-room is dark. A sound of snoring is heard. There is a persistent knocking at door now. FRANK, *who has been asleep, stirs on cot. We are dimly aware that he is sitting up now, as knocking persists, a voice asking:*

VOICE: Is there anybody in there? Mr. Elgin? [*Lights go on around mirror;* FRANK *has toddled over to switch and stands there blinking, the knocking persisting.*] Are you in there, Mr. Elgin? Frank? [*Knocking stops and several voices are joined in con-ference outside door.* FRANK *realizes where he is and what is happening. He is fully clothed, including top coat, and shows in everything the evidence of having been drunk until now, past two in the afternoon. He mutters under his breath.*]
FRANK: Oh, my God . . . my God. . . . [*He does not know what to do first. Tries to brush his hair back with nervous hands; nothing will help him at this mo-ment, particularly as he is being hunted and pushed by further knocking on door.*]
VOICES: [*Including* LARRY. COOK *and* UNGER.] Is the key in there with you? Open up, Frank! Is the key in there with him? [*Looking around, realizing that he is trapped,* FRANK *clears his throat.*]
FRANK: Yes, yes . . . what is it?
VOICE: This is Larry, Mr. Elgin. May I come in?
FRANK: Yes, Larry, yes . . . just a mo-ment, please. . . . [*Sotto voice.*] Oh, my God. . . . [*He hangs up his coat; it slips to the floor. Shaking himself, dabbing pitifully at his face and hair, he finally opens door.* LARRY *and* COOK *are standing there,* UNGER *behind them.*] What's wrong? What's wrong, boys? [*They come in and look at him;* FRANK *blusters with a crooked smile.*] Well, where's the fire . . . ?
LARRY: It's past two o'clock, Mr. Elgin. . . . Your door was locked and the key wasn't on the rack.

FRANK: I was napping in here. Tired. [*Tries to light cigarette, but his hands shake so that* LARRY *quietly steps in and holds out a match for him.*]
COOK: There was a one o'clock call, for the new scene!
FRANK: Ow, ow! Completely slipped my mind! Walked around. Got tired. Slept in here and just forgot—
COOK: You mean you "slept it off" in here! You're so loaded you can't stand straight right now!
LARRY: [*Restrainingly.*] Mr. Cook . . . [FRANK *drops into chair at makeup shelf.*]
UNGER: What the dickens happened to you?
FRANK: [*Snarling.*] Nothing happened to me! I have a cold! Had a couple of beers and some food—

COOK:		Look at him! Smells like the sovereign state of Kentucky in person! [FRANK *has put his head in his hands; the world is whirling for him.*]
UNGER:	*Together*	Where's Bernie?
LARRY:		We've sent for him.

COOK: [*Fervidly, stepping in.*] Well, this does it! Thank my lucky stars this does it! That wife of yours can help you start pack-ing! [*Only* LARRY *sees* GEORGIE *has come in at door. Head down,* FRANK *does not see her.*]
LARRY: Mr. Cook, I can't let you talk to an actor that way.

COOK: [*Not believing his ears.*] You can't what?

LARRY: [*White-faced.*] You're the boss, Mr. Cook, but you can't talk that way to an actor in any show I'm on. I won't permit it.

COOK: *You* won't permit it?!

LARRY: There is a lady in the room, too. I'll have to ask you to keep quiet until Bernie gets here. . . .

COOK: [*Grimly.*] We'll see what he says when *he* gets here!

[*He walks out of the room.* UNGER *follows him, after shaking his head dolefully at* GEORGIE. FRANK *has not looked up.* LARRY *approaches him in a kindly way.*]

LARRY: Can I get you some coffee, Frank? [FRANK *does not answer or lift his head.*]

GEORGIE: Don't get him coffee, Larry—it makes him sicker.

LARRY: [*Pausing.*] I'll get you a bromo-seltzer. . . . [*Looks at* GEORGIE *and leaves room, closing door.* GEORGIE *does not move.*]

GEORGIE: Where were you all night? [FRANK *stands and reels over to cot, falling to a seated position there, saying with averted eyes.*]

FRANK: Get me some water. Let it run. . . . [*She crosses to sink with a still face.*]

GEORGIE: It's not very cold. . . . [*Then.*] Watch that cigarette, Frank. You'll have us all on fire in a minute. [*He drops cigarette underfoot and grinds it dead, saying bitterly.*]

FRANK: I missed the reading and that's *all* I did miss! [*She crosses and gives him water.*] Where's Bernie?

GEORGIE: I don't know. [*She turns.* BERNIE *has pushed door open; he snaps on room lights. Behind him are* COOK *and* UNGER. FRANK *drops his eyes, and his soul drops its head within.* BERNIE *comes to* C. *of room; he turns squarely on a line with* GEORGIE *and speaks in a low but tense voice.*]

BERNIE: When did you see your husband last, Mrs. Elgin?

GEORGIE: [*Eyeing him warily.*] Past two this morning.

BERNIE: Where?

GEORGIE: In this room. . . .

BERNIE: Did he go back to the hotel with you?

GEORGIE: No, he wanted to go for food. I was tired.

BERNIE: What did you tell me when I phoned you in your room today?

GEORGIE: You asked me where Frank was. I said I didn't know. You asked me if he'd had a good night's sleep. I hoped he had, I said.

BERNIE: Why did you lie? [*This scene is so painful to* UNGER *that he slips out.*]

GEORGIE: I am not aware, Mr. Dodd, that I lied!

BERNIE: You didn't think it was important to tell me that Frank hadn't been home all night?

GEORGIE: Suppose he'd been with another woman?

BERNIE: You're being deliberately evasive and childish! [*A tap at door, a voice saying: "It's Larry. . . ."* BERNIE *barks back without turning, "Wait outside!"*] Where did you get him a bottle after midnight?

GEORGIE: Where did I—? [*She is so astounded that she is unable to resist a strange, strained laugh.*]

COOK: What the heck's so funny? I resent that!

BERNIE: [*Turning to him.*] There's only one thing to do, Phil—

COOK: And, yes sir, I'm going right out to the box-office to do it! [*He walks out quickly;* BERNIE *pauses, then says, without looking at* GEORGIE.]

BERNIE: There is still one person too many in this room. [GEORGIE *smiles faintly; she walks out, closing door. We don't know what* BERNIE *is going to do, but now he breaks a momentary silence quietly.*] What about this . . . ? [*Head down,* FRANK *does not answer.* BERNIE *waits; then we see that he is really very emotional about this incident, for now his voice vibrates when he speaks.*] I'm in a mood to cut my throat in public. God a'mighty, human beings are funny people. . . . [*Pausing, abruptly harsh.*] Sit up! Don't act as if I'm beating you up! Don't make me the victimizer! Sit up! [*It seems for a moment that* BERNIE *may hit* FRANK; *instead he turns and walks away.*]

FRANK: Don't bawl me out, Bernie. . . . I'll stay till you get somebody else. . . .

BERNIE: I'm tired right down to my bones. . . . [*Then, strongly, turning.*] That wife of yours—she—!

FRANK: No, not my wife. Why kid around? It's all my fault—I'm no good.

[*This is said with such empty hopelessness that it activates* BERNIE *once again.*]

BERNIE: You're guilty as hell! But I want you to do something for the kid—

FRANK: What kid?

BERNIE: *This* kid! Stop being naive: stop protecting her!

FRANK: Bernie, she's weak. She—

BERNIE: She's driven you to drink for ten years and you call her weak? You might be magnificent in this part, but it would have to start with her! She goes back to New York on the 'five-o-five'!

FRANK: [*Weakly.*] Bernie, kid, I can't leave her. Left her once—she cuts her wrists. She'd cut her wrists again.

BERNIE: [*Angrily.*] She goes back today!

FRANK: [*A nervous whisper.*] Bernie, she's weak. . . .

BERNIE: I'll talk to her. If we go on together, you move in with me for the duration!

FRANK: But, Mr. Cook—he doesn't want me and—

BERNIE: [*Flashing.*] I'm not so sure *I* want you!

FRANK: [*Fumblingly.*] Bernie, you decide. . . .

[BERNIE *has gone to door without even listening to* FRANK, *who has not moved from his isolated spot on cot.* BERNIE *crisply calls, "Mrs. Elgin!" When she enters she closes door and goes directly to* FRANK *with a fizzy drink which he takes but does not drink.*]

GEORGIE: Take this. . . .

[BERNIE *begins talking from behind her. She turns to him, a wary hatred in her eyes.*]

BERNIE: Frank stays—you go! The management will take care of your expenses. Frank may follow you in a day or two—I'm not sure. Just now he's moving in with me.

GEORGIE: As crisp as lettuce, aren't you . . . ? [*Then.*] You want me to go back, Frank? [*Then, of his silence.*] That means yes. . . . I'll go and pack. [*Crossing to go.*] But I want to know one thing: why do you hold on to this sack of trouble?

BERNIE: [*Coldly.*] I will answer that, for Frank's sake. I'm interested in theater, not show business. I could make a fortune in films, but that's show "biz" to me.

GEORGIE: What do you call this play, Literature?

BERNIE: That's true: it's show business, trying hard to be theater. And a man like Elgin, giving his best performance—he has the magic to transform a mere show to Theater with a capital T!

GEORGIE: [*Quietly.*] Let us hope. . . . [*With a sad smile she starts for door, but* BERNIE *steps up quickly, blocking her way.*]

BERNIE: One moment. Tell Frank he has nothing to worry about.

GEORGIE: ? ? ?

BERNIE: He thinks you may go drastic. Its happened before, I understand. [FRANK *turns, nervously murmuring, "Bernie . . ."*]

GEORGIE: What's happened before?

BERNIE: Phoney suicide attempts.

FRANK: [*Nervously.*] Bernie, she wants to help. . . .

GEORGIE: [*Wearily, closing her eyes.*] Mr. Dodd . . . we had a town idiot when I was a child . . . he kept insisting that elephant's tusks come from piano keys. You are very obtuse and wilful, for a man who so relishes his own humanity.

BERNIE: What are you talking about?

FRANK: [*Weakly.*] Bernie, she has to pack. . . .

BERNIE: What are you trying to tell me, Mrs. Dodd?

GEORGIE: Don't call me Mrs. Dodd. Suicide attempts are Frank's department. [*Back to door, pausing,* BERNIE *walks down to* FRANK.]

BERNIE: Show me your wrists, Frank. . . . [*Waiting.*] Show me your wrists. [*Then, louder.*] I asked you to show me your wrists! [*Agonized,* FRANK *slowly raises his wrists;* BERNIE *looks down for several intense seconds and the story is plain. Sickened,* BERNIE *turns away, his face to the wall. Behind him* FRANK's *head slips down into his hands; he sobs without control.* BERNIE *slowly turns to look across at* GEORGIE, *who is on the other side of the room, face averted.*] I must ask you several questions. . . .

GEORGIE: Michael on angel wings couldn't talk to me with your face.

BERNIE: [*Pausing.*] Frank may have to go back with you, unless you answer. He's been lying to me. . . .

GEORGIE: He's incapable of the truth, as commonly understood.

BERNIE: You were "Miss America" in the late '30s?

GEORGIE: He told you that? I can't believe my ears. [*Then, turning, thinking.*] Did . . . I burn down a house in Great

Neck? Or a hotel suite? Did I need a nurse to watch me while he was tending work?

BERNIE: [*Nodding.*] Umm. . . .

GEORGIE: You didn't recognize any of it, from the play you admired him in, "Werba's Millions?" [*She slowly sits, the heart completely out of her. Frank has not lifted his face from his hands. Her eyes wet with years,* GEORGIE *talks on, spent, scarcely knowing what she is saying.*] You don't know what it is . . . meet, marry, elope . . . nineteen, romantic, real cute, raised on too many books. Oh, my, I had such a naive belief in Frank's worldliness and competence. Yes, I saw he drank . . . but that was only a pathetic hint of frailty in a wonderful glowing man. It was touching and sweet—it made me love him more. He could reform—I'd do it for him. Well, finally . . . there wasn't much left to take over. . . . [*Pausing, turning.*] Send him back to the hotel—he needs some rest. [BERNIE *hesitates before moving briskly to door and calling for* LARRY, *who immediately appears.*]

LARRY: Yes, Bernie . . . ?

BERNIE: Is Lucas out there? Is he "up" in Judge Murray's part?

LARRY: Yes, he is. . . .

BERNIE: Could he go on tonight?

LARRY: [*Hesitantly.*] Yes, I think he could. . . . [*Thinking, to himself,* BERNIE *murmurs, "Dunno what I'll do."* FRANK *says, eyes to floor.*]

FRANK: I'll play if I get another chance. . . .

[BERNIE'S *face tightens; says harshly, with a vicious jab of his thumb.*]

BERNIE: Take him back to the hotel! Dismiss the company—check with me around five!

LARRY: Yes, sir, Bernie. [*Almost awed,* LARRY *picks up* FRANK'S *coat.* FRANK *stands slowly, looking at* GEORGIE. *Without looking at him, she quietly says.*]

GEORGIE: Go on, Frank. I won't leave without seeing you. . . . [*Taking his coat,* FRANK *leaves;* LARRY *follows, closing door. Silence:* BERNIE *tense and tender, smarting and apologetic;* GEORGIE *abstracted and drained.*]

BERNIE: [*Finally.*] May I smoke?

GEORGIE: May you smoke? What is that, homage to a lady? That will never make me forgive you, Mr. Dodd, for what you've said and done. [*He pauses, not looking at her, not lighting cigarette.*]

BERNIE: I'm very confused and troubled . . . what about Frank?

GEORGIE: Those lies are his big, respectable reason for having gone to pieces.

BERNIE: Why did he go to pieces?

GEORGIE: That's no subject to discuss at this minute.

BERNIE: I don't know where to begin apologizing, Mrs. Dodd.

GEORGIE: I'm a real lemon-drop. You can begin by not calling me Mrs. Dodd. [*Standing, she flicks him a look and begins buttoning her coat.*]

BERNIE: Have you ever left him . . . ?

GEORGIE: Twice left, twice returned. He's a helpless child. . . . [*Wryly, lifting her purse.*] Anyone taking a cab to New York?

BERNIE: But if he's as helpless as you say—

GEORGIE: He's not helpless now—he has you.

BERNIE: [*Earnestly, voice quivering.*] Listen, he had to be watched and handled. You can do that—no one else—I didn't know it before.

GEORGIE: [*Bitterly.*] Then you've learned something—ripeness is all!

BERNIE: Listen, Georgie, if—

GEORGIE: [*Opening up.*] I don't intend to stay! Even the cat's dragged me up and down the stairs in this theater!

BERNIE: [*Unhappily.*] But the man needs you—he has to be watched—! [GEORGIE *turns from door and now he gets it.*]

GEORGIE: *You* take on the job with waving banners and twelve hours later hand it back? *You're telling me!?* [*She throws her purse on cot and begins circling him. Helpless, he makes an attempt here and there to stop her torrential anger.*] Yes, he has to be watched—he has to be nursed, guarded and coddled! But not by me, my very young friend!

BERNIE: Please—

GEORGIE: I'm going back to New York, to the fiesta of a quiet room. For the first time in twelve years I won't have to wonder where he is—he'll be in the strong, sober hands of Mr. Bernie Dodd!

BERNIE: [*Ineffectually.*] Georgie, listen—

GEORGIE: Can you stand him up on his feet? Because that's where all my prayers have gone—to see that one holy hour when he can stand alone! [*Avoiding him as he tries to grab her.*] And I might forgive even you, Mr. Dodd, if you can keep him up long enough for me to get out from under!

All I want is my own name and a modest job to buy the sugar for my coffee!

BERNIE: [*Temper slipping.*] Wait—if you'll listen—!

GEORGIE: [*Evading him.*] You can't believe that, can you, you goddam man! You can't believe a woman's crazy-out-of-her-mind to live alone! In one room! By herself!

[BERNIE *is so aroused by her that he has grabbed her by one arm. She pulls away; he grabs with his other hand and whirls her around.*]

BERNIE: Dammit, listen to me! You're knocking all the apologies out of my head! [*Now he has pulled her in close to him and is holding her by both arms.*] Now, listen, Lady Brilliance: you have to stay—he doesn't play unless you stay! It's a time for promotion, not more execution! But I can't take the chance *if you don't stay!* [*A quick tense moment follows,* GEORGIE *frozen in his arms, her hands against his chest.*]

GEORGIE: Why are you holding me? [*Then, pushing.*] I said you are holding me! [*Abruptly, not releasing her, he kisses her fully on the mouth. Then they both step apart and after a moment he walks to a chair and sits, turned from her, one hand up to his face.* GEORGIE *says, thinly.*] I . . . [*Then she seems to come out of sleep.*] What is that toughness of yours? A pose . . . ? [BERNIE *has not changed his position, except to put one hand over his eyes; it is some time before he can trust himself to speak.*] To be so mad at someone you didn't even know . . . ? [*Then.*] No one

has looked at me as a woman for years and years. . . . [BERNIE *turns abruptly, facing her; she eyes his scowling face.*] You want to beat me up again, don't you?

BERNIE: No, I deserve anything you say . . . no excuses, no excuses. . . . [*Then, manner changing.*] Now I need your answer. For Frank's sake, I want you to stay.

GEORGIE: Wanting, wanting, always wanting!

BERNIE: [*Humble for him.*] I'm asking. . . . [*A tap at door and* COOK *irritably bustles in.*]

COOK: Where are you, Bernie? I'm waiting—Ray Newton is on the phone—he's available. He can catch the sleeper and be here in the morning.

BERNIE: I'll be right there.

COOK: He's on the box-office phone.

BERNIE: [*Sharply.*] I'll be right there. [COOK *glowers quickly and goes.* BERNIE *stands.*] I have to go out now and battle him. He's armed with plenty of facts and weapons. Will you stay?

GEORGIE: [*Pausing.*] Yes. [*He starts for door, face rigid; she stops him.*]

GEORGIE: You kissed me . . . don't let it give you any ideas, Mr. Dodd.

BERNIE: [*Quietly.*] No, Mrs. Elgin. . . . [*He walks out, quietly closing door.* GEORGIE *stands for a full moment, as if listening, an air of impenetrable unreality about her. Her hand slowly moves up to her face. Her fingers touch her lips.*]

SLOW CURTAIN

Scene Three

TIME: *Five weeks later*
PLACE: FRANK'S *dressing-room, in a New York theater*

Out of sight, the curtain will drop presently on the second act of the play at its New York opening. FRANK'S *dressing-room door opens directly onto the stage:* GEORGIE, *as she is doing now, can stand in the doorway and listen to the play. We, too, can hear a stretch of dialogue from time to time; and later, when curtain drops, we will hear the applause.*

There is a hushed, tip-top quality about everything. RALPH, FRANK'S *dresser, enters, hanging a garment on wall and handing* GEORGIE *several telegrams.*

RALPH: A few more telegrams.

GEORGIE: Thanks. How is it going on the other side of the stage?

RALPH: A big man, Mrs. Elgin, he's a big man—it's a positive honor to be working for him.

[GEORGIE *smiles.* RALPH *exits with loaded powder puff.* GEORGIE *leafs through wires, reaching for her glasses; one wire interests her and she doesn't see* BERNIE *enter. When she turns she is startled to see* BERNIE *there, himself tense and nervous, all ears for the stage, hanging his overcoat on a hook. He is in a strange and complex mood of cynicism and gloom, begrudging but not without hope, nervous and painful, with a quality of "riding" everyone and everything.*]

GEORGIE: Where've you been, Bernie, out front?

BERNIE: Out front. On an opening night, the world's most useless man.

GEORGIE: How is Frank?

BERNIE: [*Admitting nothing.*] His first act wasn't bad. How's it been back here?

GEORGIE: Quiet. Mr. Cook came back but I wouldn't let him in.

BERNIE: More telegrams? [GEORGIE *is putting one up at mirror.*]

GEORGIE: This one is from Mr. Unger's aunt.

[BERNIE *strolls towards makeup shelf; she seems to evade him, going to door and listening again.* BERNIE *drops into chair.*]

BERNIE: Why don't you go out front?

GEORGIE: On a New York opening night! Not me. I don't sit out there with all those nabobs and critics. I hear very well right from here.

BERNIE: That's the advantage of an onstage dressing-room. [LARRY *appears in doorway, a fierce working fool in shirt sleeves, minus his usual deference.*]

LARRY: Shh! Shh! Please! Quiet, dammit! Shh! [*He goes without concession, closing door.* GEORGIE *grimaces.*]

GEORGIE: That's the *disadvantage.* [*Then worried, crossing.*] Isn't Frank's performance pleasing you . . . ?

BERNIE: [*Annoyed.*] He's erratic, in and out—the bursts aren't coming! We'll see. . . .

GEORGIE: Don't let him see your long face when he comes off.

BERNIE: [*With a mock bow.*] State Department Sadie—I forgot.

GEORGIE: Depressed, aren't you . . . ?

BERNIE: [*Readily agreeing.*] Depressed and mean. [*Sighing and fiddling with a powder can.*] Well, it's been a long nine weeks. A job is a home to a homeless man.

Now the job is finished . . . where do I go from here? [*Wryly, turning.*] I'm told—it has been intimated to me—that you call me Bernardo the Great.

GEORGIE: Haven't you been a magician to Frank? To both of us, in fact?

[BERNIE *gets up and crosses impatiently to his coat.*]

BERNIE: He can thank *you* for anything that's happened.

GEORGIE: [*Sincerely.*] No, he can thank *you,* Bernie.

BERNIE: [*Sourly.*] Here we go, jockeying for position again. [*Turning, abruptly tense.*] Georgie, five weeks ago I kissed a woman, a married woman; and now I love a woman, a married woman, and don't know where to turn. [*He steps in and takes her arms, his voice ardent but low.*] Lady, lady, close to you this way. . . .

GEORGIE: [*Gently.*] Bernie . . .

BERNIE: Who knows what'll happen after tonight—rehearsals are over—I may never see you again!

GEORGIE: Bernie . . . [*She is holding him off, her hands to his chest. He desists, smiling wryly.*]

BERNIE: Okay. [*Then, nervously snapping his fingers.*] I didn't say before what this must mean to you. No matter what happens to this show tonight . . . he'll have offers galore. [*Then.*] Are you leaving him?

GEORGIE: [*Quietly.*] Don't you think the subject can wait?

BERNIE: [*With abrupt flare.*] No, it happens to be on my mind! You've been evading me for weeks!

GEORGIE: You're unregenerate, Bernie—you'll never change. In a minute we'll be at each other's throats. [*She has not spoken unkindly, but he is ready to push to a fight, it would seem.*]

BERNIE: I don't mind a fight about something real! You could be a home for me—that's real! [*Then, as abruptly, he lapses gloomily, sitting on a stool.* FRANK'S *voice is heard lifted in a scene.*] Excuse me for blowing my wig. I can't escape that voice tonight . . . it follows me everywhere I go. [*Smirking.*] Listen to him . . . he's ready to give that dark sterling silver quality to the best available parts. He needs you, dear.

GEORGIE: You're Frank's friend—you're thinking of his future—I like that. But what about mine . . . ?

BERNIE: [*Gloomily.*] Right, right, only right . . . I can't tell you what to do, can I? But how can a man be so disgruntled and still live? [*Face averted, he runs a nervous hand through his hair. She moves to him sympathetically.*]

GEORGIE: I hate to see you this way, troubled, contrite—[*He gets to his feet and moves away, saying harshly.*]

BERNIE: Lecture me no lectures!

GEORGIE: Now, why don't you stop clenching your fists to hide your tenderness and pity? [*Then, smiling.*] Put your eyes down before they burn a hole in me. . . .

BERNIE: [*Staring at her.*] Are you leaving him?

GEORGIE: Don't be wilful, dear. You see, you'll go on—[*She stops, for* BERNIE *has abruptly turned his head and is listening sharply to the stage play; then he bounds to doorway, ears even bigger;* GEORGIE *joins him, not knowing what is wrong. Off-stage we hear running feet and excited whispers.* FRANK'S *voice has risen high, bellowing and angry.* BERNIE *brings an excited, half hysterical* NANCY *into dressing-room. Dresser appears in doorway, waiting for orders.*]

BERNIE: [*To* NANCY, *impatiently.*] Shh, quiet! What happened? Shh!

NANCY: [*Sobbing.*] He began to hit me, Bernie . . . on stage. I can't bear it! I don't know what he's doing out there—he's even changed the lines!

BERNIE: [*Mordant and cutting.*] Quiet, quiet, this is an opening night! [*Turning, harshly.*] Close the door, Ralph—get back to your job! [RALPH *obeys; excitedly* NANCY *continues.*]

NANCY: He's—he's—his eyes are red—he looks right at you and doesn't see you! He—I began to cry—he took me and shook me like a doll!

BERNIE: [*Sharply.*] Come on now, it didn't hurt that much! That's the scene!

NANCY: To shake me and slap me like that? And to change the lines? I didn't know what to answer him!

BERNIE: Don't raise your voice—the curtain is up. [*She sullenly rubs her smarting face;* GEORGIE *anxiously returns.*]

GEORGIE: Are you all right, dear?

NANCY: Yes, I'm all right, Mrs. Elgin . . . I'm all right. . . .

BERNIE: Now stop sulking, junior miss—go up and change for your last act.

NANCY: [*Standing.*] Yes, I will, Bernie,

I will . . . it was just such a shock, Mrs. Elgin.

GEORGIE: We understand, dear. . . .

BERNIE: I hope that's the biggest shock you ever get. Go on, now. [NANCY *goes to door, wary of* BERNIE'S *mood.*]

BERNIE: Come here.

NANCY: [*Turning.*] Me?

BERNIE: Come here. . . . [*She slowly comes to him; unbending, he kisses her unsmilingly. She is happy again.*] Go up and change.

NANCY: Yes, I will, Bernie, yes . . . gee. . . . [*She goes. Scowling,* BERNIE *goes to door and looks out,* GEORGIE *following him.*]

GEORGIE: It was spooky—he's wild out there—he almost knocked her down.

BERNIE: [*Impatiently.*] I've been waiting *forty minutes* for that burst! If he can play scenes like that, let him do what he wants. [*They stand at door listening out; they can hear* FRANK. *After a moment* BERNIE *murmurs.*] Here comes the curtain. . . . [*Out of sight the curtain has come down on the second act. Applause is strong. Sounds of swarming stagehands are heard.* BERNIE *and* GEORGIE *step aside;* FRANK *enters like a man in a perspiring trance, heavy and hoarse, keyed into the just completed scene.*]

FRANK: Close that window. . . .

GEORGIE: There's no window in here. . . . [FRANK IS *breathing heavily, like a boxer between two late rounds.* BERNIE, *waving* RALPH *away, closes door.*]

FRANK: I'm dripping wet. . . .

GEORGIE: [*Warily.*] Get your clothes off. . . . [*He throws off her attentions with a lifted arm and, half sobbing, waves an embittered fist at the world.*]

FRANK: I couldn't hold myself back! Belted, belted! Did I hurt the kid? [*Seeing* BERNIE.] Bernie, I couldn't help it, Bernie! I started to go and I couldn't help it!

BERNIE: Sit down and take it easy.

GEORGIE: Sit down, Frank, sit down.

FRANK: I'm sorry, kid, forgive me . . . it just came out that way! That's what he should do there, the Judge—no one wants him, not even his grandchild! And suddenly I got the image—they're caging a lion—like you shove him in the face! Like they do in the circus, with chairs and brooms! And I couldn't hold it back. . . .

BERNIE: [*Firmly.*] I didn't want you to hold it back! [*Exhausted,* FRANK *sits down.*]

GEORGIE: Now get your jacket off. [*Standing behind him, she peels off dinner jacket and hangs it up. Intermission music starts far away.* FRANK *takes off his collar and tie.*]

FRANK: This is limp . . . I'll need a fresh one. . . . [*Then.*] I hope I didn't hurt that kid.

BERNIE: Don't worry—she's fine.

FRANK: [*Sighing, relieved.*] Well, nobody's sore at anybody, then. . . . Golly, I was wild out there for a minute. They made me sore out front, too—they're sitting on their hands.

BERNIE: [*Mordantly.*] They may be very moved.

FRANK: [*Growling but pleased.*] Don't kid the ugly man. . . .

BERNIE: [*Soberly.*] I'm not kidding—your performance can only be a big surprise.

FRANK: That's swell—I hope so! Say, did you see that hospital scene? She's good, that Mabel Beck! [*Turning.*] Here are some more wires. Someone must remember Poppa. Here's one from Sue Lewis . . . ". . . renewal of a great career. Am out front rooting. Much affection and regards. . . ." [*Wire seems to affect* FRANK *in a strange way; he looks at* GEORGIE *furtively, something on his mind, before saying briskly.*] Let's see . . . what am I wearing next?

GEORGIE: The smoking jacket, dear.

FRANK: [*To* BERNIE.] Jo-Jo, the dog-faced boy—I wish I had four hands. Well, as long as you excused me for going wild. . . .

BERNIE: [*Starting for door.*] Keep going wild and I'll bless you in Macy's window. Here's Philip Cook, Esquire—he'll do *even more* than *I* will in Macy's window! Be back. [BERNIE *exits, leaving the newly-arrived* COOK *in the room.*]

FRANK: How is it out front, Mr. Cook?

COOK: I only know what I read in the papers. How do you feel?

FRANK: Good, good—pluperfect good. [*Seated,* FRANK *is sipping milk at shelf.*]

COOK: The reactions in the lobby are pretty good. You hungry?

FRANK: This? It's for my voice.

COOK: [*Uneasily.*] Frank, a lot of things . . . are said in the heat and toil of the day. I hope you'll accept my apologies. . . .

FRANK: Sure, we all know how those things can happen. [*With a sudden thought, turning.*] Of course, you include my wife, too, in your apologies?

COOK: [*Quickly.*] Of course, Mrs. Elgin, I include you, too—of course!

FRANK: Then start by taking your hat off—you're not at a smoker, Mr. Cook. [COOK *is very thrown by this attitude;* GEORGIE *silently watches the scene.*] This is the first polite word you've had for either one of us. And I think I know why. You—

COOK: Frank, it's human—if we have to protect a show—naturally—

FRANK: You want me to sign a run-of-the-play contract before the morning papers are out, for half of what I'm worth.

COOK: [*Removing his hat.*] I'm really very sorry, Frank, and you have to believe me on a thing like that. As to different contractual arrangements . . . it *was* on my mind. . . . [*Bowing stiffly, he slithers sideways out of the room.*]

FRANK: I guess *that* put a pimple on his nose. [*Then, alarmed.*] I hope I didn't say too much. . . .

GEORGIE: [*Laughing.*] He thinks you're wonderful in the show, but he wouldn't have the grace to say so. Just you keep your self respect, the way you have it out on that stage tonight. And remember, Frank, don't forget—it isn't necessary to be liked by every Tom, Dick, and Harry Truman, even if he's president! [*She has brought down his smoking-jacket and he stands and slips into it, humming his favorite little tune.*]

FRANK: You're a real scrapper—I've always admired your nerve.

GEORGIE: Still some shine on your face.

FRANK: I'll fix it. [*Thoughtfully, going to mirror.*] That was nice of Sue, that wire. . . .

GEORGIE: [*Levelly.*] Yes, it was. . . . [*Then.*] You're handsome tonight.

FRANK: [*Slowly, turning.*] Am I . . . ? [*Seriously.*] Well, after tonight—catch this one and tuck it in your memory book—you'll never again have to ask why you married me.

[GEORGIE *asks quietly, as she puts handkerchief in his pocket.*]

GEORGIE: Won't I . . . ? [*A serious moment is about to take place, but* BERNIE *breaks it by returning with a tap on the door first.* FRANK *turns for his collar.*]

BERNIE: Friend Mabel sends her love.

FRANK: [*Abruptly.*] Don't wanna be a

pest, kid, but can I show you something? No collar and tie—just a collar button.

BERNIE: You mean go on that way?

FRANK: Yes, that's the way they arrest him, without a collar—from collar button to collar button in thirty years! Get it?

BERNIE: [Half smiling.] It's a real point —leave it in. [RALPH appears briefly in doorway, saying, "They're ready, Mr. Elgin." FRANK has gone back to shelf and is fingering a telegram as he looks at himself in mirror. LARRY's call of "Places, places. Third act, please. Places," is heard outside until it brings him to doorway.]

LARRY: You ready, Frank?

FRANK: [Unturning.] Yes, thanks, kid, all ready. . . . [BERNIE grabs LARRY by arm as he is about to go.]

BERNIE: Larry, don't take the curtain up till they're all seated—the front rows in particular.

LARRY: [Grinning.] If the front rows had the balcony's manners . . . what a world this could be! [He goes; his third act cry is heard as a distant echo for quite some time. FRANK turns, speaking with hesitant nervousness.]

FRANK: Georgie . . . I can be wrong most of the time . . . but any idea you have, if you want to leave me—don't. [BERNIE seems about to leave at doorway, but FRANK stops him by crossing over.] I'm deliberately talking in front of a third person. Maybe I should do it more often— sometimes it's a big relief to fall on your face in public. [Turning.] Am I wrong, Georgie? Aren't you setting up Sue Lewis to put in your place? Don't leave me, darling. Give me a chance. I love you. . . .

[GEORGIE pauses for her answer; one of her hands creeps up to lapel of FRANK's coat.]

GEORGIE: Frank, I certainly didn't want to bring up any of this tonight. But you did . . . so let's have the whole truth. I married you for happiness, Frank . . . and, if necessary, I'll leave you for the same reason. Right now I don't know where I stand.

FRANK: [Humbly.] You don't . . . ?

[GEORGIE drops her hand, steps back a little, carefully picking her way.]

GEORGIE: No. Because neither of us has really changed. And yet I'm sure that both our lives are at some sort of turning point . . . there's some real new element of hope here . . . I don't know what. But I'm

uncertain . . . and you, Frank, have to be strong enough to bear that uncertainty. . . .

FRANK: [Hushed.] I think I know what you mean. . . . [LARRY looks in just long enough to say, "We're waiting, Frank." FRANK says, nervously.] They're waiting, dear. I . . . I don't know how to say this . . . but no matter what happens, you have saved me, Georgie . . . you and Bernie. [Kissing her, then pulling himself together.] I think I have a chance. [He turns and exits firmly. After a moment, BERNIE seems about to say something to GEORGIE, but she is moved and withdrawn. BERNIE slips out, muttering.]

BERNIE: I'd better show my face on stage a moment—rah-rah stuff. [UNGER, wearing a dinner-jacket, enters, almost brushing BERNIE; he is jubilant.]

UNGER: Frank is magnificent! He's really showing me what my play is all about!

GEORGIE: [Smiling.] He's on-stage— they're going up.

UNGER: You don't look like a veteran of all the wars tonight! You must be damned proud! I know my aunt is—we're sitting together. She's showing all the proprietary interest of a mother hen.

GEORGIE: [Quietly.] Give your aunt my regards.

UNGER: I will. . . . [He comes to her sweetly, wanting to kiss her or touch her hands. She attempts the same, but it is clumsy and fizzles out; he goes. GEORGIE slowly walks to door; she is thoughtful and inward as she looks out. BERNIE returns, his spirits slightly lifted. Intermission music dies away. LARRY's cautioning voice is heard: "Quiet back-stage, please, we're going up . . . quiet, please . . ."]

BERNIE: Everything ship-shape. . . .

GEORGIE: It was sweet of you to send him all those wires.

BERNIE: [Impassively.] Who told you?

GEORGIE: Guessed. How many did you send?

BERNIE: Nine or ten. And you?

GEORGIE: Four or five.

BERNIE: There she goes . . . ! [Curtain has gone up. GEORGIE and BERNIE are looking out. A strained pause is followed by a rumble of applause.]

BERNIE: [Mordantly.] Applauding a third act entrance . . . surprise follows surprise. Well, this is the act where he wraps up the show and walks off with the town. [*He has gone to get his topcoat from hook;* GEORGIE *is leaning against door jamb, saying to herself.*]

GEORGIE: He's handsome tonight. . . .

BERNIE: [*Turning down to her.*] I'll go out front and watch. Goodnight, Georgie. [*But she has crossed to make-up shelf, saying.*]

GEORGIE: He'll come off dripping again. . . . [*Humming* FRANK'S *snatch of tune, she is picking up some kleenex tissues and a towel; when she turns* BERNIE *has moved in closer to her, almost forcibly making her aware of his presence.*]

BERNIE: Goodnight, Georgie. [*They are face to face; she speaks gently.*]

GEORGIE: Goodnight, Bernardo.

BERNIE: [*Wryly.*] I don't know . . . maybe a magician *does* live in this frail, foolish body, but he certainly can't work wonders for himself! You'll never leave him. . . . [*He has been fishing in a pocket; now he jerks his hand out, almost angrily, it would seem.*] I keep running out of cigarettes!

GEORGIE: [*Gently.*] You smoke too much.

BERNIE: [*Mockingly.*] You are impertinent, Madame! [*Then, longingly.*] And steadfast. And loyal . . . reliable. I like that in a woman!

GEORGIE: [*Hand on his arm.*] Wrestle, Bernie . . . you may win a blessing. But stay unregenerate. Life knocks the sauciness out of us soon enough. [*Lonely, arch and rueful, he looks at her a moment before stepping in and kissing her lightly on the lips. Then he turns, throws his folded coat over one shoulder and slowly leaves room. For a moment she wears a sad and yearning look; finally a towel in her hand calls her back to reality. She crosses and takes* FRANK'S *robe off wall and starts for door. Meanwhile* FRANK'S *stage voice is heard, playing a quiet but powerful scene. A thought makes* GEORGIE *stop. She goes back to dressing shelf, takes down* SUE'S *telegram, considers it quickly, comes to a decision, crumples it into a ball and throws it into trash-basket; and then, head up, slowly walks out of the room with* FRANK'S *robe across one arm.*]

SLOW CURTAIN

TENNESSEE WILLIAMS

WILLIAMS IN ART AND MORALS: AN ANXIOUS FOE OF UNTRUTH [1] by Don Ross

ROSS: Some people accuse you of filling your plays with sordid characters. Are they right?

WILLIAMS: I don't think Blanche Du Bois was sordid. I think she was rather noble. I don't think deeply troubled people are sordid. . . . Tell me who was sordid in *The Glass Menagerie?* In *The Rose Tattoo* Serafina was earthy and sensual. These things can be very beautiful, I have always thought. . . .

ROSS: Are you a moralist?

WILLIAMS: I would say so. I have a distinct moral attitude. I wouldn't say message. I'm not polemical, but I have a distinct attitude toward good and evil in life and people. I think any of my plays examined closely will indicate what I regard as evil. I think I regard hypocrisy and mendacity as almost the cardinal sins. It seems they are the ones to which I am most hostile. . . . The moral contribution of my plays is that they expose what I consider to be untrue. But I don't want to pretend that I'm a great moral evangelist. I'm an entertainer and a playwright—a profession that is at least partly entertainer.

ROSS: Are your plays optimistic or pessimistic?

WILLIAMS: I think it's very necessary to discover those things in life one can believe in. . . . In that sense I am mostly optimistic. I believe very strongly in the existence of good. I believe that honesty, understanding, sympathy and even sexual passion are good. So I don't think I'm a pessimist altogether. I find life a mysterious and terrifying experience.

[1] Don Ross, from "Williams in Art and Morals: An Anxious Foe of Untruth," *New York Herald Tribune,* CXVI (March 3, 1957), Sec. 4, p. 1. Reprinted by permission of the *New York Herald Tribune* and MCA Artists, Ltd.

THE TIMELESS WORLD OF A PLAY [2]

. . . Plays in the tragic tradition offer us a view of certain moral values in violent juxtaposition. Because we do not participate, except as spectators, we can view them clearly, within the limits of our emotional equipment. These people on the stage do not return our looks. We do not have to answer their questions nor make any sign of being in company with them, nor do we have to compete with their virtues nor resist their offenses. All at once, for this reason, we are able to *see* them! Our hearts are wrung by recognition and pity. . . .

[yet] So successfully have we disguised from ourselves the intensity of our own feelings, the sensibility of our own hearts, that plays in the tragic tradition have begun to seem untrue. For a couple of hours we may surrender ourselves to a world of fiercely illuminated values in conflict, but when the stage is covered and the auditorium lighted, almost immediately there is a recoil of disbelief . . . we have convinced ourselves once more that life has as little resemblance to the curiously stirring and meaningful occurrences on the stage as a jingle has to an elegy of Rilke.

This modern condition of his theater audience is something that an author must know in advance. The diminishing influence of life's destroyer, time, must be somehow worked into the context of his play. Perhaps it is a certain foolery, a certain distortion toward the grotesque, which will solve the problem for him. Perhaps it is only restraint, putting a mute on the strings that would like to break all bounds. But almost surely, unless he contrives in some way to relate the dimensions of his tragedy to the dimensions of a world in which time is *included* —he will be left among his magnificent debris on a dark stage, muttering to himself: "Those fools . . ."

[2] Tennessee Williams, from "The Timeless World of a Play," *The Rose Tattoo* (New York, 1951), pp. viii-ix. Copyright 1951 by Tennessee Williams. Reprinted by permission of New Directions.

TENNESSEE WILLIAMS

The Rose Tattoo

AUTHOR'S PRODUCTION NOTES

The locale of the play is a village populated mostly by Sicilians somewhere along the Gulf Coast between New Orleans and Mobile. The time is the present.

As the curtain rises we hear a Sicilian folk-singer with a guitar. He is singing. At each major division of the play this song is resumed and it is completed at the final curtain.

The first lighting is extremely romantic. We see a frame cottage, in a rather poor state of repair, with a palm tree leaning dreamily over one end of it and a flimsy little entrance porch, with spindling pillars, sagging steps and broken rails, at the other end. The setting seems almost tropical, for, in addition to the palm trees, there are tall canes with feathery fronds and a fairly thick growth of pampas grass. These are growing on the slope of an embankment along which runs a highway, which is not visible, but the cars passing on it can occasionally be heard. The house has a rear door which cannot be seen. The facing wall of the cottage is either a transparency that lifts for the interior scenes, or is cut away to reveal the interior.

The romantic first lighting is that of late dusk, the sky a delicate blue with an opalescent shimmer more like water than air. Delicate points of light appear and disappear like lights reflected in a twilight harbor. The curtain rises well above the low tin roof of the cottage.

We see an interior that is as colorful as a booth at a carnival. There are many religious articles and pictures of ruby and gilt, the brass cage of a gaudy parrot, a large bowl of goldfish, cutglass decanters and vases, rose-patterned wallpaper and a rose-colored carpet; everything is exclamatory in its brightness like the projection of a woman's heart passionately in love. There is a small shrine against the wall between the rooms, consisting of a prie-dieu and a little statue of the Madonna in a starry blue robe and gold crown. Before this burns always a vigil light in its ruby glass cup. Our purpose is to show these gaudy, childlike mysteries with sentiment and humor in equal measure, without ridicule and with respect for the religious yearnings they symbolize.

An outdoor sign indicates that SERAFINA, *whose home the cottage is, does* "SEWING." *The interior furnishings give evidence of this vocation. The most salient feature is a collection of dressmaker's dummies. There are at least seven of these life-size mannequins, in various shapes and attitudes. [They will have to be made especially for the play as their purpose is not realistic. They have pliable joints so that their positions can be changed. Their arms terminate at the wrist. In all their attitudes there is an air of drama, somewhat like the poses of declamatory actresses of the old school.] Principal among them are a widow and a bride who face each other in violent attitudes, as though having a shrill argument, in the parlor. The widow's costume is complete from black-veiled hat to black slippers. The bride's featureless head wears a chaplet of orange blossoms from which is depended a flowing veil of white marquisette, and her net gown is trimmed in white satin—lustrous, immaculate.*

Most of the dummies and sewing equipment are confined to the dining room which is also SERAFINA'S *work room. In that room there is a tall cupboard on top of which are several dusty bottles of imported Sicilian Spumanti.*

SALVATORE.	TERESA.
VIVI.	FATHER DE LEO.
BRUNO.	A DOCTOR.
ASSUNTA.	MISS YORKE.
ROSA DELLE ROSE.	FLORA.
SERAFINA DELLE ROSE.	BESSIE.
ESTELLE HOHENGARTEN.	JACK HUNTER.
THE STREGA.	THE SALESMAN.
GIUSEPPINA.	ALVARO MANGIACAVALLO.
PEPPINA.	A MAN.
VIOLETTA.	ANOTHER MAN.
MARIELLA.	

ACT ONE

It is the hour that the Italians call "prima sera," the beginning of dusk. Between the house and the palm tree burns the female star with an almost emerald lustre.

The mothers of the neighborhood are beginning to call their children home to supper, in voices near and distant, urgent and tender, like the variable notes of wind and water. There are three children: BRUNO, SALVATORE, *and* VIVI, *ranged in front of the house, one with a red paper kite, one with a hoop, and the little girl with a doll dressed as a clown. They are in attitudes of momentary repose, all looking up at something—a bird or a plane passing over—as the mothers' voices call them.*

BRUNO: The white flags are flying at the Coast Guard station.

SALVATORE: That means fair weather.

VIVI: I love fair weather.

GIUSEPPINA: Vivi! Vieni mangiare! [1]

PEPPINA: Salvatore! Come home!

VIOLETTA: Bruno! Come home to supper!

[*The calls are repeated tenderly, musically.*]

[*The interior of the house begins to be visible.* SERAFINA DELLE ROSE *is seen on the parlor sofa, waiting for her husband* ROSARIO's *return. Between the curtains is a table set lovingly for supper; there is wine in a silver icebucket and a great bowl of roses.*]

[SERAFINA *looks like a plump little opera singer in the role of Madame Butterfly. Her black hair is done in a high pompadour that glitters like wet coal. A rose is held in place by glittering jet hairpins. Her voluptuous figure is sheathed in pale rose silk. On her feet are dainty slippers with glittering buckles and French heels. It is apparent from the way she sits, with such plump dignity, that she is wearing a tight girdle. She sits very erect, in an attitude of forced composure, her ankles daintily crossed and her plump little hands holding a yellow paper fan on which is painted a rose. Jewels gleam on her fingers, her wrists and her ears and about her throat. Expectancy shines in her eyes. For a few* moments she seems to be posing for a picture.*]

[ROSA DELLE ROSE *appears at the side of the house, near the palm tree.* ROSA, *the daughter of the house, is a young girl of twelve. She is pretty and vivacious, and has about her a particular intensity in her every gesture.*]

SERAFINA: Rosa, where are you?

ROSA: Here, Mama.

SERAFINA: What are you doing, cara? [2]

ROSA: I've caught twelve lightning bugs.

[*The cracked voice of* ASSUNTA *is heard, approaching.*]

SERAFINA: I hear Assunta! Assunta!

[ASSUNTA *appears and goes into the house, Rosa following her in.* ASSUNTA *is an old woman in a gray shawl, bearing a basket of herbs, for she is a fattuchiere, a woman who practises a simple sort of medicine. As she enters the children scatter.*]

ASSUNTA: Vengo, vengo. Buona sera. Buona sera. [3] There is something wild in the air, no wind but everything's moving.

SERAFINA: I don't see nothing moving and neither do you.

ASSUNTA: Nothing is moving so you can see it moving, but everything is moving, and I can hear the star-noises. Hear them? Hear the star-noises?

SERAFINA: Naw, them ain't the star-noises. They're termites, eating the house

---

[1] Come and eat!

[2] Dear.

[3] I'm coming, I'm coming. Good evening. Good evening.

up. What are you peddling, old woman, in those little white bags?

ASSUNTA: Powder, wonderful powder. You drop a pinch of it in your husband's coffee.

SERAFINA: What is it good for?

ASSUNTA: What is a husband good for! I made it out of the dry blood of a goat.

SERAFINA: Davero! [4]

ASSUNTA: Wonderful stuff! But be sure you put it in his coffee at supper, not in his breakfast coffee.

SERAFINA: My husband don't need no powder!

ASSUNTA: Excuse me, Baronessa. Maybe he needs the opposite kind of a powder, I got that, too.

SERAFINA: Naw, naw, *no* kind of powder at all, old woman. [*She lifts her head with a proud smile.*]

[*Outside the sound of a truck is heard approaching up on the highway.*]

ROSA: [*Joyfully.*] Papa's truck!

[*They stand listening for a moment, but the truck goes by without stopping*].

SERAFINA: [*To* ASSUNTA.] That wasn't him. It wasn't no 10-ton truck. It didn't rattle the shutters! Assunta, Assunta, undo a couple of hooks, the dress is tight on me!

ASSUNTA: Is it true what I told you?

SERAFINA: Yes, it is true, but nobody needed to tell me. Assunta, I'll tell you something which maybe you won't believe.

ASSUNTA: It is impossible to tell me anything that I don't believe.

SERAFINA: Va bene! Senti, Assunta!—I knew that I had conceived on the very night of conception! [*There is a phrase of music as she says this.*]

ASSUNTA: Ahhhh?

SERAFINA: Senti! That night I woke up with a burning pain on me, here, on my left breast! A pain like a needle, quick, quick, hot little stitches. I turned on the light, I uncovered my breast!—On it I saw the rose tattoo of my husband!

ASSUNTA: Rosario's tattoo?

SERAFINA: On me, on my breast, his tattoo! And when I saw it I knew that I had conceived . . .

[SERAFINA *throws her head back, smiling proudly, and opens her paper fan.* ASSUNTA *stares at her gravely, then rises and hands her basket to* SERAFINA.]

ASSUNTA: Ecco! [5] *You* sell the powders! [*She starts toward the door.*]

SERAFINA: You don't believe that I saw it?

ASSUNTA: [*Stopping.*] Did Rosario see it?

SERAFINA: I screamed. But when he woke up, it was gone. It only lasted a moment. But I *did* see it, and I *did* know, when I seen it, that I had conceived, that in my body another rose was growing!

ASSUNTA: Did he believe that you saw it?

SERAFINA: No. He laughed.—He laughed and I cried . . .

ASSUNTA: And he took you into his arms, and you stopped crying!

SERAFINA: Si! [6]

ASSUNTA: Serafina, for you everything has got to be different. A sign, a miracle, a wonder of some kind. You speak to Our Lady. You say that she answers your questions. She nods or shakes Her head at you. Look, Serafina, underneath Our Lady you have a candle. The wind through the shutters makes the candle flicker. The shadows move. Our Lady seems to be nodding!

SERAFINA: She gives me signs.

ASSUNTA: Only to you? Because you are more important? The wife of a barone? Serafina! In Sicily they called his uncle a baron, but in Sicily everybody's a baron that owns a piece of the land and a separate house for the goats!

SERAFINA: They said to his uncle "Voscenza!" [7] and they kissed their hands to him! [*She kisses the back of her hand repeatedly, with vehemence.*]

ASSUNTA: His uncle in Sicily!—So—but here what's he do? Drives a truck of bananas?

SERAFINA: [*Blurting out.*] No! *Not* bananas!

ASSUNTA: Not bananas?

SERAFINA: Stai zitta [*She makes a warning gesture.*]—No—Vieni qui, Assunta! [8] [*She beckons her mysteriously. Assunta approaches.*]

ASSUNTA: Cosa dici? [9]

SERAFINA: On top of the truck is bananas! But underneath—something else!

ASSUNTA: Che altre cose? [10]

---

[4] Really!
[5] There!   [6] Yes.   [7] "Your Excellency!"
[8] Keep quiet—No—Come here, Assunta!
[9] What are you saying?   [10] What else?

SERAFINA: Whatever it is that the Brothers Romano want hauled out of the state, he hauls it for them, underneath the bananas! [*She nods her head importantly.*] And money, he gets so much it spills from his pockets! Soon I don't have to make dresses!

ASSUNTA: [*Turning away.*] Soon I think you will have to make a black veil!

SERAFINA: Tonight is the last time he does it! Tomorrow he quits hauling stuff for the Brothers Romano! He pays for the 10-ton truck and works for himself. We live with dignity in America, then! Own truck! Own house! And in the house will be everything electric! Stove—deep-freeze—*tutto!* [11]—But tonight, stay with me . . . I can't swallow my heart!—Not till I hear the truck stop in front of the house and his key in the lock of the door!—When I call him, and him shouting back, *"Sì, sono qui!"* [12] In his hair, Assunta, he has—oil of roses. And when I wake up at night—the air, the dark room's—full of—roses . . . Each time is the first time with him. Time doesn't pass . . .

[*ASSUNTA picks up a small clock on the cupboard and holds it to her ear.*]

ASSUNTA: Tick, tick, tick, tick.—You say the clock is a liar.

SERAFINA: No, the clock is a fool. I don't listen to it. My clock is my heart and my heart don't say tick-tick, it says love-love! And now I have two hearts in me, both of them saying love-love!

[*A truck is heard approaching, then passes. SERAFINA drops her fan. ASSUNTA opens a bottle of spumanti with a loud pop. SERAFINA cries out.*]

ASSUNTA: Stai tranquilla! Calmati! [13] [*She pours her a glass of wine.*] Drink this wine and before the glass is empty he'll be in your arms!

SERAFINA: I can't—swallow my heart!

ASSUNTA: A woman must not have a heart that is too big to swallow!

[*She crosses to the door.*]

SERAFINA: Stay with me!

ASSUNTA: I have to visit a woman who drank rat poison because of a heart too big for her to swallow.

[*ASSUNTA leaves. SERAFINA returns indolently to the sofa. She lifts her hands to her great swelling breasts and murmurs aloud.*]

SERAFINA: Oh, it's so wonderful, having *two* lives in the body, not *one* but two! [*Her hands slide down to her belly, luxuriously.*] I am heavy with life, I am big, big, big with life! [*She picks up a bowl of roses and goes into the back room.*]

[*ESTELLE HOHENGARTEN appears in front of the house. She is a thin blonde woman in a dress of Egyptian design, and her blonde hair has an unnatural gloss in the clear, greenish dusk. ROSA appears from behind the house, calling out.*]

ROSA: Twenty lightning bugs, Mama!

ESTELLE: Little girl? Little girl?

ROSA: [*Resentfully.*] Are you talking to me? [*There is a pause.*]

ESTELLE: Come here. [*She looks ROSA over curiously.*] You're a twig off the old rose-bush.—Is the lady that does the sewing in the house?

ROSA: Mama's at home.

ESTELLE: I'd like to see her.

ROSA: Mama?

SERAFINA: Dimi? [14]

ROSA :There's a lady to see you.

SERAFINA: Oh. Tell her to wait in the parlor. [*ESTELLE enters and stares curiously about. She picks up a small framed picture on the cupboard. She is looking at it as SERAFINA enters with a bowl of roses. SERAFINA speaks sharply.*] That is my husband's picture.

ESTELLE: Oh!—I thought it was Valentino.—With a mustache.

SERAFINA: [*Putting the bowl down on the table.*] You want something?

ESTELLE: Yes. I heard you do sewing.

SERAFINA: Yes, I do sewing.

ESTELLE: How fast can you make a shirt for me?

SERAFINA: That all depends. [*She takes the picture from ESTELLE and puts it back on the cupboard.*]

ESTELLE: I got the piece of silk with me. I want it made into a shirt for a man I'm in love with. Tomorrow's the anniversary of the day we met . . . [*She unwraps a piece of rose-colored silk which she holds up like a banner.*]

SERAFINA: [*Involuntarily.*] Che bella stoffa! [15] Oh, that would be wonderful stuff for a lady's blouse or for a pair of pyjamas!

---

[11] *Everything!*   [12] Yes, I am here!
[13] Take it easy! Be calm!

[14] Tell me?   [15] What lovely **material**!

ESTELLE: I want a man's shirt made with it.

SERAFINA: Silk this color for a shirt for a *man*?

ESTELLE: This man is wild like a Gypsy.

SERAFINA: A woman should not encourage a man to be wild.

ESTELLE: A man that's wild is hard for a woman to hold, huh? But if he was tame—would the woman want to hold him? Huh?

SERAFINA: I am a married woman in business. I don't know nothing about wild men and wild women and I don't have much time—so . . .

ESTELLE: I'll pay you twice what you ask me.

[*Outside there is the sound of the goat bleating and the jingle of its harness; then the crash of wood splintering.*]

ROSA: [*Suddenly appearing at the door.*] Mama, the black goat is loose! [*She runs down the steps and stands watching the goat.* SERAFINA *crosses to the door.*]

THE STREGA: [*In the distance.*] Hyeh, Billy, hyeh, hyeh, Billy!

ESTELLE: I'll pay you three times the price that you ask me for it.

SERAFINA: [*Shouting.*] Watch the goat! Don't let him get in our yard! [*To* ESTELLE.]—if I ask you five dollars?

ESTELLE: I will pay you fifteen. Make it twenty; money is not the object. But it's got to be ready tomorrow.

SERAFINA: Tomorrow?

ESTELLE: Twenty-five dollars! [SERAFINA *nods slowly with a stunned look.* ESTELLE *smiles.*] I've got the measurements with me.

SERAFINA: Pin the measurements and your name on the silk and the shirt will be ready tomorrow.

ESTELLE: My name is Estelle Hohengarten.

[*A little boy races excitedly into the yard.*]

THE BOY: Rosa, Rosa, the black goat's in your yard!

ROSA: [*Calling.*] Mama, the goat's in the yard!

SERAFINA: [*Furiously, forgetting her visitor.*] Il becco della strega!—Scusi![16] [*She runs out onto the porch.*] Catch him, catch him before he gets at the vines!

[16] The goat of the witch! Excuse me!

[ROSA *dances gleefully.* THE STREGA *runs into the yard. She has a mop of wild grey hair and is holding her black skirts up from her bare hairy legs. The sound of the goat's bleating and the jingling of his harness is heard in the windy blue dusk.*]

[SERAFINA *descends the porch steps. The high-heeled slippers, the tight silk skirt and the dignity of a baronessa make the descent a little gingerly. Arrived in the yard, she directs the goat-chase imperiously with her yellow paper fan, pointing this way and that, exclaiming in Italian.*]

[*She fans herself rapidly and crosses back of the house. The goat evidently makes a sudden charge. Screaming,* SERAFINA *rushes back to the front of the house, all out of breath, the glittering pompadour beginning to tumble down over her forehead.*]

SERAFINA: Rosa! you go in the house! Don't look at the Strega!

[*Alone in the parlor,* ESTELLE *takes the picture of* ROSARIO. *Impetuously, she thrusts it in her purse and runs from the house, just as* SERAFINA *returns to the front yard.*]

ROSA: [*Refusing to move.*] Why do you call her a witch?

[SERAFINA *seizes her daughter's arm and propels her into the house.*]

SERAFINA: She has a white eye and every finger is crooked! [*She pulls* ROSA's *arm.*]

ROSA: She has a cataract, Mama, and her fingers are crooked because she has rheumatism!

SERAFINA: Malocchio—the evil eye—that's what she's got! And her fingers are crooked because she shook hands with the devil. Go in the house and wash your face with salt water and throw the salt water away! *Go in! Quick!* She's coming!

[*The boy utters a cry of triumph.*]

[SERAFINA *crosses abruptly to the porch. At the same moment the boy runs triumphantly around the house leading the captured goat by its bell harness. It is a middle-sized black goat with great yellow eyes.* THE STREGA *runs behind with the broken rope. As the grotesque little procession runs before her—*THE STREGA, *the goat and the children—*SERAFINA *cries out shrilly.*]

She crouches over and covers her face.
THE STREGA *looks back at her with a derisive cackle.*]
SERAFINA: Malocchio! Malocchio! [17]
[17] Evil eye! Evil eye!

[*Shielding her face with one hand,* SERAFINA *makes the sign of the horns with the other to ward off the evil eye. And the scene dims out.*]

Scene Two

It is just before dawn the next day. FATHER DE LEO, *a priest, and several black-shawled women, including* ASSUNTA, *are standing outside the house. The interior of the house is very dim.*

GUISEPPINA: There is a light in the house.

PEPPINA: I hear the sewing machine!

VIOLETTA: There's Serafina! She's working. She's holding up a piece of rose-colored silk.

ASSUNTA: She hears our voices.

VIOLETTA: She's dropped the silk to the floor and she's . . .

GUISEPPINA: Holding her throat! I think she . . .

PEPPINA: Who's going to tell her?

VIOLETTA: Father De Leo will tell her.

FATHER DE LEO: I think a woman should tell her. I think Assunta must tell her that Rosario is dead.

ASSUNTA: It will not be necessary to tell her. She will know when she sees us.

[*It grows lighter inside the house.* SERAFINA *is standing in a frozen attitude with her hand clutching her throat and her eyes staring fearfully toward the sound of voices.*]

ASSUNTA: I think she already knows what we have come to tell her!

FATHER DE LEO: Andiamo, Signore! [1] We must go to the door.

[*They climb the porch steps.* ASSUNTA *opens the door.*]

SERAFINA: [*Gasping.*] Don't speak!

[*She retreats from the group, stumbling blindly backwards among the dressmaker's dummies. With a gasp she turns and runs out the back door. In a few moments we see her staggering about outside near the palm tree. She comes down in front of the house, and stares blindly off into the distance.*]

SERAFINA: [*Wildly.*] Don't speak!

[*The voices of the women begin keening in the house.* ASSUNTA *comes out and approaches* SERAFINA *with her arms extended.* SERAFINA *slumps to her knees, whispering hoarsely:* "Don't speak!" ASSUNTA *envelopes her in the gray shawl of pity as the scene dims out.*]

[1] Let's go, ladies.

Scene Three

It is noon of the same day. ASSUNTA *is removing a funeral wreath on the door of the house. A doctor and* FATHER DE LEO *are on the porch.*

THE DOCTOR: She's lost the baby. [AS-SUNTA *utters a low moan of pity and crosses herself.*] Serafina's a very strong woman and that won't kill her. But she is trying not to breathe. She's got to be watched and not allowed out of the bed. [*He removes a hypodermic and a small package from his bag and hands them to* ASSUNTA.]—This is morphia. In the arm with the needle if she screams or struggles to get up again.

ASSUNTA: Capisco! [1]

[1] I understand.

FATHER DE LEO: One thing I want to make plain. The body of Rosario must not be burned.

THE DOCTOR: Have you seen the "body of Rosario"?

FATHER DE LEO: Yes, I have seen his body.

THE DOCTOR: Wouldn't you say it was burned?

FATHER DE LEO: Of course the body was burned. When he was shot at the wheel of the truck, it crashed and caught fire. But deliberate cremation is not the same thing. It's an abomination in the sight of God.

THE DOCTOR: Abominations are something I don't know about.

FATHER DE LEO: The Church has set down certain laws.

THE DOCTOR: But the instructions of a widow have to be carried out.

FATHER DE LEO: Don't you know why she wants the body cremated? So she can keep the ashes here in the house.

THE DOCTOR: Well, why not, if that's any comfort to her?

FATHER DE LEO: Pagan idolatry is what I call it!

THE DOCTOR: Father De Leo, you love your people but you don't understand them. They find God in each other. And when they lose each other, they lose God and they're lost. And it's hard to help them.—Who is that woman?

[ESTELLE HOHENGARTEN has appeared before the house. She is black-veiled, and bearing a bouquet of roses.]

ESTELLE: I am Estelle Hohengarten.

[Instantly there is a great hubbub in the house. The women mourners flock out to the porch, whispering and gesticulating excitedly.]

FATHER DE LEO: What have you come here for?

ESTELLE: To say good-bye to the body.

FATHER DE LEO: The casket is closed; the body cannot be seen. And you must never come here. The widow knows nothing about you. Nothing at all.

GIUSEPPINA: We know about you!

PEPPINA: Va via! Sporcacciona! [2]

VIOLETTA: Puttana! [3]

MARIELLA: Assassina! [4]

TERESA: You sent him to the Romanos.

FATHER DE LEO: Shhh!

[Suddenly the women swarm down the steps like a cloud of attacking birds, all crying out in Sicilian.

ESTELLE crouches and bows her head defensively before their savage assault. The bouquet of roses is snatched from her black-gloved hands and she is flailed with them about the head and shoulders. The thorns catch her veil and tear it away from her head. She covers her white sobbing face with her hands.]

FATHER DE LEO: Ferme! Ferme! Signore, fermate vi nel nome di Dio! [5]—Have a little respect!

[The women fall back from ESTELLE, who huddles weeping on the walk.]

ESTELLE: See him, see him, just see him . . .

FATHER DE LEO: The body is crushed and burned. Nobody can see it. Now go away and don't ever come here again, Estelle Hohengarten!

THE WOMEN: [In both languages, wildly.] Va via, va via, go away.

[ROSA comes around the house. ESTELLE turns and retreats. One of the mourners spits and kicks at the tangled veil and roses. FATHER DE LEO leaves. The others return inside, except ROSA.

[After a few moments the child goes over to the roses. She picks them up and carefully untangles the veil from the thorns.

[She sits on the sagging steps and puts the black veil over her head. Then for the first time she begins to weep, wildly, histrionically. The little boy appears and gazes at her, momentarily impressed by her performance. Then he picks up a rubber ball and begins to bounce it.

[ROSA is outraged. She jumps up, tears off the veil and runs to the little boy, giving him a sound smack and snatching the ball away from him.]

ROSA: Go home! My papa is dead!

[The scene dims out, as the music is heard again.]

2 Go away! Dirty pig!
3 Whore!   4 Murderer!

5 Stop! Stop! Ladies, stop in the name of God!

Scene Four

*A June day, three years later. It is morning and the light is
bright. A group of local mothers are storming* SERAFINA's *house,
indignant over her delay in delivering the graduation dresses for
their daughters. Most of the women are chattering continually in
Sicilian, racing about the house and banging the doors and shutters.
The scene moves swiftly and violently until the moment when*
ROSA *finally comes out in her graduation dress.*

GIUSEPPINA: Serafina! Serafina delle
Rose!

PEPPINA: Maybe if you call her "Baronessa" she will answer the door. [*With a
mocking laugh.*] Call her "Baronessa" and
kiss your hand to her when she opens the
door.

GIUSEPPINA: [*Tauntingly.*] Baronessa!
[*She kisses her hand toward the door.*]

VIOLETTA: When did she promise your
dress?

PEPPINA: All week she say, "Domani—
domani—domani." [1] But yestiddy I told
her . . .

VIOLETTA: Yeah?

PEPPINA: Oh yeah. I says to her, "Serafina, domani's the high school graduation.
I got to try the dress on my daughter *today.*"
"Domani," she says, "Sicuro! sicuro!
sicuro!" [2] So I start to go away. Then I
hear a voice call, "Signora! Signora!" So
I turn round and I see Serafina's daughter at
the window.

VIOLETTA: Rosa?

PEPPINA: Yeah, Rosa. An' you know
how?

VIOLETTA: How?

PEPPINA: *Naked!* Nuda, nuda! [*She
crosses herself and repeats a prayer.*] In
nominis padri et figlio et spiritus sancti.[3]
Aaahh!

VIOLETTA: What did she do?

PEPPINA: Do? She say, "Signora! Please,
you call this numero and ask for Jack and
tell Jack my clothes are lock up so I can't
get out from the house." Then Serafina
come and she grab-a the girl by the hair
and she pull her way from the window
and she slam the shutters right in my face!

GIUSEPPINA: Whatsa the matter the
daughter?

VIOLETTA: Who is this boy? Where did
she meet him?

PEPPINA: Boy! What boy? He's a sailor.
[*At the word "sailor" the women say
"Ahhh!"*] She met him at the high school
dance and somebody tell Serafina. That's
why she lock up the girl's clothes so she
can't leave the house. She can't even go
to the high school to take the examinations.
Imagine!

VIOLETTA: Peppina, this time *you* go to
the door, yeah?

PEPPINA: Oh yeah, I go. Now I'm
getting nervous. [*The women all crowd
to the door.*] Sera-feee-na!

VIOLETTA: Louder, louder.

PEPPINA: Apri la porta! Come on, come
on!

THE WOMEN: [*Together.*] Yeah, apri la
porta! . . . Come on, hurry up! . . .
Open up!

GIUSEPPINA: I go get-a police.

VIOLETTA: Whatsa matter? You want
more trouble?

GIUSEPPINA: Listen, I pay in advance
five dollar and get no dress. Now what she
wear, my daughter, to graduate in? A couple
of towels and a rose in the hair?

[*There is a noise inside: a shout and
running footsteps.*]

THE WOMEN: Something is going on in
the house! I hear someone! Don't I? Don't
you?

[*A scream and running footsteps are
heard. The front door opens and* SERA-
FINA *staggers out onto the porch. She
is wearing a soiled pink slip and her
hair is wild.*]

SERAFINA: Aiuto! Aiuto! [*She plunges
back into the house.*]

[MISS YORKE, *a spinsterish high school
teacher, walks quickly up to the house.
The Sicilian women, now all chattering at once like a cloud of birds, sweep
about her as she approaches.*]

[1] "Tomorrow—tomorrow—tomorrow."
[2] "Surely! surely! surely!"
[3] In the name of the Father and of the Son
and of the Holy Ghost.

MISS YORKE: You ladies know I don't understand Italian! So, please . . .

[*She goes directly into the house. There are more outcries inside.* THE STREGA *comes and stands at the edge of the yard, cackling derisively.*]

THE STREGA: [*Calling back to someone.*] The Wops are at it again!—She got the daughter lock up naked in there all week. Ho, ho, ho! She lock up all week—naked—shouting out the window tell people to call a number and give a message to Jack. Ho, ho, ho! I guess she's in trouble already, and only fifteen!—They ain't civilized, these Sicilians. In the old country they live in caves in the hills and the country's run by bandits. Ho, ho, ho! More of them coming over on the boats all the time.

[*The door is thrown open again and* SERAFINA *reappears on the porch. She is acting wildly, as if demented.*]

SERAFINA: [*Gasping in a hoarse whisper.*] She cut her wrist, my daughter, she cut her wrist! [*She runs out into the yard.*] Aiii-eeee! Aiutatemi, aiutatemi! Call the dottore! [4] [ASSUNTA *rushes up to* SERAFINA *and supports her as she is about to fall to her knees in the yard.*] Get the knife away from her! Get the knife, please! Get the knife away from—she cut her wrist with— Madonna! Madonna mia . . .

ASSUNTA: Smettila, smettila,[5] Serafina.

MISS YORKE: [*Coming out of the back room.*] Mrs. Delle Rose, your daughter has not cut her wrist. Now come back into the house.

SERAFINA: [*Panting.*] Che dice, che dice? Che cosa? Che cosa dice? [6]

MISS YORKE: Your daughter's all right. Come back into the house. And you ladies please go away!

ASSUNTA: Vieni, Serfina. Andiamo a casa.[7] [*She supports the heavy, sagging bulk of* SERAFINA *to the steps. As they climb the steps one of the Sicilian mothers advances from the whispering group.*]

GIUSEPPINA: [*Boldly.*] Serafina, we don't go away until we get our dresses.

PEPPINA: The graduation begins and the girls ain't dressed.

[SERAFINA's *reply to this ill-timed request is a long, animal howl of misery*

---

[4] Help me, help me! Call the doctor!
[5] Take it away from her, take it away from her.
[6] What are you saying, what are you saying? What is it? What is it that you're saying?
[7] Come, Serafina. Let's go home.

as she is supported into the house. MISS YORKE *follows and firmly closes the door upon the women, who then go around back of the house. The interior of the house is lighted up.*]

MISS YORKE: [*To* SERAFINA.] No, no, no, she's not bleeding. Rosa? Rosa, come here and show your mother that you are not bleeding to death.

[ROSA *appears silently and sullenly between the curtains that separate the two rooms. She has a small white handkerchief tied around one wrist.* SERAFINA *points at the wrist and cries out: "Aiieee!"*]

MISS YORKE: [*Severely.*] Now stop that, Mrs. Delle Rose!

[SERAFINA *rushes to* ROSA, *who thrusts her roughly away.*]

ROSA: Lasciami stare,[8] Mama!—I'm so ashamed I could die. This is the way she goes around all the time. She hasn't put on clothes since my father was killed. For three years she sits at the sewing machine and never puts a dress on or goes out of the house, and now she has locked my clothes up so I can't go out. She wants me to be like her, a freak of the neighborhood, the way she is! Next time, next time, I won't cut my wrist but my throat! I don't want to live locked up with a bottle of ashes! [*She points to the shrine.*]

ASSUNTA: Figlia, figlia, figlia, non devi parlare cosí! [9]

MISS YORKE: Mrs. Delle Rose, please give me the key to the closet so that your daughter can dress for graduation!

SERAFINA: [*Surrendering the key.*] Ecco la—chiave [10] . . . [ROSA *snatches the key and runs back through the curtains.*]

MISS YORKE: Now why did you lock her clothes up, Mrs. Delle Rose?

SERAFINA: The wrist is still bleeding!

MISS YORKE: No, the wrist is not bleeding. It's just a skin cut, a scratch. But the child is exhausted from all this excitement and hasn't eaten a thing in two or three days.

ROSA: [*Running into the dining room.*] Four days! I only asked her one favor. Not to let me go out but to let Jack come to the house so she could meet him!—Then she locked my clothes up!

---

[8] Let me alone.
[9] Daughter, daughter, daughter, you mustn't talk like that.
[10] There's the—key.

MISS YORKE: Your daughter missed her final examinations at the high school, but her grades have been so good that she will be allowed to graduate with her class and take the examinations later.—You understand me, Mrs. Delle Rose!

[ROSA *goes into the back of the house.*]

SERAFINA: [*Standing at the curtains.*] See the way she looks at me? I've got a wild thing in the house, and her wrist is still bleeding!

MISS YORKE: Let's not have any more outbursts of emotion!

SERAFINA: Outburst of—you make me sick! Sick! Sick at my stomach you make me! Your school, you make all this trouble! You give-a this dance where she gets mixed up with a sailor.

MISS YORKE: You are talking about the Hunter girl's brother, a sailor named Jack, who attended the dance with his sister?

SERAFINA: "Attended with sister!"—Attended with *sister!*—My daughter, she's nobody's sister!

[ROSA *comes out of the back room. She is radiantly beautiful in her graduation gown.*]

ROSA: Don't listen to her, don't pay any attention to her, Miss Yorke.—I'm ready to go to the high school.

SERAFINA: [*Stunned by her daughter's beauty, and speaking with a wheedling tone and gestures, as she crouches a little.*] O tesoro, tesoro! Vieni qua, Rosa, cara! [11]—Come here and kiss Mama one minute!—Don't go like that, now!

ROSA: Lasciami stare!

[*She rushes out on the porch.* SERAFINA *gazes after her with arms slowly drooping from their imploring gesture and jaw dropping open in a look of almost comic desolation.*]

SERAFINA: Ho solo te, solo te—in questo mondo! [12]

MISS YORKE: Now, now, Mrs. Delle Rose, no more excitement, please!

SERAFINA: [*Suddenly plunging after them in a burst of fury.*] Senti, senti, per favore!

ROSA: Don't you dare come out on the street like that!—*Mama!*

[*She crouches and covers her face in shame, as* SERAFINA *heedlessly plunges out into the front yard in her shocking deshabille, making wild gestures.*]

[11] O treasure, treasure! Come here, dear Rose!
[12] I have only you, only you—in this world.

SERAFINA: You give this dance where she gets mixed up with a sailor. What do you think you want to do at this high school? [*In weeping despair,* ROSA *runs to the porch.*] How high is this high school? Listen, how high is this high school? Look, look, look, I will show you! It's high as that horse's dirt out there in the street! [SERAFINA *points violently out in front of the house.*] Si! 'Sta fetentissima, scuola! Scuola maledetta! [13]

[ROSA *cries out and rushes over to the palm tree, leaning against it, with tears of mortification.*]

MISS YORKE: Mrs. Delle Rose, you are talking and behaving extremely badly. I don't understand how a woman that acts like you could have such a sweet and refined young girl for a daughter!—You don't deserve it!—Really . . . [*She crosses to the palm tree.*]

SERAFINA: Oh, you want me to talk refined to you, do you? Then do me one thing! Stop ruining the girls at the high school! [*As* SERAFINA *paces about, she swings her hips in the exaggeratedly belligerent style of a parading matador.*]

ASSUNTA: Piantala, Serafina! Andiamo a casa! [14]

SERAFINA: No, no, I ain't through talking to this here teacher!

ASSUNTA: Serafina, look at yourself, you're not dressed!

SERAFINA: I'm dressed okay; I'm not naked! [*She glares savagely at the teacher by the palm tree. The Sicilian mothers return to the front yard.*]

ASSUNTA: Serafina, cara? Andiamo a casa, adesso!—Basta! Basta! [15]

SERAFINA: Aspetta! [16]

ROSA: I'm so ashamed I could die, I'm so ashamed. Oh, you don't know, Miss Yorke, the way that we live. She never puts on a dress; she stays all the time in that dirty old pink slip!—And talks to my father's ashes like he was living.

SERAFINA: Teacher! Teacher, senti! [17] What do you think you want to do at this high school? Sentite! per favore! [18] You give this a dance! What kind of a spring dance is it? Answer this question, please,

[13] Yes! Stinking school! Cursed school!
[14] Stop it, Serafina! Let's go home.
[15] Serafina, dear? Let's go home, now!—Enough! Enough!
[16] Wait!   [17] Listen.
[18] Listen, please!

for me! What kind of a spring dance is it? She meet this boy there who don't even go to no high school. What kind of a boy? Guardate![19] A *sailor that wears a gold earring!* That kind of a boy is the kind of boy she meets there!—That's why I lock her clothes up so she can't go back to the high school. [*Suddenly to* ASSUNTA.] She cut her wrist! It's still bleeding! [*She strikes her forehead three times with her fist.*]

ROSA: Mama, you look disgusting! [*She rushes away.*]

[MISS YORKE *rushes after her.* SERAFINA *shades her eyes with one hand to watch them departing down the street in the brilliant spring light.*]

SERAFINA: Did you hear what my daughter said to me?—"You look—disgusting."—She calls me . . .

ASSUNTA: Now, Serafina, we must go in the house. [*She leads her gently to the porch of the little house.*]

SERAFINA: [*Proudly.*] How pretty she look, my daughter, in the white dress, like a bride! [*To all.*] Excuse me! Excuse me, please! Go away! Get out of my yard!

GIUSEPPINA: [*Taking the bull by the horns.*] No, we ain't going to go without the dresses!

ASSUNTA: Give the ladies the dresses so the girls can get dressed for the graduation.

SERAFINA: That one there she only paid for the goods. I charge for the work.

GIUSEPPINA: Ecco![20] I got the money!

THE WOMEN: We *got* the money!

SERAFINA: The names are pinned on the dresses. Go in and get them. [*She turns to* ASSUNTA.] Did you hear what my daughter called me? She called me "disgusting"!

[SERAFINA *enters the house, slamming the door. After a moment the mothers come out, cradling the white voile dresses tenderly in their arms, murmuring "carino!"[21] and "bellissimo!"[22] [As they disappear the inside light is brought up and we see Serafina standing before a glazed mirror, looking at herself and repeating the daughter's word.*]

SERAFINA: Disgusting!

[*The music is briefly resumed to mark a division.*]

[19] Watch out!   [20] There!   [21] "Lovely!"   [22] "Very beautiful!"

Scene Five

Immediately following. SERAFINA's *movements gather momentum. She snatches a long-neglected girdle out of a bureau drawer and holds it experimentally about her waist. She shakes her head doubtfully, drops the girdle and snatches the $8.98 hat off the millinery dummy and plants it on her head. She turns around distractedly, not remembering where the mirror is. She gasps with astonishment when she catches sight of herself, snatches the hat off and hastily restores it to the blank head of the dummy. She makes another confused revolution or two, then gasps with fresh inspiration and snatches a girlish frock off a dummy—an Alice blue gown with daisies crocheted on it. The dress sticks on the dummy.* SEREFINA *mutters savagely in Sicilian. She finally overcomes this difficulty but in her exasperation she knocks the dummy over. She throws off the robe and steps hopefully into the gown. But she discovers it won't fit over her hips. She seizes the girdle again; then hurls it angrily away. The parrot calls to her; she yells angrily back at the parrot: "Zitto!"*

In the distance the high school band starts playing. SERAFINA *gets panicky that she will miss the graduation ceremonies, and hammers her forehead with her fist, sobbing a little. She wriggles despairingly out of the blue dress and runs out back in her rayon slip just as* FLORA *and* BESSIE *appear outside the house.* FLORA *and* BESSIE *are two female clowns of middle years and juvenile temperament.* FLORA *is tall and angular;* BESSIE *is rather stubby. They are dressed for a gala.* FLORA *runs up the steps and bangs at the cottage door.*

BESSIE: I fail to understand why it's so important to pick up a polka-dot blouse when it's likely to make us miss the twelve o'clock train.

FLORA: Serafina! Serafina!

BESSIE: We only got fifteen minutes to get to the depot and I'll get faint on the train if I don't have m' coffee . . .

FLORA: Git a coke on th' train, Bessie.

BESSIE: Git nothing on the train if we don't git the train!

[SERAFINA *runs back out of the bedroom, quite breathless, in a purple silk dress. As she passes the millinery dummy she snatches the hat off again and plants it back on her head.*]

SERAFINA: Wrist-watch! Wrist-watch! Where'd I put th' wrist-watch? [*She hears Flora shouting and banging and rushes to the door.*]

BESSIE: Try the door if it ain't open.

FLORA: [*Pushing in.*] Just tell me, is it ready or not?

SERAFINA: Oh! You. Don't bother me. I'm late for the graduation of my daughter and now I can't find her graduation present.

FLORA: You got plenty of time.

SERAFINA: Don't you hear the band playing?

FLORA: They're just warming up. Now, Serafina, where is my blouse?

SERAFINA: Blouse? Not ready! I had to make fourteen graduation dresses!

FLORA: A promise is a promise and an excuse is just an excuse!

SERAFINA: I got to get to the high school!

FLORA: I got to get to the depot in that blouse!

BESSIE: We're going to the American Legion parade in New Orleans.

FLORA: There, there, there, there it is! [*She grabs the blouse from the machine.*] Get started, woman, stitch them bandanas together! If you don't do it, I'm a-gonna report you to the Chamber of Commerce and git your license revoked!

SERAFINA: [*Anxiously.*] What license you talking about? I got no license!

FLORA: You hear that, Bessie? *She hasn't got no license!*

BESSIE: *She ain't even got a license?*

SERAFINA: [*Crossing quickly to the machine.*] I—I'll stitch them together! But if you make me late to my daughter's graduation, I'll make you sorry some way . . .

[*She works with furious rapidity. A train whistle is heard.*]

BESSIE: [*Wildly and striking at Flora with her purse.*] Train's pullin' out! Oh, God, you made us miss it!

FLORA: Bessie, you know there's another at 12:45!

BESSIE: It's the selfish—principle of it that makes me sick! [*She walks rapidly up and down.*]

FLORA: Set down, Bessie. Don't wear out your feet before we git to th' city . . .

BESSIE: Molly tole me the town was full of excitement. They're dropping paper sacks full of water out of hotel windows.

FLORA: Which hotel are they dropping paper sacks out of?

BESSIE: What a fool question! The Monteleone Hotel.

FLORA: That's an old-fashioned hotel.

BESSIE: It might be old-fashioned but you'd be surprised at some of the modern, up-to-date things that go on there.

FLORA: I heard, I heard that the Legionnaires caught a girl on Canal Street! They tore the clothes off her and sent her home in a taxi!

BESSIE: I double dog dare anybody to try that on me!

FLORA: You?! Huh! You never need any assistance gittin' undressed!

SERAFINA: [*Ominously.*] You two ladies watch how you talk in there. This here is a Catholic house. You are sitting in the same room with Our Lady and with the blessed ashes of my husband!

FLORA: [*Acidly.*] Well, ex-cuse *me!* [*She whispers maliciously to Bessie.*] It sure is a pleasant surprise to see you wearing a dress, Serafina, but the surprise would be twice as pleasant if it was more the right size. [*To Bessie, loudly.*] She used to have a sweet figure, a little bit plump but attractive, but setting there at that sewing machine for three years in a kimona and not stepping out of the house has naturally given her hips!

SERAFINA: If I didn't have hips I would be a very uncomfortable woman when I set down.

[*The parrot squawks.* SERAFINA *imitates its squawk.*]

FLORA: Polly want a cracker?

SERAFINA: No. He don't want a cracker! What is she doing over there at that window?

BESSIE: Some Legionnaires are on the highway!

FLORA: A Legionnaire? No kidding?

[*She springs up and joins her girl friend at the window. They both laugh fatuously, bobbing their heads out the window.*]

BESSIE: He's looking this way; yell something!

FLORA: [*Leaning out the window.*] Mademoiselle from Armentieres, parley-voo!

BESSIE: [*Chiming in rapturously.*] Mademoiselle from Armentieres, parley-voo!

A VOICE OUTSIDE: [*Gallantly returning the salute.*] Mademoiselle from Armentieres, hadn't been kissed for forty years!

BOTH GIRLS: [*Together; very gaily.*] Hinky-dinky parley-voooo!

[*They laugh and applaud at the window. The Legionnaires are heard laughing. A car horn is heard as the Legionnaires drive away.* SERAFINA *springs up and rushes over to the window, jerks them away from it and slams the shutters in their faces.*]

SERAFINA: [*Furiously.*] I told you wimmen that you was not in a honky-tonk! Now take your blouse and git out! Get out on the streets where you kind a wimmen belong.—This is the house of Rosario delle Rose and those are his ashes in that marble urn and I won't have—unproper things going on here or dirty talk, neither!

FLORA: Who's talking dirty?

BESSIE: What a helluva nerve.

FLORA: I want you to listen!

SERAFINA: You are, you are, dirty talk, all the time men, men, men! You men-crazy things, you!

FLORA: Sour grapes—sour grapes is your trouble! You're wild with envy!

BESSIE: Isn't she green with jealousy? Huh!

SERAFINA: [*Suddenly and religiously.*] When I think of men I think about my husband. My husband was a Sicilian. We had love together every night of the week, we never skipped one, from the night we was married till the night he was killed in his fruit truck on that road there! [*She catches her breath in a sob.*] And maybe

that is the reason I'm not man-crazy and don't like hearing the talk of women that are. But I am interested, now, in the happiness of my daughter who's graduating this morning out of high school. And now I'm going to be late, the band is playing! And I have lost her wrist watch!—her graduation present! [*She whirls about distractedly.*]

BESSIE: Flora, let's go!—The hell with that goddam blouse!

FLORA: Oh, no, just wait a minute! I don't accept insults from no one!

SERAFINA: Go on, go on to New Orleans, you two man-crazy things, you! And pick up a man on Canal Street but not in my house, at my window, in front of my dead husband's ashes! [*The high school band is playing a martial air in the distance.* SERAFINA's *chest is heaving violently; she touches her heart and momentarily seems to forget that she must go.*] I am not at all interested, I am not interested in men getting fat and bald in soldier-boy play suits, tearing the clothes off girls on Canal Street and dropping paper sacks out of hotel windows. I'm just not interested in that sort of man-crazy business. I remember my husband with a body like a young boy and hair on his head as thick and black as mine is and skin on him smooth and sweet as a yellow rose petal.

FLORA: Oh, a *rose,* was he?

SERAFINA: Yes, yes, a rose, a rose!

FLORA: Yes, a rose of a Wop!—of a gangster!—shot smuggling dope under a load of bananas!

BESSIE: Flora, Flora, let's go!

SERAFINA: My folks was peasants, contadini,[1] but he—he came from *land*-owners! *Signorile,*[2] my husband!—At night I sit here and I'm satisfied to remember, because I had the best.—Not the third best and not the second best, but the *first* best, the *only* best!—So now I stay here and am satisfied now to remember . . .

BESSIE: Come on, come out! To the depot!

FLORA: Just wait, I wanta hear this, it's too good to miss!

SERAFINA: I count up the nights I held him all night in my arms, and I can tell you how many. Each night for twelve years. Four thousand—three hundred—and eighty. The number of nights I held him all night

---

[1] Farmers.   [2] Gentlemen.

in my arms. Sometimes I didn't sleep, just held him all night in my arms. And I am satisfied with it. I grieve for him. Yes, my pillow at night's never dry—but I'm satisfied to remember. And I would feel cheap and degraded and not fit to live with my daughter or under the roof with the urn of his blessed ashes, those—ashes of a rose— if after that memory, after knowing that man, I went to some other, some middle-aged man, not young, not full of young passion, but getting a pot belly on him and losing his hair and smelling of sweat and liquor—and trying to fool myself that *that* was love-making! I *know* what love-making was. And I'm satisfied just to remember . . . [*She is panting as though she had run upstairs.*] Go on, you do it, you go on the streets and let them drop their sacks of dirty water on you!— I'm satisfied to remember the love of a man that was mine —only mine! Never touched by the hand of *nobody! Nobody* but *me!*—Just me! [*She gasps and runs out to the porch. The sun floods her figure. It seems to astonish her. She finds herself sobbing. She digs in her purse for her handkerchief.*]

FLORA: [*Crossing to the open door.*] Never touched by nobody?

SERAFINA: [*With fierce pride.*] Never nobody but me!

FLORA: *I* know somebody that could a tale unfold! And not so far from here either. Not no further than the Square Roof is, that place on Esplanade!

BESSIE: Estelle Hohengarten!

FLORA: Estelle Hohengarten!—the black-jack dealer from Texas!

BESSIE: Get into your blouse and let's go!

FLORA: Everybody's known it but Serafina. I'm just telling the facts that come out at the inquest while she was in bed with her eyes shut tight and the sheet pulled over her head like a female ostrich! Tie this damn thing on me! It was a romance, not just a fly-by-night thing, but a steady affair that went on for more than a year.

[SERAFINA *has been standing on the porch with the door open behind her. She is in the full glare of the sun. She appears to have been struck senseless by the words shouted inside. She turns slowly about. We see that her dress is unfastened down the back, the pink slip showing. She reaches out gropingly with one hand and finds the porch column which she clings to*

while the terrible words strike constantly deeper. The high school band continues as a merciless counterpoint.]

BESSIE: Leave her in ignorance. Ignorance is bliss.

FLORA: He had a rose tattoo on his chest, the stuck-up thing, and Estelle was so gone on him she went down to Bourbon Street and had one put on her. [SERAFINA *comes onto the porch and* FLORA *turns to her, viciously.*] Yeah, a rose tattoo on her chest same as the Wop's!

SERAFINA: [*Very softly.*] Liar . . . [*She comes inside; the word seems to give her strength.*]

BESSIE: [*Nervously.*] Flora, let's go, let's go!

SERAFINA: [*In a terrible voice.*] Liar!— Lie-arrrr!

[*She slams the wooden door shut with a violence that shakes the walls.*]

BESSIE: [*Shocked into terror.*] Let's get outa here, Flora!

FLORA: Let her howl her head off. I don't care.

[SERAFINA *has snatched up a broom.*]

BESSIE: What's she up to?

FLORA: I don't care what she's up to.

BESSIE: I'm a-scared of these Wops.

FLORA: I'm not afraid of nobody!

BESSIE: She's gonna hit you.

FLORA: She'd better not hit me!

[*But both of the clowns are in retreat to the door.* SERAFINA *suddenly rushes at them with the broom. She flails* FLORA *about the hips and shoulders.* BESSIE *gets out. But* FLORA *is trapped in a corner. A table is turned over.* BESSIE, *outside, screams for the police and cries:* "Murder! Murder!" *The high school band is playing* The Stars and Stripes Forever. FLORA *breaks wildly past the flailing broom and escapes out of the house. She also takes up the cry for help.* SERAFINA *follows them out. She is flailing the brilliant noon air with the broom. The two women run off, screaming.*]

FLORA: [*Calling back.*] I'm going to have her arrested! Police, police! I'm going to have you arrested!

SERAFINA: *Have* me arrested, *have* me, you dirt, you devil, you *liar!* Li-i-arrrr!

[*She comes back inside the house and leans on the work table for a moment, panting heavily. Then she rushes back to the door, slams it and bolts it. Then she rushes to the window, slams the shutters and fastens them. The house in now dark except for the vigil light in the ruby glass cup before the Madonna, and the delicate beams admitted through the shutter slats.]*

SERAFINA: [*In a crazed manner.*] Have me—have me—arrested—dirty slut—bitch—liar! [*She moves about helplessly, not knowing what to do, with her big, stricken body. Panting for breath, she repeats the word "liar" monotonously and helplessly as she thrashes about. It is necessary for her, vitally necessary for her, to believe that the woman's story is a malicious invention. But the words of it stick in her mind and she mumbles them aloud as she thrashes crazily around the small confines of the parlor.*] Woman—Estelle—[*The sound of band*

music heard.] Band, band, already—started.—Going to miss—graduation. Oh! [*She retreats toward the Madonna.*] Estelle, Estelle Hohengarten?—"A shirt for a man I'm in love with! This man—is—wild like a gypsy."—Oh, oh, Lady—The—rose-colored—silk. [*She starts toward the dining room, then draws back in terror.*] No, no, no, no, no! I don't remember! It wasn't that name, I don't remember the name! [*The band music grows louder.*] High school—graduation—late! I'll be—late for it.—Oh, Lady, give me a—sign! [*She cocks her head toward the statue in a fearful listening attitude.*] Che? Che dice, Signora? [3] *Oh, Lady! Give me a sign!*

[*The scene dims out.*]

[3] What? What are you saying, Lady?

Scene Six

It is two hours later. The interior of the house is in complete darkness except for the vigil light. With the shutters closed, the interior is so dark that we do not know SERAFINA *is present. All that we see clearly is the starry blue robe of Our Lady above the flickering candle of the ruby glass cup. After a few moments we hear* SERAFINA's *voice, very softly, in the weak, breathless tone of a person near death.*

SERAFINA: [*Very softly.*] Oh, Lady, give me a sign . . .

[*Gay, laughing voices are heard outside the house.* ROSA *and* JACK *appear, bearing roses and gifts. They are shouting back to others in a car.*]

JACK: Where do we go for the picnic?

A GIRL'S VOICE: [*From the highway.*] We're going in three sailboats to Diamond Key.

A MAN'S VOICE: Be at Municipal Pier in half an hour.

ROSA: Pick us up here. [*She races up the steps.*] Oh, the door's locked! Mama's gone out! There's a key in that bird bath.

[JACK *opens the door. The parlor lights up faintly as they enter.*] ·

JACK: It's dark in here.

ROSA: Yes, Mama's gone out!

JACK: How do you know she's out?

ROSA: The door was locked and all the shutters are closed! Put down those roses.

JACK: Where shall I . . .

ROSA: Somewhere, anywhere!—Come here! [*He approaches her rather diffidently.*]

I want to teach you a little Dago word. The word is "bacio." [1]

JACK: What does this word mean?

ROSA: This and this and this! [*She rains kisses upon him till he forcibly removes her face from his.*] Just think. A week ago Friday—I didn't know boys existed!—Did you know girls existed before the dance?

JACK: Yes, I knew they existed . . .

ROSA: [*Holding him.*] Do you remember what you said to me on the dance floor? "Honey, you're dancing too close"?

JACK: Well, it was—hot in the Gym and the—floor was crowded.

ROSA: When my girl friend was teaching me how to dance, I asked her, "How do you know which way the boy's going to move?" And she said, "You've got to feel how he's going to move with your body!" I said, "How do you feel with your body?" And she said, "By pressing up close!"—That's why I pressed up close! I didn't realize that I was —Ha, ha! Now you're blushing! Don't go

[1] "Kiss."

away!—And a few minutes later you said to me, "Gee, you're beautiful!" I said, "Excuse me," and ran to the ladies' room. Do you know why? To look at myself in the mirror! And I saw that I was! For the first time in my life I was beautiful! You'd made me beautiful when you *said* that I was!

JACK: [*Humbly.*] You *are* beautiful, Rosa! So much, I . . .

ROSA: *You've* changed, *too.* You've stopped laughing and joking. Why have you gotten so old and serious, Jack?

JACK: Well, honey, you're sort of . . .

ROSA: What am I "sort of"?

JACK: [*Finding the right word.*] Wild! [*She laughs. He seizes the bandaged wrist.*] I didn't know nothing like this was going to happen.

ROSA: Oh, that, that's nothing! I'll take the handkerchief off and you can forget it.

JACK: How could you do a thing like that over me? I'm—nothing!

ROSA: Everybody is nothing until you love them!

JACK: Give me that handkerchief. I want to show it to my shipmates. I'll say, "This is the blood of a beautiful girl who cut her wrist with a knife because she loved me!"

ROSA: Don't be so pleased with yourself. It's mostly Mercurochrome!

SERAFINA: [*Violently, from the dark room adjoining.*] Stai zitta!—Cretina! [2]

[ROSA *and* JACK *draw abruptly apart.*]

JACK: [*Fearfully.*] I knew somebody was here!

ROSA: [*Sweetly and delicately.*] Mama? Are you in there, Mama?

SERAFINA: No, no, no, I'm not, I'm dead and buried!

ROSA: Yes, Mama's in there!

JACK: Well, I—better go and—wait outside for a—while . . .

ROSA: You stay right here!—Mama?— Jack is with me.—Are you dressed up nicely? [*There is no response.*] Why's it so dark in here?—Jack, open the shutters!—I want to introduce you to my mother . . .

JACK: Hadn't I better go and . . .

ROSA: No. Open the shutters!

[*The shutters are opened and* ROSA *draws apart the curtains between the two rooms. Sunlight floods the scene.* SERAFINA *is revealed slumped in a chair at her work table in the dining*

room near the Singer sewing machine. She is grotesquely surrounded by the dummies, as though she had been holding a silent conference with them. Her appearance, in slovenly deshabille, is both comic and shocking.]

ROSA: [*Terribly embarrassed.*] Mama, Mama, you said you were dressed up pretty! Jack, stay out for a minute! What's happened, Mama?

[JACK *remains in the parlor.* ROSA *pulls the curtains, snatches a robe and flings it over* SERAFINA. *She brushes* SERAFINA's *hair back from her sweat-gleaming face, rubs her face with a handkerchief and dusts it with powder.* SERAFINA *submits to this cosmetic enterprise with a dazed look.*]

ROSA: [*Gesturing vertically.*] Su, su, su, su, su, su, su, su, su! [3]

[SERAFINA *sits up slightly in her chair, but she is still looking stupefied.* ROSA *returns to the parlor and opens the curtains again.*]

ROSA: Come in, Jack! Mama is ready to meet you!

[ROSA *trembles with eagerness as* JACK *advances nervously from the parlor. But before he enters* SERAFINA *collapses into her slumped position, with a low moan.*]

ROSA: [*Violently.*] Mama, Mama, su, Mama! [SERAFINA *sits half erect.*] She didn't sleep good last night.—Mama, this is Jack Hunter!

JACK: Hello, Mrs. Delle Rose. It sure is a pleasure to meet you.

[*There is a pause.* SERAFINA *stares indifferently at the boy.*]

ROSA: Mama, Mama, say something!

JACK: Maybe your Mama wants me to . . . [*He makes an awkward gesture toward the door.*]

ROSA: No, no, Mama's just tired. Mama makes dresses; she made a whole lot of dresses for the graduation! How many, Mama, how many graduation dresses did you have to make?

SERAFINA: [*Dully.*] Fa niente . . . [4]

JACK: I was hoping to see you at the graduation, Mrs. Delle Rose.

ROSA: I guess that Mama was too worn out to go.

SERAFINA: Rosa, shut the front door, shut

---

[2] Shut up!—Idiot

it and lock it. There was a—policeman . . . [*There is a pause.*] What?—What?

JACK: My sister was graduating. My mother was there and my aunt was there— a whole bunch of cousins—I was hoping that you could—all—get together . . .

ROSA: Jack brought you some flowers.

JACK: I hope you are partial to roses as much as I am. [*He hands her the bouquet. She takes them absently.*]

ROSA: Mama, say something, say something simple like "Thanks."

SERAFINA: Thanks.

ROSA: Jack, tell Mama about the graduation; describe it to her.

JACK: My mother said it was just like fairyland.

ROSA: Tell her what the boys wore!

JACK: What did—what did they wear?

ROSA: Oh, you know what they wore. They wore blue coats and white pants and each one had a carnation! And there were three couples that did an old-fashioned dance, a minuet, Mother, to Mendelssohn's *Spring Song!* Wasn't it lovely, Jack? But one girl slipped; she wasn't used to long dresses! She slipped and fell on her—ho, ho! Wasn't it funny, Jack, wasn't it, wasn't it, Jack?

JACK: [*Worriedly.*] I think that your Mama . . .

ROSA: Oh, my prize, my prize, I have forgotten my prize!

JACK: Where is it?

ROSA: You set them down by the sewing sign when you looked for the key.

JACK: Aw, excuse me, I'll get them. [*He goes out through the parlor.* ROSA *runs to her mother and kneels by her chair.*]

ROSA: [*In a terrified whisper.*] Mama, something has happened! What has happened Mama? Can't you tell me, Mama? Is it because of this morning? Look. I took the bandage off, it was only a scratch! So, Mama, forget it! Think it was just a bad dream that never happened! Oh, Mama! [*She gives her several quick kisses on the forehead.* JACK *returns with two big books tied in white satin ribbon.*]

JACK: Here they are.

ROSA: Look what I got, Mama.

SERAFINA: [*Dully.*] What?

ROSA: The Digest of Knowledge!

JACK: Everything's in them, from Abracadabra to Zoo! My sister was jealous. She just got a diploma!

SERAFINA: [*Rousing a bit.*] Diploma, where is it? Didn't you get no diploma?

ROSA: Si, si, Mama! Eccolo! Guarda, guarda! [5] [*She holds up the diploma tied in ribbon.*]

SERAFINA: Va bene.—Put it in the drawer with your father's clothes.

JACK: Mrs. Delle Rose, you should be very, very proud of your daughter. She stood in front of the crowd and recited a poem.

ROSA: Yes, I did. Oh, I was so excited!

JACK: And Mrs. Delle Rose, your daughter, Rosa, was so pretty when she walked on the stage—that people went "Oooooooooo!" —like that! Y'know what I mean? They all went—"Oooooooooo!" Like a—like a—*wind* had—blown over! Because your daughter, Rosa, was so—*lovely* looking! [*He has crouched over to* SERAFINA *to deliver this description close to her face. Now he straightens up and smiles proudly at* ROSA.] How does it feel to be the mother of the prettiest girl in the world?

ROSA: [*Suddenly bursting into pure delight.*] Ha, ha, ha, ha, ha, ha! [*She throws her head back in rapture.*]

SERAFINA: [*Rousing.*] Hush!

ROSA: Ha, ha, ha, ha, ha, ha, ha, ha, ha, ha! [*She cannot control her ecstatic laughter. She presses her hand to her mouth but the laughter still bubbles out.*]

SERAFINA: [*Suddenly rising in anger.*] Pazza, pazza, pazza! Finiscila! Basta, via! [6] [ROSA *whirls around to hide her convulsions of joy. To* JACK.] Put the prize books in the parlor, and shut the front door; there was a policeman come here because of—some trouble . . . [JACK *takes the books.*]

ROSA: Mama, I've never seen you like this! What will Jack think, Mama?

SERAFINA: What do I care what Jack thinks?—You wild, wild crazy thing, you— with the eyes of your—father . . .

JACK: [*Returning.*] Yes, ma'am, Mrs. Delle Rose, you certainly got a right to be very proud of your daughter.

SERAFINA: [*After a pause.*] I am proud of the—memory of her—father.—He was a baron . . . [ROSA *takes* JACK'S *arm.*] And who are *you?* What are you?—per piacere! [7]

ROSA: Mama, I just introduced him; his name is Jack Hunter.

[5] Yes, yes, Mama! There it is. Look, look!
[6] Crazy, crazy, crazy! Stop it! Enough, go away!
[7] Please.

SERAFINA: Hunt-er?

JACK: Yes, ma'am, Hunter, Jack Hunter.

SERAFINA: What are you hunting?—Jack?

ROSA: Mama!

SERAFINA: What all of 'em are hunting? To have a good time, and the Devil cares who pays for it? I'm sick of men, I'm almost as sick of men as I am of wimmen.—Rosa, get out while I talk to this boy!

ROSA: I didn't bring Jack here to be insulted!

JACK: Go on, honey, and let your Mama talk to me. I think your Mama has just got a slight wrong—impression . . .

SERAFINA: [Ominously.] Yes, I got an impression!

ROSA: I'll get dressed! Oh, Mama, don't spoil it for me!—the happiest day of my life! [She goes into the back of the house.]

JACK: [After an awkward pause.] Mrs. Delle Rose . . .

SERAFINA: [Correcting his pronunciation.] Delle Rose!

JACK: Mrs. Delle Rose, I'm sorry about all this. Believe me, Mrs. Delle Rose, the last thing I had in mind was getting mixed up in a family situation. I came home after three months to sea, I docked at New Orleans, and came here to see my folks. My sister was going to a high school dance. She took me with her, and there I met your daughter.

SERAFINA: What did you do?

JACK: At the high school dance? We danced! My sister had told me that Rosa had a very strict mother and wasn't allowed to go on dates with boys so when it was over, I said, "I'm sorry you're not allowed to go out." And she said, "Oh! What gave you the idea I wasn't!" So then I thought my sister had made a mistake and I made a date with her for the next night.

SERAFINA: What did you do the next night?

JACK: The next night we went to the movies.

SERAFINA: And what did you do—that night?

JACK: At the movies? We ate a bag of popcorn and watched the movie!

SERAFINA: She come home at midnight and said she had been with a girl-friend studying "civics."

JACK: Whatever story she told you, it ain't my fault!

SERAFINA: And the night after that?

JACK: Last Tuesday? We went roller skating!

SERAFINA: And afterwards?

JACK: After the skating? We went to a drug store and had an ice cream soda!

SERAFINA: Alone?

JACK: At the drug store? No. It was crowded. And the skating rink was full of people skating!

SERAFINA: You mean that you haven't been alone with my Rosa?

JACK: Alone or not alone, what's the point of that question? I still don't see the point of it.

SERAFINA: We are Sicilians. We don't leave the girls with the boys they're not engaged to!

JACK: Mrs. Delle Rose, this is the United States.

SERAFINA: But we are Sicilians, and we are not cold-blooded.—My girl is a virgin! She is—or she was—I would like to know—which!

JACK: Mrs. Delle Rose! I got to tell you something. You might not believe it. It is a hard thing to say. But I am—also a—virgin . . .

SERAFINA: What? No. I do not believe it.

JACK: Well, it's true, though. This is the first time—I . . .

SERAFINA: First time you what?

JACK: The first time I really wanted to . . .

SERAFINA: Wanted to what?

JACK: Make—love . . .

SERAFINA: You? A sailor?

JACK: [Sighing deeply.] Yes, ma'am. I had opportunities to!—But I—always thought of my mother . . . I always asked myself, would she or would she not—think —this or that person was—decent!

SERAFINA: But with my daughter, my Rosa, your mother tells you okay?—go ahead, son!

JACK: Mrs. Delle Rose! [With embarrassment.]—Mrs. Delle Rose, I . . .

SERAFINA: Two weeks ago I was slapping her hands for scratching mosquito bites. She rode a bicycle to school. Now all at once—I've got a wild thing in the house. She says she's in love. And you? Do you say you're in love?

JACK: [Solemnly.] Yes, ma'am, I do, I'm in love!—very much . . .

SERAFINA: Bambini, tutti due, bambini! [8]

---

[8] Children, both of you, children!

[ROSA *comes out, dressed for the picnic.*]

ROSA: I'm ready for Diamond Key!

SERAFINA: Go out on the porch. Diamond Key!

ROSA: [*With a sarcastic curtsy.*] Yes, Mama!

SERAFINA: What are you? Catholic?

JACK: Me? Yes, ma'am, Catholic.

SERAFINA: You don't look Catholic to me!

ROSA: [*Shouting from the door.*] Oh, God, Mama, how do Catholics look? How do they look different from anyone else?

SERAFINA: Stay out till I call you! [ROSA *crosses to the bird bath and prays.* SERAFINA *turns to* JACK.] Turn around, will you?

JACK: Do what, ma'am?

SERAFINA: I said, *turn around!* [JACK *awkwardly turns around.*] Why do they make them Navy pants so tight?

ROSA: [*Listening in the yard.*] Oh, my God . . .

JACK: [*Flushing.*] That's a question you'll have to ask the Navy, Mrs. Delle Rose.

SERAFINA: And that gold earring, what's the gold earring for?

ROSA: [*Yelling from the door.*] For crossing the equator, Mama; he's crossed it three times. He was initiated into the court of Neptune and gets to wear a gold earring! He's a shellback!

[SERAFINA *springs up and crosses to slam the porch door.* ROSA *runs despairingly around the side of the house and leans, exhausted with closed eyes, against the trunk of a palm tree.* THE STREGA *creeps into the yard, listening.*]

SERAFINA: You see what I got. A wild thing in the house!

JACK: Mrs. Delle Rose, I guess that Sicilians are very emotional people . . .

SERAFINA: I want nobody to take advantage of that!

JACK: You got the wrong idea about me, Mrs. Delle Rose.

SERAFINA: I know what men want—not to eat popcorn with girls or to slide on ice! And boys are the same, only younger.— Come here. Come here!

[ROSA *hears her mother's passionate voice. She rushes from the palm tree to the back door and pounds on it with both fists.*]

ROSA: Mama! Mama! Let me in the door, Jack!

JACK: Mrs. Delle Rose, your daughter is calling you.

SERAFINA: Let her call!—Come here. [*She crosses to the shrine of Our Lady.*] Come here!

[*Despairing of the back door,* ROSA *rushes around to the front. A few moments later she pushes open the shutters of the window in the wall and climbs half in.* JACK *crosses apprehensively to* SERAFINA *before the Madonna.*]

SERAFINA: You said you're Catholic, ain't you?

JACK: Yes, ma'am.

SERAFINA: Then kneel down in front of Our Lady!

JACK: Do—do what, did you say?

SERAFINA: I said to get down on your knees in front of Our Lady!

[ROSA *groans despairingly in the window.* JACK *kneels awkwardly upon the hassock.*]

ROSA: Mama, Mama, now what?!

[SERAFINA *rushes to the window, pushes* ROSA *out and slams the shutters.*]

SERAFINA: [*Returning to* JACK.] Now say after me what I say!

JACK: Yes, ma'am.

[ROSA *pushes the shutters open again.*]

SERAFINA: I promise the Holy Mother that I will respect the innocence of the daughter of . . .

ROSA: [*In anguish.*] Ma-maaa! . . .

SERAFINA: Get back out of that window! —Well? Are you gonna say it?

JACK: Yes, ma'am. What was it, again?

SERAFINA: I promise the Holy Mother . . .

JACK: I promise the Holy Mother . . .

SERAFINA: As I hope to be saved by the Blessed Blood of Jesus . . .

JACK: As I hope to be saved by the . . .

SERAFINA: Blessed Blood of . . .

JACK: Jesus . . .

SERAFINA: That I will respect the innocence of the daughter, Rosa, of Rosario delle Rose.

JACK: That I will respect the innocence —of—Rosa . . .

SERAFINA: Cross yourself! [*He crosses himself.*] Now get up, get up, get up! I am satisfied now . . .

[ROSA *jumps through the window and rushes to* SERAFINA *with arms outflung and wild cries of joy.*]

SERAFINA: Let me go, let me breathe!

[*Outside* THE STREGA *cackles derisively.*]

ROSA: Oh, wonderful Mama, don't breathe! Oh, Jack! *Kiss* Mama! *Kiss Mama!* Mama, please kiss Jack!

SERAFINA: Kiss? Me? No, no, no, no!— Kiss my *hand* . . .

[*She offers her hand, shyly, and* JACK *kisses it with a loud smack.* ROSA *seizes the wine bottle.*]

ROSA: Mama, get some wine glasses!

[SERAFINA *goes for the glasses, and* ROSA *suddenly turns to* JACK. *Out of her mother's sight, she passionately grabs hold of his hand and presses it, first to her throat, then to her lips and finally to her breast.* JACK *snatches his hand away as* SERAFINA *returns with the glasses. Voices are heard calling from the highway.*]

VOICES OUTSIDE: Ro-osa!—Ro-osa!— Ro-osa!

[*A car horn is heard blowing.*]

SERAFINA: Oh, I forgot the graduation present.

[*She crouches down before the bureau and removes a fancily wrapped package from its bottom drawer. The car horn is honking, and the voices are calling.*]

ROSA: They're calling for us! *Coming!* Jack! [*She flies out the door, calling back to her mother.*] G'bye, Mama!

JACK: [*Following* ROSA.] Good-bye, Mrs. Delle Rose!

SERAFINA: [*Vaguely.*] It's a Bulova wrist watch with seventeen jewels in it . . [*She realizes that she is alone.*] Rosa! [*She goes to the door, still holding out the present. Outside the car motor roars, and the voices shout as the car goes off.* SERAFINA *stumbles outside, shielding her eyes with one hand, extending the gift with the other.*] Rosa, Rosa, your present! Regalo, regalo—tesoro! [9]

[*But the car has started off, with a medley of voices shouting farewells, which fade quickly out of hearing.* SERAFINA *turns about vaguely in the confusing sunlight and gropes for the door. There is a derisive cackle from the witch next door.* SERAFINA *absently opens the package and removes the little gold watch. She winds it and then holds it against her ear. She shakes it and holds it again to her ear. Then she holds it away from her and glares at it fiercely.*]

SERAFINA: [*Pounding her chest three times.*] Tick—tick—tick! [*She goes to the Madonna and faces it.*] Speak to me, Lady! Oh, Lady, give me a sign!

[*The scene dims out.*]

[9] A present, a present—my treasure!

ACT TWO

It is two hours later the same day.

SERAFINA *comes out onto the porch, barefooted, wearing a rayon slip. Great shadows have appeared beneath her eyes; her face and throat gleam with sweat. There are dark stains of wine on the rayon slip. It is difficult for her to stand, yet she cannot sit still. She makes a sick moaning sound in her throat almost continually.*

A hot wind rattles the cane-brake. VIVI, *the little girl, comes up to the porch to stare at* SERAFINA *as at a strange beast in a cage.* VIVI *is chewing a licorice stick which stains her mouth and her fingers. She stands chewing and staring.* SERAFINA *evades her stare. She wearily drags a broken grey wicker chair down off the porch, all the way out in front of the house, and sags heavily into it. It sits awry on a broken leg.*

VIVI *sneaks toward her.* SERAFINA *lurches about to face her angrily. The child giggles and scampers back to the porch.*

SERAFINA: [*Sinking back into the chair.*] Oh, Lady, Lady, Lady, give me a—sign . . . [*She looks up at the white glare of the sky.*]

[FATHER DE LEO *approaches the house.* SERAFINA *crouches low in the chair to escape his attention. He knocks at the door. Receiving no answer, he looks* out into the yard, sees her, and approaches her chair. He comes close to address her with a gentle severity.]

FATHER DE LEO: Buon giorno, Serafina.[1]

SERAFINA: [Faintly, with a sort of disgust.] Giorno . . .

FATHER DE LEO: I'm surprised to see you sitting outdoors like this. What is that thing you're wearing?—I think it's an undergarment!—It's hanging off one shoulder, and your head, Serafina, looks as if you had stuck it in a bucket of oil. Oh, I see now why the other ladies of the neighborhood aren't taking their afternoon naps! They find it more entertaining to sit on the porches and watch the spectacle you are putting on for them!—Are you listening to me?—I must tell you that the change in your appearance and behavior since Rosario's death is shocking—shocking! A woman can be dignified in her grief but when it's carried too far it becomes a sort of self-indulgence. Oh, I knew this was going to happen when you broke the Church law and had your husband cremated! [SERAFINA lurches up from the chair and shuffles back to the porch. FATHER DE LEO follows her.]—Set up a little idolatrous shrine in your house and give worship to a bottle of ashes. [She sinks down upon the steps.] —Are you listening to me?

[Two women have appeared on the embankment and descend toward the house. SERAFINA lurches heavily up to meet them, like a weary bull turning to face another attack.]

SERAFINA: You ladies, what you want? I don't do sewing! Look, I quit doing sewing. [She pulls down the "SEWING" sign and hurls it away.] Now you got places to go, you ladies, go places! Don't hang around front of my house!

FATHER DE LEO: The ladies want to be friendly.

SERAFINA: Naw, they don't come to be friendly. They think they know something that Serafina don't know; they think I got these on my head! [She holds her fingers like horns at either side of her forehead.] Well, I ain't got them! [She goes padding back out in front of the house. FATHER DE LEO follows.]

FATHER DE LEO: You called me this morning in distress over something.

SERAFINA: I called you this morning but now it is afternoon.

FATHER DE LEO: I had to christen the grandson of the Mayor.

SERAFINA: The Mayor's important people, not Serafina!

FATHER DE LEO: You don't come to confession.

SERAFINA: [Starting back toward the porch.] No, I don't come, I don't go, I—Ohhh! [She pulls up one foot and hops on the other.]

FATHER DE LEO: You stepped on something?

SERAFINA: [Dropping down on the steps.] No, no, no, no, no, I don't step on—noth'n . . .

FATHER DE LEO: Come in the house. We'll wash it with antiseptic. [She lurches up and limps back toward the house.] Walking barefooted you will get it infected.

SERAFINA: Fa niente . . .

[At the top of the embankment a little boy runs out with a red kite and flourishes it in the air with rigid gestures, as though he were giving a distant signal. SERAFINA shades her eyes with a palm to watch the kite, and then, as though its motions conveyed a shocking message, she utters a startled soft cry and staggers back to the porch. She leans against a pillar, running her hand rapidly and repeatedly through her hair. FATHER DE LEO approaches her again, somewhat timidly.]

FATHER DE LEO: Serafina?

SERAFINA: Che, che, che cosa vuole?[2]

FATHER DE LEO: I am thirsty. Will you go in the house and get me some water?

SERAFINA: Go in. Get you some water. The faucet is working.—I can't go in the house.

FATHER DE LEO: Why can't you go in the house?

SERAFINA: The house has a tin roof on it. I got to breathe.

FATHER DE LEO: You can breathe in the house.

SERAFINA: No, I can't breathe in the house. The house has a tin roof on it and I . . .

[THE STREGA has been creeping through the cane-brake pretending to search for a chicken.]

THE STREGA: Chick, chick, chick, chick,

[1] Good morning, Serafina.

[2] What, what, what do you want?

chick? [*She crouches to peer under the house.*]

SERAFINA: What's that? Is that the . . . ? Yes, the Strega! [*She picks up a flower pot containing a dead plant and crosses the yard.*] Strega! Strega! [THE STREGA *looks up, retreating a little.*] Yes, you, I mean you! You ain't look for no chick! Getta hell outa my yard! [THE STREGA *retreats, viciously muttering, back into the cane-brake.* SERAFINA *makes the protective sign of the horns with her fingers. The goat bleats.*]

FATHER DE LEO: You have no friends, Serafina.

SERAFINA: I don't want friends.

FATHER DE LEO: You are still a young woman. Eligible for—loving and—bearing again! I remember you dressed in pale blue silk at Mass one Easter morning, yes, like a lady wearing a—piece of the—weather! Oh, how proudly you walked, *too* proudly! —But now you crouch and shuffle about barefooted; you live like a convict, dressed in the rags of a convict. You have no companions; women you don't mix with. You . . .

SERAFINA: No, I don't mix with them women. [*Glaring at the women on the embankment.*] The dummies I got in my house. I mix with them better because they don't make up no lies!—What kind of women are them? [*Mimicking fiercely.*] "Eee, Papa, eeee, baby, eee, me, me, me! At thirty years old they got no more use for the letto matrimoniale,[3] no. The big bed goes to the basement! They get little beds from Sears Roebuck and sleep on their bellies!

FATHER DE LEO: Attenzione![4]

SERAFINA: They make the life without glory. Instead of the heart they got the deep-freeze in the house. The men, they don't feel no glory, not in the house with them women; they go to the bars, fight in them, get drunk, get fat, put horns on the women because the women's don't give them the love which is glory.—I did, I give him the glory. To me the big bed was beautiful like a religion. Now I lie on it with dreams, with memories only! But it is still beautiful to me and I don't believe that the man in my heart gave me horns! [*The women whisper.*] What, what are they saying? Does ev'rybody know something that

I don't know?—No, all I want is a sign, a sign from Our Lady, to tell me the lie is a lie! And then I . . . [*The women laugh on the embankment.* SERAFINA *starts fiercely toward them. They scatter.*] Squeak, squeak, squawk, squawk! Hens—like water thrown on them! [*There is the sound of mocking laughter.*]

FATHER DE LEO: People are laughing at you on all the porches.

SERAFINA: I'm laughing, too. Listen to me, I'm laughing! [*She breaks into loud, false laughter, first from the porch, then from the foot of the embankment, then crossing in front of the house.*] Ha, ha, ha, ha, ha, ha! Now ev'rybody is laughing. Ha, ha ha, ha, ha, ha!

FATHER DE LEO: Zitta ora!—Think of your daughter.

SERAFINA: [*Understanding the word "daughter."*] You, *you* think of my daughter! Today you give out the diplomas, today at the high school you give out the prizes, diplomas! You give to my daughter a set of books call the Digest of Knowledge! What does she know? How to be cheap already? —Oh, yes, that is what to learn, how to be cheap and to cheat!— You know what they do at this high school? They ruin the girls there! They give the spring dance because the girls are man-crazy. And there at that dance my daughter goes with a sailor that has in his ear a gold ring! And pants so tight that a woman ought not to look at him! This morning, this morning she cuts with a knife her wrist if I don't let her go!— Now all of them gone to some island, they call it a picnic, all of them, gone in a—boat!

FATHER DE LEO: There *was* a school picnic, chaperoned by the teachers.

SERAFINA: Oh, lo so, lo so! The man-crazy old-maid teachers!—They all run wild on the island!

FATHER DE LEO: Serafina delle Rose! [*He picks up the chair by the back and hauls it to the porch when she starts to resume her seat.*]—I command you to go in the house.

SERAFINA: Go in the house? I will. I will go in the house if you will answer one question.—Will you answer one question?

FATHER DE LEO: I will if I know the answer.

SERAFINA: Aw, you know the answer!— You used to hear the confessions of my husband. [*She turns to face the priest.*]

___
[3] Double bed.   [4] Listen to me!

FATHER DE LEO: Yes, I heard his confessions . . .

SERAFINA: [With difficulty.] Did he ever speak to you of a woman?

[A child cries out and races across in front of the house. FATHER DE LEO picks up his panama hat. SERAFINA paces slowly toward him. He starts away from the house.]

SERAFINA: [Rushing after him.] Aspettate! Aspettate un momento! [5]

FATHER DE LEO: [Fearfully, not looking at her.] Che volete? [6]

SERAFINA: Rispondetemi! [7] [She strikes her breast.] Did he speak of a woman to you?

FATHER DE LEO: You know better than to ask me such a question. I don't break the Church laws. The secrets of the confessional are sacred to me. [He walks away.]

SERAFINA: [Pursuing and clutching his arm.] I got to know. You could tell me.

FATHER DE LEO: Let go of me, Serafina!

SERAFINA: Not till you tell me, Father. Father, you tell me, please tell me! Or I will go mad! [In a fierce whisper.] I will go back in the house and smash the urn with the ashes—if you don't tell me! I will go mad with the doubt in my heart and I will smash the urn and scatter the ashes—of my husband's body!

FATHER DE LEO: What could I tell you? If you would not believe the known facts about him . . .

SERAFINA: Known facts, who knows the known facts?

[The neighbor women have heard the argument and begin to crowd around, muttering in shocked whispers at SERAFINA's lack of respect.]

FATHER DE LEO: [Frightened.] Lasciatemi, lasciatemi stare! [8]—Oh, Serafina, I am too old for this—please!—Everybody is . . .

SERAFINA: [In a fierce, hissing whisper.] Nobody knew my rose of the world but me and now they can lie because the rose ain't living. They want the marble urn broken; they want me to smash it. They want the rose ashes scattered because I had too much glory. They don't want glory like that in nobody's heart. They want—mouse-squeaking!—known facts.—Who knows the

known facts? You—padres—wear black because of the fact that the facts are known by nobody!

FATHER DE LEO: Oh, Serafina! There are people watching!

SERAFINA: Let them watch something. That will be a change for them.—It's been a long time I wanted to break out like this and now I . . .

FATHER DE LEO: I am too old a man; I am not strong enough. I am sixty-seven years old! Must I call for help, now?

SERAFINA: Yes, call! Call for help, but I won't let you go till you tell me!

FATHER DE LEO: You're not a respectable woman.

SERAFINA: No, I'm not a respectable; I'm a woman.

FATHER DE LEO: No, you are not a woman. You are an animal!

SERAFINA: Si, si, animale! Sono animale! Animale. [9] Tell them all, shout it all to them, up and down the whole block! The widow Delle Rose is not respectable, she is not even a woman, she is an animal! She is attacking the priest! She will tear the black suit off him unless he tells her the whores in this town are lying to her!

[The neighbor women have been drawing closer as the argument progresses, and now they come to FATHER DE LEO's rescue and assist him to get away from SERAFINA, who is on the point of attacking him bodily. He cries out, "Officer! Officer!" but the women drag SERAFINA from him and lead him away with comforting murmurs.]

SERAFINA: [Striking her wrists together.] Yes, it's me, it's me!! Lock me up, lock me, lock me up! Or I will—smash!—the marble . . . [She throws her head far back and presses her fists to her eyes. Then she rushes crazily to the steps and falls across them.]

ASSUNTA: Serafina! Figlia! Figlia! Andiamo a casa! [10]

SERAFINA: Leave me alone, old woman. [She returns slowly to the porch steps and sinks down on them, sitting like a tired man, her knees spread apart and her head cupped in her hands. The children steal back around the house. A little boy shoots a bean-shooter at her. She starts up with a cry. The children scatter, shrieking. She sinks down

[5] Wait! Wait a minute!
[6] What do you want?
[7] Answer me!   [8] Leave me, let me alone!

[9] Yes, yes, animal! I am an animal. An anima..
[10] Daughter! Daughter! Come home!

on the steps, then leans back, staring up at the sky, her body rocking.]

SERAFINA: Oh, Lady, Lady, Lady, give me a sign!

[*As if in mocking answer, a novelty salesman appears and approaches the porch. He is a fat man in a seersucker suit and a straw hat with a yellow, red and purple band. His face is beet-red and great moons of sweat have soaked through the armpits of his jacket. His shirt is lavender, and his tie, pale blue with great yellow polkadots, is a butterfly bow. His entrance is accompanied by a brief, satiric strain of music.*]

THE SALESMAN: Good afternoon, lady. [*She looks up slowly. The salesman talks sweetly, as if reciting a prayer.*] I got a little novelty here which I am offering to just a few lucky people at what we call an introductory price. Know what I mean? Not a regular price but a price which is less than what it costs to manufacture the article, a price we are making for the sake of introducing the product in the Gulf Coast territory. Lady, this thing here that I'm droppin' right in youah lap is bigger than television; it's going to revolutionize the domestic life of America.—Now I don't do house to house canvassing. I sell directly to merchants but when I stopped over there to have my car serviced, I seen you taking the air on the steps and I thought I would just drop over and . . .

[*There is the sound of a big truck stopping on the highway, and a man's voice, ALVARO'S, is heard, shouting.*]

ALVARO: Hey! Hey! you road hog!

THE SALESMAN: [*Taking a sample out of his bag.*] Now, lady, this little article has a deceptive appearance. First of all, I want you to notice how *compact* it is. It takes up no more space than . . .

[*ALVARO comes down from the embankment. He is about twenty-five years old, dark and very good-looking. He is one of those Mediterranean types that resemble glossy young bulls. He is short in stature, has a massively sculptural torso and bluish-black curls. His face and manner are clownish; he has a charming awkwardness. There is a startling, improvised air about him; he frequently seems surprised at his own speeches and actions, as though he had not at all anticipated them. At the*]

moment when we first hear his voice the sound of a timpani begins, at first very pianissimo, but building up as he approaches, till it reaches a vibrant climax with his appearance to SERAFINA beside the house.*]

ALVARO: Hey.

THE SALESMAN: [*Without glancing at him.*] Hay is for horses!—Now, madam, you see what happens when I press this button!

[*The article explodes in SERAFINA'S face. She slaps it away with an angry cry. At the same time ALVARO advances, trembling with rage, to the porch steps. He is sweating and stammering with pent-up fury at a world of frustrations which are temporarily localized in the gross figure of this salesman.*]

ALVARO: Hey, you! Come here! What the hell's the idea, back there at that curve? You make me drive off the highway!

THE SALESMAN: [*To SERAFINA.*] Excuse me for just one minute. [*He wheels menacingly about to face ALVARO.*] Is something giving you gas pains, Maccaroni?

ALVARO: My name is not Maccaroni.

THE SALESMAN: All right. Spaghetti.

ALVARO: [*Almost sobbing with passion.*] I am not maccaroni. I am not spaghetti. I am a human being that drives a truck of bananas. I drive a truck of bananas for the Southern Fruit Company for a living, not to play cowboys and Indians on no highway with no rotten road hog. You got a 4-lane highway between Pass Christian and here. I give you the sign to pass me. You tail me and give me the horn. You yell "Wop" at me and "Dago." "Move over, Wop, move over, Dago." Then at the goddam curve, you go pass me and make me drive off the highway and yell back "Son of a bitch of a Dago!" I don't like that, no, no! And I am glad you stop here. Take the cigar from your mouth, take out the cigar!

THE SALESMAN: Take it out for me, greaseball.

ALVARO: If I take it out I will push it down your throat. I got three dependents! If I fight, I get fired, but I will fight and get fired. Take out the cigar!

[*Spectators begin to gather at the edge of the scene. SERAFINA stares at the truck driver, her eyes like a somnambule's. All at once she utters a low cry and seems about to fall.*]

ALVARO: Take out the cigar, take out, take out the cigar!

[*He snatches the cigar from the salesman's mouth and the salesman brings his knee up violently into* ALVARO'S *groin. Bending double and retching with pain,* ALVARO *staggers over to the porch.*]

THE SALESMAN: [*Shouting, as he goes off.*] I got your license number, Maccaroni! I know your boss!

ALVARO: [*Howling.*] Drop dead! [*He suddenly staggers up the steps.*] Lady, lady, I got to go in the house!

[*As soon as he enters, he bursts into rending sobs, leaning against a wall and shaking convulsively. The spectators outside laugh as they scatter.* SERAFINA *slowly enters the house. The screen door rasps loudly on its rusty springs as she lets it swing gradually shut behind her, her eyes remaining fixed with a look of stupefied wonder upon the sobbing figure of the truck driver. We must understand her profound unconscious response to this sudden contact with distress as acute as her own. There is a long pause as the screen door makes its whining, catlike noise swinging shut by degrees.*]

SERAFINA: Somebody's—in my house? [*Finally, in a hoarse, tremulous whisper.*] What are you—doing in here? Why have you—come in my house?

ALVARO: Oh, lady—leave me alone!—Please—now!

SERAFINA: You—got no business—in here . . .

ALVARO: I got to cry after a fight. I'm sorry lady. I . . .

[*The sobs still shake him. He leans on a dummy.*]

SERAFINA: Don't lean on my dummy. Sit down if you can't stand up.—What is the matter with you?

ALVARO: I always cry after a fight. But I don't want people to see me. It's not like a man. [*There is a long pause;* SERAFINA'S *attitude seems to warm toward the man.*]

SERAFINA: A man is not no different from no one else . . . [*All at once her face puckers up, and for the first time in the play* SERAFINA *begins to weep, at first soundlessly, then audibly. Soon she is sobbing as loudly as* ALVARO. *She speaks between sobs.*]—I always cry—when somebody else is crying . . .

ALVARO: No, no, lady, *don't* cry! Why should *you* cry? I will stop. I will stop in a minute. This is not like a man. I am ashame of myself. I will stop now; please, lady . . .

[*Still crouching a little with pain, a hand clasped to his abdomen.* ALVARO *turns away from the wall. He blows his nose between two fingers.* SERAFINA *picks up a scrap of white voile and gives it to him to wipe his fingers.*]

SERAFINA: Your jacket is torn.

ALVARO: [*Sobbing.*] My company jacket is torn?

SERAFINA: Yes . . .

ALVARO: Where is it torn?

SERAFINA: [*Sobbing.*] Down the—back.

ALVARO: Oh, Dio!

SERAFINA: Take it off. I will sew it up for you. I do—sewing.

ALVARO: Oh, Dio! [*Sobbing.*] I got three dependents! [*He holds up three fingers and shakes them violently at* SERAFINA.]

SERAFINA: Give me—give me your jacket.

ALVARO: He took down my license number!

SERAFINA: People are always taking down license numbers and telephone numbers and numbers that don't mean nothing—them numbers . . .

ALVARO: Three, three dependents! Not citizens, even! No relief checks, no nothing! [SERAFINA *sobs.*] He is going to complain to the boss.

SERAFINA: I wanted to cry all day.

ALVARO: He said he would fire me if I don't stop fighting!

SERAFINA: Stop crying so I can stop crying.

ALVARO: I am a sissy. Excuse me. I am ashame.

SERAFINA: Don't be ashame of nothing, the world is too crazy for people to be ashame in it. I'm not ashame and I had two fights on the street and my daughter called me "disgusting." I got to sew this by hand; the machine is broke in a fight with two women.

ALVARO: That's what—they call a cat fight . . . [*He blows his nose.*]

SERAFINA: Open the shutters, please, for me. I can't see to work. [*She has crossed to her work table. He goes over to the window. As he opens the shutters, the light falls across his fine torso, the undershirt clinging wetly to his dark olive skin.* SERAFINA *is struck and murmurs: "Ohhh . . ." There is the sound of music.*]

ALVARO: What, lady?

SERAFINA: [*In a strange voice.*] The light on the body was like a man that lived here . . .

ALVARO: Che dice? [11]

SERAFINA: Niente.—Ma com'è strano!—Lei é Napoletano? [12] [*She is threading a needle.*]

ALVARO: Io sono Siciliano! [SERAFINA *sticks her finger with her needle and cries out.*] Che fa? [13]

SERAFINA: I—stuck myself with the—needle!—you had—better wash up . . .

ALVARO: Dov'è il gabinetto? [14]

SERAFINA: [*Almost inaudibly.*] Dietro.[15] [*She points vaguely back.*]

ALVARO: Con permesso! [16] [*He moves past her. As he does so, she picks up a pair of broken spectacles on the work table. Holding them by the single remaining side piece, like a lorgnette, she inspects his passing figure with an air of stupefaction. As he goes out, he says.*] A kick like that can have serious consequences! [*He goes into the back of the house.*]

SERAFINA: [*After a pause.*] Madonna Santa! [17]—*My husband's body,* with the head of a *clown!* [*She crosses to the Madonna.*] O Lady, O Lady! [*She makes an imploring gesture.*] Speak to me!—What are you saying!—Please, Lady, I can't hear you! Is it a sign? Is it a sign of something? What does it mean? Oh, *speak to me, Lady!* —Everything is too strange!

> [*She gives up the useless entreaty to the impassive statue. Then she rushes to the cupboard, clambers up on a chair and seizes a bottle of wine from the top shelf. But she finds it impossible to descend from the chair. Clasping the dusty bottle to her breast, she crouches there, helplessly whimpering like a child, as* ALVARO *comes back in.*]

ALVARO: Ciao! [18]

SERAFINA: I can't get up.

ALVARO: You mean you can't get down?

SERAFINA: I mean I—can't get down . . .

[11] What are you saying?
[12] Nothing.–But how strange! Are you Neapolitan?
[13] I'm Sicilian. What are you doing?
[14] Where's the bathroom?   [15] Back there.
[16] With your permission.   [17] Holy Mother!
[18] So long!

ALVARO: Con permesso,[19] Signora! [*He lifts her down from the chair.*]

SERAFINA: Grazie.[20]

ALVARO: I am ashame of what happen. Crying is not like a man. Did anyone see me?

SERAFINA: Nobody saw you but me. To me it don't matter.

ALVARO: You are simpatica, molto! [21]—It was not just the fight that makes me break down. I was like this all today! [*He shakes his clenched fists in the air.*]

SERAFINA: You and—me, too!—What was the trouble today?

ALVARO: My name is Mangiacavallo which means "Eat-a-horse." It's a comical name, I know. Maybe two thousand and seventy years ago one of my grandfathers got so hungry that he ate up a horse! That ain't my fault. Well, today at the Southern Fruit Company I find on the pay envelope not "Mangiacavallo" but "EAT A HORSE" in big print! Ha, ha, ha, very funny!—I open the pay envelope! In it I find a notice.—The wages have been *garnishee!* You know what garnishee is? [SERAFINA *nods gravely*.] Garnishee!—Eat a horse!—Road hog!—All in one day is too much! I go crazy, I boil, I cry, and I am ashame but I am not able to help it!—Even a Wop truck driver's a human being! And human beings must cry . . .

SERAFINA: Yes, they must cry. I couldn't cry all day but now I have cried and I am feeling much better.—I will sew up the jacket . . .

ALVARO: [*Licking his lips.*] What is that in your hand? A bottle of vino?

SERAFINA: This is Spumanti. It comes from the house of the family of my husband. The Delle Rose! A very great family. I was a peasant, but I married a baron!—No, I still don't believe it! I married a baron when I didn't have shoes!

ALVARO: Excuse me for asking—but where is the Baron, now? [SERAFINA *points gravely to the marble urn.*] Where did you say?

SERAFINA: Them're his ashes in that marble urn.

ALVARO: Ma! Scusatemi! Scusatemi! [22] [*Crossing himself.*]—I hope he is resting in peace.

[19] With your permission.
[20] Thanks.
[21] You are very nice, very!
[22] But! Excuse me! Excuse me!

SERAFINA: It's him you reminded me of—when you opened the shutters. Not the face but the body.—Please get me some ice from the icebox in the kitchen. I had a—very bad day . . .

ALVARO: Oh, ice! Yes—ice—I'll get some . . .

[*As he goes out, she looks again through the broken spectacles at him.*]

SERAFINA: *Non posso crederlo!* [23]—A clown of a face like that with my husband's body!

[*There is the sound of ice being chopped in the kitchen. She inserts a corkscrew in the bottle but her efforts to open it are clumsily unsuccessful.* ALVARO *returns with a little bowl of ice. He sets it down so hard on the table that a piece flies out. He scrambles after it, retrieves it and wipes it off on his sweaty undershirt.*]

SERAFINA: I think the floor would be cleaner!

ALVARO: Scusatemi!—I wash it again?

SERAFINA: Fa niente! [24]

ALVARO: I am a—clean!—I . . .

SERAFINA: Fa niente, niente!—The bottle should be in the ice but the next best thing is to pour the wine over the bottle.

ALVARO: You mean over the ice?

SERAFINA: I mean over the . . .

ALVARO: Let me open the bottle. Your hands are not used to rough work. [*She surrenders the bottle to him and regards him through the broken spectacles again.*]

SERAFINA: These little bits of white voile on the floor are not from a snowstorm. I been making voile dresses for high school graduation.—One for my daughter and for thirteen other girls.—All of the work I'm not sure didn't kill me!

ALVARO: The wine will make you feel better.

[*There is a youthful cry from outside.*]

SERAFINA: There is a wild bunch of boys and girls in this town. In Sicily the boys would dance with the boys because a girl and a boy could not dance together unless they was going to be married. But here they run wild on islands!—boys, girls, man-crazy teachers . . .

ALVARO: Ecco! [*The cork comes off with a loud pop.* SERAFINA *cries out and staggers against the table. He laughs. She laughs with him, helplessly, unable to stop, unable*

to catch her breath.]—I like a woman that laughs with all her heart.

SERAFINA: And a woman that cries with her heart?

ALVARO: I like everything that a woman does with her heart.

[*Both are suddenly embarrassed and their laughter dies out.* SERAFINA *smooths down her rayon slip. He hands her a glass of the sparkling wine with ice in it. She murmurs "Grazie."* [*Unconsciously the injured finger is lifted again to her lip and she wanders away from the table with the glass held shakily*]

ALVARO: [*Continuing nervously.*] I see you had a bad day.

SERAFINA: Sono così—stanca . . .[25]

ALVARO: [*Suddenly springing to the window and shouting.*] Hey, you kids, git down off that truck! Keep your hands off them bananas! [*At the words "truck" and "bananas"* SERAFINA *gasps again and spills some wine on her slip.*] Little buggers!—Scusatemi . . .

SERAFINA: You haul—you haul bananas?

ALVARO: Si, Signora.

SERAFINA: Is it a 10-ton truck?

ALVARO: An 8-ton truck.

SERAFINA: My husband hauled bananas in a 10-ton truck.

ALVARO: Well, he was a baron.

SERAFINA: Do you haul just bananas?

ALVARO: Just bananas. What else would I haul?

SERAFINA: My husband hauled bananas, but underneath the bananas was something else. He was—wild like a Gypsy.—"Wild—like a—Gypsy"? Who said that?—I hate to start to remember, and then not remember . . .

[*The dialogue between them is full of odd hesitations, broken sentences and tentative gestures. Both are nervously exhausted after their respective ordeals. Their fumbling communication has a curious intimacy and sweetness, like the meeting of two lonely children for the first time. It is oddly luxurious to them both, luxurious as the first cool wind of evening after a scorching day.* SERAFINA *idly picks up a little Sicilian souvenir cart from the table.*]

SERAFINA: The priest was against it.

ALVARO: What was the priest against?

[23] *I can't believe it!*   [24] It's nothing!   [25] I'm so—tired . . .

SERAFINA: Me keeping the ashes. It was against the Church law. But I had to have something and that was all I could have. [*She sets down the cart.*]

ALVARO: I don't see nothing wrong with it.

SERAFINA: You don't?

ALVARO: No! Niente! [26]—The body would've decayed, but ashes always stay clean.

SERAFINA: [*Eagerly.*] Si, si, bodies decay, but ashes always stay clean! Come here. I show you this picture—my wedding. [*She removes a picture tenderly from the wall.*] Here's me a bride of fourteen, and this—this —this! [*Drumming the picture with her finger and turning her face to* ALVARO *with great lustrous eyes.*] My husband! [*There is a pause. He takes the picture from her hand and holds it first close to his eyes, then far back, then again close with suspirations of appropriate awe.*] Annnh?—Annnnh?—Che dice!* [27]

ALVARO: [*Slowly, with great emphasis.*] Che bell' uomo! Che bell' uomo! [28]

SERAFINA: [*Replacing the picture.*] A rose of a man. On his chest he had the tattoo of a rose. [*Then, quite suddenly.*]— Do you believe strange things, or do you doubt them?

ALVARO: If strange things didn't happen, I wouldn't be here. You wouldn't be here. We wouldn't be talking together.

SERAFINA: Davvero! [29] I'll tell you something about the tattoo of my husband. My husband, he had this rose tattoo on his chest. One night I woke up with a burning pain on me here. I turn on the light. I look at my naked breast and on it I see the rose tattoo of my husband, on me, on *my* breast, *his* tattoo.

ALVARO: Strano! [30]

SERAFINA: And that was the night that— I got to speak frankly to tell you . . .

ALVARO: Speak frankly! We're grown-up people.

SERAFINA: That was the night I conceived my son—the little boy that was lost when I lost my husband . . .

ALVARO: Che cosa—strana! [31]—Would you be willing to show me the rose tattoo?

SERAFINA: Oh, it's gone now, it only lasted

a moment. But I did see it. I saw it clearly. —Do you believe me?

ALVARO: Lo credo! [32]

SERAFINA: I don't know why I told you. But I like what you said. That bodies decay but ashes always stay clean—immacolate! [33] —But, you know, there are some people that want to make everything dirty. Two of them kind of people come in the house today and told me a terrible lie in front of the ashes.—So awful a lie that if I thought it was true—I would smash the urn—and throw the ashes away! [*She hurls her glass suddenly to the floor.*] Smash it, *smash it* like that!

ALVARO: Ma!—Baronessa! [34]

[SERAFINA *seizes a broom and sweeps the fragments of glass away.*]

SERAFINA: And take this broom and sweep them out the back door like so much trash!

ALVARO: [*Impressed by her violence and a little awed.*] What lie did they tell you?

SERAFINA: No, no, no! I don't want to talk about it! [*She throws down the broom.*] I just want to forget it; it wasn't true, it was false, false, false!—as the hearts of the bitches that told it . . .

ALVARO: Yes. I would forget anything that makes you unhappy.

SERAFINA: The memory of a love don't make you unhappy unless you believe a lie that makes it dirty. I don't believe in the lie. The ashes are clean. The memory of the rose in my heart is perfect!—Your glass is weeping . . .

ALVARO: *Your* glass is weeping too.

[*While she fills his glass, he moves about the room, looking here and there. She follows him. Each time he picks up an article for inspection she gently takes it from him and examines it herself with fresh interest.*]

ALVARO: Cozy little homelike place you got here.

SERAFINA: Oh, it's—molto modesto.[35]— You got a nice place too?

ALVARO: I got a place with three dependents in it.

SERAFINA: What—dependents?

ALVARO: [*Counting them on his fingers.*] One old maid sister, one feeble-minded grandmother, one lush of a pop that's not

[26] Nothing.
[27] What are you saying!
[28] What a fine man! What a fine man!
[29] It's true. [30] Strange.
[31] What a strange thing!

[32] I believe it!
[33] Uncorrupted!
[34] But!—Baroness! [35] Very modest.

worth the powder it takes to blow him to hell.—They got the parchesi habit. They play the game of parchesi, morning, night, noon. Passing a bucket of beer around the table . . .

SERAFINA: They got the beer habit, too?

ALVARO: Oh, yes. And the numbers habit. This spring the old maid sister gets female trouble—mostly mental, I think—she turns the housekeeping over to the feeble-minded grandmother, a very sweet old lady who don't think it is necessary to pay the grocery bill so long as there's money to play the numbers. She plays the numbers. She has a perfect system except it don't ever work. And the grocery bill goes up, up, up, up, up!—so high you can't even see it!—Today the Ideal Grocery Company garnishees my wages . . . There, now! I've told you my life . . . [*The parrot squawks. He goes over to the cage.*] Hello, Polly, how's tricks?

SERAFINA: The name ain't Polly. It ain't a she; it's a he.

ALVARO: How can you tell with all them tail feathers? [*He sticks his finger in the cage, pokes at the parrot and gets bitten.*] Owww!

SERAFINA: [*Vicariously.*] Ouuu . . . [*Alvaro sticks his injured finger in his mouth.* SERAFINA *puts her corresponding finger in her mouth. He crosses to the telephone.*] I told you watch out.—What are you calling, a doctor?

ALVARO: I am calling my boss in Biloxi to explain why I'm late.

SERAFINA: The call to Biloxi is a ten-cent call.

ALVARO: Don't worry about it.

SERAFINA: I'm not worried about it. You will pay it.

ALVARO: You got a sensible attitude toward life . . . Give me the Southern Fruit Company in Biloxi—seven-eight-seven!

SERAFINA: You are a bachelor. With three dependents? [*She glances below his belt.*]

ALVARO: I'll tell you my hopes and dreams!

SERAFINA: Who? Me?

ALVARO: I am hoping to meet some sensible older lady. Maybe a lady a little bit older than me.—I don't care if she's a little too plump or not such a stylish dresser! [SERAFINA *selfconsciously pulls up a dangling strap.*] The important thing in a lady is understanding. Good sense. And I want her to have a well-furnished house and a

profitable little business of some kind . . . [*He looks about him significantly.*]

SERAFINA: And such a lady, with a well-furnished house and business, what does she want with a man with three dependents with the parchesi and the beer habit, playing the numbers!

ALVARO: Love and affection!—in a world that is lonely—and cold!

SERAFINA: It might be lonely but I would not say "cold" on this particular day!

ALVARO: Love and affection is what I got to offer on hot or cold days in this lonely old world and is what I am looking for. I got nothing else. Mangiacavallo has nothing. In fact, he is the grandson of the village idiot of Ribera!

SERAFINA: [*Uneasily.*] I see you like to make—jokes!

ALVARO: No, no joke!—Davvero! [36]—He chased my grandmother in a flooded rice field. She slip on a wet rock.—Ecco! Here I am.

SERAFINA: You ought to be more respectful.

ALVARO: What have I got to respect? The rock my grandmother slips on?

SERAFINA: Yourself at least! Don't you work for a living?

ALVARO: If I *don't* work for a living I would respect myself *more*. Baronessa, I am a healthy young man, existing without no love life. I look at the magazine pictures. Them girls in the advertisement—you know what I mean? A little bitty thing here? A little bitty thing there?

[*He touches two portions of his anatomy. The latter portion embarrasses* SERAFINA, *who quietly announces.*]

SERAFINA: The call is ten cents for three minutes. Is the line busy?

ALVARO: Not the line, but the boss.

SERAFINA: And the charge for the call goes higher. That ain't the phone of a millionaire you're using!

ALVARO: I think you talk a poor mouth. [*He picks up the piggy bank and shakes it.*] This pig sounds well-fed to me.

SERAFINA: Dimes and quarters.

ALVARO: Dimes and quarters're better than nickels and dimes. [SERAFINA *rises severely and removes the piggy bank from his grasp.*] Ha, ha, ha! You think I'm a bank robber?

[36] It's true.

SERAFINA: I think you are maleducato! [37] Just get your boss on the phone or hang the phone up.

ALVARO: What, what! Mr. Siccardi? How tricks at the Southern Fruit Com'ny this hot afternoon? Ha, ha, ha!—Mangiacavallo! —What? You got the complaint already? Sentite, per favore! [38] This road hog was— Mr. Siccardi? [He jiggles the hook; then slowly hangs up.] A man with three dependents!—out of a job . . . [There is a pause.]

SERAFINA: Well, you better ask the operator the charges.

ALVARO: Oofla! A man with three dependents—out of a job!

SERAFINA: I can't see to work no more. I got a suggestion to make. Open the bottom drawer of that there bureau and you will find a shirt in white tissue paper and you can wear that one while I am fixing this. And call for it later. [He crosses to the bureau.]—It was made for somebody that never called for it. [He removes the package.] Is there a name pinned to it?

ALVARO: Yes, it's . . .

SERAFINA: [Fiercely, but with no physical movement.] Don't tell me the name! Throw it away, out the window!

ALVARO: Perchè? [39]

SERAFINA: Throw it, throw it away!

ALVARO: [Crumpling the paper and throwing it through the window.] Ecco fatto! [40] [There is a distant cry of children as he unwraps the package and holds up the rose silk shirt, exclaiming in Latin delight at the luxury of it.] Colore di rose! Seta! Seta pura! [41]—Oh, this shirt is too good for Mangiacavallo! Everything here is too good for Mangiacavallo!

SERAFINA: Nothing's too good for a man if the man is good.

ALVARO: The grandson of a village idiot is not that good.

SERAFINA: No matter whose grandson you are, put it on; you are welcome to wear it.

ALVARO: [Slipping voluptuously into the shirt.] Sssssss!

SERAFINA: How does it feel, the silk, on you?

ALVARO: It feels like a girl's hand on me!

[There is a pause, while he shows the whiteness of his teeth.]

SERAFINA: [Holding up her broken spectacles.] It will make you less trouble.

ALVARO: There is nothing more beautiful than a gift between people!—Now you are smiling!—You like me a little better?

SERAFINA: [Slowly and tenderly.] You know what they should of done when you was a baby? They should of put tape on your ears to hold them back so when you grow up they wouldn't stick out like the wings of a little kewpie! [She touches his ear, a very slight touch, betraying too much of her heart. Both laugh a little and she turns away, embarrassed.]

[Outside the goat bleats and there is the sound of splintering timber. One of the children races into the front yard, crying out.]

SALVATORE: Mizz' Dell' Rose! The black goat's in your yard!

SERAFINA: Il becco della strega! [42]

[SERAFINA dashes to the window, throws the shutters violently open and leans way out. This time, she almost feels relief in this distraction. The interlude of the goat chase has a quality of crazed exaltation. Outside is heard the wild bleating of the goat and the jingling of his harness.]

SERAFINA: Miei pomodori! Guarda i miei pomodori! [43]

THE STREGA: [Entering the front yard with a broken length of rope, calling out.] Heyeh, Billy! Heyeh, Heyeh, Billy!

SERAFINA: [Making the sign of horns with her fingers.] There is the Strega! She lets the goat in my yard to eat my tomatoes! [Backing from the window.] She has the eye; she has the malocchio, and so does the goat! The goat has the evil eye, too. He got in my yard the night that I lost Rosario and my boy! Madonna, Madonna mia! Get that goat out of my yard! [She retreats to the Madonna, making the sign of the horns with her fingers, while the goat chase continues outside.]

ALVARO: Now take it easy! I will catch the black goat and give him a kick that he will never forget!

[ALVARO runs out the front door and joins in the chase. The little boy is clapping together a pair of tin pan lids

---

[37] Bad-mannered!   [38] Listen, please.
[39] Why?   [40] There, I did it!
[41] Rose-colored! Silk! Pure silk!

[42] The goat of the witch!
[43] My tomatoes! Watch out for my tomatoes!

*which sound like cymbals. The effect
is weird and beautiful with the wild
cries of the children and the goat's
bleating.* SERAFINA *remains anxiously
halfway between the shutters and the
protecting Madonna. She gives a furious imitation of the bleating goat, con-
torting her face with loathing. It is the
fury of woman at the desire she suf-
fers. At last the goat is captured.*]

BRUNO: Got him, got him, got him!

ALVARO: Vieni presto, Diavolo! [44]

[ALVARO *appears around the side of
the house with a tight hold on the
broken rope around the goat's neck.
The boy follows behind, gleefully clapping the tin lids together, and further
back follows* THE STREGA, *holding her
broken length of rope, her grey hair
hanging into her face and her black
skirts caught up in one hand, revealing bare feet and hairy legs.* SERAFINA
*comes out on the porch as the gro-
tesque little procession passes before
it, and she raises her hand with the
fingers making horns as the goat and*
THE STREGA *pass her.* ALVARO *turns
the goat over to* THE STREGA *and
comes panting back to the house.*]

ALVARO: Niente paura! [45]—I got to go
now.—You have been troppo gentile,[46]
Mrs. . . .

SERAFINA: I am the widow of Baron Delle
Rose.—Excuse the way I'm—not dressed
. . . [*He keeps hold of her hand as he
stands on the porch steps. She continues
very shyly, panting a little.*] I am not al-
ways like this.—Sometimes I fix myself up!
—When my husband was living, when my
husband comes home, when he was living—
I had a clean dress on! And sometimes even,
I—put a rose in my hair . . .

ALVARO: A rose in your hair would be
pretty!

SERAFINA: But for a widow—it ain't the
time of roses . . .

[*The sound of music is heard, of a
mandolin playing.*]

ALVARO: Naw, you make a mistake! It's
always for everybody the time of roses! The
rose is the heart of the world like the heart
is the—heart of the—body! But you, Baronessa—you know what I think you have
done?

SERAFINA: What—what have I—done?

ALVARO: You have put your heart in the
marble urn with the ashes.

[*Now singing is heard along with the
music, which continues to the end of
the scene.*]

And if in a storm sometime, or sometime when a 10-ton truck goes down
the highway—the marble urn was to *break!*
[*He suddenly points up at the sky.*] Look!
Look, Baronessa!

SERAFINA: [*Startled.*] Look? Look? I
don't see!

ALVARO: I was pointing at your heart,
broken out of the urn and away from the
ashes!—Rondinella felice! [47] [*He makes an
airy gesture toward the fading sky.*]

SERAFINA: Oh! [*He whistles like a bird
and makes graceful winglike motions with
his hands.*] Buffone, buffone—piantatela! [48]
I take you serious—then you make it a
joke . . . [*She smiles involuntarily at his
antics.*]

ALVARO: When can I bring the shirt
back?

SERAFINA: When do you pass by
again?

ALVARO: I will pass by tonight for supper. Volete? [49]

SERAFINA: Then look at the window tonight. If the shutters are open and there is
a light in the window, you can stop by for
your—jacket—but if the shutters are closed,
you better not stop because my Rosa will be
home. Rosa's my daughter. She has gone to
a picnic—maybe—home early—But you
know how picnics are. They—wait for the
moon to—start singing.—Not that there's
nothing wrong in two grownup people having a quiet conversation!—but Rosa's fifteen
—I got to be careful to set her a perfect
example.

ALVARO: I will look at the window.—I
will look at the win-dooow! [*He imitates a
bird flying off with gay whistles.*]

SERAFINA: Buffone!

ALVARO: [*Shouting from outside.*] Hey,
you little buggers, climb down off that
truck! Lay offa them bananas!

[*His truck is heard starting and pulling
away.* SERAFINA *stands motionless on
the porch, searching the sky with her
eyes.*]

[44] Come quick, devil!
[45] Nothing to be afraid of.   [46] Too kind.

[47] Happy little swallow!
[48] Clown, clown—stop it!
[49] Want me to?

SERAFINA: Rosario, forgive me! Forgive me for thinking the awful lie could be true!

[*The light in the house dims out. A little boy races into the yard holding triumphantly a great golden bunch of bananas. A little girl pursues him with shrill cries. He eludes her. They dash around the house. The light fades and the curtain falls.*]

ACT THREE

It is the evening of the same day. The neighborhood children are playing games around the house. One of them is counting by fives to a hundred, calling out the numbers, as he leans against the palm tree.

SERAFINA *is in the parlor, sitting on the sofa. She is seated stiffly and formally, wearing a gown that she has not worn since the death of her husband, and with a rose in her hair. It becomes obvious from her movements that she is wearing a girdle that constricts her unendurably.*

There is the sound of a truck approaching up on the highway. SERAFINA *rises to an odd, crouching position. But the truck passes by without stopping. The girdle is becoming quite intolerable to* SERAFINA *and she decides to take it off, going behind the sofa to do so. With much grunting, she has gotten it down as far as her knees, when there is the sound outside of another truck approaching. This time the truck stops up on the highway, with the sound of screeching brakes. She realizes that* ALVARO *is coming, and her efforts to get out of the girdle, which is now pinioning her legs, become frantic. She hobbles from behind the sofa as* ALVARO *appears in front of the house.*

ALVARO: [*Gaily.*] Rondinella felice! [1] I will look at win-dooooo! Signora delle Rose!

[SERAFINA'S *response to this salutation is a groan of anguish. She hobbles and totters desperately to the curtains between the rooms and reaches them just in time to hide herself as* ALVARO *comes into the parlor from the porch through the screen door. He is carrying a package and a candy box.*]

ALVARO: C'è nessuno? [2]

SERAFINA: [*At first inaudibly.*] Si, si, sono qui. [*Then loudly and hoarsely, as she finally gets the girdle off her legs.*] Si, si, sono qui! [3] [*To cover her embarrassment, she busies herself with fixing wine glasses on a tray.*]

ALVARO: I hear the rattle of glasses! Let me help you! [*He goes eagerly through the curtain but stops short, astonished.*]

SERAFINA: Is—something the matter?

ALVARO: I didn't expect to see you looking so pretty! You are a *young* little widow!

SERAFINA: You are—fix yourself up . . .

ALVARO: I been to The Ideal Barber's! I got the whole works!

SERAFINA: [*Faintly, retreating from him a little.*] You got—rose oil—in your hair . . .

ALVARO: Olio di rose! You like the smell of it? [*Outside there is a wild, distant cry of children, and inside a pause.* SERAFINA *shakes her head slowly with the infinite wound of a recollection.*]—You—don't—like —the smell of it? Oh, then I wash the smell out, I go and . . . [*He starts toward the back. She raises her hand to stop him.*]

SERAFINA: No, no, no, fa—niente.—I like the smell of it . . .

[*A little boy races into the yard, ducks some invisible missile, sticks out his tongue and yells: "Yahhhhh!" Then he dashes behind the house.*]

SERAFINA: Shall we—set down in the parlor?

ALVARO: I guess that's better than stand-

[1] Happy little swallow!
[2] No one here?
[3] Yes, yes, I'm here.

ing up in the dining room. [*He enters formally.*]—Shall we set down on the sofa?

SERAFINA: You take the sofa. I will set down on this chair.

ALVARO: [*Disappointed.*] You don't like to set on a sofa?

SERAFINA: I lean back too far on that sofa. I like a straight back behind me . . .

ALVARO: That chair looks not comfortable to me.

SERAFINA: This chair is a comfortable chair.

ALVARO: But it's more easy to talk with two on a sofa!

SERAFINA: I talk just as good on a chair as I talk on a sofa . . . [*There is a pause.* ALVARO *nervously hitches his shoulder.*] Why do you hitch your shoulders like that?

ALVARO: Oh, that!—That's a—nervous—habit . . .

SERAFINA: I thought maybe the suit don't fit you good . . .

ALVARO: I bought this suit to get married in four years ago.

SERAFINA: But didn't get married?

ALVARO: I give her, the girl, a zircon instead of a diamond. She had it examined. The door was slammed in my face.

SERAFINA: I think that maybe I'd do the same thing myself.

ALVARO: Buy the zircon?

SERAFINA: No, slam the door.

ALVARO: Her eyes were not sincere looking. You've got sincere looking eyes. Give me your hand so I can tell your fortune! [*She pushes her chair back from him.*] I see two men in your life. One very handsome. One not handsome. His ears are too big but not as big as his heart! He has three dependents.—In fact he has four dependents! Ha, ha, ha!

SERAFINA: What is the fourth dependent?

ALVARO: The one that every man's got, his biggest expense, worst troublemaker and chief liability! Ha, ha, ha!

SERAFINA: I hope you are not talking vulgar. [*She rises and turns her back to him. Then she discovers the candy box.*] What's that fancy red box?

ALVARO: A present I bought for a nervous but nice little lady!

SERAFINA: Chocolates? Grazie! Grazie! But I'm too fat.

ALVARO: You are not fat, you are just pleasing and plump. [*He reaches way over to pinch the creamy flesh of her upper arm.*]

SERAFINA: No, please. Don't make me nervous. If I get nervous again I will start to cry . . .

ALVARO: Let's talk about something to take your mind off your troubles. You say you got a young daughter?

SERAFINA: [*In a choked voice.*] Yes. I got a young daughter. Her name is Rosa.

ALVARO: Rosa, Rosa! She's pretty?

SERAFINA: She has the eyes of her father, and his wild, stubborn blood! Today was the day of her graduation from high school. She looked so pretty in a white voile dress with a great big bunch of—roses . . .

ALVARO: Not no prettier than her Mama, I bet—with that rose in your hair!

SERAFINA: She's only fifteen.

ALVARO: Fifteen?

SERAFINA: [*Smoothing her blue silk lap with a hesitant hand.*] Yes, only fifteen . . .

ALVARO: But has a boyfriend, does she?

SERAFINA: She met a sailor.

ALVARO: Oh, Dio! No wonder you seem to be nervous.

SERAFINA: I didn't want to let her go out with this sailor. He had a gold ring in his ear.

ALVARO: Madonna Santa!

SERAFINA: This morning she cut her wrist—not much but enough to bleed—with a kitchen knife!

ALVARO: Tch, tch! A very wild girl!

SERAFINA: I had to give in and let her bring him to see me. He said he was Catholic. I made him kneel down in front of Our Lady there and give Her his promise that he would respect the innocence of my Rosa! —But how do I know he was a Catholic, *really?*

ALVARO: [*Taking her hand.*] Poor little worried lady! But you got to face facts. Sooner or later the innocence of your daughter cannot be respected.—Did he—have a —tattoo?

SERAFINA: [*Startled.*] Did who have—what?

ALVARO: The sailor friend of your daughter, did he have a tattoo?

SERAFINA: Why do you ask me that?

ALVARO: Just because most sailors have a tattoo.

SERAFINA: How do I know if he had a tattoo or not!

ALVARO: *I* got a tattoo!

SERAFINA: *You* got a tattoo?

ALVARO: Si, si, veramente!

SERAFINA: What kind of tattoo you got?

ALVARO: What kind you think?

SERAFINA: Oh, I think—you have got— a South Sea girl without clothes on . . .

ALVARO: No South Sea girl.

SERAFINA: Well, maybe a big red heart with MAMA written across it.

ALVARO: Wrong again, Baronessa.

[*He takes off his tie and slowly unbuttons his shirt, gazing at her with an intensely warm smile. He divides the unbuttoned shirt, turning toward her his bare chest. She utters a gasp and rises.*]

SERAFINA: No, no, no!—Not a rose! [*She says it as if she were evading her feelings.*]

ALVARO: Si, si, una rosa!

SERAFINA: I—don't feel good! The air is . . .

ALVARO: Che fate, che fate, che dite? [4]

SERAFINA: The house has a tin roof on it!—The air is—I got to go outside the house to breathe! Scu—scusatemi! [*She goes out onto the porch and clings to one of the spindling porch columns for support, breathing hoarsely with a hand to her throat. He comes out slowly.*]

ALVARO: [*Gently.*] I didn't mean to surprise you!—Mi dispiace molto! [5]

SERAFINA: [*With enforced calm.*] Don't—talk about it! Anybody could have a rose tattoo.—It don't mean nothing.—You know how a tin roof is. It catches the heat all day and it don't cool off until—midnight . . .

ALVARO: No, no, not until midnight. [*She makes a faint laughing sound, is quite breathless and leans her forehead against the porch column. He places his fingers delicately against the small of her back.*] It makes it hot in the bedroom—so that you got to sleep without nothing on you . . .

SERAFINA: No, you—can't stand the covers.

ALVARO: You can't even stand a—nightgown! [*His fingers press her back.*]

SERAFINA: Please. There is a strega [6] next door; she's always watching!

ALVARO: It's been so long since I felt the soft touch of a woman! [*She gasps loudly and turns to the door.*] Where are you going?

SERAFINA: I'm going back in the house! [*She enters the parlor again, still with forced calm.*]

ALVARO: [*Following her inside.*] Now, now, what is the matter?

SERAFINA: I got a feeling like I have—forgotten something.

ALVARO: What?

SERAFINA: I can't remember.

ALVARO: It couldn't be nothing important if you can't remember. Let's open the chocolate box and have some candy.

SERAFINA: [*Eager for any distraction.*] Yes! Yes, open the box!

[ALVARO *places a chocolate in her hand. She stares at it blankly.*]

ALVARO: Eat it, eat the chocolate. If you don't eat it, it will melt in your hand and make your fingers all gooey!

SERAFINA: Please, I . . .

ALVARO: Eat it!

SERAFINA: [*Weakly and gagging.*] I can't, I can't, I would choke! Here, you eat it.

ALVARO: Put it in my mouth! [*She puts the chocolate in his mouth.*] Now, look. Your fingers are gooey!

SERAFINA: Oh!—I better go wash them! [*She rises unsteadily. He seizes her hands and licks her fingers.*]

ALVARO: Mmmm! Mmmmm! Good, very good!

SERAFINA: Stop that, stop that, stop that! That—ain't—nice . . .

ALVARO: I'll lick off the chocolate for you.

SERAFINA: No, no, no!—I am the mother of a fifteen-year-old girl!

ALVARO: You're as old as your arteries, Baronessa. Now set back down. The fingers are now white as snow!

SERAFINA: You don't—understand—how I feel . . .

ALVARO: You don't understand how *I* feel.

SERAFINA: [*Doubtfully.*] How do you—feel? [*In answer, he stretches the palms of his hands out toward her as if she were a fireplace in a freezing-cold room.*]—What does—that—mean?

ALVARO: The night is warm but I feel like my hands are—freezing!

SERAFINA: Bad—circulation . . .

ALVARO: No, too *much* circulation! [AL-VARO *becomes tremulously pleading, shuffling forward a little, slightly crouched like a beggar.*] Across the room I feel the sweet warmth of a lady!

SERAFINA: [*Retreating, doubtfully.*] Oh, you talk a sweet mouth. I think you talk a sweet mouth to fool a woman.

---

[4] What are you doing, what are you doing, what are you saying?
[5] I'm awfully sorry.
[6] Witch.

ALVARO: No, no, I know—I know that's what warms the world, that is what makes it the summer! [*He seizes the hand she holds defensively before her and presses it to his own breast in a crushing grip.*] Without it, the rose—the rose would not grow on the bush; the fruit would not grow on the tree!

SERAFINA: I know, and the truck—the truck would not haul the bananas! But, Mr. Mangiacavallo, that is my hand, not a sponge. I got bones in it. Bones break!

ALVARO: Scusatemi, Baronessa! [*He returns her hand to her with a bow.*] For me it is winter, because I don't have in my life the sweet warmth of a lady. I live with my hands in my pockets! [*He stuffs his hands violently into his pants' pockets, then jerks them out again. A small cellophane-wrapped disk falls on the floor, escaping his notice, but not SERAFINA's.*]—You don't like the poetry!—How can a man talk to you?

SERAFINA: [*Ominously.*] I like the poetry good. Is that a piece of the poetry that you dropped out of your pocket? [*He looks down.*]—No, no, right by your foot!

ALVARO: [*Aghast as he realizes what it is that she has seen.*] Oh, that's—that's nothing! [*He kicks it under the sofa.*]

SERAFINA: [*Fiercely.*] You talk a sweet mouth about women. Then drop such a thing from your pocket? Ve via, vigliacco! [7] [*She marches grandly out of the room, pulling the curtains together behind her. He hangs his head despairingly between his hands. Then he approaches the curtains timidly.*]

ALVARO: [*In a small voice.*] Baronessa?

SERAFINA: Pick up what you dropped on the floor and go to the Square Roof with it. Buona notte! [8]

ALVARO: Baronessa! [*He parts the curtains and peeks through them.*]

SERAFINA: I told you good night. Here is no casa privata. Io, non sono puttana! [9]

ALVARO: Understanding is—very—necessary!

SERAFINA: I understand plenty. You think you got a good thing, a thing that is cheap!

ALVARO: You make a mistake, Baronessa! [*He comes in and drops to his knees beside her, pressing his cheek to her flank.*

He speaks rhapsodically.*] So soft is a lady! So, so, so, so, so soft—is a lady!

SERAFINA: Andate via, sporcaccione, andate a casa! Lasciatemi! Lasciatemi stare! [10]

[*She springs up and runs into the parlor. He pursues. The chase is grotesquely violent and comic. A floor lamp is overturned. She seizes the chocolate box and threatens to slam it into his face if he continues toward her. He drops to his knees, crouched way over, and pounds the floor with his fists, sobbing.*]

ALVARO: Everything in my life turns out like this!

SERAFINA: Git up, git up, git up!—you village idiot's grandson! There is people watching you through that window, the—strega next door . . . [*He rises slowly.*] And where is the shirt that I loaned you? [*He shuffles abjectly across the room, then hands her a neatly wrapped package.*]

ALVARO: My sister wrapped it up for you.--My sister was very happy I met this nice lady!

SERAFINA: Maybe she thinks I will pay the grocery bill while she plays the numbers!

ALVARO: She don't think nothing like that. She is an old maid, my sister. She wants—nephews—nieces . . .

SERAFINA: You tell her for me I don't give nephews and nieces!

[*ALVARO hitches his shoulders violently in his embarrassment and shuffles over to where he had left his hat. He blows the dust off it and rubs the crown on his sleeve. SERAFINA presses a knuckle to her lips as she watches his awkward gestures. She is a little abashed by his humility. She speaks next with the great dignity of a widow whose respectability has stood the test.*]

SERAFINA: Now, Mr. Mangiacavallo, please tell me the truth about something. When did you get the tattoo put on your chest?

ALVARO: [*Shyly and sadly, looking down at his hat.*] I got it tonight—after supper . . .

SERAFINA: That's what I thought. You had it put on because I told you about my husband's tattoo.

---

[7] Go away, coward!   [8] Good night!
[9] Here is no bawdy house. Me, I'm not a whore!

[10] Go away, pig, go home! Leave me! Leave me alone!

ALVARO: I wanted to be—close to you . . . to make you—happy . . .

SERAFINA: Tell it to the marines! [*He puts on his hat with an apologetic gesture.*] You got the tattoo and the chocolate box after supper, and then you come here to fool me!

ALVARO: I got the chocolate box a long time ago.

SERAFINA: How long ago? If that is not too much a personal question!

ALVARO: I got it the night the door was slammed in my face by the girl that I give —the zircon . . .

SERAFINA: Let that be a lesson. Don't try to fool women. You are not smart enough.—Now take the shirt back. You can keep it.

ALVARO: Huh?

SERAFINA: Keep it. I don't want it back.

ALVARO: You just now said that you did.

SERAFINA: It's a man's shirt, ain't it?

ALVARO: You just now accused me of trying to steal it off you.

SERAFINA: Well, you been making me nervous!

ALVARO: Is it my fault you been a widow too long?

SERAFINA: You make a mistake!

ALVARO: *You* make a mistake!

SERAFINA: Both of us make a mistake!
[*There is a pause. They both sigh profoundly.*]

ALVARO: We should of have been friends, but I think we meet the wrong day.— Suppose I go out and come in the door again and we start all over?

SERAFINA: No, I think it's no use. The day was wrong to begin with, because of two women. Two women, they told me today that my husband had put on my head the nanny-goat's horns!

ALVARO: How is it possible to put horns on a widow?

SERAFINA: That was before, before! They told me my husband was having a steady affair with a woman at the Square Roof. What was the name on the shirt, on the slip of paper? Do you remember the name?

ALVARO: You told me to . . .

SERAFINA: Tell me! Do you remember?

ALVARO: I remember the name because I know the woman. The name was Estelle Hohengarten.

SERAFINA: Take me there! Take me to the Square Roof!—Wait, wait!

[*She plunges into the dining room, snatches a knife out of the sideboard drawer and thrusts it in her purse. Then she rushes back, with the blade of the knife protruding from the purse.*]

ALVARO: [*Noticing the knife.*] They— got a cover charge there . . .

SERAFINA: I will charge them a cover! Take me there now, this minute!

ALVARO: The fun don't start till midnight.

SERAFINA: I will start the fun sooner.

ALVARO: The floor show commences at midnight.

SERAFINA: I will commence it! [*She rushes to the phone.*] Yellow Cab, please, Yellow Cab. I want to go to the Square Roof out of my house! Yes, you come to my house and take me to the Square Roof right this minute! My number is— what is my number? Oh my God, what is my number?—64 is my number on Front Street! Subito, subito—quick!

[*The goat bleats outside.*]

ALVARO: Baronessa, the knife's sticking out of your purse. [*He grabs the purse.*] What do you want with this weapon?

SERAFINA: To cut the lying tongue out of a woman's mouth! Saying she has on her breast the tattoo of my husband because he had put on me the horns of a goat! I cut the heart out of that woman, she cut the heart out of me!

ALVARO: Nobody's going to cut the heart out of nobody!

[*A car is heard outside, and* SERAFINA *rushes to the porch.*]

SERAFINA: [*Shouting.*] Hey, Yellow Cab, Yellow Cab, Yellow—Cab . . . [*The car passes by without stopping. With a sick moan she wanders into the yard. He follows her with a glass of wine.*]—Something hurts —in my heart . . .

ALVARO: [*Leading her gently back to the house.*] Baronessa, drink this wine on the porch and keep your eyes on that star. [*He leads her to a porch pillar and places the glass in her trembling hand. She is now submissive.*] You know the name of that star? That star is Venus. She is the only female star in the sky. Who put her up there? Mr. Siccardi, the transportation manager of the Southern Fruit Company? No. She was put there by God. [*He enters the house and removes the knife from her purse.*] And yet there's some people that don't believe in nothing. [*He picks up the telephone.*] Esplanade 9-7-0.

SERAFINA: What are you doing?

ALVARO: Drink that wine and I'll settle this whole problem for you. [*On the telephone.*] I want to speak to the blackjack dealer, please, Miss Estelle Hohengarten . . .

SERAFINA: Don't talk to that woman, she'll lie!

ALVARO: Not Estelle Hohengarten. She deals a straight game of cards.—Estelle? This is Mangiacavallo. I got a question to ask you which is a personal question. It has to do with a very goodlooking truck-driver, not living now but once on a time thought to have been a very well-known character at the Square Roof. His name was . . . [*He turns questioningly to the door where* SERAFINA *is standing.*] What was his name, Baronessa?

SERAFINA: [*Hardly breathing.*] Rosario delle Rose!

ALVARO: Rosario delle Rose was the name. [*There is a pause.*]—È vero?—Mah! Che peccato [11] . . .

[SERAFINA *drops her glass and springs into the parlor with a savage outcry. She snatches the phone from* ALVARO *and screams into it.*]

SERAFINA: [*Wildly.*] This is the wife that's speaking! What do you know of my husband, what is the lie?

[*A strident voice sounds over the wire.*]

THE VOICE: [*Loud and clear.*] Don't you remember? I brought you the rose-colored silk to make him a shirt. You said, "For a man?" and I said, "Yes, for a man that's wild like a Gypsy!" But if you think I'm a liar, come here and let me show you his rose tattooed on my chest!

[SERAFINA *holds the phone away from her as though it had burst into flame. Then, with a terrible cry, she hurls it to the floor. She staggers dizzily toward the Madonna.* ALVARO *seizes her arm and pushes her gently onto the sofa.*]

ALVARO: Piano, piano,[12] Baronessa! This will be gone, this will pass in a moment. [*He puts a pillow behind her, then replaces the telephone.*]

[11] Is it true?—oh! What a shame . . .
[12] Easy, easy.
[13] I'll come right back, Baroness.
[14] Where are you, where are you?

SERAFINA: [*Staggering up from the sofa.*] The room's—going round . . .

ALVARO: You ought to stay lying down a little while longer. I know, I know what you need! A towel with some ice in it to put on your forehead—Baronessa.— You stay right there while I fix it! [*He goes into the kitchen, and calls back.*] Torno subito, Baronessa! [13]

[*The little boy runs into the yard. He leans against the bending trunk of the palm, counting loudly.*]

THE LITTLE BOY: Five, ten, fifteen, twenty, twenty-five, thirty . . .

[*There is the sound of ice being chopped in the kitchen.*]

SERAFINA: Dove siete, dove siete? [14]

ALVARO: In cucina!—Ghiaccio . . . [15]

SERAFINA: Venite qui! [16]

ALVARO: Subito, subito . . . [17]

SERAFINA: [*Turning to the shrine, with fists knotted.*] Non voglio, non voglio farlo! [18]

[*But she crosses slowly, compulsively toward the shrine, with a trembling arm stretched out.*]

THE LITTLE BOY: Seventy-five, eighty, eighty-five, ninety, ninety-five, one hundred! [*Then, wildly.*] Ready or not you shall be caught!

[*At this cry,* SERAFINA *seizes the marble urn and hurls it violently into the furthest corner of the room. Then, instantly, she covers her face. Outside the mothers are heard calling their children home. Their voices are tender as music, fading in and out. The children appear slowly at the side of the house, exhausted from their wild play.*]

GIUSEPPINA: Vivi! Vi-vi!

PEPPINA: Salvatore!

VIOLETTA: Bruno! Come home, come home!

[*The children scatter.* ALVARO *comes in with the ice-pick.*]

ALVARO: I broke the point of the ice-pick.

SERAFINA: [*Removing her hands from her face.*] I don't want ice . . . [*She looks about her, seeming to gather a fierce strength in her body. Her voice is hoarse, her body trembling with violence, eyes*

[15] In the kitchen!—Ice . . .
[16] Come here!
[17] At once, at once . . .
[18] I don't want to, I don't want to do it!

narrow and flashing, her fists clenched.]
Now I show you how wild and strong
like a man a woman can be! [*She crosses
to the screen door, opens it and shouts.*]
Buona notte,[19] Mr. Mangiacavallo!

ALVARO: You—you make me go *home*,
now?

SERAFINA: No, no; senti, cretino! [20] [*In
a strident whisper.*] You make out like
you are going. You drive the truck out of
sight where the witch can't see it. Then
you come back and I leave the back door
open for you to come in. Now, tell me
good-bye so all the neighbors can hear you!
[*She shouts.*] Arrivederci! [21]

ALVARO: Ha, ha! Capish! [22] [*He shouts
too.*] Arrivederci! [*He runs to the foot of
the embankment steps.*]

SERAFINA: [*Sill more loudly.*] Buona
notte!

ALVARO: Buona notte, Baronessa!

SERAFINA: [*In a choked voice.*] Give
them my love; give everybody—my love
. . . Arrivederci!

ALVARO: Ciao!

[ALVARO *scrambles on down the steps
and goes off.* SERAFINA *comes down
into the yard. The goat bleats. She
mutters savagely to herself.*]

SERAFINA: Sono una bestia, una bestia
feroce! [23]

[*She crosses quickly around to the back
of the house. As she disappears, the
truck is heard driving off; the lights
sweep across the house.* SERAFINA
*comes in through the back door. She
is moving with great violence, gasping
and panting. She rushes up to the
Madonna and addresses her passionately
with explosive gestures, leaning over
so that her face is level with the
statue's.*]

SERAFINA: Ora, ascolta, Signora![24] You

hold in the cup of your hand this little
house and you smash it! You break this
little house like the shell of a bird in your
hand, because you have hate Serafina?—
Serafina that *loved* you!—No, no, no, you
don't speak! I don't believe in you, Lady!
You're just a poor little doll with the paint
peeling off, and now I blow out the light
and I forget you the way you forget Serafina!
[*She blows out the vigil light.*] Ecco—
fatto! [25]

[*But now she is suddenly frightened;
the vehemence and boldness have run
out. She gasps a little and backs away
from the shrine, her eyes rolling apprehensively this way and that. The
parrot squawks at her. The goat bleats.
The night is full of sinister noises,
harsh bird cries, the sudden flapping
of wings in the cane-brake, a distant
shriek of Negro laughter.* SERAFINA
*retreats to the window and opens the
shutters wider to admit the moonlight.
She stands panting by the window
with a fist pressed to her mouth. In
the back of the house a door slams
open.* SERAFINA *catches her breath and
moves for protection behind the
dummy of the bride.* ALVARO *enters
through the back door, calling out
softly and hoarsely, with great excitement.*]

ALVARO: Dove! Dove sei, cara? [26]

SERAFINA: [*Faintly.*] Sono qui . . . [27]

ALVARO: You have turn out the light!

SERAFINA: The moon is enough . . .
[*He advances toward her. His white teeth
glitter as he grins.* SERAFINA *retreats a few
steps from him. She speaks tremulously,
making an awkward gesture toward the
sofa.*] Now we can go on with our—
conversation . . . [*She catches her breath
sharply.*]

[*The curtain comes down.*]

[19] Good night.
[20] Listen, stupid! [21] Good-bye!
[22] I understand.
[23] I'm a beast, a wild beast!
[24] Now listen, Lady!

[25] *There—it's done!*
[26] *Where, where are you, dear?*
[27] *I am here . . .*

Scene Two

It is just before daybreak of the next day. ROSA *and* JACK *appear at the top of the embankment steps.*

ROSA: I thought they would never leave. [*She comes down the steps and out in front of the house, then calls back to him.*] Let's go down there.

[*He obeys hesitatingly. Both are very grave. The scene is played as close as possible to the audience. She sits very straight. He stands behind her with his hands on her shoulders.*]

ROSA: [*Leaning her head back against him.*] This was the happiest day of my life, and this is the saddest night . . . [*He crouches in front of her.*]

SERAFINA: [*From inside the house.*] Aaaaaahhhhhhhh!

JACK: [*Springing up, startled.*] What's that?

ROSA: [*Resentfully.*] Oh! That's Mama dreaming about my father.

JACK: I—feel like a—*heel!* I feel like a rotten heel!

ROSA: Why?

JACK: That promise I made your mother.

ROSA: I hate her for it.

JACK: Honey—Rosa, she—wanted to protect you.

[*There is a long-drawn cry from the back of the house: "Ohhhh—Rosario!"*]

ROSA: She wanted me not to have what she's dreaming about . . .

JACK: Naw, naw, honey, she—wanted to—protect you . . .

[*The cry from within is repeated softly.*]

ROSA: Listen to her making love in her sleep! Is that what she wants *me* to do, just—*dream* about it?

JACK: [*Humbly.*] She knows that her Rosa *is* a rose. And wants her rose to have someone—better than *me* . . .

ROSA: *Better* than—*you!* [*She speaks as if the possibility were too preposterous to think of.*]

JACK: You see me through—rose-colored—glasses . . .

ROSA: I see you with love!

JACK: Yes, but your Mama sees me with —common sense . . . [SERAFINA *cries out again.*] I got to be going! [*She keeps a tight hold on him. A rooster crows.*] Honey, it's so late the roosters are crowing!

ROSA: They're fools, they're fools, it's early!

JACK: Honey, on the island I almost forgot my promise. Almost, but not quite. Do you understand, honey?

ROSA: Forget the promise!

JACK: I made it on my knees in front of Our Lady. I've got to leave now, honey.

ROSA: [*Clasping him fiercely.*] You'd have to break my arms to!

JACK: Rosa, Rosa! You want to drive me crazy?

ROSA: I want you not to remember.

JACK: You're a very young girl! Fifteen —fifteen is too young!

ROSA: Caro, caro, carissimo! [1]

JACK: You got to save some of those feelings for when you're grown up!

ROSA: Carissimo!

JACK: Hold some of it back until you're grown!

ROSA: I have been grown for two years!

JACK: No, no, that ain't what I . . .

ROSA: Grown enough to be married, and have a—baby!

JACK: [*Springing up.*] Oh, good—Lord! [*He circles around her, pounding his palm repeatedly with his fist and clamping his teeth together with a grimace. Suddenly he speaks.*] I got to be going!

ROSA: You want me to scream? [*He groans and turns away from her to resume his desperate circle.* ROSA *is blocking the way with her body.*]—I know, I know! You don't want me! [JACK *groans through his gritting teeth.*] No, no, you don't want me . . .

JACK: Now you listen to me! You almost got into trouble today on that island! You almost did, but not quite!—But it didn't quite happen and no harm is done and you can just—forget it . . .

ROSA: It is the only thing in my life that I want to remember!—When are you going back to New Orleans?

JACK: Tomorrow.

ROSA: When does your—ship sail?

JACK: Tomorrow.

ROSA: Where to?

[1] Dear, dear, dearest!

JACK: Guatemala.

SERAFINA: [From the house.] Aahh!

ROSA: Is that a long trip?

JACK: After Guatemala, Buenos Aires. After Buenos Aires, Rio. Then around the Straits of Magellan and back up the west coast of South America, putting in at three ports before we dock at San Francisco.

ROSA: I don't think I will—ever see you again . . .

JACK: The ship won't sink!

ROSA: [Faintly and forlornly.] No, but— I think it could just happen once, and if it don't happen that time, it never can— later . . . [A rooster crows. They face each other sadly and quietly.] You don't need to be very old to understand how it works out. One time, one time, only once, it could be—God!—to remember.—Other times? Yes—they'd be something.—But only once, God, to remember . . . [With a little sigh she crosses to pick up his white cap and hand it gravely to him.]—I'm sorry to you it didn't—mean—that much . . .

JACK: [Taking the cap and hurling it to the ground.] Look! Look at my knuckles! You see them scabs on my knuckles? You know how them scabs got there? They got there because I banged my knuckles that hard on the deck of the sailboat!

ROSA: Because it—didn't quite happen? [JACK jerks his head up and down in grotesquely violent assent to her question. ROSA picks up his cap and returns it to him again.]—Because of the promise to Mama! I'll never forgive her . . . [There is a pause.] What time in the afternoon must you be on the boat?

JACK: Why?

ROSA: Just tell me what time.

JACK: Five!—Why?

ROSA: What will you be doing till five?

JACK: Well, I could be a goddam liar and tell you I was going to—pick me a hatful of daisies in—Audubon Park.—Is that what you want me to tell you?

ROSA: No, tell me the truth.

JACK: All right, I'll tell you the truth.

I'm going to check in at some flea-bag hotel on North Rampart Street. Then I'm going to get loaded! And then I'm going to get . . . [He doesn't complete the sentence but she understands him. She places the hat more becomingly on his blond head.]

ROSA: Do me a little favor. [Her hand slides down to his cheek and then to his mouth.] Before you get loaded and before you—before you—

JACK: Huh?

ROSA: Look in the waiting room at the Greyhound bus station, please. At twelve o'clock, noon!

JACK: Why?

ROSA: You might find me there, waiting for you . . .

JACK: What—what good would that do?

ROSA: I never been to a hotel but I know they have numbers on doors and sometimes—numbers are—lucky.— Aren't they?—Sometimes?—Lucky?

JACK: You want to buy me a ten-year stretch in the brig?

ROSA: I want you to give me that little gold ring on your ear to put on my finger. —I want to give you my heart to keep forever! And ever! And ever! [Slowly and with a barely audible sigh she leans her face against him.] Look for me! I will be there!

JACK: [Breathlessly.] In all my life, I never felt nothing so sweet as the feel of your little warm body in my arms . . .

[He breaks away and runs toward the road. From the foot of the steps he glares fiercely back at her like a tiger through the bars of a cage. She clings to the two porch pillars, her body leaning way out.]

ROSA: Look for me! I will be there!

[JACK runs away from the house. ROSA returns inside. Listlessly she removes her dress and falls on the couch in her slip, kicking off her shoes. Then she begins to cry, as one cries only once in a lifetime, and the scene dims out.]

Scene Three

The time is three hours later.

We see first the exterior view of the small frame building against a night sky which is like the starry blue robe of Our Lady. It is growing slightly paler.

The faint light discloses ROSA *asleep on the couch. The covers are thrown back for it has been a warm night, and on the concave surface of the white cloth, which is like the dimly lustrous hollow of a shell, is the body of the sleeping girl which is clad only in a sheer white slip.*

A cock crows. A gentle wind stirs the white curtains inward and the tendrils of vine at the windows, and the sky lightens enough to distinguish the purple trumpets of the morning glory against the very dim blue of the sky in which the planet Venus remains still undimmed.

In the back of the cottage someone is heard coughing hoarsely and groaning in the way a man does who has drunk very heavily the night before. Bedsprings creak as a heavy figure rises. Light spills dimly through the curtains, now closed, between the two front rooms.

There are heavy, padding footsteps and ALVARO *comes stumbling rapidly into the dining room with the last bottle of Spumanti in the crook of his arm, his eyes barely open, legs rubbery, saying, "Wuh-wuh-wuh-wuh-wuh-wuh"* . . . *like the breathing of an old dog. The scene should be played with the pantomimic lightness, almost fantasy, of an early Chaplin comedy. He is wearing only his trousers and his chest is bare. As he enters he collides with the widow dummy, staggers back, pats her inflated bosom in a timid, apologetic way, remarking.]*

ALVARO: Scusami, Signora, I am the grandson of the village idiot of Ribera!

[ALVARO *backs into the table and is propelled by the impact all the way to the curtained entrance of the parlor. He draws the curtains apart and hangs onto them, peering into the room. Seeing the sleeping girl, he blinks several times, suddenly makes a snoring sound in his nostrils and waves one hand violently in front of his eyes as if to dispel a vision. Outside the goat utters a long "Baaaaaaaaaaa!" As if in response,* ALVARO *whispers, in the same bass key, "Che bella!"* [1] *The first vowel of "bella" is enormously prolonged like the "baaa" of the goat. On his rubbery legs he shuffles forward a few steps and leans over to peer more intently at the vision. The goat bleats again.* ALVARO *whispers more loudly: "Che bel-la!" He drains the Spumanti, then stag-*

gers to his knees, the empty bottle rolling over the floor. He crawls on his knees to the foot of the bed, then leans against it like a child peering into a candy shop window, repeating: "Che bel-la, che bel-la!" with antiphonal responses from the goat outside. Slowly, with tremendous effort, as if it were the sheer side of a precipice, he clambers upon the couch and crouches over the sleeping girl in a leap-frog position, saying "Che bel-la!" quite loudly, this time, in a tone of innocently joyous surprise. All at once* ROSA *wakens. She screams even before she is quite awake, and springs from the couch so violently that* ALVARO *topples over to the floor.*

[SERAFINA *cries out almost instantly after* ROSA. *She lunges through the dining room in her torn and disordered nightgown. At the sight of the man crouched by the couch a momentary stupefaction turns into a burst of savage fury. She flies at him*

[1] How beautiful!

like a great bird, tearing and clawing at his stupefied figure. With one arm ALVARO *wards off her blows, plunging to the floor and crawling into the dining room. She seizes a broom with which she flails him about the head, buttocks and shoulders while he scrambles awkwardly away. The assault is nearly wordless. Each time she strikes at him she hisses: "Sporcaccione!"* [2] *He continually groans: "Dough, dough, dough!" At last he catches hold of the widow dummy which he holds as a shield before him while he entreats the two women.*]

ALVARO: Senti, Baronessa! Signorina! I didn't know what I was doin', I was dreamin'. I was just dreamin'! I got turn around in the house; I got all twisted! I thought that you was your Mama!—Sono ubriaco! Per favore! [3]

ROSA: [*Seizing the broom.*] That's enough, Mama!

SERAFINA: [*Rushing to the phone.*] Police!

ROSA: [*Seizing the phone.*] No, no, no, no, no, no!—You want everybody to know?

SERAFINA: [*Weakly.*] Know?—Know what, cara?

ROSA: Just give him his clothes, now, Mama, and let him get out! [*She is clutching a bedsheet about herself.*]

ALVARO: Signorina—young lady! I swear I was *dreaming!*

SERAFINA: Don't speak to my daughter! [*Then, turning to* ROSA.]—Who is this man? How did this man get here?

ROSA: [*Coldly.*] Mama, don't say any more. Just give him his clothes in the bedroom so he can get out!

ALVARO: [*Still crouching.*] I am so sorry, so sorry! I don't remember a thing but that I was dreaming!

SERAFINA: [*Shoving him toward the back of the room with her broom.*] Go on, go get your clothes on, you—idiot's grandson, you!—Svelto, svelto, più svelto! [4] [ALVARO *continues his apologetic mumbling in the back room.*] Don't talk to me, don't say nothing! Or I will kill you!

[*A few moments later* ALVARO *rushes around the side of the house, his clothes half buttoned and his shirt-tails out.*]

[2] Slob!   [3] I am drunk! Please!
[4] Fast, fast, faster!

ALVARO: But, Baronessa, I *love* you! [*A tea kettle sails over his head from behind the house.* THE STREGA *bursts into laughter. Despairingly* ALVARO *retreats, tucking his shirt-tails in and shaking his head.*] Baronessa, Baronessa, I love you!

[*As* ALVARO *runs off,* THE STREGA *is heard cackling.*]

THE STREGA'S VOICE: The Wops are at it again. Had a truckdriver in the house all night!

[ROSA *is feverishly dressing. From the bureau she has snatched a shimmering white satin slip, disappearing for a moment behind a screen to put it on as* SERAFINA *comes padding sheepishly back into the room, her nightgown now covered by a black rayon kimona sprinkled with poppies, her voice tremulous with fear, shame and apology.*]

ROSA: [*Behind the screen.*] Has the man gone?

SERAFINA: That—man?

ROSA: Yes, "that man"!

SERAFINA: [*Inventing desperately.*] I don't know how he got in. Maybe the back door was open.

ROSA: Oh, yes, maybe it was!

SERAFINA: Maybe he—climbed in a window . . .

ROSA: Or fell down the chimney, maybe! [*She comes from behind the screen, wearing the white bridal slip.*]

SERAFINA: Why you put on the white things I save for your wedding?

ROSA: Because I want to. That's a good enough reason. [*She combs her hair savagely.*]

SERAFINA: I want you to understand about that man. That was a man that—that was—that was a man that . . .

ROSA: You can't think of a lie?

SERAFINA: He was a—truckdriver, cara. He got in a fight, he was chase by—policemen!

ROSA: They chased him into your bedroom?

SERAFINA: I took pity on him, I gave him first aid, I let him sleep on the floor. He give me his promise—he . . .

ROSA: Did he kneel in front of Our Lady? Did he promise that he would respect your innocence?

SERAFINA: Oh, cara, cara! [*Abandoning all pretense.*] He was Sicilian; he had rose oil in his hair and the rose tattoo of your father. In the dark room I couldn't see his clown face. I closed my eyes and dreamed that he was your father! I closed my eyes! I dreamed that he was your father . . .

ROSA: Basta, basta, non voglio sentire più niente! [5] The only thing worse than a liar is a liar that's also a hypocrite!

SERAFINA: Senti, per favore! [6] [ROSA *wheels about from the mirror and fixes her mother with a long and withering stare.* SERAFINA *cringes before it.*] Don't look at me like that with the eyes of your father! [*She shields her face as from a terrible glare.*]

ROSA: Yes, I am looking at you with the eyes of my father. I see you the way *he* saw you. [*She runs to the table and seizes the piggy bank.*] Like this, this *pig!* [SERAFINA *utters a long, shuddering cry like a cry of childbirth.*] I need five dollars. I'll take it out of this! [ROSA *smashes the piggy bank to the floor and rakes some coins into her purse.* SERAFINA *stoops to the floor. There is the sound of a train whistle.* ROSA *is now fully dressed, but she hesitates, a little ashamed of her cruelty—but only a little.* SERAFINA *cannot meet her daughter's eyes. At last the girl speaks.*]

SERAFINA: How beautiful—is my daughter! Go to the boy!

ROSA: [*As if she might be about to apologize.*] Mama? He didn't touch me—he just said—"Che bella!"

[SERAFINA *turns slowly, shamefully, to face her. She is like a peasant in the presence of a young princess.* ROSA *stares at her a moment longer, then suddenly catches her breath and runs out of the house. As the girl leaves.* SERAFINA *calls.*]

SERAFINA: Rosa, Rosa, the—wrist watch! [SERAFINA *snatches up the little gift box and runs out onto the porch with it. She starts to call her daughter again, holding the gift out toward her, but her breath fails her.*] Rosa, Rosa, the—wrist watch . . . [*Her arms fall to her side. She turns, the gift still ungiven. Senselessly, absently, she holds the watch to her ear again. She shakes it a little, then utters a faint, startled laugh.*]

[ASSUNTA *appears beside the house*

and walks directly in, as though SERAFINA *had called her.*]

SERAFINA: Assunta, the urn is broken. The ashes are spilt on the floor and I can't touch them.

[ASSUNTA *stoops to pick up the pieces of the shattered urn.* SERAFINA *has crossed to the shrine and relights the candle before the Madonna.*]

ASSUNTA: There are no ashes.

SERAFINA: Where—where are they? Where have the ashes gone?

ASSUNTA: [*Crossing to the shrine.*] The wind has blown them away.

[ASSUNTA *places what remains of the broken urn in* SERAFINA'S *hands.* SERAFINA *turns it tenderly in her hands and then replaces it on top of the prie-dieu before the Madonna.*]

SERAFINA: A man, when he burns, leaves only a handful of ashes. No woman can hold him. The wind must blow him away.

[ALVARO'S *voice is heard, calling from the top of the highway embankment.*]

ALVARO'S VOICE: Rondinella felice! [7]

[*The neighborhood women hear* ALVARO *calling, and there is a burst of mocking laughter from some of them. Then they all converge on the house from different directions and gather before the porch.*]

PEPPINA: Serafina delle Rose!

GIUSEPPINA: Baronessa! Baronessa delle Rose!

PEPPINA: There is a man on the road without the shirt!

GIUSEPPINA: [*With delight.*] Si, si! Senza camicia! [8]

PEPPINA: All he got on his chest is a rose tattoo! [*To the women.*] She lock up his shirt so he can't go to the high school? [*The women shriek with laughter. In the house* SERAFINA *snatches up the package containing the silk shirt, while* ASSUNTA *closes the shutters of the parlor windows.*]

SERAFINA: Un momento! [*She tears the paper off the shirt and rushes out onto the porch, holding the shirt above her head defiantly.*] Ecco la camicia! [9]

[*With a soft cry,* SERAFINA *drops the shirt, which is immediately snatched*

---

[5] Enough, enough, I don't want to listen to anything else.
[6] Listen, please!

[7] Happy little swallow!
[8] Yes, yes! Without a shirt!
[9] Here is the shirt!

up by PEPPINA. *At this point the music begins again, with a crash of percussion, and continues to the end of the play.* PEPPINA *flourishes the shirt in the air like a banner and tosses it to* GIUSEPPINA, *who is now on the embankment.* GIUSEPPINA *tosses it on to* MARIELLA, *and she in her turn to* VIOLETTA, *who is above her, so that the brilliantly colored shirt moves in a zig-zag course through the pampas grass to the very top of the embankment, like a streak of flame shooting up a dry hill. The women call out as they pass the shirt along.*]

PEPPINA: Guardate   questa   camicia! Coloro di rose! [10]

MARIELLA: [*Shouting up to* ALVARO.] Corragio, signor! [11]

GIUSEPPINA: Avanti, avanti, signor! [12]

VIOLETTA: [*At the top of the embankment, giving the shirt a final flourish above her.*] Corragio, corragio! The Baronessa is waiting!

[*Bursts of laughter are mingled with the cries of the women. Then they sweep away like a flock of screaming birds, and* SERAFINA *is left upon the porch, her eyes closed, a hand clasped to her breast. In the meanwhile, in-*

side the house, ASSUNTA *has poured out a glass of wine. Now she comes to the porch, offering the wine to* SERAFINA *and murmuring.*]

ASSUNTA: Stai tranquilla. [13]

SERAFINA: [*Breathlessly.*] Assunta, I'll tell you something that maybe you won't believe.

ASSUNTA: [*With tender humor.*] It is impossible to tell me anything that I don't believe.

SERAFINA: Just now I felt on my breast the burning again of the rose. I know what it means. It means that I have conceived! [*She lifts the glass to her lips for a moment and then returns it to* ASSUNTA.] Two lives again in the body! Two, two lives again, two!

ALVARO'S VOICE: [*Nearer now, and sweetly urgent.*] Rondinella felice!

[ALVARO *is not visible on the embankment but* SERAFINA *begins to move slowly toward his voice.*]

ASSUNTA: Dove vai, Serafina? [14]

SERAFINA: [*Shouting now, to* ALVARO.] Vengo, vengo, amore! [15]

[*She starts up the embankment toward* ALVARO *and the curtain falls as the music rises with her in great glissandi of sound.*]

---

[10] Look at this shirt. The color of a rose!
[11] Courage, Mister.
[12] Go on, go on.

[13] Be calm.
[14] Where are you going, Serafina?
[15] I'm coming, I'm coming, my love!

ARTHUR MILLER

THE SHADOWS OF THE GODS [1]

It is hard to imagine any playwright reading Chekhov without envying one quality of his plays. It is his balance. In this, I think he is closer to Shakespeare than any dramatist I know. There is less distortion by the exigencies of the telescoping of time in the theater, there is less stacking of the cards, there is less fear of the ridiculous, there is less fear of the heroic. His touch is tender, his eye is warm, so warm that the Chekhovian legend in our theater has become that of an almost sentimental man and writer whose plays are elegies, postscripts to a dying age. In passing, it must be said that he was not the only Russian writer who seemed to be dealing with all his characters as though he were related to them. It is a quality not of Chekhov alone but of much Russian literature, and I mention it both to relate him to this mood and to separate him from it.

Chekhov is important to us because he has been used as a club against two opposing views of drama. Sometimes he seems —as he evidently does to Walter Kerr—to have encouraged dramatists to an overly-emphasized introspection if not self-pity. To this kind of viewpoint, he is the playwright of inaction, of perverse self-analysis, of the dark blue mood. In the 'thirties he was condemned by many on the Left as lacking in militancy, and he was confused with the people he was writing about.

His plays, I think, will endure, but in one sense he is as useless as a model as the frock coat and the horse and carriage. Our civilization is immeasurably more strident than his and to try to recreate his mood would be to distort our own. But more important, I think, is that—whatever the miseries of his characters—their careers are played out against a tradition of which they are quite conscious, a tradition whose destruction is regarded by them as the setting of their woes. Whether or not it was ever objectively true is beside the point, of course; the point is that they can look back to a time when the coachman was young and happy to be a coachman, when there was a large, firmly entrenched family evenly maturing over the slow passing years, when, in a word, there was an order dominated by

[1] Arthur Miller, from "The Shadows of the Gods," *Harper's Magazine*, CCXVII (August 1958), 38–39. © Arthur Miller 1958. Reprinted by permission of MCA Artists, Ltd.

human relations. Now—to put it much more briefly than its complexity warrants—the Cherry Orchard is cut down by a real estate man, who, nice fellow that he may be, simply has to clear land for a development.

The closest we have ever gotten to this kind of relation to a tradition is in Tennessee Williams, when a disorganized refugee from a plantation arrives in our civilization some eighty years after the plantation itself has been destroyed. We cannot reproduce Chekhov if only because we are long past the time when we believe in the primacy of human relations over economic necessity. We have given up what was still in his time a live struggle. We believe—or at least take it completely for granted—that wherever there is a conflict between human relations and necessity, the outcome is not only inevitable but even progressive when necessity wins, as it evidently must.

The main point I would make here in relation to our theater, however, is that while Chekhov's psychological insight is given full play, and while his greatest interest is overwhelmingly in the spiritual life of his characters, his farthest vision does not end with their individual psychology. Here is a speech to remind you—and it is only one of a great many which do not at all fit with the conventional characterization of these allegedly wispy plays—concerned with nothing more than realistic character drawing and introspection. In *The Three Sisters* Vershinin speaks:

> What else am I to say to you at parting? What am I to theorize about? (*Laughs*) Life is hard. It seems to many of us blank and hopeless; but yet we must admit that it goes on getting clearer and easier, and it looks as though the time were not far off when it will be full of happiness. (*Looks at his watch.*) It's time for me to go! In old days men were absorbed in wars, filling all their existence with marches, raids, victories, but now all that is a thing of the past, leaving behind it a great void which there is so far nothing to fill; humanity is searching for it passionately, and of course will find it. Ah, if only it could be quickly. If, don't you know, industry were united with culture and culture with industry. . . . (*Looks at his watch.*) But, I say, it's time for me to go. . . .

In other words, these plays are not mere exercises in psychology. They are woven around a very critical point of view, a point of view not only toward the characters, but toward the social context in which they live, a point of view which—far from being some arbitrary angle, as we have come to call such things—is their informing principle. I haven't the time here to investigate the plays one by one and it is not the business of the moment. All I have said comes down to this: that with all our technical dexterity, with all our lighting effects, sets, and a theater more solvent than any I know about, yes, with all our freedom to say what we will—our theater is narrowing its vision year by year, it is repeating well what it has done well before.

I can hear already my critics complaining that I am asking for a return to what they call problem plays. That criticism is important only because it tells something important about the critic. It means that he can only conceive of man as a private entity, and his social relations as something thrown at him, something "affecting" him only when he is conscious of society. I hope I have made one thing clear to this point—and it is that society is inside of man and man is inside society, and you cannot even create a truthfully drawn psychological entity on the stage until you understand his social relations and their power to make him what he is and to prevent him from being what he is not. The fish is in the water and the water is in the fish.

ARTHUR MILLER

INTRODUCTION to the Two–Act Version of *A View from the Bridge*

A play is rarely given a second chance. Unlike a novel, which may be received initially with less than enthusiasm, and then as time goes by hailed by a large public, a play usually makes its mark right off or it vanishes into oblivion. Two of mine, *The Crucible* and *A View from the Bridge,* failed to find large audiences with their original Broadway productions. Both were regarded as rather cold plays at first. However, after a couple of years *The Crucible* was produced again off Broadway and ran two years, without a line being changed from the original. With McCarthy dead it was once again possible to feel warmly toward the play, whereas during his time of power it was suspected of being a special plea, a concoction and unaesthetic. On its second time around its humanity emerged and it could be enjoyed as drama.

At this writing I have not yet permitted a second New York production of *A View from the Bridge* principally because I have not had the desire to see it through the mill a second time. However, a year or so after its first production it was done with great success in London and then in Paris, where it ran two years. It is done everywhere in this country without any apparent difficulty in reaching the emotions of the audience. This play, however, unlike *The Crucible,* I have revised, and it was the revision which London and Paris saw. The nature of the revisions bears directly upon the questions of form and style which interest students and theater workers.

The original play produced on Broadway (Viking, 1955) was in one act. It was a hard, telegraphic, unadorned drama. Nothing was permitted which did not advance the progress of Eddie's catastrophe in a most direct way. In a Note to the published play, I wrote: "What struck me first about this tale when I heard it one night in my neighborhood was how directly, with what breathtaking simplicity, it did evolve. It seemed to me, finally, that its very bareness, its absolutely unswerving path, its exposed skeleton, so to speak, was its wisdom and even its charm and must not be tempered with. . . . These *qualities* of the events themselves, their texture, seemed to me more psychologically telling than a conventional investigation in width which would necessarily relax that clear, clean line of his catastrophe."

The explanation for this point of view lies in great part in the atmosphere of the time in which the play was written. It seemed to me then that the theater was retreating into an area of psycho-sexual romanticism, and this at the very moment when great events both at home and abroad cried out for recognition and analytic inspection. In a word, I was tired of mere sympathy in the theater. The spectacle of still another misunderstood victim left me impatient. The tender emotions, I felt, were being overworked. I wanted to write in a way that would call up the faculties of knowing as well as feeling. To bathe the audience in tears, to grip people by the age-old methods of suspense, to theatricalize life, in a word, seemed faintly absurd to me if not disgusting.

In *The Crucible* I had taken a step, I felt, toward a more self-aware drama. The Puritan not only felt, but constantly referred his feelings to concepts, to codes and ideas of social and ethical importance. Feeling, it seemed to me, had to be made of importance; the dramatic victory had to be more than a triumph over the audience's indifference. It must call up a concept, a new awareness.

I had known the story of *A View from the Bridge* for a long time. A water-front worker who had known Eddie's prototype told it to me. I had never thought to make a play of it because it was too complete, there was nothing I could add. And then a time came when its very completeness became appealing. It suddenly seemed to me that I ought to deliver it onto the stage as fact; that interpretation was inherent in the very existence of the tale in the first place. I saw that the reason I had not written it was that as a whole its meaning escaped me. I could not fit it into myself. It existed apart from me and seemed not to express anything within me. Yet it refused to disappear.

I wrote it in a mood of experiment—to see what it might mean. I kept to the *tale,* trying not to change its original shape. I wanted the audience to feel toward it as I had on hearing it for the first time—not so much with heart-wringing sympathy as with wonder. For when it was told to me I knew its ending a few minutes after the teller had begun to speak. I wanted to create suspense but not by withholding information. It must be suspenseful because one knew too well how it would come out, so that the basic feeling would be the desire to stop this man and tell him what he was really doing to his life. Thus, by knowing more than the hero, the audience would rather automatically see his life through conceptualized feelings.

As a consequence of this viewpoint, the characters were not permitted to talk about this and that before getting down to their functions in the tale; when a character entered he proceeded directly to serve the catastrophe. Thus, normal naturalistic acting techniques had to be modified. Excessive and arbitrary gestures were eliminated; the set itself was shorn of every adornment. An atmosphere was attempted in which nothing existed but the purpose of the tale.

The trouble was that neither the director, the actors, nor I had had any experience with this kind of staging. It was difficult to know how far to go. We were all aware that a strange style was called for which we were unsure how to provide.

About a year later in London new conditions created new solutions. Seemingly inconsequential details suggested these solutions at times. For one, the British actors could not reproduce the Brooklyn argot and had to create one that was never heard on heaven or earth. Already naturalism was evaporated by this much: the characters were slightly strange beings in a world of their own. Also, the pay scales of the London theater made it possible to do what I could not do in New York—hire a crowd.

These seemingly mundane facts had important consequences. The mind of Eddie Carbone is not comprehensible apart from its relation to his neighborhood, his fellow workers, his social situation. His self-esteem depends upon their estimate of him, and his value is created largely by his fidelity to the code of his culture. In New York we could have only four strategically placed actors to represent the community. In London there were at least twenty men and women surrounding the main action. Peter Brook, the British director, could then proceed to design a set which soared to the roof with fire escapes, passageways, suggested apartments, so that one sensed that Eddie was living out his horror in the midst of a certain normality, and that, invisibly and without having to speak of it, he was getting ready to invoke upon himself the wrath of his tribe. A certain size accrued to him as a result. The importance of his interior psychological dilemma was magnified to the size it would have in life. What had seemed like a mere aberration had now risen to a fatal violation of an ancient law. By the presence of his neighbors alone the play and Eddie were made more humanly understandable and moving. There was also the fact that the British cast, accustomed to playing Shakespeare, could incorporate into a seemingly realistic style the conception of the play—they moved easily into the larger-than-life attitude which the play demanded, and without the self-conscious awkwardness, the uncertain stylishness which hounds many actors without classic training.

As a consequence of not having to work at making the play seem as factual, as bare as I had conceived it, I felt now that it could afford to include elements of simple human motivation which I had rigorously excluded before—specifically, the viewpoint of Eddie's wife, and *her* dilemma in relation to him. This, in fact, accounts for almost all the added material which made it necessary to break the play in the middle for an intermission. In other words, once Eddie had been placed squarely in his social context, among his people, the mythlike feeling of the story emerged of itself, and he could be made more human and less a figure, a force. It thus seemed quite in keeping that certain details of realism should be allowed; a Christmas tree and decorations in the living room, for one, and a realistic make-up, which had been avoided in New York, where the actor was always much cleaner than a longshoreman ever is. In a word, the nature of the British actor and of the production there made it possible to concentrate more upon realistic characterization while the universality of Eddie's type was strengthened at the same time.

But it was not only external additions, such as a new kind of actor, sets, and so forth, which led to the expansion of the play. As I have said, the original was written in the hope that I would understand what it meant to me. It was only during the latter part of its run in New York that, while watching a performance one afternoon, I saw my own involvement in this story. Quite suddenly the play seemed to be "mine" and not merely a story I had heard. The revisions subsequently made were in part the result of that new awareness.

In general, then, I think it can be said that by the addition of significant psychological and behavioral detail the play became not only more human, warmer and less remote, but also a clearer statement. Eddie is still not a man to weep over; the play does not attempt to swamp an audience in tears. But it is more possible now to relate his actions to our own and thus to understand ourselves a little better not only as isolated psychological entities, but as we connect to our fellows and our long past together.

MARCH 1960

ARTHUR MILLER

A View from the Bridge

A PLAY IN TWO ACTS

CHARACTERS

LOUIS

MIKE

ALFIERI

EDDIE

CATHERINE

BEATRICE

MARCO

TONY

RODOLPHO

FIRST IMMIGRATION OFFICER

SECOND IMMIGRATION OFFICER

MR. LIPARI

MRS. LIPARI

TWO "SUBMARINES"

NEIGHBORS

ACT ONE

The street and house front of a tenement building. The front is skeletal entirely. The main acting area is the living room-dining room of EDDIE's *apartment. It is a worker's flat, clean, sparse, homely. There is a rocker down front; a round dining table at center, with chairs; and a portable phonograph.*

At back are a bedroom door and an opening to the kitchen; none of these interiors are seen.

At the right, forestage, a desk. This is MR. ALFIERI's *law office. There is also a telephone booth. This is not used until the last scenes, so it may be covered or left in view.*

A stairway leads up to the apartment, and then farther up to the next story, which is not seen.

Ramps, representing the street, run upstage and off to right and left.

As the curtain rises, LOUIS *and* MIKE, *longshoremen, are pitching coins against the building at left.*

A distant foghorn blows.

Enter ALFIERI, *a lawyer in his fifties turning gray; he is portly, good-humored, and thoughtful. The two pitchers nod to him as he passes. He crosses the stage to his desk, removes his hat, runs his fingers through his hair, and grinning, speaks to the audience.*

ALFIERI: You wouldn't have known it, but something amusing has just happened. You see how uneasily they nod to me? That's because I am a lawyer. In this neighborhood to meet a lawyer or a priest on the street is unlucky. We're only thought of in connection with disasters, and they'd rather not get too close.

I often think that behind that suspicious little nod of theirs lie three thousand years of distrust. A lawyer means the law, and in Sicily, from where their fathers came, the law has not been a friendly idea since the Greeks were beaten.

I am inclined to notice the ruins in things, perhaps because I was born in Italy. . . . I only came here when I was twenty-five. In those days, Al Capone, the greatest Carthaginian of all, was learning his trade on these pavements, and Frankie Yale himself was cut precisely in half by a machine gun on the corner of Union Street, two blocks away. Oh, there were many here who were justly shot by unjust men. Justice is very important here.

But this is Red Hook, not Sicily. This is the slum that faces the bay on the seaward side of Brooklyn Bridge. This is the gullet of New York swallowing the tonnage of the world. And now we are quite civilized, quite American. Now we settle for half, and I like it better. I no longer keep a pistol in my filing cabinet.

And my practice is entirely unromantic.

My wife has warned me, so have my friends; they tell me the people in this neighborhood lack elegance, glamour. After all, who have I dealt with in my life? Long-shoremen and their wives, and fathers and grandfathers, compensation cases, evictions, family squabbles—the petty troubles of the poor—and yet . . . every few years there is still a case, and as the parties tell me what the trouble is, the flat air in my office suddenly washes in with the green scent of the sea, the dust in this air is blown away and the thought comes that in some Caesar's year, in Calabria perhaps or on the cliff at Syracuse, another lawyer, quite differently dressed, heard the same complaint and set there as powerless as I, and watched it run its bloody course.

[EDDIE *has appeared and has been pitching coins with the men and is highlighted among them. He is forty —a husky, slightly overweight longshoreman.*]

This one's name was Eddie Carbone, a longshoreman working the docks from Brooklyn Bridge to the breakwater where the open sea begins.

[ALFIERI *walks into darkness.*]

EDDIE: [*Moving up steps into doorway.*] Well, I'll see ya, fellas.

[CATHERINE *enters from kitchen, crosses down to window, looks out.*]

LOUIS: You workin' tomorrow?

EDDIE: Yeah, there's another day yet on that ship. See ya, Louis. [EDDIE *goes into the house, as light rises in the apartment.*]

[CATHERINE *is waving to* LOUIS *from the window and turns to him.*]

CATHERINE: Hi, Eddie!

[EDDIE *is pleased and therefore shy about it; he hangs up his cap and jacket.*]

EDDIE: Where you goin' all dressed up?

CATHERINE: [*Running her hands over her skirt.*] I just got it. You like it?

EDDIE: Yeah, it's nice. And what happened to your hair?

CATHERINE: You like it? I fixed it different. [*Calling to kitchen.*] He's here, B.!

EDDIE: Beautiful. Turn around, lemme see in the back. [*She turns for him.*] Oh, if your mother was alive to see you now! She wouldn't believe it.

CATHERINE: You like it, huh?

EDDIE: You look like one of them girls that went to college. Where you goin'?

CATHERINE: [*Taking his arm.*] Wait'll B. comes in, I'll tell you something. Here, sit down. [*She is walking him to the armchair. Calling offstage.*] Hurry up, will you, B.?

EDDIE: [*Sitting.*] What's goin' on?

CATHERINE: I'll get you a beer, all right?

EDDIE: Well, tell me what happened. Come over here, talk to me.

CATHERINE: I want to wait till B. comes in. [*She sits on her heels beside him.*] Guess how much we paid for the skirt.

EDDIE: I think it's too short, ain't it?

CATHERINE: [*Standing.*] No! not when I stand up.

EDDIE: Yeah, but you gotta sit down sometimes.

CATHERINE: Eddie, it's the style now. [*She walks to show him.*] I mean, if you see me walkin' down the street—

EDDIE: Listen, you been givin' me the willies the way you walk down the street, I mean it.

CATHERINE: Why?

EDDIE: Catherine, I don't want to be a pest, but I'm tellin' you you're walkin' wavy.

CATHERINE: I'm walkin' wavy?

EDDIE: Now don't aggravate me, Katie, you are walkin' wavy! I don't like the looks they're givin' you in the candy store. And with them new high heels on the sidewalk —clack, clack, clack. The heads are turnin' like windmills.

CATHERINE: But those guys look at all the girls, you know that.

EDDIE: You ain't "all the girls."

CATHERINE: [*Almost in tears because he disapproves.*] What do you want me to do? You want me to—

EDDIE: Now don't get mad, kid.

CATHERINE: Well, I don't know what you want from me.

EDDIE: Katie, I promised your mother on her deathbed. I'm responsible for you. You're a baby, you don't understand these things. I mean like when you stand here by the window, wavin' outside.

CATHERINE: I was wavin' to Louis!

EDDIE: Listen, I could tell you things about Louis which you wouldn't wave to him no more.

CATHERINE: [*Trying to joke him out of his warning.*] Eddie, I wish there was one guy you couldn't tell me things about!

EDDIE: Catherine, do me a favor, will you? You're gettin' to be a big girl now, you gotta keep yourself more, you can't be so friendly, kid. [*Calls.*] Hey, B., what're you doin' in there? [*To* CATHERINE.] Get her in here, will you? I got news for her.

CATHERINE: [*Starting out.*] What?

EDDIE: Her cousins landed.

CATHERINE: [*Clapping her hands together.*] No! [*She turns instantly and starts for the kitchen.*] B.! Your cousins!

[BEATRICE *enters, wiping her hands with a towel.*]

BEATRICE: [*In the face of* CATHERINE'S *shout.*] What?

CATHERINE: Your cousins got in!

BEATRICE: [*Astounded, turns to* EDDIE.] What are you talkin' about? Where?

EDDIE: I was just knockin' off work before and Tony Bereli come over to me; he says the ship is in the North River.

BEATRICE: [*Her hands are clasped at her breast; she seems half in fear, half in unutterable joy.*] They're all right?

EDDIE: He didn't see them yet, they're still on board. But as soon as they get off he'll meet them. He figures about ten o'clock they'll be here.

BEATRICE: [*Sits, almost weak from tension.*] And they'll let them off the ship all right? That's fixed, heh?

EDDIE: Sure, they give them regular seamen papers and they walk off with the crew. Don't worry about it, B., there's nothin' to it. Couple of hours they'll be here.

BEATRICE: What happened? They wasn't supposed to be till next Thursday.

EDDIE: I don't know; they put them on any ship they can get them out on. Maybe the other ship they was supposed to take there was some danger— What you cryin' about?

BEATRICE: [*Astounded and afraid.*] I'm— I just—I can't believe it! I didn't even buy a new tablecloth; I was gonna wash the walls—

EDDIE: Listen, they'll think it's a millionaire's house compared to the way they live. Don't worry about the walls. They'll be thankful. [*To* CATHERINE.] Whyn't you run down buy a tablecloth. Go ahead, here. [*He is reaching into his pocket.*]

CATHERINE: There's no stores open now.

EDDIE: [*To* BEATRICE.] You was gonna put a new cover on the chair.

BEATRICE: I know—well, I thought it was gonna be next week! I was gonna clean the walls, I was gonna wax the floors. [*She stands disturbed.*]

CATHERINE: [*Pointing upward.*] Maybe Mrs. Dondero upstairs—

BEATRICE: [*Of the tablecloth.*] No, hers is worse than this one. [*Suddenly.*] My God, I don't even have nothin' to eat for them! [*She starts for the kitchen.*]

EDDIE: [*Reaching out and grabbing her arm.*] Hey, hey! Take it easy.

BEATRICE: No, I'm just nervous, that's all. [*To* CATHERINE.] I'll make the fish.

EDDIE: You're savin' their lives, what're you worryin' about the tablecloth? They probably didn't see a tablecloth in their whole life where they come from.

BEATRICE: [*Looking into his eyes.*] I'm just worried about you, that's all I'm worried.

EDDIE: Listen, as long as they know where they're gonna sleep.

BEATRICE: I told them in the letters. They're sleepin' on the floor.

EDDIE: Beatrice, all I'm worried about is you got such a heart that I'll end up on the floor with you, and they'll be in our bed.

BEATRICE: All right, stop it.

EDDIE: Because as soon as you see a tired relative, I end up on the floor.

BEATRICE: When did you end up on the floor?

EDDIE: When your father's house burned down I didn't end up on the floor?

BEATRICE: Well, their house burned down!

EDDIE: Yeah, but it didn't keep burnin' for two weeks!

BEATRICE: All right, look, I'll tell them to go someplace else. [*She starts into the kitchen.*]

EDDIE: Now wait a minute, Beatrice! [*She halts. He goes to her.*] I just don't want you bein' pushed around, that's all. You got too big a heart. [*He touches her hand.*] What're you so touchy?

BEATRICE: I'm just afraid if it don't turn out good you'll be mad at me.

EDDIE: Listen, if everybody keeps his mouth shut, nothin' can happen. They'll pay for their board.

BEATRICE: Oh, I told them.

EDDIE: Then what the hell. [*Pauses. He moves.*] It's an honor, B. I mean it. I was just thinkin' before, comin' home, suppose my father didn't come to this country, and I was starvin' like them over there . . . and I had people in America could keep me a couple of months? The man would be honored to lend me a place to sleep.

BEATRICE: [*There are tears in her eyes. She turns to* CATHERINE.] You see what he is? [*She turns and grabs* EDDIE's *face in her hands.*] Mmm! You're an angel! God'll bless you. [*He is gratefully smiling.*] You'll see, you'll get a blessing for this!

EDDIE: [*Laughing.*] I'll settle for my own bed.

BEATRICE: Go, Baby, set the table.

CATHERINE: We didn't tell him about me yet.

BEATRICE: Let him eat first, then we'll tell him. Bring everything in. [*She hurries* CATHERINE *out.*]

EDDIE: [*Sitting at the table.*] What's all that about? Where's she goin'?

BEATRICE: Noplace. It's very good news, Eddie. I want you to be happy.

EDDIE: What's goin' on?

[CATHERINE *enters with plates, forks.*]

BEATRICE: She's got a job. [*Pause.* EDDIE *looks at* CATHERINE, *then back to* BEATRICE.]

EDDIE: What job? She's gonna finish school.

CATHERINE: Eddie, you won't believe it—

EDDIE: No—no, you gonna finish school. What kinda job, what do you mean? All of a sudden you—

CATHERINE: Listen a minute, it's wonderful.

EDDIE: It's not wonderful. You'll never get nowheres unless you finish school. You can't take no job. Why didn't you ask me before you take a job?

BEATRICE: She's askin' you now, she didn't take nothin' yet.

CATHERINE: Listen a minute! I came to school this morning and the principal called me out of the class, see? To go to his office.

EDDIE: Yeah?

CATHERINE: So I went in and he says to me he's got my records, y'know? And there's a company wants a girl right away. It ain't exactly a secretary, it's a stenographer first, but pretty soon you get to be secretary. And he says to me that I'm the best student in the whole class—

BEATRICE: You hear that?

EDDIE: Well why not? Sure she's the best.

CATHERINE: I'm the best student, he says, and if I want, I should take the job and the end of the year he'll let me take the examination and he'll give me the certificate. So I'll save practically a year!

EDDIE: [*Strangely nervous.*] Where's the job? What company?

CATHERINE: It's a big plumbing company over Nostrand Avenue.

EDDIE: Nostrand Avenue and where?

CATHERINE: It's someplace by the Navy Yard.

BEATRICE: Fifty dollars a week, Eddie.

EDDIE: [*To* CATHERINE, *surprised.*] Fifty?

CATHERINE: I swear.

[*Pause.*]

EDDIE: What about all the stuff you wouldn't learn this year, though?

CATHERINE: There's nothin' more to learn, Eddie, I just gotta practice from now on. I know all the symbols and I know the keyboard. I'll just get faster, that's all. And when I'm workin' I'll keep gettin' better and better, you see?

BEATRICE: Work is the best practice anyway.

EDDIE: That ain't what I wanted, though.

CATHERINE: Why! It's a great big company—

EDDIE: I don't like that neighborhood over there.

CATHERINE: It's a block and half from the subway, he says.

EDDIE: Near the Navy Yard plenty can happen in a block and a half. And a plumbin' company! That's one step over the water front. They're practically longshoremen.

BEATRICE: Yeah, but she'll be in the office, Eddie.

EDDIE: I know she'll be in the office, but that ain't what I had in mind.

BEATRICE: Listen, she's gotta go to work sometime.

EDDIE: Listen, B., she'll be with a lotta plumbers? And sailors up and down the street? So what did she go to school for?

CATHERINE: But it's fifty a week, Eddie.

EDDIE: Look, did I ask you for money? I supported you this long I support you a little more. Please, do me a favor, will ya? I want you to be with different kind of people. I want you to be in a nice office. Maybe a lawyer's office someplace in New York in one of them nice buildings. I mean if you're gonna get outa here then get out; don't go practically in the same kind of neighborhood.

[*Pause.* CATHERINE *lowers her eyes.*]

BEATRICE: Go, Baby, bring in the supper. [CATHERINE *goes out.*] Think about it a little bit, Eddie. Please. She's crazy to start work. It's not a little shop, it's a big company. Some day she could be a secretary. They picked her out of the whole class. [*He is silent, staring down at the tablecloth, fingering the pattern.*] What are you worried about? She could take care of herself. She'll get out of the subway and be in the office in two minutes.

EDDIE: [*Somehow sickened.*] I know that neighborhood, B., I don't like it.

BEATRICE: Listen, if nothin' happened to her in this neighborhood it ain't gonna happen noplace else. [*She turns his face to her.*] Look, you gotta get used to it, she's no baby no more. Tell her to take it. [*He turns his head away.*] You hear me? [*She is *angering.*] I don't understand you; she's seventeen years old, you gonna keep her in the house all her life?

EDDIE: [*Insulted.*] What kinda remark is that?

BEATRICE: [*With sympathy but insistent force.*] Well, I don't understand when it ends. First it was gonna be when she graduated high school, so she graduated high school. Then it was gonna be when she learned stenographer, so she learned stenographer. So what're we gonna wait for now? I mean it, Eddie, sometimes I don't understand you; they picked her out of the whole class, it's an honor for her.

[CATHERINE *enters with food, which she silently sets on the table. After a moment of watching her face,* EDDIE *breaks into a smile, but it almost seems that tears will form in his eyes.*]

EDDIE: With your hair that way you look like a madonna, you know that? You're the madonna type. [*She doesn't look at him, but continues ladling out food onto the plates.*] You wanna go to work, heh, Madonna?

CATHERINE: [*Softly.*] Yeah.

EDDIE: [*With a sense of her childhood, her babyhood, and the years.*] All right, go to work. [*She looks at him, then rushes and hugs him.*] Hey, hey! Take it easy! [*He holds her face away from him to look at her.*] What're you cryin' about? [*He is affected by her, but smiles his emotion away.*]

CATHERINE: [*Sitting at her place.*] I just —[*Bursting out.*] I'm gonna buy all new dishes with my first pay! [*They laugh warmly.*] I mean it. I'll fix up the whole house! I'll buy a rug!

EDDIE: And then you'll move away.

CATHERINE: No, Eddie!

EDDIE: [*Grinning.*] Why not? That's life. And you'll come visit on Sundays, then once a month, then Christmas and New Year's, finally.

CATHERINE: [*Grasping his arm to reassure him and to erase the accusation.*] No, please!

EDDIE: [*Smiling but hurt.*] I only ask you one thing—don't trust nobody. You got a good aunt but she's got too big a heart, you learned bad from her. Believe me.

BEATRICE: Be the way you are, Katie, don't listen to him.

EDDIE: [*To* BEATRICE—*strangely and quickly resentful.*] You lived in a house all your life, what do you know about it? You never worked in your life.

BEATRICE: She likes people. What's wrong with that?

EDDIE: Because most people ain't people. She's goin' to work; plumbers; they'll chew her to pieces if she don't watch out. [*To* CATHERINE.] Believe me, Katie, the less you trust, the less you be sorry.

[EDDIE *crosses himself and the women do the same, and they eat.*]

CATHERINE: First thing I'll buy is a rug, heh, B.?

BEATRICE: I don't mind. [*To* EDDIE.] I smelled coffee all day today. You unloadin' coffee today?

EDDIE: Yeah, a Brazil ship.

CATHERINE: I smelled it too. It smelled all over the neighborhood.

EDDIE: That's one time, boy, to be a longshoreman is a pleasure. I could work coffee ships twenty hours a day. You go down in the hold, y'know? It's like flowers, that smell. We'll bust a bag tomorrow, I'll bring you some.

BEATRICE: Just be sure there's no spiders in it, will ya? I mean it. [*She directs this to* CATHERINE, *rolling her eyes upward.*] I still remember that spider coming out of that bag he brung home. I nearly died.

EDDIE: You call that a spider? You oughta see what comes outa the bananas sometimes.

BEATRICE: Don't talk about it!

EDDIE: I seen spiders could stop a Buick.

BEATRICE: [*Clapping her hands over her ears.*] All right, shut up!

EDDIE: [*Laughing and taking a watch out of his pocket.*] Well, who started with spiders?

BEATRICE: All right, I'm sorry, I didn't mean it. Just don't bring none home again. What time is it?

EDDIE: Quarter nine. [*Puts watch back in his pocket.*]

[*They continue eating in silence.*]

CATHERINE: He's bringin' them ten o'clock, Tony?

EDDIE: Around, yeah. [*He eats.*]

CATHERINE: Eddie, suppose somebody asks if they're livin' here. [*He looks at her as though already she had divulged something publicly. Defensively.*] I mean if they ask.

EDDIE: Now look, Baby, I can see we're gettin' mixed up again here.

CATHERINE: No, I just mean . . . people'll see them goin' in and out.

EDDIE: I don't care who sees them goin'

in and out as long as you don't see them goin' in and out. And this goes for you too, B. You don't see nothin' and you don't know nothin'.

BEATRICE: What do you mean? I understand.

EDDIE: You don't understand; you still think you can talk about this to somebody just a little bit. Now lemme say it once and for all, because you're makin' me nervous again, both of you. I don't care if somebody comes in the house and sees them sleepin' on the floor, it never comes out of your mouth who they are or what they're doin' here.

BEATRICE: Yeah, but my mother'll know—

EDDIE: Sure she'll know, but just don't you be the one who told her, that's all. This is the United States government you're playin' with now, this is the Immigration Bureau. If you said it you knew it, if you didn't say it you didn't know it.

CATHERINE: Yeah, but Eddie, suppose somebody—

EDDIE: I don't care what question it is. You—don't—know—nothin'. They got stool pigeons all over this neighborhood they're payin' them every week for information, and you don't know who they are. It could be your best friend. You hear? [To BEATRICE.] Like Vinny Bolzano, remember Vinny?

BEATRICE: Oh, yeah. God forbid.

EDDIE: Tell her about Vinny. [To CATHERINE.] You think I'm blowin' steam here? [To BEATRICE.] Go ahead, tell her. [To CATHERINE.] You was a baby then. There was a family lived next door to her mother, he was about sixteen—

BEATRICE: No, he was no more than fourteen, cause I was to his confirmation in Saint Agnes. But the family had an uncle that they were hidin' in the house, and he snitched to the Immigration.

CATHERINE: The kid snitched?

EDDIE: On his own uncle!

CATHERINE: What, was he crazy?

EDDIE: He was crazy after, I tell you that, boy.

BEATRICE: Oh, it was terrible. He had five brothers and the old father. And they grabbed him in the kitchen and pulled him down the stairs—three flights his head was bouncin' like a coconut. And they spit on him in the street, his own father and his brothers. The whole neighborhood was cryin'.

CATHERINE: Ts! So what happened to him?

BEATRICE: I think he went away. [To EDDIE.] I never seen him again, did you?

EDDIE: [Rises during this, taking out his watch.] Him? You'll never see him no more, a guy do a thing like that? How's he gonna show his face? [To CATHERINE, as he gets up uneasily.] Just remember, kid, you can quicker get back a million dollars that was stole than a word that you gave away. [He is standing now, stretching his back.]

CATHERINE: Okay, I won't say a word to nobody, I swear.

EDDIE: Gonna rain tomorrow. We'll be slidin' all over the decks. Maybe you oughta put something on for them, they be here soon.

BEATRICE: I only got fish, I hate to spoil it if they ate already. I'll wait, it only takes a few minutes; I could broil it.

CATHERINE: What happens, Eddie, when that ship pulls out and they ain't on it, though? Don't the captain say nothin'?

EDDIE: [Slicing an apple with his pocket knife.] Captain's pieced off, what do you mean?

CATHERINE: Even the captain?

EDDIE: What's the matter, the captain don't have to live? Captain gets a piece, maybe one of the mates, piece for the guy in Italy who fixed the papers for them, Tony here'll get a little bite. . . .

BEATRICE: I just hope they get work here, that's all I hope.

EDDIE: Oh, the syndicate'll fix jobs for them; till they pay 'em off they'll get them work every day. It's after the pay-off, then they'll have to scramble like the rest of us.

BEATRICE: Well, it be better than they got there.

EDDIE: Oh sure, well, listen. So you gonna start Monday, heh, Madonna?

CATHERINE: [Embarrassed.] I'm supposed to, yeah.

[EDDIE is standing facing the two seated women. First BEATRICE smiles, then CATHERINE, for a powerful emotion is on him, a childish one and a knowing fear, and the tears show in his eyes—and they are shy before the avowal.]

EDDIE: [Sadly smiling, yet somehow proud of her.] Well . . . I hope you have good luck. I wish you the best. You know that, kid.

CATHERINE: [*Rising, trying to laugh.*] You sound like I'm goin' a million miles!

EDDIE: I know. I guess I just never figured on one thing.

CATHERINE: [*Smiling.*] What?

EDDIE: That you would ever grow up. [*He utters a soundless laugh at himself, feeling his breast pocket of his shirt.*] I left a cigar in my other coat, I think. [*He starts for the bedroom.*]

CATHERINE: Stay there! I'll get it for you. [*She hurries out. There is a slight pause, and* EDDIE *turns to* BEATRICE, *who has been avoiding his gaze.*]

EDDIE: What are you mad at me lately?

BEATRICE: Who's mad? [*She gets up, clearing the dishes.*] I'm not mad. [*She picks up the dishes and turns to him.*] You're the one is mad. [*She turns and goes into the kitchen as* CATHERINE *enters from the bedroom with a cigar and a pack of matches.*]

CATHERINE: Here! I'll light it for you! [*She strikes a match and holds it to his cigar. He puffs. Quietly.*] Don't worry about me, Eddie, heh?

EDDIE: Don't burn yourself. [*Just in time she blows out the match.*] You better go in help her with the dishes.

CATHERINE: [*Turns quickly to the table, and, seeing the table cleared, she says, almost guiltily.*] Oh! [*She hurries into the kitchen, and as she exits there.*] I'll do the dishes, B.!

[*Alone,* EDDIE *stands looking toward the kitchen for a moment. Then he takes out his watch, glances at it, replaces it in his pocket, sits in the armchair, and stares at the smoke flowing out of his mouth.*
The lights go down, then come up on ALFIERI, *who has moved onto the forestage.*]

ALFIERI: He was as good a man as he had to be in a life that was hard and even. He worked on the piers when there was work, he brought home his pay, and he lived. And toward ten o'clock of that night, after they had eaten, the cousins came.

[*The lights fade on* ALFIERI *and rise on the street.*
Enter TONY, *escorting* MARCO *and* RODOLPHO, *each with a valise.* TONY *halts, indicates the house. They stand for a moment looking at it.*]

MARCO: [*He is a square-built peasant of* thirty-two, suspicious, tender, and quiet-voiced.*] Thank you.

TONY: You're on your own now. Just be careful, that's all. Ground floor.

MARCO: Thank you.

TONY: [*Indicating the house.*] I'll see you on the pier tomorrow. You'll go to work.

[MARCO *nods.* TONY *continues on walking down the street.*]

RODOLPHO: This will be the first house I ever walked into in America! Imagine! She said they were poor!

MARCO: Ssh! Come. [*They go to door.*] [MARCO *knocks. The lights rise in the room.* EDDIE *goes and opens the door. Enter* MARCO *and* RODOLPHO, *removing their caps.* BEATRICE *and* CATHERINE *enter from the kitchen. The lights fade in the street.*]

EDDIE: You Marco?

MARCO: Marco.

EDDIE: Come on in! [*He shakes* MARCO's *hand.*]

BEATRICE: Here, take the bags!

MARCO: [*Nods, looks to the women and fixes on* BEATRICE. *Crosses to* BEATRICE.] Are you my cousin?

[*She nods. He kisses her hand.*]

BEATRICE: [*Above the table, touching her chest with her hand.*] Beatrice. This is my husband, Eddie. [*All nod.*] Catherine, my sister Nancy's daughter. [*The brothers nod.*]

MARCO: [*Indicating* RODOLPHO.] My brother. Rodolpho. [RODOLPHO *nods.* MARCO *comes with a certain formal stiffness to* EDDIE.] I want to tell you now Eddie—when you say go, we will go.

EDDIE: Oh, no . . . [*Takes* MARCO's *bag.*]

MARCO: I see it's a small house, but soon, maybe, we can have our own house.

EDDIE: You're welcome, Marco, we got plenty of room here. Katie, give them supper, heh? [*Exits into bedroom with their bags.*]

CATHERINE: Come here, sit down. I'll get you some soup.

MARCO: [*As they go to the table.*] We ate on the ship. Thank you. [*To* EDDIE, *calling off to bedroom.*] Thank you.

BEATRICE: Get some coffee. We'll all have coffee. Come sit down.

[RODOLPHO *and* MARCO *sit, at the table.*]

CATHERINE: [*Wondrously.*] How come he's so dark and you're so light, Rodolpho?

RODOLPHO: [*Ready to laugh.*] I don't know. A thousand years ago, they say, the Danes invaded Sicily.

[BEATRICE *kisses* RODOLPHO. *They laugh as* EDDIE *enters.*]

CATHERINE: [*To* BEATRICE.] He's practically blond!

EDDIE: How's the coffee doin'?

CATHERINE: [*Brought up.*] I'm gettin' it. [*She hurries out to kitchen.*]

EDDIE: [*Sits on his rocker.*] Yiz have a nice trip?

MARCO: The ocean is always rough. But we are good sailors.

EDDIE: No trouble gettin' here?

MARCO: No. The man brought us. Very nice man.

RODOLPHO: [*To* EDDIE.] He says we start to work tomorrow. Is he honest?

EDDIE: [*Laughing.*] No. But as long as you owe them money, they'll get you plenty of work. [*To* MARCO.] Yiz ever work on the piers in Italy?

MARCO: Piers? Ts!—no.

RODOLPHO: [*Smiling at the smallness of his town.*] In our town there are no piers, only the beach, and little fishing boats.

BEATRICE: So what kinda work did yiz do?

MARCO: [*Shrugging shyly, even embarrassed.*] Whatever there is, anything.

RODOLPHO: Sometimes they build a house, or if they fix the bridge—Marco is a mason and I bring him the cement. [*He laughs.*] In harvest time we work in the fields . . . if there is work. Anything.

EDDIE: Still bad there, heh?

MARCO: Bad, yes.

RODOLPHO: [*Laughing.*] It's terrible! We stand around all day in the piazza listening to the fountain like birds. Everybody waits only for the train.

BEATRICE: What's on the train?

RODOLPHO: Nothing. But if there are many passengers and you're lucky you make a few lire to push the taxi up the hill.

[*Enter* CATHERINE; *she listens.*]

BEATRICE: You gotta push a taxi?

RODOLPHO: [*Laughing.*] Oh, sure! It's a feature in our town. The horses in our town are skinnier than goats. So if there are too many passengers we help to push the carriages up to the hotel. [*He laughs.*] In our town the horses are only for show.

CATHERINE: Why don't they have automobile taxis?

RODOLPHO: There is one. We push that too. [*They laugh.*] Everything in our town, you gotta push!

BEATRICE: [*To* EDDIE.] How do you like that!

EDDIE: [*To* MARCO.] So what're you wanna do, you gonna stay here in this country or you wanna go back?

MARCO: [*Surprised.*] Go back?

EDDIE: Well, you're married, ain't you?

MARCO: Yes. I have three children.

BEATRICE: Three! I thought only one.

MARCO: Oh, no. I have three now. Four years, five years, six years.

BEATRICE: Ah . . . I bet they're cryin' for you already, heh?

MARCO: What can I do? The older one is sick in his chest. My wife—she feeds them from her own mouth. I tell you the truth, if I stay there they will never grow up. They eat the sunshine.

BEATRICE: My God. So how long you want to stay?

MARCO: With your permission, we will stay maybe a—

EDDIE: She don't mean in this house, she means in the country.

MARCO: Oh. Maybe four, five, six years, I think.

RODOLPHO: [*Smiling.*] He trusts his wife.

BEATRICE: Yeah, but maybe you'll get enough, you'll be able to go back quicker.

MARCO: I hope. I don't know. [*To* EDDIE.] I understand it's not so good here either.

EDDIE: Oh, you guys'll be all right—till you pay them off, anyway. After that, you'll have to scramble, that's all. But you'll make better here than you could there.

RODOLPHO: How much? We hear all kinds of figures. How much can a man make? We work hard, we'll work all day, all night—

[MARCO *raises a hand to hush him.*]

EDDIE: [*He is coming more and more to address* MARCO *only.*] On the average a whole year? Maybe—well, it's hard to say, see. Sometimes we lay off, there's no ships three four weeks.

MARCO: Three, four weeks!—Ts!

EDDIE: But I think you could probably—thirty, forty a week, over the whole twelve months of the year.

MARCO: [*Rises, crosses to* EDDIE.] Dollars.

EDDIE: Sure dollars.

[MARCO *puts an arm round* RODOLPHO *and they laugh.*]

MARCO: If we can stay here a few months, Beatrice—

BEATRICE: Listen, you're welcome, Marco—

MARCO: Because I could send them a little more if I stay here.

BEATRICE: As long as you want, we got plenty a room.

MARCO: [*His eyes showing tears.*] My wife— [*To* EDDIE.] My wife—I want to send right away maybe twenty dollars—

EDDIE: You could send them something next week already.

MARCO: [*He is near tears.*] Eduardo . . . [*He goes to* EDDIE, *offering his hand.*]

EDDIE: Don't thank me. Listen, what the hell, it's no skin off me. [*To* CATHERINE.] What happened to the coffee?

CATHERINE: I got it on. [*To* RODOLPHO.] You married too? No.

RODOLPHO: [*Rises.*] Oh, no . . .

BEATRICE: [*To* CATHERINE.] I told you he—

CATHERINE: I know, I just thought maybe he got married recently.

RODOLPHO: I have no money to get married. I have a nice face, but no money. [*He laughs.*]

CATHERINE: [*To* BEATRICE.] He's a real blond!

BEATRICE: [*To* RODOLPHO.] You want to stay here too, heh? For good?

RODOLPHO: Me? Yes, forever! Me, I want to be an American. And then I want to go back to Italy when I am rich, and I will buy a motorcycle. [*He smiles.* MARCO *shakes him affectionately.*]

CATHERINE: A motorcycle!

RODOLPHO: With a motorcycle in Italy you will never starve any more.

BEATRICE: I'll get you coffee. [*She exits to the kitchen.*]

EDDIE: What you do with a motorcycle?

MARCO: He dreams, he dreams.

RODOLPHO: [*To* MARCO.] Why? [*To* EDDIE.] Messages! The rich people in the hotel always need someone who will carry a message. But quickly, and with a great noise. With a blue motorcycle I would station myself in the courtyard of the hotel, and in a little while I would have messages.

MARCO: When you have no wife you have dreams.

EDDIE: Why can't you just walk, or take a trolley or sump'm?

[*Enter* BEATRICE *with coffee.*]

RODOLPHO: Oh, no, the machine, the machine is necessary. A man comes into a great hotel and says, I am a messenger. Who is this man? He disappears walking, there is no noise, nothing. Maybe he will never come back, maybe he will never deliver the message. But a man who rides up on a great machine, this man is responsible, this man exists. He will be given messages. [*He helps* BEATRICE *set out the coffee things.*] I am also a singer, though.

EDDIE: You mean a regular—?

RODOLPHO: Oh, yes. One night last year Andreola got sick. Baritone. And I took his place in the garden of the hotel. Three arias I sang without a mistake! Thousand-lire notes they threw from the tables, money was falling like a storm in the treasury. It was magnificent. We lived six months on that night, eh, Marco?

[MARCO *nods doubtfully.*]

MARCO: Two months.

[EDDIE *laughs.*]

BEATRICE: Can't you get a job in that place?

RODOLPHO: Andreola got better. He's a baritone, very strong.

[BEATRICE *laughs.*]

MARCO: [*Regretfully, to* BEATRICE.] He sang too loud.

RODOLPHO: Why too loud?

MARCO: Too loud. The guests in that hotel are all Englishmen. They don't like too loud.

RODOLPHO: [*To* CATHERINE.] Nobody ever said it was too loud!

MARCO: I say. It was too loud. [*To* BEATRICE.] I knew it as soon as he started to sing. Too loud.

RODOLPHO: Then why did they throw so much money?

MARCO: They paid for your courage. The English like courage. But once is enough.

RODOLPHO: [*To all but* MARCO.] I never heard anybody say it was too loud.

CATHERINE: Did you ever hear of jazz?

RODOLPHO: Oh, sure! I *sing* jazz.

CATHERINE: [*Rises.*] You could sing jazz?

RODOLPHO: Oh, I sing Napolidan, jazz, bel canto—I sing "Paper Doll," you like "Paper Doll"?

CATHERINE: Oh, sure, I'm crazy for "Paper Doll." Go ahead, sing it.

RODOLPHO: [*Takes his stance after getting a nod of permission from* MARCO, *and with a high tenor voice begins singing.*]
  I'll tell you boys it's tough to be
    alone,

And it's tough to love a doll that's not your own.

I'm through with all of them,

I'll never fall again,

Hey, boy, what you gonna do?

I'm gonna buy a paper doll that I can call my own,

A doll that other fellows cannot steal.

[EDDIE *rises and moves upstage.*]

And then those flirty, flirty guys

With their flirty, flirty eyes

Will have to flirt with dollies that are real—

EDDIE: Hey, kid—hey, wait a minute—

CATHERINE: [*Enthralled.*] Leave him finish, it's beautiful! [*To* BEATRICE.] He's terrific! It's terrific, Rodolpho.

EDDIE: Look, kid; you don't want to be picked up, do ya?

MARCO: No—no! [*He rises.*]

EDDIE: [*Indicating the rest of the building.*] Because we never had no singers here . . . and all of a sudden there's a singer in the house, y'know what I mean?

MARCO: Yes, yes. You'll be quiet, Rodolpho.

EDDIE: [*He is flushed.*] They got guys all over the place, Marco. I mean.

MARCO: Yes. He'll be quiet. [*To* RODOLPHO.] You'll be quiet.

[RODOLPHO *nods.* EDDIE *has risen, with iron control, even a smile. He moves to* CATHERINE.]

EDDIE: What's the high heels for, Garbo?

CATHERINE: I figured for tonight—

EDDIE: Do me a favor, will you? Go ahead.

[*Embarrassed now, angered,* CATHERINE *goes out into the bedroom.* BEATRICE *watches her go and gets up; in passing, she gives* EDDIE *a cold look, restrained only by the strangers, and goes to the table to pour coffee.*]

EDDIE: [*Striving to laugh, and to* MARCO, *but directed as much to* BEATRICE.] All actresses they want to be around here.

RODOLPHO: [*Happy about it.*] In Italy too! All the girls.

[CATHERINE *emerges from the bedroom in low-heel shoes, comes to the table.* RODOLPHO *is lifting a cup.*]

EDDIE: [*He is sizing up* RODOLPHO, *and there is a concealed suspicion.*] Yeah, heh?

RODOLPHO: Yes! [*Laughs, indicating* CATHERINE.] Especially when they are so beautiful!

CATHERINE: You like sugar?

RODOLPHO: Sugar? Yes! I like sugar very much!

[EDDIE *is downstage, watching as she pours a spoonful of sugar into his cup, his face puffed with trouble, and the room dies.*]

[*Lights rise on* ALFIERI.]

ALFIERI: Who can ever know what will be discovered? Eddie Carbone had never expected to have a destiny. A man works, raises his family, goes bowling, eats, gets old, and then he dies. Now, as the weeks passed, there was a future, there was a trouble that would not go away.

[*The lights fade on* ALFIERI, *then rise on* EDDIE *standing at the doorway of the house.* BEATRICE *enters on the street. She sees* EDDIE, *smiles at him. He looks away. She starts to enter the house when* EDDIE *speaks.*]

EDDIE: It's after eight.

BEATRICE: Well, it's a long show at the Paramount.

EDDIE: They must've seen every picture in Brooklyn by now. He's supposed to stay in the house when he ain't working. He ain't supposed to go advertising himself.

BEATRICE: Well that's his trouble, what do you care? If they pick him up they pick him up, that's all. Come in the house.

EDDIE: What happened to the stenography? I don't see her practice no more.

BEATRICE: She'll get back to it. She's excited, Eddie.

EDDIE: She tell you anything?

BEATRICE: [*Comes to him, now the subject is opened.*] What's the matter with you? He's a nice kid, what do you want from him?

EDDIE: That's a nice kid? He gives me the heeby-jeebies.

BEATRICE: [*Smiling.*] Ah, go on, you're just jealous.

EDDIE: Of *him?* Boy, you don't think much of me.

BEATRICE: I don't understand you. What's so terrible about him?

EDDIE: You mean it's all right with you? That's gonna be her husband?

BEATRICE: Why? He's a nice fella, hard workin', he's a good-lookin' fella.

EDDIE: He sings on the ships, didja know that?

BEATRICE: What do you mean, he sings?

EDDIE: Just what I said, he sings. Right on the deck, all of a sudden, a whole song comes out of his mouth—with motions.

You know what they're callin' him now? Paper Doll they're callin' him, Canary. He's like a weird. He comes out on the pier, one-two-three, it's a regular free show.

BEATRICE: Well, he's a kid; he don't know how to behave himself yet.

EDDIE: And with that wacky hair; he's like a chorus girl or sump'm.

BEATRICE: So he's blond, so—

EDDIE: I just hope that's his regular hair, that's all I hope.

BEATRICE: You crazy or sump'm? [*She tries to turn him to her.*]

EDDIE: [*He keeps his head turned away.*] What's so crazy? I don't like his whole way.

BEATRICE: Listen, you never seen a blond guy in your life? What about Whitey Balso?

EDDIE: [*Turning to her victoriously.*] Sure, but Whitey don't sing; he don't do like that on the ships.

BEATRICE: Well, maybe that's the way they do in Italy.

EDDIE: Then why don't his brother sing? Marco goes around like a man; nobody kids Marco. [*He moves from her, halts. She realizes there is a campaign solidified in him.*] I tell you the truth I'm surprised I have to tell you all this. I mean I'm surprised, B.

BEATRICE: [*She goes to him with purpose now.*] Listen, you ain't gonna start nothin' here.

EDDIE: I ain't startin' nothin', but I ain't gonna stand around lookin' at that. For that character I didn't bring her up. I swear, B., I'm surprised at you; I sit there waitin' for you to wake up but everything is great with you.

BEATRICE: No, everything ain't great with me.

EDDIE: No?

BEATRICE: No. I got other worries.

EDDIE: Yeah. [*He is already weakening.*]

BEATRICE: Yeah, you want me to tell you?

EDDIE: [*In retreat.*] Why? What worries you got?

BEATRICE: When am I gonna be a wife again, Eddie?

EDDIE: I ain't been feelin' good. They bother me since they came.

BEATRICE: It's almost three months you don't feel good; they're only here a couple of weeks. It's three months, Eddie.

EDDIE: I don't know, B. I don't want to talk about it.

BEATRICE: What's the matter, Eddie, you don't like me, heh?

EDDIE: What do you mean, I don't like you? I said I don't feel good, that's all.

BEATRICE: Well, tell me, am I doing something wrong? Talk to me.

EDDIE: [*Pause. He can't speak, then.*] I can't. I can't talk about it.

BEATRICE: Well tell me what—

EDDIE: I got nothin' to say about it!

[*She stands for a moment; he is looking off; she turns to go into the house.*]

EDDIE: I'll be all right, B.; just lay off me, will ya? I'm worried about her.

BEATRICE: The girl is gonna be eighteen years old, it's time already.

EDDIE: B., he's taking her for a ride!

BEATRICE: All right, thats her ride. What're you gonna stand over her till she's forty? Eddie, I want you to cut it out now, you hear me? I don't like it! Now come in the house.

EDDIE: I want to take a walk, I'll be in right away.

BEATRICE: They ain't goin' to come any quicker if you stand in the street. It ain't nice, Eddie.

EDDIE: I'll be in right away. Go ahead. [*He walks off.*]

[*She goes into the house. EDDIE glances up the street, sees LOUIS and MIKE coming, and sits on an iron railing. LOUIS and MIKE enter.*]

LOUIS: Wanna go bowlin' tonight?

EDDIE: I'm too tired. Goin' to sleep.

LOUIS: How's your two submarines?

EDDIE: They're okay.

LOUIS: I see they're gettin' work alla-time.

EDDIE: Oh yeah, they're doin' all right.

MIKE: That's what we oughta do. We oughta leave the country and come in under the water. Then we get work.

EDDIE: You ain't kiddin'.

LOUIS: Well, what the hell. Y'know?

EDDIE: Sure.

LOUIS: [*Sits on railing beside EDDIE.*] Believe me, Eddie, you got a lotta credit comin' to you.

EDDIE: Aah, they don't bother me, don't cost me nutt'n.

MIKE: That older one, boy, he's a regular bull. I seen him the other day liftin' cof-fee bags over the Matson Line. They leave him alone he woulda load the whole ship by himself.

EDDIE: Yeah, he's a strong guy, that guy. Their father was a regular giant, supposed to be.

LOUIS: Yeah, you could see. He's a regular slave.

MIKE: [*Grinning.*] That blond one, though—[EDDIE *looks at him.*] He's got a sense of humor. [LOUIS *snickers.*]

EDDIE: [*Searchingly.*] Yeah. He's funny—

MIKE: [*Starting to laugh.*] Well he ain't exackly funny, but he's always like makin' remarks like, y'know? He comes around, everybody's laughin'. [LOUIS *laughs.*]

EDDIE: [*Uncomfortably, grinning.*] Yeah, well . . . he's got a sense of humor.

MIKE: [*Laughing.*] Yeah, I mean, he's always makin' like remarks, like, y'know?

EDDIE: Yeah, I know. But he's a kid yet, y'know? He—he's just a kid, that's all.

MIKE: [*Getting hysterical with* LOUIS.] I know. You take one look at him—everybody's happy. [LOUIS *laughs.*] I worked one day with him last week over the Moore-MacCormack Line, I'm tellin' you they was all hysterical. [LOUIS *and he explode in laughter.*]

EDDIE: Why? What'd he do?

MIKE: I don't know . . . he was just humorous. You never can remember what he says, y'know? But it's the way he says it. I mean he gives you a look sometimes and you start laughin'!

EDDIE: Yeah. [*Troubled.*] He's got a sense of humor.

MIKE: [*Gasping.*] Yeah.

LOUIS: [*Rising.*] Well, we see ya, Eddie.

EDDIE: Take it easy.

LOUIS: Yeah. See ya.

MIKE: If you wanna come bowlin' later we're goin' Flatbush Avenue.

[*Laughing, they move to exit, meeting* RODOLPHO *and* CATHERINE *entering on the street. Their laughter rises as they see* RODOLPHO, *who does not understand but joins in.* EDDIE *moves to enter the house as* LOUIS *and* MIKE *exit.* CATHERINE *stops him at the door.*]

CATHERINE: Hey, Eddie—what a picture we saw! Did we laugh!

EDDIE: [*He can't help smiling at sight of her.*] Where'd you go?

CATHERINE: Paramount. It was with those two guys, y'know? That—

EDDIE: Brooklyn Paramount?

CATHERINE: [*With an edge of anger, embarrassed before* RODOLPHO.] Sure, the Brooklyn Paramount. I told you we wasn't goin' to New York.

EDDIE: [*Retreating before the threat of her anger.*] All right, I only asked you. [*To* RODOLPHO.] I just don't want her hangin' around Times Square, see? It's full of tramps over there.

RODOLPHO: I would like to go to Broadway once, Eddie. I would like to walk with her once where the theaters are and the opera. Since I was a boy I see pictures of those lights.

EDDIE: [*His little patience waning.*] I want to talk to her a minute, Rodolpho. Go inside, will you?

RODOLPHO: Eddie, we only walk together in the streets. She teaches me.

CATHERINE: You know what he can't get over? That there's no fountains in Brooklyn!

EDDIE: [*Smiling unwillingly.*] Fountains? [RODOLPHO *smiles at his own naïveté.*]

CATHERINE: In Italy he says, every town's got fountains, and they meet there. And you know what? They got oranges on the trees where he comes from, and lemons. Imagine—on the trees? I mean it's interesting. But he's crazy for New York.

RODOLPHO: [*Attempting familiarity.*] Eddie, why can't we go once to Broadway—?

EDDIE: Look, I gotta tell her something—

RODOLPHO: Maybe you can come too. I want to see all those lights. [*He sees no response in* EDDIE's *face. He glances at* CATHERINE.] I'll walk by the river before I go to sleep. [*He walks off down the street.*]

CATHERINE: Why don't you talk to him, Eddie? He blesses you, and you don't talk to him hardly.

EDDIE: [*Enveloping her with his eyes.*] I bless you and you don't talk to me. [*He tries to smile.*]

CATHERINE: I don't talk to you? [*She hits his arm.*] What do you mean?

EDDIE: I don't see you no more. I come home you're runnin' around someplace—

CATHERINE: Well, he wants to see everything, that's all, so we go. . . . You mad at me?

EDDIE: No. [*He moves from her, smiling sadly.*] It's just I used to come home, you was always there. Now, I turn around, you're a big girl. I don't know how to talk to you.

CATHERINE: Why?

EDDIE: I don't know, you're runnin',

you're runnin', Katie. I don't think you listening any more to me.

CATHERINE: [Going to him.] Ah, Eddie, sure I am. What's the matter? You don't like him?

[Slight pause.]

EDDIE: [Turns to her.] You like him, Katie?

CATHERINE: [With a blush but holding her ground.] Yeah. I like him.

EDDIE: —[His smile goes.] You like him.

CATHERINE: [Looking down.] Yeah. [Now she looks at him for the consequences, smiling but tense. He looks at her like a lost boy.] What're you got against him? I don't understand. He only blesses you.

EDDIE: [Turns away.] He don't bless me, Katie.

CATHERINE: He does! You're like a father to him!

EDDIE: [Turns to her.] Katie.

CATHERINE: What, Eddie?

EDDIE: You gonna marry him?

CATHERINE: I don't know. We just been . . . goin' around, that's all. [Turns to him.] What're you got against him, Eddie? Please, tell me. What?

EDDIE: He don't respect you.

CATHERINE: Why?

EDDIE: Katie . . . if you wasn't an orphan, wouldn't he ask your father's permission before he run around with you like this?

CATHERINE: Oh, well, he didn't think you'd mind.

EDDIE: He knows I mind, but it don't bother him if I mind, don't you see that?

CATHERINE: No, Eddie, he's got all kinds of respect for me. And you too! We walk across the street he takes my arm—he almost bows to me! You got him all wrong, Eddie; I mean it, you—

EDDIE: Katie, he's only bowin' to his passport.

CATHERINE: His passport!

EDDIE: That's right. He marries you he's got the right to be an American citizen. That's what's goin' on here. [She is puzzled and surprised.] You understand what I'm tellin' you? The guy is lookin' for his break, that's all he's lookin' for.

CATHERINE: [Pained.] Oh, no, Eddie, I don't think so.

EDDIE: You don't think so! Katie, you're gonna make me cry here. Is that a workin' man? What does he do with his first money? A snappy new jacket he buys, records, a

pointy pair new shoes and his brother's kids are starvin' over there with tuberculosis? That's a hit-and-run guy, baby; he's got bright lights in his head, Broadway. Them guys don't think of nobody but theirself! You marry him and the next time you see him it'll be for divorce!

CATHERINE: [Steps toward him.] Eddie, he never said a word about his papers or—

EDDIE: You mean he's supposed to tell you that?

CATHERINE: I don't think he's even thinking about it.

EDDIE: What's better for him to think about! He could be picked up any day here and he's back pushin' taxis up the hill!

CATHERINE: No, I don't believe it.

EDDIE: Katie, don't break my heart, listen to me.

CATHERINE: I don't want to hear it.

EDDIE: Katie, listen . . .

CATHERINE: He loves me!

EDDIE: [With deep alarm.] Don't say that, for God's sake! This is the oldest racket in the country—

CATHERINE: [Desperately, as though he had made his imprint.] I don't believe it! [She rushes to the house.]

EDDIE: [Following her.] They been pullin' this since the Immigration Law was put in! They grab a green kid that don't know nothin' and they—

CATHERINE: [Sobbing.] I don't believe it and I wish to hell you'd stop it!

EDDIE: Katie!

[They enter the apartment. The lights in the living room have risen and BEATRICE is there. She looks past the sobbing CATHERINE at EDDIE, who in the presence of his wife, makes an awkward gesture of eroded command, indicating CATHERINE.]

EDDIE: Why don't you straighten her out?

BEATRICE: [Inwardly angered at his flowing emotion, which in itself alarms her.] When are you going to leave her alone?

EDDIE: B., the guy is no good!

BEATRICE: [Suddenly, with open fright and fury.] You going to leave her alone? Or you gonna drive me crazy? [He turns, striving to retain his dignity, but nevertheless in guilt walks out of the house, into the street and away. CATHERINE starts into a bedroom.] Listen, Catherine. [CATHERINE halts, turns to her sheepishly.] What are you going to do with yourself?

CATHERINE: I don't know.

BEATRICE: Don't tell me you don't know; you're not a baby any more, what are you going to do with yourself?

CATHERINE: He won't listen to me.

BEATRICE: I don't understand this. He's not your father, Catherine. I don't understand what's going on here.

CATHERINE: [*As one who herself is trying to rationalize a buried impulse.*] What am I going to do, just kick him in the face with it?

BEATRICE: Look, honey, you wanna get married, or don't you wanna get married? What are you worried about, Katie?

CATHERINE: [*Quietly, trembling.*] I don't know B. It just seems wrong if he's against it so much.

BEATRICE: [*Never losing her aroused alarm.*] Sit down, honey, I want to tell you something. Here, sit down. Was there ever any fella he liked for you? There wasn't, was there?

CATHERINE: But he says Rodolpho's just after his papers.

BEATRICE: Look, he'll say anything. What does he care what he says? If it was a prince came here for you it would be no different. You know that, don't you?

CATHERINE: Yeah, I guess.

BEATRICE: So what does that mean?

CATHERINE: [*Slowly turns her head to* BEATRICE.] What?

BEATRICE: It means you gotta be your own self more. You still think you're a little girl, honey. But nobody else can make up your mind for you any more, you understand? You gotta give him to understand that he can't give you orders no more.

CATHERINE: Yeah, but how am I going to do that? He thinks I'm a baby.

BEATRICE: Because *you* think you're a baby. I told you fifty times already, you can't act the way you act. You still walk around in front of him in your slip—

CATHERINE: Well I forgot.

BEATRICE: Well you can't do it. Or like you sit on the edge of the bathtub talkin' to him when he's shavin' in his underwear.

CATHERINE: When'd I do that?

BEATRICE: I seen you in there this morning.

CATHERINE: Oh . . . well, I wanted to tell him something and I—

BEATRICE: I know, honey. But if you act like a baby and he be treatin' you like a

baby. Like when he comes home sometimes you throw yourself at him like when you was twelve years old.

CATHERINE: Well I like to see him and I'm happy so I—

BEATRICE: Look, I'm not tellin' you what to do honey, but—

CATHERINE: No, you could tell me, B.! Gee, I'm all mixed up. See, I—He looks so sad now and it hurts me.

BEATRICE: Well look Katie, if it's goin' to hurt you so much you're gonna end up an old maid here.

CATHERINE: No!

BEATRICE: I'm tellin' you, I'm not makin' a joke. I tried to tell you a couple of times in the last year or so. That's why I was so happy you were going to go out and get work, you wouldn't be here so much, you'd be a little more independent. I mean it. It's wonderful for a whole family to love each other, but you're a grown woman and you're in the same house with a grown man. So you'll act different now, heh?

CATHERINE: Yeah, I will. I'll remember.

BEATRICE: Because it ain't only up to him, Katie, you understand? I told him the same thing already.

CATHERINE: [*Quickly.*] What?

BEATRICE: That he should let you go. But, you see, if only I tell him, he thinks I'm just bawlin' him out, or maybe I'm jealous or somethin', you know?

CATHERINE: [*Astonished.*] He said you was jealous?

BEATRICE: No, I'm just sayin' maybe that's what he thinks. [*She reaches over to* CATHERINE's *hand; with a strained smile.*] You think I'm jealous of you, honey?

CATHERINE: No! It's the first I thought of it.

BEATRICE: [*With a quiet sad laugh.*] Well you should have thought of it before . . . but I'm not. We'll be all right. Just give him to understand; you don't have to fight, you're just— You're a woman, that's all, and you got a nice boy, and now the time came when you said good-by. All right?

CATHERINE: [*Strangely moved at the prospect.*] All right. . . . If I can.

BEATRICE: Honey . . . you gotta. [CATHERINE, *sensing now an imperious demand, turns with some fear, with a discovery, to* BEATRICE. *She is at the edge of tears, as though a familiar world had shattered.*]

CATHERINE: Okay.

[*Lights out on them and up on* AL-
FIERI, *seated behind his desk.*]

ALFIERI: It was at this time that he first
came to me. I had represented his father in
an accident case some years before, and I
was acquainted with the family in a casual
way. I remember him now as he walked
through my doorway—

[*Enter* EDDIE *down right ramp.*]

His eyes were like tunnels; my first thought
was that he had committed a crime, [EDDIE
*sits beside the desk, cap in hand, looking
out.*] but soon I saw it was only a passion
that had moved into his body, like a
stranger. [ALFIERI *pauses, looks down at his
desk, then to* EDDIE *as though he were continuing a conversation with him.*] I don't
quite understand what I can do for you. Is
there a question of law somewhere?

EDDIE: That's what I want to ask you.

ALFIERI: Because there's nothing illegal
about a girl falling in love with an immigrant.

EDDIE: Yeah, but what about it if the
only reason for it is to get his papers?

ALFIERI: First of all you don't know that.

EDDIE: I see it in his eyes; he's laughin'
at her and he's laughin' at me.

ALFIERI: Eddie, I'm a lawyer. I can only
deal in what's provable. You understand
that, don't you? Can you prove that?

EDDIE: *I know what's in his mind, Mr.
Alfieri!*

ALFIERI: Eddie, even if you could prove
that—

EDDIE: Listen . . . will you listen to me
a minute? My father always said you was a
smart man. I want you to listen to me.

ALFIERI: I'm only a lawyer, Eddie.

EDDIE: Will you listen a minute? I'm
talkin' about the law. Lemme just bring out
what I mean. A man, which he comes into
the country illegal, don't it stand to reason
he's gonna take every penny and put it in
the sock? Because they don't know from one
day to another, right?

ALFIERI: All right.

EDDIE: He's spendin'. Records he buys
now. Shoes. Jackets. Y'understand me? This
guy ain't worried. This guy is *here.* So it
must be that he's got it all laid out in his
mind already—he's stayin'. Right?

ALFIERI: Well? What about it?

EDDIE: All right. [*He glances at* ALFIERI,
then down to the floor.] I'm talking to you
confidential, ain't I?

ALFIERI: Certainly.

EDDIE: I mean it don't go no place but
here. Because I don't like to say this about
anybody. Even my wife I didn't exactly
say this.

ALFIERI: What is it?

EDDIE: [*Takes a breath and glances
briefly over each shoulder.*] The guy ain't
right, Mr. Alfieri.

ALFIERI: What do you mean?

EDDIE: I mean he ain't right.

ALFIERI: I don't get you.

EDDIE: [*Shifts to another position in the
chair.*] Dja ever get a look at him?

ALFIERI: Not that I know of, no.

EDDIE: He's a blond guy. Like . . .
platinum. You know what I mean?

ALFIERI: No.

EDDIE: I mean if you close the paper fast
—you could blow him over.

ALFIERI: Well that doesn't mean—

EDDIE: Wait a minute, I'm tellin' you
sump'm. He sings, see. Which is—I mean
it's all right, but sometimes he hits a note,
see. I turn around. I mean—high. You
know what I mean?

ALFIERI: Well, that's a tenor.

EDDIE: I know a tenor, Mr. Alfieri. This
ain't no tenor. I mean if you came in the
house and you didn't know who was singin',
you wouldn't be lookin' for him you be
lookin' for her.

ALFIERI: Yes, but that's not—

EDDIE: I'm tellin' you sump'm, wait a
minute. Please, Mr. Alfieri. I'm tryin' to
bring out my thoughts here. Couple of
nights ago my niece brings out a dress which
it's too small for her, because she shot up
like a light this last year. He takes the
dress, lays it on the table, he cuts it up;
one-two-three, he makes a new dress. I
mean he looked so sweet there, like an
angel—you could kiss him he was so sweet.

ALFIERI: Now look, Eddie—

EDDIE: Mr. Alfieri, they're laughin' at
him on the piers. I'm ashamed. Paper Doll
they call him. Blondie now. His brother
thinks it's because he's got a sense of humor,
see—which he's got—but that ain't what
they're laughin'. Which they're not goin' to
come out with it because they know he's
my relative, which they have to see me if
they make a crack, y'know? But I know
what they're laughin' at, and when I think
of that guy layin' his hands on her I could
—I mean it's eatin' me out, Mr. Alfieri, because I struggled for that girl. And now he
comes in my house and—

ALFIERI: Eddie, look—I have my own children. I understand you. But the law is very specific. The law does not . . .

EDDIE: [*With a fuller flow of indignation.*] You mean to tell me that there's no law that a guy which he ain't right can go to work and marry a girl and—?

ALFIERI: You have no recourse in the law, Eddie.

EDDIE: Yeah, but if he ain't right, Mr. Alfieri, you mean to tell me—

ALFIERI: There is nothing you can do, Eddie, believe me.

EDDIE: Nothin'.

ALFIERI: Nothing at all. There's only one legal question here.

EDDIE: What?

ALFIERI: The manner in which they entered the country. But I don't think you want to do anything about that, do you?

EDDIE: You mean—?

ALFIERI: Well, they entered illegally.

EDDIE: Oh, Jesus, no, I wouldn't do nothin' about that, I mean—

ALFIERI: All right, then, let me talk now, eh?

EDDIE: Mr. Alfieri, I can't believe what you tell me. I mean there must be some kinda law which—

ALFIERI: Eddie, I want you to listen to me. [*Pause.*] You know, sometimes God mixes up the people. We all love somebody, the wife, the kids—every man's got somebody that he loves, heh? But sometimes . . . there's too much. You know? There's too much, and it goes where it mustn't. A man works hard, he brings up a child, sometimes it's a niece, sometimes even a daughter, and he never realizes it, but through the years—there is too much love for the daughter, there is too much love for the niece. Do you understand what I'm saying to you?

EDDIE: [*Sardonically.*] What do you mean, I shouldn't look out for her good?

ALFIERI: Yes, but these things have to end, Eddie, that's all. The child has to grow up and go away, and the man has to learn to forget. Because after all, Eddie—what other way can it end? [*Pause.*] Let her go. That's my advice. You did your job, now it's her life; wish her luck, and let her go. [*Pause.*] Will you do that? Because there's no law, Eddie; make up your mind to it; the law is not interested in this.

EDDIE: You mean to tell me, even if he's a punk? If he's—

ALFIERI: There's nothing you can do.

[EDDIE *stands.*]

EDDIE: Well, all right, thanks. Thanks very much.

ALFIERI: What are you going to do?

EDDIE: [*With a helpless but ironic gesture.*] What can I do? I'm a patsy, what can a patsy do? I worked like a dog twenty years so a punk could have her, so that's what I done. I mean, in the worst times, in the worst, when there wasn't a ship comin' in the harbor, I didn't stand around lookin' for relief—I hustled. When there was empty piers in Brooklyn I went to Hoboken, Staten Island, the West Side, Jersey, all over—because I made a promise. I took out of my own mouth to give to her. I took out of my wife's mouth. I walked hungry plenty days in this city! [*It begins to break through.*] And now I gotta sit in my own house and look at a son-of-a-bitch punk like that—which he came out of nowhere! I give him my house to sleep! I take the blankets off my bed for him, and he takes and puts his dirty filthy hands on her like a goddam thief!

ALFIERI: [*Rising.*] But, Eddie, she's a woman now.

EDDIE: He's stealing from me!

ALFIERI: She wants to get married, Eddie. She can't marry you, can she?

EDDIE: [*Furiously.*] What're you talkin' about, marry me! I don't know what the hell you're talkin' about!

[*Pause.*]

ALFIERI: I gave you my advice, Eddie. That's it. [EDDIE *gathers himself. A pause.*]

EDDIE: Well, thanks. Thanks very much. It just—it's breakin' my heart, y'know. I—

ALFIERI: I understand. Put it out of your mind. Can you do that?

EDDIE: I'm—[*He feels the threat of sobs, and with a helpless wave.*] I'll see you around. [*He goes out up the right ramp.*]

ALFIERI: [*Sits on desk.*] There are times when you want to spread an alarm, but nothing has happened. I knew, I knew then and there—I could have finished the whole story that afternoon. It wasn't as though there was a mystery to unravel. I could see every step coming, step after step, like a dark figure walking down a hall toward a certain door. I knew where he was heading for, I knew where he was going to end. And I sat here many afternoons asking myself why, being an intelligent man, I was so powerless to stop it. I even went to a cer-

tain old lady in the neighborhood, a very
wise old woman, and I told her, and she
only nodded, and said, "Pray for him . . ."
And so I—waited here.

[*As lights go out on* ALFIERI, *they rise
in the apartment where all are finishing dinner.* BEATRICE *and* CATHERINE
are clearing the table.]

CATHERINE: You know where they went?

BEATRICE: Where?

CATHERINE: They went to Africa once.
On a fishing boat. [EDDIE *glances at her.*]
It's true, Eddie.

[BEATRICE *exits into the kitchen with
dishes.*]

EDDIE: I didn't say nothin'. [*He goes to
his rocker, picks up a newspaper.*]

CATHERINE: And I was never even in
Staten Island.

EDDIE: [*Sitting with the paper.*] You
didn't miss nothin'. [*Pause.* CATHERINE
takes dishes out.] How long that take you,
Marco—to get to Africa?

MARCO: [*Rising.*] Oh . . . two days. We
go all over.

RODOLPHO: [*Rising.*] Once we went to
Yugoslavia.

EDDIE: [*To* MARCO.] They pay all right
on them boats?

[BEATRICE *enters. She and* RODOLPHO
stack the remaining dishes.]

MARCO: If they catch fish they pay all
right. [*Sits on a stool.*]

RODOLPHO: They're family boats, though.
And nobody in our family owned one. So
we only worked when one of the families
was sick.

BEATRICE: Y'know, Marco, what I don't
understand—there's an ocean full of fish
and yiz are all starvin'.

EDDIE: They gotta have boats, nets, you
need money.

[CATHERINE *enters.*]

BEATRICE: Yeah, but couldn't they like
fish from the beach? You see them down
Coney Island—

MARCO: Sardines.

EDDIE: Sure. [*Laughing.*] How you
gonna catch sardines on a hook?

BEATRICE: Oh, I didn't know they're
sardines. [*To* CATHERINE.] They're sardines!

CATHERINE: Yeah, they follow them all
over the ocean, Africa, Yugoslavia . . .
[*She sits and begins to look through a movie
magazine.* RODOLPHO *joins her.*]

BEATRICE: [*To* EDDIE.] It's funny,
y'know. You never think of it, that sardines

are swimming in the ocean! [*She exits to
kitchen with dishes.*]

CATHERINE: I know. It's like oranges and
lemons on a tree. [*To* EDDIE.] I mean you
ever think of oranges and lemons on a tree?

EDDIE: Yeah, I know. It's funny. [*To*
MARCO.] I heard that they paint the oranges
to make them look orange.

[BEATRICE *enters.*]

MARCO: [*He has been reading a letter.*]
Paint?

EDDIE: Yeah, I heard that they grow like
green.

MARCO: No, in Italy the oranges are
orange.

RODOLPHO: Lemons are green.

EDDIE: [*Resenting his instruction.*] I
know lemons are green, for Christ's sake,
you see them in the store they're green
sometimes. I said oranges they paint, I didn't
say nothin' about lemons.

BEATRICE: [*Sitting; diverting their attention.*] Your wife is gettin' the money all
right, Marco?

MARCO: Oh, yes. She bought medicine for
my boy.

BEATRICE: That's wonderful. You feel
better, heh?

MARCO: Oh, yes! But I'm lonesome.

BEATRICE: I just hope you ain't gonna do
like some of them around here. They're
here twenty-five years, some men, and they
didn't get enough together to go back twice.

MARCO: Oh, I know. We have many
families in our town, the children never saw
the father. But I will go home. Three, four
years, I think.

BEATRICE: Maybe you should keep more
here. Because maybe she thinks it comes so
easy you'll never get ahead of yourself.

MARCO: Oh, no, she saves. I send everything. My wife is very lonesome. [*He smiles
shyly.*]

BEATRICE: She must be nice. She pretty?
I bet, heh?

MARCO: [*Blushing.*] No, but she understand everything.

RODOLPHO: Oh, he's got a clever wife!

EDDIE: I betcha there's plenty surprises
sometimes when those guys get back there,
heh?

MARCO: Surprises?

EDDIE: [*Laughing.*] I mean, you know—
they count the kids and there's a couple
extra than when they left?

MARCO: No—no . . . The women wait,
Eddie. Most. Most. Very few surprises.

RODOLPHO: It's more strict in our town. [EDDIE *looks at him now.*] It's not so free.

EDDIE: [*Rises, paces up and down.*] It ain't so free here either, Rodolpho, like you think. I seen greenhorns sometimes get in trouble that way—they think just because a girl don't go around with a shawl over her head that she ain't strict, y'know? Girl don't have to wear black dress to be strict. Know what I mean?

RODOLPHO: Well, I always have respect—

EDDIE: I know, but in your town you wouldn't just drag off some girl without permission, I mean. [*He turns.*] You know what I mean, Marco? It ain't that much different here.

MARCO: [*Cautiously.*] Yes.

BEATRICE: Well, he didn't exactly drag her off though, Eddie.

EDDIE: I know, but I seen some of them get the wrong idea sometimes. [*To* RODOLPHO.] I mean it might be a little more free here but it's just as strict.

RODOLPHO: I have respect for her, Eddie. I do anything wrong?

EDDIE: Look, kid, I ain't her father, I'm only her uncle—

BEATRICE: Well then, be an uncle then. [EDDIE *looks at her, aware of her criticizing force.*] I mean.

MARCO: No, Beatrice, if he does wrong you must tell him. [*To* EDDIE.] What does he do wrong?

EDDIE: Well, Marco, till he came here she was never out on the street twelve o'clock at night.

MARCO: [*To* RODOLPHO.] You come home early now.

BEATRICE: [*To* CATHERINE.] Well, you said the movie ended late, didn't you?

CATHERINE: Yeah.

BEATRICE: Well, tell him, honey. [*To* EDDIE.] The movie ended late.

EDDIE: Look, B., I'm just sayin'—he thinks she always stayed out like that.

MARCO: You come home early now, Rodolpho.

RODOLPHO: [*Embarrassed.*] All right, sure. But I can't stay in the house all the time, Eddie.

EDDIE: Look, kid, I'm not only talkin' about her. The more you run around like that the more chance you're takin'. [*To* BEATRICE.] I mean suppose he gets hit by a car or something. [*To* MARCO.] Where's his papers, who is he? Know what I mean?

BEATRICE: Yeah, but who is he in the daytime, though? It's the same chance in the daytime.

EDDIE: [*Holding back a voice full of anger.*] Yeah, but he don't have to go lookin' for it, Beatrice. If he's here to work, then he should work; if he's here for a good time then he could fool around! [*To* MARCO.] But I understood, Marco, that you was both comin' to make a livin' for your family. You understand me, don't you, Marco? [*He goes to his rocker.*]

MARCO: I beg your pardon, Eddie.

EDDIE: I mean, that's what I understood in the first place, see.

MARCO: Yes. That's why we came.

EDDIE: [*Sits on his rocker.*] Well, that's all I'm askin'. [EDDIE *reads his paper. There is a pause, an awkwardness. Now* CATHERINE *gets up and puts a record on the phonograph—"Paper Doll."*]

CATHERINE: [*Flushed with revolt.*] You wanna dance, Rodolpho?

[EDDIE *freezes.*]

RODOLPHO: [*In deference to Eddie.*] No, I—I'm tired.

BEATRICE: Go ahead, dance, Rodolpho.

CATHERINE: Ah, come on. They got a beautiful quartet, these guys. Come. [*She has taken his hand and he stiffly rises, feeling* EDDIE's *eyes on his back, and they dance.*]

EDDIE: [*To* CATHERINE.] What's that, a new record?

CATHERINE: It's the same one. We bought it the other day.

BEATRICE: [*To* EDDIE.] They only bought three records. [*She watches them dance;* EDDIE *turns his head away.* MARCO *just sits there, waiting. Now* BEATRICE *turns to* EDDIE.] Must be nice to go all over in one of them fishin' boats. I would like that myself. See all them other countries?

EDDIE: Yeah.

BEATRICE: [*To* MARCO.] But the women don't go along, I bet.

MARCO: No, not on the boats. Hard work.

BEATRICE: What're you got, a regular kitchen and everything?

MARCO: Yes, we eat very good on the boats—especially when Rodolpho comes along; everybody gets fat.

BEATRICE: Oh, he cooks?

MARCO: Sure, very good cook. Rice, pasta, fish, everything.

[EDDIE *lowers his paper.*]

EDDIE: He's a cook, too! [*Looking at* RODOLPHO.] He sings, he cooks . . .

[RODOLPHO *smiles thankfully.*]

BEATRICE: Well it's good, he could always make a living.

EDDIE: It's wonderful. He sings, he cooks, he could make dresses . . .

CATHERINE: They get some high pay, them guys. The head chefs in all the big hotels are men. You read about them.

EDDIE: That's what I'm sayin'.

[CATHERINE *and* RODOLPHO *continue dancing.*]

CATHERINE: Yeah, well, I mean.

EDDIE: [*To* BEATRICE.] He's lucky, believe me. [*Slight pause. He looks away, then back to* BEATRICE.] That's why the water front is no place for him. [*They stop dancing.* RODOLPHO *turns off phonograph.*] I mean like me—I can't cook, I can't sing, I can't make dresses, so I'm on the water front. But if I could cook, if I could sing, if I could make dresses, I wouldn't be on the water front. [*He has been unconsciously twisting the newspaper into a tight roll. They are all regarding him now; he senses he is exposing the issue and he is driven on.*] I would be someplace else. I would be like in a dress store. [*He has bent the rolled paper and it suddenly tears in two. He suddenly gets up and pulls his pants up over his belly and goes to* MARCO.] What do you say, Marco, we go to the bouts next Saturday night. You never seen a fight, did you?

MARCO: [*Uneasily.*] Only in the moving pictures.

EDDIE: [*Going to* RODOLPHO.] I'll treat yiz. What do you say, Danish? You wanna come along? I'll buy the tickets.

RODOLPHO: Sure. I like to go.

CATHERINE: [*Goes to* EDDIE; *nervously happy now.*] I'll make some coffee, all right?

EDDIE: Go ahead, make some! Make it nice and strong. [*Mystified, she smiles and exits to kitchen. He is weirdly elated, rubbing his fists into his palms. He strides to* MARCO.] You wait, Marco, you see some real fights here. You ever do any boxing?

MARCO: No, I never.

EDDIE: [*To* RODOLPHO.] Betcha you have done some, heh?

RODOLPHO: No.

EDDIE: Well, come on, I'll teach you.

BEATRICE: What's he got to learn that for?

EDDIE: Ya can't tell, one a these days

somebody's liable to step on his foot or sump'm. Come on, Rodolpho, I show you a couple a passes. [*He stands below table.*]

BEATRICE: Go ahead, Rodolpho. He's a good boxer, he could teach you.

RODOLPHO: [*Embarrassed.*] Well, I don't know how to—[*He moves down to* EDDIE.]

EDDIE: Just put your hands up. Like this, see? That's right. That's very good, keep your left up, because you lead with the left, see, like this. [*He gently moves his left into* RODOLPHO's *face.*] See? Now what you gotta do is you gotta block me, so when I come in like that you—[RODOLPHO *parries his left.*] Hey, that's very good! [RODOLPHO *laughs.*] All right, now come into me. Come on.

RODOLPHO: I don't want to hit you, Eddie.

EDDIE: Don't pity me, come on. Throw it, I'll show you how to block it. [RODOLPHO *jabs at him, laughing. The others join.*] 'At's it. Come on again. For the jaw right here. [RODOLPHO *jabs with more assurance.*] Very good!

BEATRICE: [*To Marco.*] He's very good!

[EDDIE *crosses directly upstage of* RODOLPHO.]

EDDIE: Sure, he's great! Come on, kid, put sump'm behind it, you can't hurt me. [RODOLPHO, *more seriously, jabs at* EDDIE's *jaw and grazes it.*] Attaboy.

[CATHERINE *comes from the kitchen, watches.*]

Now I'm gonna hit you, so block me, see?

CATHERINE: [*With beginning alarm.*] What are they doin'?

[*They are lightly boxing now.*]

BEATRICE: [*She senses only the comradeship in it now.*] He's teachin' him; he's very good!

EDDIE: Sure, he's terrific! Look at him go! [RODOLPHO *lands a blow.*] 'At's it! Now, watch out, here I come, Danish! [*He feints with his left hand and lands with his right. It mildly staggers* RODOLPHO. MARCO *rises.*]

CATHERINE: [*Rushing to* RODOLPHO.] Eddie!

EDDIE: Why? I didn't hurt him. Did I hurt you, kid? [*He rubs the back of his hand across his mouth.*]

RODOLPHO: No, no, he didn't hurt me. [*To* EDDIE *with a certain gleam and a smile.*] I was only surprised.

BEATRICE: [*Pulling* EDDIE *down into the rocker.*] That's enough, Eddie; he did pretty good, though.

EDDIE: Yeah. [*Rubbing his fists together.*] He could be very good, Marco. I'll teach him again.

[MARCO *nods at him dubiously.*]

RODOLPHO: Dance, Catherine. Come. [*He takes her hand; they go to phonograph and start it. It plays "Paper Doll."* RODOLPHO *takes her in his arms. They dance.* EDDIE *in thought sits in his chair, and* MARCO *takes a chair, places it in front of* EDDIE, *and looks down at it.* BEATRICE *and* EDDIE *watch him.*]

MARCO: Can you lift this chair?

EDDIE: What do you mean?

MARCO: From here. [*He gets on one knee with one hand behind his back, and grasps the bottom of one of the chair legs but does not raise it.*]

EDDIE: Sure, why not? [*He comes to the chair, kneels, grasps the leg, raises the chair one inch, but it leans over to the floor.*] Gee, that's hard, I never knew that. [*He tries again, and again fails.*] It's on an angle, that's why, heh?

MARCO: Here. [*He kneels, grasps, and with strain slowly raises the chair higher and higher, getting to his feet now.* RODOLPHO *and* CATHERINE *have stopped dancing as* MARCO *raises the chair over his head.* MARCO *is face to face with* EDDIE, *a strained tension gripping his eyes and jaw, his neck stiff, the chair raised like a weapon over* EDDIE's *head—and he transforms what might appear like a glare of warning into a smile of triumph, and* EDDIE's *grin vanishes as he absorbs his look.*]

CURTAIN

ACT TWO

Light rises on ALFIERI *at his desk.*

ALFIERI: On the twenty-third of that December a case of Scotch whisky slipped from a net while being unloaded—as a case of Scotch whisky is inclined to do on the twenty-third of December on Pier Forty-one. There was no snow, but it was cold, his wife was out shopping. Marco was still at work. The boy had not been hired that day; Catherine told me later that this was the first time they had been alone together in the house.

[*Light is rising on* CATHERINE *in the apartment.* RODOLPHO *is watching as she arranges a paper pattern on cloth spread on the table.*]

CATHERINE: You hungry?

RODOLPHO: Not for anything to eat. [*Pause.*] I have nearly three hundred dollars. Catherine?

CATHERINE: I heard you.

RODOLPHO: You don't like to talk about it any more?

CATHERINE: Sure, I don't mind talkin' about it.

RODOLPHO: What worries you, Catherine?

CATHERINE: I been wantin' to ask you about something. Could I?

RODOLPHO: All the answers are in my eyes, Catherine. But you don't look in my eyes lately. You're full of secrets. [*She looks at him. She seems withdrawn.*] What is the question?

CATHERINE: Suppose I wanted to live in Italy.

RODOLPHO: [*Smiling at the incongruity.*] You going to marry somebody rich?

CATHERINE: No, I mean live there—you and me.

RODOLPHO: [*His smile vanishing.*] When?

CATHERINE: Well . . . when we get married.

RODOLPHO: [*Astonished.*] You want to be an Italian?

CATHERINE: No, but I could live there without being Italian. Americans live there.

RODOLPHO: Forever?

CATHERINE: Yeah.

RODOLPHO: [*Crosses to rocker.*] You're fooling.

CATHERINE: No, I mean it.

RODOLPHO: Where do you get such an idea?

CATHERINE: Well, you're always saying it's so beautiful there, with the mountains and the ocean and all the—

RODOLPHO: You're fooling me.

CATHERINE: I mean it.

RODOLPHO: [*Goes to her slowly.*] Catherine, if I ever brought you home with no money, no business, nothing, they would call the priest and the doctor and they would say Rodolpho is crazy.

CATHERINE: I know, but I think we would be happier there.

RODOLPHO: Happier! What would you eat? You can't cook the view!

CATHERINE: Maybe you could be a singer, like in Rome or—

RODOLPHO: Rome! Rome is full of singers.

CATHERINE: Well, I could work then.

RODOLPHO: Where?

CATHERINE: God, there must be jobs somewhere!

RODOLPHO: There's nothing! Nothing, nothing, nothing. Now tell me what you're talking about. How can I bring you from a rich country to suffer in a poor country? What are you talking about? [*She searches for words.*] I would be a criminal stealing your face. In two years you would have an old, hungry face. When my brother's babies cry they give them water, water that boiled a bone. Don't you believe that?

CATHERINE: [*Quietly.*] I'm afraid of Eddie here.

[*Slight pause.*]

RODOLPHO: [*Steps closer to her.*] We wouldn't live here. Once I am a citizen I could work anywhere and I would find better jobs and we would have a house, Catherine. If I were not afraid to be arrested I would start to be something wonderful here!

CATHERINE: [*Steeling herself.*] Tell me something. I mean just tell me, Rodolpho —would you still want to do it if it turned out we had to go live in Italy? I mean just if it turned out that way.

RODOLPHO: This is your question or his question?

CATHERINE: I would like to know, Rodolpho. I mean it.

RODOLPHO: To go there with nothing.

CATHERINE: Yeah.

RODOLPHO: No. [*She looks at him wide-eyed.*] No.

CATHERINE: You wouldn't?

RODOLPHO: No; I will not marry you to live in Italy. I want you to be my wife, and I want to be a citizen. Tell him that, or I will. Yes. [*He moves about angrily.*] And tell him also, and tell yourself, please, that I am not a beggar, and you are not a horse, a gift, a favor for a poor immigrant.

CATHERINE: Well, don't get mad!

RODOLPHO: I am furious! [*Goes to her.*]

Do you think I am so desperate? My brother is desperate, not me. You think I would carry on my back the rest of my life a woman I didn't love just to be an American? It's so wonderful? You think we have no tall buildings in Italy? Electric lights? No wide streets? No flags? No automobiles? Only work we don't have. I want to be an American so I can work, that is the only wonder here—work! How can you insult me, Catherine?

CATHERINE: I didn't mean that—

RODOLPHO: My heart dies to look at you. Why are you so afraid of him?

CATHERINE: [*Near tears.*] I don't know!

RODOLPHO: Do you trust me, Catherine? You?

CATHERINE: It's only that I— He was good to me, Rodolpho. You don't know him; he was always the sweetest guy to me. Good. He razzes me all the time but he don't mean it. I know. I would—just feel ashamed if I made him sad. 'Cause I always dreamt that when I got married he would be happy at the wedding, and laughin'—and now he's—mad all the time and nasty—[*She is weeping.*] Tell him you'd live in Italy—just tell him, and maybe he would start to trust you a little, see? Because I want him to be happy; I mean—I like him, Rodolpho—and I can't stand it!

RODOLPHO: Oh, Catherine—oh, little girl.

CATHERINE: I love you, Rodolpho, I love you.

RODOLPHO: Then why are you afraid? That he'll spank you?

CATHERINE: Don't, don't laugh at me! I've been here all my life. . . . Every day I saw him when he left in the morning and when he came home at night. You think it's so easy to turn around and say to a man he's nothin' to you no more?

RODOLPHO: I know, but—

CATHERINE: You don't know; nobody knows! I'm not a baby, I know a lot more than people think I know. Beatrice says to be a woman, but—

RODOLPHO: Yes.

CATHERINE: Then why don't she be a woman? If I was a wife I would make a man happy instead of goin' at him all the time. I can tell a block away when he's blue in his mind and just wants to talk to somebody quiet and nice. . . . I can tell when he's hungry or wants a beer before he even says anything. I know when his feet hurt him, I mean I *know* him and now I'm supposed to turn around and make a stranger out of him? I don't know why I have to do that, I mean.

RODOLPHO: Catherine. If I take in my hands a little bird. And she grows and wishes to fly. But I will not let her out of my hands because I love her so much, is that right for me to do? I don't say you must hate him; but anyway you must go, mustn't you? Catherine?

CATHERINE: [Softly.] Hold me.

RODOLPHO: [Clasping her to him.] Oh, my little girl.

CATHERINE: Teach me. [She is weeping.] I don't know anything, teach me, Rodolpho, hold me.

RODOLPHO: There's nobody here now. Come inside. Come. [He is leading her toward the bedrooms.] And don't cry any more.

[Light rises on the street. In a moment EDDIE appears. He is unsteady, drunk. He mounts the stairs. He enters the apartment, looks around, takes out a bottle from one pocket, puts it on the table. Then another bottle from another pocket, and a third from an inside pocket. He sees the pattern and cloth, goes over to it and touches it, and turns toward upstage.]

EDDIE: Beatrice? [He goes to the open kitchen door and looks in.] Beatrice? Beatrice?

[CATHERINE enters from bedroom; under his gaze she adjusts her dress.]

CATHERINE: You got home early.

EDDIE: Knocked off for Christmas early. [Indicating the pattern.] Rodolpho makin' you a dress?

CATHERINE: No. I'm makin' a blouse.

[RODOLPHO appears in the bedroom doorway. EDDIE sees him and his arm jerks slightly in shock. RODOLPHO nods to him testingly.]

RODOLPHO: Beatrice went to buy presents for her mother.

[Pause.]

EDDIE: Pack it up. Go ahead. Get your stuff and get outa here. [CATHERINE instantly turns and walks toward the bedroom, and EDDIE grabs her arm.] Where you goin'?

CATHERINE: [Trembling with fright.] I think I have to get out of here, Eddie.

EDDIE: No, you ain't goin' nowheres, he's the one.

CATHERINE: I think I can't stay here no more. [She frees her arm, steps back toward the bedroom.] I'm sorry, Eddie. [She sees the tears in his eyes.] Well, don't cry. I'll be around the neighborhood; I'll see you. I just can't stay here no more. You know I can't. [Her sobs of pity and love for him break her composure.] Don't you know I can't? You know that, don't you? [She goes to him.] Wish me luck. [She clasps her hands prayerfully.] Oh, Eddie, don't be like that!

EDDIE: You ain't goin' nowheres.

CATHERINE: Eddie, I'm not gonna be a baby any more! You—

[He reaches out suddenly, draws her to him, and as she strives to free herself he kisses her on the mouth.]

RODOLPHO: Don't! [He pulls on EDDIE's arm.] Stop that! Have respect for her!

EDDIE: [Spun round by RODOLPHO.] You want something?

RODOLPHO: Yes! She'll be my wife. That is what I want. My wife!

EDDIE: But what're you gonna be?

RODOLPHO: I show you what I be!

CATHERINE: Wait outside; don't argue with him!

EDDIE: Come on, show me! What're you gonna be? Show me!

RODOLPHO: [With tears of rage.] Don't say that to me! [RODOLPHO flies at him in attack. EDDIE pins his arms, laughing, and suddenly kisses him.]

CATHERINE: Eddie! Let go, ya hear me! I'll kill you! Leggo of him! [She tears at EDDIE's face and EDDIE releases RODOLPHO. EDDIE stands there with tears rolling down his face as he laughs mockingly at RODOLPHO. She is staring at him in horror. RODOLPHO is rigid. They are like animals that have torn at one another and broken up without a decision, each waiting for the other's mood.]

EDDIE: [To CATHERINE.] You see? [To RODOLPHO.] I give you till tomorrow, kid. Get outa here. Alone. You hear me? Alone.

CATHERINE: I'm going with him, Eddie. [She starts toward RODOLPHO.]

EDDIE: [Indicating RODOLPHO with his head.] Not with that. [She halts, frightened. He sits, still panting for breath, and they watch him helplessly as he leans toward them over the table.] Don't make me do nuttin', Catherine. Watch your step, submarine. By rights they oughta throw you back in the water. But I got pity for you. [He moves unsteadily toward the door, al-

ways facing RODOLPHO.] Just get outa here and don't lay another hand on her unless you wanna go out feet first. [*He goes out of the apartment.*]

    [*The lights go down, as they rise on* ALFIERI.]

    ALFIERI: On December twenty-seventh I saw him next. I normally go home well before six, but that day I sat around looking out my window at the bay, and when I saw him walking through my doorway, I knew why I had waited. And if I seem to tell this like a dream, it was that way. Several moments arrived in the course of the two talks we had when it occurred to me how—almost transfixed I had come to feel. I had lost my strength somewhere. [EDDIE *enters, removing his cap, sits in the chair, looks thoughtfully out.*] I looked in his eyes more than I listened—in fact, I can hardly remember the conversation. But I will never forget how dark the room became when he looked at me; his eyes were like tunnels. I kept wanting to call the police, but nothing had happened. Nothing at all had really happened. [*He breaks off and looks down at the desk. Then he turns to* EDDIE.] So in other words, he won't leave?

    EDDIE: My wife is talkin' about renting a room upstairs for them. An old lady on the top floor is got an empty room.

    ALFIERI: What does Marco say?

    EDDIE: He just sits there. Marco don't say much.

    ALFIERI: I guess they didn't tell him, heh? What happened?

    EDDIE: I don't know; Marco don't say much.

    ALFIERI: What does your wife say?

    EDDIE: [*Unwilling to pursue this.*] Nobody's talkin' much in the house. So what about that?

    ALFIERI: But you didn't prove anything about him. It sounds like he just wasn't strong enough to break your grip.

    EDDIE: I'm tellin' you I know—he ain't right. Somebody that don't want it can break it. Even a mouse, if you catch a teeny mouse and you hold it in your hand, that mouse can give you the right kind of fight. He didn't give me the right kind of fight, I know it, Mr. Alfieri, the guy ain't right.

    ALFIERI: What did you do that for, Eddie?

    EDDIE: To show her what he is! So she would see, once and for all! Her mother'll turn over in the grave! [*He gathers himself*

almost peremptorily.] So what do I gotta do now? Tell me what to do.

    ALFIERI: She actually said she's marrying him?

    EDDIE: She told me, yeah. So what do I do?

    [*Slight pause.*]

    ALFIERI: This is my last word, Eddie, take it or not, that's your business. Morally and legally you have no rights, you cannot stop it; she is a free agent.

    EDDIE: [*Angering.*] Didn't you hear what I told you?

    ALFIERI: [*With a tougher tone.*] I heard what you told me, and I'm telling you what the answer is. I'm not only telling you now, I'm warning you—the law is nature. The law is only a word for what has a right to happen. When the law is wrong it's because it's unnatural, but in this case it is natural and a river will drown you if you buck it now. Let her go. And bless her. [*A phone booth begins to glow on the opposite side of the stage; a faint, lonely blue.* EDDIE *stands up, jaws clenched.*] Somebody had to come for her, Eddie, sooner or later. [EDDIE *starts turning to go and* ALFIERI *rises with new anxiety.*] You won't have a friend in the world, Eddie! Even those who understand will turn against you, even the ones who feel the same will despise you! [EDDIE *moves off.*] Put it out of your mind! Eddie! [*He follows into the darkness, calling desperately.*]

    [EDDIE *is gone. The phone is glowing in light now. Light is out on* ALFIERI. EDDIE *has at the same time appeared beside the phone.*]

    EDDIE: Give me the number of the Immigration Bureau. Thanks. [*He dials.*] I want to report something. Illegal immigrants. Two of them. That's right. Four-forty-one Saxon Street, Brooklyn, yeah. Ground floor. Heh? [*With greater difficulty.*] I'm just around the neighborhood, that's all. Heh? [*Evidently he is being questioned further, and he slowly hangs up. He leaves the phone just as* LOUIS *and* MIKE *come down the street.*]

    LOUIS: Go bowlin', Eddie?

    EDDIE: No, I'm due home.

    LOUIS: Well, take it easy.

    EDDIE: I'll see yiz.

    [*They leave him, exiting right, and he watches them go. He glances about, then goes up into the house. The*

lights go on in the apartment. BEA-
TRICE *is taking down Christmas decorations and packing them in a box.*]

EDDIE: Where is everybody? [BEATRICE
does not answer.] I says where is everybody?

BEATRICE: [*Looking up at him, wearied
with it, and concealing a fear of him.*]
I decided to move them upstairs with
Mrs. Dondero.

EDDIE: Oh, they're all moved up there
already?

BEATRICE: Yeah.

EDDIE: Where's Catherine? She up there?

BEATRICE: Only to bring pillow cases.

EDDIE: She ain't movin' in with them.

BEATRICE: Look, I'm sick and tired of
it. I'm sick and tired of it!

EDDIE: All right, all right, take it easy.

BEATRICE: I don't wanna hear no more
about it, you understand? Nothin'!

EDDIE: What're you blowin' off about?
Who brought them in here?

BEATRICE: All right, I'm sorry; I wish
I'd drop dead before I told them to come.
In the ground I wish I was.

EDDIE: Don't drop dead, just keep in
mind who brought them in here, that's
all. [*He moves about restlessly.*] I mean I
got a couple of rights here. [*He moves,
wanting to beat down her evident disapproval of him.*] This is my house here not
their house.

BEATRICE: What do you want from me?
They're moved out; what do you want
now?

EDDIE: I want my respect!

BEATRICE: So I moved them out, what
more do you want? You got your house
now, you got your respect.

EDDIE: [*He moves about biting his lip.*]
I don't like the way you talk to me, Beatrice.

BEATRICE: I'm just tellin' you I done
what you want!

EDDIE: I don't like it! The way you talk
to me and the way you look at me. This
is my house. And she is my niece and I'm
responsible for her.

BEATRICE: So that's why you done that
to him?

EDDIE: I done what to him?

BEATRICE: What you done to him in
front of her; you know what I'm talkin'
about. She goes around shakin' all the
time, she can't go to sleep! That's what
you call responsible for her?

EDDIE: [*Quietly.*] The guy ain't right,

Beatrice. [*She is silent.*] Did you hear
what I said?

BEATRICE: Look, I'm finished with it.
That's all. [*She resumes her work.*]

EDDIE: [*Helping her to pack the tinsel.*]
I'm gonna have it out with you one of
these days, Beatrice.

BEATRICE: Nothin' to have out with
me, it's all settled. Now we gonna be like
it never happened, that's all.

EDDIE: I want my respect, Beatrice, and
you know what I'm talkin' about.

BEATRICE: What?

[*Pause.*]

EDDIE: [*Finally his resolution hardens.*]
What I feel like doin' in the bed and what
I don't feel like doin'. I don't want no—

BEATRICE: When'd I say anything about
that?

EDDIE: You said, you said, I ain't deaf.
I don't want no more conversations about
that, Beatrice. I do what I feel like doin'
or what I don't feel like doin'.

BEATRICE: Okay.

[*Pause.*]

EDDIE: You used to be different,
Beatrice. You had a whole different way.

BEATRICE: *I'm* no different.

EDDIE: You didn't used to jump me all
the time about everything. The last year
or two I come in the house I don't know
what's gonna hit me. It's a shootin' gallery in here and I'm the pigeon.

BEATRICE: Okay, okay.

EDDIE: Don't tell me okay, okay, I'm
tellin' you the truth. A wife is supposed to
believe the husband. If I tell you that guy
ain't right don't tell me he is right.

BEATRICE: But how do you know?

EDDIE: Because I know. I don't go
around makin' accusations. He give me the
heeby-jeebies the first minute I seen him.
And I don't like you sayin' I don't want
her marryin' anybody. I broke my back
payin' her stenography lessons so she could
go out and meet a better class of people.
Would I do that if I didn't want her to get
married? Sometimes you talk like I was a
crazy man or sump'm.

BEATRICE: But she likes him.

EDDIE: Beatrice, she's a baby, how is she
gonna know what she likes?

BEATRICE: Well, you kept her a baby,
you wouldn't let her go out. I told you a
hundred times.

[*Pause.*]

EDDIE: All right. Let her go out, then.

BEATRICE: She don't wanna go out now. It's too late, Eddie.

[*Pause.*]

EDDIE: Suppose I told her to go out. Suppose I—

BEATRICE: They're going to get married next week, Eddie.

EDDIE: [*His head jerks around to her.*] She said that?

BEATRICE: Eddie, if you want my advice, go to her and tell her good luck. I think maybe now that you had it out you learned better.

EDDIE: What's the hurry next week?

BEATRICE: Well, she's been worried about him bein' picked up; this way he could start to be a citizen. She loves him, Eddie. [*He gets up, moves about uneasily, restlessly.*] Why don't you give her a good word? Because I still think she would like you to be a friend, y'know? [*He is standing, looking at the floor.*] I mean like if you told her you'd go to the wedding.

EDDIE: She asked you that?

BEATRICE: I know she would like it. I'd like to make a party here for her. I mean there oughta be some kinda send-off. Heh? I mean she'll have trouble enough in her life, let's start it off happy. What do you say? Cause in her heart she still loves you, Eddie. I know it. [*He presses his fingers against his eyes.*] What're you, cryin'? [*She goes to him, holds his face.*] Go . . . whyn't you go tell her you're sorry? [CATHERINE *is seen on the upper landing of the stairway, and they hear her descending.*] There . . . she's comin' down. Come on, shake hands with her.

EDDIE: [*Moving with suppressed suddenness.*] No, I can't, I can't talk to her.

BEATRICE: Eddie, give her a break; a wedding should be happy!

EDDIE: I'm goin', I'm goin' for a walk. [*He goes upstage for his jacket.* CATHERINE *enters and starts for the bedroom door.*]

BEATRICE: Katie? . . . Eddie, don't go, wait a minute. [*She embraces* EDDIE's *arm with warmth.*] Ask him, Katie. Come on, honey.

EDDIE: It's all right, I'm— [*He starts to go and she holds him.*]

BEATRICE: No, she wants to ask you. Come on, Katie, ask him. We'll have a party! What're we gonna do, hate each other? Come on!

CATHERINE: I'm gonna get married, Eddie. So if you wanna come, the wedding be on Saturday.

[*Pause.*]

EDDIE: Okay. I only wanted the best for you, Katie. I hope you know that.

CATHERINE: Okay. [*She starts out again.*]

EDDIE: Catherine? [*She turns to him.*] I was just tellin' Beatrice . . . if you wanna go out, like . . . I mean I realize maybe I kept you home too much. Because he's the first guy you ever knew, y'know? I mean now that you got a job, you might meet some fellas, and you get a different idea, y'know? I mean you could always come back to him, you're still only kids, the both of yiz. What's the hurry? Maybe you'll get around a little bit, you grow up a little more, maybe you'll see different in a couple of months. I mean you be surprised, it don't have to be him.

CATHERINE: No, we made it up already.

EDDIE: [*With increasing anxiety.*] Katie, wait a minute.

CATHERINE: No, I made up my mind.

EDDIE: But you never knew no other fella, Katie! How could you make up your mind?

CATHERINE: Cause I did. I don't want nobody else.

EDDIE: But, Katie, suppose he gets picked up.

CATHERINE: That's why we gonna do it right away. Soon as we finish the wedding he's goin' right over and start to be a citizen. I made up my mind, Eddie. I'm sorry. [*To* BEATRICE.] Could I take two more pillow cases for the other guys?

BEATRICE: Sure, go ahead. Only don't let her forget where they came from.

[CATHERINE *goes into a bedroom.*]

EDDIE: She's got other boarders up there?

BEATRICE: Yeah, there's two guys that just came over.

EDDIE: What do you mean, came over?

BEATRICE: From Italy. Lipari the butcher—his nephew. They come from Bari, they just got here yesterday. I didn't even know till Marco and Rodolpho moved up there before. [CATHERINE *enters, going toward exit with two pillow cases.*] It'll be nice, they could all talk together.

EDDIE: Catherine! [*She halts near the exit door. He takes in* BEATRICE *too.*] What're you, got no brains? You put them up there with two other submarines?

CATHERINE: Why?

EDDIE: [*In a driving fright and anger.*] Why! How do you know they're not trackin' these guys? They'll come up for them and find Marco and Rodolpho! Get them out of the house!

BEATRICE: But they been here so long already—

EDDIE: How do you know what enemies Lipari's got? Which they'd love to stab him in the back?

CATHERINE: Well what'll I do with them?

EDDIE: The neighborhood is full of rooms. Can't you stand to live a couple of blocks away from him? Get them out of the house!

CATHERINE: Well maybe tomorrow night I'll—

EDDIE: Not tomorrow, do it now. Catherine, you never mix yourself with somebody else's family! These guys get picked up, Lipari's liable to blame you or me and we got his whole family on our head. They got a temper, that family.

[*Two men in overcoats appear outside, start into the house.*]

CATHERINE: How'm I gonna find a place tonight?

EDDIE: Will you stop arguin' with me and get them out! You think I'm always tryin' to fool you or sump'm? What's the matter with you, don't you believe I could think of your good? Did I ever ask sump'm for myself? You think I got no feelin's? I never told you nothin' in my life that wasn't for your good. Nothin'! And look at the way you talk to me! Like I was an enemy! Like I—[*A knock on the door. His head swerves. They all stand motionless. Another knock.* EDDIE, *in a whisper, pointing upstage.*] Go up the fire escape, get them out over the back fence.

[CATHERINE *stands motionless, uncomprehending.*]

FIRST OFFICER: [*In the hall.*] Immigration! Open up in there!

EDDIE: Go, go. Hurry up! [*She stands a moment staring at him in a realized horror.*] Well, what're you lookin' at!

FIRST OFFICER: Open up!

EDDIE: [*Calling toward door.*] Who's that there?

FIRST OFFICER: Immigration, open up.

[EDDIE *turns, looks at* BEATRICE. *She sits. Then he looks at* CATHERINE. *With a sob of fury* CATHERINE *streaks into a bedroom. Knock is repeated.*]

EDDIE: All right, take it easy, take it easy. [*He goes and opens the door. The* OFFICER *steps inside.*] What's all this?

FIRST OFFICER: Where are they?

[SECOND OFFICER *sweeps past and, glancing about, goes into the kitchen.*]

EDDIE: Where's who?

FIRST OFFICER: Come on, come on, where are they? [*He hurries into the bedrooms.*]

EDDIE: Who? We got nobody here. [*He looks at* BEATRICE, *who turns her head away. Pugnaciously, furious, he steps toward* BEATRICE.] What's the matter with you?

[FIRST OFFICER *enters from the bedroom, calls to the kitchen.*]

FIRST OFFICER: Dominick?

[*Enter* SECOND OFFICER *from kitchen.*]

SECOND OFFICER: Maybe it's a different apartment.

FIRST OFFICER: There's only two more floors up there. I'll take the front, you go up the fire escape. I'll let you in. Watch your step up there.

SECOND OFFICER: Okay, right, Charley. [FIRST OFFICER *goes out apartment door and runs up the stairs.*] This is Four-forty-one, isn't it?

EDDIE: That's right. [SECOND OFFICER *goes out into the kitchen.* EDDIE *turns to* BEATRICE. *She looks at him now and sees his terror.*]

BEATRICE: [*Weakened with fear.*] Oh, Jesus, Eddie.

EDDIE: What's the matter with *you*?

BEATRICE: [*Pressing her palms against her face.*] Oh, my God, my God.

EDDIE: What're you, accusin' me?

BEATRICE: [*Her final thrust is to turn toward him instead of running from him.*] My God, what did you do?

[*Many steps on the outer stair draw his attention. We see the* FIRST OFFICER *descending, with* MARCO, *behind him* RODOLPHO, *and* CATHERINE *and the two strange immigrants, followed by* SECOND OFFICER. BEATRICE *hurries to door.*]

CATHERINE: [*Backing down stairs, fighting with* FIRST OFFICER; *as they appear on the stairs.*] What do yiz want from them? They work, that's all. They're boarders upstairs, they work on the piers.

BEATRICE: [*To* FIRST OFFICER.] Ah, mister, what do you want from them, who do they hurt?

CATHERINE: [*Pointing to* RODOLPHO.] They ain't no submarines, he was born in Philadelphia.

FIRST OFFICER: Step aside, lady.

CATHERINE: What do you mean? You can't just come in a house and—

FIRST OFFICER: All right, take it easy. [*To* RODOLPHO.] What street were you born in Philadelphia?

CATHERINE: What do you mean, what street? Could you tell me what street you were born?

FIRST OFFICER: Sure. Four blocks away, One-eleven Union Street. Let's go fellas.

CATHERINE: [*Fending him off* RODOLPHO.] No, you can't! Now, get outa here!

FIRST OFFICER: Look, girlie, if they're all right they'll be out tomorrow. If they're illegal they go back where they came from. If you want, get yourself a lawyer, although I'm tellin' you now you're wasting your money. Let's get them in the car, Dom. [*To the men.*] Andiamo, Andiamo, let's go. [*The men start, but* MARCO *hangs back.*]

BEATRICE: [*From doorway.*] Who're they hurtin', for God's sake, what do you want from them? They're starvin' over there, what do you want! Marco!

[MARCO *suddenly breaks from the group and dashes into the room and faces* EDDIE; BEATRICE *and* FIRST OFFICER *rush in as* MARCO *spits into* EDDIE's *face.* CATHERINE *runs into hallway and throws herself into* RODOLPHO's *arms.* EDDIE, *with an enraged cry, lunges for* MARCO.]

EDDIE: Oh, you mother's—!

[FIRST OFFICER *quickly intercedes and pushes* EDDIE *from* MARCO, *who stands there accusingly.*]

FIRST OFFICER: [*Between them, pushing* EDDIE *from* MARCO.] Cut it out!

EDDIE: [*Over the* FIRST OFFICER's *shoulder, to* MARCO.] I'll kill you for that, you son of a bitch!

FIRST OFFICER: Hey! [*Shakes him.*] Stay in here now, don't come out, don't bother him. You hear me? Don't come out, fella. [*For an instant there is silence. Then* FIRST OFFICER *turns and takes* MARCO's *arm and then gives a last, informative look at* EDDIE. *As he and* MARCO *are going out into the hall,* EDDIE *erupts.*]

EDDIE: I don't forget that, Marco! You hear what I'm sayin'?

[*Out in the hall,* FIRST OFFICER *and* MARCO *go down the stairs. Now, in the street,* LOUIS, MIKE, *and several neighbors including the butcher,* LIPARI—*a stout, intense, middle-aged man—are gathering around the stoop.* LIPARI, *the butcher, walks over to the two strange men and kisses them. His wife, keening, goes and kisses their hands.* EDDIE *is emerging from the house shouting after* MARCO. BEATRICE *is trying to restrain him.*]

EDDIE: That's the thanks I get? Which I took the blankets off my bed for yiz? You gonna apologize to me, Marco! *Marco!*

FIRST OFFICER: [*In the doorway with* MARCO.] All right, lady, let them go. Get in the car, fellas, it's over there.

[RODOLPHO *is almost carrying the sobbing* CATHERINE *off up the street, left.*]

CATHERINE: He was born in Philadelphia! What do you want from him?

FIRST OFFICER: Step aside, lady, come on now . . .

[*The* SECOND OFFICER *has moved off with the two strange men.* MARCO, *taking advantage of the* FIRST OFFICER's *being occupied with* CATHERINE, *suddenly frees himself and points back at* EDDIE.]

MARCO: That one! I accuse that one!

[EDDIE *brushes* BEATRICE *aside and rushes out to the stoop.*]

FIRST OFFICER: [*Grabbing him and moving him quickly off up the left street.*] Come on!

MARCO: [*As he is taken off, pointing back at* EDDIE.] That one! He killed my children! That one stole the food from my children!

[MARCO *is gone. The crowd has turned to* EDDIE.]

EDDIE: [*To* LIPARI *and wife.*] He's crazy! I give them the blankets off my bed. Six months I kept them like my own brothers!

[LIPARI, *the butcher, turns and starts up left with his arm around his wife.*]

EDDIE: Lipari! [*He follows* LIPARI *up left.*] For Christ's sake, I kept them, I give them the blankets off my bed!

[LIPARI *and wife exit.* EDDIE *turns and starts crossing down right to* LOUIS *and* MIKE.]

EDDIE: Louis! *Louis!*

[LOUIS *barely turns, then walks off and exits down right with* MIKE. *Only*

BEATRICE *is left on the stoop.* CATHER-
INE *now returns, blank-eyed, from
offstage and the car.* EDDIE *calls after
LOUIS and MIKE.*]

EDDIE: He's gonna take that back. He's
gonna take that back or I'll kill him! You
hear me? I'll kill him! I'll kill him! [*He
exits up street calling.*]

[*There is a pause of darkness before
the lights rise, on the reception room
of a prison.* MARCO *is seated;* ALFIERI,
CATHERINE, *and* RODOLPHO *standing.*]

ALFIERI: I'm waiting, Marco, what do
you say?

RODOLPHO: Marco never hurt anybody.

ALFIERI: I can bail you out until your
hearing comes up. But I'm not going to
do it, you understand me? Unless I have
your promise. You're an honorable man,
I will believe your promise. Now what do
you say?

MARCO: In my country he would be dead
now. He would not live this long.

ALFIERI: All right, Rodolpho—you come
with me now.

RODOLPHO: No! Please, Mister. Marco—
promise the man. Please, I want you to
watch the wedding. How can I be married
and you're in here? Please, you're not going
to do anything; you know you're not.

[MARCO *is silent.*]

CATHERINE: [*Kneeling left of* MARCO.]
Marco, don't you understand? He can't
bail you out if you're gonna do something
bad. To hell with Eddie. Nobody is gonna
talk to him again if he lives to a hundred.
Everybody knows you spit in his face,
that's enough, isn't it? Give me the satisfaction—I want you at the wedding. You
got a wife and kids, Marco. You could be
workin' till the hearing comes up, instead
of layin' around here.

MARCO: [*To* ALFIERI.] I have no chance?

ALFIERI: [*Crosses to behind* MARCO.]
No, Marco. You're going back. The hearing
is a formality, that's all.

MARCO: But him? There is a chance, eh?

ALFIERI: When she marries him he can
start to become an American. They permit
that, if the wife is born here.

MARCO: [*Looking at* RODOLPHO.] Well—
we did something. [*He lays a palm on*
RODOLPHO'S *arm and* RODOLPHO *covers it.*]

RODOLPHO: Marco, tell the man.

MARCO: [*Pulling his hand away.*] What
will I tell him? He knows such a promise
is dishonorable.

ALFIERI: To promise not to kill is not
dishonorable.

MARCO: [*Looking at* ALFIERI.] No?

ALFIERI: No.

MARCO: [*Gesturing with his head—this
is a new idea.*] Then what is done with
such a man?

ALFIERI: Nothing. If he obeys the law,
he lives. That's all.

MARCO: [*Rises, turns to* ALFIERI.] The
law? All the law is not in a book.

ALFIERI: Yes. In a book. There is no
other law.

MARCO: [*His anger rising.*] He degraded
my brother. My blood. He robbed my children, he mocks my work. I work to come
here, mister!

ALFIERI: I know, Marco—

MARCO: There is no law for that? Where
is the law for that?

ALFIERI: There is none.

MARCO: [*Shaking his head, sitting.*] I
don't understand this country.

ALFIERI: Well? What is your answer?
You have five or six weeks you could work.
Or else you sit here. What do you say
to me?

MARCO: [*Lowers his eyes. It almost
seems he is ashamed.*] All right.

ALFIERI: You won't touch him. This is
your promise.

[*Slight pause.*]

MARCO: Maybe he wants to apologize
to me. [MARCO *is staring away.* ALFIERI
takes one of his hands.*]

ALFIERI: This is not God, Marco. You
hear? Only God makes justice.

MARCO: All right.

ALFIERI: [*Nodding, not with assurance.*]
Good! Catherine, Rodolpho, Marco, let us
go.

[CATHERINE *kisses* RODOLPHO *and*
MARCO, *then kisses* ALFIERI'S *hand.*]

CATHERINE: I'll get Beatrice and meet
you at the church. [*She leaves quickly.*]

[MARCO *rises.* RODOLPHO *suddenly embraces him.* MARCO *pats him on the
back and* RODOLPHO *exits after*
CATHERINE. MARCO *faces* ALFIERI.]

ALFIERI: Only God, Marco.

[MARCO *turns and walks out.* ALFIERI
with a certain processional tread leaves
the stage. The lights dim out.

The lights rise in the apartment.*
EDDIE *is alone in the rocker, rocking
back and forth in little surges. Pause.
Now* BEATRICE *emerges from a bed-*

room. She is in her best clothes, wearing a hat.]

BEATRICE: [*With fear, going to* EDDIE.] I'll be back in about an hour, Eddie. All right?

EDDIE: [*Quietly, almost inaudibly, as though drained.*] What, have I been talkin' to myself?

BEATRICE: Eddie, for God's sake, it's her wedding.

EDDIE: Didn't you hear what I told you? You walk out that door to that wedding you ain't comin' back here, Beatrice.

BEATRICE: Why! What do you want?

EDDIE: I want my respect. Didn't you ever hear of that? From my wife?

[CATHERINE *enters from bedroom.*]

CATHERINE: It's after three; we're supposed to be there already, Beatrice. The priest won't wait.

BEATRICE: Eddie. It's her wedding. There'll be nobody there from her family. For my sister let me go. I'm going for my sister.

EDDIE: [*As though hurt.*] Look, I been arguin' with you all day already, Beatrice, and I said what I'm gonna say. He's gonna come here and apologize to me or nobody from this house is goin' into that church today. Now if that's more to you than I am, then go. But don't come back. You be on my side or on their side, that's all.

CATHERINE: [*Suddenly.*] Who the hell do you think you are?

BEATRICE: Sssh!

CATHERINE: You got no more right to tell nobody nothin'! Nobody! The rest of your life, nobody!

BEATRICE: Shut up, Katie! [*She turns* CATHERINE *around.*]

CATHERINE: You're gonna come with me!

BEATRICE: I can't Katie, I can't . . .

CATHERINE: How can you listen to him? This rat!

BEATRICE: [*Shaking* CATHERINE.] Don't you call him that!

CATHERINE: [*Clearing from* BEATRICE.] What're you scared of? He's a rat! He belongs in the sewer!

BEATRICE: Stop it!

CATHERINE: [*Weeping.*] He bites people when they sleep! He comes when nobody's lookin' and poisons decent people. In the garbage he belongs!

[EDDIE *seems about to pick up the table and fling it at her.*]

BEATRICE: No, Eddie! Eddie! [*To* CATHERINE.] Then we all belong in the garbage. You, and me too. Don't say that. Whatever happened we all done it, and don't you ever forget it, Catherine. [*She goes to* CATHERINE.] Now go, go to your wedding, Katie, I'll stay home. Go. God bless you, God bless your children.

[*Enter* RODOLPHO.]

RODOLPHO: Eddie?

EDDIE: Who said you could come in here? Get outa here!

RODOLPHO: Marco is coming, Eddie. [*Pause.* BEATRICE *raises her hands in terror.*] He's praying in the church. You understand? [*Pause.* RODOLPHO *advances into the room.*] Catherine, I think it is better we go. Come with me.

CATHERINE: Eddie, go away, please.

BEATRICE: [*Quietly.*] Eddie. Let's go someplace. Come. You and me. [*He has not moved.*] I don't want you to be here when he comes. I'll get your coat.

EDDIE: Where? Where am I goin'? This is my house.

BEATRICE: [*Crying out.*] What's the use of it! He's crazy now, you know the way they get, what good is it! You got nothin' against Marco, you always liked Marco!

EDDIE: I got nothin' against Marco? Which he called me a rat in front of the whole neighborhood? Which he said I killed his children! Where you been?

RODOLPHO: [*Quite suddenly, stepping up to* EDDIE.] It is my fault, Eddie. Everything. I wish to apologize. It was wrong that I do not ask your permission. I kiss your hand. [*He reaches for* EDDIE's *hand, but* EDDIE *snaps it away from him.*]

BEATRICE: Eddie, he's apologizing!

RODOLPHO: I have made all our troubles. But you have insult me too. Maybe God understand why you did that to me. Maybe you did not mean to insult me at all—

BEATRICE: Listen to him! Eddie, listen what he's tellin' you!

RODOLPHO: I think, maybe when Marco comes, if we can tell him we are comrades now, and we have no more argument between us. Then maybe Marco will not—

EDDIE: Now, listen—

CATHERINE: Eddie, give him a chance!

BEATRICE: What do you want! Eddie, what do you want!

EDDIE: I want my name! He didn't take my name; he's only a punk. Marco's got my name—[*To* RODOLPHO.] and you can run tell him, kid, that he's gonna give it back to me in front of this neighborhood, or we have it out. [*Hoisting up his pants.*] Come on, where is he? Take me to him.

BEATRICE: Eddie, listen—

EDDIE: I heard enough! Come on, let's go!

BEATRICE: Only blood is good? He kissed your hand!

EDDIE: What he does don't mean nothin' to nobody! [*To* RODOLPHO.] Come on!

BEATRICE: [*Barring his way to the stairs.*] What's gonna mean somethin'? Eddie, listen to me. Who could give you your name? Listen to me, I love you, I'm talkin' to you, I love you; if Marco'll kiss your hand outside, if he goes on his knees, what is he got to give you? That's not what you want.

EDDIE: Don't bother me!

BEATRICE: You want somethin' else, Eddie, and you can never have her!

CATHERINE: [*In horror.*] B.!

EDDIE: [*Shocked, horrified, his fists clenching.*] Beatrice.

[MARCO *appears outside, walking toward the door from a distant point.*]

BEATRICE: [*Crying out, weeping.*] The truth is not as bad as blood, Eddie! I'm tellin' you the truth—tell her good-by forever!

EDDIE: [*Crying out in agony.*] That's what you think of me—that I would have such a thought? [*His fists clench his head as though it will burst.*]

MARCO: [*Calling near the door outside.*] Eddie Carbone!

[EDDIE *swerves about; all stand transfixed for an instant. People appear outside.*]

EDDIE: [*As though flinging his challenge.*] Yeah, Marco! Eddie Carbone. Eddie Carbone. Eddie Carbone. [*He goes up the stairs and emerges from the apartment.* RODOLPHO *streaks up and out past him and runs to* MARCO.]

RODOLPHO: No, Marco, please! Eddie, please, he has children! You will kill a family!

BEATRICE: Go in the house! Eddie, go in the house!

EDDIE: [*He gradually comes to address the people.*] Maybe he came to apologize to me. Heh, Marco? For what you said about me in front of the neighborhood? [*He is incensing himself and little bits of laughter even escape him as his eyes are murderous and he cracks his knuckles in his hands with a strange sort of relaxation.*] He knows that ain't right. To do like that? To a man? Which I put my roof over their head and my food in their mouth? Like in the Bible? Strangers I never seen in my whole life? To come out of the water and grab a girl for a passport? To go and take from your own family like from the stable—and never a word to me? And now accusations in the bargain! [*Directly to* MARCO.] Wipin' the neighborhood with my name like a dirty rag! I want my name, Marco. [*He is moving now, carefully, toward* MARCO.] Now gimme my name and we go together to the wedding.

BEATRICE *and* CATHERINE: [*Keening.*] Eddie! Eddie, don't! Eddie!

EDDIE: No, Marco knows what's right from wrong. Tell the people, Marco, tell them what a liar you are! [*He has his arms spread and* MARCO *is spreading his.*] Come on, liar, you know what you done! [*He lunges for* MARCO *as a great hushed shout goes up from the people.* MARCO *strikes* EDDIE *beside the neck.*]

MARCO: Animal! You go on your knees to me!

[EDDIE *goes down with the blow and* MARCO *starts to raise a foot to stomp him when* EDDIE *springs a knife into his hand and* MARCO *steps back.* LOUIS *rushes in toward* EDDIE.]

LOUIS: Eddie, for Christ's sake!

[EDDIE *raises the knife and* LOUIS *halts and steps back.*]

EDDIE: You lied about me, Marco. Now say it. Come on now, say it!

MARCO: Anima-a-a-l!

[EDDIE *lunges with the knife.* MARCO *grabs his arm, turning the blade inward and pressing it home as the women and* LOUIS *and* MIKE *rush in and separate them, and* EDDIE, *the knife still in his hand, falls to his knees before* MARCO. *The two women support him for a moment, calling his name again and again.*]

CATHERINE: Eddie I never meant to do nothing bad to you.

EDDIE: Then why—Oh, B.!

BEATRICE: Yes, yes!

EDDIE: My B.! [*He dies in her arms, and* BEATRICE *covers him with her body.* ALFIERI, *who is in the crowd, turns out to the audience. The lights have gone down, leaving him in a glow, while behind him the dull prayers of the people and the keening of the women continue.*]

ALFIERI: Most of the time now we settle for half and I like it better. But the truth is holy, and even as I know how wrong he was, and his death useless, I tremble, for I confess that something perversely pure calls to me from his memory—not purely good, but himself purely, for he allowed himself to be wholly known and for that I think I will love him more than all my sensible clients. And yet, it is better to settle for half, it must be! And so I mourn him—I admit it—with a certain . . . alarm.

CURTAIN

JEAN-CLAUDE VAN ITALLIE

A REVIEW of *America Hurrah* by Robert Brustein[1]

Just a few days ago, a director friend was trying to convince me that America stood on the brink of a theatrical renaissance that would produce at least ten dramatists of the first rank in the next few years. At the time I found this notion fairly preposterous but I am much more willing to entertain it now, having just returned from Jean-Claude van Itallie's three-play sequence, AMERICA HURRAH. I think I would respond to Mr. van Itallie's work under any circumstances—he speaks, if these plays are typical of him, more directly to my own particular obsessions than any other contemporary American playwright—but the important thing to note is that he does not function in isolation. The workshop and cabaret groups with which he has been associated have been collaborating with a surprising number of promising experimental dramatists, and one of these groups—the Open Theatre—has partly determined the development of his style.

The Open Theatre production of AMERICA HURRAH, in fact, is inseparable from the plays themselves, and the difficulty of the reviewer is in finding ways to praise the playwright without helping to deliver him over to the cultural cannibals. For if Mr. van Itallie provides the mind, spirit, and creative impulse of the evening, the Open Theatre actors provide the technique and invention, formed over three years of experimental work in histrionic transformation, and it would be criminal if the playwright's success led to any dissolution of this collaboration. With AMERICA HURRAH, the concept of theatrical unity finally becomes meaningful in this country and the American theatre takes three giant steps towards maturity.

The triumph of this occasion is to have found provocative theatrical images for the national malaise we have been suffering in Johnsonland these last three years: the infection of violence, calamity, indifference, gratuitous murder, and (prob-

[1] "Three Views of America." Copyright © 1966 by Robert Brustein. Reprinted from THE THIRD THEATRE, by Robert Brustein, by permission of Alfred A. Knopf, Inc. Originally published in *The New Republic*, 3 December, 1966, pp. 31-33.

ably the cause of all these) brutalizing war. In his first and most abstract short play, INTERVIEW, Mr. van Itallie examines, through a form of verbal and physical choreography, the mechanization of life in modern urban America. The setting is chalk white, broken by aluminum lines; four nervous job applicants from various classes of life are questioned by four bland interviewers in smiling shiny masks. The interview begins to reduce the applicants to a gaping, blinking chorus, and when they retreat into the air, the street completes the process. A young girl trying to find her way to Fourteenth Street runs a gauntlet of spastics, creeps, drunks, bizarre couples; a telephone operator is given cancer surgery with the actors transforming themselves into a failing respiratory machine; one unhappy man is given the usual ritual advice by his analyst ("Blah, blah, blah, blah, HOSTILE. Blah, blah, blah, blash, PENIS. Blah, blah, blah, blah, MOTHER. Blah, blah, blah, blah, MONEY.") while another is given customary silence by his priest; a candidate for governor dispenses hollow rhetoric on the subject of rats, red tape, foul air, and Vietnam; and the play ends with the entire cast marching in place, their mouths opening and closing in a dehumanized language ("My fault" "Excuse me" "Can you help me?" "Next") from which all emotion has been evacuated. Joseph Chaikin, who founded the Open Theatre, has directed with keen imagination, finding the exact mechanical equivalents for the automatic movement of the play.

TV and MOTEL, both directed by the gifted Jacques Levy, are more particularized works, and both make their points through the interesting device of juxtaposition. TV, for example, which takes place in a television rating room, juxtaposes the eventless activities of three tired employees of the company with melodramatic scenes from familiar television programs (performed behind them by actors whose faces have been made up with video lines). The effect of this is to make a commonplace office reality act as a simple counterpoint to the grotesqueries taking place on the screen, thus obviating any need for satiric exaggeration (which mars most satire on the medium). While the office workers quarrel, joke, hold a birthday party, choke on chicken bones, etc., the television people enact the fantasies, crimes, and aberrations of contemporary America. Wonderboy, aided by his Wondervision, saves a housewife threatened by her monster husband; a news program tells of the accidental killing of 60 peasants in a friendly Vietnamese village, followed by a commercial for cigarettes; the Lily Heaven show brings us a loudmouthed pop singer with a Pepsodent smile, singing an endless finale to endless applause; a Billion Dollar movie about World War II ends with the reconciliation of two stiff lovers ("I've learned a lot. . . . Maybe that's what war is for."); Billy Graham addresses a crusade in Houston ("If we could look through the ceiling of this wonderful new air-conditioned stadium we could see the stars"), trying to reconcile great wealth with evangelical Christianity; a situation comedy, continually interrupted by canned laughter, revolves around the momentous question of why daughter isn't going to the prom. By the conclusion of the play, the three employees have become completely assimilated into the video action, though they haven't even been watching it, thus demonstrating, I assume, how mass culture has the power to break down our reality, whether we allow it to or not.

Mr. van Itallie's final short play is the most exciting of the evening, for it is based on a metaphor so powerful that it may well become the objective correlative of the Johnson age. Entitled MOTEL, it too is based on juxtapositions—of civilization and savagery, harmony and disorder, the nostalgic past and the terrifying present. Verbally, MOTEL is a monologue spoken by a female motelkeeper—the homey voice belongs to Ruth White, but the body is that of an enormous aproned doll with a huge carnival mask atop it, complete with hair rollers and glasses. The speech drones on about rooms ("rooms of marble and rooms of cork, all letting forth an avalanche"), rooms throughout history, and particularly this motel room with its antimacassars, hooked rugs, plastic flowers from Japan, television sets, toilets that automatically flush. As the motelkeeper proudly catalogues the room's possessions, the door opens with a blinding flash of headlights and a young couple enters—two more Artaudian mannikins on raised shoes, their huge heads bobbing, their bodies moving with the jerky menace of animated monsters. Gradually, they undress for the night, coming together for a grotesque papier mâché embrace, rubbing their cardboard bodies, then turn on the TV and, to the accompaniment of wild rock-and-roll, go about the cheerful destruction of the room: ripping off the toilet seat, breaking the bed springs, pulling down doors and windows, scrawling obscenities and pornographic drawings with lipstick on the walls, and finally tearing the motelkeeper apart, head and all. Vladimir Nabokov effectively used motel culture, in Lolita, as an image of the sordidness and tastelessness in the depths of our land; Mr. van Itallie uses it as an image of our violence, our insanity, our need to defile.

He has, in short, discovered the deepest poetic function of the theatre which is not, like most American dramatists, to absorb the audience into the author's own personal problems under the pretext that they are universal, but rather to invent metaphors which can poignantly suggest a nation's nightmares and afflictions. These metaphors solve nothing, change nothing, transform nothing, but they do manage to relax frustration and assuage loneliness by showing that it is still possible for men to share a common humanity—even if this only means sharing a common revulsion against what is mean and detestable. It is for this reason that I am exhilarated by these plays and by what they augur for the future of the American theatre.

JEAN-CLAUDE VAN ITALLIE

America Hurrah

Three One-Act Plays

Interview

TV

Motel

Interview

A Fugue for Eight Actors

CHARACTERS

FIRST INTERVIEWER.
FIRST APPLICANT.
SECOND APPLICANT.
THIRD APPLICANT.
The set is white and impersonal.

FOURTH APPLICANT.
SECOND INTERVIEWER.
THIRD INTERVIEWER.
FOURTH INTERVIEWER.

Two subway stairs are at the back of the stage. On the sides there is one entrance for Applicants and another entrance for Interviewers.

The only furniture or props needed are eight grey blocks.

The actors, four men and four women, are dressed in black-and-white street clothes. During the employment agency section only, Interviewers wear translucent plastic masks.

There is an intermittent harpsichord accompaniment: dance variations (minuet, Virginia reel, twist) on a familiar American tune. But much of the music (singing, whistling, humming) is provided by the actors on stage. It is suggested, moreover, that as a company of actors and a director approach the play they find their own variations in rhythmic expression. The successful transition from one setting to the next depends on the actors' ability to play together as a company and to drop character instantaneously and completely in order to assume another character, or for a group effect.

[*The* FIRST INTERVIEWER *for an employment agency, a young woman, sits on stage as the* FIRST APPLICANT, *a Housepainter, enters.*]

FIRST INTERVIEWER: [*Standing.*] How do you do?

FIRST APPLICANT: [*Sitting.*] Thank you, I said, not knowing where to sit.

[*The characters will often include the audience in what they say, as if they were being interviewed by the audience.*]

FIRST INTERVIEWER: [*Pointedly.*] Won't you sit down?

FIRST APPLICANT: [*Standing again quickly, afraid to displease.*] I'm sorry.

FIRST INTERVIEWER: [*Busy with imaginary papers, pointing to a particular seat.*] There. Name, please?

FIRST APPLICANT: Jack Smith.

FIRST INTERVIEWER: Jack what Smith?

FIRST APPLICANT: Beg pardon?

FIRST INTERVIEWER: Fill in the blank space, please. Jack blank space Smith.

FIRST APPLICANT: I don't have any.

FIRST INTERVIEWER: I asked you to sit down. [*Pointing.*] There.

FIRST APPLICANT: [*Sitting.*] I'm sorry.

FIRST INTERVIEWER: Name, please?

FIRST APPLICANT: Jack Smith.

FIRST INTERVIEWER: You haven't told me your MIDDLE name.

FIRST APPLICANT: I haven't got one.

FIRST INTERVIEWER: [*Suspicious but writing it down.*] No middle name.

[SECOND APPLICANT, *a woman, a Floorwasher, enters.*]

FIRST INTERVIEWER: How do you do?

SECOND APPLICANT: [*Sitting.*] Thank you, I said, not knowing what.

FIRST INTERVIEWER: Won't you sit down?
SECOND APPLICANT: [*Standing.*] I'm sorry.
FIRST APPLICANT: I am sitting.
FIRST INTERVIEWER: [*Pointing.*] There. Name, please?
SECOND APPLICANT: [*Sitting.*] Jane Smith.
FIRST APPLICANT: Jack Smith.
FIRST INTERVIEWER: What blank space Smith?
SECOND APPLICANT: Ellen.
FIRST APPLICANT: Haven't got one.
FIRST INTERVIEWER: What job are you applying for?
FIRST APPLICANT: Housepainter.
SECOND APPLICANT: Floorwasher.
FIRST INTERVIEWER: We haven't many vacancies in that. What experience have you had?
FIRST APPLICANT: A lot.
SECOND APPLICANT: Who needs experience for floorwashing?
FIRST INTERVIEWER: You will help me by making your answers clear.
FIRST APPLICANT: Eight years.
SECOND APPLICANT: Twenty years.
[THIRD APPLICANT, *a Banker, enters.*]
FIRST INTERVIEWER: How do you do?
SECOND INTERVIEWER: I'm good at it.
FIRST APPLICANT: Very well.
THIRD APPLICANT: [*Sitting.*] Thank you, I said, as casually as I could.
FIRST INTERVIEWER: Won't you sit down?
THIRD APPLICANT: [*Standing again.*] I'm sorry.
SECOND APPLICANT: I am sitting.
FIRST APPLICANT: [*Standing again.*] I'm sorry.
FIRST INTERVIEWER: [*Pointing to a particular seat.*] There. Name, please?
FIRST APPLICANT: Jack Smith.
SECOND APPLICANT: Jane Smith.
THIRD APPLICANT: Richard Smith.
FIRST INTERVIEWER: What EXACTLY Smith, please?
THIRD APPLICANT: Richard F.
SECOND APPLICANT: Jane Ellen.
FIRST APPLICANT: Jack None.
FIRST INTERVIEWER: What are you applying for?
FIRST APPLICANT: Housepainter.
SECOND APPLICANT: I need money.
THIRD APPLICANT: Bank president.
FIRST INTERVIEWER: How many years have you been in your present job?
THIRD APPLICANT: Three.
SECOND APPLICANT. Twenty.

FIRST APPLICANT: Eight.
[FOURTH APPLICANT, *a Lady's Maid, enters.*]
FIRST INTERVIEWER: How do you do?
FOURTH APPLICANT: I said thank you, not knowing where to sit.
THIRD APPLICANT. I'm fine.
SECOND APPLICANT: Do I have to tell you?
FIRST APPLICANT: Very well.
FIRST INTERVIEWER: Won't you sit down?
FOURTH APPLICANT: I'm sorry.
THIRD APPLICANT: [*Sitting again.*] Thank you.
SECOND APPLICANT: [*Standing again.*] I'm sorry.
FIRST APPLICANT: [*Sitting.*] Thanks.
FIRST INTERVIEWER: [*Pointing to a particular seat.*] There. Name, please?
[FOURTH APPLICANT *sits.*]
ALL APPLICANTS: Smith.
FIRST INTERVIEWER: What Smith?
FOURTH APPLICANT: Mary Victoria.
THIRD APPLICANT: Richard F.
SECOND APPLICANT: Jane Ellen.
FIRST APPLICANT: Jack None.
FIRST INTERVIEWER: How many years' experience have you had?
FOURTH APPLICANT: Eight years.
SECOND APPLICANT: Twenty years.
FIRST APPLICANT: Eight years.
THIRD APPLICANT: Three years four months and nine days not counting vacations and sick leave and the time both my daughters and my wife had the whooping cough.
FIRST INTERVIEWER: Just answer the questions, please.
FOURTH APPLICANT: Yes, sir.
THIRD APPLICANT: Sure.
SECOND APPLICANT: I'm sorry.
FIRST APPLICANT: That's what I'm doing.
[SECOND INTERVIEWER, *a young man, enters and goes to inspect Applicants. With the entrance of each Interviewer, the speed of the action accelerates.*]
SECOND INTERVIEWER: How do you do?
FIRST APPLICANT: [*Standing.*] I'm sorry.
SECOND APPLICANT: [*Sitting.*] Thank you.
THIRD APPLICANT: [*Standing.*] I'm sorry.
FOURTH APPLICANT: [*Sitting.*] Thank you.
SECOND INTERVIEWER: What's your name?
FIRST INTERVIEWER: Your middle name, please.

FIRST APPLICANT: Smith.

SECOND APPLICANT: Ellen.

THIRD APPLICANT: Smith, Richard F.

FOURTH APPLICANT: Mary Victoria Smith.

FIRST INTERVIEWER: What is your exact age?

SECOND INTERVIEWER: Have you any children?

FIRST APPLICANT: I'm thirty-two years old.

SECOND APPLICANT: One son.

THIRD APPLICANT: I have two daughters.

FOURTH APPLICANT: Do I have to tell you that?

FIRST INTERVIEWER: Are you married, single, or other?

SECOND INTERVIEWER: Have you ever earned more than that?

FIRST APPLICANT: No.

SECOND APPLICANT: Never.

THIRD APPLICANT: Married.

FOURTH APPLICANT: Single, NOW.

[THIRD INTERVIEWER, *a woman, enters.*]

THIRD INTERVIEWER: How do you do?

FIRST APPLICANT: [*Sitting.*] Thank you.

SECOND APPLICANT: [*Standing.*] I'm sorry.

THIRD APPLICANT: [*Sitting.*] Thank you.

FOURTH APPLICANT: [*Standing.*] I'm sorry.

[FOURTH INTERVIEWER, *a man, appears on the heels of* THIRD INTERVIEWER.]

FOURTH INTERVIEWER: How do you do?

FIRST APPLICANT: [*Standing.*] I'm sorry.

SECOND APPLICANT: [*Sitting.*] Thank you.

THIRD APPLICANT: [*Standing.*] I'm sorry.

FOURTH APPLICANT: [*Sitting.*] Thank you.

ALL INTERVIEWERS: What is your Social Security Number, please?

[*Applicants do the next four speeches simultaneously.*]

FIRST APPLICANT: 333 dash 6598 dash 5590765439 dash 003.

SECOND APPLICANT: 999 dash 5733 dash 699075432 dash 11.

THIRD APPLICANT: [*Sitting.*] I'm sorry. I left it home. I can call if you let me use the phone.

FOURTH APPLICANT: I always get it confused with my Checking Account Number.

[INTERVIEWERS *do the next four speeches in a round.*]

FIRST INTERVIEWER: Will you be so kind as to tell me a little about yourself?

SECOND INTERVIEWER: Can you fill me in on something about your background please?

THIRD INTERVIEWER: It'd be a help to our employers if you'd give me a little for our files.

FOURTH INTERVIEWER: Now what would you say, say, to a prospective employer about yourself?

[APPLICANTS *address parts of the following four speeches, in particular, directly to the audience.*]

FIRST APPLICANT: I've been a Union member twenty years, I said to them, if that's the kind of thing you want to know. Good health, I said. Veteran of two wars. Three kids. Wife's dead. Wife's sister, she takes care of them. I don't know why I'm telling you this, I said smiling. [*Sits.*]

SECOND APPLICANT: [*Standing.*] So what do you want to know, I told the guy. I've been washin' floors for twenty years. Nobody's ever complained. I don't loiter after hours, I said to him. Just because my boy's been in trouble is no reason, I said, no reason—I go right home, I said to him. Right home. [*Sits.*]

THIRD APPLICANT: [*Standing.*] I said that I was a Republican and we could start right there. And then I said that I spend most of my free time watching television or playing in the garden of my four-bedroom house with our two lovely daughters, aged nine and eleven. I mentioned that my wife plays with us too, and that her name is Katherine, although, I said casually, her good friends call her Kitty. I wasn't at all nervous. [*Sits.*]

FOURTH APPLICANT: [*Standing.*] Just because I'm here, sir, I told him, is no reason for you to patronize me. I've been a lady's maid, I said, in houses you would not be allowed into. My father was a gentleman of leisure, AND what's more, I said, my references are unimpeachable.

FIRST INTERVIEWER. I see.

SECOND INTERVIEWER: All right.

THIRD INTERVIEWER: That's fine.

FOURTH INTERVIEWER: Of course.

[APPLICANTS *do the following four speeches simultaneously.*]

FIRST APPLICANT: Just you call anybody at the Union and ask them. They'll hand me a clean bill of health.

SECOND APPLICANT: I haven't been to jail if that's what you mean. Not me. I'm clean.

THIRD APPLICANT: My record is impeccable. There's not a stain on it.

FOURTH APPLICANT: My references would permit me to be a governess, that's what.

FIRST INTERVIEWER: [*Going to* FIRST APPLICANT *and inspecting under his arms.*] When did you last have a job housepainting?

SECOND INTERVIEWER: [*Going to* SECOND APPLICANT *and inspecting her teeth.*] Where was the last place you worked?

THIRD INTERVIEWER: [*Going to* THIRD APPLICANT *and inspecting him.*] What was your last position in a bank?

FOURTH INTERVIEWER: [*Going to* FOURTH APPLICANT *and inspecting her.*] Have you got your references with you?

[APPLICANTS *do the following four speeches simultaneously, with music under.*]

FIRST APPLICANT: I've already told you I worked right along till I quit.

SECOND APPLICANT: Howard Johnson's on Fifty-first Street all last month.

THIRD APPLICANT: First Greenfield International and Franklin Banking Corporation Banking and Stone Incorporated.

FOURTH APPLICANT: I've got a letter right here in my bag. Mrs. Muggintwat only let me go because she died.

[INTERVIEWERS *do the next four speeches in a round.*]

FIRST INTERVIEWER: [*Stepping around and speaking to* SECOND APPLICANT.] Nothing terminated your job at Howard Johnson's? No franks, say, missing at the end of the day, I suppose?

SECOND INTERVIEWER: [*Stepping around and speaking to* THIRD APPLICANT.] It goes without saying, I suppose, that you could stand an FBI Security Test?

THIRD INTERVIEWER: [*Stepping around and speaking to* FOURTH APPLICANT.] I suppose there are no records of minor thefts or, shall we say, borrowings from your late employer?

FOURTH INTERVIEWER: [*Stepping around and speaking to* FIRST APPLICANT.] Nothing political in your Union dealings? Nothing Leftist, I suppose? Nothing Rightist either, I hope.

[APPLICANTS *and* INTERVIEWERS *line up for a square dance. Music under the following.*]

FIRST APPLICANT: [*Bowing to* FIRST INTERVIEWER.] What's it to you, buddy?

SECOND APPLICANT: [*Bowing to* SECOND INTERVIEWER.] Eleanor Roosevelt wasn't more honest.

THIRD APPLICANT: [*Bowing to* THIRD INTERVIEWER.] My record is lily-white, sir!

FOURTH APPLICANT: [*Bowing to* FOURTH INTERVIEWER.] Mrs. Thumbletwat used to take me to the bank and I'd watch her open her box!

[*Each* INTERVIEWER, *during his next speech, goes upstage to form another line.*]

FIRST INTERVIEWER: Good!

SECOND INTERVIEWER: Fine!

THIRD INTERVIEWER: Swell!

FOURTH INTERVIEWER: Fine!

[APPLICANTS *come downstage together; they do the next four speeches simultaneously and directly to the audience.*]

FIRST APPLICANT: I know my rights. As a veteran. AND a citizen. I know my rights. AND my cousin is very well-known in certain circles, if you get what I mean. In the back room of a certain candy store in the Italian district of this city my cousin is VERY well known, if you get what I mean. I know my rights. And I know my cousin.

SECOND APPLICANT: [*Putting on a pious act, looking up to heaven.*] Holy Mary Mother of God, must I endure all the sinners of this earth? Must I go on a poor washerwoman in this City of Sin? Help me, oh my God, to leave this earthly crust, and damn your silly impudence, young man, if you think you can treat an old woman like this. You've got another thought coming, you have.

THIRD APPLICANT: I have an excellent notion to report you to the Junior Chamber of Commerce of this city of which I am the Secretary and was in line to be elected Vice President and still will be if you are able to find me gainful and respectable employ!

FOURTH APPLICANT: Miss Thumblebottom married into the Twiths and if you start insulting me, young man, you'll have to start in insulting the Twiths as well. A Twith isn't a nobody, you know, as good as a Thumbletwat AND they all call me their loving Mary, you know.

ALL INTERVIEWERS: [*In a loud raucous voice.*] Do you smoke?

[*Each* APPLICANT, *during his next speech, turns upstage.*]

FIRST APPLICANT: No thanks.

SECOND APPLICANT: Not now.

THIRD APPLICANT: No thanks.

FOURTH APPLICANT: Not now.

ALL INTERVIEWERS: [*Again in a harsh voice and bowing or curtsying.*] Do you mind if I do?

FIRST APPLICANT: I don't care.

SECOND APPLICANT: Who cares?

THIRD APPLICANT: Course not.

FOURTH APPLICANT: Go ahead.

[*Interviewers form a little group off to themselves.*]

FIRST INTERVIEWER: I tried to quit but couldn't manage.

SECOND INTERVIEWER: I'm a three-pack-a-day man, I guess.

THIRD INTERVIEWER: If I'm gonna go I'd rather go smoking.

FOURTH INTERVIEWER: I'm down to five a day.

[APPLICANTS *all start to sneeze.*]

FIRST APPLICANT: Excuse me, I'm gonna sneeze.

SECOND APPLICANT: Have you got a hanky?

THIRD APPLICANT: I have a cold coming on.

FOURTH APPLICANT: I thought I had some tissues in my bag.

[APPLICANTS *all sneeze.*]

FIRST INTERVIEWER: Gesundheit.

SECOND INTERVIEWER: God bless you.

THIRD INTERVIEWER: Gesundheit.

FOURTH INTERVIEWER: God bless you.

[APPLICANTS *all sneeze simultaneously.*]

FIRST INTERVIEWER: God bless you.

SECOND INTERVIEWER: Gesundheit.

THIRD INTERVIEWER: God bless you.

FOURTH INTERVIEWER: Gesundheit.

[APPLICANTS *return to their seats.*]

FIRST APPLICANT: Thanks, I said.

SECOND APPLICANT: I said thanks.

THIRD APPLICANT: Thank you, I said.

FOURTH APPLICANT: I said thank you.

[INTERVIEWERS *stand on their seats and say the following as if one person were speaking.*]

FIRST INTERVIEWER: Do you

SECOND INTERVIEWER: speak any

THIRD INTERVIEWER: foreign

FOURTH INTERVIEWER: languages?

FIRST INTERVIEWER: Have you

SECOND INTERVIEWER: got a

THIRD INTERVIEWER: college

FOURTH INTERVIEWER: education?

FIRST INTERVIEWER: Do you

SECOND INTERVIEWER: take

THIRD INTERVIEWER: shorthand?

FOURTH INTERVIEWER: Have you

FIRST INTERVIEWER: any

SECOND INTERVIEWER: special

THIRD INTERVIEWER: qualifications?

FIRST INTERVIEWER: Yes?

FIRST APPLICANT: [*Stepping up to* INTERVIEWERS.] Sure, I can speak Italian, I said. My whole family is Italian so I oughta be able to, and I can match colors, like green to green, so that even your own mother couldn't tell the difference, begging your pardon, I said, I went through the eighth grade. [*Steps back.*]

SECOND INTERVIEWER: Next.

SECOND APPLICANT: [*Stepping up to Interviewers.*] My grandmother taught me some Gaelic, I told the guy. And my old man could rattle off in Yiddish when he had a load on. I never went to school at all excepting church school, but I can write my name good and clear. Also, I said, I can smell an Irishman or a Yid a hundred miles off. [*Steps back.*]

THIRD INTERVIEWER: Next.

THIRD APPLICANT: [*Stepping up to* INTERVIEWERS.] I've never had any need to take shorthand in my position, I said to him. I've a Z.A. in business administration from Philadelphia, and a Z.Z.A. from M.Y.U. night school. I mentioned that I speak a little Spanish, of course, and that I'm a whiz at model frigates and warships. [*Steps back.*]

FOURTH INTERVIEWER: Next.

FOURTH APPLICANT: [*Stepping up to* INTERVIEWERS.] I can sew a straight seam, I said, hand or machine, and I have been exclusively a lady's maid although I CAN cook and will too if I have someone to assist me, I said. Unfortunately, aside from self-education, grammar school is as far as I have progressed. [*Steps back.*]

[*Each* INTERVIEWER, *during his next speech, bows or curtsies to the* APPLICANT *nearest him.*]

FIRST INTERVIEWER: Good.

SECOND INTERVIEWER: Fine.

THIRD INTERVIEWER: Very helpful.

FOURTH INTERVIEWER: Thank you.

[*Each* APPLICANT, *during his next speech, jumps on the back of the* INTERVIEWER *nearest him.*]

FOURTH APPLICANT: You're welcome, I'm sure.

THIRD APPLICANT: Anything you want to know.

SECOND APPLICANT: Just ask me.

FIRST APPLICANT: Fire away, fire away.

[*The next eight speeches are spoken simultaneously, with* APPLICANTS *on* INTERVIEWERS' *backs.*]

FIRST INTERVIEWER: Well unless there's anything special you want to tell me, I think—

SECOND INTERVIEWER: Is there anything more you think I should know about before you—

THIRD INTERVIEWER: I wonder if we've left anything out of this questionnaire or if you—

FOURTH INTERVIEWER: I suppose I've got all the information down here unless you can—

FIRST APPLICANT: I've got kids to support, you know, and I need a job real quick—

SECOND APPLICANT: Do you think you could try and get me something today because I—

THIRD APPLICANT: How soon do you suppose I can expect to hear from your agency? Do you—

FOURTH APPLICANT: I don't like to sound pressureful, but you know I'm currently on unemploy—

[Each APPLICANT, during his next speech, jumps off INTERVIEWER's back.]

FIRST APPLICANT: Beggin' your pardon.

SECOND APPLICANT: So sorry.

THIRD APPLICANT: Excuse me.

FOURTH APPLICANT: Go ahead.

[Each INTERVIEWER, during his next speech, bows or curtsies and remains in that position.]

FIRST INTERVIEWER: That's quite all right.

SECOND INTERVIEWER: I'm sorry.

THIRD INTERVIEWER: I'm sorry.

FOURTH INTERVIEWER: My fault.

[Each APPLICANT, during his next speech, begins leap-frogging over INTERVIEWERS' backs.]

FIRST APPLICANT: My fault.

SECOND APPLICANT: My fault.

THIRD APPLICANT: I'm sorry.

FOURTH APPLICANT: My fault.

[Each INTERVIEWER, during his next speech, begins leap-frogging too.]

FIRST INTERVIEWER: That's all right.

SECOND INTERVIEWER: My fault.

THIRD INTERVIEWER: I'm sorry.

FOURTH INTERVIEWER: Excuse me.

[The leap-frogging continues as the preceding eight lines are repeated simultaneously. Then the INTERVIEWERS confer in a huddle and come out of it.]

FIRST INTERVIEWER: Do you enjoy your work?

FIRST APPLICANT: Sure, I said, I'm proud. Why not? Sure I know I'm no Rembrandt, I said, but I'm proud of my work, I said to him.

SECOND APPLICANT: I told him it stinks. But what am I supposed to do, sit home and rot?

THIRD APPLICANT: Do I like my work, he asked me. Well, I said, to gain time, do I like my work? Well, I said, I don't know.

FOURTH APPLICANT: I told him right straight out: for a sensible person, a lady's maid is the ONLY POSSIBLE way of life.

SECOND INTERVIEWER: Do you think you're irreplaceable?

ALL APPLICANTS: Oh, yes indeed.

ALL INTERVIEWERS: Irreplaceable?

ALL APPLICANTS: Yes, yes indeed.

THIRD INTERVIEWER: Do you like me?

FIRST APPLICANT: You're a nice man.

SECOND APPLICANT: Huh?

THIRD APPLICANT: Why do you ask?

FOURTH APPLICANT: It's not a question of LIKE.

FIRST INTERVIEWER: Well, we'll be in touch with you.

[This is the beginning of leaving the the agency. Soft music under. APPLICANTS and INTERVIEWERS push their seats into two masses of four boxes, one on each side of the stage. APPLICANTS leave first, joining hands to form a revolving door.

All are now leaving the agency, not in any orderly fashion. INTERVIEWERS start down one of the subway stairs at the back of the stage and APPLICANTS start down the other. The following speeches overlap and are heard indistinctly as crowd noise.]

FOURTH INTERVIEWER: What sort of day will it be?

FIRST APPLICANT: I bet we'll have rain.

SECOND APPLICANT: Cloudy, clearing in the afternoon.

THIRD APPLICANT: Mild, I think, with some snow.

FOURTH APPLICANT: Precisely the same as yesterday.

SECOND APPLICANT: Can you get me one?

FIRST INTERVIEWER: See you tomorrow.

THIRD APPLICANT: When will I hear from you?

SECOND INTERVIEWER: We'll let you know.

FOURTH APPLICANT: Where's my umbrella?

THIRD INTERVIEWER: I'm going to a movie.

FIRST APPLICANT: So how about it?

FOURTH INTERVIEWER: Good night.

THIRD APPLICANT: Can you help me, Doctor, I asked.

[When all of the actors are offstage, the FOURTH INTERVIEWER makes a siren sound and the following speeches continue from downstairs as a loud crowd noise for a few moments; they overlap so that the stage is empty only briefly.]

FIRST INTERVIEWER: It'll take a lot of work on your part.

SECOND INTERVIEWER: I'll do what I can for you.

THIRD INTERVIEWER: Of course I'll do my best.

FIRST INTERVIEWER: God helps those who help themselves.

FIRST APPLICANT: I have sinned deeply, Father, I said.

FIRST INTERVIEWER: You certainly have. I hope you truly repent.

SECOND INTERVIEWER: In the name of the Father, etcetera, and the Holy Ghost.

THIRD INTERVIEWER: Jesus saves.

FOURTH APPLICANT: I said can you direct me to Fourteenth Street, please?

FIRST INTERVIEWER: Just walk down that way a bit and then turn left.

SECOND INTERVIEWER: Just walk down that way a bit and then turn right.

THIRD INTERVIEWER: Take a cab!

FOURTH APPLICANT: Do you hear a siren?

ALL INTERVIEWERS: What time is it?

FIRST APPLICANT: Half-past three.

SECOND APPLICANT: It must be about four.

THIRD APPLICANT: Half-past five.

FOURTH APPLICANT: My watch has stopped.

FIRST INTERVIEWER: Do you enjoy your work?

SECOND INTERVIEWER: Do you think you're irreplaceable?

THIRD INTERVIEWER: Do you like me?

[The actor who played the FOURTH INTERVIEWER comes on stage while continuing to make the loud siren noise. The actress who played the FOURTH APPLICANT comes on stage and speaks directly to the audience.]

FOURTH APPLICANT: Can you direct me to Fourteenth Street, please, I said. I seem to have lost my—I started to say, and then I was nearly run down.

[The remaining actors return to the stage to play various people on Fourteenth Street: ladies shopping, a panhandler, a man in a sandwich board, a peddler of "franks and orange," a snooty German couple, a lecher, a pair of sighing lovers, and so on. The actors walk straight forward toward the audience and then walk backwards to the rear of the stage. Each time they approach the audience, they do so as a different character. The actor will need to find the essential vocal and physical mannerisms of each character, play them, and help them immediately to assume another character. The FOURTH APPLICANT continues to address the audience directly, to involve them in her hysteria, going up the aisle and back.]

FOURTH APPLICANT: I haven't got my Social Security—I started to say, I saw someone right in front of me and I said, could you direct me please to Fourteenth Street, I have to get to Fourteenth Street, please, to get a bargain, I explained, although I could hardly remember what it was I wanted to buy. I read about it in the paper today, I said, only they weren't listening and I said to myself, my purpose for today is to get to—and I couldn't remember, I've set myself the task of—I've got to have—it's that I can save, I remembered, I can save if I can get that bargain at—and I couldn't remember where it was so I started to look for my wallet which I seem to have mislaid in my purse, and a man—please watch where you're going, I shouted with my purse half-open, and I seemed to forget—Fourteenth Street, I remembered, and you'd think with all these numbered streets and avenues a person wouldn't get lost—you'd think a person would HELP a person, you'd think so. So I asked the most respectable looking man I could find, I asked him, please can you direct me to Fourteenth Street. He wouldn't answer. Just wouldn't. I'm lost, I said to myself. The paper said—the television said—they said, I couldn't remember what they said. I turned for help: "Jesus Saves" the sign said, and a man was carrying it, both sides of his body, staring straight ahead. "Jesus Saves" the sign said.

[*The passers-by jostle her more and more.*]

FOURTH APPLICANT: I couldn't remember where I was going. "Come and be saved" it said, so I asked the man with the sign, please, sir, won't you tell me how to, dear Lord, I thought, anywhere, please, sir, won't you tell me how to—can you direct me to Fourteenth Street, PLEASE!

[*The passers-by have covered the FOURTH APPLICANT. All actors mill about until they reach designated positions on the stage where they face the audience, a line of women and a line of men, students in a gym class. The SECOND INTERVIEWER has stayed coolly out of the crowd during this last; now he is the Gym Instructor.*]

GYM INSTRUCTOR: I took my last puff and strode resolutely into the room. Ready men, I asked brightly. And one and two and three and four and one and two and keep it up.

[*The GYM INSTRUCTOR is trying to help his students mold themselves into the kind of people seen in advertisements and the movies. As he counts to four the students puff out their chests, smile, and look perfectly charming. As he counts to four again, the students relax and look ordinary.*]

GYM INSTRUCTOR: You wanna look like the guys in the movies, don't you, I said to the fellahs. Keep it up then. You wanna radiate that kinda charm and confidence they have in the movies, don't you, I said to the girls. Keep it up then, stick 'em out, that's what you got 'em for. Don't be ashamed. All of you, tuck in your butts, I said loudly. That's the ticket, I said, wishing to hell I had a cigarette. You're selling, selling all the time, that right, miss? Keep on selling, I said. And one and two and three and four and ever see that guy on TV, I said. What's his name, I asked them. What's his name? Aw, you know his name, I said, forgetting his name. Never mind, it'll come to you, I said. He comes in here too. See that, I said, grabbing a guy out of line and showing 'em his muscle. See that line, I said, making the guy feel good, know what that is? It's boyishness, I said. You come here, I said, throwing him back into the line, and it'll renew your youthfulness, I said, taking a deep breath. And one and two and three and four and smile, I said,

smiling. Not so big, I said, smiling less. You look like creeps, I said, when you smile that big. When you smile, hold something back. Make like you're holding back something big, I said, a secret, I said. That's the ticket. And one and two and three and four and . . . [*Accelerating the rhythm to a double count.*] Anybody got a cigarette, I said suddenly, without thinking. I was just kidding, I said then, sheepishly. One and two and three and four, I said, wishing I had a cigarette. And one and two and three and four . . .

[*The rapid movements of the gym class become the vibrations of passengers on a moving subway train. The actors rush to the boxes stage left, continuing to vibrate. Two of the actors stand on the boxes and smile like subway advertisements while the others, directly in front of them, are pushed against each other on the crowded train. They make an appropriate soft subway noise, a kind of rhythmic hiss and, as the subway passengers, form their faces into frozen masks of indifference.*]

SECOND APPLICANT: [*Squeezing her way to an uncomfortable front seat and speaking half to herself.*] God forgive me . . . you no-good chump, I said to him, I used to love you . . . not now. Not now . . . God forgive me . . . God forgive me for being old. Not now, I said. I wouldn't wipe the smell off your uncle's bottom now, not for turnips, no. God forgive me . . . Remember how we used to ride the roller coaster out at Coney Island, you and me? Remember? Holding hands in the cold and I'd get so scared and you'd get so scared and we'd hug each other and buy another ticket . . . Remember? . . . Look now, I said. Look at me now! God forgive you for leaving me with nothing . . . God forgive you for being dead . . . God forgive me for being alive . . .

[*The actress who played the THIRD INTERVIEWER slips out of the subway as though it were her stop and sits on a box, stage right, as a TELEPHONE OPERATOR. The other actors form a telephone circuit by holding hands in two concentric circles around the boxes, stage left; they change the hissing sound of the subway into the whistling of telephone circuits.*]

TELEPHONE OPERATOR: Just one moment and I will connect you with Information.

[*The* TELEPHONE OPERATOR *alternates her official voice with her ordinary voice; she uses the latter when she talks to her friend Roberta, another operator whom she reaches by flipping a switch. When she is talking to Roberta, the whistling of the telephone circuit changes into a different rhythm and the arms of the actors, which are forming the circuit, move into a different position.*]

TELEPHONE OPERATOR: Just one moment and I will connect you with Information. Ow! Listen, Roberta, I said, I've got this terible cramp. Hang up and dial again, please; we find nothing wrong with that number at all. You know what I ate, I said to her, you were there. Baked macaroni, Wednesday special, maple-nut fudge, I said. I'm sorry but the number you have reached is not—I can feel it gnawing at me at the bottom of my belly, I told her. Do you think it's serious, Roberta? Appendicitis? I asked. Thank you for giving us the area code but the number you have reached is not in this area. Roberta, I asked her, do you think I have cancer? One moment, please, I'm sorry the number you have reached—ow! Well, if it's lunch, Roberta, I said to her, you know what they can do with it tomorrow. Ow! One moment, please, I said. Ow, I said, Roberta, I said, it really hurts.

[*The* TELEPHONE OPERATOR *falls off her seat in pain. The whistling of the telephone circuit becomes a siren. Three actors carry the* TELEPHONE OPERATOR *over to the boxes, stage left, which now serve as an operating table. Three actors imitate the* TELEPHONE OPERATOR's *breathing pattern while four actors behind her make stylized sounds and movements as surgeons and nurses in the midst of an operation. The* TELEPHONE OPERATOR's *breathing accelerates, then stops. After a moment the actors begin spreading over the stage and making the muted sounds of a cocktail party: music, laughter, talk. The actors find a position and remain there, playing various aspects of a party in slow motion and muted tones. They completely ignore the* FIRST INTERVIEWER *who, as a* GIRL AT THE PARTY, *goes from person to person as if she were in a garden of living statues.*]

GIRL AT THE PARTY: [*Rapidly and excitedly.*] And then after the ambulance took off I went up in the elevator and into the party. Did you see the accident, I asked, and they said they did, and what did he look like, and I said he wore a brown coat and had straight brown hair. He stepped off the curb right in front of me. We had been walking up the same block, he a few feet ahead of me, this block right here, I said, but she wasn't listening. Hi, my name is Jill, I said to somebody sitting down and they looked at me and smiled so I said his arm was torn out of its socket and his face was on the pavement gasping but I didn't touch him and she smiled and walked away and I said after her, you aren't supposed to touch someone before—I WANTED to help, I said, but she wasn't listening. When a man came up and said was it someone you knew and I said yes, it was someone I knew slightly, someone I knew, yes, and he offered me a drink and I said no thanks, I didn't want one, and he said well how well did I know him, and I said I knew him well, yes, I knew him very well. You were coming together to the party, he said. Yes, I said, excuse me. Hi, my name is Jill, did you hear a siren, and they said oh you're the one who saw it, was he killed? [*Becoming resigned to the fact that no one is listening.*] And I said yes I was, excuse me, and went back across the room but couldn't find another face to talk to until I deliberately bumped into somebody because I had to tell them one of us couldn't come because of the accident. It was Jill. Jill couldn't come. I'm awfully sorry, I said, because of the accident. She had straight brown hair, I said, and was wearing a brown coat, and two or three people looked at me strangely and moved off. I'm sorry, I said to a man, and I laughed, and moved off. I'm dead, I said to several people and started to push them over, I'm dead, thank you, I said, thank you, please, I said, I'm dead, until two or three of them got hold of my arms and hustled me out. I'm sorry, I said, I couldn't come because of the accident. I'm sorry. Excuse me.

[*The* GIRL AT THE PARTY *is lowered to the floor by two of the men and then all fall down except the actor who played the* FOURTH INTERVIEWER. *He remains seated as a* PSYCHIATRIST. *The*

THIRD APPLICANT, *on the floor, props his head up on his elbow and speaks to the audience.*]

THIRD APPLICANT: Can you help me, Doctor, I asked him.

[*The* PSYCHIATRIST *crosses his legs and assumes a professional expression.*]

THIRD APPLICANT: Well, it started, well it started, I said, when I was sitting in front of the television set with my feet on the coffee table. Now I've sat there hundreds of times, thousands maybe, with a can of beer in my hand. I like to have a can of beer in my hand when I watch the beer ads. But now for no reason I can think of, the ad was making me sick. So I used the remote control to get to another channel, but each channel made me just as sick. The television was one thing and I was a person, and I was going to be sick. So I turned it off and had a panicky moment. I smelled the beer in my hand and as I vomited I looked around the living room for something to grab on to, something to look at, but there was just our new furniture. I tried to get a hold of myself. I tried to stare straight ahead above the television set, at a little spot on the wall I know. I've had little moments like that before, Doctor, I said, panicky little moments like that when the earth seems to slip out from under, and everything whirls around and you try to hold onto something, some object, some thought, but I couldn't think of anything. Later the panic went away, I told him, it went away, and I'm much better now. But I don't feel like doing anything anymore, except sit and stare at the wall. I've lost my job. Katherine thought I should come and see you. Can you help me, Doctor, I asked him.

PSYCHIATRIST:

Blah, blah, blah, blah, blah, blah, HOS-
TILE.
Blah, blah, blah, blah, blah, blah,
PENIS.
Blah, blah, blah, blah, blah, blah,
MOTHER.
[*Holding out his hand.*]
Blah, blah, blah, blah, blah, blah,
MONEY.

[*The* THIRD APPLICANT *takes the* PSY-
CHIATRIST's *hand and gets up, extending his left hand to the next actor. This
begins a grand right and left with all*

the actors all over the stage.]

ALL: [*Chanting as they do the grand right and left.*]

Blah, blah, blah, blah, blah, blah, HOS-
TILE.
Blah, blah, blah, blah, blah, blah,
PENIS.
Blah, blah, blah, blah, blah, blah,
MOTHER.
Blah, blah, blah, blah, blah, blah,
MONEY.
Blah, blah, blah, blah, blah, blah, HOS-
TILE.
Blah, blah, blah, blah, blah, blah,
PENIS.
Blah, blah, blah, blah, blah, blah,
MOTHER.
Blah, blah, blah, blah, blah, blah,
MONEY.

[*Forming couples and locking hands with arms crossed, continuing to move, but in a smaller circle.*]

Blah, blah, blah, blah, blah, blah, blah.
Blah, blah, blah, blah, blah, blah, blah.

[*Now they slow down to the speed of a church procession. The women bow their heads, letting their hair fall forward over their faces. The "blah, blah, blah" continues, but much more slowly while some of the women accompany it with a descant of "Kyrie Eleison." After they have gone around in a circle once this way, the actor who played the* FOURTH INTERVIEWER *sits with his back to the audience as a Priest. The* FIRST APPLICANT *kneels next to him, facing the audience as if in a confessional booth. The other six actors are at the back of the stage in two lines, swaying slightly, heads down. The women are in front with their hair still over their faces.*]

FIRST APPLICANT: [*Crosses himself perfunctorily and starting to speak; his manner is not impassioned; it is clear that he comes regularly to repeat this always fruitless ritual.*] Can you help me, Father, I said, as I usually do, and he said, as usual, nothing. I'm your friend, the housepainter, I said, the good housepainter. Remember me, Father? He continued, as usual, to say nothing. Almost the only color you get to paint these days, Father, I said, is white. Only

white, Father, I said, not expecting any more
from him than usual, but going on anyway.
The color I really like to paint, Father, is
red, I said. Pure brick red. Now there's a
confession, Father. He said nothing. I'd like
to take a trip to the country, Father, I said,
and paint a barn door red, thinking that
would get a rise out of him, but it didn't.
God, I said then, deliberately taking the
Lord's name in vain, the result of taking a
three-inch brush and lightly kissing a coat
of red paint on a barn door is something
stunning and beautiful to behold. He still
said nothing. Father, I said, springing it on
him, Father, I'd like to join a monastery.
My wife's sister, she could take care of the
kids. Still nothing. Father, I said again, I'd
like to join a monastery. Can you help me,
Father? Nothing. Father, I said, I've tried
lots of things in my life, I've gone in a lot
of different directions, Father, and none of
them seems any better than any other,
Father, I said. Can you help me, Father, I
said. But he said nothing as usual, and
then, as usual, I went away.

[*The* FIRST APPLICANT *and the* FOURTH
INTERVIEWER, *who haven't moved at
all during the confession, move upstage
to join the others as the music starts
up violently in a rock beat. The actors
do a rock version of the Virginia reel.*]

SECOND INTERVIEWER: [*Loudly.*] My
[*All bow to partners.*]

FOURTH APPLICANT: [*Loudly.*] fault.
[*All dos-à-dos.*]

SECOND APPLICANT: [*Loudly.*] Excuse
[*All circle around.*]

FOURTH INTERVIEWER: [*Loudly.*] me.
[*All peel off.*]

FIRST INTERVIEWER: [*Loudly.*] Can you
SECOND APPLICANT: [*Loudly.*] help
FIRST APPLICANT: [*Loudly.*] me?
FOURTH INTERVIEWER: [*Loudly.*] Next.

[*All continue dancing, joining hands at
the center to form a revolving door
again. They repeat the preceding eight
speeches. Then the* SECOND INTER-
VIEWER *speaks rapidly, as a* SQUARE
DANCE CALLER.]

SQUARE DANCE CALLER: Step right up,
ladies and gents, and shake the hand of the
next governor of this state. Shake his hand
and say hello. Tell your friends you shook
the hand of the next governor of the state.
Step right up and shake his hand. Ask him

questions. Tell him problems. Say hello.
Step right up, shake his hand, shake the
hand, ladies and gents, of the next governor of the state. Tell your folks: I shook
his hand. When he's famous you'll be proud.
Step right up, ladies and gents, and shake
his hand. Ask him questions. Tell him problems. Say hello. Step right up, ladies and
gents. Don't be shy. Shake the hand of
the next governor of this state.

[*The actors have formed a crowd,
downstage right, facing the audience.
They give the impression of being but a
few of a great number of people, all
trying to squeeze to the front to see
and speak to the political candidate.
The* FOURTH INTERVIEWER, *now a*
POLITICIAN, *stands on a box, stage left,
facing the audience. The* SECOND IN-
TERVIEWER *stands by the crowd and
keeps it in order.*]

POLITICIAN: Thank you very much, I
said cheerfully, and good luck to you, I said,
turning my smile to the next one.

[*The* FIRST INTERVIEWER, *panting as
the* GIRL AT THE PARTY, *squeezes out
of the crowd and rushes up to the*
POLITICIAN, *who smiles at her benign-
ly.*]

POLITICIAN: Our children ARE our most
important asset, I agreed earnestly. Yes they
are, I said solemnly. Children, I said, with
a long pause, are our most important asset.
I only wish I could, madame, I said earnestly, standing tall, but rats, I said regretfully,
are a city matter.

[*The* FIRST INTERVIEWER *returns to
the crowd while the* THIRD INTERVIEW-
ER, *as the* TELEPHONE OPERATOR,
rushes up to the POLITICIAN. *She ap-
peals to him, making the same noise
she made when her stomach hurt her.*]

POLITICIAN: Nobody knows more about
red tape than I do, I said knowingly, and I
wish you luck, I said, turning my smile to
the next one.

[*The* THIRD INTERVIEWER *returns to
the crowd and the* FOURTH APPLICANT
goes up to the POLITICIAN.]

POLITICIAN: I certainly will, I said, with
my eyes sparkling, taking a pencil out of
my pocket. And what's your name, I said,
looking at her sweetly and signing my name
at the same time. That's a lovely name, I
said.

[*The* FOURTH APPLICANT *returns to the crowd while the* THIRD APPLICANT, *as an* OLDER MAN, *shakes the* POLITICIAN's *hand.*]

POLITICIAN: Yes sir, I said, those were the days. And good luck to you, sir, I said respectfully but heartily, and look out for the curb, I said, turning my smile to the next one.

[*The* THIRD APPLICANT *returns to the crowd and the* SECOND APPLICANT *approaches the* POLITICIAN.]

POLITICIAN: Indeed yes, the air we breathe is foul, I said indignantly. I agree with you entirely, I said wholeheartedly. And if my opponent wins it's going to get worse, I said with conviction. We'd all die within ten years, I said. And good luck to you, madame, I said politely, and turned my smile to the next one.

[*The* FIRST APPLICANT *approaches him, his cap in his hand.*]

POLITICIAN: Well, I said confidingly, getting a bill through the legislature is easier said than done, and answering violence, I said warningly, with violence, I said earnestly, is not the answer, and how do you do, I said, turning my smile to the next one.

[*Next, two* SIGHING LOVERS—*we saw them on Fourteenth Street—played by the* FIRST *and* SECOND INTERVIEWERS, *approach the* POLITICIAN.]

POLITICIAN: No, I said, I never said my opponent would kill us all. No, I said, I never said that. May the best man win, I said manfully.

[*Half-hearted cheers. The* FIRST *and* SECOND INTERVIEWERS *return to the crowd.*]

POLITICIAN: I do feel, I said without false modesty, that I'm better qualified in the field of foreign affairs than my opponents are, yes, I said, BUT, I said, with a pause for emphasis, foreign policy is the business of the President, not the Governor, therefore I will say nothing about the war, I said with finality.

[*The crowd makes a restive sound, then freezes.*]

POLITICIAN: Do you want us shaking hands, I asked the photographer, turning my profile to the left. Goodbye, I said cheerfully, and good luck to you too.

[*The crowd makes a louder protest, then freezes.*]

POLITICIAN: I'm sorry, I said seriously, but I'll have to study that question a good deal more before I can answer it.

[*The crowd makes an angry noise, then freezes.*]

POLITICIAN: Of course, I said frowning, we must all support the President, I said as I turned concernedly to the next one.

[*The crowd makes a very angry sound, then freezes.*]

POLITICIAN: I'm sorry about the war, I said. Nobody could be sorrier than I am, I said sorrowfully. But I'm afraid, I said gravely, that there are no easy answers. [*Smiles, pleased with himself.*] Good luck to you too, I said cheerfully, and turned my smile to the next one.

[*The Politician topples from his box, beginning his speech all over again. Simultaneously, all the other actors lurch about the stage, speaking again in character: the* SHOPPER ON FOURTEENTH STREET, *the* GYM INSTRUCTOR, *the* SUBWAY RIDER, *the* TELEPHONE OPERATOR, *the* GIRL AT THE PARTY, *the* ANALYSAND, *and the* HOUSEPAINTER. *Simultaneously, they all stop and freeze, continue again, freeze again, then continue with music under. The* SECOND INTERVIEWER, *acting as policeman, begins to line them up in a diagonal line, like marching dolls, one behind the other. As they are put into line they begin to move their mouths without sound, like fish in a tank. The music stops. When all are in line the* SECOND INTERVIEWER *joins them.*]

SECOND INTERVIEWER: My
FOURTH APPLICANT: fault.
SECOND APPLICANT: Excuse
FOURTH INTERVIEWER: me.
FIRST INTERVIEWER: Can you
SECOND APPLICANT: help
FIRST APPLICANT: me?
FOURTH INTERVIEWER: Next.

[*All continue marching in place, moving their mouths, and shouting their lines as the lights come slowly down.*]

SECOND INTERVIEWER: My
FOURTH APPLICANT: fault.
SECOND APPLICANT: Excuse
FOURTH INTERVIEWER: me.
FIRST INTERVIEWER: Can you
SECOND APPLICANT: help
FIRST APPLICANT: me?
FOURTH INTERVIEWER: Next.

TV
Niblock/Bough, Fundamental Photographs

TV

The youth Narcissus mistook his own reflection in the water for another person . . . He was numb. He had adapted to his extension of himself and had become a closed system.

MARSHALL MC LUHAN

THE CAST:

HAL.

SUSAN.

GEORGE.

An Actress plays HELEN FARGIS, THE PRESIDENT'S WIFE, A UGP RESEARCHER, A MEMBER OF THE ROCK AND ROLL GROUP, A PEACE MARCHER, LILY HEAVEN, THE HEADACHE SUFFERER, A SINGER IN THE EVANGELIST CHOIR, and MOTHER in "My Favorite Teenager"

An Actor plays HARRY FARGIS, FIRST NEWS ANNOUNCER, STEVE, THE PRESIDENT, A UGP RESEARCHER, A MEMBER OF THE ROCK AND ROLL GROUP, WEATHER ANNOUNCER, HE in the Billion Dollar Movie, EVANGELIST, and FATHER in "My Favorite Teenager"

An Actor plays WONDERBOY, SECOND NEWS ANNOUNCER, THE MAN IN THE CIGARETTE COMMERCIAL, BILL, UGP ANNOUNCER, A MEMBER OF THE ROCK AND ROLL GROUP, ONE YOUNG MAN FROM NEW YORK CITY, LILY HEAVEN'S ANNOUNCER, RON CAMPBELL, JOHNNY HOLLAND, and A SINGER IN THE EVANGELIST CHOIR

An Actress plays THE WOMAN IN THE CIGARETTE COMMERCIAL, THE PRESIDENT'S OLDER DAUGHTER, A UGP RESEARCHER, A MEMBER OF THE ROCK AND ROLL GROUP, A PEACE MARCHER, FAMOUS TELEVISION PERSONALITY, CAROL, SHE in the Billion Dollar Movie, and A SINGER IN THE EVANGELIST CHOIR

An Actress plays SALLY, THE PRESIDENT'S YOUNGER DAUGHTER, THE SPANISH TEACHER, A UGP RESEARCHER, A MEMBER OF THE ROCK AND ROLL GROUP, ANNIE KAPPELHOFF, LADY ANNOUNCER, LUCI, A SINGER IN THE EVANGELIST CHOIR, and DAUGHTER in "My Favorite Teenager"

The set is white and impersonal. There are two doors on the stage right wall: one leads to the rest rooms, the other to the hall.
Downstage right is the control console in a television viewing room. It faces the audience.
Above the console, also facing the audience, is a screen. Projected on it, from the rear, is the logo of a television station.
Downstage left is a water cooler, a closet for coats, and a telephone.
Downstage right is a bulletin board. Upstage center is a table with a coffee maker on it.
HAL and SUSAN are seated at the console, SUSAN in the middle chair. They are both in their twenties. HAL is playing, as he often will, with his penknife: whittling pencils, paring his nails, or throwing it at the bulletin board. SUSAN is involved with the papers on the console, with sharpening pencils, and so forth.

At the back of the stage, on the left, are the five actors who will portray what will appear on television. For the moment they have no light on them and their backs are to the audience.

To indicate the correlation of the events and dialogue on television with those which occur in the viewing room, the play is printed in two columns.

HAL: So what do you say?

SUSAN: I don't know.

HAL: That doesn't get us very far, does it?

SUSAN: Well it's such a surprise, your asking. I was planning to work on my apartment.

HAL: I'll help you, after the movie.

SUSAN: That's too late. One thing I have to have is eight hours' sleep. I really have to have that.

[GEORGE *enters: he is older than* HAL *and* SUSAN, *and is in charge of the viewing room.*]

HAL: Hi, George.

SUSAN: Hello, George.

GEORGE: [*To* SUSAN.] Is that a new dress?

SUSAN: [*Nodding toward* HAL.] He didn't even notice.

[GEORGE *puts his coat and jacket in the closet and puts on a cardigan sweater.*]

GEORGE: How many check marks have you made, Hal?

HAL: I don't know, George. I don't count.

SUSAN: I got it on Fourteenth Street. I love going into places like that because they're so cheap.

GEORGE: If you don't make at least a hundred check marks, they'll dock you. That's what the totals count column is for.

SUSAN: [*Looking at herself in a mirror.*] Have I lost any weight?

GEORGE: Where would you lose it from?

HAL: George, how come they haven't asked us for a detailed report in nearly three weeks?

GEORGE: How should I know?

HAL: Think they're forgetting about us, George?

SUSAN: I was trying to tell in the Ladies, but the fluorescent light in there just burns your eyes.

HAL: I've never been to the Ladies. You think I'd like it?

GEORGE: This viewing room is the backbone of the rating system.

HAL: He said that to you LAST month, George. Things move fast.

GEORGE: Are you trying to make me nervous?

HAL: Maybe.

GEORGE: Well don't, because my stomach is not very good this morning.

SUSAN: I want to know seriously, and I mean seriously, do you think I've lost any weight?

GEORGE: Where from?

HAL: Why don't you let yourself go?

SUSAN: What do you mean?

HAL: Just let nature take its course.

SUSAN: What if nature wants you to be a big fat slob?

HAL: Then be a big fat slob.

SUSAN: Thanks.

[HAL, SUSAN, *and* GEORGE *sit down and get ready for the day's work.* GEORGE *turns a dial on the console which turns on TV. Two of the People On Television turn around to play* HELEN *and* HARRY FARGIS.

All of the People On Television are dressed in shades of gray. They make no costume changes and use no real props. Their faces are made up with thin horizontal black lines to suggest the way they might appear to a viewer. They are playing television images. Their style of acting is cool, not pushy. As television characters, they have only a few facial masks, such as "cute," "charming," or "serious," which they use infallibly, like signals, in the course of each television segment.

After each television segment, the People involved in it will freeze where they are until it is time for them to become another character.

As the play progresses, the People On Television will use more and more of the stage. The impressions should be that of a slow invasion of the viewing room. HAL, SUSAN, *and* GEORGE *will simply move around the People On Television when that becomes necessary. Ultimately, the control console itself will be taken over by television characters, so that the distinction between what is on television and what is occurring in the viewing room will be lost completely.*

The attention of the audience should be focused not on a parody of television, but on the relationship of the life that appears on television to the life that goes on in the viewing room.

All of the actors will need to be constantly aware of what is happening on all parts of the stage, in order to give and take the attention of the audience to and from each other, and also in order to demonstrate the influence of the style of certain television segments on the behavior of HAL, SUSAN, *and* GEORGE.]

HAL: Why try to look like somebody else?

[*Slide on screen: Wonderboy's face.*]
[HELEN *and* HARRY FARGIS *are at home.* HELEN *is baking cookies.*]

HELEN: Harry, what are you working on in the garage?

SUSAN: I'm trying to look like myself, thin. Very thin.

HAL: [*Offering him one.*] Want a cigarette, George?
GEORGE: No, thanks.

HAL: Just one?
GEORGE: No.

SUSAN: Hal, why don't you try to help George instead of being so cruel?

HAL: I'm just offering him a cigarette.

GEORGE: [*As* HAL *takes the cigarette away.*] Give me one.
SUSAN: Hal, that's utter torture for George.

GEORGE: Give me one.

SUSAN: Don't, George. He's just playing cat and mouse.

HAL: That's right, George. Don't have one. I'm just playing cat and mouse. [*Lights a cigarette.*]

GEORGE: Just give it to me, will you?

SUSAN: Try to control yourself for just another half hour, George.
GEORGE: No.

SUSAN: Why not?
GEORGE: Because I don't wanna control myself for just another half hour.
HAL: Whatever you want, George. [*Hands a cigarette to* GEORGE.]

HARRY: If I succeed in my experiments, nobody in the world will be hungry for love. Ever again.

HELEN: Hungry for love? Harry, you make me nervous.
HELEN: You really do.

HARRY: Men will put down their arms.

HELEN: You haven't been to work for a week now. You'll lose your job.

HARRY: You don't understand. This is more important.
HELEN: Oh, Harry. I don't understand you at all any more. I really don't.

[HARRY *goes back to the garage.* HELEN *mumbles to herself as she cleans up the kitchen.*]
HELEN: I don't know.

HELEN: I just don't know. He used to be so docile.

HELEN: And now I just don't know—
HARRY: [*Calling from garage.*] Helen!
HELEN: Harry?

HARRY: Helen, my experiments.
HELEN: Harry, what?

HARRY: A terrible mistake.
HELEN: Harry, your voice—

HARRY: [*His voice getting lower and gruffer.*] For the love of heaven, Helen, keep away from me.
HELEN: What happened?

HARRY: I can't restrain myself anymore. I'm coming through the garage door. [*Comes through the garage door, wearing a monster mask; his voice is now very deep and gruff.*] I'm irresistibly attracted to you, Helen, irresistibly.

HELEN: Eeeeeeeeeeeeeeeeeeeek!

HARRY: [*Stepping toward her.*] Helen, I love you. [*Goes to embrace her.*]

HELEN: Harry, you're hideous. Eeeeek! Eeeeeeeeeeeeek! Eeeeeeeeeeeeek!

[*As* HELEN *screams,* WONDERBOY *is discovered, in mufti, doing his homework.*]

SUSAN: What was the point of that, Hal?

HAL: No point.

WONDERBOY: Two superquantums plus five uranium neutrons, and I've got the mini-sub fuel. Hooray. Boy, will my friends in the U.S. Navy be pleased. Hey, what's that? Better use my wonder-vision. Helen Fargis seems to be in trouble. Better change to Wonderboy. [*As if throwing open his shirt.*] And fly over there in a flash. [*Jumping as if flying.*] I guess I'm in the nick of time. [*With one super-powerful punch in the jaw he subdues* HARRY, *the monster.*]

HELEN: Oh, Wonderboy, what would have happened if you hadn't come? But what will happen to IT?

WONDERBOY: I'll fly him to a distant zoo where they'll take good care of him.

HELEN: Oh, Wonderboy, how can I ever repay you?

SUSAN: The president of the company has an Eames chair.

WONDERBOY: Are those home-baked cookies I smell?

[HELEN *smiles at* WONDERBOY *through her tears; he puts his arm around her shoulders.*]

WONDERBOY: Tune in tomorrow, boys and girls, when I'll subdue a whole country full of monsters.

[*Slide: "Winners Eat Wondrex."*]

GEORGE: How do you know that?

WONDERBOY: And in the meantime, remember: winners eat Wondrex. [*Smiles and jumps in the air, as if flying away.*]

[*Slide: little girls with shopping bags.*]

SUSAN: Jennifer showed it to me.

GEORGE: You asked to see it?

SUSAN: Don't worry George. He wasn't there. I just had this crazy wild impulse as I was passing his office. I wanted to see what it looked like. Isn't that wild?

FIRST NEWS ANNOUNCER: Little girls with big shopping bags means back to school season is here again. Among the many shoppers in downtown New York were Darlene, nine, Lila, four, and Lucy Gladden, seven, of Lynbrook, Long Island.

[*Slide: the Vice President.*]

FIRST NEWS ANNOUNCER: In Washington, D.C., as he left John Foster Dulles Airport, as President Johnson's favorite.

[*Slide: second view of the Vice President.*]

HAL: Did you sit in it?

SUSAN: I didn't dare. What would I have said if he'd come in?
[GEORGE *goes to the rest room.*]

HAL: I love you, Mr. President of my great big company, and that's why I'm sitting in your nice warm leather arm chair.
SUSAN: You're perverted. I don't want to be a person working in a company who's never seen her president.

SUSAN: [*To Hal, who has gotten up.*] While you're up—
HAL: What?
SUSAN: You know. Get me a Coke. [*Titters at her own joke.*]
[HAL *goes out through the hall door.* GEORGE *returns from the rest room.*]

GEORGE: [*Turning TV sound off.*] Can I come over tonight?

SUSAN: Not tonight. [*Goes to bulletin board.*]

GEORGE: [*Following her.*] Why not tonight?
SUSAN: Because I don't feel like it.
GEORGE: You have a date?
SUSAN: What business is that of yours? Don't think because—
GEORGE: Who with?
SUSAN: None of your business.
GEORGE: What about late, after you get back, like one o'clock?
SUSAN: That's too late. I need lots of sleep.
GEORGE: I'll call first.
SUSAN: You'd better.
[*Whenever* HAL, SUSAN, *and* GEORGE *have nothing else to do, they stare straight ahead, as if at a television screen.* GEORGE *and* SUSAN *do this now.*

FIRST NEWS ANNOUNCER: Representative, the Vice President said he was bursting with confidence.
[*Slide: first view of Vietnamese mourners.*]

SECOND NEWS ANNOUNCER: U.S. spokesmen in Saigon said families would be given adequate shelter and compensation. Our planes are under strict orders not to return to base with any bombs. The United States regrets that a friendly village was hit. The native toll was estimated at sixty.
[*Slide: second view of Vietnamese mourners.*]

SECOND NEWS ANNOUNCER: This was high, explained spokesmen, in answer to questions, because of the type of bomb dropped. These are known as Lazy Dogs. Each Lazy Dog bomb contains ten thousand slivers of razor-sharp steel.
[*Slide: third view of Vietnamese mourners.*]
[*Volume off.*]
[*Slide: a pack of Longford cigarettes superimposed on a lake.*]
[*Two People On Television do a silent commercial for Longford cigarettes: a man lights a woman's cigarette and she looks pleased.*]

[*Slide on the screen: "The Endless Frontier."*]

HAL *comes back with two Cokes.*
GEORGE *goes to the telephone and dials
it.*]
GEORGE: Hello, dear. Yes, I'm here. Listen, I'm afraid I have to take the midnight to three shift.
[HAL *turns TV volume on.*]

GEORGE: I've got to. The night supervisor is out.

GEORGE: And I've already said I would.

GEORGE: Listen, let's talk about it over dinner, huh? I'll be out after you go to sleep and in before you wake up so what's the difference? Listen, let's talk about it over dinner, I said. Listen, I love you. Goodbye. [*Hangs up.*]
HAL: [*Watching TV intently but talking to* GEORGE.] You have to take the midnight to three shift, George? That's really too bad.

HAL: Got a call while I was out?

GEORGE: [*Snapping TV volume off.*] Do either of you want to take on some evening overtime this week?
SUSAN: Which?
GEORGE: Five to midnight Tuesday and Thursday.

HAL: Thursday.
SUSAN: Oh, all right, I'll take Tuesday.
HAL: Did you want Thursday?
SUSAN: I'd like to get the apartment finished.
HAL: Then give me Tuesday.
SUSAN: Not if you HAVE something on Thursday.
HAL: No sweat.
SUSAN: Oh, I know. It was that talk with that man.

[HAL *turns TV volume on.*]
GEORGE: [*Snapping TV volume off.*] What talk with what man?
SUSAN: A man he has to talk to.
GEORGE: About a job?
HAL: I probably won't even see him.

[SALLY *and* BILL *are two characters in the Western.*]

SALLY: Don't go, Bill.
BILL: I've got to.

SALLY: Oh, Bill.
[BILL *leaves.*]
SALLY: Oh, Bill.

[SALLY *fixes her hair in the mirror.*]

[SALLY *is surprised by* STEVE, *the villain, who has just been waiting for* BILL *to ride off.*]

SALLY: Steve!

STEVE: Bill's dead, Sally.
SALLY: I don't believe you.
[*Volume off.*]
[STEVE *tries to embrace* SALLY. *She slaps him hard as he approaches her. He tries it again. She slaps him again. He tries it a third time. She gets him a third time. Then he grabs and kisses her despite her terrible struggling.*]

[BILL, *his arm wounded, appears again. Seeing* STEVE *with* SALLY, *he draws and aims.*]
BILL: Sally, duck!
[*Volume off.*]

[SALLY *ducks.* BILL *shoots* STEVE, *then goes to* SALLY *to make sure she's all right.* STEVE, *however, is not badly wounded and he reaches for* BILL'S *gun. The gun falls to the floor and they fight.* SALLY *tries to get into the fight but is pushed away.*]

GEORGE: What kind of job?
HAL: For the government. I tell you I probably won't see him.
GEORGE: If you quit, Hal, I'll need three weeks' notice. If you care about severance pay.
HAL: [*Turning TV volume on.*] I haven't seen him yet, even.
GEORGE: Or about me.

HAL: I wasn't going to mention it.
SUSAN: I'm sorry. It was my fault.
GEORGE: [*Turning volume off.*] Just don't spring anything on me. If you don't like the job, leave. But don't spring anything on me because I can't take it, you know that.

HAL: George, I'm NOT quitting.
SUSAN: He likes this job too much, George.
HAL: I love it more than my own life. I wouldn't leave it for all the world. Honest Injun, George. [*Turns volume on.*]

GEORGE: Can you imagine what I'd have to go through to train another person? Can you?

SUSAN: Listen, I just remembered a joke. There's this writing on the subway. "I love grills" it says on the wall. So somebody crosses out "grills" and writes in "girls." "I love girls" it says now. And then somebody else writes in, "What about us grills?" [*Laughs and laughs over this.*]

SUSAN: What about us grills? Isn't that fantastic?

HAL: What's the matter with you?

SUSAN: [*Still laughing.*] I think that's the funniest thing I ever heard.
HAL: Shhhh.

[BILL *is losing his fight with* STEVE *because of his wounded arm.* STEVE *is about to get the gun.*]

SALLY: [*Warningly.*] Bill!

[*Volume off.*]
[*In the nick of time,* SALLY *shoots* STEVE *in the back with a rifle. As he falls he makes a mute appeal to her. He is dead now and she is appalled at what she's done.*]

SALLY: [*Embracing* BILL.] Oh, Bill!

BILL: I love you, Sally.
SALLY: [*Touched.*] Oh, Bill.
BILL: Let's move to another town.
SALLY: [*Delighted*] Oh Bill.
[BILL *and* SALLY *ride off together into the dusk.*]

[*Slide: the President and his family.*]
SECOND NEWS ANOUNCER: The President is accompanied by his wife, Lady Bird Johnson, and by his two daughters, Lynda Bird Johnson and Luci Baines Johnson Nugent, who lives in nearby Austin with her husband Patrick Nugent, President Johnson's son-in-law.
[*Slide: second view of the President and his family.*]
[*The President appears at a podium reading a speech. He is indeed accompanied by his wife and daughters.*]
[*Slide: the President alone.*]

[SUSAN *continues laughing.*]
HAL: Shhhhh. Stop it.
SUSAN: I can't.

PRESIDENT: We will stamp out aggression wherever and whenever.

SUSAN: I can't stop. Get the water.
[GEORGE *gets up to get some water.* HAL *wants to watch TV and can't hear it at at all because of* SUSAN's *laughter.*]

PRESIDENT: We will tighten our defenses and fight, to guarantee the peace of our children, our children's children, and their children.

HAL: This is easier. [*Slaps* SUSAN *very hard on the face.*]
SUSAN: Ow!

PRESIDENT: That all men are not well-intentioned or well-informed or even basically good, is unfortunate.

SUSAN: Just who do you think you are!

PRESIDENT: But these people will not be indulged.
[*Applause by the* PRESIDENT's *family. No sound in this play need be put on tape; all of it can be provided by the People On Television.*]

HAL: Are you finished?
SUSAN: I couldn't help it.

PRESIDENT: Those who are our friends will declare themselves publicly. The others, we will not tolerate.
[*Slide: second view of the President alone.*]

SUSAN: Sadist.

PRESIDENT: Belief in American success and victory is the cornerstone of our faith.

SUSAN: Why didn't anyone get water?
GEORGE: Don't look at me.

PRESIDENT: Whatever else may chance to happen on far-off shores, nothing, I repeat nothing, will be allowed to disturb the serenity of our cities and suburbs, and when we fight we fight for a safer and more comfortable America, now and in years to come. Thank you.
[*Slide: third view of the President and his family.*]

SUSAN: You don't slap people because they're sick.
HAL: Every day we go through the same thing. You laugh. We bring you water. You spill the water all over everybody, and half an hour later you stop.

SECOND NEWS ANNOUNCER: The President and his family will now be cheered by the cadet corps.
[*The President and his family respond to cheers like mechanical dolls. Turning his back, the* SECOND NEWS ANNOUNCER *provides us with one hummed bar of "So Hello Lyndon."*]

SUSAN: Give me the water, George. I'm going to take a pill.

GEORGE: What makes you laugh like that?

[HAL *lowers the volume but does not turn it off.*]

SUSAN: I'm a hysteric. I mean I'm not constantly hysterical but sometimes I get that way. I react that way, through my body. You're a compulsive, Hal, a nasty little compulsive.

HAL: [*Turning volume off.*] How do you know?

SUSAN: I've discussed it with my analyst. Hysterics react through their bodies. Compulsives react compulsively.

GEORGE: What does he say about me?

SUSAN: He doesn't.

GEORGE: Hmph.

HAL: How long have you been going now? Twenty-seven years?

SUSAN: A year, wise guy.

HAL: How long do you expect to be going?

SUSAN: It might take another two or three years.

GEORGE: I know people who have gone for ten or twelve years.

HAL: Don't you think that's a lot?

GEORGE: If you need it, you need it. It's a sickness like any other sickness. It's got to be looked after.

HAL: What did they do in the old days?

GEORGE: [*Turning volume up.*] They stayed sick.

SUSAN: My analyst has been going to HIS analyst for twenty-five years.

HAL: How do you know?

SUSAN: He told me.

[*A Spanish Teacher appears.*]
[*Slide: the Spanish Teacher's face.*]

[*Volume low.*]
SPANISH TEACHER: Buenos dias muchachos and muchachas. Hello, boys and girls. Muchachos. Boys. Muchachas. Girls. Aqui es la casa. Here is the house. Casa. House.

[*Volume off.*]

[*The* SPANISH TEACHER *finishes the lesson.*]
[*Efficient researchers walk back and forth across the stage, checking things, nodding at each other curtly, and so on.*]
[*Slide: the efficient researchers.*]

[*Volume up.*]
UGP ANNOUNCER: Who are they? They are a community of devotion.
[*Slide: "*UGP*" in very Germanic lettering.*]
UGP ANNOUNCER: Men and women whose lives are dedicated to the researching of more perfect products for you. Get the benefit of a community of devotion. Look for the letters UGP whenever you buy a car, radio, television set, or any of a thousand other products. Their tool: devotion. Their goal: perfection.
[*Slide: a civil rights demonstration.*]

FIRST NEWS ANNOUNCER: Three men were critically injured during a civil rights

GEORGE: Can you feel the tranquilizer working?
SUSAN: A little bit. I think so.

GEORGE: Maybe I should have one too.

SUSAN: [*Turning volume off.*] Are you upset?
GEORGE: I can feel my stomach.
SUSAN: [*Reaching into her bag to give him a pill.*] Here.
GEORGE: I'd like some coffee.
HAL: I'd like some lunch.
SUSAN: Lunch! I'll get it.
    [*Dashes into her coat and is almost out the door.*]
HAL: Hey.
SUSAN: Rare with onion and a danish. I know. So long, you guys.
HAL: [*Throwing his penknife into the bulletin board.*] Think she's all right?
GEORGE: People wouldn't say this was a crazy office or anything like that.
HAL: Nope.
GEORGE: She's really a nice girl, isn't she?
HAL: [*Doing calisthenics.*] Yup.
GEORGE: You like her, don't you?
HAL: Yup.
GEORGE: I mean you don't just think she's a good lay, do you?
HAL: What makes you think I lay her?
GEORGE: Well, don't you?
HAL: George, that's an old trick.
GEORGE: I'm just trying to find out if you really like her.
HAL: Why do you care?
GEORGE: I feel protective.
HAL: That's right. She's half your age, isn't she?
GEORGE: Not exactly half.
HAL: How old are you, George, exactly?
GEORGE: Forty-three.
HAL: [*Crossing to water cooler.*] Humph.
GEORGE: What's that mean?
HAL: I was just wondering what it was like to be forty-three.
GEORGE: It stinks.

demonstration in Montgomery, Alabama today.

[*Slide: the Vice President.*]
FIRST NEWS ANNOUNCER: This afternoon the Vice President arrived in Honolulu. As he stepped off the plane he told newsmen things are looking up.
[*Slide: a map of China.*]
FIRST NEWS ANNOUNCER: The Defense Department today conceded that United States aircraft may have mistakenly flown over Chinese territory last month. It regrets the incident.
[*Volume off.*]

[*Slide: a rock and roll group.*]
[*A rock and roll group is seen singing and playing.*]

HAL: That's what I thought.

GEORGE: You'll be forty-three sooner than you think.

HAL: I'll never be forty-three.

GEORGE: Why not?

HAL: I don't intend to live that long.

GEORGE: You have something?

HAL: No. I just don't intend to live that long.

[Returns to console and turns volume on.]

[The rock and roll group bows.]
[Slide: a group of peace marchers.]
[A group of peace marchers appears.]

GEORGE: [Sits.] You're probably a socialist.

HAL: A socialist?

GEORGE: A socialist at twenty and a Republican at forty. Everybody goes through that cycle.

FIRST NEWS ANNOUNCER: A group of so-called peaceniks marched down the center mall of the capital today, singing:
[The peace marchers sing "We Shall Overcome."]

FIRST NEWS ANNOUNCER: One young man from New York City predicted:

ONE YOUNG MAN FROM NEW YORK CITY: The Washington Monument's going to burst into bloom and—
[It is as if the sound were cut off on the word he was going to say, but we can read "Fuck" on his lips.]

[Slide: ANNIE KAPPELHOFF.]

FIRST NEWS ANNOUNCER: A little girl, Annie Kappelhoff, had her own opinion:

ANNIE: [As if leading a cheer.] Burn yourselves, not your draft cards, burn yourselves, not your draft cards—
[The sound is cut off on ANNIE, too, as she continues the same cheer.]

GEORGE: It's healthy.

FIRST NEWS ANNOUNCER: Later in the day Annie was the star of her own parade. She's head-cheerleader of Wilumet High School in Maryland. Today Annie cheered her team on to victory, thirty to nothing, over neighboring South Dearing. Annie is also an ardent supporter of the young American Nazi party, and hopes to become a model. And now, a message.
[Slide: a jar of K-F soap-cream.]

FAMOUS TV PERSONALITY: Are you one of those lucky women who has all the time in the world?

HAL: Are you a Republican, George?

GEORGE: That's right.

HAL: You know I have a lot of friends who won't even speak to Republicans.

GEORGE: I'd rather not discuss politics.

HAL: Why not?

GEORGE: Because we probably don't see eye to eye.

HAL: So?

FAMOUS TV PERSONALITY: Or are you like most of us: busy, busy, busy all day long with home or job so that when evening comes you hardly have time to wash your face, much less transform yourself into the living doll he loves.

GEORGE: So I'd rather not discuss it. And my stomach's upset.

FAMOUS TV PERSONALITY: Well then, K-F is for you. More than a soap. More than a cream. It's a soap-cream. You apply it in less time than it takes to wash your face and it leaves your skin tingling with loveliness. Try it. And for an extra super thrill, use it in the shower.

[*Slide:* LILY HEAVEN.]

LILY HEAVEN'S ANNOUNCER: The Lily Heaven Show, ladies and gentlemen, starring that great star of stage, screen, and television: Lily Heaven.

[*Out through imaginary curtains comes* LILY HEAVEN, *very starlike. She greets her audience in her own inimitable way. She sings a line from a popular American love song.*]

[There is a special knock on the viewing room door.]

HAL: What's that?

GEORGE: Nothing.

[GEORGE *turns volume off.*]

HAL: What do you mean, nothing?

GEORGE: [*Calling.*] One minute.

HAL: [*Getting panicky.*] One minute until what?

[GEORGE *turns out the lights in the viewing room.*]

HAL: I knew it. What's going on?

GEORGE [*Calling.*] Okay.

HAL: Okay what? What? What?

SUSAN: [*Coming through the door with a cake with lighted candles on it.*] Okay this, stupid.

HAL: Oh my God, you're crazy.

SUSAN and GEORGE: One, two, three. [Singing.]

Happy Birthday to you,
Happy Birthday to you,
Happy Birthday dear Ha-al,
Happy Birthday to you.
[*Susan kisses Hal on the lips.*]

SUSAN: Happy Birthday. You had no idea, did you?

HAL: No.

GEORGE: Happy Birthday.

HAL: Thanks a lot.

SUSAN: Make a wish and blow.

[HAL *blows on the candles but doesn't get them all.*]

SUSAN: Well, almost.

[GEORGE *turns the viewing room lights on again, and* SUSAN *gets two presents from the closet.*]

SUSAN: People thought I was crazy walk-

[*Volume off.*]
[*Slide: a second view of Lily Heaven.*]

ing down the hall with this cake and this lunch in a paper bag. And I was petrified one of you would swing the door open while I was waiting in the corridor and knock me down and the cake and everything. I was almost sure you'd guessed, Hal, when I put the presents in my locker this morning.

HAL: I hadn't.

SUSAN: I love birthdays. I know it's childish but I really do. Look at the card on George's.

HAL: It's cute.

SUSAN: Open it.

[HAL *opens the package. It's a tie.*]

HAL: Well thanks, George. I can use this. [*Makes a mock noose of it around his neck.*]

GEORGE: You're welcome.

SUSAN: [*Looking at the label as if she hadn't seen it before.*] It's a good tie.

GEORGE: What'd you expect?

[GEORGE *is biting into an egg salad sandwich.* HAL *starts to open the second present.*]

SUSAN: [*Stopping* HAL.] Save mine for when we eat the cake, so the birthday will last longer.

HAL: George, there's egg salad all over the dials.

GEORGE: [*Turning volume on.*] Sorry.

SUSAN: Here's a napkin. I'll make some coffee.

GEORGE: Good.

[LILY HEAVEN *finishes singing and bows.*]

LILY HEAVEN: So long, everybody.

LILY HEAVEN: This is Lily Heaven saying so long.

[*Applause from part of* LILY HEAVEN'S *audience, played by the People On Television, who stand behind her.*]

LILY HEAVEN: [*As if each sentence were her last.*] Here's wishing you a good week before we meet again. From all of us here to all of you out there: so long. Thanks a lot and God bless you. This is Lily signing off. I only hope that you enjoyed watching us as much as we enjoyed being here. So long. It's been wonderful being with you. Really grand, and I hope you'll invite us into your living room again next week. I only wish we could go on but I'm afraid it's time to say so long, so from the actors and myself, from the staff here, I want to wish you all a very very good week. This is your Lily saying so long to you. So long. So long. So long. So long. Have a happy, and so long. Till next week. Bye. So long. Bye. So long.

[GEORGE *and* HAL *are mesmerized by* LILY HEAVEN. SUSAN *is paying no attention but is fussing with the coffee things and putting paper bags, as party hats, on* HAL *and* GEORGE.]

GEORGE: Give me another of those tranquilizers, please. The first one doesn't seem to have done a thing.

[HAL *turns the volume off.* SUSAN *has plugged in the hot plate and coffee maker. She also has some real coffee and a jar of dried cream, some sugar and sugar substitute in little bags stolen from a luncheonette, napkins and little wooden stick-stirrers.*]

HAL: [*Who has been opening his present.*] Say, this is nice.

SUSAN: It's an art book.

HAL: I can see that.

GEORGE: Hal especially interested in art?

SUSAN: A person doesn't have to be especially interested in art to like it.

HAL: It must have cost a lot, Susan. Here, George. [*Passes* GEORGE *a piece of cake.*]

SUSAN: Well, as a matter of fact, I got it on sale at Marboro.

HAL: If I had a place for it everything would be fine. Cake, Susan?

SUSAN: [*To* GEORGE.] Hal still doesn't have a place.

GEORGE: What kind of place are you looking for?

HAL: I'd like to find an apartment with more than one small room for under a hundred dollars.

SUSAN: Do you want to live in the Village?

HAL: Makes no difference.

GEORGE: Don't live down there.

SUSAN: Why not?

GEORGE: It's too crowded.

SUSAN: It's not so crowded, and in the Village you can see a lot of wonderful faces.

GEORGE: Yes, well frankly I've been working for a living for twenty-one years and I resent having to support a lot of bums on relief.

SUSAN: That's not the Village. That's the Bowery.

GEORGE: Let's not talk about it.

SUSAN: Why not?

GEORGE: I already told Hal that people with differing points of view shouldn't talk about politics. And I shouldn't be eating this cake either.

[*Snaps volume on.*]

[*Slide: a weather map.*]

WEATHER ANNOUNCER: And now, the weather.

[*Volume off.*]

[*Slide: Miracle Headache Pills.*]
[*Still without volume, an advertisement for Miracle Headache Pills: a woman is seen before and after taking the pills.*]

[LADY ANNOUNCER *begins to speak, still without volume.*]

[*Slide: First Federal Savings Bank.*]

LADY ANNOUNCER: And now First Federal Savings and Kennel-Heart Dog Food present Luncheon With Carol, a program especially designed for the up-to-date woman. Our topic for today: I Quit. And here's Carol.

[*Slide:* CAROL *and* RON CAMPBELL.]

CAROL: Hello, ladies. This is Carol. I have as my guest today Mr. Ron Campbell just back from an eighteen month tour of duty in Vietnam. Mr. Campbell was a member of the famed Green Berets. He is a holder of the Bronze Star and the South Vietnamese Order of Merit; he has been nominated for the U.S. Silver Star. A few weeks ago he was offered a field commission as captain. But instead of accepting, what did you do, Ron?

RON: I quit.

CAROL: That's right, you quit. Tell us why you quit, Ron, when you were obviously doing so ˙well.

RON: I didn't like being there.

CAROL: You didn't?

RON: No.

CAROL: [*Cheerfully.*] I see.

RON: We're committing mass murder.

CAROL: [*Interested.*] Yes?

RON: We're trying to take over a people that don't want to be taken over by anybody.

CAROL: Now, Ron, American boys are out there dying so somebody must be doing something wrong somewhere.

RON: Whoever in Hanoi or Peking or Washington is sending men out to be killed, THEY'RE doing something wrong.

CAROL: [*Interested in his opinion, tolerant.*] I see.

RON: You do? Well I was there for a year and a half and every day I saw things that would make you sick. Heads broken, babies smashed against walls—

CAROL: [*Deeply sympathetic.*] I KNOW.

RON: You know?

CAROL: War is horrible.

RON: Listen—

CAROL: Thank you, Ron. We've been talking this afternoon, ladies, with Ron Campbell, war hero.

RON: Will you let me say something, please?

CAROL: [*Tolerating him, kindly.*] And a fascinating talk it's been, Ron, but I'm afraid our time is up.

RON: One—

CAROL: [*With her special smile for the ladies.*] Ladies, see you all tomorrow.

SUSAN: [*Dreamily.*] I think I'm floating further and further left.

GEORGE: You don't know a thing about it.

SUSAN: I was listening to Norman Thomas last night—

LADY ANNOUNCER: This program was brought to you by First Federal Savings and Kennel-Heart Dog Food. The opinions expressed on this program are not necessarily those of anyone connected with it. A dog in the home means a dog with a heart.
[*Slide: Kennel-Heart Dog Food.*]
LADY ANNOUNCER: Kennel-Heart. Bow-wow. Wow.
[*Slide: "Billion Dollar Movie."*]

GEORGE: I'm going to the Men's Room.

SUSAN: Poor George.
HAL: You still haven't told me about tonight.
SUSAN: Told you what about tonight?

[*A very English man and a very English woman appear in the movie.*]
HE: Sarah.
SHE: Yes, Richard.

HAL: Are we going to the movies or are we not going to the movies?

HE: Our old apartment.

SUSAN: I don't know. I can't make up my mind.

SHE: Yes, Richard. It's still here.

HAL: That's just fine.

HE: It seems very small to me.
SHE: It does to me, too.

SUSAN: I want to work on my apartment.
HAL: Okay.

HE: Do you think we can live in it again?
SHE: Not in the old way.

SUSAN: I should really get it done.

HE: In a better way.

HAL: You're right.

SHE: You've changed too, Richard, for the better.
HE: So have you, darling, for the better.

SUSAN: Suppose I let you know by the end of the afternoon?
HAL: Suppose we forget I ever suggested it.

SHE: I've learned a lot.
HE: Maybe that's what war is for.
    [*The People On Television hum "White Cliffs of Dover" under the following.*]
SHE: The brick wall in front of the window is gone.
HE: We'll rebuild for the future.

SUSAN: Oh, all right, I'll go. Happy?
HAL: I'm so happy I could put a bullet through my brain.

SHE: I hope there is never any more war. Ever, ever again.
HE: Amen.
    [*Slide: "The End."*]
    [*The People On Television sing, meaningfully, the last line of "White Cliffs*

SUSAN: Sugar?

HAL: You're like my grandmother.

SUSAN: How?

HAL: She asked me if I took sugar every day we lived together. It was very comforting.

HAL: Hal, she used to say to me, my grandmother, you're going to be a big man.

HAL: Everybody's going to love you. She used to sing that song to me: "Poppa's gonna buy you a dog named Rover, and if that dog don't bark, Poppa's gonna buy you a looking glass, and if that looking glass should break, you're still the sweetest little boy in town."

SUSAN: That's nice.

[GEORGE enters and goes directly to telephone.]

GEORGE: Hello, darling? Listen, I've gotten out of it. Isn't that good news? The midnight shift.

GEORGE: I'm looking forward to being home nice and comfy with you.

GEORGE: You know my stomach is killing me. Sure I will. Wait a minute.

[GEORGE takes out a pencil.]

GEORGE: Toothpaste. Cauliflower. That's a good idea.

GEORGE: Large face cream. Why large? No, I don't care. I was just asking.

GEORGE: Okay. Listen, I'm really looking forward to seeing you.

of Dover": "Tomorrow, just you wait and see."]

[FIRST NEWS ANNOUNCER appears.]

[Slide: baseball player.]

FIRST NEWS ANNOUNCER: Baseball's Greg Pironelli, fifty-six, died today of a heart attack in St. Petersburg, Florida. He hit a total of four hundred and eighty home runs and had a lifetime batting average of three forty-one.

[Slide: a baseball game.]

FIRST NEWS ANNOUNCER: In 1963, the year he was elected to baseball's hall of fame in Cooperstown, New York, Pironelli suffered his first stroke. Pironelli owned a Florida-wide chain of laundries.

[Slide: "Johnny Holland Show."]

JOHNNY: We're back.

[Slide: JOHNNY and LUCI.]

JOHNNY: That's a very pretty dress you've got on, Luci.

LUCI: Thank you, Johnny.

JOHNNY: How does it feel living in Austin after all the excitement of the big wedding?

LUCI: It feels fine.

JOHNNY: Do you miss your father?

LUCI: Oh sure, I miss him.

JOHNNY: [Awkward pause.] I guess your heart belongs to Daddy, huh?

LUCI: That's right.

JOHNNY: [Awkward pause.] Is your father hard to get along with?

LUCI: Oh, no. When I want something I just march right in, cuddle up in his lap, and give him a great big kiss.

[Slide: a second view of Johnny and Luci.]

GEORGE: No, I haven't been drinking, and it's rotten of you to ask.

GEORGE: Okay, okay. Bye. [*Hangs up telephone.*]

SUSAN: Have a little coffee, George.
GEORGE: No, thanks.
HAL: Oh, come on, George, have a little coffee.
GEORGE: A sip.

SUSAN: Sugar or superine?
GEORGE: Sugar.

SUSAN: George.
GEORGE: Don't take care of me. I said sugar.
SUSAN: Whatever you want, George.

SUSAN: George, what are you eating now?
GEORGE: Chicken sandwich.
SUSAN: Give me a bite.
[HAL *plays with his penknife.* SUSAN *eats another piece of cake.* GEORGE *eats his chicken sandwich.*]

[GEORGE *starts to cough.*]

JOHNNY: [*Awkward pause.*] So you'd say your father is affectionate?
LUCI: Very affectionate.

JOHNNY: [*Awkward pause.*] Does he ever ask your advice about important matters?

LUCI: Well, one day I told him what I thought, good and proper, about all those nervous nellies interfering with my Daddy's war.
[JOHNNY *does a double take of scandalized amusement to the audience.*]
[*Slide: Johnny doing double take.*]
JOHNNY: And what did he say?
LUCI: He laughed.

JOHNNY: It's lovely talking to you, Luci.

LUCI: It's nice talking to you too, Johnny.
JOHNNY: We'll be back.
[*Slide: "Johnny Holland Show."*]

[*An* EVANGELIST *appears with his choir, which is singing "Onward Christian Soldiers."*]
[*Slide: the* EVANGELIST.]
EVANGELIST: If we could look through the ceiling of this wonderful new air-conditioned stadium we could see the stars. Nonetheless I have heard them in faraway countries, I have heard them criticize, criticize us and the leaders we know and love.

EVANGELIST: Why? Well I will tell you why. They criticize us because we are rich, as if money itself were evil. Money, the Bible says, is the root of evil, not evil itself. I have seen a roomful of men and women, powerful Hollywood celebrities at four o'clock A.M. in the morning, listening to me with tears streaming down their faces crying out to me that they had lost touch with God.

EVANGELIST: "In God We Trust" is on our coins, ladies and gentlemen —

SUSAN: What's the matter, George?

[GEORGE *motions her away and continues to cough.*]

HAL: [*Turning volume off.*] Spit it out, George.

SUSAN: Hal, leave him alone.

HAL: George, spit it out. [*Thumps* GEORGE *on the back.*]

SUSAN: Hal! George, is it epilepsy?

HAL: It's something in his throat.

SUSAN: Try to tell us what it is, George.

HAL *and* GEORGE: Chicken!

HAL: He has a chicken bone stuck in his throat.

SUSAN: Oh my God. Well give him some water.

[GEORGE's *choking is getting worse.*]

HAL: Water will wash right by it. Let me look.

[*Holds* GEORGE's *head and looks into his mouth.*]

Don't move, George. I want to take a look.

[*Looks in* GEORGE's *mouth.*]

There it is.

SUSAN: [*Also looking.*] Ugh, it's stuck in his throat. I'll get some water.

[HAL *and* SUSAN *let go of* GEORGE, *who falls to the floor.*]

HAL: Not water.

SUSAN: Why not?

HAL: Because water will wash right past the thing. It needs something to push it out.

SUSAN: Like what?

HAL: Like bread.

SUSAN: Bread? Bread will get stuck on the bone and he'll choke.

HAL: You're wrong.

SUSAN: I'm right.

HAL: Bread will push it right down.

SUSAN: Water will do that.

HAL: You're wrong.

SUSAN: It's you that's wrong and won't admit it.

HAL: I'm going to give him some bread.

SUSAN: I won't allow it.

HAL: YOU won't allow it?

SUSAN: It'll kill him.

HAL: He's choking right now and I'm going to give him some of this bread.

SUSAN: Give him water.

HAL: I said bread.

SUSAN: [*Starting to walk past* HAL.] And I said water.

[*Slide: a second view of the* EVANGE-LIST.]
[*The Evangelist choir sings "Onward Christian Soldiers."*]

[*Volume off.*]

HAL: [*Grabbing her arm.*] Bread.

SUSAN: Water. Ow, you're hurting me.
[GEORGE *is having a very bad time.* HAL *and* SUSAN *turn to look at him, speaking softly.*]

SUSAN: Let's call the operator.

HAL: It would take too long.

SUSAN: And he wouldn't like anyone to see him.

HAL: Why not?

SUSAN: I don't know.
[*At this point* GEORGE *finally coughs the thing up, and his cough subsides into an animal pant.*]

SUSAN: [*Going to him, patting him.*] Poor George.

HAL: It's over.

SUSAN: No thanks to you.

HAL: Nor you.

SUSAN: [*Putting* GEORGE's *head on her breast.*] He might have choked. Poor George.

GEORGE: [*Pushing her away.*] Fuck!
[GEORGE *lurches against the console on his way to the bathroom, accidentally turning on the volume.*]

EVANGELIST CHOIR: [*Still singing "Onward Christian Soldiers."*] "With the cross of Jesus—"

[HAL *changes channels from the* EVANGELIST's *meeting to* "My Favorite Teenager."]

[*Slide:* MOTHER, FATHER, *and* DAUGHTER *in* "My Favorite Teenager."]

SUSAN: [*Sitting in her chair.*] Poor George.

MOTHER: Why aren't you going?

DAUGHTER: [*Sitting in* GEORGE's *chair at the control console.*] Because I told Harold Sternpepper he could take me.

MOTHER: Yes, and—

DAUGHTER: Well, Harold Sternpepper is a creep. Everybody knows that.
[*The remaining People On Television make the sound of canned laughter.*]

HAL: [*Sitting in his chair.*] What movie are we going to?

MOTHER: So, why—

DAUGHTER: Oh, because I was mad at Gail.
[*Canned laughter.*]

SUSAN: I don't know.

MOTHER: What about Johnny Beaumont?

HAL: What about George?

SUSAN: What about him?

HAL: Well, I guess it's none of my business.

DAUGHTER: What about him?

MOTHER: Well, I guess it's none of my business.

GEORGE: [*Returning.*] What's the matter?

SUSAN: Nothing.
GEORGE: Going somewhere?

SUSAN: We're going to the movies.

[HAL *and* SUSAN *and* GEORGE *are slowing down because they are mesmerized by* "My Favorite Teenager."]
GEORGE: What movie are you going to?

GEORGE: Mind if I come along?

SUSAN: Oh, George, you don't really want to.

GEORGE: I'd be pleased as punch.

SUSAN: Hal, say something.

HAL: [*To* GEORGE.] You look bushed to me, George.
GEORGE: Who's bushed?

[GEORGE *sits in his chair.*]

[HAL, SUSAN, *and* GEORGE *are completely mesmerized by the TV show.*]

FATHER: What's the matter?
[*Slide: second view of* MOTHER, FATHER, *and* DAUGHTER *in* "My Favorite Teenager."]
DAUGHTER: Nothing.
FATHER: Why aren't you dressed for the prom?
DAUGHTER: I'm not going to the prom.

FATHER: Why not? Why isn't she going, Grace?
MOTHER: Don't ask me. I just live here.

[*Canned laughter.*]
FATHER: Why doesn't anybody tell me anything around here?
[*Canned laughter.*]
DAUGHTER: [*Getting up from* GEORGE's *chair.*] Oh, why don't you two leave me alone? I'm not going because nobody's taking me.

FATHER: [*Sitting in* GEORGE's *chair.*] Nobody's taking my little girl to the junior prom? I'll take her myself.
DAUGHTER: [*Stifling a yelp of horror.*] Oh no, Daddy, don't bother. I mean how would it look, I mean—
FATHER: I'd be pleased as punch.
DAUGHTER: [*Aside to* MOTHER.] Help.
[*Canned laughter.*]
MOTHER: [*To* FATHER.] Now, dear, don't you think for your age—
[*Canned laughter.*]

FATHER: My age?
[*Canned laughter.*]
FATHER: [*Standing and doing a two-step.*] I'd like to see anybody laugh at my two-step.
[*Canned laughter.*]
DAUGHTER: [*In despair.*] Oh, Daddy. Mother, DO something.
[*Canned laughter.*]
MOTHER: [*Putting her arm around* GEORGE's *shoulders.*] I think it's a very nice idea. And maybe I'll go with Harold Sternpepper.
[*Canned laughter.*]
DAUGHTER: [*Loudly, sitting on* HAL's *knee.*] Oh, Mother, oh, Daddy, oh no!
[*The canned laughter mounts. Music.*]
[*Slide:* "My Favorite Teenager."]

[*Now they all speak like situation-comedy characters.*]
HAL: What movie shall we go to?
GEORGE: Let's talk about it over dinner.
HAL: Who said anything about dinner?

[*All of the People On Television do canned laughter now. They are crowded around the control console.*]

SUSAN: Isn't anybody going to ask me what I want to do?

[*Canned laughter.*]

GEORGE: Sure, what do you want, Susan?
HAL: It's up to you.

[*Slide:* HAL, SUSAN, *and* GEORGE *with the same facial expressions they now have on the stage.*]

SUSAN: Well, have I got a surprise for you two. I'M going home to fix up my apartment and you two can have dinner TOGETHER.

[HAL, SUSAN, *and* GEORGE *join in the canned laughter. Then, lights off. Slide off. Curtain call: all are in the same position, silent, their faces frozen into laughing masks.*]

MOTEL
Niblock/Bough, Fundamental Photographs

Motel

A Masque for Three Dolls

. . . after all our subtle colour and nervous rhythm, after the faint mixed tints of Conder, what more is possible? After us the Savage God.

W. B. Yeats

CHARACTERS

MOTEL-KEEPER
MAN
WOMAN
MOTEL-KEEPER'S VOICE

Lights come up on the MOTEL-KEEPER *doll. The intensity of the light will increase as the play continues.*

The MOTEL-KEEPER *doll is large, much larger than human size, but the impression of hugeness can come mainly from the fact that her head is at least three times larger than would be normal in proportion to her body. She is all gray. She has a large full skirt which reaches to the floor. She has squarish breasts. The hair curlers on her head suggest electronic receivers.*

The MOTEL-KEEPER *doll has eyeglasses which are mirrors. It doesn't matter what these mirrors reflect at any given moment. The audience may occasionally catch a glimpse of itself, or be bothered by reflections of light in the mirrors. It doesn't matter; the sensory nerves of the audience are not to be spared.*

The motel room in which the MOTEL-KEEPER *doll stands is anonymously modern, except for certain "homey" touches. A neon light blinks outside the window. The colors in the room, like the colors in the clothes on the* MAN *and* WOMAN *dolls, are violent combinations of oranges, pinks, and reds against a reflective plastic background.*

The MOTEL-KEEPER'S VOICE, *which never stops, comes from a loudspeaker, or from several loudspeakers in the theatre. The* VOICE *will be, at first, mellow and husky and then, as the light grows harsher and brighter, the* VOICE *will grow harsher too, more set in its pattern, hard finally, and patronizing and petty.*

An actor on platform shoes works the MOTEL-KEEPER *doll from inside it. The actor can move only the doll's arms or its entire body. As the* VOICE *begins, the arms move, and then the* MOTEL-KEEPER *doll fusses about the room in little circles.*

MOTEL-KEEPER'S VOICE: I am old. I am an old idea: the walls; that from which it springs forth. I enclose the nothing, making then a place in which it happens. I am the room: a Roman theatre where cheers break loose the lion; a railroad carriage in the forest at Compiègne, in 1918, and in 1941. I have been rooms of marble and rooms of cork, all letting forth an avalanche. Rooms of mud and rooms of silk. This room will be slashed too, as if by a scimitar, its contents spewed and yawned out. That is what happens. It is almost happening, in fact. I am this room.

[*As the* MOTEL-KEEPER'S VOICE *continues, the doors at the back of the room open and headlights shine into the eyes of the audience; passing in front of the headlights, in silhouette, we see two more huge dolls, the* MAN *and the* WOMAN.]

MOTEL-KEEPER'S VOICE: It's nice; not so fancy as some, but with all the conveniences. And a touch of home. The antimacassar comes from my mother's house in Boise. Boise, Idaho. Sits kind of nice, I think, on the Swedish swing. That's my own idea, you know. All modern, up-to-date, that's it—no motel on this route is more up-to-date. Or cleaner. Go look, then talk me a thing or two.

[*The* WOMAN *doll enters. Her shoulders are thrown way back, like a girl posing for a calendar. Her breasts are particularly large and perfect, wiggleable if possible. She has a cherry-lipstick smile, blond hair, and a garish patterned dress.*
Both the MAN *and the* WOMAN *dolls are the same size as the* MOTEL-KEEPER *doll, with heads at least three times larger than would be normal for their bodies. The* MAN *and the* WOMAN *dolls, however, are flesh-colored and have more mobility. The actors inside these dolls are also on platform shoes. There is absolutely no rapport between the* MOTEL-KEEPER *and the* MAN *and* WOMAN. *All of the* MOTEL-KEEPER'S *remarks are addressed generally. She is never directly motivated by the actions of the* MAN *and* WOMAN *dolls.*
As the WOMAN *doll enters, she puts down her purse and inspects the room. Then she takes off her dress, revealing lace panties and bra.*]

MOTEL-KEEPER'S VOICE: All modern here but, as I say, with the tang of home. Do you understand? When folks are fatigued, in a strange place? Not that it's old-fashioned. No. Not in the wrong way. There's a push-button here for TV. The toilet flushes of its own accord. All you've got to do is get off. Pardon my mentioning it, but you'll have to go far before you see a thing like that on this route. Oh, it's quite a room. Yes. And reasonable. Sign here. Pardon the pen leak. I can see you're fatigued.

[*The* WOMAN *doll goes into the bathroom.*]

MOTEL-KEEPER'S VOICE: Any children? Well, that's nice. Children don't appreciate travel. And rooms don't appreciate children. As it happens it's the last one I've got left.

I'll just flip my vacancy switch. Twelve dollars, please. In advance that'll be. That way you can go any time you want to go, you know, get an early start. On a trip to see sights, are you? That's nice. You just get your luggage while I unlock the room. You can see the light.

[*The* MAN *doll enters carrying a suitcase. He has a cigar and a loud Florida shirt. He closes the door, inspects the room, and takes off his clothes, except for his loudly patterned shorts.*]

MOTEL-KEEPER'S VOICE: There now. What I say doesn't matter. You can see. It speaks for itself. The room speaks for itself. You can see it's a perfect 1966 room. But a taste of home. I've seen to that. A taste of home. Comfy, cozy, nice, but a taste of newness. That's what. You can see it. The best stop on route Six Sixty-Six. Well, there might be others like it, but this is the best stop. You've arrived at the right place. This place. And a hooked rug. I don't care what, but I've said no room IS without a hooked rug.

[*Sound of the toilet flushing.*]

MOTEL-KEEPER'S VOICE: No complaints yet. Never. Modern people like modern places. Oh yes. I can tell. They tell me. And reasonable. Very very reasonable rates. No cheaper rates on the route, not for this. You receive what you pay for.

[*Sound of the toilet flushing again.*]

MOTEL-KEEPER'S VOICE: All that driving and driving and driving. Fatigued. You must be. I would be. Miles and miles and miles.

[*The* MAN *doll begins an inspection of the bed. He pulls at the bedspread, testing its strength.*]

MOTEL-KEEPER'S VOICE: Fancy. Fancy your ending up right here. You didn't know and I didn't know. But you did. End up right here. Respectable and decent and homelike. Right here.

[*The* WOMAN *doll comes back from the bathroom to get her negligee from her purse. She returns to the bathroom.*]

MOTEL-KEEPER'S VOICE: All folks everywhere sitting in the very palm of God. Waiting, whither, whence.

[*The* MAN *doll pulls the bedspread, blankets, and sheets off the bed, tearing them apart. He jumps hard on the bed.*]

MOTEL-KEEPER'S VOICE: Any motel you might have come to on Six Sixty-Six. Any motel. On that vast network of roads Whizzing by, whizzing by. Trucks too. And cars from everywhere. Full up with folks, all sitting in the very palm of God. I can tell proper folks when I get a look at them. All folks.

[*The* MAN *doll rummages through the suitcase, throwing clothes about the room.*]

MOTEL-KEEPER'S VOICE: Country roads, state roads, United States roads. It's a big world and here you are. I noticed you got a license plate. I've not been to there myself. I've not been to anywhere myself, excepting town for supplies, and Boise. Boise, Idaho.

[*Toilet articles and bathroom fixtures, including toilet paper and the toilet seat, are thrown out of the bathroom. The* MAN *doll casually tears pages out of the Bible.*]

MOTEL-KEEPER'S VOICE: The world arrives to me, you'd say. It's a small world. These plastic flowers here: "Made in Japan" on the label. You noticed? Got them from the catalogue. Cat-al-ogue. Every product in this room is ordered.

[*The* MAN *doll pulls down some of the curtains. Objects continue to be thrown from the bathroom.*]

MOTEL-KEEPER'S VOICE: Ordered from the catalogue. Excepting the antimacassars and the hooked rug. Made the hooked rug myself. Tang of home. No room is a room without. Course the bedspread, hand-hooked, hooked near here at town. Mrs. Harritt. Betsy Harritt gets materials through another catalogue. Cat-al-ogue.

[*The* WOMAN *doll comes out of the bathroom wearing her negligee over her panties and bra. When the* MAN *doll notices her, he stops his other activities and goes to her.*]

MOTEL-KEEPER'S VOICE: Myself, I know it from the catalogue: bottles, bras, breakfasts, refrigerators, cast iron gates, plastic posies,

[*The* WOMAN *doll opens her negligee and the* MAN *doll pulls off her bra. The* MAN *and* WOMAN *dolls embrace. The* WOMAN *doll puts lipstick on her nipples.*]

MOTEL-KEEPER'S VOICE: paper subscriptions, Buick trucks, blankets, forks, clitterclack darning hooks, transistors and antimacassar, vinyl plastics,

[*The* MAN *doll turns on the TV. It glares viciously and plays loud rock and roll music.*]

MOTEL-KEEPER'S VOICE: crazy quilts, paper hairpins, cats, catnip, club feet, canisters, banisters, holy books, tattooed toilet articles, tables, tea cozies,

[*The* MAN *doll writes simple obscene words on the wall. The* WOMAN *doll does the same with her lipstick.*]

MOTEL-KEEPER'S VOICE: pickles, bayberry candles, South Dakotan Kewpie Dolls, fiberglass hair, polished milk, amiable grandpappies, colts, Galsworthy books, cribs, cabinets, teeter-totters,

[*The* WOMAN *doll has turned to picture-making. She draws a crude cock and coyly adds pubic hair and drops of come.*]

MOTEL-KEEPER'S VOICE: and television sets. Oh I tell you it, I do. It's a wonder. Full with things, the world, full up. Shall I tell you my thought? Next year there's a shelter to be built by me, yes. Shelter motel. Everything to be placed under the ground. Signs up in every direction up and down Six Sixty-Six.

[*The* MAN *and* WOMAN *dolls twist.*]

MOTEL-KEEPER'S VOICE: Complete Security, Security While You Sleep Tight, Bury Your Troubles At This Motel, Homelike, Very Comfy, and Encased In Lead, Every Room Its Own Set, Fourteen Day Emergency Supplies $5.00 Extra,

[*The rock and roll music gets louder and louder. A civil-defense siren, one long wail, begins to build. The* MAN *and* WOMAN *dolls proceed methodically to greater and greater violence. They smash the TV screen and picture frames. They pull down the remaining curtains, smash the window, throw bits of clothing and bedding around, and finally tear off the arms of the* MOTEL-KEEPER *doll.*]

MOTEL-KEEPER'S VOICE: Self-Contained Latrine Waters, Filters, Counters, Periscopes and Mechanical Doves, Hooked Rugs, Dearest Little Picture Frames for Loved Ones— Made in Japan—through the catalogue. Cat-a-logue. You can pick items and products: cablecackles—so nice—cuticles, twice-twisted combs with corrugated calisthenics, meatbeaters, fish-tackles, bug bombs, toasted terra-cotta'd Tanganyikan switch blades, ochre closets, ping-pong balls, didies, Capri-

corn and Cancer prognostics, crackers, total
uppers, stick pins, basting tacks . . .

> [*The* MOTEL-KEEPER'S VOICE *is drown-
> ed out by the other sounds—siren and
> music—which have built to a deafening
> pitch and come from all parts of the
> theatre. The door opens again and
> headlights shine into the eyes of the
> audience. The actor inside the* MOTEL-
> KEEPER *doll has slipped out of it. The*
> MAN *and* WOMAN *dolls tear off the*
> head of the MOTEL-KEEPER *doll, then
> throw her body aside. Then, one by
> one, the* MAN *and* WOMAN *dolls leave
> the motel room and walk down the
> aisle. Fans blow air through the de-
> bacle on stage onto the audience. After
> an instant more of excruciatingly loud
> noises: blackout and silence. It is pref-
> erable that the actors take no bow after
> this play.*]

ED BULLINS

Ed Bullins, former cultural director of San Francisco's Black House, is currently playwright in residence at Harlem's New Lafayette Theatre. He is quoted in *Ebony* (September, 1968) as saying "Most of my plays are about black people who have been crushed by the system, turned into gross distortions of what they can and should be, because they were denied knowledge of themselves and a place to grow." To William Couch, Jr. he said that theater must "transmit the revolution, for revolution is the metaphor of the times." He then defined what he meant by revolution in the theater: "The revolutionary nature of this theater is not of style and technique but of theme and character. . . . Honesty . . . is what the writer should be after." (William Couch, Jr., *New Black Playwrights: An Anthology* [Louisiana State University Press: Baton Rouge, 1968, p. xxi.]) Ed Bullins' plays to date are collected in *Five Plays by Ed Bullins* (The Bobbs-Merrill Co.: Indianapolis, 1969).

A Son, Come Home

CHARACTERS

MOTHER, EARLY 50's
SON, 30 YEARS OLD
THE GIRL
THE BOY

The BOY *and the* GIRL *wear black tights and shirts. They move the action of the play and express the* MOTHER'S *and the* SON'S *moods and tensions. They become various embodiments recalled from memory and history: they enact a number of personalities and move from mood to mood.*

The players are Black.

At rise: Scene: Bare stage but for two chairs positioned so as not to interfere with the actions of the BOY *and the* GIRL.

The MOTHER *enters, sits in chair and begins to use imaginary iron and board. She hums a spiritual as she works.*

MOTHER: You came three times . . . Michael? It took you three times to find me at home?

[*The* GIRL *enters, turns and peers through the cracked, imaginary door.*]

SON'S VOICE: [*Offstage.*] Is Mrs. Brown home?

GIRL: [*An old woman.*] What?

MOTHER: It shouldn't have taken you three times. I told you that I would be here by two and you should wait, Michael.

[*The* SON *enters, passes the* GIRL *and takes his seat upon the other chair. The* BOY *enters, stops on other side of the imaginary door and looks through at the* GIRL.]

BOY: Is Mrs. Brown in?

GIRL: Miss Brown ain't come in yet. Come back later . . . She'll be in before dark.

MOTHER: It shouldn't have taken you three times . . . You should listen to me, Michael. Standin' all that time in the cold.

SON: It wasn't cold, Mother.

MOTHER: I told you that I would be here by two and you should wait Michael.

BOY: Please tell Mrs. Brown that her son's in town to visit her.

GIRL: You little Miss Brown's son? Well, bless the Lord.

[*Calls over her shoulder.*]

Hey, Mandy, do you hear that? Little Miss Brown upstairs got a son . . . a great big boy . . . He's come to visit her.

BOY: You'll tell her, won't you?

GIRL: Sure, I'll tell her.

[*Grins and shows gums.*]

I'll tell her soon as she gets in.

MOTHER: Did you get cold, Michael?

SON: No, Mother. I walked around some . . . sightseeing.

BOY: I walked up Twenty-third Street toward South. I had phoned that I was coming.

MOTHER: Sightseeing? But this is your home, Michael . . . always has been.

BOY: Just before I left New York I phoned that I was taking the bus. Two hours by bus, that's all. That's all it takes. Two hours.

SON: This town seems so strange. Different than how I remember it.

MOTHER: Yes, you have been away for a good while . . . How long has it been, Michael?

BOY: Two hours down the Jersey Turnpike, the trip beginning at the New York Port Authority Terminal . . .

SON: . . . and then straight down through New Jersey to Philadelphia . . .

GIRL: . . . and home . . . Just imagine . . . little Miss Brown's got a son who's come home.

SON: Yes, home . . . an anachronism.

MOTHER: What did you say, Michael?

BOY: He said . . .

GIRL: [*Late teens.*] What's an anachronism, Mike?

SON: Anachronism: 1: an error in chronology; *esp:* a chronological misplacing of persons, events, objects, or customs in regard to each other 2: a person or a thing that is chronologically out of place—anachronistic/ *also* anachronic/ *or* anachronous—anachronistically/ *also* anachronously.

MOTHER: I was so glad to hear you were going to school in California.

BOY: College.

GIRL: Yes, I understand.

MOTHER: How long have you been gone, Michael?

SON: Nine years.

BOY: Nine years it's been. I wonder if she'll know me . . .

MOTHER: You've put on so much weight, son. You know that's not healthy.

GIRL: [*20 years old.*] And that silly beard . . . how . . .

SON: Oh . . . I'll take it off. I'm going on a diet tomorrow.

BOY: I wonder if I'll know her.

SON: You've put on some yourself, Mother.

MOTHER: Yes, the years pass. Thank the Lord.

BOY: I wonder if we've changed much.

GIRL: Yes, thank the Lord.

SON: The streets here seem so small.

MOTHER: Yes, it seems like that when you spend a little time in Los Angeles.

GIRL: I spent eighteen months there with your aunt when she was sick. She had nobody else to help her . . . she was so lonely. And you were in the service . . . away. You've always been away.

BOY: In Los Angeles the boulevards, the avenues, the streets . . .

SON: . . . are wide. Yes, they have some wide ones out West. Here, they're so small and narrow. I wonder how cars get through on both sides.

MOTHER: Why, you know how . . . we lived on Darby Street for over ten years, didn't we?

SON: Yeah, that was almost an alley.

MOTHER: Did you see much of your aunt before you left Los Angeles?

SON: What?

GIRL: [*Middle-aged woman.*] [*To* BOY.] Have you found a job yet, Michael?

MOTHER: Your aunt. My sister.

BOY: Nawh, not yet . . . Today I just walked downtown . . . quite a ways . . . this place is plenty big, ain't it?

SON: I don't see too much of Aunt Sophie.

MOTHER: But you're so much alike.

GIRL: Well, your bags are packed and are sitting outside the door.

BOY: My bags?

MOTHER: You shouldn't be that way, Michael. You shouldn't get too far away from your family.

SON: Yes, Mother.

BOY: But I don't have any money. I had to walk downtown today. That's how much money I have. I've only been here a week.

GIRL: I packed your bags, Michael.

MOTHER: You never can tell when you'll need or want your family, Michael.

SON: That's right, Mother.

MOTHER: You and she are so much alike.

BOY: Well, goodbye, Aunt Sophie.

GIRL: [*Silence.*]

MOTHER: All that time in California and you hardly saw your aunt. My baby sister.

BOY: Tsk tsk tsk.

SON: I'm sorry, Mother.

MOTHER: In the letters I'd get from both of you there'd be no mention of the other. All these years. Did you see her again?

SON: Yes.

GIRL: [*On telephone.*] Michael? Michael who? . . . Ohhh . . . Bernice's boy.

MOTHER: You didn't tell me about this, did you?

SON: No, I didn't.

BOY: Hello, Aunt Sophie. How are you?

GIRL: I'm fine, Michael. How are you? You're looking well.

BOY: I'm getting on okay.

MOTHER: I prayed for you.

SON: Thank you.

MOTHER: Thank the Lord, Michael.

BOY: Got me a job working for the city.

GIRL: You did now.

BOY: Yes, I've brought you something.

GIRL: What's this, Michael . . . ohhh . . . it's money.

BOY: It's for the week I stayed with you.

GIRL: Fifty dollars. But, Michael, you didn't have to.

MOTHER: Are you still writing that radical stuff, Michael?

SON: Radical?

MOTHER: Yes . . . that stuff you write and send me all the time in those little books.

SON: My poetry, Mother?

MOTHER: Yes, that's what I'm talking about.

SON: No.

MOTHER: Praise the Lord, son. Praise the Lord. Didn't seem like anything I had read in school.

BOY: [*On telephone.*] Aunt Sophie? . . . Aunt Sophie? . . . It's me, Michael . . .

GIRL: Michael?

BOY: Yes . . . Michael . . .

GIRL: Oh . . . Michael . . . yes . . .

BOY: I'm in jail, Aunt Sophie . . . I got picked up for drunk driving.

GIRL: You did . . . how awful . . .

MOTHER: When you going to get your hair cut, Michael?

BOY: Aunt Sophie . . . will you please come down and sign my bail. I've got the money . . . I just got paid yesterday . . . They're holding more than enough for me

. . . but the law says that someone has to sign for it.

MOTHER: You look almost like a hoodlum, Michael.

BOY: All you need to do is come down and sign . . . and I can get out.

MOTHER: What you tryin' to be . . . a savage or something? Are you keeping out of trouble, Michael?

GIRL: Ohhh . . . Michael . . . I'm sorry but I can't do nothin' like that . . .

BOY: But all you have to do is sign . . . I've got the money and everything.

GIRL: I'm sorry . . . I can't stick my neck out.

BOY: But, Aunt Sophie . . . if I don't get back to work I'll lose my job and everything . . . please . . .

GIRL: I'm sorry, Michael . . . I can't stick my neck out . . . I have to go now . . . Is there anyone I can call?

BOY: No.

GIRL: I could call your mother. She wouldn't mind if I reversed the charges on her, would she? I don't like to run my bills up.

BOY: No, thanks.

MOTHER: You and your aunt are so much alike.

SON: Yes, Mother. Our birthdays are in the same month.

MOTHER: Yes, that year was so hot . . . so hot and I was carrying you . . .

[As the MOTHER speaks the BOY comes over and takes her by the hand and leads her from the chair, and they stroll around the stage, arm in arm. The GIRL accompanies them and she and the BOY enact scenes from the MOTHER's mind.]

. . . carrying you, Michael . . . and you were such a big baby . . . kicked all the time. But I was happy. Happy that I was having a baby of my own . . . I worked as long as I could and bought you everything you might need . . . diapers . . . and bottles . . . and your own spoon . . . and even toys . . . and even books . . . And it was so hot in Philadelphia that year . . . Your Aunt Sophie used to come over and we'd go for walks . . . sometimes up on the avenue . . . I was living in West Philly then . . . in that old terrible section they called "The Bottom." That's where I met your father.

GIRL: You're such a fool, Bernice. No

nigger . . . man or boy's . . . ever going to do a thing to me like that.

MOTHER: Everything's going to be all right, Sophia.

GIRL: But what is he going to do? How are you going to take care of a baby by yourself?

MOTHER: Everything's going to be all right, Sophia. I'll manage.

GIRL: You'll manage? How? Have you talked about marriage?

MOTHER: Oh, please, Sophia!

GIRL: What do you mean "please?" Have you?

MOTHER: I just can't. He might think . . .

GIRL: Think! That dirty nigger better think. He better think before he really messes up. And you better too. You got this baby comin' on. What are you going to do?

MOTHER: I don't know . . . I don't know what I can do.

GIRL: Is he still tellin' you those lies about . . .

MOTHER: They're not lies.

GIRL: Haaaa . . .

MOTHER: They're not.

GIRL: Some smooth-talkin' nigger comes up from Georgia and tell you he escaped from the chain gang and had to change his name so he can't get married 'cause they might find out . . . What kinda shit is that, Bernice?

MOTHER: Please, Sophia. Try and understand. He loves me. I can't hurt him.

GIRL: Loves you . . . and puts you through this?

MOTHER: Please . . . I'll talk to him . . . Give me a chance.

GIRL: It's just a good thing you got a family, Bernice. It's just a good thing. You know that, don't cha?

MOTHER: Yes . . . yes, I do . . . but please don't say anything to him.

SON: I've only seen my father about a half dozen times that I remember, Mother. What was he like?

MOTHER: Down in The Bottom . . . that's where I met your father. I was young and hinkty then. Had big pretty brown legs and a small waist. Everybody used to call me Bernie . . . and me and my sister would go to Atlantic City on the weekends and work as waitresses in the evenings and sit all afternoon on the black part of the beach at Boardwalk and Atlantic . . . getting blacker

. . . and having the times of our lives. Your father probably still lives down in The Bottom . . . perched over some bar down there . . . drunk to the world . . . I can see him now . . . He had good white teeth then . . . not how they turned later when he started in drinkin' that wine and wouldn't stop . . . he was so nice then.

BOY: Awwww, listen, kid. I got my problems too.

GIRL: But Andy . . . I'm six months gone . . . and you ain't done nothin'.

BOY: Well, what can I do?

GIRL: Don't talk like that . . . What can you do? . . . You know what you can do.

BOY: You mean marry you? Now lissen, sweetheart . . .

GIRL: But what about our baby?

BOY: Your baby.

GIRL: Don't talk like that! It took more than me to get him.

BOY: Well . . . look . . . I'll talk to you later, kid. I got to go to work now.

GIRL: That's what I got to talk to you about too, Andy. I need some money.

BOY: Money! Is somethin' wrong with your head, woman? I ain't got no money.

GIRL: But I can't work much longer, Andy. You got to give me some money. Andy . . . you just gotta.

BOY: Woman . . . all I got to *ever* do is die and go to hell.

GIRL: Well, you gonna do that, Andy. You sho are . . . you know that, don't you? . . . You know that.

MOTHER: . . . Yes, you are, man. Praise the Lord. We all are . . . All of us . . . even though he ain't come for you yet to make you pay. Maybe he's waitin' for us to go together so I can be a witness to the retribution that's handed down. A witness to all that He'll bestow upon your sinner's head . . . A witness! . . . That's what I am, Andy! Do you hear me? . . . A witness!

SON: Mother . . . what's wrong? What's the matter?

MOTHER: Thank the Lord that I am not blinded and will see the fulfillment of divine . . .

SON: Mother!

MOTHER: Oh . . . is something wrong, Michael?

SON: You're shouting and walking around . . .

MOTHER: Oh . . . it's nothing, son. I'm just feeling the power of the Lord.

SON: Oh . . . is there anything I can get you, Mother?

MOTHER: No, nothing at all.

[*She sits again and irons.*]

SON: Where's your kitchen? . . . I'll get you some coffee . . . the way you like it. I bet I still remember how to fix it.

MOTHER: Michael . . . I don't drink anything like that no more.

SON: No?

MOTHER: Not since I joined the service of the Lord.

SON: Yeah? . . . Well, do you mind if I get myself a cup?

MOTHER: Why, I don't have a kitchen. All my meals are prepared for me.

SON: Oh . . . I thought I was having dinner with you.

MOTHER: No. There's nothing like that here.

SON: Well, could I take you out to a restaurant? . . . Remember how we used to go out all the time and eat? I've never lost my habit of liking to eat out. Remember . . . we used to come down to this part of town and go to restaurants. They used to call it home cooking then . . . now, at least where I been out West and up in Harlem . . . we call it soul food. I bet we could find a nice little restaurant not four blocks from here, Mother. Remember that old man's place we used to go to on Nineteenth and South? I bet he's dead now . . . but . . .

MOTHER: I don't even eat out no more, Michael.

SON: No?

MOTHER: Sometimes I take a piece of holy bread to work . . . or some fruit . . . if it's been blessed by my Spiritual Mother.

SON: I see.

MOTHER: Besides . . . we have a prayer meeting tonight.

SON: On Friday?

MOTHER: Every night. You'll have to be going soon.

SON: Oh.

MOTHER: You're looking well.

SON: Thank you.

MOTHER: But you look tired.

SON: Do I?

MOTHER: Yes, those rings around your eyes might never leave. Your father had them.

SON: Did he?

MOTHER: Yes . . . and cowlicks . . . deep cowlicks on each side of his head.

SON: Yes . . . I remember.

MOTHER: You do?

[*The* BOY *and the* GIRL *take crouching positions behind and in front of them. They are in a streetcar. The* BOY *behind the* MOTHER *and* SON, *the* GIRL *across the aisle, a passenger.*]

MOTHER: [*Young woman.*] [*To the* BOY.] Keep your damn hands off him, Andy!

BOY: [*Chuckles.*] Awww, c'mon . . . Bernie. I ain't seen him since he was in the crib.

MOTHER: And you wouldn't have seen neither of us . . . if I had anything to do with it . . . Ohhh . . . why did I get on this trolley?

BOY: C'mon . . . Bernie . . . don't be so stuckup.

MOTHER: Don't even talk to us . . . and stop reaching after him.

BOY: Awww . . . c'mon . . . Bernie. Let me look at him.

MOTHER: Leave us alone. Look . . . people are looking at us.

[*The* GIRL *across the aisle has been peeking at the trio but looks toward front at the mention of herself.*]

BOY: Hey, big boy . . . do you know who I am?

MOTHER: Stop it, Andy! Stop it, I say . . . Mikie . . . don't pay any attention to him . . . you hear?

BOY: Hey, big boy . . . know who I am? . . . I'm your daddy. Hey, there . . .

MOTHER: Shut up . . . shut up, Andy . . . you nothin' to us.

BOY: Where you livin' at . . . Bernie? Let me come on by and see the little guy, huh?

MOTHER: No! You're not comin' near us . . . ever . . . you hear?

BOY: But I'm his father . . . look . . . Bernie . . . I've been an ass the way I've acted but . . .

MOTHER: He ain't got no father.

BOY: Oh, come off that nonsense, woman.

MOTHER: Mikie ain't got no father . . . his father's dead . . . you hear?

BOY: Dead?

MOTHER: Yes, dead. My son's father's dead.

BOY: What you talkin' about? . . . He's the spittin' image of me.

MOTHER: Go away . . . leave us alone, Andrew.

BOY: See there . . . he's got the same name as me. His first name is Michael after your father . . . and Andrew after me.

MOTHER: No, stop that, you hear?

BOY: Michael Andrew . . .

MOTHER: You never gave him no name . . . his name is Brown . . . Brown. The same as mine . . . and my sister's . . . and my daddy . . . You never gave him nothin' . . . and you're dead . . . go away and get buried.

BOY: You know that trouble I'm in . . . I got a wife down there, Bernie. I don't care about her . . . what could I do?

MOTHER: [*Rises, pulling up the* SON.] We're leavin' . . . don't you try and follow us . . . you hear, Andy? C'mon . . . Mikie . . . watch your step now.

BOY: Well . . . bring him around my job . . . you know where I work. That's all . . . bring him around on payday.

MOTHER: [*Leaving.*] We don't need anything from you . . . I'm working . . . just leave us alone.

[*The* BOY *turns to the* GIRL.]

BOY: [*Shrugs.*] That's the way it goes . . . I guess. Ships passing on the trolley car . . . Hey . . . don't I know you from up around 40th and Market?

[*The* GIRL *turns away.*]

SON: Yeah . . . I remember him. He always had liquor on his breath.

MOTHER: Yes . . . he did. I'm glad that stuff ain't got me no more . . . Thank the Lord.

GIRL: [*35 years old.*] You want to pour me another drink, Michael?

BOY: [*15 years old.*] You drink too much, Mother.

GIRL: Not as much as some people I know.

BOY: Well, me and the guys just get short snorts, Mother. But you really hide some port.

GIRL: Don't forget you talkin' to your mother. You gettin' more like your father every day.

BOY: Is that why you like me so much?

GIRL: [*Grins drunkenly.*] Oh, hush up now, boy . . . and pour me a drink.

BOY: There's enough here for me too.

GIRL: That's okay . . . when Will comes in he'll bring something.

SON: How is Will, Mother?

MOTHER: I don't know . . . haven't seen Will in years.

SON: Mother.

MOTHER: Yes, Michael.

SON: Why you and Will never got married? . . . You stayed together for over ten years.

MOTHER: Oh, don't ask me questions like that, Michael.

SON: But why not?

MOTHER: It's just none of your business.

SON: But you could be married now . . . not alone in this room . . .

MOTHER: Will had a wife and child in Chester . . . you know that.

SON: He could have gotten a divorce, Mother . . . Why . . .

MOTHER: Because he just didn't . . . that's why.

SON: You never hear from him?

MOTHER: Last I heard . . . Will had cancer.

SON: Oh, he did.

MOTHER: Yes.

SON: Why didn't you tell me? . . . You could have written.

MOTHER: Why?

SON: So I could have known.

MOTHER: So you could have known? Why?

SON: Because Will was like a father to me . . . the only one I've really known.

MOTHER: A father? And you chased him away as soon as you got big enough.

SON: Don't say that, Mother.

MOTHER: You made me choose between you and Will.

SON: Mother.

MOTHER: The quarrels you had with him . . . the mean tricks you used to play . . . the lies you told to your friends about Will . . . He wasn't much . . . when I thought I had a sense of humor I us'ta call him just plain Will. But we was his family.

SON: Mother, listen.

MOTHER: And you drove him away . . . and he didn't lift a hand to stop you.

SON: Listen, Mother.

MOTHER: As soon as you were big enough you did all that you could to get me and Will separated.

SON: Listen.

MOTHER: All right, Michael . . . I'm listening.

[Pause.]

SON: Nothing.

[Pause. Lifts an imaginary object.]

Is this your tambourine?

MOTHER: Yes.

SON: Do you play it?

MOTHER: Yes.

SON: Well?

MOTHER: Everything I do in the service of the Lord I do as well as He allows.

SON: You play it at your meetings.

MOTHER: Yes, I do. We celebrate the life He has bestowed upon us.

SON: I guess that's where I get it from.

MOTHER: Did you say something, Michael?

SON: Yes. My musical ability.

MOTHER: Oh . . . you've begun taking your piano lessons again?

SON: No . . . I was never any good at that.

MOTHER: Yes, three different teachers and you never got past the tenth lesson.

SON: You have a good memory, Mother.

MOTHER: Sometimes, son. Sometimes.

SON: I play an electric guitar in a combo.

MOTHER: You do? That's nice.

SON: That's why I'm in New York. We got a good break and came East.

MOTHER: That's nice, Michael.

SON: I was thinking that Sunday I could rent a car and come down to get you and drive you up to see our show. You'll get back in plenty of time to rest for work Monday.

MOTHER: No, I'm sorry. I can't do that.

SON: But you would like it, Mother. We could have dinner up in Harlem, then go down and . . .

MOTHER: I don't do anything like that any more, Michael.

SON: You mean you wouldn't come to see me play even if I were appearing here in Philly?

MOTHER: That's right, Michael. I wouldn't come. I'm past all that.

SON: Oh, I see.

MOTHER: Yes, thank the Lord.

SON: But it's my life, Mother.

MOTHER: Good . . . then you have something to live for.

SON: Yes.

MOTHER: Well, you're a man now, Michael . . . I can no longer live it for you. Do the best with what you have.

SON: Yes . . . Yes, I will, Mother.

GIRL'S VOICE: [Offstage.] Sister Brown . . . Sister Brown . . . hello.

MOTHER: [Uneasy; peers at watch.] Oh . . . it's Mother Ellen . . . I didn't know it was so late.

GIRL: [*Enters.*] Sister Brown . . . how are you this evening?

MOTHER: Oh, just fine, Mother.

GIRL: Good. It's nearly time for dinner.

MOTHER: Oh, yes, I know.

GIRL: We don't want to keep the others waiting at meeting . . . do we?

MOTHER: No, we don't.

GIRL: [*Self-assured.*] Hello, son.

SON: Hello.

MOTHER: Oh, Mother . . . Mother . . .

GIRL: Yes, Sister Brown, what is it?

MOTHER: Mother . . . Mother . . . this is . . . this is . . .

[*Pause.*]

. . . this is . . .

SON: Hello, I'm Michael. How are you?

MOTHER: [*Relieved.*] Yes, Mother . . . This is Michael . . . my son.

GIRL: Why, hello, Michael. I've heard so much about you from your mother. She prays for you daily.

SON: [*Embarrassed.*] Oh . . . good.

GIRL: [*Briskly.*] Well . . . I have to be off to see about the others.

MOTHER: Yes, Mother Ellen.

GIRL: [*As she exits; chuckles.*] Have to tell everyone that you won't be keeping us waiting, Bernice.

[*Silence.*]

SON: Well, I guess I better be going, Mother.

MOTHER: Yes.

SON: I'll write.

MOTHER: Please do.

SON: I will.

MOTHER: You're looking well . . . Thank the Lord.

SON: Thank you, so are you, Mother.

[*He moves toward her and hesitates.*]

MOTHER: You're so much like your aunt. Give her my best . . . won't you?

SON: Yes, I will, Mother.

MOTHER: Take care of yourself, son.

SON: Yes, Mother. I will.

[*The* SON *exits. The* MOTHER *stands looking after him as the lights go slowly down to . . .*]

BLACKNESS